FINANCIAL ACCOUNTING
A Managerial Perspective
SIXTH EDITION

R. Narayanaswamy
Indian Institute of Management Bangalore

PHI Learning Private Limited
Delhi-110092
2021

₹ 695.00

FINANCIAL ACCOUNTING: A Managerial Perspective, Sixth Edition
R. Narayanaswamy

© 2021 by PHI Learning Private Limited, Delhi. Previous editions © 2014, 2011, 2008, 2005, 2002.

ISBN-978-81-203-5343-5 (Print Book)
ISBN-978-93-90669-08-0 (e-Book)

Published by Asoke K. Ghosh, PHI Learning Private Limited, Rimjhim House, 111, Patparganj Industrial Estate, Delhi-110092 and Printed by Rajkamal Electric Press, Plot No. 2, Phase IV, HSIDC, Kundli-131028, Sonepat, Haryana.

To
My Family and My Students

CONTENTS

Introduction   1
Interview with Mr. N. R. Narayana Murthy,
Infosys Limited   5

Part One
THE BASICS OF FINANCIAL STATEMENTS

1. Business and Accounting Basics

Speed Read   11
The Pitfalls of Reductionism   11
Understanding Business Organizations   12
Forms of Business Organization   13
Accounting, Markets and Governance   18
What is Accounting   21
Users of Accounting Information   24
Accounting Principles   30
Institutions that Regulate Accounting   32
Ind AS, IFRS and US GAAP   33
Accounting Policies   35
The World of the Accountant   36
Fraud and Ethical Issues in Accounting   38
Recap   40
Review Problem   40
Assignment Material   41

2. Financial Statements

Speed Read   46
Dodgy Reporting?   46
The Accounting Equation   47
Effects of Transactions   49
Financial Statements   53
Financial Statement Analysis: The Basics   56
Form and Content of Company Financial Statements   57
Recap   61
Review Problem   62
Assignment Material   65

3. Transaction Processing

Speed Read   73
Gandhiji, Rockefeller and Accounting   73
The Accounting System   74
Commonly Used Accounts   75
The Double-entry System   76

Comprehensive Illustration: Vogue Company   80
Recording Transactions   87
Ledger   88
Trial Balance   90
Errors in Accounting Records   91
Technology in Accounting   94
Internal Control Systems   95
Recap   97
Review Problem   98
Assignment Material   100

4. Measuring Income

Speed Read   112
How Much Does that Car Cost?   112
Income Measurement Basics   113
Accrual System and Cash System   115
Income Measurement Principles   115
Income Measurement Mechanics   119
Adjusting Entries   119
Financial Statements of a Service Organization   126
Income Measurement for a Merchandising
    Organization   130
Revenue from Sales   131
Cost of Goods Sold   136
Operating Expenses   139
Financial Statements of a Merchandising
    Organization   140
Financial Statement Analysis: Profitability of
    Operations   146
The Accounting Cycle   146
Closing Entries and Reversing Entries   147
Special Cases of Revenue Recognition   149
Earnings Quality   152
Recap   155
Review Problem   156
Assignment Material   159

Part Two
MEASURING AND REPORTING ASSETS, LIABILITIES, AND EQUITY

5. Inventories

Speed Read   181
Phantom Wheat   181
Current Assets   182
Inventory Valuation and Income Measurement   182

Effect of Inventory Error   183
Determining the Physical Inventory   185
Inventory Costs   186
Cost Formulas   187
Inventory Valuation   191
Conservatism, Neutrality, and Prudence   192
Comparability   193
Estimating Inventory Value   193
Perpetual Inventory System   196
Manufacturing Costs   198
Financial Analysis of Inventories   199
Managing the Operating Cycle   200
Recap   203
Review Problem   204
Assignment Material   205

6. Long-lived Assets

Speed Read   214
Double Your Assets in Troubled Times, Effortlessly   214
Long-lived Assets in Perspective   215
Cost of Acquisition   216
Depreciation   219
Depreciation Methods   221
Capital and Revenue Expenditure   230
Depreciation for Income Tax Purposes   232
Derecognition of Property, Plant and Equipment   233
Myths About Depreciation   236
Revaluation of Property, Plant and Equipment   238
Intangible Assets   239
Natural Resources   243
Impairment of Long-lived Assets   247
Financial Analysis of Property, Plant and
    Equipment   248
Investment Property   249
Recap   251
Review Problem   251
Assignment Material   252

7. Financial Assets

Speed Read   264
When the Party Ends...   264
Financial Instruments   265
Financial Assets   265
Fair Value   266
Cash   266
Trade Receivables   267
Credit Losses   267
Transfer of Trade Receivables   271
Bills Receivable   272
Financial Analysis of Receivables   276
Financial and Operating Investments   277
Accounting for Financial Investments   278
Derivative Financial Instruments   283
Impairment of Financial Assets   284
Recap   287
Review Problem   287
Assignment Material   288

8. Operating Investments

Speed Read   299
A Limousine Crowds into a Runabout   299
Equity Investments for Business Purposes   300
Subsidiaries   300
Consolidated Financial Statements   302
Business Combination   303
Consolidated Financial Statements and Business
    Combination Illustrated   305
Joint Arrangements   311
Accounting for Joint Arrangements   312
Associates   313
The Equity Method: One-line Consolidation   313
Separate Financial Statements   316
Recap   318
Review Problem   318
Assignment Material   319

9. Operating Liabilities

Speed Read   328
Tax Works for Your Business   328
Liabilities in Perspective   329
Operating Liabilities and Financial Liabilities   329
Current Liabilities   330
Definite Liabilities and Estimated Liabilities   330
Income Taxes   333
Current Tax   333
Deferred Tax   335
Employee Benefits   344
Contingent Liabilities   346
Recap   348
Review Problem   348
Assignment Material   349

10. Financial Liabilities

Speed Read   359
Oops! My Bond Prices Have Gone Up   359
Financial Liabilities in Perspective   360
Measurement of Financial Liabilities   360
Debentures Payable   361
Issuing Debentures   361
Redeemable Preference Shares   364
Derecognition of Debentures   365
Debenture Redemption Fund   365
Compound Financial Instruments   366
Mortgages Payable   368
Leases   369
Off-balance Sheet Financing   372
Recap   374
Review Problem   374
Assignment Material   375

11. Equity

Speed Read   382
Letter from a Failed Business Tycoon   382
The Corporate Organization   383
Share Capital   384

Accounting for Share Capital 385
Preference Share Capital 387
Reserves and Surplus 389
Foreign Currency Transactions and Translations 390
Buyback of Shares and Treasury Stock Operation 394
Bonus Shares 396
Dividends 397
Share-based Compensation 398
Statement of Changes in Equity 400
Non-controlling Interest 400
Earnings Per Share 401
Recap 405
Review Problem 405
Assignment Material 406

Interview with Mr. P. R. Ramesh, Deloitte India 417

Part Three
ANALYZING AND INTERPRETING FINANCIAL STATEMENTS

12. Balance Sheet and Statement of Profit and Loss

Speed Read 423
The House of Debt 423
Objectives of Financial Statement Analysis 424
Public Sources of Information 425
Standards of Comparison 425
Techniques of Financial Statement Analysis 427
Profitability Analysis 431
Liquidity Analysis 435
Solvency Analysis 438
Capital Market Standing 441
Recap 444
Review Problem 445
Assignment Material 446

13. Statement of Cash Flows

Speed Read 458
Give It Back 458
Statement of Cash Flows in Perspective 459
Purpose and Structure of the Statement of Cash Flows 459
Computing Net Cash Flow from Operating Activities 464
Computing Net Cash Flow from Investing Activities 469
Computing Net Cash Flow from Financing Activities 471
Reporting Cash Flows 473
Interpreting the Statement of Cash Flows 475
Cash Flow Ratios 477
Recap 479

Review Problem 479
Assignment Material 482

14. Financial Statements of Banks

Speed Read 497
Reversing the Decline 497
Understanding Banks 498
Bank Regulation 498
Legal Framework for Financial Statements 500
Balance Sheet 500
Statement of Profit and Loss 506
The Drivers of a Bank's Performance 508
Capital Adequacy 514
Basel III Regulations 515
Off-balance Sheet Activities 522
Recap 523
Review Problem 524
Assignment Material 525

15. Earnings Analysis and Qualitative Information

Speed Read 531
Wah Taj? 531
Earnings Quality 532
Advanced Profitability Analysis: Focus on Operations 538
Earnings Management 541
Segment Performance 545
Pro Forma Financial Measures 547
Free Cash Flow 549
Economic Value Added 550
Corporate Disclosure Policy 551
Efficient Market Hypothesis and Financial Statement Analysis 552
Understanding Annual Reports and Earnings Releases 553
Corporate Governance and Financial Reporting 554
Auditors, Analysts and the Press 555
Recap 556
Review Problem 557
Assignment Material 557

Interview with Professor Suraj Srinivasan, Harvard Business School 569

Appendix A   Ind AS and IFRS 573
Appendix B   Dr. Reddy's Laboratories Limited Consolidated Financial Statements 574
Appendix C   Time Value of Money 577
Appendix D   Summary of Formulas 586
Answer Hints for Selected Problems 589
Index 591

Preface

What are Financial Statements?

Financial statements tell the story of an organization in numbers. Business organizations, governments, and not-for-profit organizations prepare financial statements. At first look, financial statements are a mass of numbers with some incomprehensible words thrown in. But the story is hidden there waiting to be read.

Who Should Read this Book?

Those who want to work with organizations should be able to read financial statements. Investors, lenders, analysts, managers, employees, trade unions, alliance partners, journalists, competitors, consultants, suppliers, customers, government administrators, tax officers, regulators, politicians, activists, donors, lawyers, expert witnesses, judges, and police officers need to grasp the essential information in financial statements.

About This Book

This book is designed as a first-level course offered in business schools, universities, and professional programmes. Its distinctive features include the following:

- Developing the accounting model from the basics of business.
- Stress on the *why* of accounting rather than the *how* of bookkeeping.
- Emphasis on financial analysis from the beginning.
- Attention to accounting regulations and legal requirements.
- Problems and cases that strengthen conceptual foundation and encourage critical thinking.

Anyone who follows plain English and knows basic math (+, −, ×, ÷) can read this book.

New to This Edition

- **Chapters:** Chapter 7 Financial Assets, Chapter 9 Operating Liabilities, Chapter 10 Financial Liabilities, and Chapter 15 Earnings Analysis and Qualitative Information.
- **Topics:** Accounting fraud and red flags, cash flow ratios, economic value added, foreign currency accounting, and joint arrangements.
- **Expanded coverage:** Earnings quality, earnings management, and pro forma measures.
- **Standards:** IFRS, Ind AS, and Indian GAAP comparisons for key items in financial statements.
- **Real-world cases:** Amazon, Lanco, National Spot Exchange, Olympus, Suzlon, Valeant Pharmaceuticals, TCS, and Toshiba.
- **Interview:** Professor Suraj Srinivasan, Harvard Business School.
- **Pedagogical features:** Application, Discussion Question, Forensic Corner, Ladder, One-minute Quiz, Quick Question, Real World, and Speed Read.
- **Examples:** New examples in Chapter Vignette, Earnings Quality Analysis, and Financial View.
- **New Material and Revision:** Additional and revised text and figures in almost all chapters.

Student Resources

Interactive Study Guide available at www.phindia.com/narayanaswamy6e provides valuable support.

Instructor Resources

Instructor's Manual is available to adopting instructors from the publisher.

Disclaimer

All cases and examples in this book are intended to illustrate business and accounting practices of organizations purely for the purpose of classroom discussions. They are not meant to pass judgment on the practices followed by the organizations.

I welcome suggestions and feedback. My e-mail address is narayan@iimb.ernet.in

R. Narayanaswamy

Keeping the Student in Mind

➤ A tone-setting **vignette** at the start of every chapter motivates the students to think about the significance of the chapter.

THE PITFALLS OF REDUCTIONISM

Business is in some ways quite simple; it has clearly defined aims. The aim is to make money. So you have a measure against which to judge all the subsidiary actions which add up to the overall result.

These words are from *The Power of Yes*, a play by Sir David Hare, the well-known British dramatist. How right is the comment? Anyone who has run a business—any business—would know that business is far from simple. Even a small business—something seemingly as straightforward as selling vegetables from a pushcart—requires complex operations. Again, the idea that business is just about making money is naïve. If a business pursues profit mindlessly by

➤ **Figures** simplify ideas

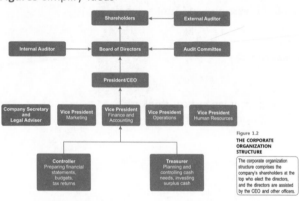

Figure 1.2
THE CORPORATE ORGANIZATION STRUCTURE

The corporate organization structure comprises the company's shareholders at the top who elect the directors, and the directors are assisted by the CEO and other officers.

➤ **Test Your Understanding** helps the student try a short problem on a specific point.

Describe the business of the following organizations:
- (a) Airbnb
- (b) Paytm
- (c) Selco India
- (d) The Lending Club
- (e) Healthcare Global
- (f) Bombay Dyeing

TEST YOUR UNDERSTANDING 1.1
Business Organizations

➤ **Review Problem** covers the key points in a chapter in a numerical form.

Review Problem

Akhil, Binoy, Chhavi and Devika formed a partnership. Their partnership agreement provided that the profits would be divided among the partners in the ratio of 4:3:2:1. The agreement was silent on allocating losses. At the end of its first year, the partnership had losses of ₹100,000. Before allocating losses, the partners' capital balances were: Akhil, ₹70,000; Binoy, ₹50,000; Chhavi, ₹35,000; and Devika, ₹8,200. Devika has no personal assets. After losses were allocated to the partners, assets were sold and liabilities were paid, the partnership had ₹63,200 in cash.

Required

How would the cash be distributed among the partners?

Solution to the Review Problem

	Akhil	Binoy	Chhavi	Devika
Capital balance	₹70,000	₹50,000	₹35,000	₹8,200
Allocation of losses	(40,000)	(30,000)	(20,000)	(10,000)
Balance	30,000	20,000	15,000	(1,800)
Distribution of Devika's deficiency	(800)	(600)	(400)	1,800
Balance	29,200	19,400	14,600	0
Distribution of remaining assets	29,200	19,400	14,600	

➤ **Speed Read** is a précis of the chapter in 100 words.

SPEED READ

Business organizations provide products and services. Businesses may be proprietorships, partnerships or companies. Efficient markets need high quality accounting information. Accounting is the most widely spoken language of business. Investors, lenders, managers, governments and others should be able to make sense of financial statements. In order to remain strong, flourishing businesses and mighty empires need good accounting and financial control. India's growing

➤ **Handhold** reinforces understanding.

HANDHOLD 1.2
Liability of Sole Proprietor

Consider the following cases.

Case A: Manasi started a proprietorship business with an investment of ₹10,000. After one year, the business has ₹15,000 in cash and ₹3,000 in unpaid bills. Manasi has no personal cash or debt.

Case B: Sunil started a proprietorship business with an investment of ₹10,000. After one month, the business has ₹15,000 in cash and owes ₹20,000 in unpaid bills. Sunil has personal cash of ₹8,000 and no personal debt.

This is what happens in each case.

Case A: The business has enough cash to pay its bills. Manasi doesn't need to bring in any cash. She is solvent. The business will continue.

Case B: The business is short of ₹5,000 for paying its bills. Sunil must bring in ₹5,000 from personal cash in order to pay the bills in full. After the payment, he is solvent. The business will continue. Since we are concerned with the current position, the initial investment is irrelevant.

➤ **Recap** contains a crisp summary of the chapter for a quick review just before the exam.

RECAP

- Business organizations provide products and services.
- Sole proprietorship, partnership, company and limited liability partnership are the common forms of business organization.
- Capital market channels savings into investment. High quality accounting reports are a must for orderly markets and good governance.
- Accounting is a principal means of communicating financial information.
- The accounting information system applies accounting principles, standards and policies to transactions and other events to produce financial statements.
- Financial accounting provides information to outsiders; management accounting provides information to insiders.
- Users of financial statements include owners, lenders, employees, managers, governments, and regulators.
- Accounting is the language of business. The conventions, assumptions, concepts and rules which define accepted accounting practice constitute generally accepted accounting principles (GAAP).

➤ **Interview** has insights from leading practitioners and thinkers.

Interview with
Professor Suraj Srinivasan,
Harvard Business School

Professor Suraj Srinivasan is the Philip J. Stomberg Professor of Business Administration at Harvard Business School.

Question: Audit committees are expected to monitor the financial reporting and control systems of companies. What should the audit committee members do to avoid unpleasant surprises?

Answer: The task of audit committees starts with developing a good understanding of the strategy of the business, the key drivers of performance, and the risks in the business model. Directors should ensure that they have a deep knowledge of whether the strategy is ensuring sustainable growth and profitability. This will allow the audit committee to focus on how the company's internal systems are geared to managing the key risks and how external financial reporting communicates the key success and risk factors to investors. Risks can arise from competition, technology, and other factors external to the firm or from internal factors such as weak controls systems, high-powered incentives, and risky investment decisions. The audit committee needs to have a systematic process to consider these risks, ask the right questions, and assess the answers. A focus merely on compliance issues carries the danger of blinding the audit committee to bigger risks that are strategic in nature.

Where Numbers Have Life

➢ **Discussion Question** encourages the students to think deeply about an issue.

DISCUSSION QUESTION 1.2

Should business go public or remain private?

....

....

....

➢ **Real World** illustrates an idea with a live case.

REAL WORLD
Is Smart Debt an Oxymoron?

Is it possible to borrow wisely? Suzlon Energy manufactures wind turbines. Suzlon literally means 'smart debt': *suz* from the Gujarati *suz-buz* (intelligence or smartness) and *lon*, the Gujarati way of saying loan. In the early 2000s, the company was cited in the international media as an example of a successful emerging market giant. The company's chairman and managing director, Tulsi Tanti, pushed aggressively for growth. Suzlon set up manufacturing facilities around the world and acquired Hansen Transmissions International, Belgium and REpower Systems, Germany. The expansion was financed by debt of about ₹130 billion in foreign currency convertible bonds (FCCBs). In its enthusiasm to acquire Repower, Suzlon seemed to have overpaid for it and ended up with 94 per cent of the stake. The economic crisis following the collapse of Lehman Brothers in September 2008 adversely affected the company's wind power markets in the US and Europe. Nearly 60 per cent of the company's order book came from REpower. All of these contributed to Suzlon defaulting on the redemption of an instalment of FCCBs. Possibly, wind energy was (and still is) a good business, but it was brought down by debt. Too much debt would appear to be not such a smart idea.

Source: Company annual reports.

➢ **Financial View** presents the business implications of financial numbers and practices.

FINANCIAL VIEW
Maruti Suzuki's Inventory Management

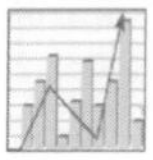

Maruti Suzuki is a leading passenger car maker in India. The company depends heavily on its suppliers, since 80 per cent of the car by value is procured in the form of components and raw material. So efficient inventory management is crucial to the company's operations and financial performance. Maruti's 2016 annual report claims that the company "continued its partnership with suppliers in value analysis/value enhancement (VA/VE) projects. Joint efforts were also made in yield improvement. Along with this, the Company worked on the localisation of parts imported by vendors to mitigate risk arising out of foreign exchange exposure and to bring down input cost." Let's see how we can evaluate this claim using information available in the financial statements. Maruti's inventories of components and raw materials were ₹17,317 million in 2016 and ₹13,189 million in 2015. The cost of material consumed was ₹362,007 million in 2016. The inventory turnover was 24 times, equivalent to 15 days' consumption being carried in inventories. How does Maruti manage with such a low inventory? Can other manufacturers follow Maruti's example?

Inventory management is a lot more than just reducing inventories. Good suppliers who deliver quality parts in time at a reasonable cost are critical. It involves educating and monitoring vendors, giving them technical and managerial support, developing and sustaining long-term relationships and paying them fair prices on time. This often means sticking with the same vendors over a long period. As a result, both Maruti and its vendors benefit over the long term. These are the features of a JIT (just-in-time) inventory system. Accountants and bankers think of inventories as assets. The fact is that high inventory levels usually hide serious problems in quality, production process, labour, transportation, and vendors. While some inventory is often unavoidable, especially in Indian conditions, high inventories are financially inefficient and not an assurance of ready availability of materials and parts. Interestingly, Maruti's inventory holding of 11 days in 2015 was better than in 2016.

➢ **Earnings Quality Analysis** examines the effect of business activities and accounting policies on the prediction of future profits.

EARNINGS QUALITY ANALYSIS
Non-interest Income

In 2016, HDFC Bank earned 11.17 per cent of total revenue from commission, exchange and brokerage. Interest income requires investment in advances. Non-interest income such as commission, exchange and brokerage requires no investment and frees the bank from credit risk and interest rate risk. Fee income from investment banking, securities underwriting, sales of third party products and so on have greater growth potential. Also, these activities don't consume capital. There are some negatives, though. Lending relationships are built over long periods are difficult to break. A borrower would stick to its bank that has stood by it during difficult times. Activities that generate fee income don't engender the same loyalty. Also, these activities require high set-up costs and continuing fixed or semi-fixed costs that increase the degree of operating leverage. Therefore, while these activities don't increase financial leverage, they may increase the volatility of earnings. Further, sales of third party products such as insurance and mutual funds could cannibalize the bank's deposits and open the bank to charges of mis-selling.

➢ **One-Minute Quiz** gingers up the student.

ONE-MINUTE QUIZ 1.2
Agency Costs

You have to appoint a new chief executive for five years. How can you reduce the chances of moral hazard? There may be more than one correct answer.

(a) Relate pay to performance.
(b) Require external auditing.
(c) Screen the job applications with the help of a reputable consultant.
(d) Require a degree from a top school.

➢ **Quick Question** is the interactive tutor.

QUICK QUESTION
Cash account balance

Can the cash account have a credit balance?

➢ **Forensic Corner** draws attention to the methods fraudsters use.

FORENSIC CORNER
Understanding Fraud

There are many kinds of fraud. Here are a few.

- *Misappropriation of assets:* Embezzlement of cash, inventories, shares and equipment and procurement fraud.
- *Accounting fraud:* Manipulation of the numbers in the financial statements, e.g. reporting non-existent revenues and assets and suppressing expenses and liabilities.
- *Bribery:* Taking cash or other consideration in return for doing a favour (or sometimes for even doing one's duty!).
- *Money laundering:* Disguising the proceeds of crime as legitimate assets.

Fraud causes financial, legal and reputational damage. Organizations should devise systems to prevent, detect and report fraud. Businesses have collapsed due to fraud, causing problems for customers and suppliers and immense suffering to employees. Consider these examples of known or alleged accounting fraud.

- *Ricoh India:* Reporting fictitious sales, cash, receivables and inventories.
- *Satyam:* Reporting fictitious sales, cash and receivables.
- *Enron:* Using off-balance sheet entities to hide debts.

➢ **Ladder** simplifies tricky ideas.

LADDER
Face Value Has No Meaning

Suppose a company issues shares for cash at ₹100 each, made up of the share capital of ₹10 and securities premium of ₹90. Would it have mattered if the issue price was split as the capital of ₹1 and premium of ₹99, or any other arbitrary split of ₹100? The short answer is "No". The share issue increases cash (and equity) by ₹600. This is because both share capital and securities premium are part of shareholders' equity. Therefore, the transaction has the same effect on the accounting equation, regardless of how the company breaks up the issue price between capital and premium. How does a company decide on the break-up? First, it decides on the face value. A company is free to choose its face value. Tata Steel has a face value of ₹10, RPG Life Sciences ₹8, Infosys ₹5, Wipro ₹2 and TCS ₹1. Next, it determines the issue price based on the valuation of the shares. Last, the company arrives at the premium as the excess of the issue price over the face value. Whatever may be the break-up of the issue price, the shareholder is obliged to pay the amount when demanded by the company. Also, when a company is liquidated, its assets are sold and liabilities are paid off. Any remaining amount is paid to the shareholders without distinguishing between share capital and securities premium. When a dividend is stated as a percentage of share capital, the dividend amount will depend on the paid-up value. When a dividend is stated as a per share amount, the face value does not matter.

➢ **IFRS, IND AS, AND INDIAN GAAP** provides comparisons for key items.

IFRS, IND AS AND INDIAN GAAP
Revenue Recognition

Indian GAAP is the set of "accounting standards" (AS) notified by the government in 2006. Ind AS is the set of "Indian Accounting Standards" notified by the government on February 16, 2015 and March 30, 2016. IFRS is the set of IFRS/IAS issued by the IASB. The comparison below gives the key differences between these systems.

IFRS	Ind AS	Indian GAAP
IAS 11, IAS 18	Ind AS 11, Ind AS 18	AS 7, AS 9
▪ Sales discount deducted from revenue.		Sales discount treated as an expense.
▪ Percentage of completion method used for service transactions.		Completed contract method used for service transactions.
▪ Revenue from multiple element arrangements or bundled offers recognized based on the substance of the contract.		No specific guidance.
▪ Customer loyalty programmes treated similar to multiple element arrangements.		No specific guidance.
▪ Gain or loss from non-monetary barter transactions not considered.		No specific guidance.

➢ **Application** guides the student on how to read accounting policies.

APPLICATION
Revenue Recognition

Let's see how media, entertainment and sports companies apply the principles of revenue recognition.

Revenue	Explanation
▪ Advertising income and broadcast fees are recognised when the related commercial or programme is telecast. *(Sun TV)*	▪ Revenue is earned by advertising and broadcasting.
▪ Subscription fees billed to cable operators are determined based on management's best estimates of the number of subscription points to which the service is provided. *(Sun TV)*	▪ Presumably, there will be an adjustment for any difference after cable operators report the actual number of subscription points.
▪ Revenues from sale of movie distribution/sub-distribution rights are recognized on the theatrical release of the related movie. *(Sun TV)*	▪ Revenue is earned when a movie is released, regardless of how well it does in the box office.
▪ Revenues from the theatrical distribution of movies are recognized as they are exhibited, based on box office collections reported by the exhibitors after deduction of taxes and exhibitor's share of net collections. *(Sun TV)*	▪ There is no assured revenue from a movie release. Revenue is the company's share of collections.

➢ **Research Insight** provides answers from academic research to managers' questions.

RESEARCH INSIGHT
Accrual

Researchers have studied the role of accrual accounting and its incremental usefulness over the cash system. Cash accounting is a simple system of reporting cash receipts and payments. Accrual accounting requires considerable management judgment and expertise to determine if a revenue has been earned but not received or if an expense has been incurred but not paid as of the reporting date.

Research by Professor Patricia Dechow[3] indicates that the greater the importance of accrual accounting, (a) the shorter the performance measurement interval; (b) the greater the volatility of the firm's working capital requirements and investment and financing activities; and (c) the longer the firm's operating cycle. Under each of these circumstances, cash flows suffer more severely from timing and matching problems that reduce their ability to reflect the firm's performance. The results of empirical tests are consistent with these predictions.

To understand this research, look at the following examples:

(i) *Short reporting period:* Suppose a firm buys an expensive piece of equipment with a long life in the first quarter of a fiscal year. If the firm reports quarterly and follows the cash system, it will expense the equipment in that quarter. Since the firm uses up only a small part of the productive capacity of the equipment in that quarter, there will be significant revenues in the future, but there will be no expense for the use of the equipment. As a result, there will be a mismatch between the firm's accomplishments and efforts. As the reporting period increases, the distortion will decrease. The matching will be perfect over the life of the equipment.

Practice Reinforces Learning

➤ **Questions** help revise the chapter quickly.

| Questions |

1. What is the purpose of a business?
2. What are the advantages of a company over a partnership?
3. How is a limited liability partnership different from a partnership?
4. How does limited liability encourage entrepreneurship?
5. Who appoints a company's auditors?
6. Give examples of costly signals that well-managed companies can send.
7. Why should a manager know accounting?
8. Give examples of economic decisions that are based on accounting information.
9. Who sets accounting standards in India?
12. Who sets accounting standards in India?
13. Do you think the *money measurement assumption* is realistic?
14. Why do we need *accounting standards* in addition *to accounting principles*?
15. Distinguish between *accounting standards* and *accounting policies*.
16. Why is historical cost still used in many countries?
17. Who issues *International Financial Reporting Standards* (IFRS)?
18. What are the responsibilities of a company's chief financial officer, controller and treasurer?

➤ **Business Decision Cases** involve working with unstructured information and encourage students to identify and think about questions that may not be obvious.

| Business Decision Cases |

Sudipto Bhattacharyya is a professor of accounting in a leading business school. He has received the following message from a former student:

Dear Professor Bhattacharyya,

I belong to the MBA Class of 1997 and was your student in the financial accounting course. Currently, I am Vice President, Sales and Operations in the India office of findomega.com, the well-known Internet search engine listed in the National Stock Exchange of India. I need your advice on how to get out of a mess in my workplace.

As you would know, findomega.com provides targeted advertising as part of its search services. It works as follows. When a user searches the Internet using our engine, findomega.com provides the requested information. In addition, it gives the names and related web links of five advertisers (who are our customers) for the products or services that the user may be potentially interested in. If the user clicks on any of those web links, we charge the customer concerned. Otherwise, we do not charge our customers. Of course, we never charge the Internet search user anything. Lately, we have localized the search and have made it possible to get information based on postal code and street name. This is generating a lot of additional revenue for us.

BDC 4.1
Findomega.com

➤ **Financial Analysis** has ideas that students can explore in projects and papers.

| Financial Analysis |

FA 1.1
The Satyam Accounting Scandal

Search the Internet for reports about the accounting scandal in Satyam.

Required
1. Explain the essential elements of the scandal based on your understanding of accounting at this stage.
2. Prepare a report comparing the Satyam scandal with accounting scandals in the US highlighting any similarities and differences between them.

FA 1.2
Investment Advice

The job of an investment adviser is to recommend profitable investment opportunities. These include stocks, bonds, real estate, commodities, and art. The adviser should maximize the return (or profit) from an investment keeping in view the related risks (or the chances of loss or a low profit). Your friend is looking at options for investing a large fortune she has inherited from her uncle. She has heard that lately the stock market has been doing well and the stock prices of many companies have zoomed. She wants you, a financial wizard in the making (or so she thinks!), to tell her how to invest.

Required
1. Prepare a report setting out the information an individual should have in order to decide on investing in stocks and where the information will be available.

➤ **The Online Interactive Study Guide** available at www.phindia.com/narayanaswamy6e has sheets for solving problems, besides a number of self-test questions.

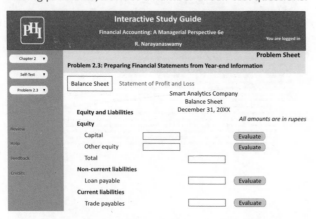

➤ **Problems** have numerical problems that students can solve to master application of the principles.

| Problems |

More * indicates higher difficulty.

On February 11, 20XX, Annamalai started Fauna Enterprise, a nature tourism business as a proprietorship with an investment of ₹25,000. On September 30, 20XX, the business had cash of ₹35,000 and unpaid bills of ₹45,000. On that date, Annamalai had personal cash of ₹8,000 and a used computer worth ₹3,500 (bought at a cost of ₹10,000) and owed ₹7,500 in personal bank loan.

Problem 1.1
Liability of Sole Proprietor *

Required
1. How much is Annamalai required to pay?
2. How much is Annamalai able to pay?
3. Is Annamalai solvent or insolvent?

On July 3, 20XX, Shankar and Tanvi set up Paintbrush & Co. as equal partners to teach art investing ₹25,000 each. On December 19, 29XX, the business had ₹95,000 in cash and ₹130,000 in unpaid bills. On that date, Shankar had personal cash of ₹22,000 and a house worth ₹150,000 (bought for ₹60,000) and owed ₹130,000 on a mortgage loan. Tanvi had personal cash of ₹1,000 and jewellery worth ₹87,000 (bought for ₹18,000) and personal bank loan of ₹85,000.

Problem 1.2
Liability of Partners *

Required
1. How much are Shankar and Tanvi required to pay?
2. How much are Shankar and Tanvi able to pay?
3. Are Shankar and Tanvi solvent?

➤ **Interpreting Financial Reports** have cases based on published financial reports, press reports, and other sources that throw light on real-world accounting.

| Interpreting Financial Reports |

All cases and examples in this book are intended to illustrate business and accounting practices of organizations purely for the purpose of classroom discussions. They are not meant to pass judgment on the practices followed by the organizations

Once upon a time, Kingfisher Airlines was one of the largest aviation companies in India. The company's jaunty slogan "Welcome to a world without passengers" was meant to say that the passenger is "made to feel like a guest and not just a passenger". Unfortunately for the company, the slogan soon acquired its literal meaning.

IFR 1.1
Kingfisher Airlines Limited

Kingfisher Airlines was set up in 2003 by the United Breweries Group. It started operations in 2005. Kingfisher Airlines shut down operations in 2012. It never made a profit all its life. In August 2015, United Bank of India declared Vijay Mallya, the company's promoter and chairman, a 'wilful defaulter' – a term used by the Reserve Bank of India to describe a borrower who has the capacity to repay but doesn't, diverts funds for other purposes, siphons off funds or disposes or removes assets furnished as security. The company owed more than ₹80 billion in unpaid loans to banks in India. Besides, the airports, tax authorities and employees, among others, had claims against the company for unpaid amounts.

Mr. Mallya left India for the United Kingdom in March 2016. Television channels and newspapers demanded that he return to India and repay the company's loans and other dues.

Required
Using publicly available information, answer the following questions:
1. Who is obliged to repay a company's debts: the company, promoters, shareholders, or directors?
2. Are there circumstances under which promoters or directors could be asked to repay the loans taken by the company?
3. What options do the banks have for recovery of the loans in a case like this one?
4. What are the rights of a company's shareholders against the promoter in a case like this one?

➤ **Review Problems** have solved numerical problems to reinforce the understanding of the concepts.

| Review Problem |

Akhil, Binoy, Chhavi and Devika formed a partnership. Their partnership agreement provided that the profits would be divided among the partners in the ratio 4:3:2:1. The agreement was silent on allocating losses. At the end of its first year, the partnership had losses of ₹100,000. Before allocating losses, the partners' capital balances were: Akhil, ₹70,000; Binoy, ₹50,000; Chhavi, ₹35,000; and Devika, ₹8,200. Devika has no personal assets. After losses were allocated to the partners, assets were sold and liabilities were paid, the partnership had ₹63,200 in cash.

Required
How would the cash be distributed among the partners?

Solution to the Review Problem

	Akhil	Binoy	Chhavi	Devika
Capital balance	₹70,000	₹50,000	₹35,000	₹8,200
Allocation of losses	(40,000)	(30,000)	(20,000)	(10,000)
Balance	30,000	20,000	15,000	(1,800)
Distribution of Devika's deficiency	(800)	(600)	(400)	1,800
Balance	29,200	19,400	14,600	0
Distribution of remaining assets	29,200	19,400	14,600	

Notes:
1. Profits and losses are distributed in the same ratio, unless there is agreement to the contrary.
2. Insolvent partner's deficiency is distributed among the solvent partners in the ratio in which losses are distributed.
3. Remaining assets are distributed in the ratio in which profits are distributed.

Acknowledgements

I thank my colleagues, students, friends, and other well-wishers for their critical observations and encouraging words on the Fifth Edition.

I am grateful to the following eminent individuals for sharing their thoughts on accounting, auditing, governance, and related matters with me for the benefit of the readers of this book:

N. R. Narayana Murthy	Executive Chairman of the Board, Infosys Limited
P. R. Ramesh	Chairman of the Board of Deloitte India and Partner, Deloitte Haskins & Sells LLP
Suraj Srinivasan	The Philip J. Stomberg Professor of Business Administration at Harvard Business School

I thank the following colleagues for their valuable feedback:

Manoj Anand	Indian Institute of Management Lucknow	**Krishna Prasad**	Justice K. S. Hegde Institute of Management Nitte
Debarati Basu	Indian Institute of Management Bangalore	**M. Durga Prasad**	T. A. Pai Management Institute Manipal
Vrishali Bhat	T. A. Pai Management Institute Manipal	**K. K. Ramesh**	Indian Institute of Management Kozhikode
Madhumita Chakraborty	Indian Institute of Management Lucknow	**Latha Ramesh**	Christ University Bangalore
Chanchal Chatterjee	International Management Institute Kolkata	**Srinivasan Rangan**	Indian Institute of Management Bangalore
Dinesh Gupta	University Business School Chandigarh	**Padmini Srinivasan**	Indian Institute of Management Bangalore
Pankaj Gupta	Jaipuria Institute of Management Noida	**Ullas Rao**	Heriot-Watt University Dubai Campus
Narahari Hansoge	Indian Institute of Management Tiruchirappalli	**M. Ravisundar**	ICICI Securities Mumbai
V. Hariprasad	Indian Institute of Management Indore	**Rajiv Shah**	T. A. Pai Management Institute Manipal
Bhawana Jain	Amrita School of Business Coimbatore	**Manish Singh**	L. M. Institute of Management Lucknow
M. Kannadhasan	Indian Institute of Management Raipur	**Rajesh, S. P.**	Chinmaya Institute of Technology Kannur
Krishna M.	Birla Institute of Technology and Science Pilani	**V. Sridevi**	IFIM Business School Bangalore
N. R. Parasuraman	S. D. M. Institute for Management Development Mysore	**Ashok Thampy**	Indian Institute of Management Bangalore
P. Padmanabha Pillai	National Law School of India University Bangalore	**Ashish Varma**	Institute of Management Technology Ghaziabad
Samveg Patel	Goa Institute of Management Goa	**Sushma Vishnani**	Jaipuria Institute of Management Lucknow
Nandan Prabhu	School of Management Manipal University	**Vandana Zachariah**	Loyola Institute of Business Administration Chennai

Kavitha Sandeep and G Thiyaghamurthi provided valuable secretarial and administrative support at the Institute.

As in the past, the Publishers, PHI Learning, and their editorial and production team, in particular, Shivani Garg and Ajai Kumar Lal Das had to live with my never-ending changes in the content and style of the manuscript. I cannot thank them enough.

I owe a deep debt of gratitude to Indian Institute of Management Bangalore for the superior library, computing, and other resources and the right ambience for the work.

This book would not have been possible without the whole-hearted cooperation and support that I received at home. My wife, Geeta, and my daughter, Vasudha, showed understanding and patience whenever I was busy working on the manuscript.

R. Narayanaswamy

Introduction

A Fairy Tale

Welcome to Utopia, the land where everyone is good. So the people there trust one another. There are two kinds of Utopians: the Investopians, frugal people who save money for which they have no immediate use; and the Corporatopians, industrious people who forever need money for doing business. The Investopians hand over their savings to the Corporatopians, who are smart businessmen and businesswomen. When the Corporatopians make a lot of money, they gladly give the Investopians much bigger amounts, greatly appreciating their generosity and good nature. The Investopians and the Corporatopians live happily and never fight. The spirit of comity and goodwill on display between them inspires a healing and oneness throughout Utopia. So the Utopians have nothing to do except frolic in fields of lilies where pixies dance in mid-air, the sound of a harp wafting from a hill . . . .

Everyone else should know financial reporting.

This book is about understanding, analyzing and interpreting financial statements and related reports: balance sheet, statement of profit and loss, statement of cash flows, statement of changes in equity, accounting policies, explanatory notes, schedules, and auditors' report. Let us see some examples from the real world to get a flavour of accounting.

Tata's Mystery

Tata Sons Limited is the holding company of the Tata Group. On October 24, 2016, the company's board removed its chairman, Cyrus P. Mistry and named Ratan N. Tata as the interim chairman. Mr. Mistry had succeeded Mr. Tata as chairman in 2012. After his removal, Mr. Mistry questioned the company's decisions during Mr. Tata's tenure. Examples:

- Tata Motors had employed aggressive accounting to capitalize a substantial proportion of the product development expenses, creating a future liability.
- Tata Motors Finance extended credit with lax risk assessment and the losses exceeded ₹40 billion.
- Tata Steel's European steel business faced potential impairments in excess of $10 billion, only some of which had been taken.
- Indian Hotels had acquired the Sea Rock property at a highly inflated price and housed it in an off-balance sheet structure. The company had to write down nearly its entire net worth over the past three years.
- A forensic investigation in Air Asia revealed fraudulent transactions of ₹220 million involving non-existent parties in India and Singapore.

Question: Did the companies violate any accounting norms?

Strange Reaction

For the quarter ended June 30, 2016, Punjab National Bank was expected to report a loss but posted a profit of ₹3.06 billion. Yet PNB shares plunged nearly 3 per cent soon after earnings announcement. Bank of Baroda reported a loss of ₹33.42 billion for the quarter ended December 31, 2015, compared with a profit of ₹3.34 billion for the year-ago quarter. But the stock zoomed 22 per cent on the bank's announcement.

Question: What can we understand from the market reaction?

King-size Problems

Kingfisher Airlines diminished (to put it mildly) the empire of Vijay Mallya, the flamboyant tycoon. It never made a profit since it was set up in 2005 and stopped flying in 2012, because it could not repay its bank loans of ₹80 billion. Mr. Mallya became the poster child for India's bad loans problem. Chased by the banks and various government agencies, he went into "forced exile" in the UK.

Question: What went wrong?

Life after Debt

Not long ago Suzlon, the world's fifth largest wind turbine manufacturer, was thought to be a basket case. It was drowning in debt of over ₹120 billion. Its ambitious acquisitions did not work. In early 2016, the company was on track to profitability. Its debt had come down by one-third.

Question: How did Suzlon bounce back?

Stuffed in the Wrong Folder

On October 5, 2016, the United States Securities and Exchange Commission (SEC) announced that Credit Suisse AG had agreed to pay a $90 million penalty. Credit Suisse had at times overstated net new assets (NNA), a measure of success in attracting new business. The bank reclassified assets owned by its clients and given to it for safekeeping as managed by the bank. Banks earn more fee income from assets under management than from those held under custody. The SEC found that the bank took an "undisclosed results-driven approach" to determining NNA in order to meet certain targets established by senior management. According to the SEC's orders, the chief operating officer of the firm's private banking division pressured employees to classify certain high net worth and ultra-high net worth client assets as NNA despite concerns raised by employees most knowledgeable about a particular client's intent.

Question: Why did the officer ask his staff to misclassify assets? And why didn't the staff protest?

A Law Firm's Troubles

Slater & Gordon, an Australian law firm, acquired Quindell Professional Services, a British firm. S&G was one of the world's first law firms to list. Soon after the acquisition, it ran into accounting problems. Legal accounting has its quirks. The firm bills in different ways: by the hour in some cases, and on a "No Win, No Fee" basis in others. The revenue and profit numbers had to be restated following a review of the firm's accounting policies by PwC.

Question: How should S&G reckon revenue?

A Store Chain for £1. Anyone?

In April 2016, Sir Philip Green sold BHS, the department store chain he bought for £200 million at the turn of the century, for £1. Note: *This is not a typo.*

Question: Are we missing something here?

This book will help you develop the skills to think about questions like the ones above.

The Environment of Financial Reporting

Many economic forces operate on firms that produce financial reports. These forces determine the amount of information that a firm provides and how the firm measures and presents the information. The following figure illustrates the major economic forces.

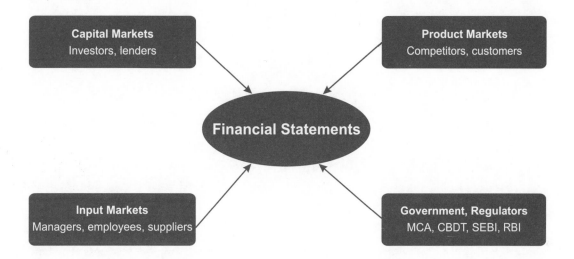

The impact of the economic forces – capital markets, product markets, labour and other markets, and regulation – varies. For example, investors often want more information about a firm, whereas the firm's managers would want to give out less information because of the presence of competitors. Thus, financial statements are the product of the interplay of the forces that drive firms.

The Road Ahead

The above examples will give you a glimpse of the nature and purpose of financial reporting. Let us see what lies ahead. This book has three parts.

Part One, consisting of Chapters 1 to 4, describes the financial statements and income measurement and explains the basics of financial statement analysis. After completing this part, you can find out for yourself whether Slater & Gordon's revenue was unreal.

Part Two, made up of Chapters 5 to 11, introduces the reader to the principles and standards that underlie a firm's accounting policies and the managerial and other considerations that shape the policies. When you have understood the material in this part, you should be able to solve the mystery of Tata's accounting and the truth behind the store sold for £1.

Part Three, containing Chapters 12 to 15, explains the tools and techniques that are useful in analyzing financial statements. With the help of these you should be in a position to understand why Kingfisher Airlines collapsed, how Suzlon was revived, whether the market reacted "irrationally" to PNB and BoB, and what drove the officer and staff at Credit Suisse to overstate performance.

Interview with Mr. N. R. Narayana Murthy, Infosys Limited

Mr. N. R. Narayana Murthy is Founder, Infosys Limited.

"I want our shareholders to treat us first as trustworthy people and then as smart people. Our desire is to deliver whatever we promise".

Question: How important is financial reporting to a technology company like Infosys?

Answer: First of all, the *raison d'être* of a corporation is to maximize the shareholder value on a sustainable basis, while ensuring fairness, transparency and accountability to every one of the stakeholders: customers, investors, employees, vendor-partners, the government of the land, and the society. The annual report and the quarterly report that Infosys produces are definitive instruments for the investor community to understand our strategy, performance, compliance with the generally accepted accounting principles, revenue recognition policies, risk mitigation procedures, systems and controls, human resources policies, and segmentation of revenue. In other words, it is a single window for our investors to look into our operations and our aspirations. It is our view and not the view of the analysts. It is a statutory document. Obviously, companies will have to ensure that it is truthful and it does not communicate any false hope. Also, when you deal with customers, they want to know your strategy, your position in the market, financial strength; who your directors are; your stock movement; and your segmentation of revenue. In other words, even though prospective customers do not buy your shares, they want to ensure that they have good understanding of your financial strength because they are hinging their future on you to some extent.

So, the financial reporting document is very important.

Question: What is the disclosure philosophy of Infosys?

Answer: Well, the tenets of our philosophy have been *When in doubt, disclose* and *Under-promise and over-deliver*, throughout the 20 years of our listed existence. However, we missed our targets during 2011–2013. In other words, in the last 80 quarters, we have taken the view that we will get market data on what the future is likely to be, we will assess our strengths, weaknesses and our readiness to take advantage of market opportunities, and then we will come out with a view of the future that every member of the board has agreed with. We want to make sure that we can deliver whatever we have agreed upon. We do not make our decisions based on what the analysts say or the public expects.

Question: How can financial reporting become a part of a company's business strategy?

Answer: The annual report covers the major aspects of our business operations. Our prospects and our customers use this document as the definitive instrument to assess our viability in the future because of our strategy, our operation and our financial strength. Quite often, our success in selling to our customers and prospects depends on their perception of our strength. This document is very helpful in our investors' and customers' understanding of our strategy. I have seen many of our customers refer to specific pages of the document and ask us to detail out what we have said about the company's plans.

Question: Does the practice of earnings guidance result in excessive pressure on managers' performance?

Answer: Yes and no. My view has been that management is all about our ability to make considered judgments under a situation of competing pressures, and competing priorities. So, we, managers, must accept that there will be pressures. There are different opinions on whether the earnings guidance should be quarterly, six-monthly or yearly, and whether it should be only for the top line or both the top and the bottom line. I am not sure whether the quarterly guidance for both top line and bottom line is any worse than other guidance schemes. My one belief is that it is all about the mindset of the management. Because of globalization, there is tremendous growth and competition in the marketplace. Companies are growing much faster today than they were growing 15 years ago. So, I am not a great believer in the perception that quarterly guidance leads to any extra pressure on the management. What kind of a CEO are you if you do not have a plan to achieve a certain revenue and a certain profit in the next three months? But, if you know what your future is likely to be in the next three months and if you do not share it with your investors at large, then you are creating asymmetry of information, particularly in a company where there are several owner-managers. That is not fair to the investors at large. I will give an example. In 2001, we announced that we would grow by 30 per cent. The previous year, we had grown by 100 per cent. So, I stood up and said, "There is considerable fog on the windshield and we can only promise 30 per cent." Our stock price came down from ₹5,000 + to ₹1,500 or ₹1,600. I did not lose my sleep. Our view was that we had a fairly good system of collection of data, and we had people in the trenches with a very good view of what was likely to happen. Our forecasting, analytics and tools confirmed that the only sales growth figure we could give our investors was 30 per cent. We told our investors that Infosys was not the company to invest in if they were looking for higher than 30 per cent sales growth. Many of them left. Our share price came down to ₹1,500 or ₹1,600. So, the problem does not lie in giving quarterly guidance. The challenge lies in dealing with the short-term mindset of investors.

Question: Does providing voluntary financial disclosures result in competitive disadvantage to companies like yours?

Answer: Providing voluntary disclosures, transparency and following principles of good governance have always created goodwill for the company. We were the first Indian company to give revenue segmentation details, details of our attrition, hiring and many other performance data. I believe that transparency is a hygiene factor for us. We are not transparent just because it enhances market capitalization. I have always believed and acted according to the adage: *When in doubt, disclose.*

Question: Many technology companies have argued against expensing stock options. What is your view?

Answer: I personally believe that there should be some norm for allocating stock options. That is, the regulator should fix a certain cap on the number of options as a percentage of the total number of outstanding stocks. There should be no other restrictions including expensing of options. If we can incentivize our employees to perform better, then our earnings per share will likely be better. So, even though we dilute the total number of shares by a percentage, the overall benefit to the investors is likely to be much more than that percentage. I have found that stock ownership by employees brings better focus on cost control in the company. For example, right from the beginning, people at Infosys understood that every rupee saved went to the bottom line and that translated to something like ₹25 in market capitalization. So, options do create an incentive for employees to control cost.

Question: How do the shareholders of a company benefit from the presence of independent directors on the board?

Answer: The shareholders benefit in many ways. Good corporate governance is minimization of agency costs. The role of the independent directors, if exercised properly, is to ensure that agency costs are minimized. Second, the independent directors ensure that the owner-managers do not benefit from the asymmetry of information through insider trading. They are expected to prevent any related party transactions. They review the strategy of the company and suggest changes. They would be the ombudsmen and ombudswomen for risk mitigation. After all, risk mitigation is extremely important to protect your shareholders. Independent directors also ensure that there are proper procedures and controls. But whether this happens in practice depends on how cooperative the owner-managers are and how competent the independent directors are.

Question: Given that many retail investors do not have any formal accounting training, would it not be better for them to have a summary annual report?

Answer: This is a question that we have debated often. Determining the level of detail to disclose is not easy. At the end of the day, shareholder democracy is like democracy in a nation. Every vote is as important whether the voter is rich or poor, educated or illiterate, powerful or weak, and urban or rural. Therefore, it is best to provide as detailed information as possible to every shareholder. If a shareholder is not as conversant in accounting as he would like to be, let him take the report to an expert and get the expert's opinion on critical issues. The only disadvantage of providing a detailed report is the cost of paper and cost of printing. Let the shareholders decide what they want. Who am I to decide? After all, we are spending their own money for printing the annual report.

Question: Does quarterly reporting discourage risk-taking as the horizon is very short?

Answer: No. There will be activities that are going to take a long time. It is important for the management of a corporation to tell the investors that they would be taking up a major initiative, that it would bring down the profits by x percentage in the ensuing n_1 years, and that the profits would likely be increasing by a multiple of x percentage in the ensuing n_2 years following the period of reduced profits. This is what investing for a better future is all about and the shareholders will accept it. The problem is that, in most cases, most CEOs are not certain whether their investments will indeed bear fruit. So, they want to make investment in a clandestine manner, so that they mask their failures and they look great if they succeed. Consequently, they do not even want to report such investments.

Question: Has globalization raised the standards of corporate governance in India?

Answer: Corporate governance is all about maximizing shareholder value on a sustainable basis, while ensuring fairness, transparency and accountability to customers, investors, employees, vendor-partners, the government of the land, and the society. Today, international investors have multiple choices of countries for investing – US, Europe, India, China, Australia, South East Asia, Africa and South America. Therefore, they compare us with the rest of the world before they take any decision to invest in us. Therefore, we must benchmark ourselves on a global basis. Thanks to globalization and opening up of our borders, we have multinational corporations operating in India. In general, these multinational corporations have up-to-date corporate governance practices. Therefore, Indian companies are also forced to adopt those practices. Today, our employees have global skills, aspirations and opportunities. Therefore, they seek opportunities in the best companies. If we want to retain them, we have to adopt such global best practices and perhaps improve upon them. So, because of globalization, I believe that our benchmarking in terms of how we handle our employees, customers and investors has improved. Most importantly, the importance of the price-earnings ratio has dawned on Indian businessmen. They realize that every rupee they save translates to multiple rupees in market capitalization. So, they realize that it is much better not to blur the distinction between corporate resources and personal resources.

PART ONE

THE BASICS OF FINANCIAL STATEMENTS

In this Part, you will learn the fundamentals of business and accounting from scratch.

Chapters 1– 4 introduce accounting using examples from service and trading organizations.

Chapter 1 describes business organizations and capital markets. It introduces accounting principles, standards and policies.

Chapter 2 explains the effect of business transactions and the content of financial statements and discusses the basics of financial statement analysis.

Chapter 3 shows how to process business transactions and store accounting information in formal records for efficient retrieval.

Chapter 4 develops the accounting measure of profit and brings out the difficulties in measuring revenues and expenses and allocating them to specific accounting periods.

CHAPTER 1

Business and Accounting Basics

LEARNING OBJECTIVES

After studying this chapter, you should be able to:

1. Understand the activities of business organizations.
2. Describe and evaluate the common forms of business organization.
3. Explain the importance of accounting in markets and governance.
4. Define accounting and explain its role in making economic and business decisions.
5. Identify the major users of accounting information.
6. Understand the role of accounting principles in measurement.
7. Describe the institutions that regulate and influence accounting in India.
8. Explain the relevance of Indian and international accounting standards.
9. Explain the role of accounting policies in measuring performance.
10. Appreciate the role of accountants in business and non-business organizations.
11. Understand the importance of ethics in accounting.

THE PITFALLS OF REDUCTIONISM

Business is in some ways quite simple; it has clearly defined aims. The aim is to make money. So you have a measure against which to judge all the subsidiary actions which add up to the overall result.

These words are from *The Power of Yes*, a play by Sir David Hare, the well-known British dramatist. How right is the comment? Anyone who has run a business—any business—would know that business is far from simple. Even a small business—something seemingly as straightforward as selling vegetables from a pushcart—requires complex operations. Again, the idea that business is just about making money is naïve. If a business pursues profit mindlessly by sacrificing quality and safety, it will disappear soon. Also, measuring how much money a business made—the subject of this book—can be quite complicated.

The financial crisis underscores the position that business is neither 'simple' nor is its only aim 'to make money'. If it were that clear-cut, Bear Stearns and Lehman Brothers wouldn't have evaporated.

Do a small experiment to find out whether business is simple and its aim is to make money: Try to sell something, *anything*, to someone you don't know. If you succeed, try to sell to the same person a second time.

SPEED READ

Business organizations provide products and services. Businesses may be proprietorships, partnerships or companies. Efficient markets need high quality accounting information. Accounting is the most widely spoken language of business. Investors, lenders, managers, governments and others should be able to make sense of financial statements. In order to remain strong, flourishing businesses and mighty empires need good accounting and financial control. India's growing interaction with the world requires convergence with international standards. Fraudulent and unethical accounting erodes trust in accounting. The best way to avoid fraud is to say no to it the first time.

Understanding Business Organizations

Peter Drucker, the great management philosopher, said: "With respect to the definition of business purpose and business mission, there is only one focus, one starting point. It is the customer. The customer delivers the business." Business organizations bring together materials, technology, people, and money in order to satisfy their customers' needs and thereby seek to earn a profit.

Business organizations provide products and services. They convert *inputs* into *outputs* by applying *processes*. The conventional view is that a product has form and substance, and the seller transfers it physically to the buyer. Soaps, pens, cars, computers, and medicines are examples of products that we use in our everyday lives. **Merchandising** (or **trading**) **organizations** such as Pantaloons, Wal-Mart, and Amazon buy and sell products; they don't make them. These organizations connect producers with consumers. **Manufacturing organizations** make products that vary greatly in complexity from butter and cheese (Amul) to intricate electronics (Sony) to mighty aircraft (Boeing).

A service is work done by one person that benefits another. Unlike products, services don't have form or substance. The recipient of a service can experience it personally but can't transfer it to another person. Repairing cars, hairstyling, writing computer programs, performing cardiac surgery, providing legal advice, managing hotels, and transporting passengers are familiar examples of services. **Service organizations** such as the State Bank of India, Goldman Sachs, and Lakme Beauty Salon provide professional or personal services. Increasingly, the line between products and services is disappearing. Is the iPhone, the iPad, or the Sony PlayStation a product or service? These would seem to be more of a service packaged as a product. Many of us would think of a car as a product but a significant portion of the cost of a car is the cost of embedded software that controls fuel mix, brakes and air conditioning.

HANDHOLD 1.1
Business Organizations

Business organizations provide goods and services ranging from toothpaste to fly-by-wire aircraft. Consider the following examples to get a sense of how business organizations affect our lives.

Amazon	Internet retail
Cipla	Medicines
Deloitte	Accounting, auditing, and business advice
Indigo Airlines	Air transportation
Netflix	Streaming TV shows and movies
Uber	Car-hailing service

Business organizations perform complex operations. Yet, in essence they are *cash generating-cum-dispensing machines*: they receive cash from customers for providing goods and services and pay suppliers for materials, equipment, labour, electricity and transportation. To illustrate this idea, let us think of a biotechnology firm – we will call it Nzyme Company – that produces fermentation agents for food and beverages. It hires buildings and equipment and employs scientists and other professionals. The company receives cash for sales in three ways: (a) collections for past sales, (b) receipts from current sales; and (c) advance payments for future sales. The company pays staff salaries and other benefits and pays for materials, office and factory space, electricity, laboratory supplies, and equipment. It pays income tax and other taxes to the government. It distributes a part of the surplus cash to its owners in the form of dividends. Figure 1.1 presents the activities of this business. As you can imagine, business operations are far more involved.

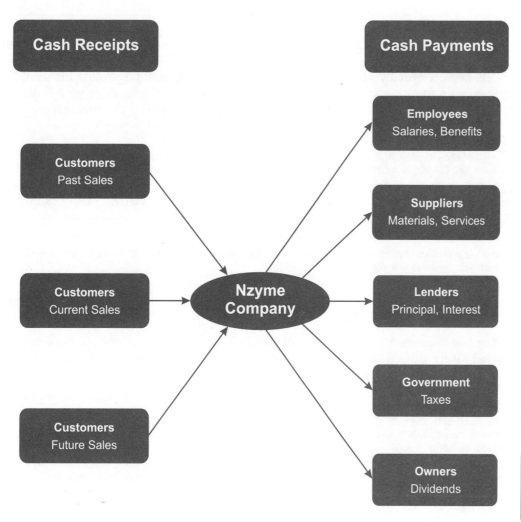

Figure 1.1
THE BUSINESS ORGANIZATION AS A CASH MACHINE

Business organizations are cash generating-cum-dispensing machines, often with leads and lags in receiving and paying cash.

TEST YOUR UNDERSTANDING 1.1
Business Organizations

Describe the business of the following organizations:
 (a) Airbnb
 (b) Paytm
 (c) Selco India
 (d) The Lending Club
 (e) Healthcare Global
 (f) Bombay Dyeing

Are business organizations good or evil?

DISCUSSION QUESTION 1.1

....
....
....

Forms of Business Organization

Learning Objective

LO 2 Describe and evaluate the common forms of business organization.

From commercial and legal angles, business may be organized in many ways. The common forms of organizing business are sole proprietorship, partnership, company, and limited liability partnership.

Sole Proprietorship

In **sole proprietorship**, a single individual carries on a business. He keeps all the profits the business earns. The sole proprietor's liability is unlimited, i.e. if the business doesn't do well, he is personally liable for paying off the debts. He could even lose his shirt. The proprietorship form is usually appropriate when the business is small or very small and is not expected to grow much. There is no specific law to regulate proprietorships.

<table>
<tr><td>

HANDHOLD 1.2
Liability of Sole
Proprietor

</td><td>

Consider the following cases.

Case A: Manasi started a proprietorship business with an investment of ₹10,000. After one year, the business has ₹15,000 in cash and owes ₹3,000 in unpaid bills. Manasi has no personal cash or debt.

Case B: Sunil started a proprietorship business with an investment of ₹10,000. After one month, the business has ₹15,000 in cash and owes ₹20,000 in unpaid bills. Sunil has personal cash of ₹8,000 and no personal debt.

This is what happens in each case.

Case A: The business has enough cash to pay its bills. Manasi doesn't need to bring in any cash. She is solvent. The business will continue.

Case B: The business is short of ₹5,000 for paying its bills. Sunil must bring in ₹5,000 from personal cash in order to pay the bills in full. After the payment, he is solvent. The business will continue. Since we are concerned with the current position, the initial investment is irrelevant.

</td></tr>
</table>

The law requires the proprietor to make good any deficiency in the business from his personal assets. If his assets fall short of the deficiency, he will be declared insolvent. The key point to note is that the law doesn't treat the proprietor as different from his business.

<table>
<tr><td>

**TEST YOUR
UNDERSTANDING 1.2**
Liability of Sole
Proprietor

</td><td>

Consider the following cases.

Case C: Preeti started a proprietorship with an investment of ₹10,000. After one year, the business has ₹15,000 in cash and ₹20,000 in unpaid bills. Preeti has personal cash of ₹2,000 and no personal debt.

Case D: Akshay started a proprietorship with an investment of ₹10,000. After three months, the business has ₹15,000 in cash and ₹20,000 in unpaid bills. Akshay has personal cash of ₹2,000 and personal debt of ₹500.

    In each case determine how much cash, if any, the proprietor must bring in.

</td></tr>
</table>

Partnership

A **partnership** has a minimum of two and a maximum of 100 persons trading together as one firm. There is no upper limit for professional practices. The partners share the firm's profits and losses equally, unless they agree otherwise. Each partner has unlimited liability for all the debts and obligations of the firm and is further responsible for the liabilities in the firm of his fellow partner or partners. This is because partnership is a mutual agency, i.e. every partner is an agent of the other partners. The Indian Partnership Act regulates partnership businesses. The regulation is minimal; even registration with the government is not a must. The partnership agreement can be oral or written. Usually, partnerships are formed by people who know and trust each other. Traditionally, many professional practices of architects, lawyers, and accountants are partnerships.

<table>
<tr><td>

HANDHOLD 1.3
Liability of Partners

</td><td>

Now consider the following cases.

Case E: Ajay and Pankaj started an equal partnership with an investment of ₹10,000 each. After two months, the business has ₹25,000 in cash and ₹18,000 in unpaid bills. Neither Ajay nor Pankaj has personal cash or debt.

Case F: Sneha and Sunayana started an equal partnership with an investment of ₹10,000 each. After three years, the business has ₹25,000 in cash and ₹30,000 in unpaid bills. Sneha and Sunayana have personal cash of ₹5,000 each and have no personal debt.

This is what happens in each case.

Case E: The business has enough cash to pay its bills. Neither Ajay nor Pankaj needs to bring in any cash. Both are solvent. The partnership and the business will continue.

</td></tr>
</table>

Case F: The business is short of ₹5,000 for paying its bills. Sneha and Sunayana must bring in ₹2,500 each from personal cash in order to pay the bills in full. Both are solvent. The partnership and the business will continue.

The law requires the partners to make good their agreed share of the deficiency in the business from their personal assets. If a partner's assets fall short of his share of the deficiency, he will be declared insolvent. The other partner(s) must make good the deficiency. The key point to note is that the law doesn't treat the partners as different from their business. Insolvency of a partner ends the partnership and the business.

Consider the following cases.

Case G: Tejas and Vinod started an equal partnership with an investment of ₹10,000 each. After one month, the business has ₹25,000 in cash and ₹30,000 in unpaid bills. Tejas has personal cash of ₹5,000; Vinod has personal cash of ₹2,500. Both have no personal debt.

Case H: Juhi and Vani started an equal partnership with an investment of ₹10,000 each. After nine months, the business has ₹25,000 in cash and ₹30,000 in unpaid bills. Juhi has personal cash of ₹8,000; Vani has personal cash of ₹500. Both have no personal debt.

In each case determine how much cash, if any, the partners must bring in.

TEST YOUR UNDERSTANDING 1.3
Liability of Partners

Company

A **company** is a legal entity unlike a sole proprietorship or partnership. Under the law, it has most of the rights of a natural person. For example, a company can buy, sell, lend and borrow. The Companies Act 2013 governs the functioning of companies. Companies must, among other things, prepare audited financial statements.

A **one-person company** has a single shareholder with limited liability. A **private limited company** must have a minimum of two shareholders and can have up to 200 shareholders. Private companies' shares are not available to the public. They have "Private Limited" as part of their names (e.g. FANUC India Private Limited). A **public limited company** must have a minimum of seven shareholders; there is no maximum. Public companies' shares are available to the public. In addition, they may be listed for trading on a stock exchange. Public companies have "Limited" as part of their names (e.g. Hindustan Unilever Limited).

The shareholders of a company undertake to contribute an agreed amount to the company's capital. This limits the liability of the members to pay the company's debts. Even if the company can't meet its debts, it can't ask for an amount above the agreed amount. Since a company's shareholders are usually strangers, they wouldn't like to assume unlimited liability for the other shareholders. Limited liability is now so common that business would be unthinkable without it.

Consider the following cases.

HANDHOLD 1.4
Liability of Shareholders

Case I: Darshak and Kshitij started a company with an agreed share capital of ₹10,000 each. They contributed ₹8,000 each. After one year, the company has ₹25,000 in cash and ₹18,000 in unpaid bills. Neither Darshak nor Kshitij has personal cash or debt.

Case J: Himanshu and Manoj started a company with an agreed share capital of ₹10,000 each. They contributed ₹10,000 each. After two months, the business has ₹25,000 in cash and ₹30,000 in unpaid bills. Himanshu and Manoj have personal cash of ₹5,000 each and have no personal debt.

This is what happens in each case.

Case I: The company has enough cash to pay its bills. Neither Darshak nor Kshitij needs to bring in any cash. Both are solvent. The business will continue.

Case J: The business is short of ₹5,000 for paying its bills. Both Himanshu and Manoj have contributed their agreed share capital. Since their liability is limited to the agreed amount, they need not bring in any cash. Both are solvent. The business ends and the company is liquidated. Bills for ₹5,000 will go unpaid.

The law requires the shareholders to contribute the amount agreed to by them. If the company's assets fall short of its liabilities, the shareholders have no legal obligation to make good the deficiency. As a result, the deficiency will go unpaid. The company will be liquidated. The shareholders will continue to be solvent. The key point to note is that the law treats the shareholders as different from their company.

Case K: Amit and David started a company with an agreed share capital of ₹10,000 each. They contributed ₹10,000 each. The business has ₹25,000 in cash and ₹30,000 in unpaid bills. Amit has personal cash of ₹5,000; David has personal cash of ₹2,500. Both have no personal debt.

Case L: Gaurav and Venkat started a company with an agreed share capital of ₹10,000 each. They contributed ₹8,000 each. The business has ₹25,000 in cash and ₹30,000 in unpaid bills. Gaurav has personal cash of ₹8,000; Venkat has personal cash of ₹500. Both have no personal debt.

In each case determine how much cash, if any, the shareholders must bring in.

Limited Liability Partnership

A limited liability partnership (LLP), created by the Limited Liability Partnership Act 2008, is a hybrid between a company and a partnership. It is a separate legal entity with perpetual existence, similar to a company. Only individuals can be partners in a partnership, but an LLP can have individuals or corporate bodies as partners. Barring fraud, the liability of the partners is limited to their shareholdings and the partners are not personally liable. An LLP must have at least two partners; there is no upper limit. Every partner of an LLP is an agent of the LLP, but is generally not bound by anything done by the other partners. An LLP may designate one or more partners as managing or executive partner for compliance with legal requirements. The LLP form is especially suitable for professional services firms. In order to meet competition from international firms, Indian firms must become bigger and better, and that means they should be able to have more than 100 partners (the limit for a partnership). Also, the partners of an LLP will have protection from professional negligence litigation. LLPs combine the flexibility of a partnership with limited liability. Many accounting and law partnerships are becoming LLPs.

Legal Formalities for a Company

Forming a company is more complicated than forming a proprietorship or partnership business. The founders (known as 'promoters' in India) of a proposed company must register it with the Registrar of Companies in the state in which the company's registered office is to be located. They must submit the memorandum of association which should include the name of the company, its objects, a statement of the limited liability of its members, the amount of share capital, and how the share capital is divided into shares. The company must also submit the articles of association which cover internal matters, such as meetings, voting, and issue of new shares. Once the legal formalities for formation of a company have been complied with, the Registrar issues a certificate of incorporation, bringing the company into existence as a separate legal entity.

Although companies are fewer in number than proprietary or partnership enterprises, they carry on a large part of the economic activity, especially large-scale trading, manufacturing and services. The main advantages of the company form of business over sole proprietary and partnership forms are limited liability, free transferability of ownership, perpetual existence, professional management, and ease of raising capital.

The Corporate Organization

The corporate organization structure consists of the shareholders, board of directors, and corporate officers. The shareholders appoint the board of directors to manage the company. Corporate officers assist the board of directors in carrying out its responsibilities to the shareholders. Figure 1.2 shows the typical organization structure of a company.

At the apex of the corporate organization are its shareholders who are the owners of a company. The capital of a company is divided into units of ownership called shares. The shares of a public company are freely transferable from one person to another. Individual shareholders generally own small numbers of shares, while institutional shareholders, such as banks, insurance companies, and mutual funds, may hold a substantial portion of the share capital. The shareholders appoint the company's directors and determine their

remuneration. They delegate the authority to manage the company to the board of directors. The shareholders appoint an individual auditor or an audit firm as the external auditor.

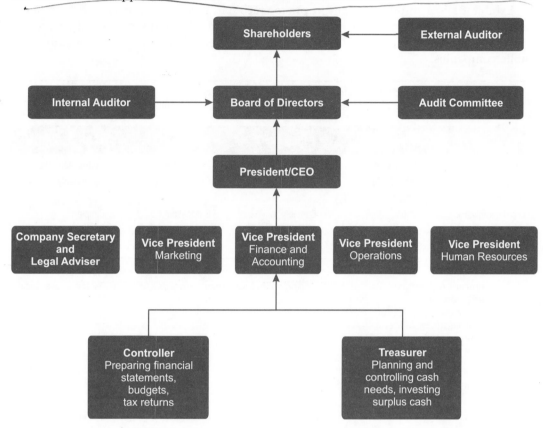

Figure 1.2
THE CORPORATE ORGANIZATION STRUCTURE

The corporate organization structure comprises the company's shareholders at the top who elect the directors, and the directors are assisted by the CEO and other officers.

The primary duties of the board of directors are to conduct the business of the company and to protect the interests of the shareholders. The directors are mainly concerned with formulating policies and monitoring the performance of the officers. Specific duties of the board include approving major contracts, recommending dividends for approval by shareholders, and fixing the salaries of officers. Typically, the board consists of company officers and outsiders.

The board of directors appoints officers to conduct the company's everyday business. Executives usually included in this group are the **chief executive officer** (president or managing director), several vice-presidents, a treasurer, a controller, and a company secretary. The **chief financial officer** (or vice-president, finance and accounting) has overall responsibility for financial management and accounting and auditing matters. The **controller** is the chief accounting officer of the company and is responsible for the maintenance of accounting records and preparation of financial statements, budgets, and tax returns. The **treasurer** is the custodian of the company's funds and is responsible for planning and controlling the company's cash position. The **company secretary** maintains minutes for meetings of directors and shareholders, represents the company in many legal matters and ensures compliance with laws. The **internal auditor** reviews the company's financial and other decisions and reports his findings to the board. The designations of the officers may differ from company to company.

Who appoints a company's external auditor? For how long?

QUICK QUESTION
External auditor

Selecting a Form of Business Organization

Before you choose a form of business organization, you should consider a number of factors such as the owner's need for control, growth plans, capital requirements, government regulation, and taxation. Businesses often start as proprietorships or partnerships and grow to become large corporations.

Exhibit 1.1 is a run-through of proprietorship, partnership, company, and LLP. Other forms of business organization in India include the Hindu undivided family, statutory corporation, mutual association, and cooperative society. This book deals mainly with public companies.

EXHIBIT 1.1
Forms of Business
Organization

Businesses differ in ease of starting, flexibility in decision-making, access to capital requirement, extent of regulation, and liability.			
	Proprietorship	**Partnership**	**Company**	**LLP**
Getting started	Instant start	Near-instant start	Takes time	Near-instant start
Decision-making	Highly flexible	Reasonably flexible	Constrained	Reasonably flexible
Raising capital	Difficult	Difficult	Easy	Difficult
Legal compliance	Simple	Simple	Burdensome	Simple
Owners' liability	Unlimited	Unlimited	Limited	Limited
Suitability	Small business	Mid-sized business	Large business	Professional services

ONE-MINUTE QUIZ 1.1
Accounting Records

Who is primarily responsible for the maintenance of accounting records? There may be more than one correct answer.
(a) Chief executive officer.
(b) Chief financial officer.
(c) Controller.
(d) Treasurer.

DISCUSSION QUESTION 1.2

Should business go public or remain private?

....

....

....

> ## Accounting, Markets and Governance

Learning Objective

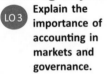

LO 3 Explain the importance of accounting in markets and governance.

Let us do a thought experiment. Suppose you have identified a highly cost-effective technology for generating solar power. This project requires an initial investment of ₹100 million. Your own savings and even generous support from your relatives and friends are not anywhere near this amount. You know that many individuals are interested in clean energy projects. You approach them with your detailed project proposal, colourful promotional material, and superb multimedia presentation. Many of them tell you about how they invested in ventures relying on entrepreneurs' promises of wonderful returns but finally did not get back even their initial investment. "Of course, we don't mean to question your intentions or competence," they add politely, as they lead you to the door. "Just that we don't know whom to trust." You have a good project but you can't find the money for it. The anecdote may sound familiar to many entrepreneurs. But as we will see shortly, the story doesn't necessarily have to end this way.

The Lemons Principle and the Problem of Adverse Selection

The inability of an entrepreneur to find funds is a classic case of the working of the **lemons principle**: the presence of people in the market offering inferior goods tends to drive the market out of existence, if it is difficult to separate good quality from bad. The principle was first formally stated by George A. Akerlof, Professor of Economics at the University of California, Berkeley in one of the most cited economics papers – the paper won him the Nobel Prize.[1]

To understand how the lemons principle works, think of the market for used cars. Potential buyers know less about the quality of used cars than the sellers, a condition referred to as *information asymmetry*. If we assume that half the used cars are of good quality and the rest are bad (known as 'lemons' in the used-car market), buyers have a 50:50 chance of getting a good car or a lemon. Assume that the worth of a good car is ₹100,000 and that of a lemon is ₹50,000. The price the buyers would be willing to pay would be roughly equal to the weighted average of the prices for good cars and lemons. In our example, this would be ₹75,000, calculated as follows: ₹100,000 × 0.5 + ₹50,000 × 0.5. As this average price is less than the true worth of good cars, some sellers of good cars will leave the market. However, sellers of lemons will remain because the price is attractive: after all, their cars are worth ₹50,000, but they stand a chance of getting ₹75,000. The market now has a larger proportion of lemons, say 60 per cent. As a result, the average price will fall below the previous average. In our example, the average price will now become ₹70,000. Some more sellers of good cars will now leave the market. This process repeats until the market has only lemons. When this happens, buyers refuse to buy used cars.

The lemons principle is at work in **adverse selection**, a process by which 'undesirable' buyers or sellers are more likely to participate in a market. It can be applied to a variety of settings including the capital market. The capital market consists of entrepreneurs (sellers of business ideas) and savers or potential investors (buyers of those ideas). An entrepreneur may be either good or bad. As savers are unable to spot good entrepreneurs, they offer a weighted average price for the investments. That price would be too low for good entrepreneurs and they will leave the market, as a result of which there will be a larger proportion of bad entrepreneurs in the market. In the end, there will be only bad entrepreneurs, but savers will refuse to part with their funds and the capital market will break down. In a corporate setting, firms and managers substitute for entrepreneurs.

Signalling Quality

All of us know that vibrant capital markets exist in Mumbai, London, New York and in many other financial centres of the world. So, what makes these markets work despite the lemons principle? We find the answer in a well-known paper by Michael Spence, Professor of Economics at Stanford University – he was awarded the Nobel Prize for this research.[2] Professor Spence argued that job applicants with superior skills or abilities would invest time and resources in acquiring superior educational qualifications in order to distinguish themselves from less skilled applicants. This is **signalling**.

Signals should be costly in order to be effective. If signals are costless, everyone can send them; so the signal is of no use. For example, if you want to become a successful academic, you will invest time and resources in getting admission to the PhD programme of a good university and complete the programme. This is a costly signal because a less competent person has a low chance of completing a doctorate from such an institution. In the used-car example, a seller of a good car could give a performance warranty for a certain period of time. Signalling mitigates information asymmetry. Here are two recent examples of signalling:

---

[1] George A. Akerlof, The market for 'lemons': Quality uncertainty and the market mechanism, *Quarterly Journal of Economics*, August 1970. Interestingly, one of the illustrations of the lemons principle in the paper relates to the practice of adulterating rice with stones by Indian shopkeepers and the resultant costs of dishonesty to the buyer and to honest business.

[2] Michael Spence, Job market signalling, *Quarterly Journal of Economics*, August 1973.

- In August 2014, Tesla Motors increased the warranty on Model S electric motors to match that of the battery pack. So the company's most popular model now has an 8-year, infinite mile warranty on both the battery pack and motors. There is also no limit on the number of owners during the warranty period.
- In February 2015, Huawei, the Chinese technology group, appointed former BP chief executive Lord Browne to head a UK board of directors that will oversee British operations to dispel concerns over its corporate governance.

Extending Professor Spence's idea of educational signalling to the capital market, good entrepreneurs and managers can differentiate themselves in a number of ways, such as consistently paying higher dividends, giving credible guarantees of higher returns, appointing reputable accounting firms to audit their financial statements, having respectable outsiders as independent directors, and conforming to superior standards of accounting and disclosure. All these are costly signals because incompetent or dishonest managers can't mimic these signals in much the same way an unintelligent person can't complete PhD from a top school.

High quality financial reporting mitigates the problem of adverse selection by reducing information asymmetry and thus facilitates orderly functioning of the capital market, making it possible for entrepreneurs to raise funds at reasonable rates and investors to earn fair returns. Accounting standards, managerial behaviour, and audit quality determine the quality of accounting information. A well-organized capital market guided by reliable public information encourages people to save and invest, leading to greater production of goods and services and higher employment, and thus contributes significantly to the economic advancement of people. On the contrary, when markets are driven by manipulated financial numbers or wild expectations, they are prone to frequent speculative bubbles that inevitably burst and cause enormous damage to investor wealth and confidence. Enron has become the byword for accounting manipulation. India had Satyam. The dotcom bubble of the 1990s is an example of investors going by hopes of incredible growth prospects rather than sound business and financial information. When Bernard Madoff's Ponzi scheme failed, the investors lost $20 billion. Bitcoins, emu farms and the Saradha chit fund are other examples of Ponzi schemes. In a Ponzi scheme, early investors are paid high returns with money invested by later investors. The promise of high returns lures more investors. Since the returns are unrealistic, the scheme is bound to collapse soon.

Moral Hazard and Corporate Governance

Moral hazard describes a situation where a decision-maker takes unwarranted risks or puts in inadequate effort because he or she has been provided with some kind of safety net. For example, individuals may not park their cars securely or drive carefully when their cars are insured; financial traders often gamble to earn large bonuses, because the penalty for losing money is mild. Suppose you have invested in a business. With your cash now firmly in their pockets, the managers may not only stop exerting themselves to the point of being indifferent to selection of projects but may even give themselves an executive jet, high managerial pay and generous perquisites, and huge separation benefits. This is an example of moral hazard.

The separation of ownership and management in the corporate form increases the chances of managers pursuing their goals and interests, rather than those of the shareholders. This results in **agency costs**, a term for the ill-effects of the disconnect between managers' and shareholders' interests. The following quote from Adam Smith's classic sums up this point:

> The directors of such [public] companies, however, being the managers rather of other people's money than of their own, it can't well be expected that they should watch over it with the same anxious vigilance with which the partners in a private co-partnership frequently

watch over their own. Like the stewards of a rich man, they are apt to consider attention to small matters as not for their master's honour, and very easily give themselves a dispensation from having it. Negligence and profusion, therefore, must always prevail, more or less, in the management of the affairs of such a company.[3]

Accounting plays an important role in dealing with this problem by disciplining managerial actions. Executive compensation contracts specify performance standards in accounting terms, such as net profit and return on investment. If a minimum level of profitability is specified, managers would select only projects that are at or above that level and reject 'bad' projects. As a result, accounting becomes a key instrument for motivating, directing, monitoring and evaluating managerial performance and, thus, ensuring good corporate governance. Insurance companies levy substantial additional premium after a claim to discourage careless driving; shareholders stipulate clawback of traders' bonuses to restrain them from taking excessive risks.

Financial markets exist to transfer capital from investors to entities that need funding and to provide liquidity. By providing high quality information in a timely manner, accounting enables business organizations to raise capital on fair terms and makes them utilize the capital efficiently.

You have to appoint a new chief executive for five years. How can you reduce the chances of moral hazard? There may be more than one correct answer.

(a) Relate pay to performance.
(b) Require external auditing.
(c) Screen the job applications with the help of a reputable consultant.
(d) Require a degree from a top school.

ONE-MINUTE QUIZ 1.2
Agency Costs

Considering that managers' and owners' interests are quite different, why has the corporate form survived?

DISCUSSION QUESTION 1.3

....

....

....

What is Accounting

Accounting is as old as human civilization. Early accounting records have been found in archaeological sites in Mesopotamia, India, Egypt, Greece, Rome, and other places. Historically, accounting acted as a check on the working of village councils and local business organizations. People would assemble in a common area to hear the statement of revenue and expenses read out by the village leader. Over time, they appointed a respectable individual as their representative to hear the statement and ask questions. That person was known as the auditor. The word "auditor" comes from the Latin root "audire" meaning to hear. In many temples in India, the administrator reads out the statement of daily collections and expenses in the shrine of the deity. Thus, accounting is relevant to both secular and religious institutions.

Accounting is one of the fastest-growing professions and ranks among the most popular fields of study. It offers interesting, challenging, and rewarding careers. Business enterprises, government agencies, charities, and individuals need information to make sound decisions. The accounting system provides relevant and reliable financial information to interested parties.

Accounting is often called the *language of business*. The function of a language is to facilitate communication among individuals in a society. Accounting is the common

Learning Objective

LO 4 Define accounting and explain its role in making economic and business decisions.

_____
[3] Adam Smith, *The Wealth of Nations*.

language used to communicate financial information in the world of business. Clearly, individuals who aspire to be professional accountants should be experts in accounting. Many others, such as investors, managers, employees, civil servants, police investigators, lawyers, judges, doctors and regulators, have to constantly deal with business organizations. All of them should have good knowledge of accounting terms, principles and techniques.

At the beginning of my full-time and executive MBA classes I ask the students: "Why should you know accounting?" Here are some typical responses (besides the unstated one, "It is in the curriculum, so I have no choice."):

- Since a company's financial statements affect stock prices, a manager should know accounting.
- I plan to be in corporate strategy. Without accounting numbers strategy won't make sense.
- I want to be an investment banker. I want to use accounting information to value firms.
- I was in marketing. Profitability analysis was an important part of my job. I want to learn it formally.
- I am going to do a start-up. I want to manage the accounting and finance function of my business.
- Using financial numbers I can analyze cases in marketing, operations and strategy better.
- The law requires the CEO and the CFO, to certify the financial statements. As a CEO, I should know what the items in the statements mean.

Managers have a responsibility to provide truthful, relevant and timely information. The MBA Oath initiated by the students of Harvard Business School has this to say on reporting:

> I will report the performance and risks of my enterprise accurately and honestly.

After what happened in the technology bubble of the 1990s and the global financial crisis in 2008, managers need to reassure everyone that their enterprises' financial reports are trustworthy. For this, they should have a sound understanding of financial statements.

Accounting is a principal means of communicating financial information to owners, lenders, managers, and many others who have an interest in an enterprise. It is not an end in itself. Indeed, this book presents accounting as *an information development and communication function that supports economic decision-making*.

The Accounting Information System

Accounting is an information system. Like any system, it converts inputs into outputs using processes. Business transactions and events are the input of the accounting system. Investment by owner, sale of goods, payment of salaries, collection from customers, payment of taxes, and loss of goods are examples of transactions and events.

The accounting process involves applying policies, assumptions, laws, and mechanics. To get a sense of the accounting process consider these sample questions:

- What should be the life of a computer for accounting purposes?
- Does a business earn revenue on receipt of customer order, delivery of goods or services, or payment by customer?
- What information should a business disclose to its investors?
- What is the income tax rate for a business?

You can answer them by applying accounting principles to the related transaction. The next step is to record the transaction appropriately. The output of the accounting information system includes the financial statements, management commentary, tax returns, and regulatory filings. Figure 1.3 depicts the accounting information system.

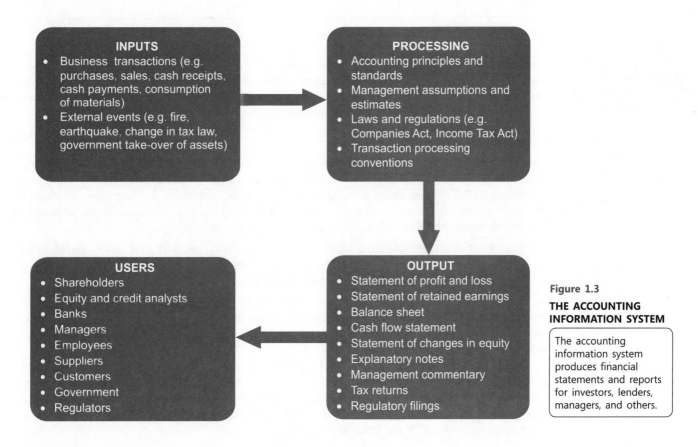

Figure 1.3

THE ACCOUNTING INFORMATION SYSTEM

The accounting information system produces financial statements and reports for investors, lenders, managers, and others.

Accounting Information and Economic Decisions

Accounting information is useful in making a number of decisions that affect the income or wealth of individuals and organizations. Accounting reports, or *general purpose financial reports*, are designed to meet the common information needs of most decision-makers. The information given in a language can be useful only to persons who understand that language. For example, if a restaurant's menu is in Italian, a customer should know enough Italian to be able to make sense of the items and their ingredients. In the same way, decision-makers should understand the language of accounting and its intricacies. Accounting is an indispensable part of their life.

Financial and Management Accounting

The accounting system provides information to persons inside and outside the enterprise. Financial accounting is the preparation and communication of financial information for use primarily by those outside the enterprise. Its chief purpose is to provide information about the performance of the enterprise's management to its owners. Management accounting is the preparation and communication of financial and other information to help managers plan and control operations. Management accounting information is more detailed and timely than what is available to external users

Which of the following is likely to be the subject of a financial accounting report? There may be more than one correct answer.

    (a) Waste caused by abnormal evaporation.

    (b) Cost of carrying excessive inventories.

    (c) Amount spent on research and development activities.

    (d) Sales forecast.

ONE-MINUTE QUIZ 1.3

Financial and Management Accounting

Users of Accounting Information

Learning Objective

LO 5 Identify the major users of accounting information.

Financial reports have diverse users. Investors and lenders are the most obvious users. Other users include analysts, advisers, managers, employees, trade unions, suppliers, customers, governments, regulatory agencies, and the public. Business enterprises increasingly report on their economic, social and environmental impact.

Investors

Investors are the major recipients of the financial statements of business enterprises. They may be retail investors with small shareholdings or large mutual funds, hedge funds or private equity firms. As chief providers of risk capital, investors are keen to understand the profitability of their investments and the associated risks, i.e. the likelihood of loss or low profit. Investors want accurate and timely financial statements.

- A joint ASSOCHAM and Grant Thornton survey revealed that cases of financial fraud have risen in India over the last few years and have become one of the main factors deterring foreign companies from investing in India.[4]

Accounting information enables investors to identify promising investment opportunities. Investors need information to decide which investments to buy, hold or sell. They also require information to monitor management performance and assess the ability of an enterprise to pay dividends.

While present investors have a legal right to receive periodic financial reports, potential investors too are interested in financial information. Private equity funds are on the lookout for investing in ailing businesses they can restructure and sell at a substantial profit. Hedge funds use accounting and other information to earn high profits. Activist investors seek to force managers to act in the interests of shareholders.

Lenders

Lenders such as banks and debenture holders want to know about the financial stability of a business that approaches them for funds. They are interested in information that would enable them to determine whether their borrowers will be able to repay the loans and pay the related interest on time.

Banks use credit evaluation benchmarks based on information derived from financial statements when deciding on the amount of the loan, interest rate, repayment period, and security. They also use the information for monitoring the financial condition of borrowers. Thus, many lenders stipulate dos and don'ts, or *covenants*, for borrowers that often require the use of accounting information. For example, a loan agreement may impose an upper limit on a borrower's total debt from all sources or compel the borrower to keep a minimum level of cash. If a borrower fails to comply with the stipulations, the lender may raise the interest rate, ask for additional security, and even demand repayment of the loan.

- Banks run the risk of lending based on fraudulent financial statements. A consortium of banks ordered forensic audit into the books of account of Bhushan Steel. The development followed the arrest of Bhushan Steel's Vice-Chairman and Managing Director Neeraj Singal by the CBI in the alleged cash-for-loan scam, involving Syndicate Bank Chairman S.K. Jain. The forensic audit would investigate whether the company used loans for the right purpose or there was diversion of funds.[5]

Analysts and Advisers

Equity analysts, bond analysts, stockbrokers, and credit rating agencies offer a wide array of

---

[4] Grant Thornton and ASSOCHAM, *Financial and Corporate Frauds,* July 2016, New Delhi.
[5] Bankers order forensic audit of Bhushan Steel, *The Hindu,* August 19, 2014.

information services. These specialists serve the needs of investors by providing them with skilled analyses and interpretation of financial reports. Analysts also collect information through face-to-face meetings and conference calls with company executives and field visits. *Sell-side analysts* work for brokerages, banks and research firms who use their reports to make recommendations to their clients. In contrast, *buy-side analysts* are employed in mutual funds and other investment firms and produce research reports for in-house use by their employers. Proxy advisory firms tell shareholders whether they should support or oppose resolutions proposed by the board of directors.

Managers and Directors

Managers not only prepare the financial statements but also use the statements. For example, they need financial information for planning and controlling operations, making special decisions and formulating major plans and policies. They monitor the key financial indicators of the business and compare their firm's performance with their competitors'. They may be interested in acquiring other firms.

Increasingly, managers receive a commission or bonus related to profit or other accounting measures. A CEO compensation survey of 380 companies in India shows that more than half of the CEO pay is tied to performance.[6] So managers have a natural interest in understanding how those numbers are computed.

Further, when faced with a hostile takeover attempt, managers communicate additional information with a view to boosting their firm's stock price. As you can imagine, managerial motives in financial reporting can vary depending on the context of the business, and can conflict with those of investors and other users of financial statements.

Under the Companies Act, a company's directors are responsible for financial reporting. Their responsibilities include applying accounting standards and policies, maintaining accounting records, preventing and detecting fraud, preparing the financial statements on a going concern basis, laying down internal financial controls, and devising systems for compliance with laws and regulations. Therefore, directors need a good understanding of accounting.

In the fiscal year ended March 31, 2016 (FY16), many leading banks reported losses or drastically lower profits. This resulted mainly from the substantially higher provisions for bad loans resulting from the Reserve Bank of India's asset quality review (AQR). Axis Bank bucked the trend by reporting a net profit of ₹73 billion in FY16, an increase of nearly 12 per cent over FY15. Since all banks swim in the same pool, this raised a few eyebrows. Along with its fourth quarter results for FY16 (Q4FY16), Axis Bank released a 'watch list' of standard loans of ₹226 billion. The bank had stated earlier that though the RBI had given two quarters to disclose and provide for the additional loans, it had taken the full impact in Q3FY16 itself. A commentator questioned whether the bank was trying to keep reporting consistent rise in profits as it increases the share price and justifies huge management remuneration in the form of salary, bonus and stock options.[7]

FINANCIAL VIEW
Questioning Performance

Employees and Trade Unions

Employees are keen to know about their employer's general operations, stability and profitability. Current employees have a natural interest in the financial condition of an enterprise because their jobs and salaries depend on its financial performance. Profitable businesses attract adverse notice when their employees are not seen to be benefiting from their success.

- When McDonald's Corporation reported a 35 per cent increase in profits for the first quarter of 2016, its wage increase of $1 over the local minimum wage was seen as feeble.[8]

---

[6] Saumya Bhattacharya, As companies get performance-driven, India Inc CEOs could soon lose comfort of fixed pay, *The Economic Times*, April 26, 2016.

[7] Hemendra Hazari, "Axis Bank's watch list – Guardrails or illusion?", *The Wire*, June 3, 2016.

[8] Editorial, At McDonald's, fat profits but lean wages, The New York Times, April 28, 2016.

Potential employees may use financial information in order to gauge an enterprise's prospects. Past employees, who depend on their former employer for their post-retirement benefits, such as pensions and health care, have a continuing interest in its performance and prospects. Trade unions use financial reports for negotiating enhancements in wages, bonus and other benefits. Union leaders are often as good as, if not better than, analysts at dissecting financial statements.

- Unions understand that their members can't do well unless their employers prosper. For instance, the All India Bank of Baroda Officers' Association's tagline is "Grow with the bank – Our bank grows, we grow."

Suppliers and Trade Financiers

Suppliers regard a firm as an outlet for their products and services. They use financial information to assess the likelihood of the enterprise continuing to buy from them, especially if it is a major customer. Suppliers plan their production and capacity on the basis of expected demand. Trade financiers provide short-term financial support. Suppliers and trade financiers want information to determine whether the enterprise will pay them on the dot. While lenders take a long-term view, suppliers and trade financiers usually focus on the enterprise's near-term financial condition.

Customers

Present, prospective and past customers need information to evaluate the financial strength of their suppliers. Customers would like to be certain that they can count on their suppliers for future purchases and after-sales support. This is particularly important for products and services that are proprietary. For example, car owners depend on the manufacturer for warranty repairs and continued supply of spare parts. Computer software users look to the software firm for periodic upgrade of the product. When an airline keeps losing money, customers begin to worry about the possibility of flight cancellations, the fate of their mileage points and even aircraft safety. Insurance policyholders need confidence that their insurer will have the financial resources to pay their claims.

- When Satyam Computer Services was hit by an accounting scandal, some of its important clients were concerned and began to review their contracts and look at other suppliers.

However, when suppliers make large profits, customers may suspect that they are being fleeced. For example, if your mobile phone company makes huge profits, you would like the company to cut call charges. Companies have to respond to customers' perceptions of profiteering by behaving in morally acceptable ways.

- Pharmaceutical companies routinely face criticism for "price gouging". In 2015, Gilead Science's hepatitis C drugs, Harvoni and Solvani, are seen as "miracle drugs", offering cure rates of over 94 per cent. But the cost of a pill at $1,125, or a 12-week treatment cost of $94,500, attracted the adverse comments from politicians and doctors. Pharmaceutical companies argue that high drug prices allow them to find new treatments.

Auditors

Auditors provide assurance on the reliability of accounting information. Their reputation depends on the quality of their clients' financial statements. They would not want to certify the financial statements of companies suspected of fraudulent or questionable accounting practices. Increasingly, auditors are sued or pulled up for negligence. Professional indemnity insurance has become a must for auditors and the premium is higher for those seen to be having risky clients. Auditors may resign when they think the risks are unacceptable.

- In July 2016, Deloitte resigned as the auditor of 1Malaysia Development Berhad (1MDB) when there were investigations into alleged money laundering by the Malaysian fund in several countries. The fund said that its audited financial statements for 2013 and 2014 shouldn't be relied on.

Government and Regulatory Authorities

The three levels of government in India – central, state and local – allocate resources and are concerned with the activities of enterprises. They require information in order to regulate the business practices of enterprises, determine taxation policies, investigate crime, and provide a basis for national income and similar statistics.

The Ministry of Corporate Affairs (MCA) is among those in the Government of India that take a keen interest in the financial affairs of business enterprises. The Serious Fraud Investigation Office (SFIO) attached to the MCA investigates corporate fraud. The Ministry of Finance is concerned with tax administration and the working of the economy. The two major tax authorities in India are the Central Board of Direct Taxes (CBDT) and the Central Board of Excise and Customs (CBEC). The CBDT administers the income tax law. The CBEC administers central excise and customs duties, service tax, and goods and services tax. Increasingly, tax authorities deal with complex transactions involving international taxation and transfer pricing. Proper accounting and recordkeeping are essential for effective tax administration.

- Multinational companies use transfer pricing to determine revenue earned in different countries. Tax authorities are concerned that the companies may be using transfer pricing to move their profits from high-tax countries to low-tax countries. For instance, in 2016, Facebook agreed to report sales linked to its British operations, primarily from digital advertising, through UK subsidiary, instead of booking its British revenues through its subsidiary in low-tax Ireland. Other tech giants such as Google and Apple have also been faulted for paying low or no taxes.

A number of regulatory agencies are government or quasi-government bodies, such as the Securities and Exchange Board of India (SEBI), the Reserve Bank of India (RBI), the Insurance Regulatory and Development Authority of India (IRDAI), the Telecom Regulatory Authority of India (TRAI), and the Competition Commission of India (CCI). These agencies use financial reports in order to identify abuses and violations and to protect the interests of investors and consumers. SEBI stipulates extensive disclosures in the financial statements and offer documents. IRDAI requires life and non-life insurance companies to provide public disclosures of accounting practices, valuation of investments, and pension and post-retirement obligations, so that policyholders and investors can understand the financial health of their insurer. Others such as stock exchanges have a legitimate interest in financial reports of publicly held enterprises to ensure efficient operation of capital markets.

The Public

The activities of business enterprises affect the members of the public in a variety of ways. For example, businesses employ people from the local community and patronize local suppliers; so the prosperity of the local community depends on their success. It is said that whenever the software industry slows down, business in upmarket restaurants and pubs in Bengaluru falls. Financial statements assist the public by providing information about the trends and recent developments in the prosperity of the enterprise and the range of its activities. Political parties, public affairs groups, consumer groups, newspapers and magazines, television channels, anti-globalization and anti-business activists and environment protection groups have a general interest in the affairs of business enterprises. The nature and extent of their interest often vary considerably. They use the information in the financial statements to put forward their point of view. Extractive industries such as oil, gas and mining are frequent targets of attack on the basis of their profits that activist groups argue are ill-gotten. Of course, investment banks are always under attack for a variety of reasons.

- When there was a blowout in the Deep Horizon well in the Gulf of Mexico in 2010, the profits of BP and other large oil companies came under public scrutiny.

Exhibit 1.2 summarizes the major users of accounting information and their information needs. Whether someone is a legitimate user of accounting information differs from one country to another. For example, in the US and the UK, financial statements are meant primarily for shareholders and lenders. But countries in Continental Europe, such as Germany, France and Sweden, explicitly recognize employees and trade unions as having a stake in financial reports.

REAL WORLD
Scandals in Sports

Sports scandals have become as gripping as sports.

- The goal of Fédération Internationale de Football Association (FIFA) is the "constant improvement of football". Lately, FIFA has been in the news for other things. In October 2015, the Swiss authorities opened a criminal investigation into a Swiss Franc 2 million payment from FIFA to Michel Platini, the president of Uefa. The Swiss authorities' investigations focused on the payment made in 2011 by Sepp Blatter, FIFA's president for 17 years, to Mr. Platini, allegedly for work performed between 1999 and 2002. Domenico Scala, the head of FIFA's audit committee, said the agreement had not been recorded in FIFA's accounts until the payment occurred. "That is a serious omission, and both parties were members of FIFA's executive committee and knowingly approved each year financial statements, which were incorrect by SFr2m. That could be seen as falsification of the accounts", said Mr. Scala. In the midst of all of this, Mr. Blatter was re-elected for another term as FIFA's president in May 2015 but he changed his mind a few days later saying that he would lay down his mandate. In 2016, FIFA announced reforms "designed to help FIFA in rebuilding and restoring trust after the difficult challenges of the past year." In June 2016, KPMG, FIFA's auditor for over ten years resigned stating that the new management was not serious about reform.

- Closer home, the Board of Control for Cricket in India (BCCI) was embroiled in allegations of misdeeds. It began as a betting scandal in the Indian Premier League but the financial affairs of BCCI and State cricket associations came under scrutiny. The cricket associations in Delhi, Assam, Goa and Jammu and Kashmir reportedly committed irregularities in financial reporting and tax payment. The Supreme Court appointed a committee headed by R M Lodha, a former Chief Justice of India, to recommend measures to reform the sports body. In 2016, the committee suggested revamping of BCCI's accounting, auditing, internal control and governance.

Investors, lenders and many others use accounting information to make important economic decisions.

EXHIBIT 1.2
Users of Accounting Information

Users	Examples	Queries/Concerns
Investors, analysts, advisers	Retail investors Mutual funds, private equity funds, hedge funds Equity analysts and bond analysts Credit rating agencies Investment banks Shareholder activists Proxy advisory firms	■ Should I buy, hold or sell the company's shares? ■ Will the investment yield good dividends regularly? ■ Is the enterprise in which I have invested, or thinking of investing, performing well? ■ Are there governance problems in the company? ■ Are the shares a good medium- to long-term investment?
Lenders	Banks Bank depositors Debenture holders Leasing companies	■ Can my borrower pay the principal and interest on time? ■ What should be the security and interest rate for a loan?
Managers and directors	Chief executive officers Chief finance officers Marketing managers Production managers Profit centre heads	■ How is my business performing relative to my competitors? ■ What projects should I invest in? ■ Do the financial reports communicate my firm's true value? ■ Will it be profitable for me to buy out my business?
Employees, trade unions	Factory and office workers Trade unions Trade union federations	■ How much increase in wages and bonus can my employer afford? ■ Can my employer continue to be in business? ■ Can my employer honour its future obligations for pension, health and other post-retirement benefits?
Suppliers, trade financiers	Suppliers of materials, services and utilities Short-term financiers	■ Will my customer be a major source of business? ■ Can my customer pay for its purchases on time?
Customers	Present, past and prospective customers	■ Is my supplier a reliable and competitive source? ■ Can I count on my supplier to provide spare parts for equipment? ■ Does my supplier have the financial resources to honour its warranty obligations?
Auditors	Present, past and prospective auditors	■ How reliable are my client's internal control systems? ■ Are the financial statements likely to be affected by fraud? ■ Are the shareholders and creditors likely to sue us for audit failure?
Government, regulatory authorities	Income tax officers Excise, customs, and service tax officers Commercial tax officers Ministry of Finance Ministry of Corporate Affairs Securities and Exchange Board of India Reserve Bank of India Competition Commission of India Stock exchanges Insurance Regulatory and Development Authority	■ Is a business evading income tax, excise duty, service tax, sales tax or other government levies? ■ Should the government subsidize an industry, increase taxes, or give it protection from dumping? ■ Does a bank follow prudent financial norms? ■ Does a business make required disclosures of its financial affairs? ■ Does a business make abnormal profits by stifling competition in its industry? ■ Does an insurance company follow prudential norms?
The public	Local community Political parties Public affairs groups Consumer groups Environmental activists	■ Does a business exploit local suppliers, small businesses or labour? ■ Does a business earn profits by compromising on product safety or damaging the environment? ■ Is a business abusing its monopoly by overcharging its customers?

ONE-MINUTE QUIZ 1.4
Users of Financial
Statements

Who gives recommendations to outsiders to buy or sell investments? There may be more than one correct answer.

(a) Buy-side analysts.
(b) Sell-side analysts.
(c) Crediting rating analysts.
(d) Proxy advisory firms.

**DISCUSSION
QUESTION 1.4**

How can companies help non-professional users understand their financial statements and related information?

....

....

....

Accounting Principles

Learning Objective

LO 6 Understand the role of accounting principles in measurement.

Accounting, the language of business, facilitates communication of financial information. Like any language, accounting has rules. These include assumptions, principles, standards and conventions. Accounting records transactions and events. Some transactions involve an exchange, such as buying equipment for cash, selling goods on credit, and collecting cash from customers. Others involve a one-way transfer, such as giving or receiving a gift and paying income tax. Events such as earthquake and expropriation of assets by the government result in a loss.

Accounting records transactions and events that result in a present benefit or obligation. No doubt, launching new brands, appointing talented managers, and identifying profitable business opportunities are important for a business. Unfortunately, accounting doesn't have the tools to measure and report on them.

The information contained in financial reports should be reliable and intelligible. Besides, we should be able to make meaningful comparisons between a firm's past financial history and the financial information of other firms. Therefore, we need a body of concepts and a set of practices to guide business enterprises in preparing financial reports. The conventions, assumptions, concepts and rules which define accepted accounting practice constitute **generally accepted accounting principles (GAAP)**. GAAP represents the fundamental positions that have been generally agreed upon, often tacitly and ambiguously, by accountants and encompasses contemporary permissible accounting practice. GAAP assures us of the reliability and comparability of accounting information. Unlike the laws of physics or chemistry, accounting principles and practices are not the product of any laboratory research. They have evolved in response to the needs of the users of information.

We will begin with the following conventions or assumptions that underlie accounting measurement in GAAP: reporting entity, going concern, periodicity and money measurement.

Reporting Entity

A **reporting entity** is the subject of a set of financial statements. Accountants treat a business as separate from its owners and other related firms. The reporting entity defines the scope of the activities to be included in the financial statements. It may be a business, a legal entity, a group, or a segment.

- *Business:* The financial statements of a proprietorship or partnership business should deal with only the business enterprise's transactions and should exclude the proprietor's or partners' personal financial affairs. Suppose Seema owns a boutique. She should keep separate accounting records for her business activities in order to know how the business is doing. Her personal revenues, expenses, possessions and debts should not appear in the business records.

- *Legal entity:* Companies are legal entities. The law requires each legal entity to prepare financial statements. For example, Hindustan Unilever Limited (HUL) and its subsidiary, Pond's Exports Limited, are separate legal entities, though they are part of the same group. Therefore, HUL and its subsidiaries prepare their *standalone financial statements*. So each of them is a reporting entity.

- *Group:* A reporting entity can be a group of interconnected enterprises. Thus, the Hindustan Unilever Group prepares *consolidated financial statements* for the group by combining the financial statements of the individual companies, such as HUL and Pond's Exports Limited. The consolidated financial statements of the Anglo-Dutch Unilever Group comprise the likes of the Hindustan Unilever Group from around the world.

- *Segment:* Business or geographical segments can be reporting entities. For example, HUL reports the performance of its businesses such as soaps and detergents, personal products, and beverages. The business segments of Tata Consultancy Services are banking, financial services and insurance, manufacturing, retail and distribution, and telecom. IBM provides information on a geographical basis for the Americas, Europe/Middle East/Africa and Asia Pacific.

Going Concern

Unless there is substantial evidence to the contrary, accountants assume that a business is a continuing enterprise or **going concern**. The assumption makes sense because many businesses survive difficult economic circumstances. The going concern assumption is critical to the users of an entity's financial statements.

- In 2015, the auditors of GMR Infrastructure Limited (the developer of the Delhi airport) questioned whether the company was a going concern because of disputes and arbitration proceedings involving group companies.

- In 2009, the auditors of General Motors, the automobile company, warned about the company's viability to continue as a going concern without more US government loans, making it difficult for the company to negotiate with its lenders. GM's shares fell by 15 per cent as a result.

When preparing financial statements, management should review the going concern assumption. It should disclose any material uncertainties related to events or conditions that may cast significant doubt on the ability of the business to continue as a going concern. Suppose an enterprise has to repay a ₹100 million loan in the next three months but doesn't have that much cash and won't be able to raise the amount by the payment date. The management hopes that the lender will renew the loan for a two-year period. If the renewal is in doubt, there is a going concern uncertainty that must be disclosed. Persistent losses may call for a going concern rethink. When an entity doesn't prepare its financial statements on a going concern basis, it should disclose that fact, the basis used, and the reason why it is not regarded as a going concern. Going concern exceptions are rare in India, though there are always reports of a few companies in serious trouble.

HANDHOLD 1.5
Going Concern

Historical Cost

Historical cost is the amount of cash paid to acquire an asset. The historical cost assumption is an extension of the going concern assumption. It requires assets not meant for sale to be presented at their cost of acquisition. If a business is likely to be closed down, it doesn't matter how much it paid for an asset. What is relevant then would be the estimated market value of the asset. Increasingly, accounting is moving towards recording fair value instead of historical cost for some assets. You will learn about both historical cost accounting and fair value accounting in this book.

Periodicity

Businesses may have a long life. However, owners need information about the profitability of their business, and they expect to get dividends at regular intervals. Lenders need continuing assurance about the financial soundness of the business. Employees and managers get bonus computed on periodic profit. The government levies tax based on income for each year. The periodicity assumption breaks up the life of an enterprise into time periods in order to provide information for these purposes. Annual reporting is required everywhere. In addition, in some countries (e.g. India and US), listed companies must report quarterly. In Europe, semi-annual reporting is more common.

Money Measurement

The money measurement assumption means that only transactions and events that can be measured in money are recorded. We know that employee skills, management quality, research and development, and in-house brands are critical to the success of a business. However, accountants don't have reliable methods for measuring their value. As a result, these items are not reported in the financial statements. Also, accountants assume that the rupee is a stable measuring unit much the same way the metre or the litre is. So they add the cost of a building bought in 1970 with the cost of a building bought today. Of course, we know that because of inflation, a rupee today can't buy what a rupee could in 1970. Here again, accountants lack the tools for making adjustments for such price changes.

You will develop an understanding of GAAP as you progress through this book.

TEST YOUR
UNDERSTANDING 1.5
Accounting Principles

Do you think the following practices violate any accounting principles?

(a) A business records an expense for the electricity charges for the owner's home.

(b) A business buys a car at an auction for ₹40,000 and records it at that amount. One week later, the price of the car is ₹50,000, and the business records the car at the new market value.

(c) A business records a smartphone purchased for the owner's personal use as an asset of the business.

Institutions that Regulate Accounting

Learning Objective

LO 7 Describe the institutions that regulate and influence accounting in India.

Many Indian and international institutions influence accounting standards and practices in India. Figure 1.4 presents the major institutions that influence and shape Indian accounting.

Figure 1.4
INSTITUTIONS THAT INFLUENCE INDIAN ACCOUNTING

Many institutions including the government, the securities regulator, the accounting profession, and international organizations influence Indian accounting.

The **Ministry of Corporate Affairs (MCA)**, Government of India administers the Companies Act 2013. The Act lays down the form and content of financial reports of companies. The MCA articulates the government's view on financial reporting and accounting requirements. The government prescribes accounting and auditing standards in consultation with the **National Financial Reporting Authority (NFRA)**. The fifteen-member NFRA recommends accounting and auditing standards and enforces compliance.

The **Securities and Exchange Board of India (SEBI)** regulates companies listed in stock exchanges in India. It prescribes the type and amount of information provided in company prospectuses for issue of securities. SEBI introduced cash flow statements, quarterly financial results, and consolidated financial statements. The **Institute of Chartered Accountants of India (ICAI)**, constituted under the Chartered Accountants Act 1949, regulates chartered accountants (CAs). Its recommendations on accounting and auditing have a significant persuasive influence on practice.

The **Ministry of Finance**, Government of India administers the tax laws through the CBDT and the CBEC. Tax rules and accounting principles have different objectives but they have similarities. Tax treatment is an important influence on accounting. The **Reserve Bank of India (RBI)** regulates the functioning of banks and finance companies. The RBI specifies accounting and reporting requirements for them. Lately, the RBI has been requiring banks to increase provisions for bad loans. The **Insurance Regulatory and Development Authority of India (IRDAI)** regulates the functioning of the insurance business in India and lays down accounting and disclosure rules for insurance companies. The **Comptroller and Auditor-General of India (CAG)** audits the accounts of the Government of India, State governments, government organizations and public sector enterprises and reports to Parliament. The CAG appoints the auditors of government companies.

The **International Accounting Standards Board (IASB)** develops a single set of accounting standards for businesses around the world. The IASB issues **International Financial Reporting Standards (IFRS)** and **International Accounting Standards (IAS)**, commonly known as IFRS. The IASB works with national regulators to achieve worldwide convergence. The **International Federation of Accountants (IFAC)** works in areas such as education, ethics, and auditing. The **International Organization of Securities Commissions (IOSCO)** is an association of national securities regulators. IOSCO is influential in improving accounting regulation in securities markets around the world.

Ind AS, IFRS and US GAAP

As we noted earlier, GAAP is the collection of accounting conventions, assumptions, concepts and rules. The sources of Indian GAAP (IGAAP) include the Companies Act 2013, accounting standards, and the ICAI's pronouncements. **Accounting standards** specify the acceptable methods from the wide array of accounting choices allowed by GAAP.

Learning Objective

LO 8 Explain the relevance of Indian and international accounting standards.

Indian Accounting Standards

The global financial crisis in 2008 highlighted the need for strengthening the international financial regulatory system. In September 2009, the Group of 20 countries (G20) – that includes India – called on international accounting bodies to work for a single set of high quality, global accounting standards and complete their convergence project by June 2011. In February 2011, the MCA notified the converged standards, known as the **Indian Accounting Standards (Ind AS)**. The MCA proposed to implement them in phases beginning April 1, 2011. However, the government never announced the date for implementation of the standards. Meanwhile, there were significant changes in IFRS. As a result, the standards became outdated. In the Union Budget 2014 presented to Parliament on July 10, 2014, the Finance Minister stated that there was an urgent need to converge the current Indian accounting standards with IFRS. He proposed adoption of the new Indian Accounting Standards (Ind AS) from the financial year 2015-16 voluntarily and from the financial year 2016-17 mandatorily.

On February 16, 2015 and March 30, 2016, the MCA notified Ind AS under the Companies Act 2013. These would replace Accounting Standards (AS) issued by the government in 2006. Companies may opt to comply with Ind AS for financial statements for accounting periods beginning on or after April 1, 2015. All listed companies and some unlisted companies must comply with Ind AS for accounting periods beginning on or after April 1, 2016. The RBI and the IRDAI have directed banks and insurers to comply with Ind AS for financial statements for accounting periods beginning from April 1, 2018.

Ind AS and IFRS

The MCA's notifications on Ind AS contains some "carve-outs" from international standards. "Convergence" enables the Indian authorities to carve out exceptions to IFRS when they are applied in India. In contrast, "adoption" would require accepting IFRS without changes. The government intends to follow IFRS with modifications. As a result, *financial statements prepared in accordance with Ind AS will not be IFRS-compliant.* This would lead to some problems in comparing them with IFRS financial statements. Appendix A has the list of Ind AS and corresponding IFRS/IAS.

Convergence with IFRS is likely to bring about major changes in Indian financial reporting. IFRS follows the fair value measurement basis, whereas Indian standards largely follow historical cost. Indian companies may face significant problems in their transition to IFRS because of the absence of active markets for some assets in India. Also, companies must improve their documentation of management decisions and judgments on financial reporting. In this book you will learn about Ind AS and IFRS.

IFRS and US GAAP

In the US, the Financial Accounting Standards Board (FASB) issues accounting standards, the principal source of US GAAP. IFRS and US GAAP are the two accounting systems competing for international acceptance. These differ in terms of the amount of detail, quality of application and acceptability across nations. US GAAP is more detailed and is thought to be applied more consistently. IFRS has more worldwide acceptability. IFRS and US GAAP are similar in many areas, but they differ significantly in others. The good news is that the IASB and the FASB are working towards convergence of their standards. In 2007, the United States Securities and Exchange Commission (SEC) agreed to allow non-US companies that raise capital in the US to follow IFRS instead of US GAAP. A common set of accounting standards around the world will reduce accounting and auditing costs for businesses and make international financial comparisons easier. IFRS is mandatory in the European Union, Australia, Canada and New Zealand and in many other countries.

Principles-based standards place greater reliance on substance and lay down the broad principles that govern the accounting and disclosure requirements. In contrast, rules-based standards prescribe detailed conditions and stipulations and place greater reliance on bright lines, industry-specific guidelines, and exceptions. As one commentator put it, "If you tell your child to be at home at a reasonable hour, you are using a principles-based guideline. But if you tell your child to be home by 11 p.m. and then provide for 15 different contingencies that might justify a different time, you are using rules-based guidelines." Many consider US GAAP to be rules-based and IFRS to be principles-based. It would be fair to say that in the continuum from details to principles, US GAAP is closer to details. Because of the US legal environment, American managers and auditors face a much greater risk of shareholder lawsuits. The prescriptive nature of US standards makes it easier for them to defend their assumptions and judgments.

Is "One world, one accounting" realistic?

....

....

....

DISCUSSION QUESTION 1.5

Accounting Policies

Accounting policies are the methods, procedures and practices used in preparing the financial statements. GAAP lays down the general considerations for good accounting. Accounting standards specify the acceptable methods from the alternatives allowed by GAAP and identify the issues that require to be examined. Accounting policies state how a firm has selected and applied the accounting methods allowed by the accounting standards.

Figure 1.5 illustrates how accounting principles, standards and policies are related.

Learning Objective

LO 9 Explain the role of accounting policies in measuring performance.

Accounting Topic	Accounting Principle	Accounting Standard	Accounting Policy
1. Equipment cost	Match costs and benefits.	*Expensing methods:* ■ Equal expense in all years. ■ Higher expense in earlier years, lower amounts in later years. ■ Expense related to actual output.	• Select an expensing method. • Estimate the expected period of use considering: ■ Expected usage; ■ Replacement policy; ■ Technological change; ■ Industry practices; ■ Legal requirements and government regulations.
2. Employee benefits	Recognize future obligations of current commitments.	*Employee benefits:* ■ Paid leave. ■ Provident fund. ■ Gratuity. ■ Pension.	• Estimate the following: ■ Salary growth rate. ■ Life expectancy. ■ Discount rate ■ Return on the related investments.
3. Financial assets	Value assets based on the investor's intention.	*Investment classification:* ■ Meant for trading. ■ Not meant for trading.	• State criteria for classification. • Explain how fair value is determined.
4. Oil exploration activities	Match costs and benefits.	*Expensing methods:* ■ Full cost. ■ Successful efforts.	• Select an expensing method. • Estimate the value of the benefits considering: ■ Likelihood of finding oil; ■ Contractual arrangements for sharing the benefits; ■ Quantity of oil; ■ Quality/grade of oil; ■ Cost of production; ■ Market prices; ■ Legal requirements and government regulations.

Figure 1.5
ACCOUNTING PRINCIPLES, ACCOUNTING STANDARDS AND ACCOUNTING POLICIES

Accounting principles are fundamental positions. Accounting standards specify the acceptable methods. Accounting policies describe how an enterprise has applied the standards.

As you can see, accounting principles are quite broad; accounting standards give them shape; and accounting policies describe the management's judgment, assumptions and estimates in applying the standards. Managers of different firms may, and often do, differ in their views. This results in different numbers in the financial statements. Regulators are often tempted to lay down uniform rules for all firms. A one-size-fits-all approach should be avoided in order to let the managers produce informative financial statements. Instead, regulators should require documented evidence that the managers have considered the relevant factors and have made reasonable judgments. Investors should know an enterprise's accounting policies. Therefore, managers should disclose their accounting policies.

Economic Performance and Accounting Performance

Accounting seeks to report economic performance. Measuring economic phenomena is not easy. There are two problems with accounting measurement:

1. *Error:* Accounting tools and techniques are far from perfect. So they measure economic performance with error. For instance, accounting standards generally treat research and development spending as current expense and not as investment for the future. This is because of the uncertainty about the outcome of R & D projects. If some projects succeed, this accounting would lead to understatement of current performance and overstatement of future performance. Such distortion is unavoidable given the current state of the development of accounting measurement methods.

2. *Bias:* Error results from the state of accounting technology; bias is attributable to individuals' beliefs. The need for management judgment, assumptions and estimates leaves scope for discretion. Some managers are optimistic, while some are cautious. For example, Manager A may estimate that 15 per cent of the sales will require warranty repairs, while Manager B may reckon that figure to be 5 per cent. Institutional mechanisms such as audit committee, board of directors and external auditors can identify and undo managerial bias to an extent but not fully. Also, audit committee and board members and auditors too have their biases.

The following equation sums up this discussion:

$$\text{Accounting performance} = \text{Economic performance} + \text{Error} + \text{Bias}$$

While using accounting information, we should keep in mind the distortion inherent in the measurement process.

The World of the Accountant

Learning Objective

LO 10 Appreciate the role of accountants in business and non-business organizations.

Accountants are an integral part of organizations and society. Economic progress, social harmony and political stability are built on the foundation of sound accounting and financial control. Good accounting and financial discipline have underpinned mighty empires and flourishing businesses. Often, it is bad accounting more than powerful enemies or clever competitors that has destroyed them. Accountants play an important role in society and offer a wide range of services to business organizations, governments and not-for-profit organizations.

Auditing (or **assurance**) involves the examination of financial statements and generally forms an important part of the work of CAs. The external auditor reports whether the financial statements give a "true and fair view" of a company's financial affairs. Credible financial reports are essential for society to have trust in organizations. The work of external auditors is critical to the functioning of capital markets. Consider the following comment:

- Auditing is not just a business; it is an important public service. Without confidence in the…numbers, the machinery of capitalism can become gummed up, with serious consequences for society.[9]

---

[9] From the *Financial Times*. August 24, 2016. FT View: Accountancy's Big Four need more competition. © The Financial Times Limited 2016. All Rights Reserved.

Forensic accounting and risk management Forensic accountants uncover fraud. They require high-level computer and investigation skills. Risk management aims at identifying potential weaknesses and failures in financial systems. Growing white-collar crime has led to high demand for forensic accountants and risk management specialists. The Central Bureau of Investigation (CBI) and the SFIO engage forensic accountants to probe financial crime.

- In 2016, the CBI engaged forensic auditors to investigate allegations of fraud in sanctioning bank loans to Kingfisher Airlines.

Tax services include the preparation of tax returns and planning business activities with a view to minimizing taxes. While tax evasion is unlawful, tax planning is perfectly legitimate. But the line between the two is hazy.

Advisory services Designing information systems, improving inventory control, and advising on restructuring are examples of consulting assignments. Accounting firms are now "professional services firms".

Bankruptcy Bankruptcy administrators don't have the glamour of investment bankers. But when the music stops and a business is wound up, its bankruptcy administrators stand to gain. For example, fees paid to lawyers and accountants for unwinding Lehman Brothers in the US and Europe were estimated to surpass $2 billion. The Insolvency and Bankruptcy Code 2016 has increased opportunities in bankruptcy practice.

Management accounting Management accountants provide information to management for making business decisions and formulating long-term policies. Management accounting information has use in several areas including cost control, product costing, capital investment appraisal, profitability analysis, corporate planning, budgeting, pricing policies, and cash flow and liquidity management.

Internal auditing involves reviewing internal controls, assessing compliance with established policies, ascertaining the extent to which assets are safeguarded, and recommending improvements to operations. The Companies Act 2013 requires companies to appoint an internal auditor.

Information systems A rapidly growing field for accountants is the design and development of information systems for processing accounting data. Since large corporations make extensive use of technology for processing transactions, a good working knowledge of computer hardware and software is indispensable for specialization in this field. **Information system auditors** examine the adequacy of security in computerized accounting systems.

Government accounting Government organizations such as the Indian Railways, India Post, Police, Tax and Defence have large operations. Their operations should be cost effective, so that taxes and other levies can be kept low. Efficient and proper handling of revenues and expenses requires extensive systems for recording transactions and preparation of financial reports. The Controller-General of Accounts is the head of the Central government's accounting function and is part of the Ministry of Finance.

Not-for-profit accounting Religious organizations, hospitals for the poor and advocacy groups are not profit-oriented. They survive on donations and endowments. These organizations need financial reports and controls in order to assure their donors that the funds are utilized efficiently. Strange as it may sound, they are as prone to fraud and embezzlement as business organizations are.

Academic accounting Accounting is not only a profession but also a field of intellectual enquiry, similar to medicine, law, architecture and engineering. Academic accountants apply economic and behavioural theories to financial reporting, management accounting and other areas.

RESEARCH INSIGHT
Accounting and Stock Prices

Here are some questions you might be already asking: 1. Do accounting numbers influence stock prices? 2. How important is accounting to the capital market? 3. Are accounting reports a timely source of information to the capital market? Professors Ray Ball and Philip Brown investigated these questions and reported their findings in a paper that holds the world record for being the most cited research in accounting.[10] They found that stock prices reacted to firms' announcements of financial results. However, most of the changes in the stock prices occurred prior to the month in which annual results were announced. They noted that one-half or more of all the information is captured in that year's net profit. However, about 85 to 90 per cent of the change is captured by more prompt media that would include accounting and non-accounting sources of information. Thus, while the capital market anticipates much of the information contained in the annual financial statements, full anticipation does not occur.

DISCUSSION QUESTION 1.6

Should auditors be prohibited from providing non-audit services?

....

....

....

Fraud and Ethical Issues in Accounting

Learning Objective

LO 11 Understand the importance of ethics in accounting.

With more managers trying to cut ethical corners to accomplish enterprise objectives, ethical standards in business are declining. This has serious implications for the accounting profession. Fraudulent accounting and weak internal control systems have been the principal causes of many recent corporate scandals, including the ones that affected Adelphia, Enron, Lehman Brothers, Reebok India, Ricoh India, Satyam, Tesco, Toshiba, Tyco, WorldCom, and Xerox. Falling ethical standards often, but not always, result from high pressure to perform and exceed market expectations. Increasingly, managerial compensation is linked to profit and other accounting measures of performance. Hence, the temptation to manipulate the accounting reports is at times irresistible.

Stock-based incentive methods such as stock options have the unintended effect of inducing managers to boost their company's stock prices by unethical methods. Further, analysts and fund managers expect companies to produce instant results forcing managers to tweak the quarterly or annual earnings numbers rather than focus on the long-term growth of the business. Booking incomplete or fictitious sales as revenues, improperly deferring current expenses to future periods, and making unwarranted changes in accounting policies are examples of accounting tricks that have been used often to manipulate the earnings. Keep an eye on the possibility of manipulation and fraud while you examine the financial statements.

- Even venerable institutions are not immune to pressure. In 2016, Wells Fargo, a retail bank and the world's most valuable bank by market capitalization (i.e. market value of shares), was fined $185 million for opening millions of accounts without customers' knowledge by staff racing to meet sales targets. Staff faked email addresses to create accounts and even went as far as to create PIN numbers for customers without telling them. According to the US Consumer Financial Protection Bureau, about 5,300 Wells Fargo employees lost their jobs as a result of their misconduct since 2011. Interestingly, Wells Fargo was largely free from the scandals that hit investment banks. Almost $9 billion was wiped out off the bank's market capitalization soon after the regulator's disclosure.

Accountants frequently encounter ethical dilemmas. For example, a controller may be caught in a conflict between professional standards and the expectations of a superior. An external auditor may be caught in a conflict between a client's wishes and the requirements

---

[10] Ray Ball and Philip Brown, An empirical evaluation of accounting income numbers, *Journal of Accounting Research*, Autumn, 1968.

of an accounting standard. In the face of sudden decreases in revenue or market share, unrealistic budget pressures, particularly for short-term results, or financial pressure resulting from bonus plans that depend on short-term economic performance, managers are often tempted to bend the accounting rules.

Unfortunately, many ethical questions that arise in practice can't be answered by adhering to GAAP or following the rules of the profession. The accountant must decide on the basis of the facts and circumstances of each case whether it is necessary "to blow the whistle" or not. Ethical questions often involve conflicting considerations, and balancing these pressures is far from easy. For example, though the accountant may be ethically obliged to inform an external agency of a wrongful act committed by a client, the code of conduct for accountants prohibits the accountant from revealing confidential information about a client. Nevertheless, it is important for the accountant to recognize an ethical dilemma, identify and evaluate the various alternatives available for resolving the dilemma, and select the most ethical alternative considering all the circumstances and consequences. While deciding on the appropriate course of action, the accountant should consider taking appropriate legal advice.

In case you are still unconvinced, note that the punishment for accounting and financial fraud is too severe. Jeff Skilling, Enron's former chief executive, was sentenced to 24 years in prison, while Bernie Ebbers of WoldCom was jailed for 25 years. Bernard Madoff, the fraudster who ran a Ponzi scheme, was sentenced to 150 years in jail. Closer home, Satyam's directors and auditors have been convicted for fraudulent accounting and sentenced to imprisonment (however, they have appealed). Accountants and managers would be tempting fate, if they engage in fraudulent reporting.

There are many kinds of fraud. Here are a few.

FORENSIC CORNER
Understanding Fraud

- *Misappropriation of assets:* Embezzlement of cash, inventories, shares and equipment and procurement fraud.
- *Accounting fraud:* Manipulation of the numbers in the financial statements, e.g. reporting non-existent revenues and assets and suppressing expenses and liabilities.
- *Bribery:* Taking cash or other consideration in return for doing a favour (or sometimes for even doing one's duty!).
- *Money laundering:* Disguising the proceeds of crime as legitimate assets.

Fraud causes financial, legal and reputational damage. Organizations should devise systems to prevent, detect and report fraud. Businesses have collapsed due to fraud, causing problems for customers and suppliers and immense suffering to employees. Consider these examples of known or alleged accounting fraud.

- *Ricoh India:* Reporting fictitious sales, cash, receivables and inventories.
- *Satyam:* Reporting fictitious sales, cash and receivables.
- *Enron:* Using off-balance sheet entities to hide debts.
- *WoldCom:* Overstating assets and understating expenses.
- *Bernard Madoff:* Defrauding investors in a Ponzi scheme.
- *Toshiba:* Reporting sales before completion of contracts.
- *Autonomy:* Reporting fictitious sales and misclassification of expenses.
- *Lehman Brothers:* Selling and buying back securities to understate liabilities.
- *Sino-Forestry:* Overstating forest holdings.

Can accounting fraud be eliminated?

DISCUSSION QUESTION 1.7

....

....

....

RECAP

- Business organizations provide products and services.
- Sole proprietorship, partnership, company and limited liability partnership are the common forms of business organization.
- Capital market channels savings into investment. High quality accounting reports are a must for orderly markets and good governance.
- Accounting is a principal means of communicating financial information.
- The accounting information system applies accounting principles, standards and policies to transactions and other events to produce financial statements.
- Financial accounting provides information to outsiders; management accounting provides information to insiders.
- Users of financial statements include owners, lenders, employees, managers, governments, and regulators.
- Accounting is the language of business. The conventions, assumptions, concepts and rules which define accepted accounting practice constitute generally accepted accounting principles (GAAP).
- Accounting measurement assumptions – reporting entity, going concern, historical cost, periodicity, and money measurement – are important in understanding the information in the financial statements.
- A number of institutions such as the Ministry of Corporate Affairs, the Securities and Exchange Board of India, the Institute of Chartered Accountants of India, the Income Tax Authorities, and the Reserve Bank of India regulate and influence accounting in India.
- Accounting standards narrow down the choice of available acceptable methods.
- Accounting policies state how a firm has applied the accounting methods.
- Accounting performance measurement is affected by error and bias.
- The International Accounting Standards Board develops a single set of accounting standards known as the International Financial Reporting Standards (IFRS).
- Many countries follow the IFRS. Indian Accounting Standards (Ind AS) are India's version of IFRS.
- Accountants provide a variety of services to businesses, governments and not-for-profit organizations.
- Fraud and ethical compromises diminish the value of accounting information.

Review Problem

Akhil, Binoy, Chhavi and Devika formed a partnership. Their partnership agreement provided that the profits would be divided among the partners in the ratio of 4:3:2:1. The agreement was silent on allocating losses. At the end of its first year, the partnership had losses of ₹100,000. Before allocating losses, the partners' capital balances were: Akhil, ₹70,000; Binoy, ₹50,000; Chhavi, ₹35,000; and Devika, ₹8,200. Devika has no personal assets. After losses were allocated to the partners, assets were sold and liabilities were paid, the partnership had ₹63,200 in cash.

Required

How would the cash be distributed among the partners?

Solution to the Review Problem

	Akhil	Binoy	Chhavi	Devika
Capital balance	₹70,000	₹50,000	₹35,000	₹8,200
Allocation of losses	(40,000)	(30,000)	(20,000)	(10,000)
Balance	30,000	20,000	15,000	(1,800)
Distribution of Devika's deficiency	(800)	(600)	(400)	1,800
Balance	29,200	19,400	14,600	0
Distribution of remaining assets	29,200	19,400	14,600	

Notes:

1. Profits and losses are distributed in the same ratio, unless there is agreement to the contrary.
2. Insolvent partner's deficiency is distributed among the solvent partners in the ratio in which losses are distributed.
3. Remaining assets are distributed in the ratio in which profits are distributed.

ASSIGNMENT MATERIAL

Questions

1. What is the purpose of a business?

2. What are the advantages of a company over a partnership?

3. How is a limited liability partnership different from a partnership?

4. How does limited liability encourage entrepreneurship?

5. Who appoints a company's auditors?

6. Give examples of costly signals that well-managed companies can send.

7. Why should a manager know accounting?

8. Give examples of economic decisions that are based on accounting information.

9. Who are the important users of financial reports?

10. How does *financial accounting* differ from *management accounting*?

11. What do you understand by *generally accepted accounting principles*?

12. Who sets accounting standards in India?

13. Do you think the *money measurement assumption* is realistic?

14. Why do we need *accounting standards* in addition *to accounting principles*?

15. Distinguish between *accounting standards* and *accounting policies*.

16. Why is historical cost still used in many countries?

17. Who issues *International Financial Reporting Standards* (IFRS)?

18. What are the responsibilities of a company's chief financial officer, controller and treasurer?

19. How does internal auditing differ from external auditing?

20. What do forensic accountants do?

21. Why do managers engage in fraudulent accounting?

Problems

∗ Least difficult   ∗∗∗∗∗ Most difficult

Problem 1.1
Liability of Sole Proprietor ∗

On February 11, 20XX, Annamalai started Fauna Enterprise, a nature tourism business as a proprietorship with an investment of ₹25,000. On September 30, 20XX, the business had cash of ₹35,000 and unpaid bills of ₹45,000. On that date, Annamalai had personal cash of ₹8,000 and a used computer worth ₹3,500 (bought at a cost of ₹10,000) and owed ₹7,500 in personal bank loan.

Required

1. How much is Annamalai required to pay?
2. How much is Annamalai able to pay?
3. Is Annamalai solvent or insolvent?

Problem 1.2
Liability of Partners ∗

On July 3, 20XX, Shankar and Tanvi set up Paintbrush & Co. as equal partners to teach art investing ₹25,000 each. On December 19, 29XX, the business had ₹95,000 in cash and ₹130,000 in unpaid bills. On that date, Shankar had personal cash of ₹22,000 and a house worth ₹150,000 (bought for ₹60,000) and owed ₹130,000 on a mortgage loan. Tanvi had personal cash of ₹1,000 and jewellery worth ₹87,000 (bought for ₹18,000) and personal bank loan of ₹85,000.

Required

1. How much are Shankar and Tanvi required to pay?
2. How much are Shankar and Tanvi able to pay?
3. Are Shankar and Tanvi solvent?

Problem 1.3
Liability of Sole
Proprietor ✳✳

On October 20, 20XX, Raj started Darlings, a kennel as a proprietorship with an investment of ₹15,000. On November 17, 20XX, the business had cash of ₹9,000 and unpaid bills of ₹5,000. On that date, Raj had personal cash of ₹7,000 and a car worth ₹17,000 (bought at a cost of ₹40,000) and owed ₹29,000 in personal bank loan.

Required

1. How much is Raj required to pay?
2. How much is Raj able to pay?
3. Is Raj solvent or insolvent?

Problem 1.4
Liability of Partners ✳✳

On January 19, 20XX, Anand and Ramesh set up Olive Restaurant as equal partners to serve Italian cuisine investing ₹12,000 each. On October 31, 29XX, the business had ₹60,000 in cash and ₹70,000 in unpaid bills. On that date, Anand had personal cash of ₹5,000 and a piece of land worth ₹100,000 (bought for ₹10,000) and owed ₹120,000 on a personal bank loan. Ramesh had personal cash of ₹9,000, silver worth ₹50,000 (bought for ₹25,000) and personal bank loan of ₹10,000.

Required

1. How much are Anand and Ramesh required to pay?
2. How much are Anand and Ramesh able to pay?
3. Are Anand and Ramesh solvent or insolvent?

Problem 1.5
Accounting Principles ✳✳

Maria, a bank lending officer, is studying the financial statements of Vault, a proprietorship selling dry fruits. She notes the following in her review:
(a) Rent expense includes rent for the proprietor's home.
(b) The company has moved from credit to cash-on-delivery terms with suppliers.
(c) The cost of land was recorded as ₹100,000, its estimated market value, rather than its purchase price of ₹60,000 two years ago.
(d) A measuring balance costing ₹10,000 was expensed immediately, though it is expected to be used for five years.
(e) The value of a new manager was recorded as ₹500,000 based on the advice of the headhunter.

Required

Explain whether Vault's financial statements violate, or potentially violate, any accounting principles or assumptions.

Problem 1.6
Liability of Partners ✳✳✳

On June 3, 20XX, Ahmed, Benjamin and Chaman started Geo as equal partners to provide weather reports to farmers investing ₹20,000 each. On December 11, 29XX, the business had ₹20,000 in cash and ₹50,000 in unpaid bills. On that date, Ahmed had personal cash of ₹30,000 and a diamond ring worth ₹90,000 (bought for ₹70,000) and owed ₹50,000 on a personal bank loan. Benjamin had personal cash of ₹10,000 and a painting worth ₹18,000 (bought for ₹60,000) and owed ₹15,000 on a personal bank loan. Chaman had personal cash of ₹6,000 and owed ₹4,000 on a personal bank loan.

Required

1. How much are Ahmed, Benjamin and Chaman required to pay?
2. How much are Ahmed, Benjamin and Chaman able to pay?
3. Are Ahmed, Benjamin and Chaman solvent or insolvent?

Problem 1.7
Liability of
Shareholders ✳✳✳

On March 18, 20XX, Harish and Tanmay started Crescendo Limited, a concert-booking service as equal shareholders with a total share capital of ₹100,000. Each of them contributed ₹40,000 and agreed to contribute the balance when called. On August 12, 20XX, the company had ₹150,000 in cash and ₹180,000 in unpaid bills. On that date, Harish had personal cash of ₹90,000 and owed ₹50,000 on a personal bank loan. Tanmay had personal cash of ₹30,000 and owed ₹22,000 on a personal bank loan.

Required

1. How much are Harish and Tanmay required to pay?
2. How much are Harish and Tanmay able to pay?
3. Are Harish and Tanmay solvent or insolvent?

Business Decision Cases

BDC 1.1
Learn-the-Ropes

Ramya and Hari, her husband, plan to start an edutech enterprise. Learn-the-Ropes, the proposed venture, will help students to supplement their classroom learning. It will offer online courses in

STEM (science, technology, engineering and mathematics) disciplines. Ramya and Hari have made some savings from their consulting jobs. They think the business is not likely to involve much capital investment, but there will have to be considerable upfront spending on developing the course platform. Their estimate of the spending in the first year is around ₹250 million. It will take at least one year to earn any revenue. Profits are not expected to kick in until the end of second year. Also, the business is highly competitive and there are many online course providers, including established providers of mass open online courses (MOOCs) such as Coursera, edX, Udacity and Khan's Academy, not to mention the thousands of free videos on YouTube. Besides, traditional tuition centres are beginning to create online content. Given all of these, Learn-the-Ropes may need to approach venture capital firms for investment before long.

You recently met with Ramya and Hari in an alumni networking event and are impressed by their idea. They have asked you, a budding manager with ambitions to make it big in life, to think about how to go about selecting a suitable form of business for their proposed business. If you do a good job, you stand a good chance of being offered an attractive job ahead of your campus placement. If all goes well, you could even end up owning a part of the business in course of time.

Required

Prepare a report describing the suitability of the various forms of business organization for Learn-the-Ropes. Your report should be specific to the needs and circumstances of the business, rather than being a dissertation on business organizations, that Ramya and Hari can use as a starting point for thinking about their business.

> ## Interpreting Financial Reports

Once upon a time, Kingfisher Airlines was one of the largest aviation companies in India. The **IFR 1.1** company's jaunty slogan "Welcome to a world without passengers" was meant to say that the **Kingfisher Airlines** passenger is "made to feel like a guest and not just a passenger". Unfortunately for the company, **Limited** the slogan soon acquired its literal meaning.

Kingfisher Airlines was set up in 2003 by the United Breweries Group. It started operations in 2005. Kingfisher Airlines shut down operations in 2012. It never made a profit all its life. In August 2015, United Bank of India declared Vijay Mallya, the company's promoter and chairman, a 'wilful defaulter' – a term used by the Reserve Bank of India to describe a borrower who has the capacity to repay but doesn't, diverts funds for other purposes, siphons off funds or disposes or removes assets furnished as security. The company owed more than ₹80 billion in unpaid loans to banks in India. Besides, the airports, tax authorities and employees, among others, had claims against the company for unpaid amounts.

Mr. Mallya left India for the United Kingdom in March 2016. Television channels and newspapers demanded that he return to India and repay the company's loans and other dues.

Required

Using publicly available information, answer the following questions:

1. Who is obliged to repay a company's debts: the company, promoters, shareholders, or directors?
2. Are there circumstances under which promoters or directors could be asked to repay the loans taken by the company?
3. What options do the banks have for recovery of the loans in a case like this one?
4. What are the rights of a company's shareholders against the promoter in a case like this one?

Infosys is a leading information technology services company listed in Indian stock exchanges and in **IFR 1.2** the New York Stock Exchange, Euronext London and Euronext Paris. The company's 2016 directors' **Infosys Limited** report contains the following statement:

> The financial statements are prepared in accordance with the Generally Accepted Accounting Principles (GAAP) under the historical cost convention on accrual basis except for certain financial instruments, which are measured at fair values. GAAP comprises mandatory accounting standards as prescribed under Section 133 of the Companies Act 2013 ('the Act'), read with Rule 7 of the Companies (Accounts) Rules 2014, the provisions of the Act (to the extent notified) and guidelines

issued by the Securities and Exchange Board of India (SEBI). There are no material departures from the prescribed accounting standards in the adoption of the accounting standards.

The directors confirm that:

- In preparation of the annual accounts for the financial year ended March 31, 2016, the applicable standards have been followed.
- They have selected such accounting policies and applied them consistently and made judgments and estimates that are reasonable and prudent so as to give a true and fair view of the state of affairs of the Company at the end of the financial year and of the profit and loss of the Company for that period.
- They have taken proper and sufficient care towards the maintenance of adequate accounting records in accordance with the provisions of the Act for safeguarding the assets of the Company and for preventing and detecting fraud and other irregularities.
- They have prepared the annual accounts on a going concern basis.
- They have laid down internal financial controls, which are adequate and operating effectively.
- They have devised proper systems to ensure compliance with the provisions of all applicable laws and such systems are adequate and operating effectively.

Required

Describe the responsibilities of the various agencies or parties in relation to the company's financial reporting and allied matters and explain how the above statement benefits them.

Financial Analysis

FA 1.1
The Satyam Accounting Scandal

Search the Internet for reports about the accounting scandal in Satyam.

Required

1. Explain the essential elements of the scandal based on your understanding of accounting at this stage.
2. Prepare a report comparing the Satyam scandal with accounting scandals in the US highlighting any similarities and differences between them.

FA 1.2
Investment Advice

The job of an investment adviser is to recommend profitable investment opportunities. These include stocks, bonds, real estate, commodities, and art. The adviser should maximize the return (or profit) from an investment keeping in view the related risks (or the chances of loss or a low profit). Your friend is looking at options for investing a large fortune she has inherited from her uncle. She has heard that lately the stock market has been doing well and the stock prices of many companies have zoomed. She wants you, a financial wizard in the making (or so she thinks!), to tell her how to invest.

Required

1. Prepare a report setting out the information an individual should have in order to decide on investing in stocks and where the information will be available.
2. List the benefits and risks of alternative investment opportunities and explain how studying the information in the financial statements would be useful in making an informed decision.

Answers to One-minute Quiz

    1.1 c.
    1.2 a, b.
    1.3 c.
    1.4 b.

Answers to Test Your Understanding

    1.1 (a) Accommodation booking; (b) Online payments; (c) Solar energy; (d) Peer-to-peer lending; (e) Cancer care.
    1.2 *Case C:* The business is short of ₹5,000 for paying its bills. Preeti must bring all of her personal cash of ₹5,000. Even then, bills of ₹3,000 will go unpaid. Preeti is insolvent. The business ends.

Case D: The business is short of ₹5,000 for paying its bills. Akshay can bring in ₹1,500 after paying his personal debt. Even then, bills of ₹3,500 will go unpaid. Akshay is insolvent. The business ends.

1.3 *Case G:* The business is short of ₹5,000 for paying its bills. Tejas must bring in ₹2,500 from personal cash. Vinod must bring in all of his personal cash of ₹2,500. The business can now pay the bills in full. Both are solvent. The partnership and the business continue.

Case H: The business is short of ₹5,000 for paying its bills. Initially, Juhi must bring in ₹2,500 from personal cash. Vani must bring in all of her personal cash of ₹500. Even with these, bills of ₹2,000 will remain unpaid. So Juhi must bring in an additional ₹2,000 (being Vani's deficiency of ₹2,000) from personal cash. Juhi is solvent; Vani is insolvent. The partnership and the business end.

1.4. *Case K:* The business is short of ₹5,000 for paying its bills. Both Amit and David have contributed their agreed share capital. Since their liability is limited to the agreed amount, they need not bring in any cash. Both are solvent. The business ends and the company is liquidated. Bills for ₹5,000 will go unpaid.

Case L: The business is short of ₹5,000 for paying its bills. Gaurav and Venkat have contributed ₹8,000 out of their agreed contribution of ₹10,000 each. So they can be required to contribute up to ₹2,000 each, if called. Gaurav must bring in ₹2,000 from personal cash. Gaurav has no further liability. Venkat must bring all of his personal cash of ₹500. Venkat's deficiency of ₹1,500 is a debt payable by him to the company. Gaurav is solvent; Venkat is insolvent. The business ends and the company is liquidated. Bills for ₹2,500 will go unpaid.

1.5 (a) Violates the reporting entity assumption. Business transactions should be separated from the owner's personal affairs. (b) Violates the going concern assumption coupled with the historical cost principle. Assets should be recorded at their cost of purchase, regardless of their subsequent market value. (c) Violates the reporting entity assumption. Business transactions should be separated from the owner's affairs.

CHAPTER 2

Financial Statements

LEARNING OBJECTIVES

After studying this chapter, you should be able to:

1. Explain the accounting equation.
2. Analyze the effects of transactions on the accounting equation.
3. Describe the financial statements and explain how they are interrelated.
4. Appreciate the basics of financial statement analysis.
5. Understand the main items in a company's financial statements.

SPEED READ

The accounting equation captures the essence of accounting. It expresses the relation between assets, liabilities and equity. Transactions affect the accounting equation. Financial statements report the effects of transactions concisely. They tell us the story of a business in numbers. A good knowledge of accounting is necessary to appreciate the story. The law specifies the form and content of company financial statements. Financial statement analysis helps us to understand the performance of a business.

DODGY REPORTING?

Innocent: Revenue is the most important number in the financial statements.

Sceptic: I agree. What is revenue?

Innocent: How silly? It's another name for sales.

Sceptic: Well, I thought as much. But a news report made me wonder if there is more to revenue than adding up customers' bills.

Innocent: You mean there is more than one revenue number?

Sceptic: That's not what I meant. It may have to be tweaked in certain contexts.

Innocent: Isn't that dangerous? It can lead to disputes.

Sceptic: It can and it does. So when a contract provides for sharing revenue between parties, it should be clear about what revenue means.

A report of the Comptroller and Auditor-General of India (CAG) tabled in Parliament on March 11, 2016 indicated a loss of ₹124.88 billion due to understatement of revenue by India's top six telcos – Aircel, Airtel, Idea, Reliance, TATA and Vodafone.[1] According to the report, the companies understated ₹460.46 billion in gross revenue, resulting in short payment of ₹37.52 billion in licence fee and ₹14.60 billion in spectrum usage charge. The interest charge on the short payment was ₹72.76 billion. The report identified practices such as exclusion of the value of promotional schemes, interest income, commission or discount paid to distributors, and netting of discounts granted to post-paid subscribers. The CAG said that even 16 years after the introduction of the revenue share regime, the government could not assure the correctness and completeness of revenue from telcos. The government said that it would recover the amounts from the companies.

---

[1] Comptroller and Auditor-General of India, Sharing of Revenue by Private Telecom Service Providers during the years 2006–07 to 2009–10, Union Government (Communication and IT Sector), No. 4 of 2016.

The Accounting Equation

The **accounting equation** shows the relationship between the economic resources of a business and the claims against those resources. At all times, the following relationship holds:

Learning Objective

LO 1 Explain the accounting equation.

Economic resources = Claims

Economic resources are assets. The claims consist of creditors' claims, or *liabilities*, and owners' claims, or *equity*. (Recall that a business is separate from its owner for accounting purposes. So the owner too has a claim on the business.) The accounting equation may now be modified as follows:

Assets = Liabilities + Equity

We can analyze any business transaction, regardless of its size and complexity, in terms of its effect on the accounting equation. The **balance sheet** shows the position of assets, liabilities and equity.

Assets

An **asset** is a resource that gives benefits to its owner. An enterprise should consider a resource its asset if (a) it controls the resource, and (b) the resource is expected to give benefits.

- Swati enjoys the sight of trees, plants and flowers in a public park (*benefits*). But she can't prevent others from going to the park (*no control*). So the park is not her asset.
- Jayesh is the unquestioned master of his broken car (*control*). But he can't use it (*no benefits*). So the car is not his asset.

An asset has the capacity to provide benefits to its owner in the form of sales, savings, comfort, safety or speed. It is expected to generate cash, directly or indirectly. Clearly, cash is an asset. Items that will turn into cash or facilitate production or sales are also assets. Home mortgage loans are a bank's assets. Inventories and store buildings are a retailer's assets. An automobile company's plant and machinery are its assets.

Some assets, such as plant and machinery and inventories, have physical form. These are *tangible assets*. Assets such as patents and trademarks confer exclusive legal rights but have no physical form. So they are *intangible assets*. Others such as home mortgage loans and investments in bonds are legally enforceable claims on others. These are *financial assets*. To sum up, an asset is what an enterprise 'owns'. Think of assets as *amounts receivable* sooner or later.

What are the chief assets of Apple, Coal India, Cipla, Kotak Bank, and TCS?

QUICK QUESTION
Assets

Which of the following is an asset of Mahindra & Mahindra Limited? There may be more than one correct answer.
(a) Equipment with remaining life of three years.
(b) Investment in Mahindra Defence Systems Limited.
(c) Salaries.
(d) Tax payable.

ONE-MINUTE QUIZ 2.1
Assets

Liabilities

A **liability** is an obligation that requires to settled by giving up assets. A liability is the mirror image of an asset. Usually, it requires payment of cash. Some liabilities, such as bonds payable and trade payables, are in precise amounts. Other liabilities, such as income tax payable and pensions payable, should be estimated. Most liabilities result from contracts, e.g. amount payable for using electricity, or statutory requirements, e.g. amount payable for employer's contribution to provident fund. A liability may also arise from a constructive obligation that an enterprise regards as payable even without a legally enforceable claim. For instance, a store may allow full refund for goods returned even after the contractual period; this may give rise to a liability. In sum, a liability is what an enterprise 'owes'. Think of liabilities as *payable*.

QUICK QUESTION
Liabilities

What are the chief liabilities of Barclays Bank, Bharat Electronics, Larsen & Toubro, Oil and Natural Gas Corporation, and Volkswagen?

ONE-MINUTE QUIZ 2.2
Liabilities

Which of the following is a liability of Wipro Limited? There may be more than one correct answer.
  (a) Warranty payable.
  (b) Technical know-how.
  (c) Salaries payable.
  (d) Incomplete projects requiring further spending.

Equity

Equity is net assets, i.e. the difference between an enterprise's assets and its liabilities. The equity of a business enterprise increases through investments by owners and profits from operations and decreases through distributions to owners and losses from operations. Think of equity as the *residual*.

The equity of a company is called **shareholders' equity**. Its components include share capital, securities premium, and retained earnings. **Share capital** is the amount contributed by the shareholders towards a company's capital. **Securities premium** (or **share premium**) is the excess of shareholders' contribution over share capital.

The activities of a business result in revenues and expenses. **Revenues are amounts** charged to customers for goods and services provided. For instance, airlines earn revenue by transporting passengers and cargo. **Expenses are the costs of earning revenues.** The expenses of running an airline include aircraft lease rent, fuel, staff salaries, interest costs, and income tax. **Net profit** is the excess of revenues over expenses; **net loss** is the excess of expenses over revenues.

Dividends are distributions to shareholders. Profits increase equity; losses, dividends and share buybacks decrease equity. **Retained earnings** represent the profit kept in the business. You will learn more about the components of equity as you progress.

QUICK QUESTION
Equity

What are the chief revenues and expenses of Balaji Telefilms, Facebook, ITC, L'Oréal, and Manchester United?

ONE-MINUTE QUIZ 2.3
Equity

Which of the following is an equity item of Tata Steel Limited? There may be more than one correct answer.
  (a) Cash.
  (b) Dividend payable.
  (c) Amounts receivable from customers.
  (d) Income tax expense.

LADDER
Understanding Equity

We see assets all the time, e.g. cash, buildings, computers, and phones. We can't see liabilities, still we can imagine them as requiring us to part with cash, e.g. bank loan payable, salaries payable, and tax payable. We can neither see nor imagine equity. When a business sells goods worth ₹1,000 for cash, it earns a revenue of ₹1,000. Revenue is a component of equity. So equity increases and cash increases. The increase in cash is straightforward. What does the increase in equity mean? Revenue belongs to the owner. When a business earns revenue, the owner's claim increases. In our example, the business owes its owner ₹1,000 more. As an exercise, explain the effect of the following transaction: *A business pays salaries of ₹300.*

What happens when an enterprise buys equipment with cash? An answer sometimes heard in class is that equity decreases. This results from a misunderstanding of equity. The effect of this transaction is that equipment increases and cash decreases. *The transaction has no other effect on the accounting equation.* Equity would change when a firm (a) earns revenue, (b) incurs expense, (c) pays dividend, or (d) receives capital from, or returns capital to, owner. None of these happens when an enterprise buys equipment with cash.

(a) Hot Chocolate has assets of ₹87,000 and liabilities of ₹53,000. How much is its equity?

$$\text{Equity} = \text{Assets} - \text{Liabilities} = ₹87,000 - ₹53,000 = ₹34,000$$

HANDHOLD 2.1
Accounting Equation

(b) Abraham Company's September 30 balance sheet contained the following items: Cash, ₹5,000; Trade receivables, ₹17,000; Supplies, ₹9,000; Equipment, ₹19,000; Building, ₹21,800; Land, ₹21,000; Loan payable, ₹12,000; Expenses payable, ₹x; Abraham's equity, ₹77,300. What is the amount of expenses payable?

To find out expenses payable, substitute the known items in the equation, Assets = Liabilities + Equity: Cash, 5,000 + Trade receivables, 17,000 + Supplies, 9,000 + Equipment, 19,000 + Building, 21,800 + Land, 21,000 = Loan payable, 12,000 + Expenses payable, x + Abraham's equity, 77,300. Therefore, Expenses payable = ₹3,500.

(c) On March 31, 20XX, Coffee Corner's equity is twice its liabilities. Its assets are ₹81,000. Prepare its balance sheet.

Assets = 81,000 = Liabilities + Equity = Liabilities + (2 × Liabilities) = 3 × Liabilities. Therefore, liabilities = ₹27,000. Coffee Corner's balance sheet is as follows:

Coffee Corner's Balance Sheet, March 31, 20XX

Assets...	₹81,000
Liabilities...	27,000
Equity...	54,000
Total liabilities and equity	81,000

Give an example of a transaction that has the following effect on the accounting equation:

(a) Increases an asset and increases a liability.
(b) Increases an asset and decreases another asset.
(c) Increases an asset and increases equity.
(d) Decreases an asset and decreases a liability.
(e) Decreases an asset and decreases equity.

TEST YOUR UNDERSTANDING 2.1
Effect on Accounting Equation

Effects of Transactions

We will now see how the accounting equation works. On March 1, 20XX, Suresh starts Softomation as a proprietorship for providing software services. The business engaged in the following transactions in March:

Learning Objective
LO 2 Analyze the effects of transactions on the accounting equation.

Owner invests On March 1, 20XX, Suresh invests ₹50,000 in cash. The first balance sheet of the new business will show cash of ₹50,000 and equity of ₹50,000. (The items affected by the transaction appear in italics):

Balance Sheet, March 1, 20XX			
Liabilities and Equity		**Assets**	
Equity......................................	*₹50,000*	*Cash*	*₹50,000*
	50,000		50,000

The Indian convention is to show liabilities and equity on the left side and assets on the right side.

Takes a loan On March 2, Suresh takes an interest-free loan of ₹20,000 from his friend, Manish for Softomation. This transaction increases both assets (cash) and liabilities (loan payable):

Balance Sheet, March 2, 20XX			
Liabilities and Equity		**Assets**	
Loan payable	₹20,000	*Cash*	₹70,000
Equity	50,000		
	70,000		70,000

Buys equipment for cash On March 3, Softomation pays ₹58,000 for a computer. This transaction decreases one asset (cash) and increases another asset (equipment):

Balance Sheet, March 3, 20XX			
Liabilities and Equity		**Assets**	
Loan payable..	₹20,000	*Cash*	₹12,000
Equity	50,000	*Equipment*	58,000
	70,000		70,000

Buys supplies on credit On March 6, Softomation purchases supplies for ₹6,000 on credit. The effect is that both assets (supplies) and liabilities (trade payables[2]) increase:

Balance Sheet, March 6, 20XX			
Liabilities and Equity		**Assets**	
Loan payable..	₹20,000	Cash	₹12,000
Trade payables..	6,000	*Supplies*	6,000
Equity	50,000	Equipment	58,000
	76,000		76,000

Sells for cash On March 9, Softomation sells its first software to a retail store and receives ₹12,000 in fee. Revenue increases the owner's claim on the business. So the cash sale increases both assets (cash) and equity:

Balance Sheet, March 9, 20XX			
Liabilities and Equity		**Assets**	
Loan payable..	₹20,000	*Cash*	₹24,000
Trade payables..	6,000	Supplies	6,000
Equity..	62,000	Equipment	58,000
	88,000		88,000

Pays supplier On March 12, Softomation pays on account for the supplies bought on credit on March 6, ₹2,000.[3] As a result, both assets (cash) and liabilities (trade payables) decrease:

Balance Sheet, March 12, 20XX			
Liabilities and Equity		**Assets**	
Loan payable..	₹20,000	*Cash*	₹22,000
Trade payables..	4,000	Supplies	6,000
Equity	62,000	Equipment	58,000
	86,000		86,000

---

[2] Creditors and accounts payable are other terms for trade payables.
[3] 'On account' means part payment of an amount due.

Takes supplies home   On March 17, Suresh takes supplies costing ₹1,000 for personal use. The reporting entity assumption requires separation of personal and business activities. So we should treat this use as a withdrawal of capital by the owner, and not as a business expense.[4] As a result, both assets (supplies) and equity decrease:

Balance Sheet, March 17, 20XX			
Liabilities and Equity		**Assets**	
Loan payable..	₹20,000	Cash..	₹22,000
Trade payables......................................	4,000	*Supplies*...	*5,000*
Equity...	*61,000*	Equipment...	58,000
	85,000		85,000

Returns supplies On March 23, Softomation returned supplies costing ₹1,900 and received full refund. As a result, one asset (cash) increases and another asset (supplies) decreases:

Balance Sheet, March 23, 20XX			
Liabilities and Equity		**Assets**	
Loan payable..	₹20,000	Cash..	₹23,900
Trade payables......................................	4,000	*Supplies*...	*3,100*
Equity...	61,000	Equipment...	58,000
	85,000		85,000

Pays expense On March 26, Softomation pays employees' salaries of ₹4,000 and office rent of ₹1,200. Expenses reduce the owner's claim on the business, the opposite of the effect of revenue. This transaction decreases both assets (cash) and equity:

Balance Sheet, March 26, 20XX			
Liabilities and Equity		**Assets**	
Loan payable..	₹20,000	*Cash*..	*₹18,700*
Trade payables......................................	4,000	Supplies...	3,100
Equity...	*55,800*	Equipment...	58,000
	79,800		79,800

Sells on credit On March 29, Softomation completes a software for a shoe store. The customer will pay the agreed fee of ₹8,000 a week later. In this case, Softomation has done the work but has not received the fee. Even so, we count it as revenue.[5] The effect of this transaction is that both assets (trade receivables[6]) and equity increase:

Balance Sheet, March 29, 20XX			
Liabilities and Equity		**Assets**	
Loan payable..	₹20,000	Cash..	₹18,700
Trade payables......................................	4,000	*Trade receivables*	*8,000*
Equity...	*63,800*	Supplies...	3,100
		Equipment...	58,000
	87,800		87,800

---

[4] Even if we mistakenly treated the item as a business expense, the effect on equity would not be different. But the profit would be lower by ₹1,000.

[5] We are getting a little ahead of the story. In Chapter 4, you will see why we considered the revenue though cash was not received.

[6] Debtors and accounts receivable are other terms for trade receivables.

Withdraws cash   On March 30, Suresh withdraws ₹3,500 for personal use. The reporting entity assumption requires separation of personal and business activities. So we should treat this payment as a withdrawal of capital by the owner, and not as a business expense.[7] This transaction decreases both assets (cash) and equity:

Balance Sheet, March 30, 20XX			
Liabilities and Equity		**Assets**	
Loan payable..	₹20,000	Cash...	₹15,200
Trade payables....................................	4,000	Trade receivables	8,000
Equity...	60,300	Supplies..	3,100
		Equipment...	58,000
	84,300		84,300

Uses supplies On March 31, Softomation uses supplies costing ₹1,400. This is an expense. Expenses reduce the owner's claim on the business. This transaction decreases both assets (supplies) and equity:

Balance Sheet, March 31, 20XX			
Liabilities and Equity		**Assets**	
Loan payable..	₹20,000	Cash...	₹15,200
Trade payables....................................	4,000	Trade receivables.................................	8,000
Equity...	58,900	Supplies..	1,700
		Equipment...	58,000
	82,900		82,900

To sum up, the transactions are as follows:

20XX

Mar.   1   Suresh begins business with cash, ₹50,000.

2   Takes a loan from Manish, ₹20,000.

3   Buys a computer for cash, ₹58,000.

6   Buys supplies on credit, ₹6,000.

9   Sells software for cash, ₹12,000.

12   Pays for a part of the supplies bought on March 6, ₹2,000.

17   Uses supplies for personal purpose, ₹1,000.

23   Returns defective supplies for immediate refund, ₹1,900.

26   Pays salaries, ₹4,000, and office rent, ₹1,200.

29   Sells software on credit, ₹8,000.

30   Withdraws cash for personal use, ₹3,500.

31   Uses supplies for business purpose, ₹1,400.

Exhibit 2.1 presents the effect of these transactions on the accounting equation. *The balances that change appear in italics.*

---

7 Even if we mistakenly treated the item as a business expense, the effect on equity would not be different. But the profit would be lower by ₹3,500.

(amounts in rupees)

EXHIBIT 2.1
Effect of Transactions on Accounting Equation

Date		Assets				=	Liabilities		+	Equity
		Cash	Trade Receivables	Supplies	Equipment		Trade Payables	Loan Payable		Suresh's Capital
March	1	+ 50,000								+50,000
Balance		50,000								50,000
March	2	+ 20,000						+ 20,000		
Balance		70,000						20,000		50,000
March	3	− 58,000			+58,000					
Balance		12,000			58,000			20,000		50,000
March	6			+ 6,000			+ 6,000			
Balance		12,000		6,000	58,000		6,000	20,000		50,000
March	9	+ 12,000								+12,000
Balance		24,000		6,000	58,000		6,000	20,000		62,000
March	12	− 2,000					− 2,000			
Balance		22,000		6,000	58,000		4,000	20,000		62,000
March	17			− 1,000						− 1,000
Balance		22,000		5,000	58,000		4,000	20,000		61,000
March	23	+ 1,900		− 1,900						
Balance		23,900		3,100	58,000		4,000	20,000		61,000
March	26	− 5,200								− 5,200
Balance		18,700		3,100	58,000		4,000	20,000		55,800
March	29		+ 8,000							+ 8,000
Balance		18,700	8,000	3,100	58,000		4,000	20,000		63,800
March	30	− 3,500								− 3,500
Balance		15,200	8,000	3,100	58,000		4,000	20,000		60,300
March	31			− 1,400						− 1,400
Balance		15,200	8,000	1,700	58,000		4,000	20,000		58,900

What is the effect of the transaction 'Paid rent for last month' on the accounting equation?

	Assets	Liabilities	Equity
(a)	Decrease	Decrease	Decrease
(b)	Decrease	Decrease	No effect
(c)	Decrease	No effect	Decrease
(d)	No effect	Decrease	Decrease

ONE-MINUTE QUIZ 2.4
Accounting Equation

Revenues increase equity; expenses and drawings (or dividends) decrease equity. Therefore, we can rewrite the accounting equation, *Assets = Liabilities + Equity*, as follows:

Assets = Liabilities + Capital + Revenues – Expenses – Drawings (or Dividends)

Give examples of transactions and explain how they would affect the accounting equation.

DISCUSSION QUESTION 2.1

....

....

....

Financial Statements

Financial statements provide information about an enterprise's financial position and financial performance. Financial statements present the financial effects of transactions and other events by grouping them into broad classes, or **elements**. Assets, liabilities and equity are the elements related to the measurement of financial position. Revenues and expenses are the elements related to the measurement of performance. There are four major financial statements:

Learning Objective

LO 3 Describe the financial statements and explain how they are interrelated.

1. The *balance sheet* shows the financial position at a point in time.
2. The *statement of profit and loss* reports the financial performance in a period.
3. The *statement of changes in equity* explains how equity changed as a result of net profit, dividends, return of capital and other transactions in a period.
4. The *statement of cash flows* summarizes the cash inflows and outflows resulting from operating, investing and financing activities in a period.

Balance sheet reports *stock*, i.e. the position at a point in time. The other statements report *flow*, i.e. change in a period. Exhibit 2.2, Panel A to Panel D, presents Softomation's financial statements. Note that there is no specific form for the financial statements of proprietorship and partnership businesses.

EXHIBIT 2.2
Softomation's Financial Statements

> Financial statements present the financial position and financial performance of a business.

Panel A

SOFTOMATION Balance Sheet, March 31, 20XX	
Assets	
Cash	₹15,200
Trade receivables	8,000
Supplies	1,700
Equipment	58,000
Total assets	82,900
Liabilities	
Trade payables	₹ 4,000
Loan payable	20,000
Total liabilities	24,000
Equity	
Capital, Suresh	50,000
Retained earnings	8,900
Total equity	58,900
Total liabilities and equity	82,900

Panel B

SOFTOMATION Statement of Profit and Loss For the month ended March 31, 20XX	
Revenues	
Revenue from services	₹20,000
Expenses	
Salaries expense	4,000
Rent expense	1,200
Supplies expense	1,400
	6,600
Net profit	13,400

Panel C

SOFTOMATION Statement of Changes in Equity			
	Capital	**Retained Earnings**	**Total**
Balance, March 1, 20XX	₹	₹	₹
Capital introduced	50,000		50,000
Net profit		13,400	13,400
Withdrawn		(4,500)	(4,500)
Balance, March 31, 20XX	50,000	8,900	58,900

Panel D

SOFTOMATION Statement of Cash Flows For the month ended March 31, 20XX		
Cash flows from operating activities		
Cash received from customers	₹12,000	
Cash paid to suppliers and employees..	(5,300)	
Net cash provided by operating activities		₹ 6,700
Cash flows from investing activities		
Purchase of equipment..	(58,000)	
Net cash used in investing activities...		(58,000)
Cash flows from financing activities		
Proprietor's investment	50,000	
Proprietor's drawings	(3,500)	
Loan from Manish...	20,000	
Net cash provided by financing activities...		66,500
Net increase in cash		15,200
Beginning balance		0
Ending balance		15,200

Understanding Softomation's Financial Statements

Balance sheet The **balance sheet** presents an enterprise's assets, liabilities and equity *at a point in time*. It's similar to a snapshot. As shown in Exhibit 2.2: Panel A, at the end of March 20XX Softomation has assets totalling ₹82,900, equal to the total of liabilities of ₹24,000 and equity of ₹58,900.

Statement of profit and loss The **statement of profit and loss,** also known as *profit and loss account* or *income statement,* summarizes the revenues and expenses *for a period*. It's like a video. The statement tells us about a firm's financial performance. From Exhibit 2.2: Panel B, we note that in March 20XX Softomation earned a revenue of ₹20,000 from services, spent ₹6,600 to earn that revenue and made a net profit of ₹13,400 for the period. You might have noticed that the revenues and expenses appeared in the Equity column in Exhibit 2.1. We note that Softomation's revenues are from its business activities.

Statement of changes in equity The **statement of changes in equity** describes the changes in the equity items, e.g. share capital and retained earnings *in a period*. Changes in share capital result from introduction or withdrawal of capital by the owners. Changes in retained earnings result from net profit and distributions to the owners. Exhibit 2.2: Panel C tells us that in Softomation the changes came from both owner and non-owner transactions; the latter were routed through the statement of profit and loss. We note that Suresh withdrew ₹4,500 in cash and supplies out of Softomation's March earnings of ₹13,400 and retained ₹8,900. Since this is the first month, there is no beginning balance. Note that distribution of profit is not an expense; so it appears in the statement of changes in equity, and not in the statement of profit and loss.

Statement of cash flows The **statement of cash flows** reports the cash effects of an enterprise's (a) operations, (i.e. providing goods and services), (b) investments (i.e. buying and selling assets) and (c) financing (i.e. raising and repaying funds) *in a period*. The statement of cash flows in Exhibit 2.2: Panel D describes how Softomation starting with no cash at the beginning managed to end the month with ₹15,200 in cash. Current operations brought in ₹6,700. Investment in equipment used up ₹58,000. Suresh provided ₹46,500, net of withdrawal, and Manish provided ₹20,000.

Most transactions affect more than one financial statement. For instance, providing services for cash would affect the balance sheet (cash and equity), statement of profit and loss (revenue) and statement of cash flows (operating cash flow). Collecting past invoices would affect the balance sheet (cash and receivables) and the statement of cash flows (operating cash flow). Taking a bank loan would affect the balance sheet (cash and borrowings) and the statement of cash flows (financing cash flow).

HANDHOLD 2.2
Effect of Transactions

ONE-MINUTE QUIZ 2.5
Effect of Transactions on Financial Statements

Which of the financial statements would be affected by the transaction, 'Paid dividends'?
(a) Statement of changes in equity; statement of cash flows.
(b) Statement of profit and loss; statement of changes in equity; statement of cash flows.
(c) Balance sheet; statement of changes in equity; statement of cash flows.
(d) Balance sheet; statement of profit and loss; statement of changes in equity; statement of cash flows.

DISCUSSION QUESTION 2.2

Give examples of transactions and explain how they would affect the financial statements.

....

....

....

TEST YOUR UNDERSTANDING 2.2
Computing Profit from the Balance Sheet

On December 31, 20X1, Kiran Bakery had assets of ₹85,000 and liabilities of ₹67,000. On December 31, 20X2, the business had assets of ₹99,000 and liabilities of ₹71,000. During 20X2, Kiran invested ₹35,000 and withdrew ₹24,500. Compute Kiran Bakery's net profit for 20X2.

Financial Statement Analysis: The Basics

Learning Objective

LO 4 **Appreciate the basics of financial statement analysis.**

Suresh wants to know how his new business did in the first month. Here are some key questions:

- Is Softomation making good money from sales?
- Is Softomation earning a reasonable return on investment?
- Is Softomation using its assets efficiently?
- Are Softomation's customers taking too long to pay?
- Will Softomation be able to pay its suppliers on time?
- Is Suresh earning a reasonable return on his investment?
- Does Suresh have sufficient 'skin in the game'?
- Is Softomation's profit 'real'?
- What are Softomation's risks?

Let us do a bit of analysis to answer these questions.[8]

Is Softomation making good money from sales? Softomation made a profit of ₹13,400 on a revenue of ₹20,000. The **profit margin**, the *ratio of profit to sales*, is 67 per cent (13,400/20,000). Put differently, the business made a profit of ₹67 on ₹100 of revenue. This is impressive, because normally new businesses struggle for months, even years, before turning in a profit.

Is Softomation earning a reasonable return on investment? Softomation's investment is ₹82,900. Its **return on assets**, the *ratio of profit to assets*, is 16 per cent (13,400/82,900). It means Softomation earned ₹16 of profit for every ₹100 in investment. With no knowledge of the business, all we can say is that this is much better than the interest rate on bank deposits.

Is Softomation using its assets efficiently? Softomation's business revenue was ₹20,000 on an investment of ₹82,900 in equipment and other assets. Its **asset turnover**, the *ratio of sales to assets*, is 0.24 times. It means Softomation did business of ₹24 for every ₹100 invested. Software firms need much less assets than firms making steel or building aircraft. So Softomation's turnover would seem quite low. But these are early days and it is perhaps premature to expect full utilization. Asset turnover should improve as Softomation gets more business in future.

---

[8] It is more common to use averages for some items. In our analysis, we have used ending balance sheet numbers because there was no beginning balance sheet.

Are Softomation's customers taking too long to pay? Softomation's receivables are 40 per cent of sales (8,000/20,000). Note that the receivables relate to the sale on March 29 and it is possibly due next month or even later. It would be useful to know whether Softomation offers more generous credit than its industry peers in its anxiety to win business.

Will Softomation be able to pay its suppliers on time? Softomation owes its suppliers ₹4,000. It can pay the amount comfortably from the cash of ₹15,200.

Is Suresh earning a reasonable return on his investment? The owner's performance need not be the same as his firm's. On Suresh's investment ₹58,900 the business earned a profit of ₹13,400. The **return on equity**, the *ratio of profit to equity*, is 23 per cent (13,400/58,900). This would appear to be remarkable. Note that the return on equity would come down if the loan carried interest.

Does Suresh have sufficient 'skin in the game'? We would like to know if Suresh is in this business for the long haul. Suresh's 'skin in the game' is the equity of ₹58,900. His borrowings are ₹20,000. The **debt-to-equity ratio**, the *ratio of borrowed funds to own funds*, is a measure of the dependence of the business on borrowings and the owner's commitment to the business. Softomation's debt-to-equity ratio is 0.34:1 (20,000/58,900). So the business is not too much dependent on debt. Suresh will bear the brunt of any setback to the business and therefore he has every reason to be responsible in running the business. This should be reassuring to Softomation's lenders, suppliers, customers, creditors and employees. Another way to think about the owner's commitment is to find out what portion of the profit he takes out of the business. Suresh withdrew ₹4,500 of Softomation's profit of ₹13,400. The **payout ratio**, the *ratio of dividend to profit*, is 34 per cent. While this can't be regarded as excessive, payouts are rare at the early stages of a business. A high payout would raise questions about the owner's faith in the prospects of the business. For this reason, venture capital firms do not look at payouts too kindly.

Is Softomation's profit 'real'? There is no suggestion that Suresh might have fudged Softomation's books. We trust his numbers. Rather, we would like to know whether the profit is in cash. The operations produced a net cash of ₹6,700 *vs.* profit of ₹13,400. The *ratio of cash flow from operations to profit* can tell us whether the profits are real. Softomation's ratio is just 50 per cent (6,700/13,400). High receivables is the major explanation for the large gap between the two numbers. It simply means that revenue and profit are mostly stuck in receivables. We should wait to see if the gap closes as customers start paying and the business reaches steady state.

What are Softomation's risks? We can see three risks. First, the equipment is nearly 70 per cent of the investment. No doubt, the equipment will produce sales but it will take time. If the business slows down, Softomation will be stuck with equipment that may not have a ready market. Or it may have to sell the equipment at a distress price. Second, we don't know the terms of the loan, such as when it is repayable and whether it carries interest. If repayment is spread over several years, there is no immediate cause for concern. However, if the loan is repayable in the next few months or on demand, the cash would be insufficient. Finally, the cash available may look good. But what if there had been no loan? Softomation would have faced a cash deficit. To see why, do a quick "what if" analysis by knocking off the cash receipt from the loan in the statement of cash flows.

Form and Content of Company Financial Statements

Schedule III to the Companies Act 2013 specifies the form of financial statements for companies. Companies reporting under Accounting Standards must follow the form specified in Division I to Schedule III. Listed companies and some unlisted companies reporting under Ind AS must follow the form specified in Division II. We will now see the form and content of Ind AS consolidated statements.

Learning Objective

LO 5 **Understand the main items in a company's financial statements.**

Balance Sheet

- The balance sheet has three sections: (1) assets, (2) liabilities, and (3) equity.
- It follows the accounting equation, *Assets = Liabilities + Equity*, except that equity comes before liabilities.
- The items within assets, liabilities and equity follow the order of *permanency*. Thus, items that are expected to be with the business for relatively longer periods come first and those that are expected to be converted into cash relatively quickly appear later.
- *Assets* consist of non-current assets and current assets.
- *Non-current assets* are kept for use in the company's business and not for conversion into cash as part of the operations. These include long-term assets, such as tangible assets, intangible assets, financial assets and deferred tax assets.
  - *Tangible assets: Property, plant and equipment* consists of land, buildings, plant and machinery, office equipment, computers, furniture and vehicles. *Capital work-in-progress* is facilities that are under construction.
  - *Intangible assets* include goodwill, software, sub-contracting rights, and intellectual property rights (e.g. copyrights and patents).
  - *Financial assets* are contractual rights to receive definite amounts. Examples are long-term investments, trade receivables and loans.
  - *Deferred tax assets* result from differences between accounting profit and taxable profit that are expected to be realized in future periods.
- *Current assets* are regularly converted into cash as part of the operations or within 12 months from the balance sheet date. These include inventories and financial assets.
  - *Inventories* include raw materials, semi-finished products and finished goods.
  - *Financial assets* include cash, short-term investments and trade receivables.
- *Equity* includes of equity share capital and other equity.
  - *Equity share capital* represents the original and subsequent shares issued to the shareholders.
  - *Other equity* includes retained earnings, i.e. profit not distributed to shareholders.
- *Non-controlling interest* refers to the interests of minority shareholders in the company's subsidiaries.
- *Liabilities* consist of non-current liabilities and current liabilities.
- *Non-current liabilities* are payable after one year from the balance sheet date. These include financial liabilities, provisions and deferred tax liabilities.
  - *Financial liabilities* are contractual obligations to pay definite amounts, e.g. borrowings.
  - *Provisions* include estimated employee benefits payable such as gratuity, pensions and paid leave.
  - *Deferred tax liabilities* result from differences between accounting profit and taxable profit that are expected to be paid in future periods.
- *Current liabilities* are payable as part of the operations or within one year from the balance sheet date. These include financial liabilities, provisions and income tax liabilities.
  - *Financial liabilities* include trade payables, bills payable and security deposits payable.
  - *Provisions* include estimated employee benefits payable such as gratuity, pensions and paid leave.
  - *Current tax liabilities* is income tax payable for the current period.

Statement of Profit and Loss

- The statement of profit and loss has three sections: (1) income (top line), (2) expenses (middle line), and (2) profit (bottom line).
- *Income* consists of revenue from operations and other income.
  - *Revenue from operations,* or turnover, is revenue from sale of goods and services.
  - *Other income* includes interest, dividend and other non-operating income.
- *Expenses* include cost of materials consumed, employee benefits expense, finance costs, depreciation and amortization expense, and other expenses.
  - *Cost of materials consumed* is the cost of raw materials used up in the operations.
  - *Purchases of stock in trade* refers to the purchase of finished goods for resale.
  - *Changes in inventories of finished goods, stock-in-trade and work-in-progress* refers to the increase or decrease in these over the reporting period.
  - *Employee benefits expense* includes employees' salaries and other benefits.
  - *Finance costs* include interest and other borrowing costs.
  - *Depreciation and amortization expense* is the charge for the use of non-current assets.
  - *Other expenses* consist of expenses not mentioned above. Examples are repairs and maintenance, power and fuel, advertising and sales promotion, and insurance.
- *Tax expense* refers to income tax.
- *Profit for the period* = Income − Expenses.
- *Other comprehensive income* items are gains and losses not included in income and expenses.
- *Comprehensive income* is the sum of profit and other comprehensive income.

Statement of Changes in Equity

- The statement of changes in equity describes changes in equity including share capital and retained earnings.
- *Equity share capital* is increased by issue of additional shares and decreased by share buyback.
- *Retained earnings* is increased by profit for the period and decreased by loss for the period and dividends.
- *Other comprehensive income* changes as a result of gains and losses.

Statement of Cash Flows

- The statement of cash flows has three sections: operating, investing, and financing.
- *Operating activities* are for production of goods and services.
- *Investing activities* relate to acquisition and disposal of long-term assets and investments.
- *Financing activities* result in changes in equity and borrowings.

Financial statements tell the story of a business in numbers. At this stage, your aim should be to get an overview of the financial statements. You will study the principles and procedures followed in the preparation, analysis and interpretation of the financial statements in later chapters. *You will find it greatly useful to keep referring to company annual reports as you progress through this book.* Appendix B has the financial statements of Dr. Reddy's Laboratories Limited.

Why do profit and cash flow from operating activities differ?

QUICK QUESTION
Profit and cash flow

Where would you expect to find purchase of property, plant and equipment in the statement of cash flows? **QUICK QUESTION**
Statement of cash flows

DISCUSSION QUESTION 2.3

Do the financial statements omit some important assets of a business?

....

....

....

REAL WORLD
The Overwhelming Report

Until the early 1990s, the company annual report was a simple document with the financial statements, the directors' report, the chairman's statement and the auditors' report. Back then, annual reports hardly exceeded 30 pages. Over the years, reports have become much longer. Consider the size of the annual reports of some well-known companies for the year 2016.

Company	Number of Pages
Larsen & Toubro Limited	412
Reliance Industries Limited	404
Oil and Natural Gas Corporation Limited	396
Bharti Airtel Limited	360
Tata Steel Limited	300
State Bank of India	290
Tata Motors Limited	288
Bharat Heavy Electricals Limited	276
ICICI Bank Limited	252
HDFC Bank Limited	220
Hindustan Unilever Limited	208

Still, Indian investors have reason to be grateful, because some foreign companies have much longer reports. For instance, the Deutsche Bank's 2015 annual report runs to more than *600* pages. It is highly doubtful whether any investor, professional or lay, ever reads the full report. The reports have lots of photographs and charts. The text is full of jargon and acronyms, much of which would be unintelligible to many shareholders. There is hardly any meaningful analysis of performance. Increasingly, annual reports have become public relations documents and are, indeed, written by PR companies. Soon, shareholders may be required to attend a speed reading course and preferably acquire a degree in jargon. The annual report should communicate. These days it is used more to impress and obfuscate.

FORENSIC CORNER
Smelling Fraud

It is never a bad idea to be on your guard, particularly when you are looking at numbers churned out by individuals who may have an axe to grind, endorsed by worthies who may not understand them and certified by those who may be heavily conflicted (managers, directors and auditors, since you ask). Financial statements don't come with the caveat "Fraudulent accounting not ruled out here". The Russian saying "Trust, but verify" is sound advice for all those who use financial statements.

You should actively look for "red flags", unusual trends and patterns that may indicate deeper problems warranting further investigation. Red flags don't necessarily imply fraud, but ignoring them would be risky. Here are a few red flags that should make you pause, think and question:

- *Qualified audit report*: Audit reports are usually written as boilerplate. That is all the more reason why you should be sceptical when the auditors cite concerns, reservations or disagreements.

- *Auditor resignation or removal*: Auditors don't give up or turn down clients unless there is a serious dispute. They may quit when they are pressured to go along with aggressive accounting, or they think the control systems are weak and their risk is unacceptably high, or they are not given relevant information. Management may remove auditors who are unwilling to bend the rules.

- *Audit committee chair or independent director resignation*: The audit committee chair or an independent director usually resigns only when they fundamentally disagree with the management on a vital matter.

- *CFO resignation*: CFOs may leave for justifiable reasons, such as better career, health problems, spouse's job, children's education, less polluted city and so on. Sometimes they resign because of a difference of opinion with the management over business decisions and financial reporting matters.

- *Contravention of the law*: Good citizens follow the law scrupulously. Run-ins with the police may indicate a fatal flaw in one's character. Persistent problems with the law enforcement agencies, such as tax authorities, anti-corruption or anti-money laundering agencies, or regulators may be the proverbial tip of the iceberg. It is highly improbable that companies that have suppressed tax or paid bribes are holy when it comes to accounting.

- *Promise of excessively high profitability*: Companies in highly competitive industries must struggle to earn a decent profit. Monopolies are severely constrained by rules on profitability. So a business offering excessively high returns to investors should explain credibly where its profits come from.

- *Payment problems*: Persistent default in paying suppliers and employees may be a sign of sales or profitability problems. Downgrading of credit rating is an important indicator of cash flow mismatch or excessive debt.

- *High performance pressure and huge financial incentives*: Performance-based pay cuts both ways. In good times it encourages people to do their best. In bad times it brings out the worst in them. Companies that award highly differentiated bonuses run the risk of fraudulent reporting.

Lead indicators such as payment problems and aggressive organizational culture are particularly useful in avoiding or substantially reducing the loss caused by fraud.

RECAP

- The accounting equation states that at a given time, the sum of assets must equal the sum of liabilities and equity: *Assets = Liabilities + Equity*. The equation helps us to understand the effect of transactions.
- There are four major financial statements:
  - The *balance sheet* presents an enterprise's assets, liabilities and equity.
  - The *statement of profit and loss* lists an enterprise's revenues and expenses.
  - The *statement of changes in equity* describes the changes in the components of equity.
  - The *statement of cash flows* lists the major items of cash receipts and cash payments.
- There is no specific form for the financial statements of proprietorship and partnership businesses.
- Companies must prepare their financial statements following the requirements of Schedule III to the Companies Act.
- Key items in the financial statements are as follows:
  - *Balance sheet:* Assets: Non-current assets; Current assets
  - *Balance sheet:* Equity: Equity share capital; Other equity. Non-controlling interests
  - *Balance sheet:* Liabilities: Non-current liabilities; Current liabilities
  - *Statement of profit and loss:* Income: Revenue from operations; Other income
  - *Statement of profit and loss:* Expenses: Raw materials consumed; Employee benefits; Interest; Depreciation and amortization; Tax
  - *Statement of profit and loss:* Profit for the period; Other comprehensive income; Comprehensive income
  - *Statement of changes in equity:* Equity share capital; Retained earnings; Other comprehensive income
  - *Statement of cash flows:* Operating activities; Investing activities; Financing activities

Review Problem

On January 1, 20XX, Manohar started QualPhoto Company. The following transactions took place during the first month:

Jan. 1   Manohar invested ₹30,000 cash in the company's share capital (shares of ₹10 each).
      2   Bought supplies of photographic materials on credit, ₹9,000.
      5   Bought photographic equipment for cash, ₹12,000.
      7   Received fees for photographic services, ₹15,000.
      13 Paid creditor for supplies, ₹5,000.
      18 Manohar invested further ₹12,000 cash in the company's share capital.
      22 Billed customers for services, ₹19,000.
      27 Paid office rent, ₹2,500, and electricity charges, ₹1,200.
      30 Paid dividends, ₹4,000.
      31 Prepared the monthly payroll to be paid on February 1, ₹11,500.

Required
1. Analyze the effect of these transactions on the accounting equation.
2. Prepare the balance sheet, statement of profit and loss, statement of changes in equity and statement of cash flows.

Solution to the Review Problem
1. Effect of transactions

(amounts in rupees)

		Assets			=	Liabilities	+	Equity
		Cash	Trade Receivables	Supplies	Equipment		Trade Payables		Equipment
Jan.	1	+ 30,000							+ 30,000
Balance		30,000							30,000
Jan.	2			+ 9,000			+ 9,000		
Balance		30,000		9,000			9,000		30,000
Jan.	5	– 12,000			+ 12,000				
Balance		18,000		9,000	12,000		9,000		30,000
Jan.	7	+ 15,000							+ 15,000
Balance		33,000		9,000	12,000		9,000		45,000
Jan.	13	– 5,000					– 5,000		
Balance		28,000		9,000	12,000		4,000		45,000
Jan.	18	+ 12,000							+ 12,000
Balance		40,000		9,000	12,000		4,000		57,000
Jan.	22		+ 19,000						+ 19,000
Balance		40,000	19,000	9,000	12,000		4,000		76,000
Jan.	27	– 3,700							– 3,700
Balance		36,300	19,000	9,000	12,000		4,000		72,300
Jan.	30	– 4,000							– 4,000
Balance		32,300	19,000	9,000	12,000		4,000		68,300
Jan.	31						+11,500		– 11,500
Balance		32,300	19,000	9,000	12,000		15,500		56,800

2. Financial statements

Panel A

QUALPHOTO
Balance Sheet, January 31, 20XX

	Note	In ₹ *million*
Assets		
Non-current assets		
Property, plant and equipment	1	12,000
Total non-current assets		12,000
Current assets		
Inventories	2	9,000
Financial assets		
Trade receivables		19,000
Cash		32,300
Total current assets		60,300
Total assets		72,300
Equity and Liabilities		
Equity		
Equity share capital	3	42,000
Other equity		14,800
Total equity		56,800
Liabilities		
Non-current liabilities		—
Current liabilities		
Financial liabilities		
Trade payables		15,500
Total current liabilities		15,500
Total liabilities		15,500
Total equity and liabilities		72,300

Panel B

QUALPHOTO
Statement of Profit and Loss
For the month ended January 31, 20XX

	Note	In ₹ *million*
Revenue from operations	4	34,000
Total income		34,000
Expenses		
Employee benefits expenses		11,500
Other expenses	5	3,700
Total expenses		15,200
Profit for the period		18,800

Panel C

QUALPHOTO
Statement of Changes in Equity
For the month ended January 31, 20XX

In ₹ million

	Equity Share Capital	Retained Earnings	Total
Balance, January 1, 20XX	—	—	—
Share capital issued	42,000		42,000
Profit for the period...		18,800	18,800
Dividends...		(4,000)	(4,000)
Balance, January 31, 20XX	42,000	14,800	56,800

Panel D

QUALPHOTO
Statement of Cash Flows
For the month ended January 31, 20XX

In ₹ million

Cash flows from operating activities		
Cash received from customers...	15,000	
Cash paid to suppliers and employees...............................	(8,700)	
Net cash provided by operating activities		6,300
Cash flows from investing activities		
Purchase of equipment..	(12,000)	
Net cash used in investing activities		(12,000)
Cash flows from financing activities		
Proceeds from issue of share capital.................................	42,000	
Payment of dividends...	(4,000)	
Net cash provided by financing activities...................		38,000
Net increase in cash...		32,300
Cash and cash equivalents at the beginning		0
Cash and cash equivalents at the end		32,300

Notes:
1. **Property, plant and equipment**

Particulars	Equipment	Total
Gross carrying value as of January 1, 20XX	0	0
Additions...	12,000	12,000
Gross carrying value as of January 31, 20XX	12,000	12,000
Accumulated depreciation as of January 1, 20XX.......................	0	0
Depreciation	0	0
Accumulated depreciation as of January 31, 20XX.....................	0	0
Carrying value as of January 31, 20XX..	12,000	12,000

2. **Inventories**

   Supplies... 9,000

3. **Equity share capital**

    4,200 shares of ₹10 each, fully paid   42,000

4. **Revenue from operations**

    Revenue from services   34,000

5. **Other expenses**

    Rent expense   2,500

    Electricity expense ....   <u>1,200</u>

    <u>3,700</u>

ASSIGNMENT MATERIAL

Questions

1. State the *accounting equation*.

2. Classify the following assets into tangible, intangible and financial categories: (a) aircraft; (b) copper mines; (c) deposits; (d) fishing licences; (e) franchises; (f) money market funds; (g) newspaper masthead; (h) tax-free bonds.

3. Are players' contracts a cricket club's tangible, intangible or financial assets?

4. Name the main *financial statements*.

5. How is the *statement of changes in equity* useful?

6. What can we learn from the *statement of cash flows*?

7. Why should *current assets* and *non-current assets* be disclosed separately?

8. Give alternative terms for (a) trade receivables and (b) trade payables.

9. Is employee bonus payable a current liability? Why or why not?

10. What are the components of equity?

11. Give four examples of *cash flow from financing activities*.

12. Why is it necessary to distinguish *revenue from operations* from *other income*?

13. Why is auditor resignation a red flag?

Problems

Pai World, a business owned by Anant Pai, engaged in the following activities in the first month:

Problem 2.1
Understanding the Accounting Equation ∗

  (a) Pai invested cash in the business.

  (b) Paid a rental deposit refundable on vacating the office.

  (c) Advertised on a travel website on credit.

  (d) Appointed a cashier.

  (e) Received a bank loan.

  (f) Bought a computer on part payment.

  (g) Provided services on credit.

  (h) Provided services for cash.

  (i) Paid for the advertisement in (c).

  (j) Collected payment for services provided in (g).

  (k) Paid interest on bank loan.

  (l) Paid Pai's grocery bill.

Using the format given below, state whether each activity resulted in increase or decrease in the company's assets, liabilities and equity or had no effect on them. Consider the *total effect* on assets, liabilities and equity. Item (a) has been solved as an example.

Activity	Assets	Liabilities	Equity	Explanation
a.	Increase	No effect	Increase	Cash increases assets. Investment increases equity.

Problem 2.2
Preparing a Simple Balance Sheet*

Balwant Travels had the following items on March 31, 20XX.

Building.	₹50,000	Capital, Balwant	₹40,900
Office equipment	10,000	Retained earnings	24,400
Trade receivables	5,200	Loan payable	7,100
Cash	10,000	Trade payables	2,800

Prepare the March 31, 20XX balance sheet.

Problem 2.3
Preparing Financial Statements from Year-end Information**

On January 1, 20XX, Atika Sharma set up Smart Analytics Company investing ₹100,000 in share capital. The activities of the business resulted in the following revenues and expenses for 20XX: revenue from services, ₹108,000; office rent, ₹13,100; electricity, ₹9,000; salaries, ₹12,300; cloud storage, ₹3,600. The following were the assets and liabilities of the business on December 31, 20XX: equipment, ₹80,000; supplies, ₹14,500; trade receivables, ₹13,000; cash, ₹3,900; rent deposit, ₹100,000; long-term loan payable, ₹44,000; trade payables, ₹9,200. During the year, the company paid a dividend of ₹16,800 and Ms. Sharma made a further equity investment of ₹5,000 in the business.

Prepare the 20XX balance sheet and statement of profit and loss.

Problem 2.4
Explaining Transactions**

The following table shows the effect of six transactions of Venu Hair Stylists on the accounting equation. The amounts are in rupees.

		Assets			=	Liabilities	+	Equity
	Cash	*Trade Receivables*	*Supplies*	*Equipment*		*Trade Payables*		*Venu's Capital*
Balance	10,000	12,000	4,000	15,000		13,000		28,000
(a)	+5,000							+5,000
Balance	15,000	12,000	4,000	15,000		13,000		33,000
(b)			+8,000			+8,000		
Balance	15,000	12,000	12,000	15,000		21,000		33,000
(c)		+6,500						+6,500
Balance	15,000	18,500	12,000	15,000		21,000		39,500
(d)	−1,200		+1,200					
Balance	13,800	18,500	13,200	15,000		21,000		39,500
(e)	−12,000					−12,000		
Balance	1,800	18,500	13,200	15,000		9,000		39,500
(f)	+14,000	−14,000						
Balance	15,800	4,500	13,200	15,000		9,000		39,500

Required

Write a brief explanation for each of the transactions. If several explanations are possible, write all of them.

Problem 2.5
Explaining Transactions**
Alternative to Problem 2.4

The following table shows the effect of six transactions of Hari Plumbers on the accounting equation. The amounts are in rupees.

	Assets			=	Liabilities +	Equity
	Cash	Trade Receivables	Supplies	Equipment	Trade Payables	Hari's Capital
Balance	10,000	12,900	1,100	6,000	7,000	23,000
(a)	+1,000	−1,000				
Balance	11,000	11,900	1,100	6,000	7,000	23,000
(b)	+200		−200			
Balance	11,200	11,900	900	6,000	7,000	23,000
(c)	−600				−600	
Balance	10,600	11,900	900	6,000	6,400	23,000
(d)	+2,000					+2,000
Balance	12,600	11,900	900	6,000	6,400	25,000
(e)		+1,500				+1,500
Balance	12,600	13,400	900	6,000	6,400	26,500
(f)				+1,400		+1,400
Balance	12,600	13,400	900	7,400	6,400	27,900

Required

Write a brief explanation for each of the transactions. If several explanations are possible, write all of them.

On March 1, 20XX, Sangeeta Shinde set up a loan recovery business as a sole proprietorship and concluded the following transactions in the first month:

(a) Shinde invested cash in the business, ₹20,000.
(b) Bought equipment for cash, ₹12,000.
(c) Paid rent deposit for office, ₹5,000.
(d) Provided services for cash, ₹19,000.
(e) Provided services on credit, ₹14,000.
(f) Paid salaries, ₹8,000.
(g) Collected payments for past invoices, ₹8,500.
(h) Received advance payment for services, ₹2,000.
(i) Paid rent, ₹500.

Problem 2.6
Analyzing the Effect of Transactions on Asset, Liability and Equity Items✶✶

Required

Analyze the effect of the transactions on the related asset, liability and equity items.

On September 1, 20XX, Sukriti Sood set up Skin Glow as a sole proprietorship. The business engaged in the following transactions in the first month:

(a) Sood invested ₹10,000 cash in the business.
(b) Took a bank loan, ₹30,000.
(c) Bought equipment for cash, ₹25,000.
(d) Provided services for cash, ₹12,000.
(e) Paid interest on the bank loan, ₹300.
(f) Bought supplies for cash, ₹1,000.
(g) Paid rent, ₹3,100.
(h) Received refund for return of supplies, ₹200.
(i) Paid salaries, ₹5,000.

Problem 2.7
Analyzing the Effect of Transactions on Asset, Liability and Equity Items✶✶
Alternative to Problem 2.6

Required

Analyze the effect of the transactions on the related asset, liability and equity items.

On August 1, 20XX, Satish Pande set up Trust Labs Company. The following transactions took place during the first month:

(a) Pande invested ₹20,000 cash in the company's share capital.
(b) Took a bank loan, ₹10,000.
(c) Bought equipment for cash, ₹12,000.
(d) Bought supplies for cash, ₹3,000.

Problem 2.8
Analyzing the Effect of Transactions on Asset, Liability and Equity Items and Calculating Profit✶✶✶

(e) Billed customers for services, ₹9,000.
(f) Provided services for cash, ₹10,000.
(g) Paid sales commission, ₹1,000.
(h) Paid profession tax, ₹500.
(i) Collected payments for past invoices, ₹7,000.
(j) Repaid a part of the bank loan, ₹6,000.
(k) Paid interest on bank loan, ₹150.

Required

1. Analyze the effect of the transactions on the related asset, liability and equity items.
2. Calculate the profit for August 20XX.

Problem 2.9

Analyzing the Effect of Transactions on Asset, Liability and Equity Items and Calculating Profit ✳✳✳ Alternative to Problem 2.8

On January 1, 20XX, Ajay Joshi set up Fly-by-Night Delivery Company. The following transactions took place during the first month:

(a) Joshi invested ₹10,000 cash in the company's share capital.
(b) Bought a car for cash, ₹8,000.
(c) Filled petrol for ₹1,000 on payment of ₹800; balance to be paid in two weeks.
(d) Received advance payment from a customer, ₹1,000.
(e) Bought office supplies on credit, ₹3,000.
(f) Received cash for services provided, ₹8,000.
(g) Billed customers for services, ₹6,200.
(h) Paid office rent, ₹4,000.
(i) Paid the amount due in (c).
(j) Collected payment from customers billed in (g), ₹4,900.
(k) Provided services to the customer in (d).

Required

1. Analyze the effect of the transactions on the related asset, liability and equity items.
2. Calculate the profit for January 20XX.

Problem 2.10

Entering Beginning Balances, Analyzing the Effect of Transactions on Asset, Liability and Equity Items and Calculating Profit ✳✳✳✳

In June 20XX, Prasanna set up a debt rating service as a sole proprietorship. At the end of the month, the business had the following balances: Cash, ₹3,000; Trade Receivables, ₹2,000; Office Supplies, ₹1,000; Office Equipment, ₹5,000; Trade Payables, ₹1,000; Prasanna's Capital, ₹10,000. The following transactions took place in July:

(a) Paid June salaries, ₹400.
(b) Billed clients for services, ₹2,000.
(c) Bought office equipment for cash, ₹1,000.
(d) Bought office supplies on credit, ₹100.
(e) Withdrew cash for personal use, ₹1,000.
(f) Provided services for cash, ₹18,000.
(g) Prasanna invested in the business, ₹15,000.
(h) Collected payments for past invoices, ₹1,500.
(i) Paid electricity expense, ₹300.
(j) Paid for past purchases of office supplies, ₹500.
(k) Paid July salaries, ₹400.

Required

1. Enter the beginning balances.
2. Analyze the effect of the transactions on the related asset, liability and equity items.
3. Calculate the profit for June 20XX.

Problem 2.11

Entering Beginning Balances, Analyzing the Effect of Transactions on Asset, Liability and Equity Items and Calculating Profit ✳✳✳✳ Alternative to Problem 2.10

In November 20XX, Asif Mandiwala set up a weather forecasting service. At the end of the month, he had the following balances: Cash, ₹4,100; Trade Receivables, ₹3,400; Office Supplies, ₹1,100; Office Equipment, ₹10,000; Bank Loan Payable, ₹1,900; Mandiwala's Capital, ₹16,700. The following transactions took place in December:

(a) Provided services on credit, ₹6,100
(b) Took a bank loan, ₹6,000.
(c) Paid himself office rent, ₹1,000.
(d) Collected payments from clients billed in November, ₹2,800.
(e) Used office supplies for business purposes, ₹300.
(f) Provided services for cash, ₹2,800.

(g) Paid interest on bank loan, ₹100.
(h) Bought office supplies for cash, ₹800.
(i) Billed customers for services, ₹1,700.
(j) Cancelled a bill in (i) because of customer complaint, ₹100.
(k) Paid staff salaries for November, ₹1,600.

Required

1. Enter the beginning balances.
2. Analyze the effect of the transactions on the related asset, liability and equity items.
3. Calculate the profit for December 20XX.

On February 1, 20XX, Arati Naik started Fête Company, a wedding planning service. The company had the following transactions in February:

Problem 2.12
Analyzing the Effect of Transactions on Asset, Liability and Equity Items and Preparing Financial Statements for Two Periods ✳✳✳✳✳

(a) Naik invested ₹14,000 cash in the company's share capital.
(b) Bought two pieces of office equipment for cash, ₹6,000.
(c) Provided services for cash, ₹9,000.
(d) Bought office supplies on credit, ₹1,500.
(e) Billed customers for services, ₹7,500.
(f) Used office supplies, ₹800.
(g) Collected payment from customers billed in (e), ₹6,800.
(h) Paid for office supplies bought in (d) on account, ₹1,200.
(i) Billed customers for services, ₹2,100.
(j) Paid Naik's salary, ₹6,000.
(k) Paid office rent for February, ₹600.

The following transactions took place in March 20XX:

(a) Paid office rent for March, ₹600.
(b) Collected payments for February bills, ₹1,900.
(c) Bought office supplies on credit, ₹3,000.
(d) Billed clients for services, ₹18,300.
(e) Used office supplies, ₹2,300.
(f) Issued shares to a friend for cash, ₹12,000.
(g) Bought office equipment for cash, ₹12,000.
(h) Paid for office supplies bought on credit, ₹3,100.
(i) Paid assistants' salaries, ₹6,200.
(j) Paid Naik's salary, ₹6,000.
(k) Paid a dividend, ₹1,900.

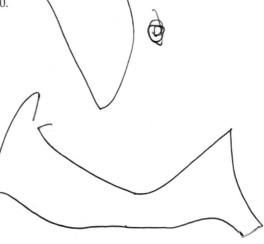

Required

1. Analyze the effect of the transactions in February 20XX on the related asset, liability and equity items.
2. Prepare the company's February 20XX balance sheet, statement of profit and loss, statement of changes in equity and statement of cash flows.
3. Enter the beginning balances for March 20XX.
4. Analyze the effect of the transactions in March 20XX on the related asset, liability and equity items.
5. Prepare the company's March 20XX balance sheet, statement of profit and loss, statement of changes in equity and statement of cash flows.

Business Decision Cases

Sampath failed the school final exam and ran away from home. He started working as a building assistant earning between ₹10,000 and ₹15,000 a month. The job was uninteresting and strenuous. Soon he learnt driving and joined a leading car fleet on revenue-sharing terms. His monthly earnings averaged ₹20,000.

BDC 2.1
Point Cabs

On April 1, 20XX, he started Point Cabs, his own taxi business. He took a bank loan of ₹500,000 and invested his savings of ₹100,000 to buy a car costing ₹600,000. In addition, he invested ₹18,000 for meeting day-to-day cash needs. All cash receipts and payments were through his bank account.

Sampath scribbled his activities in a rough notebook. The following are the entries for April:

April 1 Started business with savings of ₹118,000.
      1 Took a bank loan of ₹500,000 to be repaid in monthly instalments of ₹10,000 with interest at 18 per cent per annum.
      1 Bought a car for cash, ₹600,000.
      1 Bought an airport parking licence for April, ₹10,000.
      1 Paid for fuel, ₹3,600.
      2 Collected from customers, ₹1,700.
      3 Collected from customers, ₹1,100.
      4 Collected from customers, ₹1,300.
      5 Collected from customers, ₹3,100.
      6 Collected from customers, ₹1,200.
      7 Collected from customers, ₹1,600.
      8 Paid for fuel, ₹6,100.
      8 Collected from customers, ₹2,400.
      9 Collected from customers, ₹2,200. A customer did not pay a bill of ₹900 and will pay next month.
    10 Collected from customers, ₹1,300.
    11 Collected from customers, ₹1,700.
    11 Bought a mobile phone for cash for business use, ₹12,000.
    12 Collected from customers, ₹1,100.
    13 Collected from customers, ₹1,800.
    14 Collected from customers, ₹1,100.
    15 Collected from customers, ₹600.
    15 Paid for fuel, ₹5,300.
    16 Collected from customers, ₹1,800.
    17 Collected from customers, ₹1,900.
    17 Paid a fine for speeding, ₹500.
    18 Collected from customers, ₹1,100.
    19 Collected from customers, ₹1,100.
    20 Collected from customers, ₹4,500.
    21 Paid for fuel, ₹3,400.
    21 Collected from customers, ₹4,400.
    22 Collected from customers, ₹2,100.
    23 Collected from customers, ₹2,600.
    24 Collected from customers, ₹2,900.
    25 Collected from customers, ₹3,700. Change of ₹120 not returned will be adjusted next time.
    26 Collected from customers, ₹3,100.
    27 Filled fuel for ₹3,920 and paid ₹3,240. The balance will be paid next time.
    27 Collected from customers, ₹3,200.
    28 Collected from customers, ₹2,900.
    29 Repaired a side-view mirror damaged in an accident, ₹750.
    29 Collected from customers, ₹4,700.
    29 Paid taxi drivers' union subscription for the month, ₹500.
    30 Collected from customers, ₹4,100.
    30 Withdrew for personal purposes, ₹11,200.
    30 Paid substitute driver's salary, ₹8,000.
    30 Earned interest of ₹130 on bank balance.
    30 Paid the bank, ₹17,500.

Required
1. Analyze the effects of the transactions on the accounting equation.
2. Prepare the financial statements for April 20XX.
3. Evaluate the performance of the business.

On August 1, 20XX, Ajay and Jeevan quit as senior executives in a mutual fund to set up MoneyCare
Company, an investment advisory service. Each of them deposited ₹50,000 in MoneyCare's bank
account in exchange for 5,000 shares. Also, they raised an interest-free loan of ₹20,000 for the company
from their friend. They rented an office for the company in the city, costing ₹5,000 per month payable
on the last day of the month. At the landlord's insistence, they paid a deposit of ₹70,000, refundable
on MoneyCare vacating the place.

BDC 2.2

MoneyCare Company

They leased two computers for one year on a monthly rental of ₹6,000 per computer and
subscribed to a financial database for a fee of ₹11,000 per month. Computer rental and database
fee were payable at the beginning of the month. They appointed a secretary on a monthly salary of
₹9,000 and an assistant on a monthly salary of ₹5,000.

Depending on their credit rating, MoneyCare's customers paid in one of the following ways:

1. Before receiving service.
2. Immediately on receiving service.
3. Within one month after receiving service.

During August, MoneyCare provided services for ₹70,800 and raised invoices with the following
payment terms:

- Fifteen customers with invoices totalling ₹62,100 could pay until end of September.
- Two customers with invoices totalling ₹8,700 had to pay immediately. MoneyCare's other
  transactions in August were as follows:
  - Paid computer rental, database fee, office rent and salaries as agreed.
  - Received from customers amounts totalling ₹24,100 including ₹15,400 from customers
    who chose to pay early.
  - Paid for office supplies costing ₹1,800 but did not use them.
  - Received ₹9,000 from a customer for service to be provided in September.
  - Earned interest income of ₹460 on the bank account.

Required

1. Prepare MoneyCare's financial statements for August.
2. What do you think of the company's financial performance?

Interpreting Financial Reports

Jet Airways (India) Ltd. is a major airline in India. The following items appeared in the company's
recent financial statements:

IFR 2.1

Jet Airways (India)
Limited

1. Aircraft fuel consumed	2. Employee benefits
3. Deferred tax liability	4. Travel agents' commission
5. Purchase of investments	6. Provision for gratuity
7. Proceeds from sale of fixed assets	8. Net cash from operating activities
9. Share capital	10. Repayment of term loans and subordinated debt
11. Interest and finance charges	12. Frequent flyer points not availed of
13. Inventories	14. Aircraft lease rental
15. Wealth tax paid	16. Capital expenditure – aircraft and others
17. Dividend paid	18. Short-term borrowings
19. Unpaid dividend	20. Deposit with service tax department

Required

1. Identify the financial statement – balance sheet, statement of profit and loss, statement of
   changes in equity, or statement of cash flows – in which you would expect to see each of
   the items and indicate whether it is a revenue, expense, asset, liability, equity, operating
   cash flow, investing cash flow, or financing cash flow.
2. Give any five items that do not appear in the above list but you would expect to see in the
   financial statements.
3. Verify your answers with the help of the information in the financial statements.

FA 2.1
Understanding Financial
Statements

FA 2.2
Understanding
Auditors' Reports

Financial Analysis

Look through the financial statements of five companies, all from different industries.

Required

1. Identify items in the financial statements that are special to each company.
2. Read the notes to the financial statements to see if they explain the items adequately.

Read the auditors' reports of 25 companies. Your sample should have Indian (private sector and public sector) and foreign (US, UK, Australian) companies.

Required

1. Identify the key points from these reports and compare them across companies and countries.
2. Write in your own words what you understand from the reports.
3. In your opinion, what additional information would be useful to investors?
4. Interview auditors to find out whether they agree with your understanding of the reports and why their reports do not give the additional information.

Answers to One-minute Quiz

2.1 a, b.

2.2 a, c.

2.3 b, d. (Note: Dividend payable is an equity item because it is payable to owners, not creditors.)

2.4 b.

2.5 c.

Answers to Test Your Understanding

2.1 (a) Bought a building on credit; (b) Collected trade receivables; (c) Owner invested capital in cash; (d) Paid trade payables; (e) Owner withdrew cash from business for personal purposes.

2.2 Net profit = $\text{Equity}_{\text{Dec. 31, 20X2}} - \text{Equity}_{\text{Dec. 31, 20X1}} - \text{Investments}_{20X2} + \text{Drawings}_{20X2}$

$$= (₹99{,}000 - ₹71{,}000) - (₹85{,}000 - ₹67{,}000) - ₹35{,}000 + ₹24{,}500$$

$$= \text{Net loss, } ₹500.$$

CHAPTER

3

Transaction Processing

LEARNING OBJECTIVES

After studying this chapter, you should be able to:

1. Understand the design of the accounting system.
2. Recognize commonly used accounts.
3. Describe the double-entry system and apply the rules for debit and credit.
4. Analyze and record the effect of business transactions using debits and credits.
5. Record transactions in the journal.
6. Post journal entries to the ledger.
7. Prepare a trial balance.
8. Correct errors in accounting records.
9. Appreciate the role of technology in accounting.
10. Understand the importance of internal control systems.

GANDHIJI, ROCKEFELLER AND ACCOUNTING

Referring to Mahatma Gandhi in a book on accounting might seem odd. Wasn't Gandhiji anti-wealth? Not exactly. In his autobiography, *My Experiments with Truth*, Gandhiji talks about his personal experience with bookkeeping. He went to South Africa to argue a case mainly about accounts. His ignorance of bookkeeping came in the way of understanding the case. A lawyer was examining a witness on credit and debit entries. It was Greek to him. He was more confused when the clerk went on talking about this debited and that credited. He bought a book on bookkeeping and studied it and then understood the case. Gandhiji was known to keep a detailed record of his expenses.

John D. Rockefeller, the world's first billionaire, was known for his virtual devotion to bookkeeping. He was known to keep a small red book, called Ledger A, in which he meticulously recorded his receipts and expenditures. He owed his success as much to his accounting discipline as his business acumen.

No two individuals could have differed more in their views on wealth than Gandhiji and Rockefeller. Gandhiji was famous for choosing to be poor. Rockefeller was a perfect example of a wealthy man. Yet they were strikingly similar in their emphasis on careful accounting.

SPEED READ

Businesses have to record transactions systematically in order to prepare financial statements and other reports. The wonderful system of debits and credits is the accountant's 'robot' that processes transactions with amazing efficiency. Accounts are the building blocks of the accounting system. The journal records transactions in chronological order, while the ledger groups them. The trial balance checks the accuracy of recordkeeping. This chapter deals with the 'wiring and plumbing' of accounting – it may not be exciting or aesthetic but it is indispensable for a safe structure.

The Accounting System

Learning Objective
LO 1 Understand the design of the accounting system.

Accounting systems should respond effectively to the ever-rising demand for information from management, investors, lenders, government, regulators, and others. The starting point is to group transactions in keeping with the information needs of the users of financial statements.

An **account** is an individual record of increases and decreases in an item of interest or importance. Accounts are the building blocks of the accounting system. Let's take a few examples to understand how an account works. To know the amount of cash available, you would summarize all cash receipts and payments. To find out the salaries expense, you would put together salaries paid on various dates. To know the amount due from customers, you would need information about sales and collections. To find out the amount of goods in the store, you would assemble information about purchases and sales. In each of these examples, you need a record that enumerates transactions relating to an item that you are interested in, such as cash, salaries expense, trade receivables, and inventories. The cash account records all cash receipts and payments. The salaries expense account records salaries paid. The trade receivables account records credit sales and collections. The inventory account records purchases and sales of goods. Business organizations have accounts for revenue, expense, asset, liability and equity items.

A **ledger** is a collection of accounts. A **chart of accounts** is a complete list of the account titles used in an organization. The number of accounts and the specific account titles depend on the business. Thus, banks keep accounts for deposits, loans, interest income and interest expense. Supermarkets track store inventories. Automobile manufacturers record cost of production. An accounting system has separate accounts for asset, liability and equity items. In this chapter, we use the **general ledger**, the most commonly used type of ledger.

Exhibit 3.1 presents an illustrative chart of accounts. Accounts may have codes. Often the accounting staff refer to account codes rather than account titles. In the chart below, the first digit tells us whether an account is an asset, liability or equity item and the next two digits identify the specific item. Thus, all asset accounts begin with 1, liability accounts begin with 2, and so on. Every organization should develop a chart of accounts that is most appropriate for its purposes. For example, a large company may use a 10-digit system in order to identify the division or business unit, plant, product line, and so on. The chart of accounts is much more detailed than the line items that appear in financial statements.

EXHIBIT 3.1
Chart of Accounts

A chart of accounts lists the account titles and codes used by an organization.

Account Title	Code	Account Title	Code
Assets		**Revenues and Other Income**	
Buildings	101	Sale of goods	401
Office equipment	102	Revenue from services	402
Office supplies	103	Interest income	403
Trade receivables	104	Gain on sale of assets	404
Cash	105	**Expenses and Losses**	
Prepaid rent	106	Cost of goods sold	501
Liabilities		Salaries expense	502
Borrowings	201	Office supplies expense	503
Trade payables	202	Electricity expense	504
Unearned revenue	203	Advertisement expense	505
Equity		Telephone expense	506
Share capital	301	Rent expense	507
Securities premium	302	Insurance expense	508
Retained earnings	303	Interest expense	509
Currency translation reserve	304	Income tax expense	510
Dividends	305	Loss on sale of assets	511

Special ledgers are used to record the details of accounts in the general ledger. For example, the trade receivables ledger has the accounts of the individual receivable accounts of customers. The balance of the trade receivables account in the general ledger should be equal to the sum of the individual receivable accounts. Special ledgers are often kept for trade payables, property, plant and equipment, and inventories.

Commonly Used Accounts

Let's now see some commonly used accounts. Assets are what a business owns. Land, buildings, equipment, trade receivables, bills receivable, cash, prepaid expense, unbilled revenue and interest receivable are examples of asset accounts. Liabilities are what a business owes. Salaries payable, warranty payable, trade payables, bills payable, bonds payable, tax payable, unearned revenue, and interest payable are examples of liability accounts. Equity is the owners' claim on the business. Share capital, retained earnings, sales revenue, interest income, cost of goods sold, advertisement expense, interest expense, drawings, and dividends are examples of equity accounts.

Learning Objective

LO 2 Recognize commonly used accounts.

The accounting system builds an organization's memory. An organization remembers what is recorded in its accounts. There will be no trace of what is not recorded. Writer and Nobel laureate, Garcia Gabriel Marquez says, "What matters in life is not what happens to you but what you remember and how you remember it." The accounting system determines what activities an organization 'remembers' and 'how' it remembers them.

The number of accounts and specific account titles used by an enterprise depend on the nature and complexity of the enterprise's business. For example, an automobile company will keep detailed accounts for its plant and equipment, whereas a bank will need meticulous information about its various deposits, investments and loans, and its cash kept in various forms. Again, a small bakery that sells for cash can possibly manage with a few accounts, while a large multinational company will have thousands of accounts.

In deciding on the level of detail in the accounts, a firm should also consider relevant legal requirements. For example, the Companies Act requires disclosure of directors' remuneration; the Income Tax Act disallows many kinds of entertainment expenses. It is necessary to keep separate accounts for such items.

Recognition is the process of recording an item that meets the definition of an element (revenue, expense, asset, liability, or equity). Derecognition is the process of removing an item that no longer meets the definition of an element.

State whether the following are asset, liability or equity accounts:

(a) Directors' fees

(b) Cost of materials consumed

(c) Gain on sale of investments

(d) Provision for leave wages

(e) Security deposit with Customs

(f) Work-in-progress

TEST YOUR UNDERSTANDING 3.1
Classifying Accounts

Which of the following statements about account is correct? There may be more than one correct answer.

(a) An account records all increases and decreases in an item.

(b) The trade payables account describes credit purchases and payments to suppliers of goods and services.

(c) The Companies Act has a model chart of accounts.

(d) An accountant records important increases and decreases in an item.

ONE-MINUTE QUIZ 3.1
Account

DISCUSSION
QUESTION 3.1

Should revenues and expenses relating to an enterprise's core and peripheral activities be collected in separate accounts?

....

....

....

The Double-entry System

Learning Objective

LO 3 Describe the double-entry system and apply the rules for debit and credit.

In Chapter 2, we analyzed the effect of transactions on the accounting equation. Recall that each transaction affects two columns. For example, receiving cash from customers for past invoices increases cash and decreases trade receivables. Thus, we record each transaction in two accounts so that the accounting equation, *Assets = Liabilities + Equity*, is always in balance. This balancing is as important to the accountant as safe landing is to an airline pilot: the number of times an aircraft takes off must equal the number of times it lands (needless to add, safely). This principle of duality is valid regardless of the complexity of a transaction. The **double-entry system** records every transaction with equal debits and credits. As a result, the total of debits must equal the total of credits. Luca Pacioli (pronounced pot-chee-oh-lee), an Italian monk, first articulated the double-entry system in 1494 in his book titled *Summa de Arithmetica, Geometria, Proportioni et Proportionalita* (which means "Everything about Arithmetic, Geometry, and Proportions").[1]

The T Account

The common form of an account has three parts:

1. Title describing the asset, liability or equity account.
2. Debit side, or left side.
3. Credit side, or right side.

This form of account is called a **T account** because it looks like the letter T, as shown below.

<table>
<tr><td colspan="2" align="center">Title of Account</td></tr>
<tr><td align="center">Left = Debit</td><td align="center">Right = Credit</td></tr>
</table>

Debits and credits Accountants use the terms *debit* and *credit*, respectively, to refer to the left side and right side of an account. To debit an account is to enter an amount on the left side of an account and to credit an account is to enter an amount on the right side of an account. Note that in accounting debit and credit do not have any value connotations such as bad and good. They are simply the accountant's terms for left and right – and nothing more.

The T account explained In the illustration in Chapter 2, Softomation received and paid cash. We record these transactions in the cash account below, with receipts on the left or debit side and payments on the right or credit side:

---

[1] Luca Pacioli was the best friend and teacher of Leonardo da Vinci, the renowned painter, scientist and inventor, and taught him mathematics and geometry. Pacioli is believed to have helped the artist with the painting of *The Last Supper*. Interestingly, Pacioli also penned the world's oldest magic text, *De Viribus Quantitatis* (On the Powers of Numbers). It would appear that accounting skill and tricks have had something in common for a long time.

Cash					
Date	Explanation	Amount	Date	Explanation	Amount
20XX			20XX		
March 1	Owner's investment	50,000	March 3	Cash purchase of computer	58,000
2	Loan from Manish	20,000	12	Payment to suppliers	2,000
9	Cash sales	12,000	26	Salaries	4,000
23	Refund for supplies returned	1,900	26	Office rent	1,200
			30	Drawings	3,500
	Total	83,900		**Total**	68,700
31	Balance	15,200			

The debit and credit totals, or footings in accounting jargon, are an intermediate step in determining the cash at the end of the month. The difference between the total debits and the total credits is the balance.

- If the total debits exceed the total credits, the account has a **debit balance**.
- If the total credits exceed the total debits, the account has a **credit balance**.

The cash account has a debit balance of ₹15,200 (₹83,900 – ₹68,700). It represents the cash available on March 31. You would have observed that the cash account has the same information as that in the cash column in Exhibit 2.1.

Standard Form of Account

The T account is a convenient way to record transactions. In practice, accountants use the *standard form*, given in Exhibit 3.2. The standard form shows the balance after every transaction and is, therefore, more useful and efficient than the T account. Your bank statement is an everyday example of the standard form.

> The standard form is more efficient than the T form. The bank statement follows the standard form.

EXHIBIT 3.2
Standard Form of Account

Cash					
Date	Explanation	Post. Ref.	Debit	Credit	Balance
20XX					
March 1	Owner's investment		50,000		50,000
2	Loan from Manish		20,000		70,000
3	Cash purchase of computer			58,000	12,000
9	Cash sales		12,000		24,000
12	Payment to suppliers			2,000	22,000
23	Refund for supplies returned		1,900		23,900
26	Salaries			4,000	19,900
26	Office rent			1,200	18,700
30	Drawings			3,500	15,200

LADDER
Opposite Entries

Here is a common question that comes up in the early stages of an accounting course: We record receipts as debits and payments as credits in the cash account. But the bank *credits* our account when we deposit money and *debits* our account when we withdraw money. It's confusing, isn't it? Answer: The cash account in our records is the mirror image of our deposit account kept by the bank. While our deposits with the bank are our assets, they are the bank's liabilities. The bank credits our account when we deposit cash because it owes us more; it debits our account for withdrawals because it owes us less.

Debit and Credit Rules

Under the double-entry system, we enter increases in assets on the debit side of the account, and increases in liabilities and equity on the credit side. Figure 3.1 describes the recording procedure in terms of the accounting equation:

Figure 3.1
DEBIT AND CREDIT RULES

Debit and credit rules for assets are the mirror image of those for liabilities and equity.

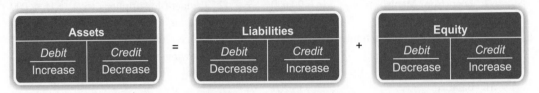

The rules for debit and credit for assets, liabilities, and equity are as follows:

1. *Assets*: Debit increase in asset to asset account. Credit decrease in asset to asset account.
2. *Liabilities and equity*: Credit increase in liability or equity to liability or equity account. Debit decrease in liability or equity to liability or equity account.

From Chapter 2, you know the following expanded form of the accounting equation:

Assets = Liabilities + Capital + Revenues – Expenses – Drawings (or Dividends)

We can rewrite this equation as follows:

Assets + Expenses + Drawings (or Dividends) = Liabilities + Capital + Revenues

We can now extend the rules for recording increase and decrease in equity to revenues, expenses, drawings, and dividends. Thus, we credit revenues to increase them; we debit expenses, drawings, and dividends to increase them. Figure 3.2 summarizes the rules for debit and credit.

Figure 3.2
DEBIT AND CREDIT RULES

Debit and credit rules follow the expanded accounting equation.

Effect	Assets, Expenses, Drawings, Dividends	Liabilities, Capital, Revenues
Increase	Debit	Credit
Decrease	Credit	Debit

The double-entry system is the workhorse of accounting. Shortly, you will be able to appreciate its great value in organizing and processing information. Though debits and credits may seem irksome, knowing them is a big help in communicating with accountants. However, the significance of the double-entry system goes far beyond its usefulness as a system of accounting mechanics. The German economic historian, Werner Sombart, noted that capitalism derives from the spirit of double-entry bookkeeping.

ONE-MINUTE QUIZ 3.2
Debits and Credits

Which of the following statements about debits and credits is correct? There may be more than one correct answer.
  (a) Debit balance represents something unfavourable; credit balance represents something favourable.
  (b) Debit is left and credit is right.
  (c) Balance is the net of debits and credits in an account.
  (d) A transaction must have equal debits and credits.

Consider the following two accounts.

HANDHOLD 3.1
Figuring out Transactions
from Accounts

Equipment	
10,000	

Cash

	10,000

The debit in the equipment account indicates purchase of equipment. The credit in the cash account indicates payment of cash. Therefore, the transaction is: Bought equipment for cash, ₹10,000.

Vineeta started Gastros, a food-ordering service. Her first six transactions, (a) to (f), appear in the accounts below. Identify the transactions.

TEST YOUR UNDERSTANDING 3.2
Figuring out Transactions from Accounts

Equipment

(a)	10,000		

Supplies

(b)	2,500		

Trade Receivables

(d)	6,000	(f)	4,900

Cash

(a)	5,000	(c)	1,200
(f)	4,900	(e)	1,500

Prepaid Insurance

(c)	1,200		

Share Capital

		(a)	15,000

Trade Payables

		(b)	2,500

Revenue from Services

		(d)	6,000

Salaries Expense

(e)	1,500		

Salma sets up FreeHand Company, a creative writing school. Let us take the company's first two transactions to illustrate the four steps in processing transactions: (1) analysis; (2) rules; (3) entry; (4) accounts. Italics signify change. We have the following four steps for each transaction:

HANDHOLD 3.2
Processing Transactions

Step 1	**ANALYSIS**	Study the changes in asset, liability and equity items.
Step 2	**RULES**	State the debit and credit rules relevant to the transaction.
Step 3	**ENTRY**	Record the transaction showing the accounts to debit and credit.
Step 4	**ACCOUNTS**	Present the related accounts after recording the transaction.

April 1	Salma invests cash in FreeHand Company's share capital, ₹10,000
ANALYSIS	Asset (Cash) increased. Equity (Share Capital) increased.
RULES	Debit asset to record increase. Credit equity to record increase.
ENTRY	Apr. 1 Cash.. 10,000 Share Capital............................. 10,000

ACCOUNTS	**Cash**			**Share Capital**		
	Apr. 1	10,000			Apr. 1	10,000

April 3	Takes a bank loan carrying interest of 12 per cent per year, ₹5,000.		
ANALYSIS	Asset (Cash) increased. Liability (Bank Loan) increased.		
RULES	Debit asset to record increase. Credit liability to record increase.		
ENTRY	April 3 Cash...		5,000	
	Bank Loan			5,000

	Cash				Bank Loan	
ACCOUNTS	Apr. 1	10,000			Apr. 3	5,000
	3	5,000				

The balance is the result of recording more increase than decrease. We debit asset, expense, drawing, and dividend accounts to record increase, and credit to record decrease in those accounts. As a result, asset and expense accounts usually have *debit balances*. Since we credit liability, share capital and revenue accounts to record increase and debit to record decrease, these accounts usually have *credit balances*. The usual type of balance for an account is its normal balance. Figure 3.3 summarizes the normal balances for the various types of accounts.

Figure 3.3

NORMAL BALANCES

Normal balance appears on the same side (debit or credit) of an account in which increase in the account appears.

Type of Account	Increase Recorded by	Normal Balance
Asset	Debit	Debit
Liability	Credit	Credit
Equity		
Share capital	Credit	Credit
Revenue	Credit	Credit
Expense	Debit	Debit
Drawing / Dividend	Debit	Debit

Can the cash account have a credit balance?

QUICK QUESTION
Cash account balance

**TEST YOUR
UNDERSTANDING 3.3**
Normal Balances

Indicate the normal balance of the accounts in *Test Your Understanding 3.1*.

**DISCUSSION
QUESTION 3.2**

We don't need to learn double-entry accounting when we can use accounting software. Do you agree?

....
....
....

Comprehensive Illustration: Vogue Company

Learning Objective

LO 4 Analyze and record the effect of business transactions using debits and credits.

To illustrate the procedure for recording transactions, let us set up Vogue Company, a business that supplies new designs for dresses. In this illustration, you will learn how to record a transaction in terms of debits and credits.

June 1	Rakesh invested cash in Vogue Company's share capital, ₹50,000.		
ANALYSIS	Asset (Cash) increased. Equity (Share Capital) increased.		
RULES	Debit asset to record increase. Credit equity to record increase.		
ENTRY	June 1 Cash...		50,000	
	Share Capital..			50,000

	Cash				Share Capital	
ACCOUNTS	June 1	50,000			June 1	50,000

June 2	Bought office supplies for cash, ₹2,000.
ANALYSIS	Asset (Office Supplies) increased. Asset (Cash) decreased.
RULES	Debit expense to record increase. Credit asset to record decrease.
ENTRY	June 2　Office Supplies ....　2,000 　　　　　　　Cash..　　　　　2,000

ACCOUNTS	Office Supplies		Cash		
	June 2	2,000	June 1	50,000	June 2　2,000

June 3	Paid office rent for June, ₹1,500.
ANALYSIS	Expense (Rent Expense) increased. Asset (Cash) decreased.
RULES	Debit asset to record increase. Credit asset to record decrease.
ENTRY	June 3　Rent Expense ....　1,500 　　　　　　　Cash..　　　　　1,500

ACCOUNTS	Rent Expense		Cash		
	June 3	1,500	June 1	50,000	June 2　2,000
					3　1,500

June 4	Bought equipment from Agrawal Company for cash, ₹3,000.
ANALYSIS	Asset (Equipment) increased. Asset (Cash) decreased.
RULES	Debit asset to record increase. Credit asset to record decrease.
ENTRY	June 4　Equipment ....　3,000 　　　　　　　Cash..　　　　　3,000

ACCOUNTS	Equipment		Cash		
	June 4	3,000	June 1	50,000	June 2　2,000
					3　1,500
					4　3,000

June 5	Signed an agreement with EthnicWear for developing a special design. The agreement provided for payment of a fee of ₹2,000 by EthnicWear on completion of the work.
ANALYSIS	Signing an agreement with a customer is not a transaction since it does not create any asset or revenue. Vogue will earn the revenue when it completes the design.

June 6	Paid for a one-year fire insurance policy that will expire May 31, next year, ₹720.
ANALYSIS	Asset (Prepaid Insurance) increased. Asset (Cash) decreased.
RULES	Debit asset to record increase. Credit asset to record decrease.
ENTRY	June 4　Prepaid Insurance ....　720 　　　　　　　Cash..　　　　　720

ACCOUNTS	Prepaid Insurance		Cash		
	June 6	720	June 1	50,000	June 2　2,000
					3　1,500
					4　3,000
					6　720

June 7	Sold design for cash, ₹2,000.
ANALYSIS	Asset (Cash) increased. Revenue (Revenue from Services) increased.
RULES	Debit asset to record increase. Credit revenue to record increase.

ENTRY	June 7 Cash... 2,000	
	Revenue from Services	2,000

ACCOUNTS

Cash					Revenue from Services		
June 1	50,000	June 2	2,000			June 7	2,000
7	2,000	3	1,500				
		4	3,000				
		6	720				

June 8	Received from Kidswear, a customer, for services to be provided later, ₹1,500.
ANALYSIS	Asset (Cash) increased. Liability (Unearned Revenue) increased.
RULES	Debit asset to record increase. Credit liability to record increase.

ENTRY	June 8 Cash... 1,500	
	Unearned Revenue	1,500

ACCOUNTS

Cash					Unearned Revenue		
June 1	50,000	June 2	2,000			June 8	1,500
7	2,000	3	1,500				
8	1,500	4	3,000				
		6	720				

June 9	Bought office supplies on credit from Mohan Company, ₹3,500.
ANALYSIS	Asset (Office Supplies) increased. Liability (Trade Payables) increased.
RULES	Debit asset to record increase. Credit liability to record increase.

ENTRY	June 9 Office Supplies 3,500	
	Trade Payables	3,500

ACCOUNTS

Office Supplies				Trade Payables		
June 2	2,000				June 9	3,500
9	3,500					

June 10	Billed Shah Company for designs completed, ₹9,000.
ANALYSIS	Asset (Trade Receivables) increased. Revenue (Revenue from Services) increased.
RULES	Debit asset to record increase. Credit revenue to record increase.

ENTRY	June 10 Trade Receivables.. 9,000	
	Revenue from Services...................................	9,000

ACCOUNTS

Trade Receivables				Revenue from Services		
June 10	9,000				June 7	2,000
					10	9,000

June 14	Paid Mohan Company on account, ₹1,000.[2]
ANALYSIS	Liability (Trade Payables) decreased. Asset (Cash) decreased.
RULES	Debit liability to record decrease. Credit asset to record decrease.

ENTRY	June 14 Trade Payables 1,000	
	Cash...	1,000

ACCOUNTS

Trade Payables				Cash			
June 14	1,000	June 9	3,500	June 1	50,000	June 2	2,000
				7	2,000	3	1,500
				8	1,500	4	3,000
						6	720
						14	1,000

---

[2] 'On account payment' is a part payment.

June 18	Received from Shah Company on account, ₹4,000.		
ANALYSIS	Asset (Cash) increased. Asset (Trade Receivables) decreased.		
RULES	Debit asset to record increase. Credit asset to record decrease.		
ENTRY	June 18 Cash..	4,000	
	Trade Receivables...		4,000

		Cash				**Trade Receivables**		
	June 1	50,000	June 2	2,000	June 10	9,000	June 18	4,000
ACCOUNTS	7	2,000	3	1,500				
	8	1,500	4	3,000				
	18	4,000	6	720				
			14	1,000				

June 21	Appointed an office manager on a monthly salary of ₹1,500.
ANALYSIS	Appointing an employee is not a transaction since it does not create any expense or liability. Vogue will record an expense after the office manager has provided services.

June 22	Used office supplies, ₹1,800.		
ANALYSIS	Expense (Office Supplies Expense) increased. Asset (Office Supplies) decreased.		
RULES	Debit expense to record increase. Credit asset to record decrease.		
ENTRY	June 22 Office Supplies Expense..................................	1,800	
	Office Supplies...		1,800

	Office Supplies Expense			**Office Supplies**		
ACCOUNTS	June 22	1,800		June 2	2,000	June 22	1,800
				9	3,500	

June 25	Completed designs for Gupta Company for ₹3,000 and received ₹1,000 in part payment.		
ANALYSIS	Asset (Trade Receivables) increased. Asset (Cash) increased. Revenue (Revenue from Services) increased.		
RULES	Debit assets to record increase. Credit revenue to record increase.		
ENTRY	June 25 Cash..	1,000	
	Trade Receivables...	2,000	
	Revenue from Services.............................		3,000

		Cash				**Trade Receivables**		
	June 1	50,000	June 2	2,000	June 10	9,000	June 18	4,000
	7	2,000	3	1,500	25	2,000		
ACCOUNTS	8	1,500	4	3,000	**Revenue from Services**			
	18	4,000	6	720			June 7	2,000
	25	1,000	14	1,000			10	9,000
							25	3,000

June 27	Paid telephone bill, ₹200.		
ANALYSIS	Expense (Telephone Expense) increased. Asset (Cash) decreased.		
RULES	Debit expense to record increase. Credit asset to record decrease.		
ENTRY	June 27 Telephone Expense	200	
	Cash..		200

	Telephone Expense			**Cash**		
	June 27	200		June 1	50,000	June 2	2,000
				7	2,000	3	1,500
ACCOUNTS				8	1,500	4	3,000
				18	4,000	6	720
				25	1,000	14	1,000
						27	200

June 28	Paid office assistant's June salary, ₹800.
ANALYSIS	Expense (Salaries Expense) increased. Asset (Cash) decreased.
RULES	Debit expense to record increase. Credit asset to record decrease.
ENTRY	June 28 Salaries Expense... 800
	Cash... 800

	Salaries Expense		Cash			
	June 28	800	June 1	50,000	June 2	2,000
			7	2,000	3	1,500
ACCOUNTS			8	1,500	4	3,000
			18	4,000	6	720
			25	1,000	14	1,000
					27	200
					28	800

June 29	Paid electricity bill, ₹150.
ANALYSIS	Expense (Electricity Expense) increased. Asset (Cash) decreased.
RULES	Debit expense to record increase. Credit asset to record decrease.
ENTRY	June 29 Electricity Expense 150
	Cash... 150

	Electricity Expense		Cash			
	June 29	150	June 1	50,000	June 2	2,000
			7	2,000	3	1,500
			8	1,500	4	3,000
ACCOUNTS			18	4,000	6	720
			25	1,000	14	1,000
					27	200
					28	800
					29	150

June 30	Paid dividend, ₹2,200.
ANALYSIS	Dividends (Dividends) increased. Asset (Cash) decreased.
RULES	Debit dividends to record increase. Credit asset to record decrease.
ENTRY	June 30 Dividends... 2,200
	Cash... 2,200

	Dividends		Cash			
	June 30	2,200	June 1	50,000	June 2	2,000
			7	2,000	3	1,500
			8	1,500	4	3,000
			18	4,000	6	720
ACCOUNTS			25	1,000	14	1,000
					27	200
					28	800
					29	150
					30	2,200

Exhibit 3.3 presents Vogue's ledger for June. The accounts are grouped into asset, liability and equity categories.

Asset Accounts				EXHIBIT 3.3

EXHIBIT 3.3
VOGUE COMPANY:
Ledger

Equipment

June	4	3,000		
Balance		**3,000**		

Office Supplies

June	2	2,000	June	22	1,800
	9	3,500			
		5,500			1,800
Balance		**3,700**			

Trade Receivables

June	10	9,000	June	18	4,000
	25	2,000			
		11,000			4,000
Balance		**7,000**			

Cash

June	1	50,000	June	2	2,000
	7	2,000		3	1,500
	8	1,500		4	3,000
	18	4,000		6	720
	25	1,000		14	1,000
				27	200
				28	800
				29	150
				30	2,200
		58,500			11,570
Balance		**46,930**			

Prepaid Insurance

June	6	720		
Balance		**720**		

Assets = 3,000 + 3,700 + 7,000 + 46,930 + 720 = 61,350

Liability Accounts				

Trade Payables

June	14	1,000	June	9	3,500
		1,000			3,500
			Balance		**2,500**

Unearned Revenue

			June	8	1,500
			Balance		**1,500**

Liabilities = 2,500 + 1,500 = 4,000

Equity Accounts				

Share Capital

			June	1	50,000
			Balance		**50,000**

Dividends

June	30	2,200		
Balance		**2,200**		

Revenue from Services

	June	7	2,000
		10	9,000
		25	3,000
	Balance		**14,000**

Rent Expense

June	3	1,500	
Balance		**1,500**	

Telephone Expense

June	27	200	
Balance		**200**	

Salaries Expense

June	28	800	
Balance		**800**	

Electricity Expense

June	29	150	
Balance		**150**	

Office Supplies Expense

June	22	1,800	
Balance		**1,800**	

Equity = 50,000 + 14,000 − 4,450 − 2,200 = 57,350

Verification of the Accounting Equation

Assets		=	Liabilities		+	Capital		+
Equipment........................	3,000		Trade payables	2,500		Share capital..............	50,000	
Office supplies.................	3,700		Unearned revenue..................	1,500				
Trade receivables.............	7,000							
Cash	49,930							
Prepaid insurance.............	720							
	61,350	=		4,000	+		50,000	+

Revenue		−	Expenses		−	Dividends		
Revenue from services	14,000		Rent expense...........................	1,500		Dividends...................	2,200	
			Telephone expense	200				
			Salaries expense	800				
			Electricity expense..................	150				
			Office supplies expense	1,800				
	14,000	−		4,450	−		2,200	

TEST YOUR UNDERSTANDING 3.4
Processing Transactions

Continuing with Handhold 3.2, FreeHand engaged in the following transactions:

April	4	Hired a computer on a monthly rental of ₹1,000.
	8	Provided services for cash, ₹4,000.
	12	Billed customers for services, ₹8,000.
	17	Received cash for services to be provided in May, ₹1,000.
	21	Bought supplies on credit, ₹400.
	25	Collected on account from customers billed on April 12, ₹5,000.
	29	Paid computer rental, ₹1,000.
	30	Paid interest on bank loan for April, ₹50.

Analyze the transactions, apply the debit-credit rules and record the entries.

When can the trade receivables account have a credit balance?

Recording Transactions

Journal

The journal is a chronological record of an enterprise's transactions. The word 'journal' derives from the Latin word *diurnalis* meaning "diurnal" which implies "of or during the day time". The journal is called the *book of original entry* or *primary book* because this is the accounting record where we first record transactions. It provides in one place a complete record of all transactions with necessary explanation. A journal entry has transaction date, individual accounts, debit and credit amounts, and narration. Journalizing is the process of recording transactions in the journal. *Day book* is another term for journal.

Learning Objective

LO 5 — Record transactions in the journal.

Companies usually maintain several kinds of journals. The nature of operations and the frequency of a particular type of transaction in a company determine the number and design of journals. This book describes the **general journal**, the most common type of journal. It has separate columns to record the following information about each transaction:

1. Date;
2. Individual accounts;
3. Debit and credit amounts;
4. Brief explanation of the transaction; and
5. Posting reference.

Exhibit 3.4 illustrates the general journal using two transactions of Vogue Company.

The general journal has columns for date, debit and credit accounts, and related amounts.

EXHIBIT 3.4
VOGUE COMPANY:
Journal

Date	Description	Post. Ref. [5]	Debit	Credit
20XX		Page 1		
June 1 [1]	Cash [2]		50,000 [3]	
	Share capital [2]			50,000 [3]
	Invested cash [4]			
				Page 3
	Compound entry			
25 [1]	Cash [2]		1,000 [3]	
	Trade Receivables [2]		2,000 [3]	
	Revenue from Services [2]			3,000 [3]
	Provide services on part payment [4]			

General Journal — Page 1

The procedure for recording transactions in the general journal is as follows:
1. Enter the year, month, and date of the transaction in the Date column.
   - There is no need to repeat the year and month for subsequent entries until the start of a new page, or a new month.
2. Write the account titles under the Description column.
   - Enter the account to debit on the first line of the entry next to the left margin. If there are several accounts to debit, enter them one after the other.
   - Enter the account to credit on the line below the account(s) to debit and *indent* it to set the account apart from the account(s) to debit. If there are several accounts to credit, enter them one after the other.
   - Use the account titles from the company's chart of accounts.
   - A *compound entry* has more than one debit and/or credit items.
3. Enter the amount of the debit in the Debit column alongside the account to debit and the amount of the credit in the Credit column alongside the account to credit.
4. Write a brief explanation of the transaction.
5. Post. Ref. (Posting Reference) is left blank at the time of making the journal entry.

Special journals are used to record transactions of specific types. For example, the *purchases journal* records credit purchases, the *sales journal* records credit sales and the *cash book* records cash receipts and payments.

QUICK QUESTION
Special journal

Is a special journal a journal or a ledger?

DISCUSSION QUESTION 3.3

Does it make sense to keep only the journal and no ledger?

....

....

....

Ledger

Learning Objective

LO 6 Post journal entries to the ledger.

Posting is the process of transferring information from the journal to the ledger. We enter each amount in the Debit column in the journal on the debit side of the appropriate account and each amount on the Credit column in the journal on the credit side of the appropriate account. The frequency of posting could be daily, weekly, or monthly, depending on the number of transactions.

Posting has the following steps:

1. Locate in the ledger the account(s) to debit.
2. Enter the date of the transaction in the account.
3. Enter the relevant journal page number in the Post. Ref. column of the account.
4. Enter the debit amount appearing in the journal in the Debit column of the account.
5. Enter the account code or the ledger folio number in the Post. Ref. column of the journal.
6. Repeat steps 1 to 5 for the account(s) to credit.

Exhibit 3.5 illustrates these steps separately for the debit and credit parts of a journal entry. Entering the account code in the "Post. Ref." column of the journal is the last step in posting. It indicates that the accountant has transferred all the information in the journal entry to the ledger. In addition, the account codes in this column are a convenient means for locating any additional information about an amount appearing in an account. Since this book does not use account codes, you don't have to complete this column.

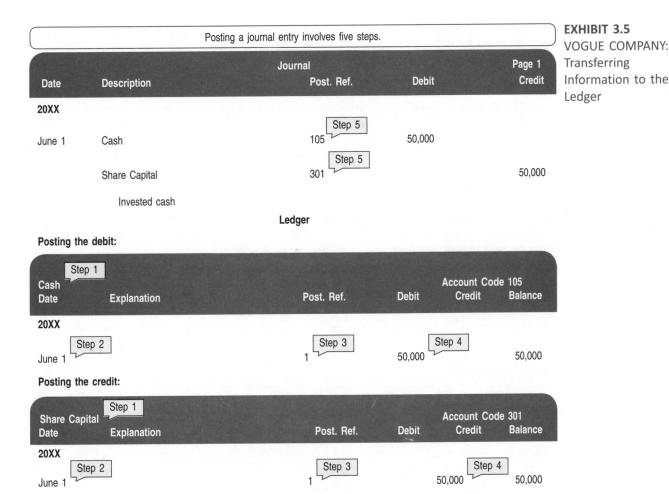

EXHIBIT 3.5
VOGUE COMPANY: Transferring Information to the Ledger

The next step in the recording process is the preparation of trial balance.

Which of the following statements about the journal is correct? There may be more than one correct answer.

ONE-MINUTE QUIZ 3.3
Journal and Ledger

(a) The number of accounts debited in a journal entry must equal the number of accounts credited in the entry.
(b) The total amount debited in a journal entry must equal the total amount credited in the entry.
(c) Transactions are first recorded in the journal and then in the ledger.
(d) At the end of a day, the journal will show the balance of the accounts.

For a beginner in accounting, recording the effect of a transaction can be confusing at times. Recall that an account is a record of increases and decreases in an item. We use journal entries to record *changes* in an account. To illustrate, suppose a business has cash of ₹2,100 and a receivable of ₹1,000 from a customer, besides other items. The customer pays ₹600, a part of the receivable of ₹1,000. The journal entry, *Debit Cash 600; Credit Trade Receivables 600*, records this transaction. As a result, Cash increases by ₹600 and Trade Receivables decreases by ₹600. The new balance of Trade Receivables is ₹400, i.e. beginning balance, ₹1,000 – collection, ₹600. The new balance of Cash is ₹2,700, i.e. beginning balance, ₹2,100 + collection, ₹600. *We do not record a journal entry for the balance amount.* The balance is the difference between the debit and the credit totals. Transaction entries record *delta* (Δ), the mathematical shorthand for change. So remember that journal entries record changes, not balances.

LADDER
Transaction and Balance

Materiality

The **materiality threshold** (also known as the **materiality principle**) saves us from having to make tedious calculations or disclosing needless detail, not warranted in most cases.

An item is material if it is sufficiently large or important for users of the information to be influenced by it.

The materiality threshold helps in balancing the costs and benefits of disclosures and accounting methods. Materiality questions are pervasive in financial reporting. For instance: Should all inventory items be physically verified? Should every piece of equipment be recorded as an asset and depreciated or can items of low value be expensed at the time of acquisition? How operating segments should be selected for reporting? Can expenses be grouped into categories? The answers will depend on the facts and circumstances of each case. For example, a payment of ₹10,000 is most probably not material for a business that reports a profit of ₹250 million. However, it could very well be material for a business reporting a profit of ₹250,000. Schedule III requires disclosure of any item of income or expenditure which exceeds 1 per cent of the revenue from operations or ₹100,000, whichever is higher. Judgment is required in determining materiality.

DISCUSSION QUESTION 3.4

Should small amounts of fines and penalties be disclosed?

....

....

....

Trial Balance

Learning Objective

LO 7 Prepare a trial balance.

The **trial balance** is a list of account balances. Pacioli is said to have advised that the bookkeeper should not go to sleep at night until the debits equalled the credits. Exhibit 3.6 shows a trial balance for Vogue Company. The trial balance lists each account in the ledger that appears in Exhibit 3.3, with the debit balances in the left column, and the credit balances in the right column. Each column has a total, and the two totals must be equal. When this happens, the trial balance is said to be "in balance."

EXHIBIT 3.6

VOGUE COMPANY: Trial Balance, June 30, 20XX

The trial balance lists ledger balances on a specified date. It is a basic check on bookkeeping.		
Equipment	₹ 3,000	
Office supplies	3,700	
Trade receivables	7,000	
Cash	46,930	
Prepaid insurance	720	
Trade payables		2,500
Unearned revenue		1,500
Share capital		50,000
Dividends	2,200	
Revenue from services		14,000
Rent expense	1,500	
Telephone expense	200	
Salaries expense	800	
Electricity expense	150	
Office supplies expense	1,800	
Total	68,000	68,000

We are quite pleased that the debits equalled the credits in the Vogue Company illustration. This is because we followed double entry meticulously and recorded the transactions and amounts accurately.

Errors in Accounting Records

A trial balance that balances is a necessary condition for error-free accounting but it is not a sufficient condition. This means that it can be trusted to detect some types of error but not others. All errors should be corrected, whether they affect the trial balance or not. In most cases, a <u>correcting entry</u> would be necessary to fix the error. The three steps in correcting errors are:

Learning Objective

LO 8 Correct errors in accounting records.

1. Understand the erroneous entry.
2. Visualize the correct entry.
3. Record the correcting entry.

Errors that Don't Affect the Trial Balance

First, let us see some errors that *don't affect* the trial balance. Suppose the accountant made the following errors in the Vogue Company illustration:

Error Type	Example	Effect
Incorrect classification	1. June 3: Recorded rent paid as telephone expense.	• Rent expense less, and telephone expense more, by ₹1,500.
Omission	2. June 10: Omitted the credit sale.	• Trade receivables and revenue less by ₹9,000.
Repetition	3. June 2: Recorded the purchase twice.	• Cash balance less, and office supplies more, by ₹2,000.
Compensating error	4. June 7: Recorded ₹200 in both cash and revenue.	• Cash and revenue less by ₹1,800.

Suppose we notice the errors at the month-end. Let's now see how to correct the above errors.

June 3: Recording rent paid as telephone expense, ₹1,500. This resulted in understating rent expense by ₹1,500 and overstating telephone expense by a like amount. The following entry corrects the error:

| June 30 | Rent Expense... | 1,500 | |
| | Telephone Expense.. | | 1,500 |

June 10: Omitting the credit sale, ₹9,000. This resulted in understating both trade receivables and revenue by ₹9,000. We correct the error by recording the transaction:

| June 30 | Trade Receivables .... | 9,000 | |
| | Revenue from Services.. | | 9,000 |

June 2: Recording the purchase twice, ₹2,000. This resulted in understating cash, and overstating office supplies, by ₹2,000. We correct the error by cancelling the duplicate entry:

| June 30 | Cash.. | 2,000 | |
| | Office Supplies .... | | 2,000 |

June 7: Recording ₹200 in both cash and revenue. This resulted in understating both cash and revenue by ₹1,800. We correct the error by recording the difference:

| June 30 | Cash.. | 1,800 | |
| | Revenue from Services .... | | 1,800 |

The above journal entries are posted and the account balances are recalculated.

Errors that Affect the Trial Balance

Now, we will see how to correct errors that *affect* the trial balance. Suppose the accountant made the following errors in the Vogue Company illustration:

Error Type	Example	Effect
Omitting a debit	5. June 25: Omitted the debit to trade receivables.	• Trade receivables less by ₹2,000.
Omitting a credit	6. June 6: Omitted the credit to cash.	• Cash more by ₹720.
Recording a debit as a credit	7. June 7: Credited instead of debiting cash.	• Cash less by ₹4,000.
Recording a credit as a debit	8. June 25: Debited instead of crediting revenue from services.	• Revenue from services less by ₹6,000.
Recording different amounts in debit and credit	9. June 4: Debited equipment ₹3,000 and credited cash ₹300.	• Cash more by ₹2,700.
Transposing digits	10. June 22: Debited office supplies expense ₹8,100 instead of ₹1,800.	• Office supplies expense more by ₹6,300.

Since these errors contravene double entry, the trial balance will not balance. We initially note the difference as suspense. Let us take three examples from the above.

June 25: Omitting the debit to trade receivables, ₹2,000. As a result, trade receivables has a balance of ₹5,000, which is ₹2,000 less than the correct June 30 balance. So the trial balance debit total would be ₹2,000 less than the credit total. Initially, we take the difference to the debit of an account called Suspense. The following entry corrects the error:

June 30   Trade Receivables 2,000
           Suspense   2,000

After posting the above entry, Trade Receivables has a debit balance of ₹7,000 and Suspense has zero balance, as shown below:

Trade Receivables

June 10	9,000	June 18	4,000
	9,000		**4,000**
Incorrect balance	5,000		
June 30 Correcting entry	*2,000*		
Correct balance	*7,000*		

Suspense

June 30 Difference in trial balance	2,000	*June 30 Correcting entry*	*2,000*

June 7: Crediting instead of debiting cash, ₹2,000. As a result, cash has a balance of ₹42,930, which is ₹4,000 less than the correct June 30 balance. So the trial balance debit total would be less than the credit total by ₹4,000. Initially, we take the difference to the debit of Suspense. The following entry corrects the error:

June 30   Cash 4,000
           Suspense   4,000

After posting the above entry, Cash has a debit balance of ₹46,930 and Suspense has zero balance, as shown below:

Cash

June 1	50,000	June 2		2,000
8	1,500	3		1,500
18	4,000	4		3,000
25	1,000	6		720
		7		2,000
		14		1,000
		27		200
		28		800
		29		150
		30		2,200
	56,500			13,570
Incorrect balance	42,930			
June 30 Correcting entry	4,000			
Correct balance	46,930			

Suspense

June 30 Difference in trial balance	4,000	June 30 *Correcting entry*	4,000

June 22: Crediting office supplies expense ₹8,100 instead of ₹1,800. As a result, office supplies has a balance of ₹8,100, which is ₹6,300 more than the correct June 30 balance. So the trial balance debit total would be more than the credit total by ₹6,300. Initially, we take the difference to the credit of Suspense. The following entry corrects the error:

June 30 Suspense...	6,300	
Office Supplies Expense...		6,300

After posting the above entry, Office Supplies Expense has a debit balance of ₹1,800 and Suspense has zero balance, as shown below:

Office Supplies Expense

June 22	8,100		
Incorrect balance	8,100		
		June 30 Correcting entry	*6,300*
Correct balance	1,800		

Suspense

June 30 Correcting entry	*6,300*	June 30 Difference in trial balance	6,300

A better alternative to correcting errors is not to make them in the first place. That said, learning how to correct errors is arguably the best test of your grasp of the double-entry system.

Which of the following statements about the trial balance is correct? There may be more than one correct answer.
  (a) If a trial balance balances, it implies that the debits and credits in the accounts are equal.
  (b) If a trial balance balances, it means that the transactions in a period have been recorded.
  (c) Crediting unearned revenue instead of revenue earned will cause a trial balance difference.
  (d) Debiting trade payables instead of trade receivables will cause a trial balance difference.

ONE-MINUTE QUIZ 3.4
Trial Balance and Errors

Prepare correcting entries for the remaining errors in the Vogue Company illustration.

TEST YOUR UNDERSTANDING 3.5
Correcting Errors

Technology in Accounting

Rapid changes in technology have a profound effect on accounting. We will now look at how three major advances in technology — cloud computing, blockchain technology, and machine learning — are changing the work of accountants.

Cloud Computing

Cloud computing eliminates the need to buy, run and maintain in-house technology infrastructure, such as servers and software. Instead, cloud applications are made available over the Internet. Users share applications, while the software vendor manages the applications and the storage space.

Cloud computing includes SaaS (Software-as-a-service), IaaS (Infrastructure-as-a-service), and Platform-as-a-service (PaaS). The vendor owns the software and runs it in its data centre. The customer does not buy the software or server, but rents it for a periodic fee. Many customers can access the same software and server at a time. Many applications such as payroll, sales tax and VAT, income tax return preparation, invoice management, and enterprise resource planning (ERP) run on cloud.

Cloud computing firms claim a number of benefits for their products, such as quick implementation, anytime access anywhere with an Internet connection, lower initial investment in hardware and software, no or low maintenance costs, reduced support costs, easy and regular upgrades, and disaster recovery and back-up capabilities. Cloud computing risks and difficulties include safety of users' data, unscheduled downtime, low Internet bandwidth, and data ownership and migration.

Blockchain Technology

Blockchain is a shared public database for recording transactions in a way that does not allow the record to be altered at a later date. Blockchain technology underpins bitcoin, the cryptocurrency. The technology has the potential to transform accounting systems.

Managers can trust their own books because of the checks built in double-entry bookkeeping. Gaining the trust of outsiders is a different and difficult matter. To illustrate, suppose that Seller Company has a receivable of ₹10,000 from Buyer Company. This would make sense only if Buyer Company has a payable of ₹10,000 to Seller Company. Currently, Seller Company sends and records the invoice and other documents and accountants review the records to make sure that it is all fine. In contrast, the blockchain has both the transaction and a *shared ledger* for that transaction. Using blockchain, Seller and Buyer share the same data. There is one ledger for this transaction that is shared between the two companies. Since both Seller and Buyer are looking at exactly the same data, we can certainly say Buyer owes Seller ₹10,000.

Using blockchain technology, businesses can record their transactions directly in a joint register. The entries are distributed and cryptographically sealed. So falsifying or destroying transactions to conceal activity is practically impossible. It is an electronic verification system.

The law requires tamper-proof recordkeeping. It is easy to detect modification in physical records. Electronic records are vulnerable because they can't be seen physically. Using blockchain it is possible to generate hash string of the file. It is the digital fingerprint of that file. That fingerprint is immutably timestamped into the blockchain. At anytime it is possible to prove the integrity of the file by again generating the fingerprint and comparing it with the fingerprint stored in the blockchain. Entire processes carried out in many departments or companies can be traced. This generates an audit trail for the use of external auditors and others interested in following through the life cycle of a transaction from say placing a purchase order to paying the vendor.

Finally, blockchain allows for *smart contracts,* i.e. a computer program that executes on its own. For instance, an invoice will get paid automatically after confirming that goods have been received as specified and there is sufficient bank balance.

Machine Learning

Machine learning, a branch of artificial learning, uses computer programs called algorithms to extract patterns from data and make predictions. Many accounting and auditing procedures are amenable to machine learning. For instance, algorithms can check travel claims and supplier invoices and raise a red flag on suspected fraud cases. It is impossible for auditors to verify the large numbers of transactions. In the past auditors looked at samples of data. Using machine learning technologies auditors can analyze entire journals looking for entries recorded by unexpected people or at odd times. Also, auditors are increasingly trawling the unstructured data in emails, blog posts, posts on Facebook or LinkedIn, or tweets to get a sense of deviant behaviour. The use of analytics can produce significant cost savings and improve the reliability of auditing.

Internal Control Systems

Internal control is a process intended to assure that an organization works to achieve its goals efficiently, produces reliable financial statements, complies with relevant laws and regulations and manages its major risks. The board of directors and management require good internal control systems. Equally, outsiders such as shareholders, regulators, and government benefit from internal controls. An internal control system extends beyond matters that relate directly to the functions of the accounting system. Internal controls comprise accounting controls and administrative controls, as illustrated in Exhibit 3.7.

Learning Objective

LO 10 Understand the importance of internal control systems.

EXHIBIT 3.7
Accounting Controls and Administrative Controls

Internal controls go beyond the accounting system.	
Accounting Controls	**Administrative Controls**
Objective ■ To safeguard assets and reliability of financial records. ■ To provide reasonable assurance that — all transactions are authorized by management and are promptly and properly recorded. — access to assets is permitted only in accordance with management's authorization.	■ Maintain and improve operational efficiency and adhere to management policies.
Examples (a) Stores can issue materials only when an employee produces a proper requisition. (b) Employees must submit travel claims and get them approved by the higher authority for payment of travel expenses.	(a) Sales managers must meet quarterly and annual targets for sales volume, product mix, profitability, and advertising expense. (b) Employees must prepare reports describing the purpose and result of official travel and get them approved by the higher authority.

In many cases, an administrative control is the starting point for establishing accounting control. For example, a requirement that every employee must submit a report describing the purpose and result of an official travel is related to the accounting control for payment of official travel expense. In practice, some controls may be meant for both managerial decision-making and custody of property. For instance, a product cost classification may be used for recording the value of inventories (an accounting matter), as also for product pricing (an administrative matter).

Administrative controls span different functional areas and are dealt with in courses in management accounting, operations management, and marketing management. Since the accountant is responsible for establishing systems for the safeguarding of assets and the reliability of records, a study of the elements of accounting controls is an important part of a course in financial accounting. The Companies Act requires the directors of a listed company to state that they have laid down "internal financial controls" to be followed by the company and the controls are adequate and are operating effectively.

Features of a Good Internal Control System

We will now see some of the features of a good internal control system.

Separation of duties The organizational structure should provide for the segregation of functional responsibilities. No individual should be responsible for all phases of a transaction. Segregation of operations, custody, and accounting significantly reduce the chances of fraud, since fraud would become more difficult if two or more individuals have to collude.

- In a sale transaction, one employee may enter the quantity of the item sold, a second employee may input its price, and a third may post the invoice to the customer's ledger.

Authorizing and recording transactions A competent official in the organization must authorize transactions, preferably by signing or initialling documents. Then the accounting department must record the transactions, by first classifying them on the basis of a carefully devised scheme and then summarizing them according to the classification. There are several mechanisms to verify the correctness of the recording process. For example, preparation of a trial balance is a check on the proper recording of debits and credits.

Sound administrative practices All major instructions and procedures should be in writing. Many organizations have manuals that describe the procedures to be followed by employees in carrying out their duties. They lay down the standards of work and specify the responsibilities of individual managers. Also, they prepare budgets and circulate them to key managers.

Sound personnel policies Reliable and competent personnel are fundamental to the success of a control system. The organization should verify past experience cited in job applications and investigate significant gaps in experience. At times, it may turn out that a candidate was serving a jail sentence during an unexplained gap in employment. Mass recruitment is risky, because it does not allow for proper pre-employment screening. Wherever necessary, an organization should engage the services of specialist investigation agencies. (In fact, some organizations employ detectives to verify the background of selected candidates.) There should be periodical rotation of employees on different jobs and regular supervision of their work. Many organizations require employees in key positions to take vacation every year in order to let them have a well-deserved break and find out in their absence what they were doing. Fidelity bonds insure the company against employee theft.

Internal audit Human ingenuity is inexhaustible. Dishonest employees find out ways of defrauding the organization despite the existence of many controls. The organization should always be alert to possibilities of embezzlements, frauds, and errors. Managers should regularly investigate the systems they are working with. Internal auditors are not directly involved in operations and they should perform regular reviews of internal control systems. They can evaluate both the overall efficiency of operations and the effectiveness of the internal control system. According to an Ernst & Young survey, 41 per cent of respondents said that they employed internal audit to detect fraud.[3] The Companies Act requires companies to appoint an internal auditor, who shall be a CA or a cost accountant.

---

[3] Ernst & Young, *Fraud and Corporate Governance: Changing Paradigm in India*, 2012.

Can journal entries be weapons of mass destruction? Satyam Computer Services is the most high profile case of the collapse of accounting, auditing and corporate governance involving an Indian company. On January 7, 2009, B. Ramalinga Raju, chairman and executive of Satyam, resigned after admitting that he had manipulated the accounts for several years in order to show hugely inflated profits and fictitious assets totaling $1 billion. On that day, Satyam's stock plunged to ₹40.25 at the National Stock Exchange, after opening at ₹179, and touched a low of ₹6.30 on January 9, 2009, the next trading day. Reacting to this development, the Sensex crashed 7 per cent. As a news report put it, it was "a unique case of upheavals at a single company pulling down the Indian stock market."[4]

Fictitious accounting entries were at the core of the fraud. The following entries illustrate the fraud:

(a)	Trade Receivables	1,000	
	Revenue from Services...		1,000
(b)	Cash	1,000	
	Trade Receivables...		1,000

In reality, the company did not provide any services for ₹1,000 and certainly did not collect anything for those made-up customers. There was an elaborate scheme of manipulation of computerized accounting records in breach of established control systems.

Cash, unlike receivables, can be verified easily. Cash is either there or not there. How did the company conjure up the cash? Answer: The company produced fake bank deposit documents.

RECAP

- The accounting system organizes information systematically.
- An *account* is a record of increases and decreases in an asset, liability or equity item.
- Accounts can be in *T form* or *standard form*. Debit is left and credit is right.
- *Ledger* is a collection of accounts.
- *Chart of accounts* is a complete list of the account titles used in an organization.
- *Journal* is a chronological record of transactions.
- *Trial balance* is a list of account balances.
- Debit and credit rules:
  - *Assets, expenses, dividends:* Debit to increase. Credit to decrease.
  - *Liabilities, capital, revenues:* Credit to increase. Debit to decrease.
- Transaction processing steps:
  1. Analyze the changes in asset, liability, capital, revenue, expense and dividend items.
  2. Enter the transaction in the journal applying the debit and credit rules.
  3. Post the journal entry to the related accounts in the ledger.
  4. At the end of a period, balance the accounts and list them in a trial balance.
- Asset, expense and dividend accounts normally have normal balances. Liability, capital and revenue accounts normally have credit balances.
- Errors are the result of incorrect journalizing, incorrect posting and incorrect balancing.
- Error correction steps:
  1. Understand the incorrect entry.
  2. Visualize the correct entry.
  3. Record the correcting entry.
- Technological changes such as cloud computing, blockchain technology and machine learning are changing the way accounting and auditing is done.
- Good internal control systems ensure the reliability of the accounting system.

---

[4] Satyam spooks market, *Business Line*, January 8, 2009.

Review Problem

Ganesh started Woodcraft Company on September 1, 20XX. The transactions for the month are as follows:

Sep. 1   Invested cash in share capital, ₹10,000.
     4   Paid two months' rent in advance for a shop, ₹2,000.
     5   Bought equipment for cash, ₹1,200.
     7   Bought supplies on credit, ₹700.
   10   Received payment for remodelling a kitchen, ₹8,600.
   14   Paid for an advertisement, ₹1,400.
   17   Received payment for furnishing an office, ₹11,200.
   23   Billed customers for work done, ₹13,100.
   25   Paid assistant's wages, ₹1,500.
   28   Paid electricity charges, ₹240.
   29   Received payment from customers billed on September 23, ₹4,800.
   30   Paid a dividend, ₹2,500.

Required

1. Prepare journal entries for the above transactions.
2. Post the journal entries to the ledger.
3. Prepare a trial balance.

Solution to the Review Problem

1. Journal entries

General Journal   Page 1

Date	Description	Post. Ref.	Debit	Credit
20XX				
Sep. 1	Cash..		10,000	
	Share Capital..			10,000
4	Prepaid Rent...		2,000	
	Cash..			2,000
5	Equipment		1,200	
	Cash..			1,200
7	Supplies..		700	
	Trade Payables..			700
10	Cash		8,600	
	Revenue from Services			8,600
14	Advertisement Expense.................................		1,400	
	Cash..			1,400
17	Cash		11,200	
	Revenue from Services			11,200
23	Trade Receivables...		13,100	
	Revenue from Services			13,100
25	Salaries Expense		1,500	
	Cash..			1,500
28	Electricity Expense		240	
	Cash..			240
29	Cash		4,800	
	Trade Receivables...			4,800
30	Dividends..		2,500	
	Cash..			2,500

2. General Ledger

Equipment

Date	Explanation	Post. Ref.	Debit	Credit	Balance
20XX					
Sep. 5		1	1,200		1,200

Supplies

Date	Explanation	Post. Ref.	Debit	Credit	Balance
20XX					
Sep. 7		1	700		700

Trade Receivables

Date	Explanation	Post. Ref.	Debit	Credit	Balance
20XX					
Sep. 23		1	13,100		13,100
29		1		4,800	8,300

Cash

Date	Explanation	Post. Ref.	Debit	Credit	Balance
20XX					
Sep. 1		1	10,000		10,000
4		1		2,000	8,000
5		1		1,200	6,800
10		1	8,600		15,400
14		1		1,400	14,000
17		1	11,200		25,200
25		1		1,500	23,700
28		1		240	23,460
29		1	4,800		28,260
30		1		2,500	25,760

Prepaid Rent

Date	Explanation	Post. Ref.	Debit	Credit	Balance
20XX					
Sep. 4		1	2,000		2,000

Trade Payables

Date	Explanation	Post. Ref.	Debit	Credit	Balance
20XX					
Sep. 7		1		700	700

Share Capital

Date	Explanation	Post. Ref.	Debit	Credit	Balance
20XX					
Sep. 1		1		10,000	10,000

Dividends

Date	Explanation	Post. Ref.	Debit	Credit	Balance
20XX					
Sep. 30		1	2,500		2,500

Revenue from Services

Date	Explanation	Post. Ref.	Debit	Credit	Balance
20XX					
Sep. 10		1		8,600	8,600
17		1		11,200	19,800
23		1		13,100	32,900

Salaries Expense

Date	Explanation	Post. Ref.	Debit	Credit	Balance
20XX					
Sep. 25		1	1,500		1,500

Electricity Expense

Date	Explanation	Post. Ref.	Debit	Credit	Balance
20XX					
Sep. 28		1	240		240

Advertisement Expense

Date	Explanation	Post. Ref.	Debit	Credit	Balance
20XX					
Sep. 14		1	1,400		1,400

3. **Trial balance**

WOODCRAFT COMPANY
Trial Balance, September 30, 20XX

	Debit	Credit
Equipment	₹ 1,200	
Supplies	700	
Trade receivables	8,300	
Cash	25,760	
Prepaid rent	2,000	
Trade payables		₹ 700
Share capital		10,000
Dividends	2,500	
Revenue from services		32,900
Salaries expense	1,500	
Electricity expense	240	
Advertisement expense	1,400	
Total	43,600	43,600

ASSIGNMENT MATERIAL

Questions

1. Define *account* and *ledger.*
2. What factors determine the number and types of accounts for a business?
3. "Debits = Credits." Explain.
4. Why do we enter transactions first in the *journal*?
5. State the rules of debit and credit for (a) assets, (b) liabilities, and (c) equity.
6. What is the meaning of *debit balance* and *credit balance*? Is a debit balance always favourable and a credit balance always unfavourable?
7. "Debit means increase and credit means decrease." Comment.
8. Why are the rules of debit and credit the same for liabilities and equity?
9. What is a *chart of accounts*?
10. What is a *compound entry*?
11. State whether the following are asset, liability or equity accounts: (a) Salaries expense; (b) Bills payable; (c) Supplies; (d) Dividends; (e) Cash; (f) Trade receivables; (g) Prepaid insurance; (h) Interest income; (i) Interest expense payable.
12. Why do we prepare a *trial balance*? What kinds of errors can it detect?
13. When do we open a suspense account? How do we clear it?
14. What is *cloud computing*? How will it change accounting?
15. Distinguish between *accounting control* and *administrative control.*
16. Why should the cashier not be allowed to maintain the customers ledger?
17. "A good internal control system is an assurance that no error or fraud is possible." Comment.
18. Although the computer is faster and more accurate than the human brain, frauds are more easily perpetrated in a computer environment. Do you agree?

Problems

Name the account(s) to be debited and credited for the following transactions. Item (a) has been solved as an example.

Problem 3.1
Applying Double-entry Rules*

Transaction	Debit	Credit
(a) Paid interest on bank loan	Interest Expense	Cash
(b) Used supplies...		
(c) Proprietor withdrew cash for personal purposes...................		
(d) Paid for supplies bought on credit last month.......................		
(e) Paid rent for the current month.......................................		
(f) Paid rent for the next month..		
(g) Issued additional share capital for cash.............................		
(h) Paid income tax		
(i) Received cash for services to be provided next month		
(j) Collected payment for services provided last month.............		
(k) Provided services for cash..		
(l) Paid a security deposit to the port trust.................................		
(m) Paid rent for the proprietor's home		

Harsh Shah set up Eeco-drive Company, a car brokerage. It engaged in the following transactions.

Problem 3.2
Using T Accounts*

(a) Shah invested cash in Eeco-drive's share capital, ₹25,000.
(b) Bought supplies for cash, ₹1,200.
(c) Billed customers for services, ₹4,900.
(d) Took a bank loan, ₹10,000.
(e) Paid rent for the month, ₹1,000.
(f) Paid insurance premium for the month, ₹100.

Record the transactions in T accounts.

Rhetorica Company conducts public speaking classes. The following are the account balances on March 31, 20XX:

Problem 3.3
Preparing a Trial Balance*

Building..	₹10,000	Share capital............................	₹10,000
Supplies..	900	Revenue from services........................	?
Trade receivables	2,100	Salaries expense....................................	5,800
Prepaid insurance........................	600	Electricity expense	350
Trade payables	1,700	Insurance expense.............................	50

Prepare a trial balance.

Your review of accounting records reveals the following errors.

Problem 3.4
Correcting Errors* *

(a) Cash receipt of ₹800 for services yet to be provided was debited to Cash and credited to Revenue from Services.
(b) Credit purchase of supplies of ₹1,200 was debited to Supplies and credited to Cash.
(c) Interest payment of ₹400 was debited to Bank Loan Payable and credited to Cash.
(d) Cash payment of ₹2,900 to suppliers was debited to Trade Payables, ₹9,200 and credited to Cash, ₹2,900.

Prepare correcting entries.

Ajit set up Green Shoots Company, a farming consultancy, in October 20XX. The transactions in the first month were as follows:

Problem 3.5
Transaction Analysis, T Accounts and Trial Balance* *

(a) Ajit invested cash in the company's share capital, ₹10,000.
(b) Took an interest-free loan from a friend, ₹2,000.
(c) Bought equipment for cash, ₹9,000.

(d) Paid insurance for one year, ₹480.

(e) Bought supplies on credit, ₹700.

(f) Billed customers for services, ₹1,400.

(g) Provided services for cash, ₹3,200.

(h) Received advance from a customer, ₹150.

(i) Paid for supplies in (e) on account, ₹300.

(j) Paid salary for the month, ₹800. Note: Ajit is also an employee of the company.

(k) Collected receivables, ₹1,100.

Required

1. Record the transactions directly in the accounts.
2. Prepare the October 31 trial balance.

Problem 3.6

Transaction Analysis, T Accounts and Trial Balance ✷✷ Alternative to Problem 3.5

Pradeep and Selvam set up Venus Photoshop Company in December 20XX. The transactions in the first month were as follows:

(a) Pradeep and Selvam invested cash in the company's share capital, ₹2,500 each.

(b) Took a bank loan, ₹1,000.

(c) Paid insurance for the month, ₹60.

(d) Bought supplies on credit, ₹350.

(e) Billed customers for services, ₹2,300.

(f) Used supplies, ₹270.

(g) Paid equipment rent for the month, ₹500.

(h) Collected receivables, ₹1,900.

(i) Repaid bank loan, ₹700.

(j) Paid interest on bank loan, ₹100.

(k) Paid a dividend, ₹200.

Required

1. Record the transactions directly in the accounts.
2. Prepare the December 31 trial balance.

Problem 3.7

Journal, Ledger, and Trial Balance ✷✷✷

On November 1, 20XX, Jyoti Gupta established Trailblazer Company, a leadership advisory service. The business engaged in the following transactions in the first month:

Nov. 1   Jyoti Gupta invested cash in the company's share capital, ₹10,000.

     1   Took a bank loan, ₹3,000.

     2   Bought a camera costing ₹8,000 on down payment of ₹5,000 and gave a bill payable for the remainder.

     4   Bought software for cash, ₹1,000.

     9   Bought office supplies for cash, ₹1,100.

   11   Returned office supplies for immediate cash refund, ₹400.

   13   Provided services for cash, ₹6,900.

   16   Billed customers for services, ₹4,700.

   18   Paid rent deposit, ₹3,000.

   20   Collected receivables, ₹2,700.

   23   Paid insurance premium for three months, ₹600.

   25   Used office supplies, ₹450.

   28   Bought office supplies on credit, ₹800.

   29   Paid interest on bank loan, ₹60.

   30   Paid assistant's salary, ₹500.

Required

1. Record the transactions in the journal.
2. Post the journal entries to the ledger.
3. Prepare the November 30, 20XX trial balance.

On March 1, 20XX, Suresh Nair started SteerSafe Company, a driving school. The business engaged in the following transactions in the first month:

Problem 3.8
Journal, Ledger, and Trial Balance ✲✲✲ Alternative to Problem 3.7

Mar. 1   Suresh Nair invested cash in the company's share capital, ₹25,000.
   2   Bought a car for cash, ₹15,000.
   4   Bought car supplies for cash, ₹800.
   5   Paid subscription for six months for a magazine, ₹2,400.
   9   Provided services for cash, ₹8,100.
   14   Took a bank loan, ₹1,000.
   15   Paid car insurance premium for the month, ₹100.
   17   Billed customers for services, ₹1,700.
   19   Received advance from a customer, ₹730.
   20   Collected receivables, ₹800.
   25   Used car supplies, ₹390.
   26   Paid petrol bill for the month, ₹1,280.
   28   Bought office supplies on credit, ₹800.
   30   Paid instructor's salary, ₹1,800.
   31   Paid dividend, ₹500.

Required
1. Record the transactions in the journal.
2. Post the journal entries to the ledger.
3. Prepare the March 31, 20XX trial balance.

Whirr Company designs drones. Its latest balance sheet is as follows:

Problem 3.9
Beginning Balance Sheet, Journal, Ledger, and Trial Balance ✲✲✲✲

WHIRR COMPANY
Balance Sheet, March 31, 20XX

Equity and Liabilities
Equity
Equity share capital .... ₹30,000
Other equity: Retained earnings.. 8,180
Liabilities
Non-current liabilities
Bank loan payable.. 4,000
Current liabilities
Trade payables 5,330
Unearned revenue.. 2,100
Income tax payable 590
Total equity and liabilities.. 50,200
Assets
Non-current assets
Equipment... ₹28,000
Current assets
Supplies 2,810
Trade receivables.. 3,190
Cash... 16,200
Total assets 50,200

The company engaged in the following transactions in April:

Apr. 1   Paid March salaries, ₹1,930.

      2   Paid rent for the month, ₹500.

      5   Collected receivables, ₹2,160.

      8   Paid insurance premium for April to September, ₹720.

      9   Provided services for cash, ₹8,100.

   12   Repaid bank loan, ₹2,000.

   15   Paid for supplies bought in February, ₹2,590.

   18   Provided services for payment received in March, ₹1,490.

   20   Received advance from a customer, ₹160.

   21   Billed customers for services, ₹3,760.

   22   Used supplies, ₹2,130.

   23   Bought supplies for cash, ₹1,720.

   27   Refunded advance to a customer, ₹140.

   28   Paid income tax for last year, ₹590.

   30   Bought supplies on credit, ₹1,270.

Required

1. Record the transactions in the journal.
2. Enter the March 31 balances in the appropriate accounts from the balance sheet. Write Balance in the explanation space of the account.
3. Post the journal entries to the ledger. Open additional accounts as may be necessary.
4. Prepare the April 30, 20XX trial balance.

Problem 3.10

Beginning Balance Sheet, Journal, Ledger, and Trial Balance ✳✳✳✳
Alternative to Problem 3.9

Fenestra Company provides window cleaning and repair services. Its latest balance sheet is as follows:

FENESTRA COMPANY
Balance Sheet, September 30, 20XX

Equity and Liabilities

Equity

Equity share capital	₹10,000
Other equity: Retained earnings	1,170
Non-current liabilities	
Current liabilities	
Trade payables	2,400
Bills payable	2,000
Unearned revenue	2,020
Total equity and liabilities	17,590
Assets	
Non-current assets	
Equipment	₹12,000
Current assets	
Supplies	1,930
Trade receivables	2,710
Cash	950
Total assets	17,590

The company engaged in the following transactions in October:

Oct. 1   Paid rent for three months ending September, ₹300.

      3   Provided services for cash, ₹1,200.

      3   Provided services for payment received in August, ₹810.

      6   Collected receivables, ₹1,830.

      7   Billed customers for services, ₹7,130.

      8   Returned supplies for immediate refund, ₹490.

10   Bought supplies on credit, ₹1,720.
11   Refunded advance to a customer, ₹400.
13   Paid a September invoice for supplies, ₹2,100.
17   Received advance from a customer, ₹730.
23   Paid a bill payable, ₹1,000.
27   Paid telephone expense, ₹430.
28   Used supplies, ₹1,940.
30   Bought supplies for cash, ₹270.
31   Paid salaries, ₹550.

Required

1. Record the transactions in the journal.
2. Enter the September 30 balances in the appropriate accounts from the balance sheet. Write *Balance* in the explanation space of the account.
3. Post the journal entries to the ledger. Open additional accounts as may be necessary.
4. Prepare the October 31, 20XX trial balance.

After completing vocational education, Ramachandra set up AlignedRight Company, a plumbing service. The business carried out the following transactions in the first two months.

Problem 3.11
Journal, Ledger, and Trial Balance for Two Periods
* * * * *

Jan. 1   Ramachandra invested in the company's share capital in the form of tools, ₹2,000 and cash, ₹1,000.
      2   Took an interest-free loan from a customer, ₹10,000.
      2   Bought a car costing ₹20,000 on down payment of ₹2,000 and gave eighteen bills payable of ₹1,000 each.
      3   Bought tools for cash, ₹3,000.
      5   Received advance from a customer, ₹9,800.
      7   Provided services for cash, ₹3,700.
      8   Billed customers for services, ₹7,130.
      12   Provided services for advance received on January 5.
      15   Bought supplies for cash, ₹1,810.
      17   Used supplies, ₹1,620.
      20   Collected receivables, ₹6,920.
      24   Received advance from a customer, ₹1,300.
      27   Repaid loan, ₹1,000.
      29   Paid salaries, ₹6,310.
      31   Paid a bill payable.
Feb. 1   Paid tool repair expense, ₹150.
      2   Received advance from a customer, ₹2,400.
      4   Billed customers for services, ₹2,940.
      6   Bought supplies on credit, ₹1,790.
      7   Bought tools for cash, ₹8,000.
      12   Provided services for cash, ₹1,910.
      14   Provided services for advance received on January 24 for ₹990 and refunded the balance.
      17   Returned defective supplies to be adjusted against future purchases, ₹170.
      18   Used supplies, ₹1,540.
      22   Paid rent for January and February, ₹5,000.
      23   Collected receivables, ₹2,920.
      25   Provided services for advance received on February 2 for ₹2,750 and collected the balance.
      27   Paid petrol bill for January and February, ₹2,410.
      29   Paid salaries for January and February, ₹7,540.
      29   Paid telephone expense for January and February, ₹1,570.

Required

1. Record the January transactions in the journal.
2. Post the January journal entries to the ledger.
3. Prepare the January 31 trial balance.
4. Record the February transactions in the journal.

5. Enter the January 31 balances in the relevant accounts. Write *Balance* in the explanation space.
6. Post the February journal entries to the ledger. Open additional accounts as may be necessary.
7. Prepare the February 29 trial balance.

Problem 3.12
Journal, Ledger, and Trial Balance for Two Periods ★★★★★ Alternative to Problem 3.11

Leo set up Lovolt Company, a car electrical shop. The business carried out the following transactions in the first two months.

Aug. 1   Leo invested in the company's share capital in the form of equipment, ₹5,000 and cash, ₹2,000.
     1   Took a bank loan of ₹6,000, repayable in six monthly instalments with interest of ₹60 per month.
     2   Paid rent for two months, ₹3,500.
     4   Bought equipment costing ₹10,000 and gave an interest-free bill payable due on September 30.
     6   Bought supplies for cash, ₹2,090.
     7   Provided services for cash, ₹4,300.
     8   Received advance from a customer, ₹5,500.
   10   Used supplies, ₹910.
   12   Billed customers for services, ₹6,450.
   15   Provided services for advance received on August 8 for ₹5,900 and billed the customer for the balance.
   18   Paid towing expense for a customer's car, ₹360.
   21   Collected receivables, ₹6,550.
   24   Paid bank loan first instalment with interest.
   27   Paid salaries, ₹2,900.
   31   Paid electricity expense, ₹1,000.
Sep. 1   Bought furniture for cash, ₹1,000.
     3   Billed customers for services, ₹5,390.
     4   Received advance from customer, ₹800.
     5   Provided services for cash, ₹760.
     8   Received advance from customer, ₹1,290.
   11   Provided services for advance received on September 4 for ₹530 and refunded the balance.
   15   Bought supplies on credit, ₹1,510.
   19   Used supplies, ₹720.
   23   Collected receivables, ₹4,360.
   24   Paid bank loan second instalment with interest.
   25   Provided services for advance received on September 8 for ₹1,500 and collected the balance.
   29   Paid telephone expense for August and September, ₹980.
   29   Paid electricity expense, ₹950.
   30   Paid salaries, ₹3,000.
   30   Paid the bill payable accepted on August 4, ₹10,000.

Required

1. Record the August transactions in the journal.
2. Post the August journal entries to the ledger.
3. Prepare the August 31 trial balance.
4. Record the September 30 transactions in the journal.
5. Enter the September 30 balances in the relevant accounts. Write *Balance* in the explanation space.
6. Post the September 30 journal entries to the ledger. Open additional accounts as may be necessary.
7. Prepare the September 30 trial balance.

Business Decision Cases

BDC 3.1
Nova Materials Limited

Nova Materials is engaged in developing new materials for use in medical and aerospace industries. It is a mid-sized company planning to list in the next one or two years. The company has engaged you to design an accounting system in keeping with its responsibilities as a listed entity.

Required

1. Set out the issues that you would like to cover in your study.
2. Prepare a short presentation on your proposed accounting system to the company's board of directors and auditors.

After working for over a decade in a leading software company, Vinay and Sheela Kapoor decided to set up their own software firm, Kapoor Software Ltd. on June 1. Each of them deposited ₹30,000 in the company's bank account in exchange for 3,000 shares of ₹10 each.

BDC 3.2
Kapoor Software Limited

Amit Lal, an old friend of the Kapoors, joined the company as office manager on a monthly salary of ₹7,000, no matter how many days he showed up at work. Amit paid into the bank all customer receipts and made all payments by cheque. Although Amit had no knowledge of accounting, he carefully filed the company's letters, invoices and other papers. Also, he noted down details of cheques received and issued in his diary. The following information is available from Amit's file and diary.

June 1:

- Borrowed ₹25,000 from Canara Bank.
- Sheela ordered a computer costing ₹42,000.

June 2:

- Hired an office room on a monthly rental of ₹2,500 payable on the first day of the month and paid the rent for June.

June 3:

- Vinay appointed two programmers on a salary of ₹250 per day each for the number of days they worked.

June 6:

- Received the computer and paid ₹15,000. The balance amount is payable in equal instalments on the fifth of July, August and September.
- Ordered on Gupta & Co. supplies for ₹7,300.

June 8:

- Received supplies costing ₹3,900.

June 10:

- Raised invoices on customers, ₹29,200, for providing services.

June 16:

- One box of supplies costing ₹710 varied slightly from the purchase specification, and it was returned to Gupta & Co.; all other items were as ordered and were paid for.

June 19:

- Received cheques for ₹14,100 from customers in payment of bills.

June 20:

- Raised invoices on customers for ₹19,400 for providing services.

June 23:

- Received a cheque for ₹9,800 from a customer as payment for services to be provided in July.

June 27:

- Gupta & Co. requested me to accept the rejected supplies and said that they would be willing to give a rebate of ₹90 on the supplies to make up for the deviation. After checking with Vinay, I accepted the supplies and paid Gupta & Co.

June 28:

- Received cheques for ₹7,100 in payment of bills.

June 29:

- Vinay asked me to repay the bank loan. I paid ₹14,000 of the loan with interest of ₹340.

June 30:

- During the month, the company had 21 working days. One of the assistants reported for work on all working days and the other worked for only 17 days. I paid the June salaries.
- The inventory of supplies is worth ₹2,400.
- Received the June electricity bill for ₹450, but could not pay it.

July 1:

- Paid office rent for July.
- Paid the June electricity bill.

July 3:
  ■ Received the remaining supplies.

July 4:
  ■ Paid for the supplies.

July 5:
  ■ Paid the first instalment for the computer.

Required

1. Record the June transactions in the journal.
2. Post the journal entries to the ledger.
3. Prepare the June trial balance.
4. Prepare the June financial statements.
5. Evaluate the performance of the business.
6. The Kapoors want a dividend of ₹2 per share. Who should be concerned? Why? What is your advice?

BDC 3.3
Constellation Hotels Limited

Rashmi, an advertising executive, was staying at Constellation, a prestigious hotel, and had put her suit in the laundry bag kept in her room. While checking out of the hotel, she found that her suit had not been returned. She was due to catch a flight to attend an important meeting and she badly needed the suit. The Front Office manager apologized to her for the loss and told her that the hotel would compensate her. She mentioned an amount and the manager promptly paid her cash. He did not ask her to sign a receipt.

The hotel's internal auditor thinks that the system is vulnerable to misuse by the hotel guests and fraud by the hotel staff and asks the hotel management to follow a stringent system for establishing and paying for such losses and documenting the transaction. Excerpts from the internal audit report are as follows:

Weak internal controls:

In the course of audit, the team came across an instance of weak internal controls. At the time of checking out, a guest informed the Front Office that her suit had not been returned by Laundry Service. The Front Office staff informed the Front Office manager. The Front Office manager talked with the guest and paid her cash for the amount of loss mentioned by her.

We have the following concerns with the process followed:

(a) The fact of loss was not verified with the laundry service. Our enquiries with the laundry service staff indicated that the item was left in the guest's room. However, the housekeeping staff did not find any articles left behind after the guest left. One possibility is that the guest had put it in her luggage but perhaps forgot about it. The Front Office staff could have requested the guest to check her bags.

(b) The amount mentioned by the guest was accepted without scrutiny. The value of the loss was not established independently. The hotel should develop a method of finding out the amount of loss in such cases. If the suit was a used one, an appropriate allowance should have been made in calculating the refund.

(c) The laundry service rules require the guest to call the laundry in case of delay in delivery; in case the laundry does not respond quickly, the matter should be brought to the attention of the Front Office. The Front Office staff did not make any effort to remind the guest of her responsibility.

(d) The Front Office did not obtain any receipt from the customer for the amount paid. The Front Office manager has signed a note mentioning the amount paid.

In our view, the process is open to the following kinds of abuse (illustrative, not exhaustive):

1. Guests can claim compensation loss even if there was no loss.
2. Guests can claim amounts in excess of the loss.
3. Front office can record payment even if there was no claim.
4. Guests and Front Office can collude to pay an improper claim.

We recommend the following process for dealing with such claims in future:

(i) Guest should report the age and brand of the item in the laundry note. The laundry note format should be modified suitably.

(ii) Guest should agree to check his or her bags in the presence of the Front Office staff before a claim for loss can be considered. The hotel's rules should be modified to include this condition.

(iii) Front Office should confirm with Laundry Service that a guest claiming loss had given the item and it was not returned to the guest.

(iv) Front Office staff should obtain prior approval of Front Office Manager for payment of compensation.

(v) The amount of claim should be limited to the estimated value of the item taking into consideration the age and brand of the item.

(vi) Payment of the claim should be by bank transfer.

The hotel management worries that asking guests upset by losing their belongings to comply with detailed procedures would not only worsen the situation but also affect the hotel's reputation.

Required

1. Prepare a critique of the system suggested by the internal auditor.
2. Develop a system that in your view balances the compulsions of the business and the need for sound financial control.

Interpreting Financial Reports

Tata Consultancy Services Ltd. is a leading information technology services company listed in Indian stock exchanges. The following is the company's March 2016 Ind AS consolidated balance sheet, suitably modified for use in this case:

IFR 3.1
Tata Consultancy Services Limited

TATA CONSULTANCY SERVICES LIMITED
Balance Sheet, March 31, 2016

In ₹ million

ASSETS
Non-current assets

(a)	Property, plant and equipment	9,971
(b)	Capital work-in-progress	**A**
(c)	Intangible assets	136
(d)	Goodwill	1,669
(e)	Financial assets	
	(i) Investments	344
	(ii) Loans	2,475
	(iii) Other financial assets	1,322
(f)	Advance income tax asset	4,464
(g)	Deferred tax assets (net)	2,910
(h)	Other non-current assets	926
Total non-current assets		**B**
Current assets		
(a)	Inventories	17
(b)	Financial assets	
	(i) Investments	22,479
	(ii) Trade receivables	24,073
	(iii) Unbilled revenue	**C**
	(iv) Cash and cash equivalents	6,294
	(v) Other bank balances	493
	(vi) Loans	2,743
	(vii) Other financial assets	916
(c)	Advance income tax asset	32
(d)	Other current assets	2,175
Total current assets		63,214
Total assets		**D**

EQUITY AND LIABILITIES
EQUITY
Shareholders' funds

(a)	Share capital	197
(b)	Other equity	**E**
Equity attributable to shareholders of TCS Limited		71,072
Non-controlling interest		**F**
Total equity		71,427
Non-current liabilities		
(a)	Financial liabilities	
	(i) Borrowings	82
	(ii) Other financial liabilities	493
(b)	Employee benefit obligation	237
(c)	Provisions	**G**

(d)	Deferred tax liabilities (net)	805
(e)	Other non-current liabilities	443
Total non-current liabilities		**H**
Current liabilities		
(a)	Financial liabilities	
	(i) Borrowings	113
	(ii) Trade payables	7,541
	(iii) Other financial liabilities	2,364
(b)	Income received in advance	**I**
(c)	Current income tax liabilities (net)	805
(d)	Employee benefit obligation	1,635
(e)	Provisions	115
(f)	Other current liabilities	1,641
Total current liabilities		15,573
Total equity and liabilities		89,100

Required

Fill in the missing amounts indicated by the letters.

Financial Analysis

FA 3.1
Developing a Chart of Accounts

Study the financial statements of an Indian aviation company.

Required

1. Develop a chart of accounts that would satisfy the information needs of the typical users of the financial statements of the company.
2. Discuss the factors that you had in mind while developing the chart.

FA 3.2
Impact of Technology on Accounting and Auditing

Technological advances such as cloud computing, blockchain technology, and machine learning are changing profoundly how accounting and auditing are done.

Required

Prepare a report on how technology is expected to change accounting and auditing and the associated benefits and risks to accountants, auditors, and regulators and other users.

Answers to One-minute Quiz

3.1 a, b.
3.2 b, c, d.
3.3 b, c.
3.4 a.

Answers to Test Your Understanding

3.1 Asset: (e), (f); Liability: (d); Equity: (a), (b), (c).
3.2 (a) Vineeta invested in share capital in the form of equipment, ₹10,000 and cash, ₹5,000. (b) Bought supplies on credit, ₹2,500. (c) Paid insurance in advance, ₹1,200. (d) Billed customers for services, ₹6,000. (e) Paid salaries, ₹1,700. (f) Collected payments for past invoices, ₹4,900.
3.3 Debit: (a), (b), (e), (f). Credit: (c), (d).
3.4 April 4 This is not a transaction.
     8 *Analysis:* Asset (Cash) increased. Revenue (Revenue from Services) increased. *Rules:* Debit asset to record increase. Credit revenue to record increase. *Entry:* Debit Cash. Credit Revenue from Services.
    12 *Analysis:* Asset (Trade Receivables) increased. Revenue (Revenue from Services) increased. *Rules:* Debit asset to record increase. Credit revenue to record increase. *Entry:* Debit Trade Receivables. Credit Revenue from Services.
    17 *Analysis:* Asset (Cash) increased. Liability (Unearned Revenue) increased. *Rules:* Debit asset to record increase. Credit liability to record increase. *Entry:* Debit Cash. Credit Unearned Revenue.

21 *Analysis:* Asset (Supplies) increased. Liability (Trade Payables) increased. *Rules:* Debit asset to record increase. Credit liability to record increase. *Entry:* Debit Supplies. Credit Trade Payables.

25 *Analysis:* Asset (Cash) increased. Asset (Trade Receivables) decreased. *Rules:* Debit asset to record increase. Credit asset to record decrease. *Entry:* Debit Cash. Credit Trade Receivables.

29 *Analysis:* Expense (Computer Rental Expense) increased. Asset (Cash) decreased. *Rules:* Debit expense to record increase. Credit asset to record decrease. *Entry:* Debit Computer Rental Expense. Credit Cash.

30 *Analysis:* Expense (Interest Expense) increased. Asset (Cash) decreased. *Rules:* Debit expense to record increase. Credit asset to record decrease. *Entry:* Debit Interest Expense. Credit Cash.

3.5 June 4   Debit Suspense 2,700. Credit Cash 2,700.

        6   Debit Suspense 720. Credit Cash 720.

      25   Suspense 6,000. Credit Revenue from Services 6,000.

4

Measuring Income

LEARNING OBJECTIVES

After studying this chapter, you should be able to:

1. Define and explain net profit, revenue, and expense.
2. Explain accrual accounting and distinguish between the accrual system and the cash system.
3. Understand the principles of revenue recognition and expense recognition.
4. Define deferrals and accruals and explain the need for adjustments.
5. Prepare adjusting entries.
6. Prepare the financial statements of a service organization.
7. Identify the components of the statement of profit and loss of a merchandising organization.
8. Record merchandise sales.
9. Record merchandise purchases and calculate cost of goods sold.
10. Understand operating expenses.
11. Prepare the financial statements of a merchandising organization.
12. Analyze the profitability of operations.
13. Describe the accounting cycle.
14. Prepare closing entries and reversing entries.
15. Understand special cases of revenue recognition.
16. Explain earnings quality.

SPEED READ

Measuring performance is the raison d'être of accounting. Business activities take place all the time. This makes it difficult to trace revenues and expenses to specific periods. The accrual system is the heart of accounting. It attempts to recognize revenues when they are earned and expenses when they are incurred. Understanding the principles of revenue recognition and expense recognition helps us appreciate the meaning of the reported profit and assess the risks involved. Trading operations involve additional transactions. Separating operating items from non-operating items helps us analyze and predict performance better. Intermediate profit measures sharpen our understanding of profitability.

HOW MUCH DOES THAT CAR COST?

You come across this news item:

Audi has launched an integrated finance, service, insurance and extended warranty package in India. Called 'Audi CarLife-Advance', this initiative aims to provide the benefits of a leasing service, while still letting the customer have ownership of the vehicle. The services are available bundled under a single monthly payment.

You walk into a showroom to find out more. The salesman says his timeless lines:

Hello, Sir. Audi cars come with a two-year warranty that covers manufacturing or material defects. You can avail of a three-year warranty against any paintwork defects. As further reassurance, every car is protected by an anti-corrosion perforation warranty that can extend up to 12 years. You can continue to enjoy your peace of mind by extending the warranty period for another two years or 100,000 km at a nominal cost. The company gives a one-year comprehensive insurance and depreciation shield. You get roadside assistance free of cost – 24 × 7, 365 days, two dedicated toll numbers, multilingual services, replacement car, on-site minor repairs, despatch of spare keys in case of loss, etc. You can get an interest-free loan for the purchase. Any questions, Sir?

The company is selling a package: car, warranty, extended warranty, insurance, depreciation shield, roadside assistance, and interest-free loan. Not all the revenue is earned when the car is sold. The costs of warranty, extended warranty, depreciation shield and roadside assistance have to be estimated. Interest income would be earned over time.

Income Measurement Basics

Business enterprises are engaged in providing goods and services. The cycle of production, selling, collection and payment is a never-ending one. Serving fast food, fixing flat tyres, performing MRIs, career counselling, and selling vegetables from a pushcart often take not more than minutes or hours. At the other end of the spectrum, producing complex software, discovering and developing drugs, constructing skyscrapers, manufacturing aircraft, and building ships often take years. So, how do we measure the performance of a business organization? Figure 4.1 illustrates the cycle of activities in a typical business.

Learning Objective

LO 1 Define and explain net profit, revenue, and expense.

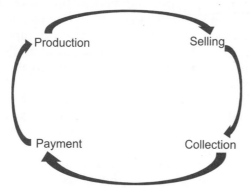

Figure 4.1
BUSINESS ACTIVITIES

Business enterprises produce goods and services, sell them, collect payment from customers and pay suppliers.

Measuring and reporting performance is undoubtedly the accountant's most important job. The most accurate way to measure performance would be to wait for a business to cease its operations. That will be when the business no longer produces anything, disposes of its assets and pays its liabilities. However, firms have to communicate their performance frequently. Managers' bonuses, dividends and income tax are based on annual profit. Listed companies must publish quarterly financial reports. For internal purposes, income is measured even more often.

In order to measure income periodically, accountants assign the results of business activities to time periods, such as a year, half year or quarter. Accounting principles, standards and policies provide the underpinning for income measurement. Periodic income measurement requires assumptions, estimates and judgments. For example, how much are unsold inventories worth? What is the life of a jig boring machine? How much of a software has been produced and how much would it cost to complete? Are customers likely to pay for credit sales? We are unlikely to get precise answers to such questions, but that is the price to pay for frequent financial reporting. Understanding the trade-offs in income measurement helps us recognize the merits and limitations of the income number.

Despite a great deal of effort, a clear definition of income remains elusive. Economists speak of income as the amount by which an entity becomes better off over a period. Unfortunately, the degree of well-offness is largely a matter of personal opinion and can seldom be objectively measured. The term 'income' has different meanings in different contexts and no single definition is likely to fit all the contexts satisfactorily.

Net Profit

Net profit, or **net income**, is what a business earns after meeting its expenses. It is the excess of income over expenses. If expenses exceed income, the difference is **net loss**. Investments by, and distributions to, owners affect the equity of a business but are not a part of net profit. The period for which a business reports net profit is its **reporting period**, **accounting period**, **financial year**, or **fiscal year**. In India, the financial year for companies is the period from April 1 to March 31. Indian companies that have foreign subsidiaries and Indian subsidiaries of foreign companies may follow a different period with the permission of the National Company Law Tribunal. Under the income tax law, companies must compute and pay tax on their income for the Government's fiscal year, April 1 to March 31.

**DISCUSSION
QUESTION 4.1**

Is more frequent reporting likely to increase the error in measuring performance?

....

....

....

Revenues and Gains

Revenue is income from providing goods and services. It comes from an enterprise's central or regular activities. Sales and service charges for a computer manufacturer and interest income and guarantee commission for a bank are common examples of revenue. Gains arise from peripheral activities. Profit on sale of used equipment and appreciation in the value of investments are examples of gains for a manufacturing organization. In India, *income* is often used as a synonym for revenue.

Revenue is straightforward when it is received immediately and in cash – it is the amount billed and received. If revenue is receivable, its fair value may be different from the amount billed. Suppose a consultant bills two customers – A and B – ₹3 million each. If A pays the amount immediately, the consultant earns a revenue of ₹3 million. If B is allowed to pay the amount in three equal annual instalments, the fair value of the revenue from B would be the discounted value of the future receipts.

Sometimes, a business may receive non-cash assets or services, or may settle its liabilities, in exchange for goods or services provided. In that case, the amount of revenue recorded is the fair value of the asset or service received, or liability settled. Thus, revenue earned in a reporting period is the sum of cash and receivables and the value of other assets and services received and liabilities reduced for the goods or services provided during that period.

Revenues increase equity *and* either increase assets or decrease liabilities. But not all increase in equity arises from revenues. For example, investment by shareholders increases equity, but it is not revenue. Again, though revenues typically increase assets, some transactions may increase assets without increasing revenues. For example, the purchase of office supplies on credit increases assets and liabilities, but does not result in revenue. Finally, revenues may decrease liabilities. For example, when a business provides services for which it has already received payment, unearned revenue – a liability – decreases and equity increases.

ONE-MINUTE QUIZ 4.1
Revenues and Gains

Which of the following is a revenue or gain? There may be more than one correct answer.
(a) Interest on government securities received by a bank.
(b) Insurance settlement in excess of the cost of inventories destroyed in flood.
(c) Premium on issue of shares.
(d) Shares in a hotel company received by an architect in return for designing the rooms.

Expenses and Losses

Expenses are costs of providing goods and services. Businesses incur expenses in order to earn revenues. Expenses relate to an enterprise's central or regular activities. Cost of goods sold, advertisement and sales promotion, warranties, travel, bank interest charge, and income tax are examples of expenses. Losses often arise from peripheral activities. Destruction of inventories and decrease in the value of a patent are examples of losses.

Expenses decrease equity *and* either decrease assets or increase liabilities. But not all decrease in equity or increase in liabilities results from expenses. For example, dividends decrease equity, but they are not expenses. Again, expenses are not the same as payments although many expenses entail payments. For example, payment to a supplier for goods bought in the past involves a payment, but it does not represent an expense. In some cases, cash may be paid out before the expense is incurred, such as advance payment of rent and payment for equipment. These payments represent assets until the benefits are received.

Which of the following is an expense or loss? There may be more than one correct answer.
  (a) Interest on bills payable.
  (b) Dividends paid to shareholders.
  (c) Decrease in the rupee value of US dollars held by a bank.
  (d) Festival advance to employees to be recovered from salary payments.

Accrual System and Cash System

Learning Objective

LO2 Explain accrual accounting and distinguish between the accrual system and the cash system.

Cash and accrual are the two systems for measuring and reporting performance. The **cash system** records revenues when cash is received from customers and records expenses when cash is paid to suppliers, employees and others. It does not consider rights to receive revenues and obligations to pay expenses. In the cash system profit equals revenues received less expenses paid. The cash system has its attractions. It is easy to understand and implement. After all, everyone knows what it means to receive or pay cash. Also, it does not require any information other than what the accounting records already have. The main problem is that it is a summary of *past* cash receipts and payments, so it is unlikely to be useful in predicting future performance.

The **accrual system** records revenues when they are earned regardless of when cash is received and records expenses when they are incurred regardless of when cash is paid. In the accrual system profit equals revenues earned less expenses incurred. The accrual system does a relatively better job of matching efforts and accomplishments. It presents the effects of transactions in the periods in which those effects occur. Since the timing of cash receipts and payments is often a matter of contract, a receipt or a payment does not tell us anything about work done or resources used. Also, since the net profit under accrual reflects anticipated cash receipts and payments, it gives a better indication of *future* cash flows and, therefore, it is more useful for decision-making. The Companies Act 2013 requires companies to follow accrual. The income tax law allows (and in some cases requires) the cash system under certain circumstances.

Traditionally, governments have followed the cash system for their own accounting, but are moving to accrual. According to the International Monetary Fund, 12 countries prepare full accrual financial statements, 52 countries are on partial accrual and 120 countries follow the cash system.[1] The countries that follow accrual include Australia, New Zealand, and the UK. In 2005, the Government of India accepted the Twelfth Finance Commission's recommendation to switch to the accrual system. It has decided to move to accrual and has issued four Indian Government Financial Reporting Standards (IGFRS). So far, 21 State governments have agreed in principle to introduce accrual accounting. Over 48 municipal bodies have switched to accrual. The Indian Railways have decided to move to accrual.

Which is better: accrual or cash? Why?

....

....

....

Income Measurement Principles

Revenue and expense are probably the best known accounting terms. We will now see how to think about them in accounting.

Revenue Recognition

Learning Objective

LO3 Understand the principles of revenue recognition and expense recognition.

Revenue recognition is the process of formally recording revenue in a reporting period. The **realization principle**, or the **revenue recognition principle**, requires that revenue

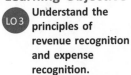

---
[1] International Monetary Fund, *Fiscal Transparency, Accountability, and Risk*, August 2, 2012.

be recognized when the revenue-earning process is complete or virtually complete. Accountants understand that earning revenue from sales or services is a continuous process. A manufacturing firm buys materials, processes them, selling the products, and collects cash from customers. The firm earns revenue as it performs each of these activities. There is uncertainty at each stage. For instance, parts may not be available in time, there may be a machine breakdown, employees may go on strike, parts may be damaged in handling, there may be no demand for the products, and so on.

The revenue earning process would be regarded as virtually complete when the firm sells the product or provides a service with assurance of payment by the customer. The realization principle probably reminds you of the proverb "Don't count your chickens before they are hatched." Uncertainty may persist even after a sale. For example, if the buyer has a right of return and wants to return the product, the seller will be obliged to take back the product and refund the amount to the buyer. Further, the buyer may not be able to pay as agreed. In all such cases, recognizing revenue at the time of sale could turn out to be premature.

The realization principle differs significantly from the view of some managers that a business earns revenue when they have performed their part. For example, marketing managers almost always claim that they have earned revenue the moment they get a customer order. (The more sanguine among them may even take a customer's smile as a confirmed order.) As an example, this is what an effusive estate agent said about earning revenue:

> I've banked deals as soon as parties accept offers instead of waiting till the point of exchange, which is…when the parties…breathe a sigh of relief.[2]

By waiting until the parties "breathe a sigh of relief", the accountant is sure to spoil the estate agent's party. Accountants and managers sometimes differ on whether revenue has been earned, leading to conflict in organizations.

But why this insistence on "completion of the earning process"? Managers have incentives to take an optimistic, rather than a realistic, view of their firm's revenue. Reporting revenue sooner would result in higher sales and profit. Good growth in sales and profit will give managers a higher remuneration, advance their career prospects in the firm, and enhance their professional reputation in the job market. Understandably, managers may wish to recognize revenue prematurely. By insisting on completion of the earning process and exchange of goods and services, the realization principle keeps in check managers' tendency to be aggressive in recognizing revenue.

The conditions for recognizing revenue from providing goods and services are as follows:

Revenue Recognition Conditions for Goods and Services
1. The price can be measured reliably.
2. The seller will receive cash or other benefits from the transaction.
3. The costs incurred and to be incurred for the transaction can be measured reliably.

Additional Condition for Services	Additional Conditions for Goods
4. The stage of completion of the transaction can be measured reliably.	4. The seller has transferred to the buyer the significant risks and rewards of ownership of the goods.
	5. The seller does not retain effective control over the goods sold.

Let us now see how to apply these conditions to services. We will see the conditions for goods later in this chapter.

---

[2] From the *Financial Times*. May 16, 2009. House & Home: Don't count your chickens. © The Financial Times Limited 2009. All Rights Reserved.

Price The contract should state the price or may lay down a method of determining the price. For example, a loan contract between a bank and a borrower may state that the interest rate shall be 12 per cent. Alternatively, the contract may specify that the interest rate will be the LIBOR (London interbank offered rate) at the start of each year during the period of the loan plus two per cent. Thus, the price should be certain or ascertainable. If the price is not clear, revenue recognition will not be possible. In our example, the contract should also specify whether the LIBOR is for one month, three months, six months, and so on. In the case of goods, the sale contract should specify the price or a method of determining the price. For example, the contract may provide that the parties shall trade crude oil at the price prevailing on the New York Mercantile Exchange on the date of sale. If the price is not clear, revenue recognition will not be possible. In our example, the contract should also specify the type of crude, such as Abu Dhabi Umm Shaif, Iran Light, Nigeria Light, and US Alaska.

The value of revenue to be recorded is the fair value of the goods or services provided to customers or the fair value of the consideration received. Fair value is the price that would be received to sell an asset in an orderly transaction. In an active market, the market price can be generally taken as the fair value.

Benefits The buyer should have paid the price or it should be certain that the buyer will pay. If collection of the revenue is not certain at the time of sale, the seller should postpone revenue recognition until collection becomes certain. However, when uncertainty about collection arises after revenue is recognized, an estimated loss is recognized at the time; the revenue originally recognized is not adjusted.

Stage of completion The stage of completion of a transaction can be measured by surveying the physical work done or by the proportion of costs incurred to date to the total estimated costs of the transaction. When the outcome of the transaction cannot be measured reliably, revenue is recognized to the extent of the costs incurred that are recoverable, and profit is not recognized. This is often the case in the early stages of a transaction. When both the outcome of the contract and the recovery of costs incurred are uncertain, the costs incurred should be recognized as an expense.

Easy Home Finance charges a processing fee of 1 per cent with every home loan application. No doubt, the company receives this amount along with the application. However, the processing fee is a revenue earned in connection with the company's lending. It should be allocated to income over the period of the loan to which it relates.	**HANDHOLD 4.1** Revenue Recognition

Another way to think about revenue recognition is to look at the balance sheet effect of earning revenue. In this view, revenue recognition is simultaneous with an increase in an asset or a decrease in a liability. For example, a business that provides services in exchange for immediate or future payment records an asset – cash or receivable – and a revenue. If it had received advance payment, it records a decrease in a liability – unearned revenue. Thus, revenue recognition and its balance sheet effect are two ways of looking at the same transaction.

Revenue recognition can be complicated. The transaction needs to be identified based on the substance of the contract. A transaction may have separately identifiable components ("multiple element arrangements"), such as a contract to develop an information system and maintain it for a certain period. The contract revenue should be allocated to the development and the maintenance components on the basis of their fair value and recognized in the periods over which these services are provided. The sale of the Audi car with warranty, extended warranty, roadside assistance, accident insurance, and interest-free loan described in the chapter vignette is another example. The automobile company should apply the conditions for revenue recognition separately to the various items.

In contrast, two or more transactions may be linked in such a way that they actually constitute a single transaction ("bundled offers"). For example, a customer enters into a contract with a phone company for a package that may include a handset, talk time, SMS, and so on. On the face of it, these are separate transactions. However, the handset is often sold at a discount and the provider expects to recover it in the form of subsequent services. In this case, the amounts paid for the handset and other services do not represent their respective fair value. The transactions have to be treated as a single transaction and revenue should be recognized based on the fair value of the components.

ONE-MINUTE QUIZ 4.3
Revenue Recognition

When should revenue be ordinarily recognized?
(a) On receiving a customer order with payment.
(b) On receiving a non-cancellable customer order with payment.
(c) On providing services to customer for cash or with assurance of payment.
(d) On receiving payment after providing services to customer.

DISCUSSION QUESTION 4.3

What is the economic role of the realization principle?

....

....

....

Expense Recognition

The **matching principle** deals with expense recognition. It requires that expenses be recognized in the reporting period in which the related revenues are earned. The objective of the matching exercise is to compare accomplishment with effort. It is easy to match an expense with a revenue when they have a cause-and-effect relationship. For example, cost of goods sold and sales commission can be matched with sales revenue. Here the matching is near-perfect. Some expenses relate to a period. Examples are salaries, insurance, rent and interest. They are charged off in that period.

Some expenses are expected to have future benefits but linking the two precisely may not be possible. Accountants attempt to allocate them in a "systematic" manner by applying approximation methods. For example, buildings and equipment are used over many years, so we record depreciation expense for such items. Finally, there are activities such as employee training, research and development, and brand building that have unpredictable outcomes. Amounts spent on such activities are expensed as incurred.

Expense recognition, similar to revenue recognition, has a balance sheet effect. Expense recognition is simultaneous with a decrease in an asset or an increase in a liability. For instance, when a business pays rent for its office, it records a rent expense and a decrease in cash, an asset. If rent has not been paid, a liability will be recorded. Thus, expense recognition and its balance sheet effect are two ways of looking at the same transaction.

Understanding the principles of revenue and expense recognition helps us appreciate the significance of the reported profit better and assess the risks involved.

ONE-MINUTE QUIZ 4.4
Expense Recognition

Rank these industries in decreasing order of complexity (i.e. most to least) in matching expenses with revenues.
(a) IT services outsourcing.
(b) Pharmaceuticals.
(c) Banking.
(d) Roadside food vending.

DISCUSSION QUESTION 4.4

"Matching revenues and expenses can never be perfect." Do you agree?

....

....

....

Income Measurement Mechanics

Accounting adjustments help in achieving the purpose of accrual accounting: *allocating revenues and expenses to appropriate periods*. Deferral is the lag in the recognition of an expense already paid or a revenue already received. It relates to past cash receipts and payments. Deferral is needed for expenses and revenues that must be apportioned between two or more reporting periods. Examples of deferral are prepaid insurance, supplies, equipment, and unearned revenue. Accrual is the recognition of an expense incurred but not paid or a revenue earned but not received. It relates to expected future cash receipts and payments. Accrual is required for unrecorded expenses and revenues. Examples of accrual are salaries payable, accrued interest expense, accrued interest income, and unbilled revenue.

Figure 4.2 illustrates the adjustment process.

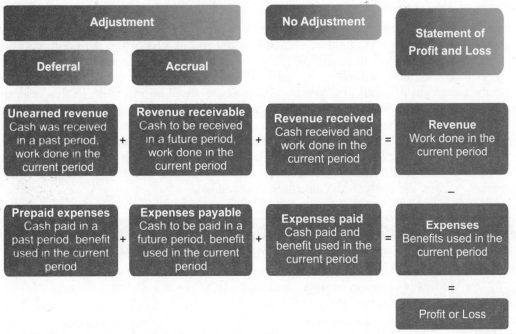

Figure 4.2
THE ADJUSTMENT PROCESS

Accounting adjustments help in allocating revenues and expenses to appropriate periods.

Learning Objective

LO 4 Define deferrals and accruals and explain the need for adjustments.

You would have noted that from Chapter 1 onwards we have been considering *revenue billed but not collected* because firms routinely record it at the transaction stage. So we are not including it in adjustments. Also, we have sometimes considered *supplies consumed* and *revenue from advance payments* at the transaction stage. More often, these require adjustment at the end of the reporting period. So we will consider them again here.

Adjusting Entries

Adjusting entries are journal entries that ensure that revenues are recorded in the period in which they are earned and expenses are recognized in the period in which they are incurred. They have two distinctive characteristics that you will find useful to remember:

1. *An adjusting entry affects both a balance sheet item (asset or liability) and a statement of profit and loss item (revenue or expense)*. For example, recording a revenue (a statement of profit and loss item) earned but not received creates a receivable (a balance sheet item) for the revenue. Again, recording an expense (a statement of profit and loss item) incurred but not paid creates a payable (a balance sheet item).

Learning Objective

LO 5 Prepare adjusting entries.

2. *An adjusting entry does not affect cash.* This should be obvious. After all, if cash is received or paid in the same period in which the expense is incurred or revenue is earned, there would be no need for an adjusting entry in the first place.

Adjusting entries record deferrals and accruals. To illustrate typical adjusting entries, we shall continue with the example of Vogue Company, introduced in Chapter 3.

Apportioning Recorded Expenses

A business often pays for benefits that last more than one reporting period. Under accrual, a payment is not necessarily an expense. Accountants usually record such items as assets to show their future benefits. At the end of the reporting period, the accountant transfers the portion of the asset that has been used during the period from asset to expense. Adjustments for prepaid expenses, office supplies, and depreciation involve apportionment of asset costs between reporting periods. An adjusting entry to apportion a recorded cost consists of a debit to an expense account and a credit to an asset account.

Prepaid expenses These are the costs of services bought and paid for but not yet used. Insurance and rent are often paid in advance. By the end of a reporting period, the portion of the services which was used during the period has become an expense and the unused portion of these items represents an asset. Without adjustments for prepaid expenses, both the statement of profit and loss and balance sheet will be incorrect. In this case, the financial statements will understate the expenses and overstate the assets and the equity.

Vogue Company has prepaid insurance. On June 6, the company paid ₹720 for a one-year fire insurance policy that will expire on May 31 next year. We recorded it by debiting an asset, *prepaid insurance*. The expenditure of ₹720 will protect the company against fire loss for one year. At the end of June, 1/12th of the protection expired; so we record it as *insurance expense*. We analyze the adjustment as follows:

Adjustment (a)		
ANALYSIS	Expense (Insurance Expense) increased. Asset (Prepaid Insurance) decreased.	
RULES	Debit expense to record increase. Credit asset to record decrease.	
ENTRY	June 30 Insurance Expense 60	
	Prepaid Insurance	60

ACCOUNTS	Insurance Expense	Prepaid Insurance
	June 30 60	June 6 720 │ *June 30* 60

The balance of ₹660 in Prepaid Insurance represents the unexpired insurance cover for the remaining 11 months. The balance of ₹60 in Insurance Expense represents the insurance cost for June. As you may have inferred, without this adjustment, Vogue would have understated expenses, and overstated net profit, assets and equity, by ₹60.

HANDHOLD 4.2
Prepaid Insurance

On October 1, Sharon Company buys a three-year insurance policy for a premium of ₹3,600 and debits prepaid insurance. The insurance benefit costs ₹100 per month (i.e. ₹3,600 ÷ 36 months). The company uses up insurance cover worth ₹300 (i.e. ₹100 × 3) in the quarter ended December 31. At December 31, the value of the unexpired insurance cover is ₹3,300 (i.e. ₹100 × 33).

The following adjusting entry records this position:

Insurance Expense.. 300
    Prepaid Insurance... 300

Office supplies Recall from Chapter 3 that at June 30, Vogue Company had office supplies of ₹3,700. Suppose the company's physical count on June 30 shows office supplies of ₹2,900. The difference represents consumption of ₹800. We record the following adjustment:

Adjustment (b)	
ANALYSIS	Expense (Office Supplies Expense) increased. Asset (Office Supplies) decreased.
RULES	Debit expense to record increase. Credit asset to record decrease.
ENTRY	June 30 Office Supplies Expense.................................... 800 Office Supplies 800

	Office Supplies Expense		Office Supplies			
ACCOUNTS	June 22	1,800	June 2	2,000	June 22	1,800
	30	800	9	3,500	30	800

Office Supplies has a balance of ₹2,900, which equals the cost of supplies on hand. Office Supplies Expense has a balance of ₹2,600, which equals the cost of supplies used in June. Without this adjusting entry, Vogue would have understated expenses, and overstated net profit, assets and equity, by ₹800.

Determine the missing amounts in the following independent cases:

TEST YOUR UNDERSTANDING 4.1
Supplies Expense

	Case A	Case B	Case C	Case D
Supplies inventory, beginning of period	₹610	₹390	₹ ?	₹450
Supplies bought during the period	950	?	280	860
Supplies inventory, end of period	530	470	160	?
Supplies expense for the period	?	960	900	820

You know that journal entries record changes in an account, not balances. Suppose an enterprise pays insurance premium of ₹720 for the next one year (at ₹60 per month) at the beginning of a fiscal year. The journal entry, *Debit Prepaid Insurance 720; Credit Cash 720*, records this transaction. At the end of the first quarter, insurance premium of ₹180 (₹60 per month × 3) has to be expensed and the prepaid insurance will now become ₹540. The journal entry, *Debit Insurance Expense 180; Credit Prepaid Insurance 180*, records this adjustment. As a result, the balance in the Prepaid Insurance account becomes ₹540. Note that the journal entry does not record the account balance.

LADDER
Expense and Prepaid Expense

As an exercise, try and explain how you will record the adjustment in the following two cases:

Case 1: The enterprise recorded the payment as follows: *Debit Insurance Expense 720; Credit Cash 720.*

Case 2: The enterprise recorded the payment as follows: *Debit Insurance Expense 180; Debit Prepaid Expense 540; Credit Cash 720.*

Depreciation Assets such as buildings, equipment, and vehicles are useful for many years. We can think of the cost of such assets as a long-term prepayment for the expected benefits. Accountants allocate the cost of an asset to current and future periods. **Depreciation** is the portion of the asset's cost allocated to a period. Since it is hard to predict the exact life of an asset, estimates are unavoidable. Accountants use a number of methods to estimate the depreciation expense. For now, we will take that the benefits are evenly distributed over an asset's life.

To illustrate, assume that Vogue Company's equipment has a useful life of five years, without any value at the end. The monthly depreciation expense is ₹50 (₹3,000/60 months). The company debits this amount to Depreciation Expense. It credits a separate account called Accumulated Depreciation for the amount allocated to the period. You will see in a moment why the company credits accumulated depreciation instead of the asset itself. The accumulated depreciation is a **contra account**, i.e. an account that appears as an offset or deduction from a related account in a financial statement. The following entry records depreciation:

Adjustment (c)	
ANALYSIS	Expense (Depreciation Expense) increased. Asset (Equipment) decreased.
RULES	Debit expense to record increase. Credit asset to record decrease.
ENTRY	June 30 Depreciation Expense .... 50 Accumulated Depreciation, Equipment....... 50

ACCOUNTS	Depreciation Expense		Accumulated Depreciation, Equipment	
	June 30	50		June 30	50

Depreciation expense appears in the statement of profit and loss. The June 30 balance sheet will now report the equipment as follows:

Equipment .... ₹3,000
Less Accumulated depreciation   50   ₹2,950

As you can see, the use of contra account permits disclosure of both the cost of the asset and the cost expired to date. The difference between the cost and the accumulated depreciation is called **book value** or **carrying amount**. It represents the unexpired cost of the asset.

Without the adjustment for depreciation, Vogue Company would have understated expenses and overstated net profit, assets and equity by, ₹50.

TEST YOUR UNDERSTANDING 4.2
Depreciation Expense

On April 1, 20X1, Ahmed Company bought a computer with an estimated useful life of 5 years for ₹10,000.
(a) Prepare the adjusting entry for depreciation on March 31, 20X2.
(b) What will be the balance in Accumulated Depreciation, Office Equipment on March 31, 20X5?

Apportioning Unearned Revenues

Businesses may receive advance payments from their customers. For example, property owners collect rent in advance, airlines receive fares ahead of travel, media companies accept magazine subscriptions for future periods, and insurance companies insist on advance payment of premium. When an enterprise collects revenue in advance, it is obliged to provide goods or services in the future. Therefore, **unearned revenue** is a liability. It is the service provider's mirror image of a prepaid expense. For example, a customer would record a prepaid insurance expense, while the insurance company record an unearned revenue. Unearned revenue becomes revenue by providing goods and services. At the end of the reporting period, an adjusting entry transfers an appropriate amount to revenue. On June 8, Vogue Company collected ₹1,500 from Kidswear for future services. Suppose on June 27 the company supplied a design for ₹900 but did not record it. The adjustment to recognize this revenue is as follows:

Adjustment (d)	
ANALYSIS	Liability (Unearned Revenue) decreased. Revenue (Revenue from Services) increased.
RULES	Debit liability to record decrease. Credit revenue to record increase.
ENTRY	June 30 Unearned Revenue .... 900 Revenue from Services............................. 900

ACCOUNTS	Unearned Revenue				Revenue from Services	
	June 30	900	June 8	1,500		June 7	2,000
						10	9,000
						25	3,000
						30	*900*

The Revenue from Services account now shows balance of ₹14,900. The balance of ₹600 in the Unearned Revenue account represents the liability for services still to be provided. Without this adjustment, Vogue Company would have understated revenue, net profit and equity and overstated liabilities by, ₹900.

Salim Property Company lets out one of its buildings on July 1 at ₹2,100 per month, collecting six months' rent in advance and credited the amount to Unearned Rent. The September 30 adjusting entry for the transaction is as follows:

HANDHOLD 4.3
Unearned Revenue

Unearned Rent	6,300	
Revenue from Rental Services		6,300

On January 1, 20X1, Business Monthly received a three-year subscription of ₹10,800 and credited it to Subscription Revenue. What adjusting entry should it record at March 31, 20X1?

TEST YOUR UNDERSTANDING 4.3
Unearned Revenue

Recording Accrued Expenses

Businesses record most expenses when they pay them. At the end of a reporting period, a business may have incurred but not paid some expenses. Expenses incurred but not paid are known as **accrued expenses**. An adjusting entry is needed to recognize these obligations. Salaries, interest, and income tax are examples of expenses that normally need an accrual adjustment.

Recall from Chapter 3 that on June 21, Vogue Company appointed an office manager on a monthly salary of ₹1,500. The manager's salary for ten days is an expense in June. Therefore, we should recognize a salary expense of ₹500 although it was not paid. We record the following adjusting entry:

Adjustment (e)			
ANALYSIS	Expense (Salaries Expense) increased. Liability (Salaries Payable) increased.		
RULES	Debit expense to record increase. Credit liability to record increase.		
ENTRY	June 30 Salaries Expense...	500	
	Salaries Payable...		500

	Salaries Expense		Salaries Payable	
ACCOUNTS	June 28	800	June 30	500
	30	500		

Sanjay Company estimates its income tax for the December 31 quarter at ₹3,500. Record the expense.

TEST YOUR UNDERSTANDING 4.4
Income Tax Payable

Recording Accrued Revenues

Usually, a business records revenue at the time it sells goods or services on credit. However, at the end of a reporting period, some revenue may remain unrecorded although it may have been earned. Earned revenue that is unrecorded is called **accrued revenue** or **unbilled revenue**. For example, suppose interest is payable on a bank deposit on January 1 and July 1 for the preceding half-year. The interest income of the depositor for three months (January 1 to March 31) is accrued revenue on March 31. Accrued revenue is an asset because it represents cash to be received from the customer after billing. Unbilled revenue is common in services and construction contracts. Billing is done after completion of project milestones. Work done between two billing dates is unbilled revenue. Accrued revenue is the mirror image of accrued expense.

Assume that Vogue Company had completed a design for a customer for a fee of ₹700 by June 30. The company will bill the customer when it supplies the design. Since the company has virtually completed the earning process, it recognizes this revenue as follows:

Adjustment (f)			
ANALYSIS	Asset (Unbilled Revenue) increased. Revenue (Revenue from Services) increased.		
RULES	Debit asset to record increase. Credit revenue to record increase.		
ENTRY	June 30 Unbilled Revenue... 700		
	Revenue from Services.............................		700

	Unbilled Revenue		**Revenue from Services**	
ACCOUNTS	*June 30* 700		June 7 2,000	
			10 9,000	
			25 3,000	
			30 900	
			30 *700*	

Unbilled Revenue is economically (but not legally) a receivable. The balance in Revenue from Services is now equal to the revenue earned in June. It represents the company's accomplishment regardless of when, or indeed whether or not, the company received cash. If this adjustment is not made, Vogue Company's revenue, net profit, assets and equity would be understated by ₹700.

LADDER
Understanding Revenue

Revenue earned in a period is the sum of the following:
1. Work done in the current period but paid for in the past.
2. Work done in the current period and paid for in the current period.
3. Work done in the current period but to be paid for in the future.

Common mistakes in revenue recognition include the following:
1. Recognizing advance payment as revenue.
2. Omitting unbilled revenue.
3. Recognizing both advance payment and subsequent invoice.
4. Recognizing both invoice and subsequent collection.

In order to avoid such errors, it is best to remember this simple point: Revenue is work done.

HANDHOLD 4.4
Accrued Revenue

On October 1, 20X5, Kate Company made a three-year bank deposit of ₹20,000 at an annual interest rate of 10 per cent payable at the time of maturity. The adjusting entry for accrued interest receivable at March 31, 20X6 is as follows:

The accrued interest receivable is ₹1,000, calculated as: ₹20,000 × 10/100 × 6/12. The adjusting entry is as follows:

Interest Receivable   1,000
    Interest Income   1,000

Figure 4.3 shows the effect of the adjustment process on revenues, expenses, assets, and liabilities.

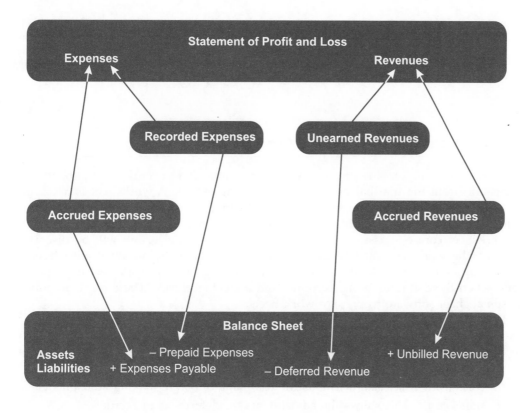

Figure 4.3

THE ADJUSTMENT PROCESS

Each accounting adjustment affects a combination of (a) a revenue and either (i) an asset or (ii) a liability or (b) an expense and either (i) an asset or (ii) a liability.

Which of the following is not an adjusting entry? There may be more than one correct answer.
(a) Debit unearned revenue, credit revenue,
(b) Debit prepaid insurance, credit cash.
(c) Debit cash, credit interest receivable.
(d) Debit equipment, credit bills payable.

ONE-MINUTE QUIZ 4.5
Adjusting Entry

Can an adjusting entry have a debit or credit to cash?

QUICK QUESTION
Adjusting entry

Researchers have studied the role of accrual accounting and its incremental usefulness over the cash system. Cash accounting is a simple system of reporting cash receipts and payments. Accrual accounting requires considerable management judgment and expertise to determine if a revenue has been earned but not received or if an expense has been incurred but not paid as of the reporting date.

RESEARCH INSIGHT
Accrual

Research by Professor Patricia Dechow[3] indicates that the greater the importance of accrual accounting, (a) the shorter the performance measurement interval; (b) the greater the volatility of the firm's working capital requirements and investment and financing activities; and (c) the longer the firm's operating cycle. Under each of these circumstances, cash flows suffer more severely from timing and matching problems that reduce their ability to reflect the firm's performance.

To understand this research, look at the following examples:

(i) *Short reporting period:* Suppose a firm buys an expensive piece of equipment with a long life in the first quarter of a fiscal year. If the firm reports quarterly and follows the cash system, it will expense the equipment in that quarter. Since the firm uses up only a small part of the productive capacity of the equipment in that quarter, there will be significant revenues in the future, but there will be no expense for the use of the equipment. As a result, there will be a mismatch between the firm's accomplishments and efforts. As the reporting period increases, the distortion will decrease. The matching will be perfect over the life of the equipment.

(ii) *Operating, investing, and financing volatility:* Mismatches can occur even if the reporting period is relatively longer (e.g. one year). Suppose a firm invests considerably different amounts in different periods and expenses any investment when acquired. Here again, the cash system will produce distorted results.

---
[3] Patricia M. Dechow, Accounting earnings and cash flows as measures of firm performance: The role of accounting accruals, *Journal of Accounting and Economics*, July 1994.

(iii) *Long operating cycle:* Suppose a firm extends credit to its customers for long periods and carries inventories over a long period, because of the nature of the production process (e.g. ship-building). Under the cash system, it will expense the cost of the materials at the time of purchase and will show the revenue much later when it receives cash. Once again, the cash system will provide an improper measure of the firm's performance.

Financial Statements of a Service Organization

Learning Objective

LO6 **Prepare the financial statements of a service organization.**

The next step is to prepare the financial statements. It is useful to put together the information from the trial balance and the adjusting entries. A **worksheet** is a columnar sheet used to summarize information needed to prepare financial statements. It is also an informal device for assembling the required information in one place. Completing the worksheet correctly assures the accountant that potential errors will be discovered. However, the worksheet can't replace the financial statements, do away with recording and posting entries, or make up for weak internal controls. The worksheet is particularly useful when there are numerous accounts and adjusting entries. These days, accountants use spreadsheet software to prepare worksheets.

The standard form of the worksheet appears in Exhibit 4.1. It has the name of the organization and the date. The worksheet can cover any period. The date is the balance sheet date. The worksheet has a column for account title. Then there are six more pairs of columns for the following:

1. *Unadjusted Trial Balance:* This is the trial balance before making adjustments.
2. *Adjustments:* This shows the adjustments for deferrals and accruals.
3. *Adjusted Trial Balance:* This shows the account balances after the adjustments.
4. *Statement of Profit and Loss:* This is for revenue and expense items.
5. *Statement of Retained Earnings:* This is for beginning and ending balances of retained earnings, net profit, and dividends.
6. *Balance Sheet:* This is for asset, liability, and equity items.

Each pair of columns consists of a debit column and a credit column, thus making a total of 12 columns for entering amounts.

We prepare the worksheet of Vogue Company in Exhibit 4.1 as follows:

1. Enter the account balances in Unadjusted Trial Balance. The amounts are taken from the trial balance in Exhibit 3.6.
2. Enter the adjustments in Adjustments. These are items (a) to (f) discussed earlier in this chapter.
3. Enter the account balances after adjustment in Adjusted Trial Balance.
4. Extend each account balance in Adjusted Trial Balance to Statement of Profit and Loss, Statement of Retained Earnings, or Balance Sheet. Revenue and expense items go to Statement of Profit and Loss. Retained earnings and dividends go to Statement of Retained Earnings.[4] Assets (including contra assets), liabilities and share capital go to Balance Sheet.
5. Total the Statement of Profit and Loss, Statement of Retained Earnings, and Balance Sheet columns. The difference between the Statement of Profit and Loss columns is the profit for the period. Extend this amount to Statement of Retained Earnings. The difference between the Statement of Retained Earnings columns is the ending balance of retained earnings. Extend this amount to Balance Sheet. Total the Balance Sheet columns.

---

[4] The statement of retained earnings is part of the statement of changes in equity.

EXHIBIT 4.1
Vogue Company: Worksheet

VOGUE COMPANY
Worksheet, June 30, 20XX

Account	Unadjusted Trial Balance Debit	Unadjusted Trial Balance Credit	Adjustments Debit	Adjustments Credit	Adjusted Trial Balance Debit	Adjusted Trial Balance Credit	Statement of Profit and Loss Debit	Statement of Profit and Loss Credit	Statement of Retained Earnings Debit	Statement of Retained Earnings Credit	Balance Sheet Debit	Balance Sheet Credit
Equipment	3,000				3,000						3,000	
Accumulated depreciation, Equipment				50 (c)		50						50
Office supplies	3,700			800 (b)	2,900						2,900	
Trade receivables	7,000				7,000						7,000	
Cash	46,930				46,930						46,930	
Prepaid insurance	720			60 (a)	660						660	
Trade payables		2,500				2,500						2,500
Unearned revenue		1,500	900 (d)			600						600
Share capital		50,000				50,000						50,000
Dividends	2,200				2,200				2,200			
Revenue from services		14,000		900 (d) 700 (f)		15,600		15,600				
Rent expense	1,500				1,500		1,500					
Telephone expense	200				200		200					
Salaries expense	800		500 (e)		1,300		1,300					
Electricity expense	150				150		150					
Office supplies expense	1,800		800 (b)		2,600		2,600					
Total	68,000	68,000										
Insurance expense			60 (a)		60		60					
Depreciation expense			50 (c)		50		50					
Salaries payable				500 (e)		500						500
Unbilled revenue			700 (f)		700						700	
Total			3,010	3,010	69,250	69,250	5,860	15,600	2,200		61,190	53,650
Net profit							9,740			9,740		
							15,600	15,600				
Retained earnings									7,540			7,540
Total									9,740	9,740	61,190	61,190

When the worksheet is done, preparing the financial statements is relatively easy. Exhibit 4.2 presents Vogue Company's financial statements. Schedule III to the Companies Act 2013 specifies the format for the balance sheet and the statement of profit and loss. The statement of cash flows follows the requirements of Ind AS 7.

EXHIBIT 4.2
Vogue Company:
Financial Statements

Panel A

VOGUE COMPANY Balance Sheet, June 30, 20XX		
	Note	
ASSETS		
Non-current assets		
Property, plant and equipment	1	₹2,950
Total non-current assets		2,950
Current assets		
Inventories	2	2,900
Financial assets		
Trade receivables		7,000
Cash and cash equivalents		46,930
Other financial assets	3	700
Other current assets	4	660
Total current assets		58,190
Total assets		61,140
EQUITY AND LIABILITIES		
EQUITY		
Equity share capital		₹50,000
Other equity		7,540
Total equity		57,540
LIABILITIES		
Non-current liabilities		—
Current liabilities		
Financial liabilities		
Trade payables		3,000
Other current liabilities	5	600
Total current liabilities		3,600
Total equity and liabilities		61,140

Panel B

VOGUE COMPANY Statement of Profit and Loss for the month ended June 30, 20XX		
	Note	
Revenue from operations	6	₹15,600
Total income		15,600
Expenses		
Employee benefits expense		1,300
Depreciation and amortization expense		50
Other expenses	7	4,510
Total expenses		5,860
Profit before tax		9,740
Tax expense		0
Profit for the period		9,740

Panel C

VOGUE COMPANY Statement of Changes in Equity			
	Equity Share Capital	Other Equity Retained Earnings	Total
Balance as of June 1, 20XX..........	₹ 0	₹ 0	₹ 0
Share issue..........	50,000		50,000
Dividends..........		(2,200)	(2,200)
Profit for the period..........		9,740	9,740
Balance as of June 30, 20XX..........	50,000	7,540	57,540

Panel D

VOGUE COMPANY Statement of Cash Flows for the month ended June 30, 20XX		
Cash flows from operating activities		
Received from customers..........	₹ 8,500	
Paid to suppliers and employees..........	(6,370)	
Net cash used in operating activities..........		₹ 2,130
Cash flows from investing activities		
Purchase of equipment..........	(3,000)	
Net cash used in investing activities..........		(3,000)
Cash flows from financing activities		
Issue of share capital..........	50,000	
Dividend paid..........	(2,200)	
Net cash provided by financing activities..........		47,800
Net increase in cash and cash equivalents..........		46,930
Cash and cash equivalents at the beginning..........		0
Cash and cash equivalents at the end..........		46,930

Notes:

1. **Property, plant and equipment**

Particulars	Equipment	Total
Gross carrying value as of June 1, 20XX..........	0	0
Additions..........	3,000	3,000
Gross carrying value as of June 30, 20XX..........	3,000	3,000
Accumulated depreciation as of June 1, 20XX..........	0	0
Additions..........	50	50
Accumulated depreciation as of June 30, 20XX..........	50	50
Carrying value as of June 30, 20XX..........	2,950	2,950

2. **Inventories**

Office supplies..........	2,900

3. **Other financial assets**

Unbilled revenue..........	700

4. **Other current assets**

Prepaid insurance..........	660

5. **Other current liabilities**

Unearned revenue..........	600

6. **Revenue from operations**

Revenue from services..........	15,600

7. **Other expenses**

Rent expense..........	1,500
Telephone expense..........	200
Electricity expense..........	150
Office supplies expense..........	2,600
Insurance expense..........	60
	4,510

There are two ways of grouping items in the statement of profit and loss: (1) natural and (2) functional. In the *natural* format, purchases and expenses are added and their total is subtracted from sales to get profit. The statement of profit and loss in Exhibit 4.2 is based on natural classification following the requirements of Schedule III to the Companies Act 2013. In the *functional* format, items are grouped according to the activities of a business, such as manufacturing, trading, marketing, and administration. Cost of goods sold (or cost of sales) is subtracted from sales to get gross profit, and operating expenses are subtracted from gross profit to get operating profit. The functional format is more user-friendly. Exhibit 4.3 presents the statement of profit and loss in this format.

EXHIBIT 4.3
Vogue Company:
Statement of Profit
and Loss in Functional
Format

VOGUE COMPANY Statement of Profit and Loss for the month ended June 30, 20XX		
	Note	
Revenue from operations	6	₹15,600
Cost of sales	7	1,300
Gross profit		14,300
Operating expenses	8	4,560
Operating profit		9,740
Notes:		
6. Revenue from operations		
Revenue from services		15,600
7. Cost of sales		
Employee benefits		1,300
8. Operating expenses		
Rent expense		1,500
Telephone expense		200
Electricity expense		150
Insurance expense		60
Office supplies expense		2,600
Depreciation and amortization expense		50
		4,560

Learning Objective

LO7 Identify the components of the statement of profit and loss of a merchandising organization.

Income Measurement for a Merchandising Organization

Merchandising (or trading) organizations earn revenue by selling goods, or **merchandise**. Figure 4.4 illustrates how goods flow from the manufacturer to the consumer through the wholesaler and the retailer. The accounting principles and methods you have learnt apply equally to these organizations. We need some additional accounts and procedures to record purchases and sales.

Figure 4.4

FLOW OF MERCHANDISE THROUGH MARKETING CHANNEL

Merchandising organizations link the manufacturer and the consumer.

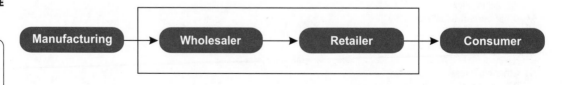

Exhibit 4.4 shows the statement of profit and loss of Vijay Electronics Limited, a wholesaler.

> The statement of profit and loss presents the revenue, cost of goods sold, and operating expenses.

VIJAY ELECTRONICS LIMITED Statement of Profit and Loss for the year ended December 31, 20X2	
Revenue from operations	₹436,820
Cost of goods sold	298,700
Gross profit	138,120
Operating expenses	75,400
Operating profit	62,720
Non-operating income/(expense), net	(3,800)
Profit before tax	58,920
Tax	26,000
Profit for the period (or net profit)	32,920

The statement of profit and loss of a merchandising organization has three components:

- Revenue from sales;
- Cost of goods sold; and
- Operating expenses.[5]

In common parlance, revenue is *top line*, costs and expenses are *middle line*, and net profit is *bottom line*. The principle of income measurement for a merchandising organization is the same as that for a service organization: *net profit results from matching expenses with revenues*. **Revenue from sales** is the primary source of revenue for a merchandising organization. **Cost of goods sold** is the cost of merchandise sold during the period. This expense is directly related to the revenue from sales. **Gross profit**, an intermediate profit measure, is the excess of revenue from sales over cost of goods sold.

Operating expenses are expenses incurred in running the business. They are normally separated by function. Selling expenses arise from activities connected with selling and distributing the goods and include storage charges, salaries for the sales staff and commissions, and cost of delivering goods to customers. Administrative expenses are those associated with general services, such as accounting, personnel, corporate office, and general administration. After calculating gross profit, we deduct operating expenses to arrive at **profit before interest and tax (PBIT), or operating profit**. Non-operating items include interest expense, interest income, dividend income and gains and losses from disposal of property, plant and equipment and investments. **Profit before tax (PBT)** is operating profit adjusted for non-operating items. **Profit for the period**, **net profit**, or **profit after tax**, is profit before tax *less* income tax.

Revenue from Sales

Management, investors, and analysts monitor sales trends. An increasing trend indicates not only sales growth but also the probability of an increase in earnings. On the other hand, a falling trend might portend a downturn in a company's fortunes. Yearly sales are compared with the previous year's sales (year on year, or "YoY"). Quarterly sales are compared with sales in the previous quarter (quarter on quarter, or "QoQ") and the year-ago quarter. Besides, sales are compared with competitors' sales. These comparisons help to spot major trends in sales. Sales are a better leading indicator of the future than profits.

- Apple's iPhones sales are slowing down, so future growth has to come from entertainment and cloud storage.

Learning Objective

LO 8 **Record merchandise sales.**

---

[5] Published financial statements of Indian companies do not usually have cost of goods sold and operating expenses. As a result, it is not possible to calculate some of the measures described in this chapter.

Once upon a time, Infosys was growing faster than peers such as TCS and Wipro. Not any more, it would appear. Look at the data.

Fiscal Year	TCS		Infosys	
	Revenue (in billions)	Growth Rate (%)	Revenue (in billions)	Growth Rate (%)
2013	₹ 630	28	404	20
2014	818	30	501	24
2015	947	16	533	6
2016	1,087	15	624	17

Source: Company reports, stock exchange websites, news reports.

In 2013, TCS was 1½ times the size of Infosys. Because of its higher growth, TCS had become 1¾ times of Infosys in 2016. Sales growth signifies relevance, competitiveness, vibrancy and innovation. In 2016, its revenue grew by ₹140 billion; Infosys's revenue grew by ₹91 billion. Since TCS was growing on a much larger base, its growth rate was lower.

Fast-growing firms command respect with employees, customers and investors.

Sales

Sales consist of cash sales and credit sales. Under accrual accounting, revenue is considered to be earned when ownership of the goods passes from the seller to the buyer. As a result, a business recognizes revenue at the time of sale even though it may collect payment later. The following are the additional conditions for the recognition of revenue from the sale of goods:

1. The seller has transferred to the buyer the significant risks and rewards of ownership of the goods.
2. The seller does not retain effective control over the goods sold.

Let us now see how to apply these conditions.

Risks and rewards of ownership The buyer should be the *economic* owner of the goods, even if there is no transfer of legal ownership. The litmus test of ownership is who will get to keep the profit if the price of the goods goes up or bear the loss if the price goes down. If the answer is 'buyer', it is a sale. Usually, the transfer of the risks and rewards of ownership occurs with physical delivery of the goods or transfer of legal title. Thus, in a vast majority of transactions delivery indicates sale (e.g. retail sales). The Indian Sale of Goods Act lays down the principles for determining when legal title is transferred. If the seller retains an insignificant risk of ownership, the transaction is a sale. For example, many supermarkets offer terms such as "money back if not completely satisfied." Here the seller recognizes the revenue and a liability for returns based on past experience and other relevant factors.

Control over the goods The spirit of a sale is that the buyer can decide what to do with the goods once the sale is over. For example, usually the seller of a piece of equipment can't tell the buyer how much to produce, at what price to sell the product, whom to sell, or how to dispose of the equipment. Legitimate exceptions include compliance with safety regulations, prohibition of resale for illegal use, and enforcement of export ban by the government.

The invoice contains the details of a sale, such as the name of the product (or service), number of units sold, unit price, total price, taxes and duties, total amount billed, and payment and shipping terms. The seller prepares the invoice at the time of sale and sends it to the buyer. A retailer prepares the invoice at the point of sale. A wholesaler prepares the invoice after the shipping department notifies the accounting department that it has shipped the goods to the retailer. Figure 4.5 shows a wholesaler's invoice.

```
                    VIJAY ELECTRONICS LIMITED
                 M-14, Connaught Circus, New Delhi 110001
                                Invoice
```

Invoice No. 1983 May 19, 20XX
Sold to: Aruna Store 19A R K Mutt Road Mylapore Chennai 600 004
P. O. No. 738 dated May 2, 20XX
Vendor Code No. 51

Terms: Net 45, FOB destination

Description	Item Code	Quantity	Price per Unit	Total
Apple iPhone 7 with standard accessories	P8	100	₹70,000	₹7,000,000
			VAT 10%	700,000
			Total	7,700,000

Terms and Conditions:
1. Our responsibility ceases as soon as our agent loads the goods on board the aircraft.
2. Any claim related to this sale shall be made within 7 days from receipt of the goods.
3. This sale is subject to National Capital Territory jurisdiction.
4. Interest will be charged @ 12% per annum for delayed payment.

Figure 4.5

A WHOLESALER'S INVOICE

An invoice contains a description of the product or service for each sale transaction, the seller prepares an invoice showing the amount payable by the buyer and other details.

Vijay Electronics records the sale transaction in Figure 4.5 as follows:

May 19	Trade Receivables	7,700,000	
	Sales		7,000,000
	VAT Payable		700,000
	Sold merchandise on credit		

The balance in the Sales account shows the total amount of cash and credit sales made in a reporting period. Since the seller may collect amounts due on credit sales in a subsequent period, there may be a significant difference between cash collections from sales and the amount of sales.

Sales Returns and Allowances

Most wholesalers and retailers allow their customers to return goods which are found to be unsatisfactory or defective. Companies following a policy of "satisfaction guaranteed" allow goods to be returned if the customer does not like them. A **sales return** is a merchandise returned by a buyer. Sometimes, the customer may find after the sale that the goods have minor defects and may agree to keep the goods if the seller allows a reduction of the sales price, called **sales allowance**. A seller may grant sales allowances for a number of reasons, including inferior quality, damage, deterioration in transit, and variation in specifications. In all cases of sales returns and allowances, the seller sends the buyer a document called **credit note**, which indicates that the balance in the customer's account is being reduced.

We could record sales returns and allowances as debits to sales because they cancel a portion of the sales. However, information about the amount of sales returns and allowances is useful to management. High returns could be an indication of the low quality of the goods or of high pressure selling. Besides, handling returned goods is a costly and time-consuming affair. For these reasons, we debit Sales Returns and Allowances, a contra-revenue account. Suppose on May 23 Vijay Electronics issues a credit note for ₹14,500 for the May 19 transaction. The following entry records this transaction:

May 23	Sales Returns and Allowances	14,500	
	Trade Receivables		14,500
	Allowance for unsatisfactory merchandise sold on May 19		

Trade Discounts

A **trade discount** is a percentage reduction granted to a customer from the specified list price or catalogue price. Trade discounts serve several purposes. Trade discounts enable firms to quote different prices to different types of customers and grant quantity discounts. Also, the cost of producing catalogues is reduced, since a seller can use a catalogue for a longer period of time and announce discounts whenever prices change. Normally, the seller does not record trade discounts in the accounts. For example, suppose the list price of a phone is ₹50,000 but the seller gives a discount of 10 per cent for buying ten phones. If you buy ten phones, the seller would record a revenue of ₹450,000.

Sales Discounts

When a company sells goods on credit, it specifies the terms of payment on the invoice. These terms vary from industry to industry. For example, the invoice in Figure 4.5 shows the terms of payment as "net 45". This is sometimes shortened as "n/45". The term "n/45" means that the entire amount of invoice is due 45 days after May 19, 20X8 (invoice date), which is not later than July 3, 20X8. If the invoice is due 10 days after the end of the month, the terms will be "n/10/eom".

Sometimes, credit terms include discount for early payment, called **cash discount**. By offering an incentive for payment before the due date, the seller is able to speed up its cash inflows. Cash discount is different from trade discount. While the former is a deduction from the invoice price for prompt payment, the latter is a deduction from the catalogue price to determine the invoice price. A cash discount is called a **sales discount** by the seller and a **purchase discount** by the buyer. Credit terms of "2/10, n/45" mean that the buyer will get a 2 per cent discount of the invoice amount for paying within 10 days of the invoice date; alternatively, the buyer can take 45 days and pay the full invoice amount without discount.

HANDHOLD 4.5
Payment Date

On January 1, 20XX, Ankita bought goods for ₹4,000 with terms "2/10, n/30". Ankita should pay the seller ₹3,920 not later than January 11, 20XX, or the full amount of ₹4,000 not later than January 31, 20XX.

The seller records sales discounts when the customer pays. The Sales Discounts account shows the amount of sales discounts. Managers can examine the amount of sales discounts to evaluate the company's credit and collection policy. Sales discounts appear in the statement of profit and loss as an expense. Suppose a sale for ₹1,000 on June 12 is on terms of "2/10, n/30". On June 22, the buyer pays ₹980. The seller records the following entries:

June 12	Trade Receivables		1,000	
	Sales			1,000
	Sold merchandise on credit			
22	Cash..		980	
	Sales Discounts..		20	
	Trade Receivables..			1,000
	Collected from customers within discount period			

Sales discount is calculated on sales *less* any sales returns and allowances.

TEST YOUR UNDERSTANDING 4.5
Payment Date

Determine the last date for payment with and without cash discount for the invoices below. It is a non-leap year.

Invoice	Date	Payment Terms
1	May 13	2/10, n/30
2	January 15	1/10/eom, n/60
3	October 30	2/eom, n/60
4	July 31	3/10/eom, n/45
5	February 12	1/10, n/60

For presentation in the statement of profit and loss, the seller deducts sales returns and allowances, trade discounts, sales discounts and taxes and duties (e.g. value added tax, sales tax, and goods and services tax), and reports only the net sales.

HANDHOLD 4.6
Calculating Revenue

Triveni Company has the following data for a quarter:
- Credit sales at catalogue prices including taxes and duties, ₹53,000.
- Trade discounts, ₹10,600.
- Cash sales, ₹9,400.
- Sales returns and allowances, ₹1,700.
- Sales discounts, ₹800.
- Value added tax/Goods and services tax, ₹9,600.

The amount of sales that would appear on the statement of profit and loss for the period is ₹40,500, calculated as follows:

Credit sales at catalogue prices		₹53,000
Cash sales		9,400
		62,400
Deduct		
Trade discounts	₹10,600	
Sales discounts	800	
Sales returns and allowances	1,700	
Value added tax/Goods and services tax	9,600	22,700
Sale of products (or net sales)		39,700

The following accounts contain five transactions keyed together with letters:

TEST YOUR UNDERSTANDING 4.6
Basic Merchandising Transactions

Sales

	(a)	12,000
	(d)	9,000

Sales Returns and Allowances

(b)	600	

Sales Discounts

(e)	90	

Trade Receivables

(a)	12,000	(b)	600
(d)	9,000	(c)	11,400
		(e)	9,000

Cash

(c)	11,400	
(e)	8,910	

Exhibit 4.5 shows Vijay Electronics' presentation of revenue, assuming sales of ₹460,120, sales returns and allowances of ₹21,900 and sales discounts of ₹1,400.

EXHIBIT 4.5
Statement of Profit and Loss: Sales

VIJAY ELECTRONICS LIMITED	
Statement of Profit and Loss for the year ended December 31, 20X2	
Revenue from operations	₹436,820

FINANCIAL VIEW
Revenue in Ecommerce
Firms

There are two types of ecommerce firms: (1) firms that buy, stock and sell goods to customers ('retail model'); (2) firms that connect sellers and customers ('marketplace model'). Retail firms own the goods and are no different from brick-and-mortar merchandisers: their revenue is the value of goods billed to customers. Marketplace firms are intermediaries; therefore, their revenue is the commission income they collect for the service they provide. Sometimes, we come across the term *gross merchandise value* (GMV). This is the value of goods sold by a retail firm. Somewhat inappropriately, the term gets used in discussions about marketplace firms giving a misleading impression of their size. For instance, consider Alibaba and Amazon. When Alibaba went public in 2015, analysts enthused about its GMV. Alibaba is a marketplace firm and its ecommerce-related revenue is its commission income. In contrast, Amazon is a retailer and it makes sense to look at its GMV. (*Note:* Amazon India is a marketplace firm.) The simple point is that *revenue is work done*. If a firm sells goods, its revenue is the value of the goods. If it facilitates sales, its revenue is the charge for that service.

QUICK QUESTION
Right of return and
revenue recognition

Can a business recognize sales revenue when its customers are allowed to return the goods?

ONE-MINUTE QUIZ 4.6
Revenue

Which of the following items is deducted from revenue for presenting in the statement of profit and loss? There may be more than one correct answer.
   (a) Trade discount.
   (b) Sales discount.
   (c) Excise duty.
   (d) Sales commission.

Cost of Goods Sold

Learning Objective

LO 9 Record merchandise purchases and calculate cost of goods sold.

The second part of a statement of profit and loss of a merchandising organization is the cost of goods sold. Merchandise inventory, or inventory, is the value of goods on hand and available for sale at a given time. Beginning inventory is inventory on hand at the beginning of a reporting period. Ending inventory is inventory at the end of a period. Ending inventory is an asset. It will become a part of cost of goods sold later period when it is sold. This year's beginning inventory was last year's ending inventory. Cost of goods available for sale is the sum of beginning inventory and net cost of purchases. Cost of goods sold is the cost to the seller of goods sold to customers and it is the largest item of expense for merchandising companies. It is determined by computing the cost of (a) the beginning inventory, (b) the net purchases, and (c) the ending inventory. For presentation in the statement of profit and loss, the buyer deducts the amount of purchase returns and allowances as well as purchase discounts, and reports only the net purchases.

Exhibit 4.6 shows the cost of goods sold section of Vijay Electronics' statement of profit and loss. The merchandise inventory on January 1, 20X2 was ₹47,300. Assume purchases of ₹326,900, purchase returns and allowances of ₹13,200 and purchase discounts of ₹1,400. So the amount of net purchases is ₹312,300. Freight paid on purchases is ₹28,100. The net cost of purchases consisting of net purchases and freight is ₹340,400. Vijay Electronics could have sold merchandise of ₹387,700 during 20X2. This is the cost of goods available for sale. On December 31, 20X2, the merchandise inventory was ₹89,000. This is the unsold inventory. Subtracting the ending inventory from the cost of goods available for sale, we get the cost of goods sold of ₹298,700.

EXHIBIT 4.6
Statement of Profit
and Loss: Cost of
Goods Sold

> Cost of goods sold includes not only the cost of purchases but also the freight in and other incidental costs.

VIJAY ELECTRONICS LIMITED Statement of Profit and Loss for the year ended December 31, 20X2		
Cost of goods sold		
Merchandise inventory, December 31, 20X1		₹47,300
Net purchases...	₹312,300	
Freight in	28,100	
Net cost of purchases		340,400
Cost of goods available for sale		387,700
Deduct Merchandise inventory, December 31, 20X2		89,000
Cost of goods sold...		298,700

Figure 4.6 illustrates the flow of goods during a reporting period. Beginning inventory and net cost of purchases, when combined, make up cost of goods available for sale. The latter is explained by cost of goods sold and ending inventory.

Figure 4.6

RELATIONSHIP BETWEEN INVENTORIES AND COST OF GOODS SOLD

> Cost of goods available for sale is the sum of beginning inventory and net cost of purchases and is accounted for by cost of goods sold and ending inventory.

The cost of goods available for sale is ₹409,210 and the ending inventory is ₹73,460. The cost of goods sold is calculated as follows:

Cost of goods sold = Cost of goods available for sale − Ending inventory

= ₹409,210 − ₹73,460 = ₹335,750

HANDHOLD 4.7
Calculating Cost of Goods Sold

The Periodic Inventory System

The amount of merchandise inventory is determined by using either the periodic inventory system or the perpetual inventory system. Under the **periodic inventory system**, the Merchandise Inventory account is updated periodically after a physical count. Hence the name. Usually, physical count takes place at the end of a period. Some stores, particularly smaller ones, use periodic inventory.

Net Cost of Purchases

The term *net cost of purchases* means purchases *less* discounts and purchase returns and allowances *plus* transport and handling costs on the purchases. Government levies, such as import duties, purchase taxes, value added tax (VAT), goods and services tax (GST), and octroi are included in the cost of purchases if they are not recoverable when the buyer sells the goods. The term *net purchases* refers to purchases *less* discounts, returns, and allowances.

Purchases

Under the periodic inventory system, a merchandising company debits the **Purchases account** to record the cost of merchandise bought for resale. Suppose Vijay Electronics purchased merchandise costing ₹50,000 on September 9. The required journal entry is:

Sep. 9   Purchases.. 50,000
              Trade Payables.. 50,000
                    Purchased merchandise on credit

Think of the Purchases account as a combination of an expense account and a temporary asset account. The balance of the account does not indicate how much of the goods has been sold. The Purchases account is used only for goods acquired for resale (after processing in the case of manufacturing organizations). Other assets such as office equipment, office supplies, and vehicles acquired for use in the business are recorded in the appropriate asset accounts.

Purchase Returns and Allowances

When a buyer finds merchandise purchased to be unsatisfactory, he may return the goods or accept an allowance on the price. The buyer sends a **debit note** to notify the seller that the latter's balance is being reduced. Depending on the terms of purchase and trade practice, the buyer may either debit the seller's account immediately or wait for the seller's acceptance of the debit note before recording the debit. Purchase returns and allowances are recorded by crediting the Purchase Returns and Allowances account, a contra-expense account, as given below:

Nov. 18	Trade Payables..	3,100	
	Purchase Returns and Allowances..		3,100
	Returned unsatisfactory merchandise to supplier		

As illustrated in Exhibit 4.6, the statement of profit and loss presents the purchases net of purchase returns. The use of a separate account for returns provides information for monitoring the efficiency of the purchase function and the quality and reliability of the suppliers. High rates of purchase returns could indicate the need for reviewing purchasing practices and eliminating certain vendors.

Purchase Discounts

Purchase discount is the mirror image of sales discount in the buyer's records. Discounts taken are recorded in the Purchase Discounts account. Suppose the terms for a purchase of ₹1,000 of goods on January 3 are 2/10, n/30. If the buyer pays the invoice latest by January 13, he can take a 2 per cent discount. Thus, the buyer must pay only ₹980 to settle the invoice. The following entry records the transactions:

Jan. 3	Purchases..	1,000	
	Trade Payables..		1,000
	Purchased merchandise on terms 2/10, n/30		
13	Trade Payables	1,000	
	Cash		980
	Purchase Discounts...		20
	Paid for merchandise within discount period		

Freight on Purchases

Transportation costs are often an important part of the cost of merchandise purchased. The cost of merchandise includes any transportation charges necessary to bring the goods to the buyer's place of business. A separate **Freight In account** is used to record inward freight charges incurred on purchases. The following entry records a freight of ₹150 paid on a purchase:

May 17	Freight In..	150	
	Cash		150
	Paid freight on merchandise purchased		

The normal balance of the Freight In account is debit. As illustrated in Exhibit 4.6, freight paid on purchases is added to net purchases to get the net cost of purchases. Freight In is an **adjunct account,** i.e. an account whose balance is added to the balance of another account. An adjunct account is the opposite of a contra account (e.g. sales returns and allowances), the balance of which is *deducted* from another account. Transit insurance on purchases is treated similar to freight in.

The invoice normally indicates whether the seller or the buyer is to pay the freight. FOB shipping point means "free on board at shipping point", i.e. the buyer incurs all transportation costs after the merchandise has been loaded on a train, truck, ship or aircraft. FOB destination means "free on board to destination", i.e. the seller ships the goods to their destination without charge to the buyer. Thus, if the terms are FOB shipping point, the buyer pays the freight; if the terms are FOB destination, the seller pays the freight. The freight terms in the invoice in Figure 4.5 are FOB destination and, therefore, Vijay Electronics must pay the freight.

Freight terms are also significant for another reason. Ownership of goods generally passes to the buyer at the FOB point. Therefore, if the terms are FOB shipping point, the buyer should include goods in transit at the year end in its ending inventory. If the terms are FOB destination, the seller should include goods in transit at the year end in its ending inventory.

Harish in Mumbai sells glass jars FOB Pune to Raghav. He places the merchandise duly packed on a truck leaving for Pune. The truck capsizes on its way and the goods are destroyed. The terms are FOB destination. So ownership would pass to Raghav when the goods reach Pune. During transit, Harish was the owner and he must bear the loss.

HANDHOLD 4.8
FOB Terms

Compute the cost of goods sold from the following information: beginning inventory, ₹11,000; purchases, ₹210,000; purchase returns and allowances, ₹7,000; purchase discounts, ₹3,000; freight in, ₹18,000; ending inventory, ₹17,000.

TEST YOUR UNDERSTANDING 4.7
Calculating Cost of Goods Sold

Inventory Losses

Merchandise inventory is lost in a variety of ways, such as spoilage, employee theft, and shoplifting. Under the periodic inventory system, inventory losses are automatically included in the cost of goods sold. To illustrate this point, let us assume the following: cost of goods available for sale, ₹100,000; spoilage, ₹2,000; ending inventory, ₹17,000. Thus, the cost of goods sold is ₹83,000 (cost of goods available for sale, ₹100,000 – ending inventory, ₹17,000). Had there been no spoilage, the ending inventory would have been ₹19,000, and the cost of goods sold would have been ₹81,000 (₹100,000 – ₹19,000), or ₹2,000 lower than that calculated earlier.

Despite their best efforts, businesses suffer inventory losses. Under the periodic inventory system, the loss is tucked away in the cost of goods sold and a measure of the loss is not available. A rough-and-ready method of computing inventory loss under the periodic inventory system is explained later in this chapter. In Chapter 5, you will see another system – the perpetual inventory system – that provides better information about inventory loss.

Which of the following items is not considered for calculating cost of goods sold? There may be more than one correct answer.
(a) Delivery expense.
(b) Freight on purchases.
(c) Purchase discount.
(d) Advertisement expense.

ONE-MINUTE QUIZ 4.7
Calculating Cost of Goods Sold

Operating Expenses

The third most important part of a statement of profit and loss of a merchandising organization is **operating expenses** (also known as *selling, general and administrative expenses* or *SGA*). These are expenses other than cost of goods sold, interest, and income tax and are incurred in running the normal business of a company. These expenses are often grouped

Learning Objective
LO 10 Understand operating expenses.

into selling and administrative expenses. **Selling expenses** include expenses of storing and preparing goods for sale, promoting sales, actually making sales, and delivering goods to customers. Examples are salaries, sales commissions, sales staff travel, advertising, store rent, depreciation on store equipment, and delivery expense. (Freight charges on purchases are included in cost of goods sold.) **Administrative expenses** are incurred in the overall management of a business and include expenses relating to office salaries, office rent, office telephone, board meetings, depreciation on office equipment, and research and development.

FINANCIAL VIEW
Understanding
Operating Expenses

For many businesses operating expenses are not very high. The Coca-Cola Company is an exception. Over the period, 2013 to 2015, the company's operating expenses were 37 per cent of revenue, just 2 per cent shy of cost of goods sold.

	Amount (in millions)			Percent of revenue		
	2015	2014	2013	2015	2014	2013
Net operating revenues	$44,294	$45,998	$46,854	100	100	100
Cost of goods sold	17,482	17,899	18,421	39	39	39
Gross profit	26,812	28,109	28,433	61	61	61
Selling, general and administrative	16,427	17,218	17,310	37	37	37
Other operating charges	1,657	1,183	895	4	3	2
Operating income	8,728	9,708	10,228	20	21	22
Advertising and selling expenses (included in SG&A)	10,001	9,911	9,685	23	22	21

Financial Statements of a Merchandising Organization

Learning Objective

LO 11 Prepare the financial statements of a merchandising organization.

As before, we will first prepare a worksheet. The worksheet for a merchandising business has additional items, such as sales, purchases and merchandise inventory. Exhibit 4.7 presents the worksheet for Vijay Electronics. The inventory of ₹47,300 that appears in the Unadjusted Trial Balance columns is the company's inventory on December 31, 20X1. We make the following adjustments:

(a) Depreciation expense, office equipment, ₹4,000

(b) Depreciation expense, store equipment, ₹6,000

(c) Expiration of prepaid insurance, ₹1,200

(d) Unpaid sales salaries, ₹2,430

(e) Unpaid office salaries, ₹1,800

(f) Unpaid store rent, ₹200

(g) Income tax payable, ₹26,000.

Exhibit 4.8 presents the financial statements of Vijay Electronics broadly in line with the requirements of Schedule III to the Companies Act 2013.[6]

---

[6] We do not have sufficient information to prepare the statement of cash flows according to the direct method.

EXHIBIT 4.7
Worksheet for a Merchandising Organization

The worksheet for a merchandising organization has merchandise inventory and other items related to trading activities.

VIJAY ELECTRONICS LIMITED
Worksheet, Dec. 31, 20X2

Account	Unadjusted Trial Balance Debit	Unadjusted Trial Balance Credit	Adjustments Debit	Adjustments Credit	Adjusted Trial Balance Debit	Adjusted Trial Balance Credit	Statement of Profit and Loss Debit	Statement of Profit and Loss Credit	Statement of Retained Earnings Debit	Statement of Retained Earnings Credit	Balance Sheet Debit	Balance Sheet Credit
Office Equipment	20,000				20,000						20,000	
Accumulated depreciation, Office Equipment		4,000		4,000 (a)		8,000						8,000
Store Furniture	30,000				30,000						30,000	
Accumulated depreciation, Store Furniture		6,000		6,000 (b)		12,000						12,000
Investments in government securities	2,000				2,000						2,000	
Merchandise inventory	47,300				47,300		47,300	89,000			89,000	
Trade receivables	7,400				7,400						7,400	
Cash	3,140				3,140						3,140	
Prepaid insurance	2,400			1,200 (c)	1,200						1,200	
Trade payables		15,200				15,200						15,200
Loan payable		10,000				10,000						10,000
Share capital		40,000				40,000						40,000
Retained earnings		9,190				9,190				9,190		
Dividends	5,000				5,000				5,000			
Sales		460,120				460,120		460,120				
Interest income		900				900		900				
Sales returns and allowances	21,900				21,900		21,900					
Purchases	326,900				326,900		326,900					
Purchases returns and allowances		13,200				13,200		13,200				
Purchases discounts		1,400				1,400		1,400				
Freight in	28,100				28,100		28,100					
Sales salaries expense	17,920		2,430 (d)		20,350		20,350					

EXHIBIT 4.7
Worksheet for a Merchandising Organization (*Contd.*)

The worksheet for a merchandising organization has merchandise inventory and other items related to trading activities.

VIJAY ELECTRONICS LIMITED
Worksheet, Dec. 31, 20X2

Account	Unadjusted Trial Balance Debit	Unadjusted Trial Balance Credit	Adjustments Debit	Adjustments Credit	Adjusted Trial Balance Debit	Adjusted Trial Balance Credit	Statement of Profit and Loss Debit	Statement of Profit and Loss Credit	Statement of Retained Earnings Debit	Statement of Retained Earnings Credit	Balance Sheet Debit	Balance Sheet Credit
Sales commission expense	8,240				8,240		8,240					
Office salaries expense	15,100		1,800 (e)		16,900		16,900					
Advertising expense	9,420				9,420		9,420					
Freight out	4,490				4,490		4,490					
Store rent expense	2,200		200 (f)		2,400		2,400					
Sales discounts	1,400				1,400		1,400					
Interest expense	4,700				4,700		4,700					
Office rent expense	2,400				2,400		2,400					
Total	560,010	560,010										
Insurance expense			1,200 (c)		1,200		1,200					
Sales salaries payable				2,430 (d)		2,430						2,430
Office salaries payable				1,800 (e)		1,800						1,800
Depreciation expense, Office equipment			4,000 (a)		4,000		4,000					
Depreciation expense, Store equipment			6,000 (b)		6,000		6,000					
Store rent payable				200 (f)		200						200
Income tax expense			26,000 (g)		26,000		26,000					
Income tax payable				26,000 (g)		26,000						26,000
Total			41,630	41,630	600,440	600,440	531,700	564,620	5,000	9,190	152,740	115,630
Net profit							32,920			32,920		
Total							564,620	564,620				
Retained earnings									37,110			37,110
Total									42,110	42,110	152,740	152,740

Panel A

VIJAY ELECTRONICS LIMITED Balance Sheet, December 31, 20X2	Note	
ASSETS		
Non-current assets		
Property, plant and equipment	1	₹30,000
Financial assets		
Investments	2	2,000
Total non-current assets		32,000
Current assets		
Inventories	3	89,000
Financial assets		
Trade receivables		7,400
Cash and cash equivalents		3,140
Other financial assets		
Other current assets	4	1,200
Total current assets		100,740
Total assets		132,740
EQUITY AND LIABILITIES		
EQUITY		
Equity share capital		₹40,000
Other equity		37,110
Total equity		77,110
LIABILITIES		
Non-current liabilities		
Financial liabilities		
Borrowings		10,000
Total non-current liabilities		10,000
Current liabilities		
Financial liabilities		
Trade payables		19,630
Income tax liabilities		26,000
Total current liabilities		45,630
Total equity and liabilities		132,740

EXHIBIT 4.8
Vijay Electronics
Limited Financial
Statements

Panel B

VIJAY ELECTRONICS LIMITED Statement of Profit and Loss for the year ended December 31, 20X2	Note	
Revenue from operations	5	₹436,820
Other income	6	900
Total income		437,720
Expenses		
Purchases of stock-in-trade		312,300
Changes in inventories of stock-in-trade	7	(41,700)
Employee benefits expense	8	37,250
Finance costs		4,700
Depreciation and amortization expense	9	10,000
Other expenses	10	56,250
Total expenses		378,800
Profit before tax		58,920
Tax expense		26,000
Profit for the period		32,920

Panel C

VIJAY ELECTRONICS LIMITED Statement of Changes in Equity for the year ended December 31, 20X2			
	Equity Share Capital	Other Equity Retained Earnings	Total
Balance as of January 1, 20X2...	₹40,000	₹ 9,190	₹ 49,190
Share issue...	0	0	0
Dividends...		(5,000)	(5,000)
Profit for the period		32,920	32,920
Balance as of December 31, 20X2...................................	40,000	37,110	77,110

Notes:

1. **Property, plant and equipment**

Particulars	Furniture	Equipment	Total
Gross carrying value as of January 1, 20X2................	30,000	20,000	50,000
Additions..		0	0
Gross carrying value as of December 31, 20X2..........	30,000	20,000	50,000
Accumulated depreciation as of January 1, 20X2........	6,000	4,000	10,000
Additions..	6,000	4,000	10,000
Accumulated depreciation as of December 31, 20X2..	12,000	8,000	20,000
Carrying value as of December 31, 20X2	18,000	12,000	30,000

2. **Investments**

Investments in government securities	2,000

3. **Inventories**

Stock-in-trade..	89,000

4. **Other current assets**

Prepaid insurance..	1,200

5. **Revenue from operations**

Sale of products	436,820

6. **Other income**

Interest income	900

7. **Changes in inventories of stock-in-trade**

Beginning inventories	47,300
Ending inventories	89,000
	(41,700)

8. **Employee benefits expense**

Office salaries...	16,900
Sales salaries	20,350
	37,250

9. **Depreciation and amortization expense**

Depreciation, Store furniture	6,000
Depreciation, Office equipment.......................................	4,000
	10,000

10. **Other expenses**

Freight in...	28,100
Advertising...	9,420
Freight out...	4,490
Insurance...	1,200
Store rent..	2,400
Office rent	2,400
Sales commission..	8,240
	56,250

The statement of profit and loss complete with the notes presented in Exhibit 4.9 follows the functional format.

VIJAY ELECTRONICS LIMITED Statement of Profit and Loss for the year ended December 31, 20X2	Note			
Revenue from operations	5			₹436,820
Cost of goods sold	6			298,700
Gross profit				138,120
Operating expenses	7			75,400
Operating profit				62,720
Non-operating income/(expense) (net)	8			(3,800)
Profit before tax				58,920
Tax expense				26,000
Net profit				32,920

EXHIBIT 4.9
Statement of Profit and Loss: Functional Classification

Notes:

5. Revenue from operations

Sale of products			436,820

6. Cost of goods sold

Beginning inventories		47,300	
Net purchases	312,300		
Freight in	28,100		
Net cost of purchases		340,400	
Cost of goods available for sale		387,700	
Ending inventories		89,000	298,700

7. Operating expenses

Marketing expenses

Sales salaries	20,350		
Advertising	9,420		
Freight out	4,490		
Store rent	2,400		
Depreciation, Store furniture	6,000		
Sales commission	8,240	50,900	

Administrative expenses

Office salaries	16,900		
Insurance	1,200		
Office rent	2,400		
Depreciation, Office equipment	4,000	24,500	75,400

8. Non-operating income/(expense)

Interest income		900	
Interest expense		(4,700)	(3,800)

How should interest payable be classified on the balance sheet?

QUICK QUESTION
Presenting interest payable

What assumptions about the users of accounting information should businesses make while designing their financial statements?

DISCUSSION QUESTION 4.5

....

....

....

Financial Statement Analysis: Profitability of Operations

In Chapter 2, you learnt the basics of financial statement analysis. We used the *ratio of profit to sales* to measure profitability. Let us now see how to analyze profitability using intermediate measures of profit. The functional form of the statement of profit and loss allows us to get the big picture and go into the detail.

Gross profit ratio, also known as gross margin, is the *ratio of gross profit to sales*. (Sales is revenue from operations, i.e. sales of products and services.) It measures the profitability of trading or manufacturing activities. It tells us what portion of revenue remained after paying for the goods sold. For instance, a gross margin of 20 per cent on sales of ₹200,000 would mean that a business earned ₹40,000 after meeting the cost of goods sold. From Exhibit 4.9, we know that Vijay Electronics earned a sales revenue of ₹436,820, incurred ₹298,700 on the goods sold and made a gross profit of ₹138,120. The gross profit ratio is nearly 32 per cent (138,120/436,820).

Operating profit ratio, or net margin, is the *ratio of operating profit to sales*. It measures the overall profitability of the activities of a business. High gross margin does not necessarily mean that the operations are profitable on the whole. Operating expenses are significant for many enterprises. For example, a business may earn a high gross margin. However, heavy advertising and sales commissions may eat away a large chunk of the margin. The operating profit ratio of Vijay Electronics is a little over 14 per cent (62,720/436,820).

Conversion ratio is the *ratio of operating profit to gross profit*. It is a direct measure of the profit 'lost in transit' because of operating expenses. The conversion ratio for Vijay Electronics is a little over 45 per cent (62,720/138,120). It means that well over half of the gross profit vanishes in marketing and administration.

Kiran Company sells goods at prices exceeding purchase prices. Can it report a net loss?

Are operating expenses, or opex, a waste of money? Opex is "overhead", spending that is not directly related to products and services. Cost of materials and factory wages can be traced to products. Marketing salaries and office air-conditioning do not result in products and services. Since opex is unrelated to sales, there is no way to tell how much is the right amount of spending. Managers have a great deal of discretion in budgeting opex items, such as advertising, IT services and R&D.

The problem is that opex tends to balloon in good times but cutting the flab is not easy. So analysts frown on high opex. They are less upset with an increase in cost of goods sold. Even so, there are forces at work that push up opex. For instance, banks spend significant sums on compliance and risk management. Automobile manufacturers spend heavily on safety and emission control. These are the outcome of tighter regulations. Inevitably, rising opex will hurt margins and analysts will only have more reasons to frown.

The Accounting Cycle

The accounting cycle comprises the sequence of accounting processes. It begins with analyzing transactions and ends with carrying forward the balances in balance sheet accounts to the next reporting period. The accounting cycle produces numerous records, entries, documents, reports, and statements. By far the most important output of the accounting cycle is the financial statements. Figure 4.7 summarizes the steps in the accounting cycle. The accountant performs the steps in the accounting cycle one after the other and repeats them in each reporting period.

Temporary accounts and permanent accounts Revenue and expense accounts are temporary accounts (or *nominal accounts*), because their balances relate only to the current reporting period. The accountant closes these accounts at the end of the reporting period by transferring their balances through statement of profit and loss to retained earnings in equity. In Exhibit 4.8, revenue from services, salaries expense, office supplies expense, and depreciation expense are examples of temporary accounts. Note that dividends is a temporary account.

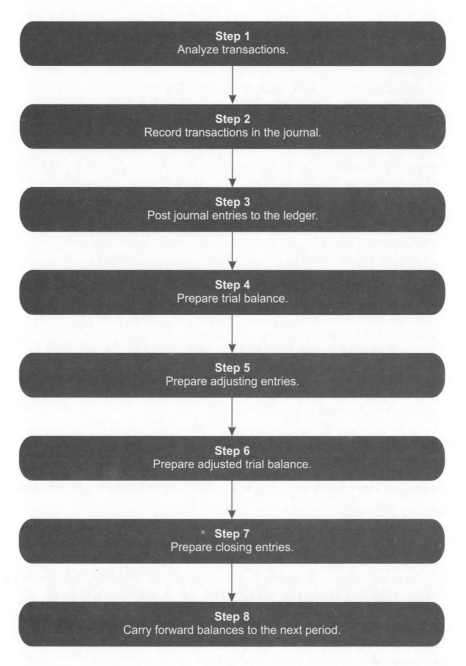

Step 1
Analyze transactions.

Step 2
Record transactions in the journal.

Step 3
Post journal entries to the ledger.

Step 4
Prepare trial balance.

Step 5
Prepare adjusting entries.

Step 6
Prepare adjusted trial balance.

Step 7
Prepare closing entries.

Step 8
Carry forward balances to the next period.

Figure 4.7
THE ACCOUNTING CYCLE

The accounting cycle has a number of accounting processes that repeat year after year.

By contrast, accounts that appear in the balance sheet are permanent accounts (or *real accounts*). The accountant carries forward the ending balances of these accounts to the next period as their beginning balances to the next period. These accounts exist as long as the specific asset, liability, or equity items recorded in the accounts exist. In Exhibit 4.8, equipment, accumulated depreciation, office supplies, and salaries payable are examples of permanent accounts. Note that depreciation expense is a temporary account but accumulated depreciation is a permanent account since the equipment continues to exist.

Closing Entries and Reversing Entries

Closing entries transfer the balances in temporary accounts to a balance sheet equity account. These amounts pertain to the current period and have no relevance to the next

Learning Objective
LO 14 Prepare closing entries and reversing entries.

period. Therefore, at the end of the reporting period, we should reset the balances in these accounts to zero. We do this by transferring their balances to the statement of profit and loss. The balance of the statement of profit and loss equals the net profit or net loss for the period.

The closing entries for Vogue Company are as follows:

June 30	Revenue from Services	15,600	
	Statement of Profit and Loss		15,600
	To close the revenue account		
30	Statement of Profit and Loss	5,860	
	Salaries Expense		1,300
	Depreciation Expense		50
	Rent Expense		1,500
	Telephone Expense		200
	Electricity Expense		150
	Office Supplies Expense		2,600
	Insurance Expense		60
	To close the expense accounts		
30	Statement of Profit and Loss	9,740	
	Statement of Retained Earnings		9,740
	To close the statement of profit and loss		
30	Statement of Retained Earnings	2,200	
	Dividends		2,200
	To close the dividends account		

A **reversing entry** is the exact reverse of an adjusting entry. The amounts and the accounts are the same; the debits and credits are just reversed. Reversing entries simplify the recording of a subsequent transaction related to an adjusting entry. Let us take the following adjusting entry for salaries payable in the Vogue Company illustration.

Adjustment (e)			
June 30	Salaries Expense	500	
	Salaries Payable		500
	To record accrued salaries		

At June 30, we closed Salaries Expense and transferred the balance to Statement of Profit and Loss. Salaries Payable appears on the June 30 balance sheet and will be carried forward to July.

The reversing entry for the above adjustment is as follows:

July 1	Salaries Payable	500	
	Salaries Expense		500
	To reverse accrued salaries		

On July 21, Vogue Company records the following entry when it pays salaries:

July 21	Salaries Expense	1,500	
	Cash		1,500
	Paid salaries for June 21 to July 20		

Because of the reversing entry, we are able to record the transaction in the normal way. Without the reversing entry, we would debit Salaries Payable instead of Salaries Expense. Note that reversing entries are only for accruals, such as salaries payable and unbilled revenue. Adjusting entries for deferrals are not reversed.

Why can't adjusting entries for deferrals be reversed?

QUICK QUESTION
Reversing entries
TEST YOUR
UNDERSTANDING 4.8
Reversing Entries
ONE-MINUTE QUIZ 4.8
Temporary Accounts

Manoj Company has an unbilled revenue of ₹700 on June 30, 20XX. On July 15, the company completed the service and billed the customer ₹1,900 for the entire work. The customer paid the bill on July 27. Record the transactions in July with and without reversing entries.

Which of the following accounts will be closed? There may be more than one correct answer.
- (a) Sales returns and allowances.
- (b) Equipment.
- (c) Accumulated depreciation, Equipment.
- (d) Salaries payable.

Special Cases of Revenue Recognition

We will now see revenue recognition in cases that have special terms of sale, construction contracts, franchises, and leases.

Learning Objective
LO 15 Explain special cases of revenue recognition.

Special Terms of Sale

Accountants recognize revenue from sale of goods on the basis of the intention of the contracting parties and the legal provisions for transfer of title to the goods. They have to go beyond the legal form of a transaction and find out whether it meets the conditions for revenue recognition. Sales transactions are structured in complex ways for business, tax, and regulatory reasons. Revenue recognition should be based on the economic substance of a transaction. That means determining whether the significant risks and rewards of ownership have been transferred to the buyer, the price is certain and the buyer will pay. We will now consider some special terms of sale to decide when to recognize revenue.

Bill and hold sales In 'bill and hold' sales delivery is delayed at the buyer's request, but the buyer takes title and accepts billing. Revenue is generally recognized when the buyer takes title, if it is probable that (a) delivery will be made, (b) the item is on hand, identified, and ready for delivery to the buyer, (c) the buyer acknowledges the deferred delivery instructions, and (d) the usual payment terms apply.

Conditional sales Goods may be shipped subject to conditions to be fulfilled by the seller or the buyer, such as the ones described below:
- *Installation and inspection* If the contract requires installation by the seller and inspection by the buyer, the seller normally recognizes revenue when the buyer accepts delivery and installation and inspection are complete.
- *On approval* In a sale on approval, the buyer has to communicate his acceptance or rejection of the goods within a specified time period. If there is uncertainty about the possibility of return, revenue is recognized when the buyer accepts the goods or the specified time period for rejection has elapsed without any communication from the buyer.
- *Consignment* In a consignment "sale", the recipient (consignee) undertakes to sell the goods on behalf of the shipper (consignor). The consignor is the owner of the goods and the consignee is the consignor's agent. The consignor recognizes revenue when the consignee sells the goods to a third party.
- *Cash on delivery* Revenue is recognized when the goods are delivered and cash is received by the seller or its agent.

Lay away sales In a lay away sale, goods will be delivered when the buyer makes the final payment in a series of instalments. Revenue from such sales is recognized when the goods are delivered. However, when past experience indicates that most such sales are consummated, revenue may be recognized when a significant deposit is received provided the goods are on hand, identified, and ready for delivery to the buyer.

Sale and repurchase agreements In a sale and repurchase agreement, the seller concurrently agrees to repurchase the same goods at a later date, or the seller has an option to repurchase the goods, or the buyer has an option to require the repurchase of the goods by the seller. Even though legal title may have been transferred, the seller retains the risks and rewards of ownership. Sale and repurchase agreements are usually product financing arrangements in which the seller raises a loan with the goods being given as collateral. The cash inflow to the buyer is a loan receipt and not a revenue. The difference between repurchase and sale prices represents the finance charge for the loan. The transaction does not give rise to revenue.

Sales to distributors, dealers, or others for resale Revenue from such sales is generally recognized when the risks and rewards of ownership have passed. However, when the buyer is acting, in substance, as an agent, the sale is treated as a consignment "sale".

Instalment sales Revenue from instalment sale of goods has two parts: (1) the cash price or the price for immediate payment, and (2) interest on future instalments. The revenue representing the cash price should be recognized at the date of sale. This is just like recognizing revenue from a normal cash or credit sale. The interest element should be recognized as revenue as it is earned, using the effective interest method.

Subscription to publications When the items are of similar value in each time period, revenue is recognized on a straight-line basis over the period in which the items are despatched. When the items vary in value from period to period, revenue is recognized on the basis of the sales value of the item despatched in relation to the total estimated sales value of all items covered by the subscription.

TEST YOUR UNDERSTANDING 4.9
Revenue Recognition

On August 1, Manohar Company sold goods costing ₹14,000 to Vijay Company for ₹15,000. Manohar Company will repurchase these goods on December 1 for ₹16,800. How should Manohar Company treat this transaction?

Franchises

A franchise is a contractual arrangement under which the franchiser grants the franchisee the right to manufacture or sell certain products or services, to use certain trademarks, or to perform certain functions, usually within an agreed area. The franchiser protects his unique concept or product through a patent, copyright or trademark. NIIT, Holiday Inn, and McDonald's are examples of some popular franchises. Franchising has been growing rapidly in India in recent years.

Franchisers derive their revenue from two sources:
1. Sale of initial franchises; and
2. Continuing franchise operations.

The initial franchise fee may be recorded as revenue only when the franchiser makes substantial performance of the service he is obliged to provide, i.e. when the franchiser has no obligation to refund any cash received and has performed all the initial services required under the contract. Initial services provided by the franchiser usually cover assistance in site selection and acquisition of plant and display signs. Continuing franchise fees may be recognized as revenue when the franchiser earns the right to receive them.

Leases

A **lease** is an agreement that allows the use of an asset for a certain period of time. The owner of the asset is the **lessor** and the user of the asset is the **lessee**. Shortage of capital, attractive tax incentives, and easy availability have made leasing a booming industry in India and abroad. The substance of the leasing arrangement determines the accounting by lessors for lease rentals and profit. There are two types of lease: *operating lease* and *finance lease*.

Operating lease is a short-term rental arrangement such as renting office space, car or photocopier. The lessor has to depreciate the asset on operating lease in accordance with its normal depreciation policy for similar assets and recognize rentals as revenue on a systematic basis representing the pattern of the earnings process implicit in the lease. A straight-line basis may be appropriate in many cases. Estimating the residual value is an important task in accounting for an asset on operating lease.

Finance lease is a lease that transfers substantially economic ownership of an asset. The lessor (usually a leasing company) transfers the risks and rewards of ownership of an asset to the lessee. A finance lease is usually non-cancellable for a specified period and secures for the lessor the recovery of his capital outlay plus a return for the funds invested. Finance leasing is, in substance, a financing arrangement. Therefore, the income from it should be recognized in proportion to the amount outstanding from the lessee. Usually, the residual value of a leased asset in a finance lease will not be significant.

Sales-type leases are entered into by manufacturers and dealers who use leasing as a means of promoting their products. Unlike a finance lease, in a sales-type lease, the lessor has to account for the profit on sale. Otherwise, accounting is similar in both these leases.

We will discuss lessee accounting in Chapter 10.

Construction Contracts

A **construction contract** is a contract for the building of an asset. Long-term construction contracts differ from sales of goods in that the revenue-earning process in these contracts is usually spread over several financial years. Examples include contracts for construction of bridges, tunnels, dams, ships, aircraft, buildings, and complex pieces of equipment.

Under the **percentage of completion method**, contract revenue and contract costs are recognized by reference to the stage of completion of the contract activity at the end of the reporting period. The advantage of this method is that it reflects revenues and costs in periods in which the related economic activity occurs. When the outcome of a contract can be estimated reliably, the percentage of completion method should be used. Otherwise, the contract revenue should be recognized only to the extent of costs incurred which are expected to be recovered. When it is probable that the total contract costs will exceed the total contract revenue, the expected loss is recognized as an expense immediately.

Suppose Ace Construction Company enters into a contract for construction of a bridge in 20X7 at a fixed price of ₹2,500,000. The details of the progress of the contract are as follows:

	20X7	20X8	20X9
Costs incurred to date	₹620,000	₹1,664,000	₹2,080,000
Progress billings to date	180,000	740,000	1,120,000
Cash received to date	130,000	900,000	1,570,000
Estimated further costs	1,380,000	416,000	–0–

We compute the percentage completed and revenue recognized as follows:

	20X7	20X8	20X9
Contract price	₹2,500,000	₹2,500,000	₹2,500,000
Deduct Estimated total costs:			
Costs incurred to date	620,000	1,664,000	2,080,000
Estimated further costs	1,380,000	416,000	–0–
	2,000,000	2,080,000	2,080,000
Estimated gross profit	500,000	420,000	420,000
Percentage of completion:			

$$\frac{\text{Costs incurred to date}}{\text{Estimated total costs}} \qquad \frac{620,000}{2,000,000}=31\% \qquad \frac{1,664,000}{2,080,000}=80\% \qquad \frac{2,080,000}{2,080,000}=100\%$$

Revenue recognized:

20X7:	₹2,500,000 × 31% = ₹775,000		
20X8:		₹2,500,000 × 80% = ₹2,000,000	
Deduct recognized in 20X7		775,000	
20X9:			₹2,500,000 × 100% = ₹2,500,000
Deduct recognized in 20X6 and 20X7			2,000,000
	775,000	1,225,000	500,000

In 20X7, Ace Construction should report a gross profit of ₹155,000, calculated as follows: revenue, ₹775,000 – costs, ₹620,000. The gross profit would be ₹181,000 in 20X8 and ₹84,000 in 20X9. You should verify these numbers to make sure that you understand the method. If, as a result of uncertainties, Ace Construction cannot estimate the percentage of completion reliably, it will not recognize any revenue or profit in either 20X7 or 20X8. In 20X9, it will recognize the entire revenue and profit on completion of the contract.

Earnings Quality

Learning Objective

LO 16 Explain earnings quality.

Separating revenues and expenses from gains and losses tells us how much of the net profit comes from regular business operations. **Earnings quality** refers to the probability of earnings trends continuing. Earnings are said to be of *high quality* if, among others, they are derived primarily from continuing operations that are not volatile from year to year. Therefore, high quality earnings are more predictable than low quality earnings. High quality earnings come from predictable revenues and expenses. Low quality earnings come from gains and losses which are, by nature, less foreseeable and so are more difficult to predict. For example, we would expect a consumer durables company to earn profit by selling refrigerators, washing machines and dishwashers. We are unlikely to be impressed if its profit comes significantly from trading in shares and selling its surplus land. Profit from such activities are not only difficult to predict but also may be aimed at camouflaging the management's inability to sell its products. Again, a steel company may have suffered a big loss from the sale of an unprofitable plant. As a result, the company may appear to be unprofitable. However, by getting rid of the loss-making plant, the company is poised to become profitable in the future. Thus, great care is needed in interpreting reported performance.

Whether an item is a revenue or gain or an expense or loss depends on the major activities of a business. For example, buying and selling shares are ordinary activities for banks and venture capital companies but result in gains and losses for non-financial firms. Distinguishing revenues and expenses from gains and losses is important for understanding how much of an enterprise's profit is derived from activities that are related to its main business and therefore can be counted on. Analysts spare no effort to understand the performance of the core business by winnowing out gains and losses. Figure 4.8 illustrates the idea of earnings quality.

Components of Profit

- **Recurring Business Activities:**
  - ◆ Revenue from sales and services
  - ◆ Cost of goods sold
  - ◆ Advertisement and sales promotion
  - ◆ Warranty costs
  - ◆ Income tax
- **One-time Gains and Losses**
  - ◆ Gain or loss from sale of property, plant and equipment and investments
  - ◆ Appreciation or depreciation in the value of investments
  - ◆ Loss from fire and flood
  - ◆ Government and regulatory penalties

Net profit is entirely from one-time gains and losses		Net profit is entirely from recurring business activities
Very Low	**Moderate**	**Very High**

Earnings Quality

Figure 4.8

THE EARNINGS QUALITY SPECTRUM

Earnings quality varies from very low to very high depending on whether profit comes from recurring business activities or one-time gains and losses.

EARNINGS QUALITY ANALYSIS
The Story behind a Profit

ICICI Bank, India's second largest bank, reported a net profit of ₹7.02 billion for the quarter ended March 31, 2016. Television channels and newspapers screamed: "ICICI Q4 net profit falls 76 per cent". The culprit was the "exceptional item" for "collective contingency and related reserve" of ₹36 billion made on "a prudent basis...over and above provisions made for non-performing and restructured loans as per RBI guidelines". The story is more nuanced than that, since a couple of other items in the financial statements too require attention.

The profit included a gain of ₹6.12 billion on sale of shares of ICICI Prudential Life Insurance Company Limited and ₹15.08 billion on sale of shares of ICICI Lombard General Insurance Company Limited. In addition, there was a "deferred tax adjustment" that reduced income tax expense by ₹21.99 billion. Together, the three items contributed ₹43.19 billion. They considerably cushioned the ₹36-billion hole caused by the "exceptional item". Had the gains not been taken, the profit of ₹7.02 billion would have turned into a loss of ₹36.17 billion – and the headlines would have been very different.

Which of the following items included in net profit indicates low earnings quality? There may be more than one correct answer.
- (a) Compensation received for infringement of trademark.
- (b) Income tax refund for past years.
- (c) Interest on income tax refund for past years.
- (d) Loss of a large receivable.

ONE-MINUTE QUIZ 4.9
Earnings Quality

Revenue recognition is the most common accounting fraud in the U.S., according to a study by the Committee of Sponsoring Organizations, an ethics and advocacy group.[7] Revenue frauds accounted for over 60 per cent of the cases in 1998-2007, versus 50 per cent in 1987-1997. This was done by creating fictitious revenue transactions or by recording revenues prematurely. The techniques included the following:

- Fake sales generated by using falsified inventory records, shipping documents, and invoices.
- Conditional sales treated as sales.

FORENSIC CORNER
Revenue Recognition Fraud

---

[7] Committee of Sponsoring Organizations, Fraudulent Financial Reporting 1998-2007: An Analysis of U.S. Public Companies, Mark S. Beasley, Joseph V. Carcello, Dana R. Hermanson and Terry L. Neal, May 2010.

- Round-tripping of goods or recording loans as sales.
- Bill and hold transactions treated as sales.
- Prematurely recognizing revenue after the goods were ordered but before they were shipped to the customer.
- Keeping the accounting records open beyond the balance sheet date to record sales of the subsequent period in the current period.
- Accelerating the estimated stage of completion while using the percentage of completion method.
- Recognizing revenue by shipping goods never ordered by the customer or by shipping defective goods and recording goods at full, rather than discounted, prices.
- Recognizing revenue for consignment shipments (commonly known as "channel stuffing") or shipments of goods for customers to consider on a trial basis.

According to a report prepared by India Ratings, established companies in FMCG (fast-moving consumer goods), automobiles and pharmaceuticals could be pushing goods to distributors so as to book higher revenue.

Revenue recognition frauds may also involve delaying, rather than advancing, revenue. This is "cookie jar" accounting in which today's revenue is pushed into the future for use in weak quarters.

Revenue recognition frauds result from deliberate intent (such as Satyam), complexity of business operations (e.g. long-term contracts, bundling of several products and services) or a plain misunderstanding of the accounting principles and standards by the operating staff. Non-financial executives who are an important part of the revenue recognition process need to be educated on revenue recognition policies.

Red flags signalling revenue recognition fraud:

- A big increase in trade receivables relative to earlier periods.
- A high proportion of old receivables.
- Complex business structures (related parties, a web of domestic and overseas subsidiaries).
- A low receivable turnover.
- A large difference between revenue and collections.

APPLICATION
Revenue Recognition

Let's see how media, entertainment and sports companies apply the principles of revenue recognition.

Revenue	Explanation
▪ Advertising income and broadcast fees are recognised when the related commercial or programme is telecast. *(Sun TV)*	▪ Revenue is earned by advertising and broadcasting.
▪ Subscription fees billed to cable operators are determined based on management's best estimates of the number of subscription points to which the service is provided. *(Sun TV)*	▪ Presumably, there will be an adjustment for any difference after cable operators report the actual number of subscription points.
▪ Revenues from sale of movie distribution/sub-distribution rights are recognized on the theatrical release of the related movie. *(Sun TV)*	▪ Revenue is earned when a movie is released, regardless of how well it does in the box office.
▪ Revenues from the theatrical distribution of movies are recognized as they are exhibited, based on box office collections reported by the exhibitors after deduction of taxes and exhibitor's share of net collections. *(Sun TV)*	▪ There is no assured revenue from a movie release. Revenue is the company's share of collections.
▪ Revenues from multiuse tickets are recognized ratably over the estimated usage period. The estimated usage periods are derived from historical usage patterns. *(The Walt Disney Company)*	▪ Since the tickets can be used many times, usage has to be estimated from past patterns.

- Merchandise licensing advances and guaranteed royalty payments are recognized based on the contractual royalty rate when the licensed product is sold by the licensee. Non-refundable advances and minimum guarantee royalty payments in excess of royalties earned are generally recognized as revenue at the end of the contract period. *(The Walt Disney Company)*

- Minimum guaranteed revenue is recognized over the term of the sponsorship agreement. *(Manchester United)*

- Distributions from the FA Premier League comprise a fixed element (which is recognized evenly as domestic home league matches are played), facility fees for live coverage and highlights of domestic home and away matches (which are recognized when the respective match is played), and merit awards (which are only recognized when they are known at the end of each football season). *(Manchester United)*

- Match day revenue is recognized based on matches played throughout the year with revenue from each match being recognized only after the match to which the revenue relates has been played. *(Manchester United)*

- Revenue from merchandise licensing is earned when the licensee sells the goods. Since there is no continuing obligation after the contract period, non-refundable advances and any guaranteed shortfall in royalties become revenue.

- Revenue is allocated to the reporting periods in the agreement.

- *Fixed element* is allocated to the reporting periods in the agreement. *Facility fees* are earned when a match is played. *Merit awards* are announced at the end of a season and recognized in that reporting period.

- Revenue from ticket sales, catering, etc. is earned when a match is played.

Indian GAAP is the set of "accounting standards" (AS) notified by the government in 2006. Ind AS is the set of "Indian Accounting Standards" notified by the government on February 16, 2015 and March 30, 2016. IFRS is the set of IFRS/IAS issued by the IASB. The comparison below gives the key differences between these systems.

IFRS, IND AS AND INDIAN GAAP
Revenue Recognition

IFRS	Ind AS	Indian GAAP
IAS 11, IAS 18	Ind AS 11, Ind AS 18	AS 7, AS 9
■ Sales discount deducted from revenue.		Sales discount treated as an expense.
■ Percentage of completion method used for service transactions.		Completed contract method used for service transactions.
■ Revenue from multiple element arrangements or bundled offers recognized based on the substance of the contract.		No specific guidance.
■ Customer loyalty programmes treated similar to multiple element arrangements.		No specific guidance.
■ Gain or loss from non-monetary barter transactions not considered.		No specific guidance.
■ Discounting of revenues to present value required where receipt is deferred.		Discounting not required.

RECAP

- Accountants assign the results of activities of business organizations to time periods, such as a year, half-year or quarter. Periodic income measurement requires assumptions, estimates and judgments.
- Net profit (or net income) = Revenues − Expenses.
- In the cash system revenues and expenses are recorded when cash is received or paid. The *accrual system* records revenues when they are earned and expenses when they are incurred.
- The *accrual system* is the heart of financial accounting.
- Revenue is recognized when the revenue-earning process is complete or virtually complete.
- Expenses are recognized in the reporting period in which the related revenues are earned.
- Determining when to recognize revenues and expenses involves judgment.
- The adjustment process involves converting the account balances into accrual numbers. Deferrals and accruals need adjustments.

- A sale is complete when the seller transfers ownership of the product to the buyer and has no further obligation to the buyer.
- Sales returns and incentives are reduced from revenue.
- Accounting for purchases mirrors accounting for sales.
- Freight terms state who pays the freight and when title to the goods passes. In FOB origin, the buyer pays the freight and becomes the owner of the goods when the seller despatches the goods. In FOB destination, the seller pays the freight and owns the goods until they reach the destination.
- Operating expenses are expensed when they are incurred.
- Gross profit is the difference between revenue and cost of goods sold. Operating profit is the difference between gross profit and operating expenses.
- *High quality earnings* come from core operations.

Review Problem

Backbay Company provides local mail delivery service in the financial district of Mumbai. The trial balance of the company is as follows:

BACKBAY COMPANY
Trial Balance, February 28, 20XX

Office equipment	₹ 7,000	
Accumulated depreciation, Office equipment		₹ 1,000
Office supplies	3,800	
Trade receivables	1,900	
Cash	770	
Prepaid rent	2,400	
Trade payables		1,100
Unearned revenue		400
Share capital		10,000
Retained earnings		2,100
Dividends	1,400	
Revenue from services		7,200
Salaries expense	3,800	
Telephone expense	730	
	21,800	21,800

Additional information:

(a) Prepaid rent represents rent for February to April.
(b) The inventory of office supplies at the end of February was ₹3,200.
(c) Revenue earned for services performed but not yet billed at the end of February was ₹1,600.
(d) Revenue earned for services performed, paid for in advance, was ₹210.
(e) Depreciation on office equipment for February was ₹250.
(f) Accrued salaries at the end of February were ₹540.

Required

1. Post adjusting entries directly to the T accounts.
2. Prepare an adjusted trial balance.
3. Prepare the February statement of profit and loss and balance sheet.

Solution to the Review Problem

1. Posting adjusting entries

Office Equipment

Balance	7,000	

Accumulated Depreciation, Office Equipment

		Balance	1,000
		(e)	250
		Balance	*1,250*

Office Supplies

Balance	3,800	*(b)*	600
Balance	*3,200*		

Trade Receivables

Balance	1,900		

Cash

Balance	770		

Prepaid Rent

Balance	2,400	*(a)*	
Balance	*1,600*		

Unbilled Revenue

(c)	1,600		

Trade Payables

		Balance	1,100

Unearned Revenue

(d)	210	Balance	400
		Balance	*190*

Salaries Payable

		(f)	540

Share Capital

		Balance	10,000

Retained Earnings

		Balance	2,100

Dividends

Balance	1,400		

Revenue from Services

		Balance	7,200
		(c)	*1,600*
		(d)	*210*
		Balance	*9,010*

Salaries Expense

Balance	3,800		
(f)	*540*		
Balance	*4,340*		

Office Supplies Expense

(b)	600		

Telephone Expense

Balance	730		

Rent Expense

(a)	800		

Depreciation Expense

(e)	250		

2. Adjusted trial balance

BACKBAY COMPANY		
Adjusted Trial Balance, February 28, 20XX		
Office equipment..	₹7,000	
Accumulated depreciation, Office equipment..		₹1,250
Office supplies..	3,200	
Trade receivables...	1,900	
Cash...	770	
Prepaid rent...	1,600	
Unbilled revenue..	1,600	
Trade payables..		1,100
Unearned revenue		190
Salaries payable..		540
Share capital...		10,000
Retained earnings		2,100
Dividends	1,400	
Revenue from services..		9,010
Salaries expense..	4,340	
Office supplies expense	600	
Telephone expense	730	
Rent expense..	800	
Depreciation expense	250	
	24,190	24,190

3. Financial statements

BACKBAY COMPANY	
Balance Sheet, February 28, 20XX	
ASSETS	
Non-current assets	
Property, plant and equipment..	₹ 5,750
Current assets	
Inventories..	3,200
Financial assets	
Trade receivables..	1,900
Cash and cash equivalents...	770
Other current assets..	3,200
Total current assets...	9,070
Total assets...	14,820
EQUITY AND LIABILITIES	
EQUITY	
Equity share capital	₹10,000
Other equity..	2,990
Total equity	12,990
LIABILITIES	
Current liabilities	
Financial liabilities	
Trade payables...	1,640
Other current liabilities..	190
Total current liabilities..	1,830
Total equity and liabilities..	14,820

BACKBAY COMPANY
Statement of Profit and Loss
For the month ended February 28, 20XX

Revenue from operations...	₹9,010
Expenses	
Employee benefits expense...	4,340
Depreciation and amortization expense..	250
Other expenses...	2,130
Total expenses...	6,720
Profit before tax	2,290
Tax expense..	0
Profit for the period	2,290

ASSIGNMENT MATERIAL

Questions

1. Define the terms: *net profit, revenue,* and *expense.*
2. Why is periodic income measurement necessary?
3. What is *accrual accounting*? How does it differ from cash accounting?
4. "The matching principle poses major challenges for the accountant." Do you agree?
5. What do you understand by *deferrals* and *accruals*? Give two examples.
6. "Expenses are used-up assets." Explain.
7. What is a *contra account*? Give an example of a contra account used in the adjusting process.
8. What is an *accrued expense*? Give two examples.
9. Differentiate between *temporary accounts* and *permanent accounts*. Give two examples.
10. What are the objectives of the closing process?
11. What is a *reversing entry*? How do reversing entries make the bookkeeping process easier?
12. Adjustments are recorded for the following items: (a) services provided but not billed; (b) depreciation expense; (c) services provided for amounts received earlier;

(d) interest expense payable; (e) supplies expense. Which of these can be reversed?
13. Give five examples of account titles that are specific to a retailer.
14. Explain the difference between *trade discount* and *cash discount*.
15. Explain why the amount of collections from customers during a period may differ from the net sales appearing on the statement of profit and loss.
16. How is the cost of goods sold determined under the periodic inventory system?
17. Give two examples of contra accounts in a merchandising organization.
18. What is an *adjunct account*? Give an example of an adjunct account for a wholesaler.
19. Is Sales Returns and Allowances an expense account? Explain.
20. Complete the following relationships:
    (a) Cost of goods sold + Gross profit = ?
    (b) Operating profit + Operating expenses = ?
    (c) Cost of goods available for sale – Net cost of purchases = ?
    (d) Ending inventory + Cost of goods sold = ?
    (e) Net cost of purchases – Net purchases = ?

Problems

The following are some of the year-end balances of Shobha Company:

Problem 4.1
Computing Revenue and Expenses from Cash Receipts and Payments *

	20X2	20X1
Unbilled revenue	₹2,100	₹1,800
Interest receivable..	570	680
Unearned revenue	1,100	1,600
Prepaid rent..	5,900	7,900
Salaries payable..	1,200	850
Interest payable..	730	810

The statement of cash flows for 20X2 has the following information:

Fees received	₹21,710
Interest received..	2,030
Rent paid..	11,600
Salaries paid	6,820
Interest paid...	1,840

Note: There was no refund of fee to any customer in 20X2.

Required

Compute the following for 20X2:
1. Fee revenue.
2. Interest income.
3. Rent expense.
4. Salaries expense.
5. Interest expense.

Problem 4.2
Adjusting Entries *

The following information is available on December 31, 20XX:

(a) The company's inventory of office supplies on November 30 was ₹2,850. The company bought supplies costing ₹4,710 in December. The inventory of office supplies on December 31 totalled ₹1,930.

(b) The company paid rent for six months at ₹2,500 per month in advance on December 1 and charged it to Prepaid Rent.

(c) The company had not paid the December salary of ₹4,900 at the month end.

(d) On December 9, a customer paid an advance of ₹9,300 for future services. The company provided services worth ₹7,100 to the customer in December.

(e) The company made a three-year bank deposit of ₹20,000 on December 1. The deposit carried interest at 12 per cent per annum.

(f) The company bought equipment costing ₹13,000 on November 1. The equipment had an estimated useful life of 10 years, at the end of which it was expected to fetch ₹1,000.

(g) Income tax payable for the year is estimated at ₹2,100.

Required

Prepare adjusting entries on December 31, 20XX.

Problem 4.3
Preparation of Financial
Statements *

The adjusted trial balance of Quick Car Service Limited is as follows:

QUICK CAR SERVICE LIMITED		
Adjusted Trial Balance, December 31, 20X8		
Equipment..	₹18,000	
Accumulated depreciation, Equipment...		₹ 3,600
Supplies..	1,900	
Trade receivables..	4,210	
Cash...	1,170	
Prepaid rent..	5,100	
Unbilled revenue...	3,020	
Trade payables...		2,160
Unearned revenue		970
Salaries payable...		1,310
Share capital...		25,000
Retained earnings		2,160
Dividends..	3,800	
Revenue from services..		20,050
Salaries expense...	9,720	
Supplies expense..	2,160	
Telephone expense..	970	
Rent expense..	2,400	
Depreciation expense	1,800	
Income tax expense	1,000	
	55,250	55,250

Required

Prepare the 20X8 balance sheet and statement of profit and loss.

Problem 4.4
Completing Worksheet *

Account	Adjusted Trial Balance		Statement of Profit and Loss		Balance Sheet	
	Debit	Credit	Debit	Credit	Debit	Credit
Merchandise inventory.............................	?					
Sales...		64,100				
Sales returns and allowances....................	1,200					
Purchases...	43,290					
Purchase returns and allowances.............		370				
Purchase discounts...................................		410				
Freight in..	3,280					
Sales discounts..	560					
Income tax expense.................................	4,500					
Income tax payable..................................		900				

The beginning and ending merchandise inventories were ₹3,900 and ₹4,200, respectively.

Required

Extend the account balances to their proper columns after entering the inventory amounts in the worksheet.

Chen Company had the following transactions with Chang Company:

Problem 4.5
Recording Purchases and Sales *

Apr. 3 Purchased ₹2,000 of merchandise; terms 2/10, n/30.
    9 Purchased ₹9,000 of merchandise; terms 2/10, n/30.
  14 Paid the invoice for the April 3 purchase.
  19 Paid the invoice for the April 9 purchase.

Required

Prepare journal entries in the records of (i) Chen Company and (ii) Chang Company.

The following is a partial list of account balances of Optica Limited for the year ended June 30, 20X6:

Problem 4.6
Preparation of Statement of Profit and Loss in Functional Form: Merchandising Organization *

Sales...	₹710,000
Sales returns and allowances...	20,000
Sales discounts..	21,000
Purchases...	583,000
Purchase returns and allowances..	68,000
Purchase discounts..	3,000
Office salaries..	48,000
Sales salaries...	96,000
Office rent..	12,000
Freight in..	43,000
Freight out..	18,000

The beginning and ending merchandise inventories were ₹47,000 and ₹69,000, respectively.

Required

Prepare the 20X6 statement of profit and loss in functional form.

A review of the accounting records of Jeet Company on March 31, 20X4 reveals the following information relevant to the preparation of year-end adjusting entries:

Problem 4.7
Adjusting Entries **

(a) There are five salaried employees. The company pays salaries on the first day of the following month. Three of the employees receive a salary of ₹2,500 per month and the other two ₹2,200 per month.

(b) The company owns a car and a computer. The car was bought on June 1, 20X2 for ₹70,000 and was estimated to be useful for ten years. The computer was acquired on February 1, 20X4 for ₹12,000 and was estimated to be useful for five years. Neither asset has any salvage value at the end of its useful life.

(c) There are two bills receivable: (i) The six-month bill for ₹20,000, dated December 1, 20X3 carries interest at 15 per cent per annum. (ii) The nine-month bill for ₹30,000, dated January 1, 20X4 carries interest at 16 per cent per annum. Interest is receivable at the time of maturity of the bills.

(d) On October 23, 20X3, the company paid ₹20,000 for advertisement campaigns in two magazines and debited Prepaid Advertisement. One of these is a monthly which was paid ₹12,000 to carry the advertisement in the following 12 issues published on the second day of every month. The other is a fortnightly that was paid ₹8,000, and it agreed to carry the advertisement in the following 20 issues published on the fifth and 20th day every month.

(e) The company pays sales commission of 2 per cent on sales on the fifth day of the month following the sales. From April 20X3 to March 31, 20X4 the company paid sales commission of ₹17,000. The sales for the year were ₹875,000. March 20X3 sales were ₹45,000.

(f) On January 12, 20X4, the company received ₹28,000 for future services. The company provided services for ₹11,000 on February 17, 20X4, but did not record it.

Required

Prepare adjusting entries on March 31, 20X4.

Problem 4.8
Adjusting Entries ✶✶
Alternative to Problem 4.7

A review of the accounting records of Suresh Company on July 31, 20X7 reveals the following information relevant to the preparation of year-end adjusting entries:

(a) There are two bills payable:
  (i) The three-month bill for ₹10,000 signed on July 1, 20X7 carries interest at 12 per cent per annum.
  (ii) The eight-month bill for ₹15,000 dated January 1, 20X7 carries interest at 14 per cent per annum.
  Interest is payable at the time of maturity of the bills.

(b) The company has two insurance policies. Policy No. F154 covers fire risk for two years and was taken on September 1, 20X6 by paying a premium of ₹12,000. Burglary risk is covered by Policy No. B113 taken on February 1, 20X7 for one year on payment of premium of ₹4,800.

(c) The Unearned Revenue account shows a balance of ₹6,000. It represents retainer fee received on March 1, 20X7 from a client for an annual maintenance contract effective from that date.

(d) There are eight salaried employees. Salaries are disbursed on the third day of the following month. Five employees receive a salary of ₹3,200 per month and the others ₹2,800 per month.

(e) Sales commissions are 3 per cent of sales, payable on the seventh day of the month following the sales. During the year ended July 31, 20X7, the company paid sales commissions totalling ₹18,400. Sales for the year were ₹670,000. July 20X6 net sales were ₹60,000.

(f) The company owns a van and a computer. The van was bought on March 1, 20X5 for ₹80,000 and was estimated to be useful for eight years. The computer was bought on March 1, 20X7 for ₹18,000 and was estimated to be useful for three years. Neither asset has any salvage value at the end of its useful life.

Required

Prepare adjusting entries on July 31, 20X7.

Problem 4.9
Recording Merchandise
Transactions ✶✶

Harcharan Company completed the following transactions in June.

June 1   Purchased merchandise on credit from Gurpreet Company, terms 2/10, n/30, FOB destination, ₹4,800.

     2   Sold merchandise on credit to Manpreet Company, terms 2/10, n/30, FOB destination, ₹7,100.

     2   Paid Inderjeet Company freight charges on merchandise sold, ₹150.

     4   Purchased office supplies on credit from Inderbir Company, terms n/30, ₹180.

     5   Issued a credit note to Manpreet Company for unsatisfactory merchandise returned, ₹300.

     6   Sold merchandise for cash, ₹1,900.

8 Purchased merchandise on credit from Krishan Company, terms 2/10, n/30, FOB shipping point, ₹6,300.

9 Paid Inderjeet Company freight charges on merchandise purchased, ₹170.

10 Sold merchandise on credit to Kartar Company, terms 2/10, n/30, FOB shipping point, ₹9,800.

11 Paid Gurpreet Company for the purchase on June 1.

12 Received a cheque from Manpreet Company for June 2 sales after allowing for the merchandise returned on June 5.

13 Issued a credit note to Kartar Company for unsatisfactory merchandise returned, ₹800.

14 Paid Inderbir Company for the purchase on June 4.

15 Issued a debit note to Krishan Company for unsatisfactory merchandise returned, ₹600.

18 Paid Krishan Company for the purchase on June 8 after allowing for the merchandise returned on June 15.

24 Purchased merchandise on credit from Gurpreet Company, terms 2/10, n/30, FOB shipping point, ₹7,200.

29 Purchased a computer for office use on credit from Maninder Company, terms n/30, ₹2,400.

30 Received a cheque from Kartar Company for June 10 sales after allowing for the merchandise returned on June 13.

Required

Prepare journal entries to record the transactions.

Bijoy Company completed the following transactions in September:

Problem 4.10
Recording Merchandise
Transactions ✱✱
Alternative to Problem 4.9

Sep. 1 Purchased merchandise on credit from Jyotirmoy Company, terms 2/10, n/30, FOB destination, ₹7,900.

3 Sold merchandise on credit to Mrinal Company, terms 2/10, n/30, FOB destination, ₹9,300.

3 Paid Subhas Company freight charges on merchandise sold, ₹210.

4 Purchased office supplies on credit from Joy Company, terms n/60, ₹510.

4 Purchased office supplies on credit from Joy Company, terms n/60, ₹510.

5 Sold merchandise for cash, ₹700.

7 Issued credit note to Mrinal Company for unsatisfactory merchandise returned, ₹500.

8 Purchased merchandise on credit from Shameek Company, terms 2/10, n/30, FOB shipping point, ₹4,200.

9 Paid Subhas Company freight charges on merchandise purchased, ₹310.

10 Sold merchandise on credit to Jayant Company, terms 2/10, n/30, FOB shipping point, ₹8,600.

11 Paid Jyotirmoy Company for the purchase on September 1.

13 Received a cheque from Mrinal Company for September 3 sales after allowing for the merchandise returned on September 7.

13 Issued credit note to Jayant Company for unsatisfactory merchandise returned, ₹200.

14 Paid Joy Company for the purchase on September 4.

15 Issued debit note to Shameek Company for unsatisfactory merchandise returned, ₹100.

18 Paid Shameek Company for the purchase on September 8 after allowing for the merchandise returned on September 15.

27 Purchased merchandise on credit from Jyotirmoy Company, terms 2/10, n/30, FOB shipping point, ₹6,100.

29 Purchased a delivery van for office use on credit from Anand Company, terms n/30, ₹11,000.

30 Received a cheque from Jayant Company for September 10 sales after allowing for the merchandise returned on September 13.

Required

Prepare journal entries to record the transactions.

In 20X3, Win Company entered into a contract to build a shopping mall at a price of ₹250 million. It completed the contract in 20X5. The following data relate to this contract:

Problem 4.11
Revenue from Construction
Contract ✱✱

	20X3	20X4	20X5
Costs incurred to date	₹92,400,000	₹194,400,000	₹297,000,000
Progress billings to date.................................	88,162,300	182,347,000	211,731,000
Cash received to date	82,103,900	167,112,000	203,780,000
Estimated further costs.................................	127,600,000	75,600,000	–0–

Required

Determine the amount of revenue that Win Company should recognize in each of the years under the percentage of completion method.

Problem 4.12
Preparation of Adjusting Entries and Financial Statements **

Leisure Centre Limited was set up on July 1, 20XX. Its trial balance on July 31, 20XX is as follows:

LEISURE CENTRE LIMITED Unadjusted Trial Balance, July 31, 20XX		
Swimming pool...	₹12,000	
Tennis court	9,600	
Supplies	3,280	
Trade receivables	2,910	
Cash..	940	
Prepaid insurance..	1,200	
Trade payables		₹ 1,290
Unearned revenue...		2,100
Share capital		15,000
Dividends...	800	
Revenue from services..		15,540
Salaries expense	2,910	
Telephone expense	290	
	33,930	33,930

The following additional information is available:
   (a) The swimming pool has an estimated life of five years and the tennis court has an estimated life of eight years. Neither has any scrap value.
   (b) The inventory of supplies on July 31 is ₹1,190.
   (c) Subscription revenue of ₹1,200 is due from members who have been admitted on a provisional basis.
   (d) Unearned subscription includes an amount of ₹300 for July.
   (e) Staff salaries for the last week totalling ₹1,290 have not been paid.
   (f) The local electricity company sent a bill for ₹280 for July after the close of the month's transactions.
   (g) Insurance premium of ₹1,200 was paid on a one-year policy effective from July 1.

Required
   1. Prepare adjusting entries and post them to T accounts.
   2. Prepare the July adjusted trial balance, balance sheet and statement of profit.

Problem 4.13
Preparation of Adjusting Entries and Financial Statements *** Alternative to Problem 4.12

Business Services Limited was set up on January 1, 20XX. Its trial balance on January 31, 20XX was as follows:

BUSINESS SERVICES LIMITED Unadjusted Trial Balance, January 31, 20XX		
Buildings	₹15,000	
Office equipment	12,000	
Office supplies	2,140	
Trade receivables	1,640	
Cash	630	
Prepaid rent	3,600	
Trade payables		₹1,020
Unearned revenue		1,600
Share capital		20,000
Dividends	1,000	
Revenue from services		16,870
Salaries expense	3,100	
Electricity expense	380	
	39,490	39,490

The following additional information is available:

(a) The building is expected to be useful for 10 years and the office equipment has an estimated useful life of four years. None of these assets are expected to have any salvage value.

(b) The inventory of office supplies on January 31 is ₹970.

(c) Services for ₹900 were provided to customers in January although no bills have been raised.

(d) Services for ₹720 were provided to customers who had made full advance payments.

(e) Salaries of staff for the second fortnight totalling ₹3,100 have not been paid.

(f) The telephone company sent a bill for ₹480 for January after the close of the month's transactions.

(g) The company paid six months' rent as advance on January 1.

Required

1. Prepare adjusting entries and post them to T accounts.
2. Prepare the January adjusted trial balance, balance sheet and statement of profit and loss.

Admark Limited was set up on April 1, 20X0. Its trial balance on March 31, 20X2 is as follows:

Problem 4.14
The Complete Accounting Cycle, Service Organization: One Period ✱✱✱✱

ADMARK LIMITED Unadjusted Trial Balance, March 31, 20X2		
Office equipment	₹10,000	
Accumulated depreciation, Office equipment		₹ 1,000
Office supplies	2,510	
Cash	5,600	
Trade payables		1,600
Unearned revenue		2,100
Share capital		10,000
Retained earningsv		2,340
Dividends	2,000	
Revenue from services		13,810
Salaries expense	5,940	
Rent expense	4,800	
	30,850	30,850

Required

1. Enter the trial balance amounts on a worksheet and complete the worksheet using the following information:
   (a) Estimated depreciation on office equipment, ₹1,000.
   (b) Inventory of office supplies, ₹930.

(c) Services provided to clients paid for in advance but not taken as revenue, ₹460.

(d) Services provided but not yet billed, ₹370.

(e) Unpaid salaries, ₹490.

(f) Unpaid cleaning expense, ₹240.

(g) Estimated income tax expense, ₹300.

2. Prepare the 20X2 balance sheet, statement of profit and loss and statement of changes in equity. There was no issue of capital in the year ended March 31, 20X2.

3. Prepare adjusting and closing entries.

Problem 4.15
The Complete
Accounting Cycle, Service
Organization: One Period
∗∗∗∗ Alternative to
Problem 4.14

Navin Packaging Limited was set up on January 1, 20X3. Its trial balance on December 31, 20X5 is as follows:

NAVIN PACKAGING LIMITED Unadjusted Trial Balance, December 31, 20X5		
Packaging equipment	₹30,000	
Accumulated depreciation, Packaging equipment		₹ 9,000
Office equipment	10,000	
Accumulated depreciation, Office equipment		3,000
Packaging supplies	6,280	
Office supplies	2,650	
Trade receivables	2,170	
Cash	8,820	
Prepaid rent	9,600	
Bills payable		2,500
Trade payables		1,360
Unearned revenue		1,800
Share capital		35,000
Retained earnings		1,350
Dividends	2,500	
Revenue from services		41,260
Salaries expense	14,910	
Electricity expense	2,340	
Advertisement expense	4,800	
Telephone expense	1,200	
	95,270	95,270

Required

1. Enter the trial balance amounts on a worksheet and complete the worksheet using the following information:

(a) Estimated depreciation on packaging equipment, ₹3,000.

(b) Estimated depreciation on office equipment, ₹1,000.

(c) Inventory of packaging supplies, ₹2,360.

(d) Inventory of office supplies, ₹1,190.

(e) Prepaid rent includes rent for January to March, 20X6 at ₹840 per month.

(f) Accrued interest on the bill payable at 15 per cent per annum from September 1, 20X5.

(g) Services provided to clients that had been paid for in advance but not taken as revenue, ₹1,040.

(h) Unbilled revenue, ₹1,390.

(i) Unpaid salaries, ₹970.

(j) Prepaid advertisement, ₹400.

(k) Unpaid telephone expense, ₹200.

(l) Estimated income tax expense, ₹1,600.

2. Prepare the 20X5 balance sheet, statement of profit and loss and statement of changes in equity. There was no issue of capital in the year ended December 31, 20X5.

3. Prepare adjusting and closing entries.

In 20XX, Anil Mathew started Mathew Adwaves Limited to provide advertising services and completed the following transactions during the first two months:

Problem 4.16
The Complete Accounting
Cycle, Service Organization:
Two Periods ✳✳✳✳✳

July 1 Began business by depositing ₹20,000 in the company's bank account in exchange for 2,000 shares of ₹10 each.

1 Paid three months' rent in advance, ₹3,000.

1 Paid the premium on a one-year insurance policy, ₹900.

5 Bought office equipment from Kiran Company, ₹6,000 and gave two bills payable for ₹3,000 each.

7 Bought office supplies for cash, ₹2,390.

8 Bought art supplies on credit from Fairdeal Company, ₹4,510.

9 Billed customers for services provided, ₹6,800.

18 Received cash for services to be provided later, ₹1,800.

27 Received cash from customers billed on July 9, ₹4,900.

29 Paid salaries for July, ₹2,100.

31 Paid Kiran Company, ₹3,000.

Aug. 1 Billed customers for services provided, ₹7,400.

3 Received cash from customers billed on July 9, ₹1,900.

5 Provided services for cash received on July 18.

9 Paid suppliers for art supplies, ₹2,100.

13 Bought art supplies on credit, ₹4,200.

17 Received cash from customers billed on August 1.

24 Bought office supplies for cash, ₹1,300.

29 Paid salaries for August, ₹2,300.

30 Paid dividend, ₹120.

31 Paid Kiran Company, ₹3,000.

Required

1. Prepare journal entries to record the July transactions.
2. Open the necessary ledger accounts and post the July journal entries.
3. Prepare a trial balance for July on a worksheet form and complete the worksheet using the following information:
   (a) One month's rent has expired, ₹1,000.
   (b) One month's insurance has expired, ₹75.
   (c) Inventory of unused office supplies, ₹1,790.
   (d) Inventory of unused art supplies, ₹1,830.
   (e) Estimated depreciation on office equipment, ₹100.
   (f) Estimated income tax, ₹120.
4. Prepare the July balance sheet, statement of profit and loss and statement of changes in equity.
5. Prepare and post the July adjusting and closing entries.
6. Prepare and post journal entries to record the August transactions.
7. Prepare a trial balance for August on a worksheet form and complete the worksheet using the following information:
   (a) One month's rent has expired, ₹1,000.
   (b) One month's insurance has expired, ₹75.
   (c) Inventory of unused office supplies, ₹1,990.
   (d) Inventory of unused art supplies, ₹3,240.
   (e) Estimated depreciation on office equipment, ₹100.
   (f) Estimated income tax, ₹915.
8. Prepare the August balance sheet, statement of profit and loss and statement of changes in equity.
9. Prepare and post the August adjusting and closing entries.

Problem 4.17

The Complete
Accounting Cycle, Service
Organization: Two Periods
✶✶✶✶✶ Alternative to
Problem 4.16

In 20XX, Raju Designs Limited completed the following transactions during the first two months:

Nov. 1   Deposited ₹50,000 in the bank in the company's bank account in exchange for 5,000 shares.
      1   Paid one month's rent, ₹2,000.
      1   Paid the premium on a one-year insurance policy, ₹2,400.
      3   Bought office equipment for cash, ₹3,000.
      5   Bought office supplies on credit, ₹3,460.
      9   Received cash for services provided, ₹4,900.
      15   Paid assistant's salary for the first fortnight, ₹700.
      18   Billed customers for services provided, ₹4,300.
      20   Paid for office supplies bought on November 5, ₹2,300.
      28   Paid electricity bill for the month, ₹270.
      29   Received cash from customers billed on November 18, ₹3,100.
      29   Paid assistant's salary for the second fortnight, ₹700.
      30   Paid dividend, ₹1,000.
Dec. 1   Paid the monthly rent, ₹2,000.
      7   Bought office supplies on credit, ₹1,900.
      9   Billed customers for services provided, ₹7,800.
      10   Received cash from customers billed on November 18, ₹1,200.
      15   Paid assistant's salary for the first fortnight, ₹700.
      18   Paid suppliers for office supplies bought on December 7, ₹1,500.
      29   Paid electricity bill for the month, ₹310.
      30   Paid assistant's salary for the second fortnight, ₹700.
      31   Paid dividend, ₹1,200.

Required

1. Prepare journal entries to record the November transactions.
2. Open the necessary ledger accounts and post the November journal entries.
3. Prepare a trial balance for July on a worksheet form and complete the worksheet using the following information:
   (a) One month's insurance has expired, ₹200.
   (b) Inventory of unused office supplies, ₹2,910.
   (c) Estimated depreciation on office equipment, ₹50.
   (d) Estimated income tax, ₹1,500.
4. Prepare the November balance sheet, statement of profit and loss and statement of changes in equity.
5. Prepare and post the November adjusting and closing entries.
6. Prepare and post journal entries to record the December transactions.
7. Prepare a trial balance for December on a worksheet form and complete the worksheet using the following information:
   (a) One month's insurance has expired, ₹200.
   (b) Inventory of unused office supplies, ₹4,050.
   (c) Estimated depreciation on office equipment, ₹50.
   (d) Estimated income tax, ₹1,400.
8. Prepare the December balance sheet, statement of profit and loss and statement of changes in equity.
9. Prepare and post the December adjusting and closing entries.

In 20XX, Kiran set up Venus Trading Limited to deal in spices and engaged in the following transactions during the first month:

Problem 4.18

The Complete Accounting
Cycle, Merchandising
Organization: One Period
✶✶✶✶✶

Oct. 1   Began business by investing cash in the company's share capital, ₹25,000.
      1   Paid two months' store rent in advance, ₹2,000.
      1   Paid premium on a one-year insurance policy, ₹600.
      2   Purchased store equipment for cash, ₹3,000.
      2   Purchased office supplies for cash, ₹4,100.
      5   Purchased merchandise on credit from Jai Hind Traders, terms 2/10, n/30, FOB destination, ₹7,000.

6   Sold merchandise on credit to Vijay Company, terms 2/10, n/30, FOB destination, ₹14,000.

10 Paid Hari Carriers freight charges on merchandise sold, ₹400.

14 Issued credit note to Vijay Company for unsatisfactory merchandise returned, ₹1,000.

15 Paid Jai Hind Traders for the purchase on October 5.

16 Received a cheque from Vijay Company for October 6 sales after allowing for the merchandise returned on October 14.

20 Sold merchandise for cash, ₹4,300.

24 Purchased merchandise on credit from Nav Bharat Traders, terms 2/10, n/30, ₹8,600.

27 Paid telephone bill for the month, ₹460.

30 Paid store salaries, ₹800, office salaries, ₹250.

31 Paid dividend, ₹5,000.

Required

1. Prepare journal entries to record the transactions.
2. Open the necessary ledger accounts and post the October journal entries.
3. Prepare a trial balance for October on a worksheet form and complete the worksheet using the following information:
   (a) Ending merchandise inventory, ₹8,720.
   (b) Inventory of unused office supplies, ₹3,580.
   (c) One month's store rent expired, ₹1,000.
   (d) One month's insurance expired, ₹50.
   (e) Estimated depreciation on store equipment, ₹50.
   (f) Estimated income tax, ₹1,000.
4. Prepare the October balance sheet, statement of profit and loss and statement of changes in equity.
5. Prepare and post the adjusting and closing entries for October.

In 20XX, Raj established Alpha Trading Limited to deal in food grains and engaged in the following transactions during the first month:

Problem 4.19
The Complete Accounting Cycle, Merchandising Organization: One Period
✶✶✶✶✶ Alternative to Problem 4.18

Feb. 1 Began business by investing cash in the company's share capital, ₹40,000.

1   Paid six months' store rent in advance, ₹12,000.

1   Paid premium on a one-year insurance policy, ₹3,600.

2   Purchased store equipment for cash, ₹18,000.

3   Purchased office supplies for cash, ₹3,700.

4   Purchased merchandise on credit from Shamlal Traders, terms 1/10, n/60, FOB shipping point, ₹9,000.

5   Paid Ibrahim Company freight on merchandise purchased, ₹860.

9   Sold merchandise on credit to Manoj Company, terms 1/10, n/60, FOB shipping point, ₹18,000.

10 Sold merchandise for cash, ₹11,600.

11 Issued debit note to Shamlal Traders for unsatisfactory merchandise returned, ₹300.

14 Paid Shamlal Traders for the purchase on February 4 after allowing for the merchandise returned on February 11.

17 Issued credit note to Manoj Company for unsatisfactory merchandise returned, ₹1,000.

19 Received cheque from Manoj Company for February 9 sales after allowing for unsatisfactory merchandise returned on February 17.

24 Purchased merchandise on credit from Nav Bharat Traders, terms 1/10, n/60, ₹19,000.

26 Paid electricity bill for the month, ₹240.

27 Paid store salaries, ₹1,200; office salaries, ₹500.

28 Paid dividend, ₹8,000.

Required

1. Prepare journal entries to record the transactions.
2. Open the necessary ledger accounts and post the February journal entries.

3. Prepare a trial balance for February on a worksheet form and complete the worksheet using the following information:
   (a) Ending merchandise inventory, ₹18,400.
   (b) Inventory of unused office supplies, ₹2,300.
   (c) One month's store rent has expired, ₹2,000.
   (d) One month's insurance has expired, ₹300.
   (e) Estimated depreciation on store equipment, ₹150.
   (f) Estimated income tax, ₹4,000.
4. Prepare the February balance sheet, statement of profit and loss and statement of changes in equity.
5. Prepare and post adjusting and closing entries for February.

Problem 4.20
Preparation of Financial Statements from Incomplete Records
★★★★★

On April 1, 20X6, Manish Mukherjee set up Realtime Consultancy Limited with a share capital of ₹30,000. He did not maintain proper accounts of the company's transactions although he barely noted some details in his personal diary. Mukherjee's secretary has kept files containing invoices raised on customers and cash memos and invoices for purchases of office supplies.

With great difficulty you have assembled the following information from Mukherjee's diary, the files kept by his secretary and the company's bank statements:

1. Cash receipts during the period are as follows:
   Advances from customers .... ₹6,500
   Collections from customers.. 38,400
2. Cash disbursements during the period are as follows:
   Rent advance for 24 months (paid on April 1, 20X6)................................. ₹12,000
   Insurance premium for 12 months (paid on April 1, 20X6)...................... 1,200
   Office equipment 18,000
   Cash purchases and payments to suppliers... 9,470
   Salaries paid to employees.. 13,200
   Electricity expense paid 1,430
   Telephone expense paid 2,200
   Dividends paid... 8,000
3. Invoices for consulting services raised during the year totalled ₹47,300. The amount excludes the value of services of ₹5,900 provided to customers who had paid advances totalling ₹6,500.
4. Invoices and cash memos for purchase of office supplies totalled ₹12,190.
5. Depreciation on office equipment is ₹2,000 per year.
6. Unpaid expenses on March 31, 20X7 are as follows:
   Salaries... ₹1,200
   Electricity... 130
   Telephone... 200
7. Inventory of office supplies on March 31, 20X7 is ₹7,480.
8. Estimated income tax for the year is ₹10,000.

Required
1. Prepare the March trial balance on a worksheet form and complete the worksheet.
2. Prepare the 20X7 balance sheet, statement of profit and loss and statement of changes in equity.

Problem 4.21
Preparation of Financial Statements from Incomplete Records
★★★★★ Alternative to Problem 4.20

On January 1, 20X3, Veena and Mohan established VM Interior Decor Limited with a share capital of ₹20,000. In early January 20X4, just a few days before the accounting records were to be sent to the CA, there was a major fire in the office, which practically destroyed all the books and vouchers. Their office assistant, however, managed to pull out a few things including some files and scribbling pads.

After poring over the documents for several hours, they have been able to put together the following information:

1. Cash receipts during 20X3:
   Advances from customers .... ₹9,100
   Collections from customers.. 57,200
   Refund for return of office supplies rejected.. 900

2. Cash disbursements during the period are as follows:

Rent advance for 3 years (paid on January 1, 20X3)	₹18,000
Insurance premium for 12 months (paid on January 1, 20X3)	3,600
Cash purchases and payments to suppliers	17,300
Salaries paid to employees	13,500
Telephone expense paid	3,300
Dividends declared and paid	15,000

3. Office equipment costing ₹12,000 was bought on credit. The amount is repayable in two equal annual instalments. The first instalment was paid during 20X3 and included in the disbursements shown above.
4. Invoices and cash memos for purchase of office supplies totalled ₹13,700.
5. Invoices for consulting services raised during the year totalled ₹63,700. The amount excludes the value of services was ₹8,300 provided to customers who had paid advances totalling ₹9,100.
6. Depreciation on office equipment was ₹1,200 per year.
7. Unpaid expenses as at December 31, 20X3 were as follows:

Salaries	₹1,500
Telephone	300

8. Inventory of office supplies on December 31, 20X3 was ₹6,900.
9. Estimated income tax for the year is ₹15,000.

Required

1. Prepare the December trial balance on a worksheet form and complete the worksheet.
2. Prepare the 20X3 balance sheet, statement of profit and loss and statement of changes in equity.

Business Decision Cases

Sudipto Bhattacharyya is a professor of accounting in a leading business school. He has received the following message from a former student:

BDC 4.1
Findomega.com

Dear Professor Bhattacharyya,

I belong to the MBA Class of 2002 and was your student in the financial accounting course. Currently, I am Vice President, Sales and Operations in the India office of findomega.com, the well-known Internet search engine listed in the National Stock Exchange of India. I need your advice on how to get out of a mess in my workplace.

As you would know, findomega.com provides targeted advertising as part of its search services. It works as follows. When a user searches the Internet using our engine, findomega.com provides the requested information. In addition, it gives the names and related web links of five advertisers (who are our customers) for the products or services that the user may be potentially interested in. If the user clicks on any of those web links, we charge the customer concerned. Otherwise, we do not charge our customers. Of course, we never charge the Internet search user anything. Lately, we have localized the search and have made it possible to get information based on postal code and street name. This is generating a lot of additional revenue for us.

My job is to contact potential customers and sell the idea of targeted advertising. Initially, businesses were not much enthusiastic, but the rising Internet penetration and smartphone use in India is making our service more attractive. When I get a customer to sign up with my company, I ask for clearance from my immediate boss who is the company's Director of Sales and Marketing, whom I report to. (My boss reports to the company's Managing Director in India, who in turn reports to the company's regional office in Hong Kong.) Once my boss approves the deal by email, I sign a contract with the customer. The contract is in a standard form that has been cleared by the Legal and Compliance Department. The signed contract goes to Accounting for billing the customer based on the number of clicks, and the customer pays within one week. My boss is very happy with my work and he thinks that I am an asset to the company. Even in this recession, I have been able to get new business though it is not always easy, and I have always met my tight performance targets.

In early December I received an interesting proposal. The prospective customer, an online travel agency, offered an innovative arrangement under which findomega.com will carry their advertisement 500 times that month. In return, the customer will carry an advertisement of our service the same number of times that month on their website at no charge. Since the company is cutting on payment for advertising and promotion, the proposal looked attractive to me. In addition, I would benefit from the additional business that would count towards my target and bonus. I emailed my boss and he promptly asked me to go ahead with the deal. I signed the contract. I had to make minor changes to the contract for the peculiarities of the arrangement since there was no precedent. The main change was that the contract required mutual billing by the two parties at the rates that my company typically charged for similar advertisements with cash payment arrangement. In order to settle the transaction, my company would record an equal amount of advertising and promotion expense.

This morning I received a memo from the Managing Director asking me to explain my signing the deal without previous approval from anyone. What has upset me is the insinuation that I have done something improper and, much worse, I have potentially benefited from the deal. The fact is that my boss knows that I got nothing from the deal. I understand that he too has received a similar memo.

I would like to add that findomega.com was set up by a group of computer programmers. It is one of the most innovative services and is the best in its league. My boss who has been with the company from its early days feels that these days the company is excessively concerned with procedures, more so after it went public a few years ago. It appears that in the past the atmosphere in the company used to be informal and that is what encouraged the employees to innovate and take big risks.

I remember that in your classes you would stress that ethical conduct is not negotiable. Do you think what I did was wrong?

Best regards,

Amit

Memo

From: Managing Director March 2, 20XX

To: Vice President, Sales and Operations

In December you signed a contract for barter advertising. The contract is not in the standard form. According to the Legal and Compliance Department, this violates company policy. The company's auditors have questioned recognizing revenue from the contract in the fourth quarter ended December 31. The Internal Audit Department has pointed out that if the contract were excluded, you would have fallen short of the quarterly target by 15 per cent. I question your motivation and sense of judgment. Please send your written explanation in three days.

Required

1. Evaluate Amit's action.
2. What is, in your opinion, the Managing Director's point about revenue recognition?
3. Do you agree with Amit that the company's procedures could stifle innovation and risk-taking?
4. Draft a response from Professor Bhattacharyya to Amit.

BDC 4.2
Platinum Trends Limited

Platinum Trends is a leader in branded jewellery. It started operations in 20X3. It sells its products to dealers in major cities in the country. Jewellery is subject to changes in fashion trends. The company bills the dealers on delivery of the products and recognizes revenue immediately. Payment terms are "2/10, n/30". All invoices are paid within the credit period and 15 per cent of the payments are received within the discount period. The dealers manage to sell a significant portion of their purchases and return the unsold products to the company. Sales returns in the industry have ranged between 19 per cent and 26 per cent in the past five years. The following table gives the company's sales and returns for the past three years (March 31 fiscal year):

Year	Sales	Sales returns	Net sales	Net profit
20X6	₹6,412	₹1,375	₹5,037	₹2,015
20X7	7,907	1,952	5,955	2,692
20X8	9,109	2,066	7,043	3,505

The dealers are allowed to return any unsold products throughout year. Over 70 per cent of the sales happen in the festival season (September to January) and the remaining sales are spread almost evenly through the year. The company accounts for sales returns during the year.

In June 20X8, Samir Jain, an analyst with Altus Securities, a reputable brokerage, questioned the company's accounting for sales returns in an equity research report titled "A Lacklustre Jewel: Dubious Accounting by Platinum Trends". Relevant extracts from the report are as follows:

Platinum Trends has consistently outperformed its industry peers. The company's sales growth of over 18 per cent and margins of 50 per cent are significantly superior to the industry median of 12 per cent and 32 per cent, respectively. The company's management is focused on the upper end of the market. Almost all of the new products introduced in the last year have done well. We believe the company's biggest strengths are its strong brand, ingenious design, and a committed dealer network.

Even so, we have an issue with Platinum Trends' accounting for sales returns. While the company accounts for all actual returns, it does not account for returns that are probable as of the balance sheet date. What this means is that products sold in a year may be returned in the following year, because they are no longer the flavour of the season. This would increase the revenue in the year of sale and reduce the revenue in the year of return.

Industry trends suggest that sales returns exceed 20 per cent. Our view is that the company's delay in recognition of returns could result in overstatement of revenue and, what is worse, allow the company to move its revenue from one period to another.

In view of the above, we recommend SELL on Platinum Trends' shares.

The company has issued the following press release in response to the research report:

Platinum Trends is the industry leader in design, innovation, and branding and has received a number of awards competing with international jewellers including Bulgari, Cartier, and Pomellato. Sales growth and margins are consistently above the industry peers. The company's shares have returned over 70 per cent over the past three years (as against the NSE 500 return of 34 per cent) and are now a matter of pride for its investors, much the same its products are for its customers. We are deeply disappointed by the negative research report of Altus Securities.

The company recognizes revenue in accordance with the two major conditions in the accounting standards:

1. The seller of goods has transferred to the buyer the significant risks and rewards of ownership of the goods and the seller retains no effective control of the goods transferred to a degree usually associated with ownership; and
2. No significant uncertainty exists regarding the amount of the consideration that will be derived from the sale of the goods.

The company has complied with both these conditions. While there is some probability that the goods may be returned by our dealers, the amount of consideration is certain. Once the company sells the products, ownership passes to the dealers and the company has no control over the goods. Therefore, the company cannot record return of such products. The company accounts for returns from its dealers immediately and refunds the amounts promptly. In our view, accounting for expected returns, as contrasted with actual returns, is fraught with risk. That kind of accounting would be based on estimation and not on facts.

Required

1. Evaluate the analyst's comment and the company's response on the company's accounting for sales returns.
2. Develop an accounting policy for revenue recognition including sales returns.

Interpreting Financial Reports

Biocon Limited was founded by Kiran Mazumdar-Shaw in 1978 to manufacture enzymes. Over the years, it has evolved into a high-profile biopharmaceutical enterprise. The company went public in 2004. In 2012, the company reported revenue of ₹20.87 billion and net profit of ₹3.38 billion (2011: sales ₹18.06 billion; net profit ₹3.40 billion).

IFR 4.1
Biocon Limited

In Biocon's 2011 annual report, the chairman's review talked about its "strategic partnership" with Pfizer as follows:

> The Biocon–Pfizer partnership is indeed a significant inflection point in our growth path. Our companies bring together a winning combination of marketing, manufacturing, and research excellence which will build a formidable global footprint in diabetes care.

> Spurred by the success of our insulins, we entered into an exciting agreement with Pfizer to address a large and lucrative global biosimilar insulin opportunity.

> The most visible and high profile partnership that we recently announced was with the world's leading pharmaceutical company, Pfizer, to commercialize our insulins portfolio. Pfizer will have exclusive and a few co-exclusive rights to commercialize these products globally, while Biocon will be responsible for the clinical development, manufacture, and supply of these biosimilar insulin products. We firmly believe this landmark partnership will drive considerable growth in the foreseeable future.

The Highlights section of the report described the terms of the agreement with Pfizer:

> In October 2010, Biocon signed a definitive global agreement with Pfizer Inc., the world's leading biopharmaceutical company, for the worldwide commercialization of Biocon's biosimilar versions of insulin and insulin analog products. Pfizer will have exclusive rights to commercialize these products globally, with certain exceptions, including co-exclusive rights for all of the products with Biocon in certain other markets. Pfizer will also have coexclusive rights with existing Biocon licensees, with respect to some of the products, primarily in a number of developing markets. Biocon will remain responsible for the clinical development, manufacture, and supply of these biosimilar insulin products, as well as for regulatory activities to secure their approval in various geographies. Biocon's recombinant human insulin formulations are approved in 27 countries in developing markets, and commercialized in 23, while glargine has been launched in its first market, India.

> Under the terms of the agreement, Pfizer will make upfront payments totaling $200 million. Biocon is also eligible to receive development and regulatory milestone payments of up to $150 million and will receive additional payments linked to Pfizer's sales of its four insulin biosimilar products across global markets.

In March 2012, Biocon and Pfizer terminated the agreement. This is what the chairman's review had to say in 2012:

> The year under review also saw the dissolution of our global partnership for Biosimilar Insulin and Insulin Analogs with pharma major, Pfizer. A change in priority within Pfizer's biosimilars division led to a preference for in house biosimilar programs that were perceived to deliver higher returns. This led the two companies to reach an agreement for amicable parting of ways which was believed to be in best mutual interest. In terms of business continuity, there will be minimal impact as Biocon will continue to develop its programs for global registrations as per plan, utilizing the retained payments received from Pfizer. We remain committed to our commercialization endeavour, albeit on a different path that will shift from a single global partner to multiple regional alliances.

> The benefit of licensing income to our PAT was sharply down to ₹390 million this fiscal from the exceptional levels recorded last fiscal of ₹990 million. However, improvements elsewhere maintained total PAT at near last year's level. Going forward, our development expenses for Insulins program will be set off against the retained payments we have received from Pfizer.

Note 41 to the 2012 financial statements described the accounting for the termination of the agreement as follows:

> In October 2010, Biocon and Pfizer entered into a global commercialization and supply agreement. Biocon was responsible for the clinical development, clinical trials and other activities to secure regulatory approval in various geographies. Pfizer had exclusive rights to commercialize Biocon's biosimilar insulin portfolio.

> Pursuant to this agreement, Biocon received upfront payment and few milestone payments. Biocon had significant obligations relating to clinical development and regulatory activities. Consequently amounts received under the global commercialization and supply agreement were being recognized in the statement of profit and loss under percentage completion method.

> In March 2012, Biocon and Pfizer terminated the global commercialization and supply agreement due to their individual priorities for their respective biosimilars businesses. Pursuant to the termination and transition agreement, the exclusive rights to commercialize reverted to Biocon and Pfizer has no further obligations to Biocon. Biocon is committed to the biosimilar insulins program and is continuing the development/clinical trial activities on a global scale.

Biocon has evaluated the prevalent regulatory framework, industry practices, and ethics/governance requirements relating to clinical trials/regulatory submissions already initiated under the global commercialization agreement and has determined that it has continuing obligations to complete the aforesaid clinical development and regulatory activities for the global markets. Accordingly, Biocon will recognize the balance amount of ₹4,929 million (net of amounts incurred towards costs of fulfilling contractual obligations) [included in Deferred revenue] received from Pfizer, in the consolidated statement of profit and loss in future periods in line with costs to be incurred towards such clinical trial and development activities.

The auditors, S.R. Batliboi Associates made the following comment on the company's accounting for the termination of the contract:

Without qualifying our opinion,

(a) we draw attention to note 41 in the consolidated financial statements regarding management's decision to defer recognition of amounts in the consolidated statement of profit and loss, pertaining to payments received pursuant to the Termination and Transition Agreement entered into with a customer for reasons as more fully discussed in the aforesaid note.

Espirito Santo Securities, a brokerage, questioned the company's accounting and argued that the company should have taken the amount of upfront fee as an exceptional item instead of deferring it to future periods commenting that the accounting policy was "aggressive". But Biocon refuted the charges stating that "the accounting method followed in the case of fees received from Pfizer is in compliance with GAAP and appropriate disclosures have been provided." It mentioned that "the licensing agreement with Pfizer was not an outright licensing deal, but a development licensing deal that mandated Biocon to incur development costs for obtaining regulatory approvals."[8]

Required

1. Evaluate Biocon's accounting for the fee received from Pfizer.
2. What do you think of the brokerage's view of the company's accounting? Specifically, is Biocon's accounting "aggressive"?
3. Comment on the auditor's position on the matter.

Valeant Pharmaceuticals has products in dermatology, eye health and neurology, among others. Its corporate headquarters is in Quebec, Canada. Its revenues were $8.25 billion in 2014.

IFR 4.2 Valeant Pharmaceuticals International, Inc

Valeant is built on acquisitions. Its acquisitions include Synergetics USA, Salix Pharmaceuticals, Solta Holdings, and Bausch + Lomb Holdings. In 2014, it made an unsuccessful attempt to buy Allergan, the owner of the Botox brand. Valeant's major investors included hedge funds, ValueAct and Pershing Square, whose boss, William Ackman, has publicly celebrated the company. Michael Pearson, Valeant's Chairman and CEO was head of the global pharmaceutical practice and head of mid-Atlantic region of McKinsey & Company, the consulting firm.

Valeant has faced criticism for its aggressive business model. Its large product price increases had come in for scrutiny and has been part of the debate on rising health care costs. For example, in August 2015, two members of the US Congress investigating generic drug price increases wrote to Valeant about two heart drugs, Isuprel and Nitropress, when it raised their prices by 525 percent and 212 percent respectively after their acquisition from Marathon Pharmaceuticals. Other drug companies have also been criticized on price increases.

Distribution Arrangements

On October 19, 2015, Southern Investigative Reporting Foundation, an organization that provides "in-depth financial investigative reporting for the common good" disclosed that a company called R&O Pharmacy in Los Angeles got a letter from Valeant's general counsel and director of business development requesting payment of $69.8 million for "invoiced amounts". Since R&O had done no business with Valeant, it forwarded the letter to its lawyer. The lawyer did not receive any reply from Valeant and filed a suit stating that R&O owed Valeant nothing.

Philidor Rx Services

Philidor is a "specialty pharmacy", term understood to mean businesses that are engaged in handling, storage, shipping, insurance approval and distribution requirements with standardized processes. Valeant had never publicly mentioned Philidor by name. In its third quarterly conference call in 2014,

---

[8] Biocon looks for life beyond Pfizer, *Business Line*, July 9, 2012.

an analyst asked for "the rough breakout between the prescription audited information and now that you get to your specialty pharmacy [Filadore]". Pearson replied that the specialty pharmacy channels "are multiple specialty pharmacies throughout the United States, but the rough script breakdown is about 40% of the volumes going through, especially pharma, and 60% is going through traditional pharmacies." Not much is known about Philidor, a private company.

Valeant's Q3 Conference Call

Valeant's Q3 2015 conference call presentation on October 19, 2015 had this question: "How does Valeant work with specialty pharmacies and what is Valeant's relationship with Philidor?". Valeant responded that it viewed its relationship with Philidor and its other specialty pharmacies as "proprietary and as one of our competitive advantages". It stated that similar to many pharmaceutical companies in the U.S., an increasing percentage of its revenue was coming from products dispensed through multiple specialty pharmacies. Further, it said that its inventory with specialty pharmacies and the title for its medicines only transferred to the pharmacy when the actual prescription is filled and that less than five per cent of its U.S. channel inventory sat in the specialty pharmacy channel. Further, it said that Valeant consolidated the financials of Philidor and that inventory held at Philidor remained on Valeant's books and was not included in Philidor's channel inventory.

Citron's Allegations

On October 21, 2015, short seller Citron Research alleged that Philidor owned R&O Pharmacy. It added that Philidor and R&O were the same company and shared management. Further, it said that the R&O website referred to themselves as Philidor. Further, it said that Valeant had created a network of "pharmacies" as clones of Philidor for the purpose of phantom sales or stuffing the channel in order to avoid scrutiny from the auditors. For good measure, it asked whether it was "Enron part deux."

Valeant's Response

In a conference call on October 26, 2015, Pearson said: "We operate our business based on the highest standards of ethics and are committed to transparency."

Market Reaction

Valeant's stock lost 25 per cent in two days after Citron's allegations. The five-year credit-default swap on Valeant's bonds climbed to 690 basis points, more than any other health care company.

Required

1. Analyze the relationship between Valeant and Philidor. Are investors' concerns about revenue recognition justified?
2. What do you think of the way Valeant responded to the allegations? Do you think the investors were convinced by Valeant's defence?

IFR 4.3
Reebok India Limited

On April 30, 2012, the German sportswear giant Adidas announced that "commercial irregularities" at its Reebok India operations could impact its past consolidated results to a pre-tax maximum of €125 million (₹8.7 billion) and restructuring costs associated with changes being brought in by the new management "including changes to commercial business practices" could lead to an additional one-off charge of €70 million. Adidas made a fourth quarter operating loss of €239 million, compared with analyst expectations for profit of €28.6 million. The announcement followed the sudden and unexplained departure in the previous week of two of Adidas India's top executives, the managing director, Subhindher Singh Prem, and the chief operating officer, Vishnu Bhagat. On May 21, the company filed a criminal complaint against the two alleging that receipts were falsified, Reebok merchandise was siphoned off, Adidas-owned goods were hidden in four different warehouses and goods were sent to non-existent distributors. On May 29, the government asked the Serious Fraud Investigation Office to investigate the matter. Prem sued Adidas for defamation and recovery of his past dues amounting to ₹127 million. Prem and four others were arrested on September 19, 2012.

The Adidas brand ranks fourth worldwide, but in India, it is the market leader. This became possible mainly because of the company's wide distribution network of over 1,000 stores. The "India growth story" played no mean part in the company's aggressive expansion. "Establish the brand now in a rapidly growing market and money will come later" seemed to be the belief. A key element of the company's business strategy was a "minimum guarantee", a promise of a minimum income to a franchisee regardless of the sales. Prem reasoned that this was necessary to encourage shop owners to stock a brand. In contrast to Reebok India's practice, global sports goods companies sell to wholesalers, who take responsibility for selling the goods. If the products sell, the wholesalers make money but the risks of not selling are also theirs. A major risk in the "minimum guarantee" model is that the franchisees may not put in their best efforts, since they were assured of a minimum income. The effect was that the profitable stores were subsidizing the loss-making ones.

In 2005, Adidas acquired Reebok for $3.8 billion, but the two businesses continued to operate as separate entities. Reebok continued to focus on growth and market share and was more aggressive. In contrast, Adidas operated in a more disciplined manner, even while continuing to use the minimum guarantee approach. In late 2010, the company decided to withdraw from the minimum guarantee model and close the loss-making stores. It became known later that a third of 1,000 outlets in India would likely be shut. Reebok's revenue was ₹7.72 billion in 2009 and ₹7.83 billion in 2010. It made a profit of ₹128 million in 2009 and a loss of ₹401 million in 2010. Suspecting that all was not well at its Indian unit, Adidas asked KPMG to conduct a forensic audit of its books.

Required

1. Describe what happened in Reebok India.
2. Was there a failure of internal controls? Explain.
3. Examine other possible reasons for the happenings.

Financial Analysis

Study the financial statements of Interglobe Aviation (Indigo Airlines), Jet Airways and Spice Jet.

FA 4.1
Accrual and Deferral in Airlines

Required

1. List the major items of accrual and deferral. Explain for each item why an accrual or deferral is necessary.
2. Compare the levels of accrual and deferral over a two-year period. What did you learn from the comparison?
3. Accrual accounting requires the board of directors and the management to make a number of estimates and judgments relating to the financial statements on a prudent and reasonable basis. As an analyst, how would you assure yourself that the three companies meet this requirement?
4. Explain the importance of your study for analyzing financial statements.

Study the financial statements of Airtel, Idea Cellular and Reliance Communications.

FA 4.2
Revenue Recognition and Matching in Telecommunication Companies

Required

1. Develop a set of critical issues in revenue recognition and matching in this business.
2. Examine the accounting policies of these companies. Are you satisfied with them? Why or why not? Explain.
3. Accrual accounting requires the board of directors and the management to make a number of estimates and judgments relating to the financial statements on a prudent and reasonable basis. As an analyst, how would you assure yourself that the three companies meet this requirement?
4. Explain the importance of your study for analyzing financial statements.

Answers to One-minute Quiz

4.1 a, b, d.
4.2 a, c.
4.3 c.
4.4 b, c, a, d.
4.5 b, c, d.
4.6 a, b, c.
4.7 a, d.
4.8 a.
4.9 a, b, c, d.

Answers to Test Your Understanding

4.1 Case A: 1,030; Case B: 1,040; Case C: 780; Case D: 490.

4.2 (a) Debit Depreciation Expense 2,000, credit Accumulated Depreciation, Office Equipment 2,000; (b) 8,000.

4.3 Debit Subscription Revenue 9,900, credit Unearned Revenue 9,900.

4.4 Debit Income Tax Expense 3,500, credit Income Tax Payable 3,500.

4.5 *With cash discount:* 1. May 23; 2. February 10; 3. October 31; 4. August 10; 5. February 22. *Without cash discount:* 1. June 12; 2. March 16; 3. December 29; 4. September 14; 5. April 13.

4.6 (a) Sold merchandise on credit, ₹12,000; (b) Accepted merchandise returned by customer, ₹600; (c) Collected amount due on invoice, ₹11,400; (d) Sold merchandise on credit, ₹9,000. (e) Collected amount due on invoice, ₹8,910, after allowing cash discount of ₹90.

4.7 Cost of goods sold = ₹11,000 + ₹210,000 − ₹7,000 − ₹3,000 + ₹18,000 − ₹17,000 = ₹212,000.

4.8 *With reversing entries:* July 1 Debit Revenue from Services 700, credit Unbilled Revenue 700; July 15 Debit Trade Receivables 1,900, credit Revenue from Services 1,900; July 27 Debit Cash 1,900, credit Trade Receivables 1,900. *Without reversing entries:* July 1 No entry because there is no reversal; July 15 Debit Trade Receivables 1,900, credit Revenue from Services 1,200, credit Unbilled Revenue 700; July 27 Debit Cash 1,900, credit Trade Receivables 1,900.

4.9 This is a sale and repurchase transaction. In substance, there is no sale. Manohar Company should treat the amount received as a loan and the difference between the sale and repurchase prices as interest on the loan.

PART TWO

MEASURING AND REPORTING ASSETS, LIABILITIES, AND EQUITY

In this Part, we move from mechanics to decision-making. We examine the principles and standards on which firms base their accounting policies and the managerial and other considerations that shape their policies. Our focus is on managers' accounting policy choices for measuring assets, liabilities and equity and their effect on reported profit, and how managers make those choices.

Chapter 5 analyzes the principles of inventory valuation and how alternative methods affect the reported net profit.

Chapter 6 discusses accounting for acquisition, depreciation, and disposal of tangible and intangible assets and natural resources.

Chapter 7 explains the valuation and presentation of financial investments.

Chapter 8 discusses investments in subsidiaries, joint arrangements and associates.

Chapter 9 considers liabilities related to operations and the role of managers' assumptions and estimates in measuring them.

Chapter 10 discusses debentures, mortgages and leases.

Chapter 11 examines share capital, reserves, foreign currency transactions and foreign operations, share-based compensation and earnings per share.

CHAPTER

5

Inventories

LEARNING OBJECTIVES

After studying this chapter, you should be able to:

1. Describe current assets.
2. Define inventories and apply the matching principle to inventory valuation.
3. Analyze the effect of an inventory error.
4. Describe how to measure the physical inventory.
5. Distinguish between product costs and period expenses.
6. Apply the inventory costing methods.
7. Explain the lower-of-cost-or-market principle of inventory valuation.
8. Appreciate the role of conservatism, neutrality, and prudence in financial reporting.
9. Explain the significance of comparability.
10. Estimate the value of inventory by the retail inventory and standard cost methods.
11. Explain the perpetual inventory system.
12. Compute the cost of goods sold for a manufacturing organization.
13. Evaluate the efficiency of inventory management using financial analysis.
14. Understand the importance of managing the operating cycle.

PHANTOM WHEAT

In April 2016, the Reserve Bank of India (RBI) directed banks to provide for losses on food grain-related loans to the government of Punjab. And thereby hangs a tale. Earlier in the month, there were reports that food grains worth ₹120 billion (₹200 billion according to some reports) had gone 'missing' from Punjab's warehouses. The government, however, responded that the inventories were all fully accounted for and any discrepancy required reconciliation between its agencies and the Food Corporation of India (FCI). Banks had given loans secured by the goods. The FCI denied liability because the goods were not with it. The RBI asked banks to provide for 15 per cent of the gap – the difference between the amount of the loans and the value of food grains in the warehouses – in two quarters at 7.5 per cent per quarter. Banks argued that loans to government entities were considered safe but the RBI insisted on provisioning. Banks saw themselves as "victims" and "fall guys" in the dispute between the FCI and the government of Punjab. Soon after, the banks stopped lending to the government of Punjab. As it happens in such cases, what happened to the missing wheat is a mystery.

SPEED READ

Current assets are converted into cash in the normal course of business. Inventories are frequently the largest item of current assets for trading and manufacturing organizations. Inventory valuation is central to income measurement. Inventory costing methods affect the reported net profit. The perpetual inventory system provides better control over inventories. Estimating inventory value is inevitable in some situations. Effective inventory management aims to avoid both excessively high and dangerously low inventories. The operating cycle of a business determines how rapidly inventories and receivables are turned into cash.

Current Assets

Learning Objective

LO 1 Describe current assets.

Assets are classified as current or non-current depending on how soon they can be converted into cash. An entity should classify an asset as a **current asset** when it expects to realize the asset, or intends to sell or consume it, in its normal operating cycle or within 12 months after the reporting period. **Operating cycle** is the time between the acquisition of assets for processing and their realization in cash. When an enterprise's normal operating cycle is not clearly identifiable, it is assumed to be 12 months. Cash, receivables, short-term financial assets, and inventories are the major current asset categories. Inventories generally constitute the largest current assets and the second largest assets (after fixed assets) in the financial statements of manufacturing organizations. An asset which is not a current asset is classified as a **non-current asset**.

ONE-MINUTE QUIZ 5.1
Current Asset

Which of the following can be classified as a current asset on the balance sheet? There may be more than one correct answer.
  (a) Bought-out components for aircraft to be manufactured and delivered in 24 months.
  (b) Cash kept with a supplier as caution deposit for 15 months.
  (c) Revolving deposit with Customs authorities for payment of customs duty.
  (d) Non-adjustable deposit with Customs authorities to be refunded when an entity stops operations.

Inventory Valuation and Income Measurement

Defining Inventories

Learning Objective

LO 2 Define inventories and apply the matching principle to inventory valuation.

Inventories are goods that are meant for eventual conversion into cash in the normal course of business. Like receivables, they are part of the operating cycle of a business. Inventories may be materials or supplies to be consumed in production (raw materials, consumable items, and packing materials), goods in the production process (semi-finished goods or work in progress), or goods held for sale (finished goods and stock-in-trade).

A merchandising organization merely buys and sells goods, barring some repacking, and reports the cost of unsold goods as merchandise inventory. A manufacturing organization buys raw materials and converts them into finished goods to be sold. As a result, it has several kinds of inventories, such as raw materials, work in progress, finished goods and stock-in-trade.

Raw materials These consist of goods yet to be introduced into the production process.
  - Steel and paint for Tata Motors.
  - Crude oil for Indian Oil.

QUICK QUESTION
Raw materials

Give examples of raw materials for Procter & Gamble, NTPC and Asian Paints.

Work in progress In any production process, some units will be in the process but are yet to be completed.
  - Partly assembled cars and car parts for Tata Motors.
  - Crude oil in the pipeline for Indian Oil.

QUICK QUESTION
Work in progress

Give examples of work in progress for L&T, Biocon and Cisco.

Finished goods Goods that have been produced completely but remaining unsold comprise the finished goods inventory of a manufacturer.
  - Fully finished cars for Tata Motors.
  - Petrol awaiting despatch at the refineries for Indian Oil.

QUICK QUESTION
Finished goods

Give examples of finished goods for ITC, Marico and L'Oreal.

Stock-in-trade These are goods bought for trading. These are the main inventories for a merchandising firm. Some manufacturing and service organizations may also keep items for trading.

- Clothes for Big Bazar (Future Retail).
- Used cars for True Value.

Other items In addition, most manufacturing firms also keep inventories of factory supplies, such as coolants, fasteners, cleaning materials, packing materials, and machinery spares. The commonly used classification for such items is *stores* and *spares*. Further, a separate inventory of manufacturing tools is maintained under the title *loose tools*. Firms that carry packing materials of significant value show them separately. In the case of a service provider, inventories include the costs of the service for which the entity has not yet recognised the related revenue. These costs consist primarily of the labour and other costs of personnel directly engaged in providing the service, including supervisory personnel, and attributable overheads. The cost of inventories of a service provider does not include profit margins or non-attributable overheads that are often factored into prices charged by service providers. Recall from Chapter 4 that to the extent revenue has been earned but not billed, a service provider recognizes the costs and the related profit as unbilled revenue. Long-term assets retired from regular use and held for sale are not inventories.

Matching Inventory Costs with Revenues

Recall from Chapter 4:

$$\text{Cost of goods sold} = \text{Cost of goods available for sale} - \text{Ending inventory}$$

$$\text{Gross profit} = \text{Net sales} - \text{Cost of goods sold}$$

The cost assigned to the ending inventory directly affects the reported profit. For instance, if we overstate the ending inventory, profit will increase. Inventory valuation affects both the statement of profit and loss and the balance sheet.

Revenue from operations arises in a continuous, repetitive process by which enterprises acquire and sell goods, and acquire further goods for additional sales. The matching principle requires matching expenses with revenues earned in a reporting period. The matching process for inventories consists of determining the amount that an enterprise should deduct from the cost of goods available for sale during the reporting period and carry forward as inventory. By doing so, it can match properly the resulting cost of goods sold with the revenue for the period. Therefore, the value of inventory at a certain date is the sum of costs attributable to the goods held by a business.

Effect of Inventory Error

An error in the value of the year-end inventory will misrepresent the cost of goods sold, gross profit, net profit, current assets, and equity. Since the ending inventory of a year becomes the beginning inventory for the next year, the error will also affect the profit for the next period. Besides, major errors in inventory values will substantially undermine the credibility of the financial statements. Since inventory is often the largest among the current assets of a business, even a 5 per cent error in inventory valuation can materially misstate the net profit. Sometimes, the effect of an error may be to convert a loss-making company into a profit-making one and *vice versa*.

Suppose a business overstates its Year 1 ending inventory by ₹1,000. The effect of this error is to overstate the profit for Year 1. As a result of the error, the enterprise will overstate Year 2 beginning inventory and understate Year 2 profit, thus offsetting the error. Exhibit 5.1 illustrates the effect of this error.

Learning Objective

LO 3 Analyze the effect of an inventory error.

EXHIBIT 5.1

Effect of Inventory Error on Two Periods

> The over (under) statement of profit resulting from an inventory error is followed by an under (over) statement of profit in the following year.

	Incorrect Ending Inventory		Correct Ending Inventory	
	20X1	20X2	20X1	20X2
Net sales	₹10,000	₹15,000	₹10,000	₹15,000
Cost of goods sold:				
Beginning inventory	2,000	2,500	2,000	1,500
Purchases	8,500	9,500	8,500	9,500
Cost of goods available for sale	10,500	12,000	10,500	11,000
Less Ending inventory	2,500	1,000	1,500	1,000
	8,000	11,000	9,000	10,000
Gross profit	2,000	4,000	1,000	5,000
Operating expenses	400	500	400	500
Net profit	1,600	3,500	600	4,500

A comparison of the correct and incorrect ending inventory columns shows that the overstatement of ₹1,000 in the ending inventory in 20X1 results in an understatement of the cost of goods sold and overstatement in both gross profit and net profit by an equal amount. The error also causes an overstatement of the 20X1 current assets, total assets and equity by ₹1,000. The error reverses in 20X2, resulting in understatement of the 20X2 gross profit and net profit by an equal amount. Note that the sum of the net profit for 20X1 and 20X2 is ₹5,100 and is unaffected by the inventory error because the 20X1 ending inventory becomes the 20X2 beginning inventory. Since the error is fully offset in 20X2, the 20X2 current assets, total assets, and equity are correct.

HANDHOLD 5.1

Inventory Error

At the time of taking physical inventory on December 31, 20X8, Fazal overlooked a barrel of coconut oil costing ₹18,200. The error would understate the 20X8 ending inventory, gross profit, net profit and equity, and overstate the cost of goods sold, each by ₹18,200. When the error reverses in 20X9, it would understate the beginning inventory and cost of goods sold and overstate the 20X9 gross profit and net profit.

TEST YOUR UNDERSTANDING 5.1

Inventory Error

The statement of profit and loss of Sapna Company for three years is as follows:

	20X1	20X2	20X3
Net sales	₹73,000	₹82,000	₹96,000
Cost of goods sold	49,000	51,000	73,000
Gross profit	24,000	31,000	23,000
Operating expenses	9,000	11,000	14,000
Net profit	15,000	20,000	9,000

The accountant recently discovered that the 20X1 ending inventory was overstated by ₹5,000. It was corrected in 20X3. How would this error and its correction affect the company's net profit and equity for each of the three years?

FINANCIAL VIEW

Inventory Retribution

The self-reversing nature of misreporting inventory is a safeguard against managerial opportunism. A manager who overvalues the ending inventory can report higher profit for that year. Unfortunately for him, this will reverse in the following year, thereby bringing down the firm's profit (and his reputation). So his game will be up soon. Managers who have a horizon beyond the current period should stay away from such practices. But the temptation is often irresistible when faced with tough quarterly earnings targets.

A manager may be able to buy time by fiddling with inventory value. The certain reversal of the increase in profit means that the problem will come back soon with a vengeance. He will have to play this game again in the next period, and again, forever. If you don't want to go down a slippery slope, don't take the first step on the slope. If you do, accounting fraud will no longer be a matter of choice; it will become an addiction and eventually a compulsion. Stay away from it.

Investors, tax authorities, and others using financial statements should be concerned about significant unexplained variation from year to year in inventory value relative to a firm's sales.

Determining the Physical Inventory

The first step in proper inventory valuation is to determine the physical inventory that belongs to the business. Under the periodic inventory system, the units on hand must be counted at the end of the reporting period to determine the ending inventory. The actual physical count of all items of inventory is commonly referred to as *taking an inventory*. Although continuous records of inventory transactions are maintained in the perpetual inventory system, physical inventory is also taken to verify the balances shown in the records.

Learning Objective

LO4 Describe how to measure the physical inventory.

Standard inventory taking procedures exist in most organizations. Pre-numbered *inventory tickets*, one for each inventory item, are issued to each department in the company. An employee counts the units (or measures, weighs, etc. as appropriate) and enters in the inventory ticket the description of the item and the number of units counted, and initials the ticket. Another employee verifies the count and initials the inventory ticket. A supervisor makes sure that inventory tickets have been tagged to all the items and may recount some items at random. All the inventory tickets are then collected and sent to the accounting department which verifies that all the pre-numbered tickets issued have been returned. The information on the inventory tickets is summarized on an inventory summary sheet for completion of the physical inventory process.

Goods in Transit

A business must include *goods in transit* in ending inventory if it owns them. The terms of shipment determine whether the buyer or the seller is the legal owner of the goods. Recall from Chapter 4:

- If the terms are *FOB shipping point*, title normally passes to the buyer when the goods are delivered to the carrier (i.e. when the carrier accepts the goods for transport).
- If the terms are *FOB destination*, title normally passes to the buyer when the goods arrive at their destination.[1]

Suppose Bina bought merchandise from Salil, *FOB shipping point*, on March 27. Salil shipped the goods on March 30, but the goods reached Bina on April 2. March 31 is the year end for both Bina and Salil. Should Bina include the goods in her ending inventory? Why or why not? What would your answer be if the terms are *FOB destination*?

HANDHOLD 5.2
FOB Terms

Since the terms are *FOB shipping point*, title passed to Bina as soon as Salil shipped the goods. Therefore, Bina should record the purchase and include the goods in her ending inventory on March 31 as goods in transit. If the terms are *FOB destination*, Salil would continue to own the goods until April 2. Therefore, he should include the goods in his ending inventory on March 31 as goods in transit. In this case, Bina should neither record the purchase nor include the goods in her ending inventory.

Vimal Company shipped merchandise to Divya Company on March 28. The merchandise reached the buyer on April 3. Specify the FOB terms under which the goods can be included in Divya Company's March 31 inventory.

TEST YOUR UNDERSTANDING 5.2
FOB Terms

Goods on Consignment

Recall from Chapter 4 that though the consignee has physical possession of the goods, the consignor owns them. Therefore, goods on consignment are part of the consignor's inventory and should be excluded from the consignee's inventory. Goods transferred to a dealer or distributor for resale, as an agent for the owner of the goods, are similar to goods on consignment. Frequently, materials belonging to a firm are issued to an outside agency to carry out manufacturing processes such as machining or painting. The firm must include these goods in its ending inventory.

---

[1] Other common shipment terms include EXW (ex works), CFR (cost and freight) and CIF (cost, insurance, and freight). The principles discussed in Chapter 4 and in this chapter should be applied to these contracts to determine the legal owner of the goods.

QUICK QUESTION
Title in online sale
You ordered a book online. The store says "free delivery". When does the book become yours?

ONE-MINUTE QUIZ 5.2
Inventory Error

The inventory department of Anima Company included twice an inventory lot costing ₹5,000 while taking the physical inventory on March 31, 20X1. Which of the following statements correctly describes the error?

	Profit for the year ended March 31, 20X1	Profit for the year ended March 31, 20X2
(a)	Overstated	Overstated
(b)	Overstated	Understated
(c)	Understated	Overstated
(d)	Understated	Understated

Inventory Costs

Learning Objective

LO 5 Distinguish between product costs and period expenses.

Pricing the inventory is one of the most contentious topics in accounting. Since the value placed on ending inventory may have a significant effect on reported net profit, users of financial statements, particularly investors, managers, and tax authorities, show a keen interest in inventory pricing. The accountant is faced with conflicting objectives for inventory valuation. Proper income determination is the guiding principle of inventory valuation for financial reporting, while minimizing income tax payable is considered the desirable objective for tax reporting. In this context, it is important to distinguish between product costs and period expenses.

Product Costs

Also known as **inventoriable costs**, these comprise all costs of purchase, costs of conversion, and other costs incurred in bringing the inventories up to their present location and condition.

Costs of purchase The costs of purchase consist of the invoice price including duties and taxes (other than those subsequently recoverable from the tax authorities), freight in, handling and other costs directly attributable to the acquisition of finished goods, materials and services. Trade discounts, purchase discounts, rebates, and other similar items are deducted in determining the costs of purchase.

Costs of conversion The costs of conversion consist of direct manufacturing costs (usually production labour cost) and indirect manufacturing costs, or production overhead. Indirect manufacturing costs include factory depreciation, helpers' wages, supervisors' salaries, factory rent, power, and factory insurance. Both fixed and variable production overheads are included. Fixed production overheads are those indirect costs of production that remain relatively constant regardless of the volume of production, such as depreciation and maintenance of factory buildings and equipment, and the cost of factory management and administration. Variable production overheads are those indirect costs of production that vary directly, or nearly directly, with the volume of production, such as indirect materials and indirect labour.

Period Expenses

Period expenses are expensed in the period in which they are incurred. Expenses incurred in general administration, storage, selling, distribution, research and development, and interest charges are period expenses. Also, losses and abnormal expenses, such as excessive waste, double freight, re-handling costs, penalties, fines, demurrage, detention charges, and idle facility expense, are treated as period expenses. The costs of normal waste (e.g. normal evaporation of petrol) are product costs. Interest charges are treated as product costs in certain situations in which the value of inventory increases with ageing (e.g. wine, timber, and rice) in accordance with Ind AS 23.[2]

Which of the following items will not be part of inventory cost? There may be more than one correct answer.

(a) Research expense.
(b) Factory canteen subsidy.
(c) Depreciation on factory equipment.
(d) Advertisement expense.

Cost Formulas

The prices of most of the merchandise change during the year. So a business buys units of a specific item of inventory at different prices on different dates. When this happens, the accountant has to assume the order in which units have been sold so that the cost of goods available for sale can be allocated between the ending inventory and the cost of goods sold. It is necessary to distinguish between physical flow and cost flow.

Learning Objective

LO 6 Apply the inventory costing methods.

Physical flow refers to the *actual* sequence in which goods are physically used or sold in the operations of the business. In contrast, **cost flow** refers to the association of costs with the *assumed* sequence in which the goods are used or sold. Four methods are commonly used to assign inventory costs:

1. Specific identification;
2. First-in, First-out (FIFO);
3. Last-in, First-out (LIFO); and
4. Weighted-average cost (WAC).

Important Note: *Ind AS 2 and IAS 2 do not permit LIFO, but we describe the method in order to cover the traditional methods. LIFO is permitted in the US.*

We will now see how these methods work using the following data:

		Units	Unit Cost	Total Cost
Jan. 1	Beginning inventory	100	₹2	₹ 200
Mar. 27	Purchase	100	3	300
June 12	Purchase	100	4	400
Sep. 19	Purchase	100	5	500
Nov. 30	Purchase	100	6	600
	Available for sale	500		2,000
	Sold	350		
Dec. 31	Ending inventory	150		

Specific Identification

This method assigns specific costs to each unit sold and each unit on hand. It may be used if the units in the ending inventory can be identified as coming from specific purchases. The specific identification method is particularly suited to inventories of high-value, low-volume items, e.g. jewellery and designer dresses. Each unit in inventory must be affixed with an identification tag. To illustrate, assume that the December 31 inventory consisted of 60 units from the March 27 purchase, 70 units from the June 12 purchase, and 20 units from the September 19 purchase. The cost of the ending inventory is computed as follows:

60 units from the purchase of March 27 at ₹3	₹180
70 units from the purchase of June 12 at ₹4	280
20 units from the purchase of September 19 at ₹5	100
Ending inventory	560

---

[2] The principles for treating borrowing costs as inventoriable costs are the same as those for including them in the cost of acquisition of property, plant and equipment, discussed in Chapter 6.

We compute the cost of goods sold by subtracting the ending inventory from the cost of goods available for sale, as follows:

Cost of goods available for sale..	₹2,000
Deduct Ending inventory	560
Cost of goods sold	1,440

The specific identification method does not involve any assumption about cost flow. It matches the cost to the physical flow of the inventory and eliminates the effect of cost flow assumptions on reported net profit. The method is costly to implement. Besides, it is unlikely to produce better information when the inventory consists of homogeneous or high-volume items.

First-in, First-out (FIFO)

The FIFO method assumes that the first units acquired are the first units sold. Therefore, the cost of the units in the ending inventory is that of the most recent purchases. Although FIFO is a cost flow assumption, physical flow too often follows the first-in, first-out sequence. In our illustration, the cost of the 150 units in the ending inventory would be ₹850, computed as follows:

50 units from the purchase of September 19 at ₹5.....................	₹250
100 units from the purchase of November 30 at ₹6..................	600
Ending inventory...	850

Under FIFO, the cost of goods sold is ₹1,150, computed as follows:

Cost of goods available for sale..	₹2,000
Deduct Ending inventory	850
Cost of goods sold	1,150

Since the cost of the ending inventory under FIFO is based on the most recent purchase prices, the inventory value reflects the conditions prevalent closer to the balance sheet. A major criticism of FIFO is that it leads to an improper matching of costs with revenues since the cost of goods sold is computed on the basis of old prices which are possibly unrealistic. For example, in times of rising prices, the application of FIFO produces the highest amount of net profit although much of this profit results from matching current revenues with low purchase prices paid in the past. Nevertheless, FIFO is one of the popular inventory costing methods.

Last-in, First-out (LIFO)

The LIFO method assumes that the last units acquired are the first units sold. Therefore, the cost of the units in the ending inventory is that of the earliest purchases. Under LIFO, the cost of the 150 units in the ending inventory would be ₹350, computed as follows:

100 units from the inventory on January 1 at ₹2......................	₹200
50 units from the purchase of March 27 at ₹3	150
Ending inventory...	350

The cost of goods sold is ₹1,650, computed as follows:

Cost of goods available for sale..	₹2,000
Deduct Ending inventory	350
Cost of goods sold	1,650

LIFO ensures that the current revenues are matched with the most recent purchase prices, thus resulting in realistic reported profits. Often, the LIFO cost of goods sold will be a good approximation of the current cost of the units sold. The chief disadvantage of LIFO is that the balance sheet value of inventories may be dated and unrealistic. *LIFO is not permitted in India.*

Weighted-average Cost (WAC)

The WAC method assumes that the goods available for sale are homogeneous. Average cost is computed by dividing the cost of goods available for sale, which consists of the cost of the beginning inventory and all purchases, by the number of units available for sale. The weighted-average unit cost, which results from this computation, is applied to the units in the ending inventory. The average may be calculated on a periodic basis, or as each additional shipment is received, depending upon the circumstances of the entity. In our illustration, the unit cost under this method would be ₹4, computed as follows:

Cost of goods available for sale..	₹2,000
Number of units available for sale..	500
Weighted-average unit cost...	4
Ending inventory: 150 units @ ₹4..	600

The cost of goods sold is ₹1,400, computed as follows:

Cost of goods available for sale..	₹2,000
Deduct Ending inventory	600
Cost of goods sold...	1,400

WAC is appropriate when the inventory units involved are homogeneous or when it is difficult to make a cost flow assumption. Besides, the cost figure for the ending inventory reported under this method is influenced by all the purchase prices paid during the year and thus evens out the effect of price increases and decreases on ending inventory value. The major criticism of WAC is that it assigns no more importance to current prices than to prices paid several months ago.

Which of the following statements about the specific identification method is correct? There may be more than one correct answer.

(a) It is appropriate for items that are produced for a specific customer order.
(b) It is appropriate for items that are bought for a specific customer order.
(c) It does not require any cost flow assumption.
(d) If the items are interchangeable, it can be used to select items so as to obtain a predetermined profit.

ONE-MINUTE QUIZ 5.4
Specific Identification

Comparing Alternative Inventory Costing Methods

Of the above four most common methods for costing inventory, the specific identification method is based on actual costs, whereas the other three methods are based on cost flow assumptions. Exhibit 5.2 presents a comparison of the effects of the methods on the firm's financial statements. We assume sales of 350 units at ₹10 each.

Profit differs systematically depending on the inventory valuation method.				
	Specific Identification	First-in, First-out (FIFO)	Last-in, First-out (LIFO)	Weighted-Average Cost (WAC)
Sales	₹3,500	₹3,500	₹3,500	₹3,500
Cost of goods sold............................				
Beginning inventory......................	200	200	200	200
Purchases.....................................	1,800	1,800	1,800	1,800
Cost of goods available for sale..	2,000	2,000	2,000	2,000
Deduct Ending inventory..............	560	850	350	600
	1,440	1,150	1,650	1,400
Gross profit	2,060	2,350	1,850	2,100

EXHIBIT 5.2
Effect of Inventory Method on Profit

From this illustration, it is clear that LIFO reports the lowest gross profit in a period of rising prices because it charges the highest costs to the goods sold. In contrast, FIFO reports the highest gross profit, because it charges the lowest costs to the goods sold. The results will be reversed in a period of falling prices. WAC, by avoiding the extremes of FIFO and LIFO, produces a gross profit somewhere between the two. It is difficult to generalize about specific identification because the results depend on the prices paid for the lots selected for sale. In a period of constant prices, the four methods will produce identical results. We now summarize in the following table the effects of FIFO, LIFO and WAC on ending inventory, the cost of goods sold, and gross profit:

Prices	Ending Inventory	Cost of Goods Sold	Gross Profit
Increasing	FIFO > WAC > LIFO	LIFO > WAC > FIFO	FIFO > WAC > LIFO
Constant	FIFO = WAC = LIFO	FIFO = WAC = LIFO	FIFO = WAC = LIFO
Decreasing	LIFO > WAC > FIFO	FIFO > WAC > LIFO	LIFO > WAC > FIFO

Which method should a business select? The answer depends on many factors, such as the effect of each method on the financial statements and income tax. A basic problem in determining the "best" inventory formula is that the ending inventory value affects both the balance sheet and the statement of profit and loss. The problem is aggravated when there is a prolonged period of increasing or decreasing prices.

Here is a summary of the methods:

- FIFO inventory value is more realistic since it is closer to current cost, but it produces a net profit unrelated to current input costs.
- LIFO does a fair job of matching current selling prices and cost of goods sold, which is closer to current replacement costs, but often produces an outdated inventory value.
- Both LIFO and WAC allow a business to manipulate net profit by changing the timing of additional purchases.

The use of LIFO in a period of rising prices produces a lower net profit, leading to a lower income tax expense and more cash availability for investment purposes. **LIFO liquidation** occurs when the year-end inventory quantity falls below the beginning level. In that event, the cost of goods sold will be charged the ridiculously low prices paid many years ago, and the business will be forced to pay income tax on the difference between the current purchase price and the old LIFO cost. Therefore, a business using LIFO must arrange for timely purchases to maintain the inventory level. Sometimes, it may lead to unnecessary inventory accumulation.

For income tax purposes, a business is free to adopt any method of inventory valuation acceptable for accounting. Once adopted, the method must be followed consistently.

Inventory Profits

It is clear from Exhibit 5.2 that LIFO reports the lowest profit in a period of inflation. Even so, it may still fall short of recovering the current cost of goods sold. Continuing with the illustration, assume that the current replacement cost is ₹8 per unit. If the company is to replace the goods sold during the year at this price, its profit is only ₹2 (i.e. ₹10 – ₹8) for every unit sold and the real gross profit is ₹700; LIFO reports an inventory profit of ₹1,150 (i.e. ₹1,850 – ₹700). As you would have thought, FIFO and WAC report much larger fictitious inventory profits of ₹1,650 (i.e. ₹2,350 – ₹700) and ₹1,400 (₹2,100 – ₹700), respectively. LIFO reports the lowest inventory profit because the LIFO cost of goods sold is based on the latest purchase prices. Since inventory profits result purely from inflation, they must be retained and reinvested in inventory. If they are distributed as taxes and dividends, there will be a reduction in capital, and the firm will run short of cash for inventory purchases.

Smart Bikes has been following FIFO since inception. Lately, the price of fibre glass-reinforced plastic, an important raw material for the company's products, has been fluctuating. What should be the company's inventory costing method?

DISCUSSION QUESTION 5.1

....

....

....

Inventory Valuation

Cost is the primary basis for valuation of inventory. However, in certain circumstances, it may be more appropriate to report inventory at an amount below cost. When the value of inventory declines by reason of damage, deterioration, obsolescence, or fall in market prices, a loss occurs. In these circumstances, we need to depart from the cost basis, and recognize the loss by writing down the ending inventory to market. This is the **lower-of-cost-or-market (LCM) principle**: Inventories should be valued at the lower of cost and net realisable value. An enterprise holds inventories for eventual conversion into cash. The practice of writing inventories down below cost is consistent with the view that assets should not be carried in excess of amounts expected to be realized from their sale or use.

Learning Objective

LO 7 Explain the lower-of-cost-or-market principle of inventory valuation.

The LCM principle provides a practical means of measuring value and determining the loss to be recognized in a reporting period. Cost is computed using a cost formula. *Market* means **net realizable value** (NRV), i.e. the normal selling price less the estimated costs of completing and selling the inventory item. Normally, we should write down inventories to net realizable value item by item. However, in some circumstances, it may be appropriate to group similar or related items. In the latter case, we compare the total cost and the total market value for each category of items. Here, the category should consist of items relating to a product line which have similar purposes or end uses. Aggregate classification such as finished goods or all the inventories is not acceptable. Exhibit 5.3 illustrates the application of the LCM principle using the two approaches.

	Cost	Market	Lower of Cost or Market	
			Item-by-item	*Group*
Group I				
Item 470	₹ 1,400	₹ 1,340	₹ 1,340	
492	1,970	1,990	1,970	
612	4,650	3,720	3,720	
688	6,380	7,040	6,380	
	14,400	14,090	13,410	₹14,090
Group II				
Item 723	₹4,920	₹5,230	₹4,920	
798	2,520	2,610	2,520	
841	3,110	2,930	2,930	
876	5,790	6,140	5,790	
	16,340	16,910	16,160	16,340
Inventory at the lower of cost or market			29,570	30,430

We can apply the LCM Principle to groups of items in some circumstances.

EXHIBIT 5.3
Applying the Lower-of-Cost-or-Market Principle

Writing down inventories to net realizable value is a principle rather than a rule. Application of the LCM principle calls for judgment so as to ensure that the write-downs do not result in an understatement of income, deliberately or otherwise. For example, normal quantities of raw materials and components held for use in production are not written down below cost if the finished goods are expected to be sold at or above the cost incurred. Similarly, inventory of maintenance supplies and consumable stores is ordinarily valued at cost. Also, a temporary decline in selling prices may not warrant the recognition of a loss. The enterprise should review the net realizable value at each reporting date. The write-down is reversed to the extent of an increase in net realizable value. In other words, the reversal is limited to the amount of the original write-down.

HANDHOLD 5.3
Lower of Cost or Market

Real View sells TV sets. The following information relates to one of the models in inventory, T24, as at March 31: cost per accounting records, ₹18,010; estimated selling price, ₹18,200; estimated selling expense, ₹230. Net realizable value is ₹17,970, calculated as: estimated selling price, ₹18,200 – estimated selling expense, ₹230. This is lower than the cost (₹18,010). Applying the LCM principle, we get an inventory value of ₹17,970.

TEST YOUR UNDERSTANDING 5.3
Lower of Cost or Market

In 20X7, Premier Technology paid ₹76,000 for a computer, shown in the books at ₹74,500 on March 31, 20X8. In late March 20X9, the computer was being sold at ₹70,000. Sales commission of 5 per cent is payable on sale, and delivery expense is estimated to be ₹500. How much, if any, should the company write down on March 31, 20X9?

The LCM principle doesn't apply to commodity broker-traders, i.e. those who buy or sell comodities for others or on their own account. They measure their inventories at fair value less costs to sell. Thus, any expected profit on their inventories is not deducted for inventory valuation.

Conservatism, Neutrality, and Prudence

Learning Objective

LO 8 Appreciate the role of conservatism, neutrality, and prudence in financial reporting.

Some cite **conservatism** in support of arbitrary write-downs below cost. This idea is sometimes expressed simplistically as "recognize all losses, but anticipate no profits". It was widely applied in the early days of accounting when lenders were the principal users of financial statements. In those days, lending decisions were made mainly on the basis of the value of assets that would be available to the lenders if the borrower defaulted. Lenders face an asymmetric loss function: while they are adversely affected by their borrowers' losses, they do not benefit from their gains. Naturally, they prefer understatement of the value of the borrower's assets to overstatement. This provided an economic logic for the practice.

In recent times, since shareholders have increasingly become the focus of financial reporting, the statement of profit and loss has emerged as the more important statement. If the ending inventory valued at below cost is sold in the next period at or above cost, the write-down understates the profit for the first period and overstates the profit for the second period. As a result, there will be distortion in reporting over time. **Neutrality**, a characteristic that makes financial statements useful, means that the information contained in financial statements must be free from bias, upward or downward. Financial statements should not aim at producing a predetermined result or outcome. Biased information will not be reliable. Neutrality is a principal qualitative characteristic of financial statements.

As a result, accountants interpret conservatism as **prudence**: a cautious attitude in making assumptions, judgments, and estimates under conditions of uncertainty such that assets or income are not overstated and liabilities or expenses are not understated. Prudence underlies accounting decisions in matters such as expected credit losses, probable useful life of plant and equipment items, product warranty claims, life expectancy of employees entitled to a pension, and tax treatment of contentious items. However, deliberate understatement of assets or income or deliberate overstatement of liabilities or expenses is not acceptable, as this would affect the reliability of financial statements.

That said, we should be aware that conservatism or prudence continues to have an important economic role in financial reporting. The managers of a company know more about the company's problems and prospects than its shareholders. When their remuneration or reappointment is related to the company's profit, they have reason to be forthcoming in sharing good news about the company's performance or prospects but may hold back bad news. As a result, accountants and shareholders require early recognition of losses, mitigating information asymmetry to an extent. Requiring managers to report losses promptly would discourage them from taking up unprofitable projects. This results in better monitoring of managers' actions by boards, investors, and analysts. Thus, timely recognition of losses is more than just good accounting; it is an important corporate governance mechanism. As you can see, conservatism in financial reporting is an important mechanism to address the moral hazard problem discussed in Chapter 1.

RESEARCH INSIGHT
Conservatism

Accounting conservatism can be viewed as asymmetric timeliness in news recognition. This means that accountants tend to report unfavourable information quickly, but delay reporting favourable information. The level of assurance required for favourable information is of a much higher order. Empirical evidence from research by Professor Sudipta Basu suggests that the timeliness of earnings is asymmetrically greater for "bad news" than for "good news" firms, indicating that firms recognize "bad news" more quickly than "good news."[3] This is in line with the general view that accountants are ready to acknowledge losses quickly, but are slow to recognize gains. The apparent lack of even-handedness in treating gains and losses is made possible by the admissibility of conservative methods and estimates in GAAP.

Comparability

Comparability (or consistency) requires the application of the same accounting policies from one reporting period to the next. If an enterprise could freely change its accounting policies, the profits would not be comparable over time. The comparability requirement safeguards users of financial statements against managers' arbitrary and opportunistic measurement and presentation. It enables investors, creditors, and other users to compare meaningfully the financial statements of an enterprise over time in order to identify trends in its financial position and performance. You have seen in Exhibit 5.2 how different inventory methods can produce different profit numbers. Further, frequent accounting changes would destroy the credibility of an enterprise's financial reports and adversely affect the reputation of its management.

Learning Objective

LO 9 Explain the significance of comparability.

While accountants frown on frequent and arbitrary changes in accounting methods, the comparability requirement does not come in the way of a change for better financial reporting. An enterprise should change an accounting policy only if the change (a) is required by an Ind AS; or (b) results in the financial statements providing reliable and more relevant information about the effects of transactions, other events or conditions on an enterprise's financial position, financial performance or cash flows.

Comparability is so important that it is a principal qualitative characteristic of financial statements. The effect of an accounting policy change on profit and the reasons for the change should be disclosed. Users of financial statements must study the footnotes carefully to understand the inventory method used and the effect of any accounting changes on profit in order to make meaningful comparisons. The need for comparability does not mean mere uniformity and should not be allowed to become an impediment to the introduction of improved accounting standards or the provision of high quality information.

Estimating Inventory Value

In the periodic inventory system, physical inventory must be taken to determine the ending inventory value. Since frequent inventory-taking disrupts normal operations and involves considerable expense, a physical inventory is usually taken at the end of the reporting period. However, management often needs to prepare quarterly or half-yearly financial statements. Besides, there are occasions when physical inventory cannot be taken and must be estimated – for instance, when the inventory has been destroyed in a fire. Estimates are also needed for insurance claims. Estimation procedures, if they are reasonable, are also a useful check on physical inventory.

Learning Objective

LO 10 Estimate the value of inventory by the retail inventory and standard cost methods.

---

[3] S. Basu, The conservatism principle and the asymmetric timeliness of earnings, *Journal of Accounting and Economics*, December 1997.

Two commonly used estimation techniques are:

- Retail inventory method; and
- Standard cost method.

Retail Inventory Method

Large merchandising firms such as supermarkets use the **retail inventory method**. They carry a large number of different items which are marked with selling prices. To determine the cost of the items in inventory, it is necessary to look up the purchase invoices. This is a formidable task for most of them. The retail inventory method helps in estimating the ending inventory value. To use this method, it is necessary to maintain records of the beginning inventory and purchases made during the period both at cost and at retail. "At retail" means the sticker prices of the inventory items.

We estimate the ending inventory as follows:

1. Compute the amount of goods available for sale both at cost and at retail.
2. Divide the goods available for sale at cost by the goods available at retail to obtain the ratio of cost to retail.
3. Deduct sales from goods available for sale at retail to determine the ending inventory at retail.
4. Multiply the ending inventory at retail by the ratio of cost to retail to convert the inventory into cost.

HANDHOLD 5.4
Retail Inventory Method

Consider the following illustration of the retail inventory method:

	At Cost	At Retail	
Beginning inventory	₹ 2,500	₹ 3,000	
Net purchases	11,500	14,500	
Goods available sale	14,000	17,500	**Step 1**
Ratio of cost to retail: 14,000/17,500 = 0.8			**Step 2**
Less Net sales		13,000	
Estimated ending inventory at retail		4,500	**Step 3**
Estimated ending inventory at cost (₹4,500 × 0.8)	3,600		**Step 4**

The retail inventory method assumes that the ending inventory consists of the same mix of goods as contained in the goods available for sale and that the selling prices of merchandise originally established do not change. In practice, the composition of inventory often varies during a period. Also, the selling prices of many items change, because of special rebates or increases in market prices. Despite these difficulties, the retail inventory method is considered a satisfactory one, and may be used to convert a physical inventory taken at retail to a cost amount. The retail method is acceptable "if the results approximate cost".

TEST YOUR UNDERSTANDING 5.4
Retail Inventory Method

The following information is available from the records of Joseph Company:

	At Cost	At Retail
Beginning inventory	₹ 700	₹ 900
Purchases	3,400	5,300
Purchase returns and allowances	100	200
Sales		4,700
Sales returns and allowances		500

Estimate the company's ending inventory at cost using the retail inventory method. Suppose the physical year-end inventory at retail was ₹1,620. What is the estimated cost of the inventory lost through shoplifting and other causes?

The **gross profit method** is a variant of the retail inventory method. It works on the assumption that the percentage of gross profit to net sales remains approximately the same from one period to another. It is not normally acceptable for financial reporting because it provides only an estimate, but it is useful in estimating inventory lost or destroyed by fire, flood or theft, when proper inventory records are not available or have been destroyed. The income tax and the sales tax authorities use this method to detect suppression of revenue.

Under the gross profit method, we estimate the amount of ending inventory as follows:

1. Compute the cost of goods available for sale.
2. Estimate the cost of goods sold by deducting the estimated gross profit from sales.
3. Deduct the estimated cost of goods sold from the cost of goods available for sale to arrive at the estimated ending inventory.

The following illustration explains the gross profit method:

HANDHOLD 5.5
Gross Profit Method

Beginning inventory		₹ 300
Net purchases		2,100
Cost of goods available for sale		2,400
Less Estimated cost of goods sold		
Net sales	₹3,000	
Less Estimated gross profit, 25% (assumed)	750	
Estimated cost of goods sold		2,250
Estimated cost of ending inventory		150

Mohan Rao's video store was totally destroyed in a fire that broke out in the morning of November 4. The following information for the period July 1 to November 3 was available:

TEST YOUR UNDERSTANDING 5.5
Gross Profit Method

Beginning inventory at cost, July 1	₹ 1200
Purchases	12,300
Purchase returns and allowances	700
Freight in	1,200
Sales	25,300
Sales returns and allowances	1,300

Estimate the cost of inventory lost assuming that Mohan Rao's gross margin was 60 per cent.

Your classmate, Ritika, is now an assistant commissioner of income tax. She recently raided a trader in Delhi on information that he was evading tax. How can she use the gross profit method to detect tax evasion?

DISCUSSION QUESTION 5.2

....

....

....

Standard Cost Method

The **standard cost method** uses a predetermined cost of making a product. Standard costs are based on the standards for material consumption and prices, labour efficiency and wage rates, and expected level of operations laid down by the management. They are reviewed and revised, as appropriate. These are used primarily for control of operational costs in management accounting. The use of standard costs results in savings in record-keeping costs and evens out wide fluctuations in the cost of goods sold.

ONE-MINUTE QUIZ 5.5
Estimating Inventory
Value

The following information is for a retail store for the year 20XX.

	At Cost	At Retail
Beginning inventory	₹ 20,000	₹ 30,000
Purchases	100,000	170,000

The net sales for the year is ₹150,000. What is the estimated inventory value at the end of the year?
- (a) ₹20,000.
- (b) ₹30,000.
- (c) ₹40,000.
- (d) ₹50,000.

Perpetual Inventory System

Learning Objective

LO 11 Explain the perpetual inventory system.

So far, the discussion of inventories has focused on the periodic inventory system. Under this system, we record purchases and determine the cost of goods sold at the end of a reporting period when a physical inventory is taken. The main disadvantage of the system is the lack of real-time information about inventory levels. Management often needs up-to-the-minute information to respond quickly to customers' enquiries, avoid shortages, and reduce interest and other expenses associated with carrying inventory.

The **perpetual inventory system** overcomes the problems of periodic inventory. Under this system, an enterprise maintains a continuous record of all purchases and sales of merchandise, resulting in constant updating of the amount of inventory on hand. With this information, it can carry out many tasks such as the following:

1. Promptly answer questions from customers and salespersons about the availability of an item.
2. Record merchandise in real time and thus avoid running out of stock.
3. Calculate the cost of goods sold and the related profit for each sale.

Not long ago, only companies that sold a limited range of products used the perpetual inventory system because the cost and effort of maintaining the system were too high for most types of businesses. However, with the availability of computing and data storage services at relatively low costs, many firms are switching to the perpetual inventory system.

Recording Accounting Entries

The perpetual inventory system updates the merchandise inventory account after each purchase and sale. We debit merchandise inventory for purchases and inward freight and credit the account for purchase returns and discounts. So, in the perpetual inventory system, we don't need accounts such as purchases, purchase returns and allowances, and freight in. For example, assume that a stationer purchases pens at ₹20 each and sells them at ₹25 each. He began the current period with six pens, which cost a total of ₹120. Exhibit 5.4 shows some typical entries made under periodic and perpetual inventory systems.

EXHIBIT 5.4
Accounting Entries under Periodic and Perpetual Inventory Systems

> Under the perpetual inventory system, entries record every purchase and sale, but under the periodic system, the updating takes place at the year end.

Periodic			Perpetual		
1. *Purchased on credit 20 pens at ₹20 each:*					
Purchases....................................	400		Merchandise Inventory.........................	400	
Trade Payables.............................		400	Trade Payables.............................		400
2. *Sold 12 pens for ₹300 cash:*					
Cash..	300		Cash..	300	

Sales		300	Sales		300
			Cost of Goods Sold	240	
			Merchandise Inventory		240
3. *Returned four pens to supplier:*					
Trade Payables	80		Trade Payables	80	
Purchase Return and Allowances		80	Merchandise Inventory		80
4. *Paid supplier in full:*					
Trade Payables	320		Trade Payables	320	
Cash		320	Cash		320
5. *Closing entries:*					
Merchandise Inventory (Ending)	200		Statement of Profit and Loss	240	
Sales	300		Cost of Goods Sold		240
Purchase Returns and Allowances	80				
Statement of Profit and Loss		580	Sales	300	
			Statement of Profit and Loss		300
Statement of Profit and Loss	520				
Merchandise Inventory (Beginning)		120			
Purchases		400			

In sum, the perpetual inventory system:

- Does not require a purchases account or a purchase return and allowances account. Here, purchases and returns and allowances are recorded in the merchandise inventory account.
- Uses a cost of goods sold account to record the cost of the merchandise sold.
- Requires no entry to record the ending inventory since a continuous record of inventory is available. The closing entries simply transfer the balance in the cost of goods sold account to the statement of profit and loss.

Entries to record sales and payment to the supplier are identical under the two systems. Also, under both inventory systems, the sales account must be closed.

Maintaining Perpetual Inventory Records

When there are many items in inventory, the merchandise inventory account serves as a control account for a subsidiary inventory ledger, also known as the **priced stores ledger**. An individual record is maintained for each item in inventory in the inventory ledger. The record is kept on a card in a manual system and in a computer file in an electronic system. In either case, the record for each item shows the number of units and cost of each purchase, the number of units and cost of each sale, and the resulting balance of inventory on hand. Exhibit 5.5 gives an example of a perpetual inventory record.

EXHIBIT 5.5
Perpetual Inventory Record, FIFO

Under FIFO, the oldest lot is charged out first. Lot-wise record-keeping is necessary.

Item Writing pad		*Location Bin 3*			*Maximum 75*			*Minimum 10*	
		Purchased			**Sold**			**Balance**	
Date	***Units***	***Cost***	***Total***	***Units***	***Cost***	***Total***	***Units***	***Cost***	***Total***
July 1							25	₹9	₹225
9	50	₹12	₹600				25	9	
							50	12	825
17				15	₹9	₹135	10	9	
							50	12	690
28				10	9	90			
				20	12	240	30	12	360

The method of inventory costing in Exhibit 5.5 is FIFO. Under LIFO, the cost of 15 writing pads sold on July 17 would be ₹180, in contrast to the FIFO figure of ₹135. The LIFO cost of the 30 writing pads sold on July 28 would be ₹360, in comparison to the FIFO cost of ₹330. The ending inventory is ₹360 under FIFO.

QUICK QUESTION
LIFO

In Exhibit 5.5, what would be the ending inventory value under LIFO?

Internal Control and Perpetual Inventory System

The perpetual inventory system enhances control over inventories. It helps prevent both stock-out and excessive inventories. Since it is possible to take a physical inventory at any time, shortages can be detected and investigated quickly.

DISCUSSION QUESTION 5.3

Realtime, an online store, has received customer complaints that when they ordered mobile phones, they received bricks instead. How should the company handle the complaints?

....

....

....

Manufacturing Costs

Learning Objective

LO 12 Explain the perpetual inventory system.

A merchandising organization has just one item of inventory: merchandise inventory. However, a manufacturing organization has several kinds of inventory, such as raw materials, work in progress, finished goods, consumable stores and spare parts, and packing materials. For a manufacturing organization, the cost of goods available for sale is the sum of the beginning inventory of finished goods and the cost of goods manufactured during the period. The cost of goods sold equals cost of goods available for sale minus the ending inventory of finished goods. The cost of goods manufactured is not published. Exhibit 5.6 shows an example of the complete cost of goods sold statement.

EXHIBIT 5.6
Cost of Goods Sold for a Manufacturing Organization

> Manufacturing costs consist of direct costs, such as materials and labour, and indirect costs, such as power and depreciation.

VIKRAM COMPANY
Statement of Cost of Goods Sold
For the year ended March 31, 20X8

Cost of goods manufactured

Raw materials inventory, March 31, 20X7			₹ 2,730
Purchases		₹14,280	
Deduct Purchase returns and allowances	₹1,040		
Purchase discounts	130	1,170	
Net purchases		13,110	
Add Freight in		1,540	
Net cost of purchases			14,650
Raw materials available for use			17,380
Deduct Raw materials inventory, March 31, 20X8			2,410
Raw materials consumed			14,970
Add Direct labour			7,690
Manufacturing overhead			
Indirect labour		2,310	
Supervisors' salaries		4,780	
Factory supplies		1,470	
Power and fuel		3,120	
Factory insurance		760	
Depreciation on plant and factory building		1,670	
Tooling expense		950	
Add Manufacturing overhead for the period			15,060

Total manufacturing costs for the period	37,720
Add Work in progress inventory, March 31, 20X7	2,590
Total manufacturing costs to account..	40,310
Deduct Work in progress inventory, March 31, 20X8	2,370
Cost of goods manufactured (or cost of production)............................	37,940

Cost of goods sold

Finished goods inventory, March 31, 20X7	4,580
Add Cost of goods manufactured..	37,940
Cost of goods available for sale...	42,520
Deduct Finished goods inventory, March 31, 20X8.............................	3,830
Cost of goods sold..	38,690

Basappa Company had a finished goods inventory of ₹2,310 at the beginning of 20X1. During the year, it manufactured goods costing ₹17,680. At the end of the year, its finished goods inventory totalled ₹1,870. Compute the company's cost of goods sold for 20X1.

TEST YOUR UNDERSTANDING 5.6
Computing Cost of Goods Sold

Financial Analysis of Inventories

A business needs inventories to meet day-to-day operating needs. Keeping some inventory is often inevitable given purchasing lead times and unexpected delays in the arrival of materials. Production stoppages and inability to meet customer requests could result if adequate inventories are not kept. However, investment in inventories represents idle funds on which a business does not earn any profit. Therefore, it is necessary to optimize inventory levels. **Inventory turnover** is a measure of the efficiency of inventory management. It is computed as follows:

Learning Objective

LO 13 Evaluate the efficiency of inventory management using financial analysis.

$$\text{Inventory turnover} = \frac{\text{Cost of goods sold}}{(\text{Beginning inventories} + \text{Ending inventories})/2}$$

Since the cost of goods sold is not reported in the financial statements, we will take it as the sum of all costs excluding interest charges and income tax.

To illustrate, assume the following data for Bhava Company:

Cost of goods sold...	₹24,000
Beginning inventories	1,000
Ending inventories..	3,000

$$\text{Inventory turnover} = \frac{24,000}{2,000} = 12 \text{ times}$$

This means that the inventories have been *turned over* or rotated 12 times during the period. In other words, the company held inventories, on average, for one month. The average holding period is computed as:

$$\text{Average holding period} = \frac{1}{\text{Inventory turnover}} \times 360$$

Inventory turnover of 12 times implies average inventory holding of one month, calculated as follows:

$$\text{Average holding period} = \frac{1}{12} \times 360 = 30 \text{ days}$$

If the cost of goods sold is not available, net sales may be used.

Marina Company's cost of goods sold for the current year is ₹5,700. The company's beginning and ending inventories are, respectively, ₹1,200 and ₹2,600. On average, for how long did the company hold inventories during the year?

TEST YOUR UNDERSTANDING 5.7
Inventory Turnover

A low holding period (or high inventory turnover) is generally an indicator of efficient inventory management, since it implies rapid movement of merchandise leading to lower investment in inventory. Conversely, a high holding period (or low inventory turnover) indicates poor management of inventory since it implies a higher investment in inventory than necessary. The average holding period for an enterprise may be compared with its past experience and with the industry average.

FINANCIAL VIEW
Maruti Suzuki's
Inventory Management

Maruti Suzuki is a leading passenger car maker in India. The company depends heavily on its suppliers, since 80 per cent of the car by value is procured in the form of components and raw material. So efficient inventory management is crucial to the company's operations and financial performance. Maruti's 2016 annual report claims that the company "continued its partnership with suppliers in value analysis/value enhancement (VA/VE) projects. Joint efforts were also made in yield improvement. Along with this, the Company worked on the localisation of parts imported by vendors to mitigate risk arising out of foreign exchange exposure and to bring down input cost." Let's see how we can evaluate this claim using information available in the financial statements. Maruti's inventories of components and raw materials were ₹17,317 million in 2016 and ₹13,189 million in 2015. The cost of material consumed was ₹362,007 million in 2016. The inventory turnover was 24 times, equivalent to 15 days' consumption being carried in inventories. How does Maruti manage with such a low inventory? Can other manufacturers follow Maruti's example?

Inventory management is a lot more than just reducing inventories. Good suppliers who deliver quality parts in time at a reasonable cost are critical. It involves educating and monitoring vendors, giving them technical and managerial support, developing and sustaining long-term relationships and paying them fair prices on time. This often means sticking with the same vendors over a long period. As a result, both Maruti and its vendors benefit over the long term. These are the features of a JIT (just-in-time) inventory system. Accountants and bankers think of inventories as assets. The fact is that high inventory levels usually hide serious problems in quality, production process, labour, transportation, and vendors. While some inventory is often unavoidable, especially in Indian conditions, high inventories are financially inefficient and not an assurance of ready availability of materials and parts. Interestingly, Maruti's inventory holding of 11 days in 2015 was better than in 2016.

QUICK QUESTION
Replacement cost

Is replacement cost better for capturing the effect of inflation on profit?

Managing the Operating Cycle

Learning Objective

LO 14 Understand the importance of managing the operating cycle.

The operating cycle is the continual conversion of cash into inventories, then into receivables and back into cash in the normal course of business. A firm buys inventories on credit or for cash, sells them on credit or for cash, collects cash from its customers, and pays its suppliers. The operating cycle time is the time it takes to get back cash.

An efficient business buys inventories when needed, converts them into receivables by smart selling, collects cash from its customers by laying down credit standards and ensuring timely payment, and manages to get a long credit period from its suppliers. The shorter the length of a firm's operating cycle, the greater the firm's efficiency in managing its current assets (receivables and inventories). The length of the operating cycle is a measure of how fast a business gets back its cash. It indicates the enterprise's efficiency in selling, collecting, and paying. The operating cycle enables us to integrate our understanding of receivables and inventories, the two major current asset items. The other important component is payables, which we will see in Chapter 10.

Figure 5.1 illustrates the operating cycle under different conditions. Figure 5.1(a) depicts a firm that has cash purchases and cash sales. The operating cycle time is the inventory holding period, i.e. the time it takes to sell the inventories. The emphasis is on selling the goods quickly. This is typical of most small businesses such as roadside vendors of fruits, vegetables, and fish. Their inventory holding period is usually zero, i.e. they sell the goods the same day. Of course, the vendors do not worry about collections since they sell for cash.

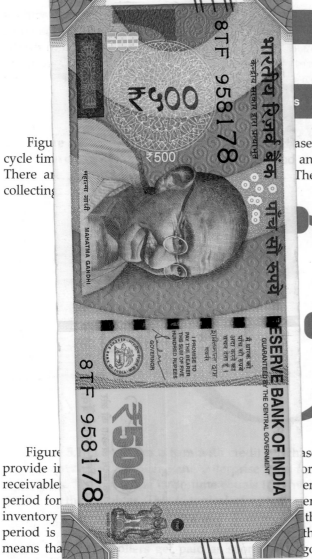

Figure 5.1(a)
OPERATING CYCLE: CASH PURCHASES AND CASH SALES

Figu...........ases and credit sales. Here, the operating cycle tim............and the credit period for the receivables. There ar............They need to worry about selling and collecting...

Figure 5.1(b)
OPERATING CYCLE: CASH PURCHASES AND CREDIT SALES

Figure...........ases and cash sales. While the suppliers provide i............or cash. So there are payables, but no receivable............entory holding period minus the credit period for............ermarkets. They should work on rapid inventory............their suppliers. If the suppliers' credit period is............the operating cycle time is zero. This means tha............goods are sold; so the enterprise does not use its cash for financing current assets. In exceptional cases, it may pay its suppliers after getting cash from sales; here the cycle time would be *negative*.[4]

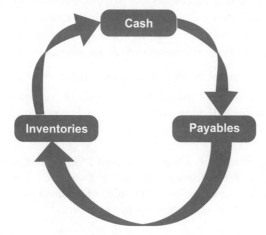

Figure 5.1(c)
OPERATING CYCLE: PURCHASES AND CASH SALES

---

[4] A *negative* operating cycle is possible. For example, Dell, the computer manufacturer, could manage that by taking advance payments from customers and delaying payments to suppliers.

Figure 5.1(d) describes a firm with credit purchases and credit sales. The enterprise's suppliers provide inventory financing and the enterprise provides credit to its customers. The operating cycle time equals the inventory holding period plus the credit period for the receivables minus the credit period for the payables. This is typical of most manufacturing and service businesses. The enterprise's bargaining power with both its customers and suppliers and its selling efficiency will determine the cycle time in this case.

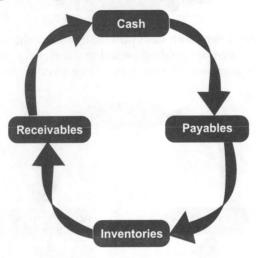

Figure 5.1(d)
OPERATING CYCLE: CREDIT PURCHASES AND CREDIT SALES

ONE-MINUTE QUIZ 5.6
Calculating the Operating Cycle

Harminder Company had 30 days' sales in inventories and 40 days' sales in receivables. What was the length of the company's operating cycle?
(a) 30 days.
(b) 35 days.
(c) 40 days.
(d) 70 days.

FORENSIC CORNER
Inventory Fraud

Inventory is the most common asset overstated, according to a study by the Committee of Sponsoring Organizations, an ethics and advocacy group.[5] Common techniques of overstatement of inventories include the following:

- Improper increase in physical inventory counts (e.g. double-counting items, adding page totals several times).
- Non-existent in-transit items included in inventories.
- Items received on consignment or other agency terms included in inventories.
- Credit purchases included in inventories but payables not recorded.
- Obsolete materials and parts not written off or written down.
- Inventory records altered when physical stocks are less than inventories.
- Items sold (e.g. bill-and-hold) not removed from inventory records.

Consider these examples of known or alleged accounting fraud.

- *Logitech:* Failing to write down the value of inventory of parts made for Revue, a device to allow internet browsing and video streaming to avoid reporting the effect of slowing sales, causing a $30.7 million, or more than 27 per cent, overstatement of operating income in fiscal 2011.
- *Phar-Mor:* Inflating inventories to hide losses from selling goods at less than purchase prices by using fake invoices for purchases, but omitted to accrue a liability and double-counted inventories. The auditors observed inventory only in four stores out of 300 and they informed *Phar-Mor* in advance which stores they would visit.

---

[5] Committee of Sponsoring Organizations, Fraudulent Financial Reporting 1998–2007: An Analysis of U.S. Public Companies, Mark S. Beasley, Joseph V. Carcello, Dana R. Hermanson and Terry L. Neal, May 2010.

Red flags signalling inventory fraud:

- A big increase in inventories relative to earlier periods.
- A high proportion of old inventories.
- Unusually low inventory turnover.
- Discrepancies in physical count.

We'll now see how companies apply the principles of inventory accounting.

Inventories	Explanation
• Raw materials, components, construction materials, stores, spares and loose tools are considered to be realisable at cost if the finished goods in which they will be used are expected to be sold at or above cost. (*Larsen & Toubro*)	• These items are not meant to be sold. They are worth the purchase price as long as the products in which they are to be used are expected to be sold at or above cost. Application of the LCM principle is not mechanical. It needs judgment.
• Finished goods in plant and work in progress involving hydro and thermal sets including gas based power plants, boilers, boiler auxiliaries, compressors and industrial turbo sets are valued at actual/estimated factory cost or at 97.5% of the realizable value, whichever is lower. (*BHEL*)	• The 2.5 per cent write-down covers estimated selling and completion costs of the inventories. Presumably, it is based on past experience and expected future conditions.
• The cost of inventories is computed on the weighted moving average basis. (*Cipla Limited*)	• Weighted moving average moderates the effect of any big change in purchase prices.

Over 75 per cent of the S&P Nifty 100 companies follow WAC. Just 8 per cent followed FIFO. The rest did not have inventories or did not disclose the method. What do you think could be the reason for the overwhelming preference for WAC?

Here are the key differences between these systems.

IFRS	Ind AS	Indian GAAP
IAS 2	Ind AS 2	AS 2
• Explicit requirement to use the same cost formula consistently for all inventories that have a similar nature and use to the entity.	No explicit requirement.	
• Reversal of past write-down of inventory value allowed.	No specific guidance.	
• Commodity broker-traders measure their inventories at fair value less costs to less.	No specific guidance.	

RECAP

- *Current assets* are intended to be converted into cash within one year or within the operating cycle.
- *Inventories* are held for sale or use in production.
- Inventory errors reverse in the next period.
- Goods in transit and goods on consignment must be included in the owner's inventory.
- *Product costs* bring inventories to their present location and condition. All other items are *period expenses*.
- The cost formulas allowed in India are *specific identification*, *FIFO*, and *WAC*. *LIFO* is not allowed in India.
- Inventories should be written down to market, if it is below cost.
- Lenders prefer understatement of the borrower's assets and profits. Both understatement and overstatement of assets and profits are unfair.
- Accounting changes would make it difficult to compare reported performance.
- Under the *perpetual inventory system*, all purchases and sales of merchandise are recorded.

- For a manufacturing organization:

  Cost of goods available for sale = Beginning inventory of finished goods + Cost of goods manufactured

  Cost of goods sold = Cost of goods available for sale – Ending inventory of finished goods.

- *Inventory turnover* measures the efficiency of inventory management.
- The shorter the *operating cycle*, the faster the speed of cash conversion.

Review Problem

Suman Company has the following inventory, purchases, and sales data for August:

Inventory:	Aug.	1	100 units @ ₹5
Purchases:	Aug.	5	600 units @ ₹6
		11	300 units @ ₹8
		23	400 units @ ₹9
Sales:	Aug.	9	400 units
		18	500 units
		28	200 units

The company uses the periodic inventory system. The physical inventory count on August 31 shows 300 units on hand.

Required

Compute the cost of the inventory on hand on August 31 and the cost of goods sold for August under each of the following methods: (1) FIFO, (2) LIFO, and (3) WAC.

Solution to the Review Problem

The cost of goods available for sale is computed as follows:

			Units	Unit Cost	Total Cost
Aug.	1	Beginning inventory	100	₹5	₹ 500
Aug.	5	Purchase	600	6	3,600
	11	Purchase	300	8	2,400
	23	Purchase	400	9	3,600
		Available for sale	1,400		10,100

1. FIFO:

Ending inventory:

300 units from the purchase on August 23 @ ₹9	₹2,700
	2,700

Cost of goods sold:

Cost of goods available for sale	₹10,100
Deduct Ending inventory	2,700
	7,400

2. LIFO:

Ending inventory:

100 units from the beginning inventory @ ₹5	₹ 500
200 units from the purchase on August 5 @ ₹6	1,200
	1,700

Cost of goods sold:

Cost of goods available for sale	₹10,100
Deduct Ending inventory	1,700
	8,400

3. WAC:

Cost of goods available for sale	₹10,100
Number of units available for sale	1,400
Weighted-average unit cost	₹7.21
Ending inventory: 300 units @ ₹7.21	₹2,163
Cost of goods sold:	
Cost of goods available for sale	₹10,100
Deduct Ending inventory..	2,163
	7,937

ASSIGNMENT MATERIAL

Questions

1. "Manipulation of inventory valuation is self-reversing." Do you agree?

2. What characteristics should an asset possess to be classified as *inventory*?

3. Can interest charges be included in *product costs*? When?

4. Why do we need inventory costing methods?

5. Which inventory costing method assumes that the goods available for sale are homogeneous?

6. Explain the income tax benefits resulting from the use of LIFO during periods of inflation if LIFO is allowed for tax purposes.

7. If goods are shipped FOB destination, should the buyer or seller pay the freight?

8. What does *market* mean in *lower of cost or market*?

9. Comment on the following statement: "While naked conservatism is unacceptable, an attitude of healthy scepticism is justified in the face of uncertainty".

10. How does *conservatism* protect shareholders from moral hazard?

11. Explain how the *comparability principle* improves the usefulness of financial statements.

12. Suppose you compute the cost of goods sold under the perpetual and the periodic inventory systems using the following inventory methods: specific identification, FIFO, LIFO, and WAC. Which of these methods will produce (a) same and (b) different amounts for cost of goods sold under the two systems?

13. How are inventories classified in the balance sheet of a manufacturing enterprise?

14. Can a company following the perpetual inventory system dispense with year-end physical inventory taking?

Problems

The following information is available from the records of Madhuri Company:

Problem 5.1
Inventory Costing Methods: Periodic Inventory System *

			Units	Unit Cost	Total Cost
July	1	Beginning inventory.................................	150	₹14	₹ 2,100
	9	Purchase..	200	15	3,000
	14	Purchase..	350	17	5,950
	23	Purchase..	200	18	3,600
	28	Purchase..	100	20	2,000
		Available for sale	1,000		16,650
		Sold..	800		
	31	Ending inventory	200		

Assume that the ending inventory on July 31 consisted of 50 units from the beginning inventory, 60 units from the July 14 purchase, and 90 units from the July 23 purchase. The company uses the periodical inventory system.

Required

Determine the cost of the ending inventory and the cost of goods sold using the following methods: (a) specific identification, (b) FIFO, (c) LIFO, and (d) WAC.

Problem 5.2

Inventory Costing Methods: Periodic Inventory System * Alternative to Problem 5.1

The records of Watawala Company contain the following information relating to the inventory item of K730 for October 20X6:

			Units	Unit Cost
Oct.	1	Beginning inventory	20	₹4
	3	Purchase	40	5
	9	Sale	10	
	14	Sale	45	
	19	Purchase	50	7
	22	Sale	30	
	26	Purchase	20	9
	28	Sale	10	
	31	Sale	5	

Required

Using the periodic inventory system, compute the cost of ending inventory and cost of goods sold. Use the FIFO and LIFO inventory costing methods.

Problem 5.3

Inventory Costing Methods: Perpetual Inventory System **

Refer to Problem 5.2. Assume that Watawala Company uses the perpetual inventory system.

Required

Compute the cost of ending inventory and cost of goods sold, using the FIFO and LIFO inventory costing methods.

Problem 5.4

Inventory Valuation: Lower of Cost or Market Principle **

Preeti Company's ending inventory includes the following items:

Product	Units on Hand	Unit Cost	Unit Price
A	200	₹10	₹11
B	170	9	7
C	210	15	22
D	40	11	9
E	4,100	3	4
F	3,700	5	2

Required

Compute the ending value by applying the lower-of-cost-market principle to (a) each item of inventory and (b) groups of similar items, assuming that products A, B, C, and D constitute one group and products E and F, the other group.

Problem 5.5

Inventory Costing Methods: Periodic Inventory System ***

Ganesh Carpets sold 190 carpets during the year at ₹3,400 each. It had a beginning inventory on April 1, 20X2 of 20 carpets at a cost of ₹2,300 each. The following purchases were made during the year ended March 31, 20X3:

May 20X2 40 carpets @ ₹2,400   September 20X2 60 carpets @ ₹2,700

July 20X2 50 carpets @ ₹2,500   February 20X3 30 carpets @ ₹2,800

The company incurred operating expenses of ₹58,000 during the year. It uses the periodic inventory system.

Required

1. Prepare a schedule to compute the cost of goods available for sale during the year.
2. Determine the ending inventory on March 31, 20X3 using (a) FIFO, (b) LIFO and (c) WAC.
3. Prepare a statement of profit and loss under each of the above inventory costing methods.

Mohan Furniture Co1mpany sold 90 chairs during 20X7 at ₹1,600 each. It had a beginning inventory on January 1, 20X7 of 20 chairs at a cost of ₹1,000 each. The following purchases were made during the year ended December 31, 20X7:

Problem 5.6
Inventory Costing
Methods: Periodic
Inventory System ✳✳✳
Alternative to Problem 5.5

      March 20 chairs @ ₹1,100   August 30 chairs @ ₹1,300

      June 10 chairs @ ₹1,200   November 20 chairs @ ₹1,400

The company incurred operating expenses of ₹16,000 during the year. It uses the periodic inventory system.

Required

1. Prepare a schedule to compute the cost of goods available for sale during the year.
2. Determine the ending inventory on December 31, 20X7 using (a) FIFO, (b) LIFO and (c) WAC.
3. Prepare a statement of profit and loss under each of the above inventory costing methods.

The beginning inventory, purchases, and sales of scarves during February are as follows:

Problem 5.7
Inventory Costing
Methods: Perpetual
Inventory System ✳✳✳

Feb.	1	Beginning inventory	20 units @ ₹140
	4	Purchases	50 units @ ₹142
	7	Sales	30 units
	10	Purchases	60 units @ ₹145
	14	Sales	20 units
	20	Purchases	30 units @ ₹147
	26	Sales	40 units
	29	Purchases	80 units @ ₹148

Required

1. Record the beginning inventory and the transactions on a perpetual inventory card using FIFO.
2. Record the beginning inventory and the transactions on a perpetual inventory card using LIFO.
3. Prepare journal entries to record the sale of 20 units at ₹160 each on February 14 to Jain Brothers and the purchase on February 29 from Vipul Company from the LIFO inventory card, assuming that both transactions were on credit.

The beginning inventory, purchases, and sales of swimming caps during November are as follows:

Problem 5.8
Inventory Costing
Methods: Perpetual
Inventory System ✳✳✳
Alternative to Problem 5.7

Nov.	1	Beginning inventory	40 units @ ₹70
	3	Purchases	80 units @ ₹71
	8	Sales	90 units
	10	Sales	10 units
	15	Purchases	40 units @ ₹73
	17	Sales	50 units
	21	Purchases	30 units @ ₹74
	26	Purchases	30 units @ ₹76
	28	Sales	20 units

Required

1. Record the beginning inventory and the transactions on a perpetual inventory card using FIFO.
2. Record the beginning inventory and the transactions on a perpetual inventory card using LIFO.
3. Prepare journal entries to record the sale of 90 units at ₹90 each on November 8 to Rohini Company and the purchase on November 26 from Tanvir Company from the LIFO inventory card, assuming that both transactions were on credit.

Problem 5.9
Inventory Valuation: Lower of Cost or Market Principle
****

Sanu Company prepared the following schedule of the company's ending inventory:

	Quantity	Cost per Unit	Price per Unit
Product Group I			
A134	210	₹450	₹480
A156	140	530	670
N278	65	480	520
P345	83	510	360
Product Group II			
R098	13	₹650	₹800
R112	17	720	760
T034	26	680	740
T041	19	610	780

Sales commission is payable on all items at 10 per cent in Product Group I and at 20 per cent in Product Group II. Delivery charges of ₹20 per unit are payable on product code R098.

Required

Compute the amount at which ending inventory is to be reported applying the LCM principle to (a) each item of inventory or (b) groups of similar items.

Problem 5.10
Inventory Valuation: Lower of Cost or Market Principle
**** Alternative to Problem 5.9

Mario Company prepared the following schedule of the company's ending inventory:

	Quantity	Cost per unit	Price per unit
Product Group I			
A087	130	₹210	₹280
C134	170	230	300
F169	100	250	260
J214	120	220	200
Product Group II			
P518	10	₹890	₹920
S098	20	850	970
U126	35	720	840
Y376	10	780	800

Sales commission is payable on all items at 10 per cent. Delivery charges of ₹10 per unit are payable on all items in Product Group II.

Required

Compute the amount at which ending inventory is to be reported applying the LCM principle to (a) each item of inventory or (b) groups of similar items.

Problem 5.11
Effect of Inventory Errors
*****

The statement of profit and loss of Fairdeal Company for the years ended March 31, 20X8 and 20X7 are as follows:

	20X8	20X7
Net sales	₹25,750	₹21,610
Cost of goods sold:		
Beginning inventory	5,230	4,790
Net purchases	19,420	18,300
Cost of goods available for sale	24,650	23,090
Ending inventory	5,410	5,230
	19,240	17,860
Gross profit	6,510	3,750
Operating expenses	2,790	2,310
Net profit	3,720	1,440

The company uses the periodic inventory system. A review of the accounting records revealed the following items:

1. Merchandise costing ₹420 was shipped to a customer on March 31, 20X7, FOB shipping point. Physical inventory had been completed before the shipping. The sale revenue of ₹530 was recognized on April 12, 20X7 when the sales invoice was prepared.

2. Merchandise costing ₹290 shipped FOB shipping point by a supplier on March 27, 20X8 was received on April 2, 20X8. The goods were not included in the inventory on March 31, but reported as purchases on April 17, 20X8 when the invoice arrived.

3. Goods received on consignment on March 25, 20X7 were kept in a separate bay. However, one lot costing ₹160 was included inadvertently in the ending inventory on March 31, 20X7.

4. On March 27, 20X7, goods costing ₹630 were shipped FOB destination to a customer. A sales invoice for ₹720 was prepared on April 6. The goods, which were in transit on March 31, 20X7, were not included in the physical inventory taken on that day.

5. The total of one of the inventory sheets was recorded in the inventory summary sheet on March 31, 20X8 as ₹1,430 instead of ₹1,340.

Required

1. Determine the correct ending inventory figures for 20X8 and 20X7. Itemize each correction to arrive at total corrections.

2. Prepare revised statement of profit and loss for the years ended March 31, 20X8 and 20X7.

3. Compute the total net profit for the two-year period, both before and after the revisions. Why are these figures similar or different?

The statement of profit and loss of Goodwill Company for the years ended December 31, 20X4 and 20X3 were as follows:

Problem 5.12
Effect of Inventory Errors ✷✷✷✷✷
Alternative to Problem 5.11

	20X4	20X3
Net sales	₹438,300	₹542,900
Cost of goods sold:		
Beginning inventory	65,900	73,200
Net purchases	398,100	481,700
Cost of goods available for sale	464,000	554,900
Ending inventory	54,300	65,900
	409,700	489,000
Gross profit	28,600	53,900
Operating expenses	31,200	28,700
Net profit (loss)	(2,600)	25,200

The company uses the periodic inventory system. A review of the accounting records revealed the following items:

1. Merchandise costing ₹3,700 was shipped to a customer on December 29, 20X3, FOB destination. The sales invoice for ₹4,300 was prepared on December 30, 20X3. The goods were received by the customer on January 3, 20X4 and were not included in the physical inventory on December 31, 20X3.

2. Merchandise costing ₹2,400 sent on consignment to a dealer was not included in the ending inventory on December 31, 20X4.

3. Merchandise costing ₹4,100 shipped FOB shipping point by a supplier on December 29, 20X3 was received on January 6, 20X4. The goods were not included in the inventory on December 31, but reported as purchases on January 9, 20X4 when the invoice arrived.

4. On December 31, 20X3, goods costing ₹4,400 were shipped FOB destination by a supplier. The goods were in transit on December 31, 20X3 and were not included in the physical inventory on that day, but were reported as purchases on January 14, 20X4 when the invoice arrived.

5. The total of one of the inventory sheets was recorded in the inventory summary sheet on December 31, 20X4 as ₹7,500 instead of ₹5,700.

Required

1. Determine the correct ending inventory figures for 20X4 and 20X3. Itemize each correction to arrive at the total corrections.
2. Prepare revised statement of profit and loss for the years ended December 31, 20X4 and 20X3.
3. Compute the total net profit for the two-year period both before and after the revisions. Why are these figures similar or different?

Problem 5.13
Inventory Valuation
Methods, Income Tax
Reporting, and Managerial
Behaviour ✳✳✳✳✳

Bashir Company sold 50,000 CDs at ₹28 during the year. Its beginning inventory consisted of 10,000 CDs at ₹18 per CD. The following purchases were made during the year: 15,000 CDs @ ₹19; 10,000 CDs @ ₹21; 20,000 CDs @ ₹22; 10,000 CDs @ ₹23. Operating expenses were ₹185,000. Income tax is payable at 30 per cent.

Required

1. Compute net profit using the FIFO and LIFO methods.
2. Which method is more advantageous to the company for (a) income tax reporting and (b) shareholder reporting? Why? What trade-offs, if any, are involved in this context? Assume that the company must use the same method for both purposes.
3. Suppose that the company makes a purchase of 15,000 CDs at ₹25 on the last day of the reporting period. How will the purchase affect the company's net profit and income tax expense under the two inventory costing methods?

Problem 5.14
Inventory Valuation
Methods, Income Tax
Reporting, and Managerial
Behaviour ✳✳✳✳✳
Alternative to
Problem 5.13

Jupiter Company sold 20,000 crates of a soft drink at ₹120 during the year. Its beginning inventory consisted of 1,000 crates at ₹70 per crate. The following purchases were made during the year: 5,000 crates @ ₹75; 8,000 crates @ ₹76; 9,000 crates @ ₹80. Operating expenses were ₹365,000. Income tax is payable at 30 per cent.

Required

1. Compute the net profit using the FIFO and LIFO methods.
2. Which method is more advantageous to the company for (a) income tax reporting, and (b) shareholder reporting? Why? What trade-offs, if any, are involved in this context? Assume that the company must use the same method for both purposes. Suppose the company makes a purchase of 4,000 crates at ₹85 on the last day of the reporting period. How will the purchase affect the company's net profit and income tax expense under the two inventory costing methods?

Business Decision Cases

BDC 5.1
Giridhar Clothing
Company

The warehouse of Giridhar Clothing Company was destroyed in a fire that broke out on the night of May 7, resulting in extensive damage to the company's inventories. Even in the best of times, the company did not maintain proper accounting records. In the past, a CA firm was engaged to prepare the financial statements based on information compiled from the company's invoice files, correspondence, and bank statements. Inventory was last taken on March 31, the end of the last reporting period. Both purchases, and sales were on FOB shipping point terms. While all purchases were on credit, there was a small amount of cash sales. There were no purchases or sales in transit on May 7. All cheques and cash received were deposited into bank every day. Payments to suppliers and transporters were by cheque. Cash was withdrawn from bank for making specific cash payments for office and warehouse rent, insurance premium, and miscellaneous office and selling expenses. The following information was culled from the company's records for the current period:

Purchase invoices filed in the folder marked *Paid Purchase Invoices* ....₹62,100
Freight invoices filed in the folder marked *Paid Freight Invoices* 2,700
Sale invoices filed in the folder marked *Paid Sale Invoices*..96,200
Purchase invoices filed in the folder marked *Unpaid Purchase Invoices*..................................11,000
Freight invoices filed in the folder marked *Unpaid Freight Invoices* 400
Sale invoices filed in the folder marked *Unpaid Sale Invoices* 3,500

Total of cheques issued for payments to suppliers and transporters 64,800

Total of cheques issued for making cash payments 8,100

Total of paying-in slips for deposits into bank account 97,400

The following information was available from the March 31 financial statements:

Merchandise inventory..₹17,200

Amounts due to suppliers for purchases..4,200

Amounts due from customers...2,900

Further examination of the folders revealed that all invoices pertaining to unpaid purchases and unpaid sales listed in the March 31 balance sheet were settled by April 15.

The insurance company's surveyor assessed the damage to the inventories at ₹500 (net of estimated salvage of ₹500), and would issue a cheque for the amount without any proof of loss. The insurance company was willing to consider a claim for a higher amount if it was supported by proper evidence. Giridhar Clothing Company's gross profit averaged 20 per cent of sales in the past two years.

Required

1. Prepare an estimate of the cost of inventory destroyed in the fire. Assume that the surveyor's estimate of salvage is reasonable.
2. What was the percentage of gross profit implicit in the insurance company's proposed settlement?
3. You are informed that selling prices went up by 2 per cent during the current period. How would your answer to Requirement 1 change in light of this information?

Galaxy Corporation started as a small clothing store on Brigade Road, Bengaluru. Over the years, it has become a large supermarket chain in southern India. In early 20X8, the owners, Sanjay and Samir, decided to make an offer for sale of a part of their shares in Galaxy. **BDC 5.2 Galaxy Corporation**

Galaxy has engaged Assure and Thrive, a reputable accounting firm, to conduct due diligence of its financial affairs. The firm has made the following observations:

- In the past two years inventories showed an unusual increase in the last few days of the fiscal year. Inventory turnover averaged from 15.1 times in the first half-year to 12.8 times in the second half-year.
- In many cases year-end purchases and related liability were not accounted for.
- The company's store personnel carried out inventory-taking.
- There were significant movements of inventories from one store to another towards the year end.
- There was no record of loss or theft of goods.
- Inventories were valued in two ways. Most items were valued using the retail inventory method. The rest were valued at the lower of cost or market. "Market" was calculated by writing down inventories held for more than six months by 25 per cent and for more than one year by 50 per cent.
- The company switched from WAC to FIFO cost in 20X6.
- The gross profit margin increased from 12.4 per cent in 20X6 to 14.7 per cent in 20X7.

Required

1. Examine the implications of the observations for the quality of Galaxy Corporation's financial statements.
2. What would your advice to a potential buyer of Galaxy Corporation's shares?

Interpreting Financial Reports

On July 31, 2013, the National Spot Exchange Limited (NSEL), a leading market for trading in commodities, announced suspension of trading in all contracts. Reports suggested that there were major violations of commodities trading regulations. Some traders had built up huge trading positions, but the exchange let them "roll over" the positions instead of forcing them to settle the positions. The fear was that if the exchange did not allow "roll over", traders would have defaulted and that would have led to a payments crisis. So the exchange allowed them to build up larger positions **IFR 5.1 National Spot Exchange Limited** thereby postponing the settlement, but the problem did not go away. It snowballed into a huge crisis estimated to be ₹56 billion. When the irregularities surfaced finally, the size of the fraud turned out to be so large that the exchange had to shut down. Deloitte, Haskins & Sells, the auditor of NSEL's parent company, Financial Technologies Limited (FTIL), withdrew their audit report stating that the financial statements had become unreliable.

Commentators pointed out that NSEL allowed trading of forward contracts though it was permitted to trade only spot contracts. There were allegations of manipulation of inventories suggesting that the physical inventories were much less than claimed. "Paired contracts" were sold by intermediaries to investors as guaranteed return instruments. There were also allegations of circuitous transactions involving NSEL and its subsidiaries. There were reports that the members were allowed to continue trading despite their defaulting on their obligations. In August 2012, the National Commodity and Derivatives Exchange Ltd (NCDEX), a rival commodity exchange, had complained to the Forward Markets Commission (FMC) that NSEL was running an arbitrage scheme. A few blamed the crisis on AS 2, the Indian accounting standard on inventories, because it did not apply to commodity broker-traders. On October 16, 2013, the Economic Offences Wing (EOW) of Mumbai Police arrested Anjani Sinha, former CEO of NSEL. Earlier, the police had arrested two other executives, Amit Mukherjee and Jai Bahukhandi. On May 7, 2014, the EOW arrested Jignesh Shah, director of NSEL and the founder chairman chief executive of FTIL.

Required

1. What was NSEL's mandate? How was it different from other commodity exchanges?
2. What was the NSEL scam about?
3. What was the role of NSEL's brokers in the scam?
4. What lessons does the scam have for auditors?
5. What was the role of regulatory agencies in the scam?
6. How can inventory accounting standards help in preventing and detecting scams of this kind?

Financial Analysis

FA 5.1

Inventory Methods

Study the inventory valuation methods of a sample of companies for five years.

Required

1. Prepare an analysis of the inventory valuation methods followed by the companies.
2. Explain any patterns in the choice of methods.
3. Why is your study important for analyzing financial statements?

FA 5.2

Inventory Accounting Changes

Study the changes in inventory accounting policies for a sample of companies for five years.

Required

1. Prepare an analysis of the changes in inventory accounting policies.
2. Explain possible managerial considerations for the changes.
3. Why is your study important for analyzing financial statements?

FA 5.3

Inventory Management

Study a sample of annual reports of companies in an industry for five years.

Required

1. Prepare an analysis of the inventory holding period of the companies.
2. Do you see any industry patterns? Explain.
3. Analyze trends in the holding period.
4. Why is your study important for analyzing financial statements?

FA 5.4

Operating Cycle

Study a sample of annual reports of companies in an industry for five years.

Required

1. Prepare an analysis of the operating cycle of the companies.
2. Do you see any industry patterns? Explain.
3. Analyze trends in the operating cycle.
4. Why is your study important for analyzing financial statements?

Answers to One-minute Quiz

5.1 a, c.
5.2 b.
5.3 a, d.
5.4 a, b, c, d.
5.5 b.
5.6 d.

Answers to Test Your Understanding

5.1 The error would overstate the net profit and equity for 20X1, and understate the net profit for 20X2, by ₹5,000. The correction would reduce the net profit and equity for 20X1, and increase the net profit for 20X2, by ₹5,000. Neither the error nor its correction would affect the net profit for 20X3 or the equity for 20X2 and 20X3.

5.2 FOB shipping point.

5.3 The carrying amount is ₹74,500. The net realizable value is ₹66,000, calculated as follows: Estimated selling price, ₹70,000 – Sales commission at 5%, ₹3,500 – Delivery expense, ₹500. LCM = ₹66,000. The write-down is ₹8,500.

5.4

	Cost	Retail
Beginning inventory	₹ 700	₹ 900
Add Net purchases	3,300	5,100
Available for sale	4,000	6,000
Ratio of cost to retail: 4,000/6,000 = 2/3		
Deduct Net sales		4,200
Estimated ending inventory at retail		1,800
Cost of inventory lost: (1,800 × 2/3 – 1,620 × 2/3)		120

5.5 July 1 to November 3:

Net sales (₹25,300 – ₹1,300)	₹24,000
Deduct Estimated gross profit, 60%	14,400
Cost of goods sold	9,600
Beginning inventory	1,200
Add Net purchases (₹12,300 – ₹700)	11,600
Add Freight in	1,200
Cost of goods available for sale	14,000
Inventory loss	4,400

5.6 Cost of goods sold = Beginning finished goods inventory, ₹2,310 + Cost of goods manufactured, ₹17,680 – Ending finished goods inventory, ₹1,870 = ₹18,120.

5.7 Average inventories = (1,200 + 2,600)/2 = 1,900; Inventory turnover = 5,700/1,900 = 3 times; Average holding period = 360/3 = 120 days.

Long-lived Assets

LEARNING OBJECTIVES

After studying this chapter, you should be able to:

1. Describe the nature and types of long-lived assets.
2. Determine the cost of acquisition of property, plant and equipment.
3. Explain depreciation.
4. Compute depreciation under popular methods.
5. Distinguish between capital expenditure and revenue expenditure.
6. Understand the difference between accounting depreciation and tax depreciation.
7. Record derecognition of property, plant and equipment.
8. Dispel the myths about depreciation.
9. Explain revaluation of property, plant and equipment.
10. Describe and account for intangible assets.
11. Account for natural resources.
12. Explain impairment of assets.
13. Analyze the utilization of property, plant and equipment.
14. Explain and account for investment property.

DOUBLE YOUR ASSETS IN TROUBLED TIMES, EFFORTLESSLY

In the fiscal year 2016, many public sector banks (PSBs) reported record losses. It would be insane for banks to acquire land, buildings or equipment in these circumstances. Strangely, the property, plant and equipment of many PSBs doubled in FY16. How did the banks manage this feat? The fact is that there was little change in their assets. The banks increased the value of the assets by writing up the amounts. The property, plant and equipment of IDBI Bank, Bank of Baroda, UCO Bank, Allahabad Bank, Vijaya Bank and Corporation Bank more than doubled because of this procedure. Revaluation produces only paper profits. So why did the banks do it? Banks were short of Basel III capital adequacy norms. By 2019 PSBs would need as much as ₹3.7 trillion of capital, of which the government should give ₹1.4 trillion. Given the government's own financial condition, there was no way it could find that kind of money. The Reserve Bank of India came up with a band-aid solution. It allowed banks to record the current value of their land and buildings and treat the resulting "gain" as part common equity Tier I capital for Basel III purposes. Banks met the Basel III requirements without lifting a finger. The government faced less pressure to invest in banks. There was universal happiness.

SPEED READ

Property, plant and equipment and intangible assets are used to provide goods and services. They represent major sources of future revenue potential. Depreciation is an important part of accrual accounting. It's often misunderstood. Whether to capitalize or expense an item can affect current and future profits. Revaluation is a departure from the historical cost system. Intangible assets are increasingly more important than tangible assets in many businesses. Natural resources come with tricky accounting issues. Efficient utilization of property, plant and equipment is essential for profitable operations.

Long-lived Assets in Perspective

A **long-lived asset**, or **fixed asset**, is held for the purpose of producing and supplying goods and services of business. Unlike inventories, long-lived assets are not acquired for resale in the normal course of business. A manufacturer often has land, buildings, plant and machinery, furniture, office equipment, patents, trademarks and know-how. Long-lived assets are non-current assets.

Learning Objective

LO 1 · Describe the nature and types of long-lived assets.

Whether an asset is a long-lived asset depends on the purpose for which it is held. For example, the land on which a company's factory stands is a long-lived asset. However, if it is for use in property development, it is a current asset. So the *intention* of holding an asset determines its classification.

Long-lived assets are of the following types:

1. **Property, plant and equipment** are tangible items held for use in the production and supply of goods and services.
   Examples: Land, buildings, plant, aircraft, vehicles, furniture, and office equipment.
2. **Intangible assets** don't have physical substance. They represent legal rights with associated economic benefits. Also, these are separately identifiable. Intangible assets exclude financial assets such as receivables and investments.
   Examples: Brand names, publishing titles, patents, licences, copyrights, and designs.
3. **Natural resources** constitute a category by themselves because of their special characteristics.
   Examples: Oil, natural gas, minerals, and forests.

Property, Plant and Equipment

Accounting for property, plant and equipment has the following objectives:

- To give investors, creditors, management, and tax and regulatory authorities accurate information about these assets;
- To account for use and disposal of these assets; and
- To plan for acquisitions through realistic budgeting.

Accounting for property, plant and equipment involves the following issues:

- Determining the cost of acquisition of an item of property, plant and equipment.
- Allocating the cost of the item to several reporting periods.
- Recording the disposal of the item.

Figure 6.1

THE PROPERTY, PLANT AND EQUIPMENT LIFE CYCLE

Figure 6.1 describes the accounting issues that arise in the life cycle of an item of property, plant and equipment.

The life cycle of an item of property, plant, and equipment consists of acquisition, consumption, and disposal.

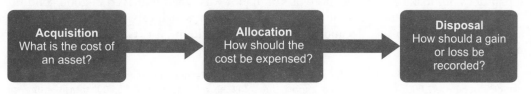

Acquisition
What is the cost of an asset?

Allocation
How should the cost be expensed?

Disposal
How should a gain or loss be recorded?

Give examples of property, plant and equipment for a restaurant.

Which of the following should be classified as property, plant and equipment? There may be more than one correct answer.

(a) Land on which factory building stands.
(b) Land held for constructing a factory in future.
(c) Land used as a playground by employees.
(d) Land held for sale.

QUICK QUESTION
Property, plant and equipment

ONE-MINUTE QUIZ 6.1
Classification of Assets

Cost of Acquisition

Learning Objective

LO 2 Determine the cost of acquisition of property, plant and equipment.

Traditionally, the accounting profession has placed considerable emphasis on the objectivity of valuation. You may recall from Chapter 1 that the case for the historical cost system rests on the going concern assumption. Accountants prefer cost as the basis of valuation of property, plant and equipment because cost is easier to measure and verify than other measures, such as market value. Also, cost would often approximate the service value of an asset in an arm's length transaction. The general principle is that an enterprise can recognize the cost of an item of property, plant and equipment as an asset only if it is probable that the item will give future economic benefits to the enterprise and the cost of the item can be measured reliably. Items acquired for safety or environmental reasons, e.g. electrostatic precipitators used in a cement plant to reduce emissions, also qualify for recognition as property, plant and equipment, because without them it will not be possible to use the main asset.

The cost of property, plant and equipment comprises the following:

1. Purchase price, including non-refundable or non-adjustable duties and taxes, after deducting trade discounts and rebates.
2. Any directly attributable costs of bringing the asset to the location and condition for its intended use; and
3. Estimated costs of dismantling, removing and site restoration.

Examples of directly attributable costs include:

(a) Stamp duty and registration fees for transfer of title to land or building;
(b) Professional fees, e.g. fees of architects, engineers, and lawyers;
(c) Commission and brokerage for purchase;
(d) Cost of site preparation;
(e) Freight, transit insurance, and handling costs;
(f) Cost of testing; and
(g) Installation costs, such as special foundations for the plant.

Capitalization means treating a cost as part of the cost of acquisition of an asset. The principle is that expenditures that result in future economic benefits or are normal or unavoidable are capitalized, and the rest are expensed. Often, some expenditure on start-up and trial production is necessary to bring a plant to its working condition. Such pre-production expenditure is capitalized. Again, customs duty paid on imported machine is capitalized, because it is a necessary cost. Avoidable or abnormal costs are not capitalized. For example, if a machine is damaged during installation, the related repair expense is not capitalized. This is because it is possible to install a machine without damaging it and repair does not make a machine more useful than it was when it arrived in good condition. Administration and other general overhead costs do not specifically relate to acquiring an asset or bringing it to the "location and working condition" for its intended use and are not capitalized.

HANDHOLD 6.1
Acquisition Cost

Suppose the costs associated with the acquisition of a milling machine are as follows: list price, ₹20,000; trade discount, ₹1,000; non-refundable import duty, ₹4,000; refundable tax, ₹5,000; transit insurance, ₹120; freight, ₹400; installation charges, ₹1,200.

We compute the cost of acquisition of the machine as follows:

List price		₹20,000
Deduct Trade discount		1,000
Net price		19,000
Add		
Non-refundable import duty	₹4,000	
Transit insurance	120	
Freight	400	
Installation charges	1,200	5,720
Cost of acquisition		24,720

We record the acquisition of the milling machine as follows:

Plant and Machinery... 24,720

    Cash 24,720

The following expenditures relate to a chemical plant:

(a) Refundable customs duty on the plant

(b) Clearing charges paid to the port trust

(c) Demurrage for delay in clearing the consignment

(d) Freight

(e) Transit insurance

(f) Repair of some parts damaged while the plant was being unloaded at the port

(g) Cost of calibrating the plant

(h) Cost of materials spoilt during test run

(i) Cost of removal and cleaning up the site.

Which of these should be capitalized as part of the cost of the plant?

TEST YOUR UNDERSTANDING 6.1
Acquisition Cost

Borrowing costs

Borrowing costs are interest and other costs that an enterprise incurs in connection with the borrowing of funds. An enterprise should capitalize borrowing costs which are directly attributable to a **qualifying asset**, an asset that necessarily takes a substantial period of time to get ready for its intended use or sale.[1] A large petroleum refinery that takes three years to be commissioned is an example of a qualifying asset. There is no bright line for determining "substantial period of time". Determining whether an asset is a qualifying asset requires the exercise of management judgment. An asset that normally takes more than a year to be ready for use or sale will usually be a qualifying asset. Inventories, manufacturing plants, power generation facilities, intangible assets, and investment properties can be qualifying assets, depending on the circumstances.

The following table summarizes the norms for capitalization of borrowing costs.

Question	Answer	Example
What is capitalized?	Borrowing costs that are directly attributable to a qualifying asset	Interest cost on funds borrowed specifically for obtaining an asset.
What is not capitalized?	Actual or imputed costs of equity	Dividend
When does capitalization start?	From the time of incurrence of borrowing costs and expenditure on the asset	Date of payment of construction costs from loan funds
When is capitalization suspended?	During periods in which development of an asset is suspended	Construction delayed because of a dispute over title to the land
When does capitalization stop?	When substantially all the necessary activities are complete	Occupancy certificate received for a building

A company builds a thermal power plant which is expected to take 48 months to complete. It pays for the land on July 9, 20X1. The company applies for a three-year bank loan specifically for this project on July 12, 20X1. Construction work starts on July 15, 20X1. The company pays the construction agency's first bill on August 19, 20X1. It pays the second bill from the bank loan it received on September 17, 20X1. Work on the project is suspended for ten days in October 20X1, because of seasonal rains. Work resumes thereafter and is in progress on March 31, 20X2, the year end. The thermal power plant is a qualifying asset since it necessarily takes a substantial period of time to complete. The company cannot capitalize the actual or imputed costs of equity funds used to pay for the land or the first construction bill. It should capitalize interest cost incurred from September 17, 20X1 until March 31, 20X2. The short, temporary delay in October 20X1 is a necessary part of the construction process; hence the company will not suspend capitalization of interest cost.

HANDHOLD 6.2
Liability of Shareholder

---

[1] The principles for treating borrowing costs as inventoriable costs are the same as those discussed in this section.

Basket Purchases

An enterprise may buy a group of assets for a composite sum. In such cases, it should allocate the total purchase price to the various assets on the basis of **fair value**, the price of an asset in an orderly transaction between independent parties. In practice, professional valuers determine the fair value of an asset.

HANDHOLD 6.3
Basket Purchase

A firm pays a composite price of ₹25,000 for a building and the land on which it is situated. How much should we take to be the separate value of the land and the building? Suppose an expert valuer fixes the fair value of the land at ₹12,000 and of the building at ₹28,000. We allocate the purchase price as follows:

	Fair Value	Proportion of Purchase Price	Allocated Cost
Land	₹12,000	12/40 × ₹25,000	₹ 7,500
Building....................................	28,000	28/40 × ₹25,000	17,500
	40,000		25,000

A fair allocation of the purchase price is important to resolve conflicting accounting and tax considerations:

- The estimated useful lives of various assets are often different. For example, land is normally not depreciated, while buildings are depreciated over their useful lives. In our example, if the enterprise allocated ₹12,500 each to land and building, it would not depreciate an amount of ₹5,000 that was added excessively to the cost of the land, resulting in a lower depreciation expense for the building.

- Think of a firm motivated by income tax considerations. It would like to exaggerate the cost allocated to depreciable assets in order to reduce the tax expense. Therefore, the tax department is keen on a fair allocation of the lump sum purchase price.

The best way to resolve this conflict is to use fair value as the basis of allocation. Of course, there can be different views on an asset's fair value.

TEST YOUR UNDERSTANDING 6.2
Basket Purchase

Krishnan Nair bought a bakery for ₹300,000. The bakery's assets and their fair values were as follows: land, ₹180,000; building, ₹150,000; equipment, ₹50,000; furniture, ₹20,000. Allocate the purchase price to the assets.

Donated Assets

When a business gets an asset by donation, e.g. land given free or at a nominal price by the government, there is no cost of acquisition to the business. But to record the asset at zero value does not reflect the economic reality of an increase in an enterprise's assets. Therefore, the asset should be recorded at fair value.

Self-constructed Assets

When an enterprise constructs an asset using its resources, it has to arrive at the cost to be recorded. It can trace the costs of materials and labour directly to the construction. Since assigning indirect costs of construction such as power and supervision may be difficult, some companies prefer to expense them. Internal profit, i.e. the profit the company could have earned had it done the same work for a customer, can't be charged to the asset since its inclusion would violate the realization principle. Also, cost inefficiencies in the production of self-constructed assets, regardless of the reasons, should not be included as part of the cost.

Components of Assets

Sometimes, the cost of a part of an asset may be significant in relation to its total cost. Each such part must be depreciated separately. For example, an aircraft's airframe, engines, and interiors have different useful lives and maintenance requirements. The airframe has a long useful life. Engines go through periodical major and minor overhaul and require replacement after their life. Seats and galleys require frequent replacement as they wear out much faster. It is necessary to allocate the cost of the asset to its significant parts and depreciate the parts separately. Another example is an offshore drilling platform that has a life of 20 years, but its mechanical parts require replacement every three years. The mechanical parts will be treated as a component separate from the platform.

- Radiation equipment to treat cancer has a radioactive source, such as Cobalt or Iridium. The equipment may have a life of 10 to 15 years. But the radioactive source undergoes decay and has a half-life of about five years. So it has to be replaced several times over the life of the equipment. The equipment and the radioactive source have to be treated as components.

What are the arguments for and against capitalization of borrowing costs?

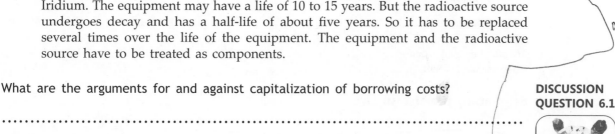

DISCUSSION QUESTION 6.1

....

....

....

Depreciation

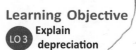

Learning Objective

LO 3 Explain depreciation

Business enterprises use property, plant and equipment over a number of reporting periods. Neither expensing the entire cost in the year of acquisition of the asset nor retaining the cost on the books until disposal of the asset provides for satisfactory measurement of periodic income. Allocation of the asset cost to the periods in which benefits from the asset are received is necessary to provide accurate information on performance.

Accountants think of depreciation as allocating the cost of an asset to the periods that are expected to benefit from the asset's use. It is the gradual conversion of cost into expense. Depreciation is the systematic allocation of the depreciable amount of an asset over its useful life. "Systematic allocation" is the key requirement. Therefore, arbitrary assignment of asset cost to reporting periods is not acceptable.

Another key implication of the definition is that it is necessary to charge depreciation even if the market value of an asset has appreciated because depreciation is a process of cost allocation, not asset valuation. Depreciation begins from the time an asset is available for use (even if it is not actually used). It continues even when the asset becomes idle or is retired from active use unless the asset is fully depreciated. Depreciation stops once the asset is classified as "held for sale" or disposed of.

Land normally has an indefinite useful life (with some exceptions such as quarries and landfill sites) and is, therefore, not depreciated. Land improvements such as parking lots are depreciable assets. For this reason, land, parking lots and buildings should be treated as separate assets. Plant and equipment have a limited useful life and are depreciated.

The depreciation accounting process involves the following steps:

1. Establishing the depreciable amount.
2. Estimating the useful life.
3. Choosing an appropriate cost allocation method.

Establishing the Depreciable Amount

The depreciable amount of an asset is its cost *less* residual value. The **residual value** of an asset is the estimated amount that an enterprise would currently realize from its disposal, after deducting the estimated costs of disposal if the asset were already of the age and condition expected at the end of its useful life. If the residual value of an asset equals or exceeds the asset's carrying amount, there will be no depreciation charge.

HANDHOLD 6.4
Depreciable Amount

The cost of acquisition of a press is ₹40,000, and its residual value is ₹4,500. The expected expenses of removal of the press at the time of disposal are ₹500. We calculate the depreciable amount of the press as follows:

Cost of acquisition..		₹40,000
Residual value..	₹4,500	
Deduct Removal expenses..	500	4,000
Depreciable amount		36,000

Estimating the Useful Life

The **useful life** (also known as *useful service life* or *useful economic life*) of an asset is the period over which an asset is expected to be available for use. For some assets, it may be taken as the number of production or similar units expected to be obtained from the asset. Useful life is not the same as physical life. The latter depends on physical wear and tear and the enterprise's maintenance policy. For example, if a plant works excessive hours, or is not subject to regular preventive maintenance, its ability to produce goods in the future will be reduced. Quite often, the useful life of an asset for an enterprise is shorter than its physical life, because of other factors, such as the following:

Factor	Explanation	Example
■ Technology	■ Technological improvements result in supersession of assets currently in use.	■ Existing computers are replaced when superior computers become available
■ Markets	■ Changes in product markets may make an asset obsolete.	■ Jute mills shut down after synthetic fibres came.
■ Regulation	■ Regulators specify limits on asset lives for environmental and safety reasons.	■ The law specifies shorter lives for nuclear power plants and trucks.
■ Contracts	■ Contractual terms constrain the use of an asset.	■ A building on leasehold land has to be demolished after the expiry of the lease.
■ Asset replacement policies	■ Companies voluntarily replace assets on safety and operating cost considerations.	■ Airlines replace their aircraft frequently to reduce operating costs and improve safety.

Often, physical life is a good starting point. An enterprise generally estimates useful life based on its past experience with similar assets and the experience of other firms in the industry. Estimating useful life requires significant managerial judgment.

HANDHOLD 6.5
Estimating Useful Life

Suppose a retail store acquires a mainframe computer. The computer manufacturer assures the store that if maintained in accordance with the prescribed standards, the machine will perform satisfactorily for five years. The store's technology consultant expects a superior computer to be introduced in three years. In the past, the store has replaced computers when they completed the life specified by the manufacturer. The store intends to replace its present computer by a new one as soon as it becomes available. Though the physical life of the asset is five years, its useful life will be taken as three years.

QUICK QUESTION
Useful life

Navin Printers has bought a high-speed laser printer. How can it estimate the printer's useful life?

Depreciation Methods

The final step in the depreciation process is to select a method of apportioning the asset's depreciable amount. Several methods are available to allocate the depreciable amount over an asset's useful life. Theoretically, the best method is the one that matches the consumption of an asset accurately with the benefits received from it in each period. These benefits can be in the form of additional revenue expected to be generated by the asset, or likely savings in the costs of material, labour, power, and so on. However, these measurements are extremely difficult. Over the years, accountants have developed a number of methods that purport to allocate an asset's cost in a systematic manner to the periods in which the asset is used.

Learning Objective
LO 4 Compute depreciation under popular methods.

The common depreciation methods are as follows:

1. Straight-line method
2. Accelerated methods
   - Written-down-value method
   - Sum-of-the-years'-digits method
3. Production-units method

Straight-line Method

The **straight-line method** (SLM) distributes the depreciable amount equally over the life of an asset. This method assumes that depreciation arises solely from the passage of time and that the effect of usage on the service value of the asset is insignificant. The yearly depreciation expense is computed by dividing the depreciable amount (cost of the asset *less* residual value) by the number of years of useful life. Assume that a bus costs ₹800,000 and is expected to realize ₹80,000 at the end of its estimated useful life of six years. The annual depreciation expense is calculated as:

$$\frac{\text{Cost} - \text{Residual value}}{\text{Useful life}} = \frac{₹800,000 - ₹80,000}{6 \text{ years}} = ₹120,000$$

The depreciation schedule for the asset under the straight-line method is as follows:

Depreciation Schedule: Straight-line Method

Year	Cost	Depreciation Expense	Accumulated Depreciation	Carrying Amount
1	₹800,000	₹120,000	₹120,000	₹680,000
2	800,000	120,000	240,000	560,000
3	800,000	120,000	360,000	440,000
4	800,000	120,000	480,000	320,000
5	800,000	120,000	600,000	200,000
6	800,000	120,000	720,000	80,000

The journal entry to record the depreciation expense in each year is as follows:

Depreciation Expense 120,000
    Accumulated Depreciation, Bus 120,000

The asset will appear in the balance sheet as follows:

Property, plant and equipment	Year 2	Year 1
Bus		
Gross block	₹800,000	₹800,000
Deduct Accumulated depreciation	240,000	120,000
Net block	560,000	680,000

The straight-line method is the simplest and the most widely used method. It is used for assets that depreciate mainly with time and are little affected by the extent of usage. For example, buildings decline in service value as they age and it is immaterial whether they are used or not. However, the service quality of most assets deteriorates over time. We know that older cars give less mileage and require frequent repairs. By assuming that assets give equal benefits in each reporting period, the straight-line method undercharges depreciation in the earlier years.

Accelerated Methods

The accelerated depreciation methods provide relatively larger amounts of depreciation in the early years of an asset's useful life and smaller amounts in later years. These methods assume that certain types of plant, equipment and vehicles are most efficient when they are new and decline in service as they age. The accelerated methods assume that depreciation depends only on time, but, unlike the straight-line method, they do not assume that the asset is equally useful in each year. Charging higher depreciation in the early years would be consistent with the matching principle if the benefits received in those years are higher.

The accelerated methods also assume that certain assets lose service value, because of rapid technological changes. In such cases, the need for early replacement justifies the use of accelerated rates. Besides, repair expenses are lower in the early years; so the sum of repair and depreciation tends to be constant over the life of the asset. We will now see two accelerated methods: (a) the written-down-value method, and (b) the sum-of-the-years'-digits method.

Written-down-value Method

In the written-down-value (WDV) method, depreciation is computed at a fixed rate on an asset's carrying amount at the beginning of a reporting period. Thus, the depreciation expense for Year 1 will be a certain per cent of the beginning carrying amount, which is cost. From Year 2 onwards, the depreciation charge would be related to the cost of the asset *less* accumulated depreciation at the beginning of the year. Since the fixed percentage is applied to the beginning carrying amount, the depreciation expense will keep decreasing from year to year. The WDV method is also known as the *diminishing-balance method*. The depreciation rate can be calculated using the following formula:

$$1 - \sqrt[n]{\frac{\text{Residual value}}{\text{Cost}}}, n \text{ being useful life in years.}$$

To illustrate the WDV method, let's take the bus example again.

$$\text{Depreciation rate} = 1 - \sqrt[6]{\frac{80,000}{800,000}}$$
$$= 31.87\% \text{ (rounded)}$$

The depreciation schedule for the asset under the WDV method is as follows:

Depreciation Schedule: Written-down-value Method

Year	Cost	Depreciation Expense	Accumulated Depreciation	Carrying Amount
1	₹800,000	₹254,960	₹254,960	₹545,040
2	800,000	173,705	428,665	371,335
3	800,000	118,345	547,010	252,990
4	800,000	80,629	627,639	172,361
5	800,000	54,933	682,572	117,428
6	800,000	37,428	720,000	80,000

Yearly depreciation is computed by applying the depreciation rate to the carrying amount at the beginning of the year. For example, depreciation expense for Year 1 = ₹800,000 × 31.87 per cent = ₹254,960. Depreciation expense for Year 2 is ₹545,040 × 31.87 per cent = ₹173,705.

The journal entries to record the depreciation expense for the first two years are as follows:

Year 1

Depreciation Expense	254,960	
Accumulated Depreciation, Bus		254,960

Year 2

Depreciation Expense	173,705	
Accumulated Depreciation, Bus		173,705

The asset will appear on the balance sheet as follows:

Property, plant and equipment	Year 2	Year 1
Bus		
Gross block	₹800,000	₹800,000
Deduct Accumulated depreciation	428,665	254,960
Net block	371,335	545,040

Since the WDV method is the only method acceptable for tax purposes for most assets, record-keeping costs are reduced by adopting the method for accounting purposes as well. However, tax depreciation rates contain an incentive element for quick replacement of assets; hence, using these rates for accounting depreciation will have the effect of writing off assets faster than can be justified by the matching principle. Therefore, even if a firm follows the WDV method, it should make independent asset life estimates for accounting.

What would be the WDV depreciation rate for an asset that has a very small residual value?

QUICK QUESTION
Depreciation rate

Sum-of-the-years'-digits Method

The **sum-of-the-years'-digits** (SYD) is method is rarely used in India. Being an accelerated depreciation method, it charges a large part of the cost of an asset in the early years. Under this method, we calculate depreciation expense for a year as the product of the depreciable amount and the factor, (k/S). The value of the numerator, k, would be n for Year 1, $(n-1)$ for Year 2, $(n-2)$ for Year 3, ..., and 1 for Year n, n being the useful life of the asset expressed in years. S equals the sum of the numbers, 1 to n, and is computed as $1 + 2 + 3 + ... + n$. The formula $n(n+1)/2$ gives the value of the denominator. Using the SYD method, we calculate depreciation expense for Year 1 as:

$$(\text{Cost} - \text{Residual value}) \times \frac{6}{\text{Sum of the digits, 1 to 6}}$$

$$= (₹800,000 - ₹80,000) \times \frac{6}{1+2+3+4+5+6}$$

Depreciation Schedule: Sum-of-the-years'-digits Method

Year	Cost	Depreciation Expense*	Accumulated Depreciation	Carrying Amount
1	₹800,000	₹205,714	₹205,714	₹594,286
2	800,000	171,429	377,143	422,857
3	800,000	137,143	514,286	285,714
4	800,000	102,857	617,143	182,857
5	800,000	68,571	685,714	114,286
6	800,000	34,286	720,000	80,000

*Depreciation for Year 1 = (800,000 – 80,000) × 6/21; for Year 2 = (800,000 – 80,000) × 5/21; and so on.

Production-units Method

The **production-units method** assumes that depreciation arises solely from the use of an asset and that time plays a trivial role in the depreciation process. Under this method, the depreciable amount of an asset is divided by the total estimated output during its useful life to obtain the unit depreciation rate. Yearly depreciation expense is calculated by multiplying the unit rate by the yearly output. For example, if the bus has an estimated useful life of 200,000 km, the unit depreciation would be worked out as follows:

$$\frac{₹720,000}{200,000 \text{ km}} = ₹3.60 \text{ per km}$$

Let's assume that the bus log shows that its usage was 10,000 km in the first year, 30,000 km in the second, 70,000 km in the third, 20,000 km in the fourth, 50,000 km in the fifth, and 20,000 km in the sixth year. The depreciation schedule under the production-units method would be as follows:

Depreciation Schedule: Production-units Method

Year	Cost	Depreciation Expense	Accumulated Depreciation	Carrying Amount
1	₹800,000	₹ 36,000	₹ 36,000	₹764,000
2	800,000	108,000	144,000	656,000
3	800,000	252,000	396,000	404,000
4	800,000	72,000	468,000	332,000
5	800,000	180,000	648,000	152,000
6	800,000	72,000	720,000	80,000

The production-units method is appropriate when it is possible to estimate the productive capacity of an asset with a fair degree of accuracy and there is a direct relationship between an asset's use and its loss of service potential. Productive capacity may be expressed in terms of the number of units of output (machines), hours (aircraft), kilometres (cars), or tonnes (mining equipment), as appropriate to the asset. Where output fluctuates widely from one period to another, the production-units method results in a better matching of costs and revenues than the straight-line method which computes a constant depreciation expense, regardless of the output.

An accurate record of asset use, such as a properly written machine log, is a prerequisite to the application of the production-units method. Very few companies follow this method, most probably because the additional data-collection costs involved in the method outweigh the benefits of better allocation of depreciation resulting from its adoption.

TEST YOUR UNDERSTANDING 6.3
Production-units Method

Manish Dairy bought a delivery van for ₹400,000. The van is expected to be sold for ₹50,000 after it has logged 175,000 km. The van logged 30,000 km in the first year. Record the depreciation expense for the year.

Comparing the Depreciation Methods

A comparison of the four methods described earlier shows that straight-line depreciation is equal over the six-year period (₹120,000). By contrast, the accelerated methods (written-down-value and sum-of-the-years'-digits) begin with much higher amounts than straight-line (212 per cent and 171 per cent of straight-line depreciation, respectively), and taper off to amounts below straight-line. The pattern generated by the production-units method follows the pattern of output, which fluctuates from year to year. The straight-line method produces a higher carrying amount than the accelerated methods in the early years. Table 6.1 compares these methods.

The differing patterns for charging depreciation have their merits and demerits.		
Method	**Merits**	**Demerits**
A. Straight-line	▪ Easy to apply. ▪ Suitable for assets that depreciate with time and are little affected by wear and tear due to usage.	▪ Undercharges depreciation in early years when assets are conceivably more productive. ▪ Smoothens income, so users may get a misleading view.
B. Accelerated methods 　▪ Sum-of-the-years'-digits 　▪ Written-down-value	▪ Charge substantially higher depreciation in early years when assets are conceivably more productive. ▪ Suitable for assets that have high rates of obsolescence.	▪ Produce lower profit in early years after asset acquisition, so managers do not like it.
C. Production-units	▪ Matches expense better by relating it to output.	▪ Produces volatility in income that may give an impression that managers have no control over the firm's performance.

TABLE 6.1

Comparison of Depreciation Methods

Figures 6.2(a) and(b) show depreciation expense and carrying amount under the straight-line and WDV methods.

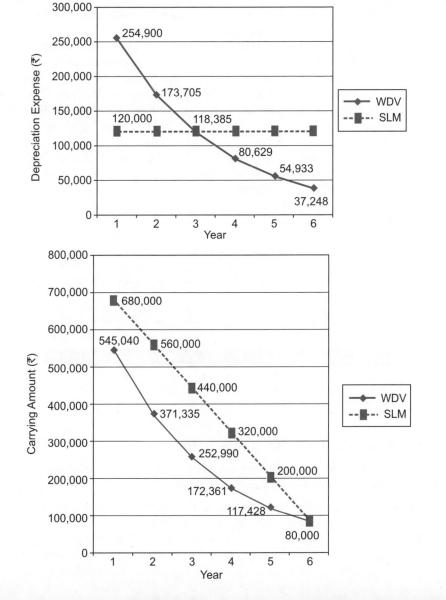

Figure 6.2(a)

STRAIGHT-LINE AND WRITTEN-DOWN-VALUE METHODS: DEPRECIATION EXPENSE

Depreciation expense under the written-down-value (WDV) method is higher in the early part of an asset's life than under the straight-line method (SLM).

Figure 6.2(b)

STRAIGHT-LINE AND WRITTEN-DOWN-VALUE METHODS: CARRYING AMOUNT

The WDV method produces a substantially lower carrying amount than the SLM. The WDV method is especially suitable for assets that have high obsolescence rates.

**TEST YOUR
UNDERSTANDING 6.4**
Depreciation Expense

Aarti Enterprise installed an air-conditioner on April 1, 20X4 at a cost of ₹600,000. The equipment was expected to be useful for five years and have a residual value of ₹40,000. Compute the depreciation expense for the year ended March 31, 20X5 under (a) straight-line, (b) WDV, and (c) SYD methods.

Selecting a Depreciation Method

Which depreciation method should an enterprise select? The method used should reflect the pattern in which the enterprise expects to consume the asset's future economic benefits. Accounting standards do not provide specific guidance on how to select the method. In line with the matching principle, the method chosen should result in a fair allocation of asset cost to the periods in which an enterprise benefits from the asset. The management is in the best position to judge the expected pattern in which the enterprise expects to realize the benefits.

While the straight-line method is the simplest of the depreciation methods, it does not match costs and revenues when the output of an asset fluctuates. In such situations, the production-units method is a better choice. The written-down-value method may result in reduced record-keeping costs if an enterprise follows the tax depreciation rates for financial reporting as well.

Factors such as the relative simplicity of a method, managerial motives, savings in record-keeping costs, tax laws, and legal requirements influence the choice of the method. Many listed companies use the straight-line method because it does not depress the reported earnings in the early years of new projects. Also, communicating the effect of the straight-line method to investors is relatively uncomplicated.

Analysts would view a company that uses accelerated depreciation as being more prudent in measuring its earnings and hence having a higher earnings quality since higher depreciation charges in the early years of an asset's life result in lower profit.

**DISCUSSION
QUESTION 6.2**

You are the chief financial officer of an airline listed on the National Stock Exchange. The airline operates on domestic and international routes. How should the airline go about selecting the depreciation method?

....

....

....

ONE-MINUTE QUIZ 6.2
Depreciation Methods

A depreciable asset has an estimated 10 per cent residual value. At the end of its estimated useful life, the carrying amount of the asset would equal zero under which of the following depreciation methods?

	Straight-line	Written-down-value
(a)	Yes	No
(b)	Yes	Yes
(c)	No	Yes
(d)	No	No

Legal Requirements Relating to Depreciation

Schedule II to the Companies Act 2013 specifies the useful life and residual value of various tangible assets. These provisions will apply as follows:

1. *Prescribed class of companies:* The useful life and residual value of an asset shall not normally be different from those specified in Schedule II. If a company uses a different useful life or residual value, it must disclose the justification for doing so. The "prescribed class of companies" would include listed companies.

2. *Other companies:* The useful life of an asset shall not be longer and residual value shall not be higher than those specified in Schedule II.

Thus, companies in the "prescribed class" can adopt shorter or longer useful life and higher or lower residual value, if they have reasons. Ordinarily, the residual value of an asset is often insignificant, but it should generally be not more than 5 per cent of the original cost of the asset. Table 6.2 gives the useful lives for selected assets from Schedule II.

TABLE 6.2

Useful Lives of Tangible Assets in Schedule II to the Companies Act 2013

Companies in the "prescribed class" can use longer or shorter useful lives, if they have justification. Other companies cannot use longer useful lives.

Assets	Useful Life (in years)
Buildings	
■ Buildings (other than factory buildings) RCC frame structure	60
■ Buildings (other than factory buildings) other than RCC frame structure	30
■ Factory buildings	30
■ Temporary structure	3
Plant and machinery	
■ Plant and machinery other than continuous process plan not covered specific industries	15
■ Continuous process plan for which no special rate has been prescribed	8
■ Refineries	25
■ Pipelines	30
■ Blast furnace	20
■ Power plant	40
■ Wind power generation unit	22
■ X-ray, CT scan, Ultrasound, ECG equipment	13
■ Road making equipment	12
Furniture and fittings	
■ General furniture and fittings	22
■ Furniture and fittings used in hotels	8
Motor vehicles	
■ Motor cycles	10
■ Buses used in a business of running them on hire	6
■ Buses other than those used in a business of running them on hire	6
Ships	
■ Ocean-going bulk carriers	25
Aircraft or helicopters	20
Office equipment	5
Computers	
■ Servers and networks	6
■ Desktops, laptops	3
■ Buses other than those used in a business of running them on hire	6

Note: Extra shift depreciation shall be charged for certain classes of assets.

Companies must disclose their depreciation method(s) and depreciation rates or useful lives of assets, if the rates followed are different from the Schedule II rates. Schedule II states that the useful life or residual value of any specific asset, as notified by a regulatory authority, shall be applied in calculating the depreciation to be provided for such asset irrespective of the requirements of Schedule II. For example, electricity companies must follow the rates and method notified by the Central Electricity Regulatory Commission.

Some Issues in Depreciation Accounting

Depreciation for Partial Reporting Periods When an asset is bought during a reporting period, depreciation for the period is proportionate to the period (or *pro rata*) it is held. Assume that an enterprise buys for ₹250,000 a machine with an estimated useful life of 10 years and residual value of ₹10,000 on January 1, 20XX and that the financial year ends on March 31, 20XX. The straight-line depreciation for three months would be for ₹6,000, calculated as follows:

$$\frac{₹250,000 - ₹10,000}{10 \text{ years}} \times \frac{1}{4} = ₹6,000$$

Assets of Low Value Items such as loose tools, dies, moulds, and spare parts have a short life and have to be replaced constantly. For practical convenience, many companies charge off assets of low value to current period's income. It is tedious to maintain records for such numerous items. The practice of writing off assets of low value is acceptable if the amounts are not material in relation to the net profit of an enterprise. This is an example of how the materiality principle may be applied.

Revising Useful Life and Residual Value Useful life and residual value estimates are seldom precise. Therefore, enterprises must review them at each reporting date. If current expectations differ from previous estimates, they must revise the estimates. New developments such as unanticipated physical damage or unforeseen obsolescence would require changing the previous estimates. Also, more experience in using the asset may suggest the need for changing the estimate. A change in accounting estimate is recognized prospectively. The enterprise expenses the depreciable amount at the time of the change over the remaining useful life of the asset.

HANDHOLD 6.6
Useful Life Revision

Vinod bought a computer for ₹100,000, with an estimated residual value of ₹10,000. At the time, it seemed that the computer would be useful for six years. After three years, he thinks that the computer will last only two more years at the end of which it is expected to realize ₹5,000. Vinod follows the straight-line method. We calculate the revised depreciation expense from Year 4 onwards as follows:

Cost	₹100,000
Deduct Estimated residual value	10,000
Original depreciable amount	90,000
Original estimated useful life (years)	6
Yearly depreciation expense: ₹90,000/6	15,000
Accumulated depreciation: ₹15,000 × 3	45,000
Carrying amount: ₹100,000 − ₹45,000	55,000
Deduct Revised estimated residual value	5,000
Revised depreciable amount	50,000
Revised useful life (years)	2
Revised yearly depreciation expense: ₹50,000/2	25,000

TEST YOUR UNDERSTANDING 6.5
Useful Life Revision

Ahmed's Diagnostic Centre bought a scanning machine for ₹120,000 with an estimated useful life of 10 years and a ₹5,000 estimated residual value. It follows the straight-line method. At the end of three years, the Centre's administrator revised the equipment's remaining useful life to five years and residual value to ₹1,000. What is the depreciation expense for the fourth year?

Changing the Depreciation Method An enterprise should apply the same depreciation method over time, so that users of financial statements can compare the numbers. The depreciation method should reflect the pattern in which the enterprise expects to consume the future economic benefits from the asset. New information could suggest a different pattern. The method must be reviewed at each reporting date. If there is a significant change in the pattern of consumption of the future benefits, the enterprise must change the method to reflect the new pattern. A change in the depreciation method is treated as a change in accounting estimate and recognized prospectively. Appropriate disclosures are required.

HANDHOLD 6.7
Depreciation Method Change

Asif bought a car for ₹500,000. The car had an estimated useful life of six years and a residual value of ₹50,000. Asif follows the straight-line method. At the beginning of the fourth year, he decides to switch to the WDV method, because he believes that it better captures the pattern of realization of the benefits from the asset. There is no change in residual value. Asif calculates the revised depreciation expense as follows:

Cost..	₹500,000
Deduct Estimated residual value..	50,000
Depreciable amount...	450,000
Estimated useful life (years)..	6
Yearly depreciation expense: ₹450,000/6..	75,000
Accumulated depreciation: ₹75,000 × 3..	225,000
Carrying amount: ₹500,000 – ₹225,000..	275,000
Depreciation rate, WDV	43.35%
Depreciation expense, year 4, WDV: ₹275,000 × 43.35%..............................	119,213

(As an exercise, verify the WDV depreciation rate.)

Cairn India, an oil and gas exploration company, changed the method of depreciation from straight-line to production-units in the year ended March 31, 2015, to comply with the Companies Act 2013. The change was done with retrospective effect from the date the related assets were acquired. As a result, there was an additional charge of ₹5,004 million disclosed as an exceptional item in the quarter ended June 30, 2014. This is a low quality earnings item, since it won't be repeated in subsequent periods. In fact, future depreciation charge will come down compared to the previous method. Cairn India's accounting for the change in the depreciation method followed AS 6, the accounting standard effective then. Note that under Ind AS the accounting method change would be prospective and the amount of additional charge would be spread over future periods.

Sources: Company reports.

EARNINGS QUALITY ANALYSIS

Depreciation Method Switch at Cairn India

Depreciating Components of an Asset When the cost of a part of an asset is significant in relation to its total cost, the cost of the asset must be allocated to its significant parts. Also, it must depreciate separately each of those parts. That means the enterprise must estimate the useful life and residual value of each such part and select a depreciation method that is appropriate for each. This involves significant managerial effort, especially for large enterprises with numerous assets. At times, a significant part of an asset may have the same useful life and depreciation method as the useful life and depreciation method of another significant part of the same asset. Such parts may be grouped for depreciation purposes.

Grand Towers Company owns buildings in which a number of companies have their offices. The management of the company divides each building into (a) foundation and frame, with a useful life of 60 years; (b) installations, with a useful life of 30 years; and (c) removable walls, with a useful life of 15 years. Grand Towers must depreciate each of these components of a building over the respective useful life of the component. Thus, partition walls will be depreciated over 15 years, even though the building foundation and frame will be around for a longer time. Similarly, installations such as some beams and load-bearing walls will be depreciated over 30 years. Useful life estimates are based on technical evaluation of engineers and architects, municipal and fire safety regulations, and the company's asset replacement policy.

HANDHOLD 6.8

Depreciating Components of an Asset

Fully Depreciated Assets An enterprise must not remove a fully depreciated asset from the accounting records, so long as it is in good working condition and continues to be used. This is necessary in order to maintain control over the asset. Also, there will be no depreciation charge for a fully depreciated asset. Since the objective of depreciation accounting is to allocate an asset's cost over its useful life, the total depreciation for an asset can't exceed its cost. The cost and accumulated depreciation should be removed when the asset is no longer used in a business.

On January 1, year 1, an entity acquires for ₹1 million a new piece of machinery with an estimated useful life of 10 years. The machine has a camshaft costing ₹300,000 that must be replaced every five years. Continued operation of the machine requires an inspection costing ₹100,000 every four years. The company uses straight-line depreciation. What is the depreciation expense for Year 1?

(a) ₹100,000
(b) ₹110,000
(c) ₹130,000
(d) ₹145,000

ONE-MINUTE QUIZ 6.3

Depreciation Expense

DISCUSSION QUESTION 6.3

According to economists, past costs being *sunk* costs are irrelevant for valuation of an asset. Is there an *economic* case for depreciation?

....

....

....

Capital and Revenue Expenditure

Learning Objective

LO 5 Distinguish between capital expenditure and revenue expenditure.

An enterprise incurs costs on an asset after its initial acquisition. If the costs meet the recognition criteria for items of property, plant and equipment, i.e. (a) probable future economic benefits and (b) reliable measurement, they can be capitalized. Otherwise, they have to be expensed. **Capital expenditures** are incurred to acquire assets. Expenditures that extend the useful life, improve the quality of output, or reduce operating costs of an existing asset beyond their originally estimated levels are capital expenditures. For example, adding rooms in a hotel increases the hotel's revenue-earning capacity, fitting air-conditioners in inter-city coaches and replacing co-axial telecommunication lines by optical fibre cables provide future benefits and their costs are capital expenditures.

Revenue expenditures are incurred for ordinary repairs, maintenance, fuel, insurance, or other items needed to maintain and use buildings, and plant and equipment. They are expensed immediately because the benefits do not last beyond that period. While relocating factories or rearranging machines for improving efficiency may have future benefits, often the related expenditures can't be separated from normal operating expenses.

Ordinary repairs are expenditures incurred to maintain assets in good working condition. These are the costs of day-to-day servicing of assets that include the costs of labour, materials, and small parts. Periodic replacements of fused bulbs and worn-out car tyres, oiling and cleaning of equipment, and painting of buildings are treated as ordinary repairs since these expenditures are fairly regular and their benefit does not last beyond the year in which they are incurred. Ordinary repairs are expensed. **Major repairs** benefit a number of periods. For example, the benefit of relining a furnace or refurbishing aircraft interiors such as seats and galleys goes beyond the current year. Hence, most businesses capitalize and depreciate those expenditures.

Some assets require regular **major inspections**. For example, civil aviation authorities stipulate major periodic inspections for faults as a condition for operating an aircraft. The dry-docking of a ship is another example. The cost of a major inspection is capitalized as a component of the related asset and depreciated over the period until the next inspection. At that time, any remaining amount relating to the previous inspection is derecognized. At the time of acquisition of an asset that requires major inspection, the estimated cost of the next major inspection is separated from the asset's cost and depreciated over the period until the next inspection. In effect, we follow the component approach for depreciation of significant parts of an asset for major repairs and major inspections.

For practical purposes, many enterprises establish policies stating what constitutes a capital or revenue expenditure. For example, small expenditures on capital items may be charged to income, because the amounts involved are frequently thought to be not material in relation to the reported profit. For example, the cost of a stapler, which may last many years, would be treated as supplies expense rather than as an asset.

HANDHOLD 6.9
Major Repair

A car bought at a cost of ₹250,000 two years ago undergoes some major repairs at a cost of ₹40,000. The useful life of the car at the time of the purchase was five years and the residual value was ₹25,000. Depreciation is charged on the straight-line basis. As a result of the repairs, the life of the car is extended by two years, while the residual value would be unchanged. The revised depreciation charge for Year 3 would be calculated as follows:

Cost	₹250,000
Deduct Residual value	25,000
Original depreciable amount	225,000
Deduct Accumulated depreciation: ₹45,000 × 2	90,000
Remaining depreciable amount	135,000
Add Major repairs	40,000
New depreciable amount	175,000
Remaining useful life (years)	5

Revised depreciation expense = ₹175,000/5 years = ₹35,000 per year

Shekhar Company bought a boiler for ₹700,000. The boiler was expected to have a useful life of eight years and a residual value of ₹60,000. After five years, the company carried out repairs costing ₹150,000. As a result, the remaining useful life of the boiler was expected to increase by two years. Its estimated residual value was not affected. The company provides straight-line depreciation. Compute the depreciation expense after the repairs.

TEST YOUR UNDERSTANDING 6.6
Major Repair

Effect of a Capital-Revenue Error

A capital expenditure goes to an asset account and does not reduce the income of the current period. The amount will be depreciated in the future periods. A revenue expenditure goes to an expense account and is deducted in computing the income of the current period. Any error in distinguishing between capital and revenue expenditures will result in distorting the reported profits of current and future reporting periods.

- Suppose a firm erroneously charges the cost of equipment to repairs. The effect of this error is to overstate current expense and understate current profit, and understate future expense (because of the absence of depreciation) and overstate future profit.

- Suppose a firm capitalizes current repairs. The effect of this error is to understate current expense and overstate current profit, and overstate future expense (because of the presence of depreciation) and understate future profit.

The effect of error in treating a capital expenditure as a revenue expenditure and *vice versa* is self-reversing, similar to an inventory error but over a longer period.

WorldCom, a US telecommunication company, collapsed in June 2012. The company had capitalized network rentals over a period of time. The amounts totalled $11 billion, according to some reports. It is a straightforward fraud that should have been detected by the company's finance officers, internal auditor and external auditor. The effect of the fraud was that earnings and cash flow from operating activities were overstated. While there was no siphoning off of cash, as has been alleged in Satyam, the financial statements turned out to be unreliable and investors were misled into making decisions that they would not have made otherwise. A major fallout of the WorldCom fraud was that Andersen, the company's external auditor, was wiped out of existence. The WorldCom fraud, together with Enron and other accounting manipulations, led to the Sarbanes-Oxley Act 2002 that imposed stringent controls and regulations on managers and auditors.

EARNINGS QUALITY ANALYSIS
WorldCom's Con Act

Conflicting Motives

The distinction between capital and revenue expenditures is not always straightforward. Hence, firms wishing to boost their profits frequently attempt to capitalize expenditures which, on closer scrutiny, may have to be written off. Auditors review the firm's treatment of nebulous expenditure items to ensure that current expenses are not capitalized. In contrast, for tax purposes most businesses, in case of doubt, choose to expense an outlay rather than capitalize it, because expensing the item has the effect of reducing their taxable income and tax expense. Of course, tax officials will scrutinize such items carefully to ensure that capital expenditure is not allowed as business expense. As may be expected, tax payers and tax officers usually differ on the appropriate treatment of many an expenditure.

Therefore, the Supreme Court and the High Courts have to decide numerous disputes leading to the development of a large body of case law on the subject.

- Now think of a firm that is highly tax-driven. It would be too happy to expense costs incurred in acquiring assets, such as brokerage and lawyer's fee, immediately and reduce its taxable income. In a few bizarre instances, companies have split up a large capital expenditure into ridiculously small amounts and expensed them in order to save tax.

Depreciation for Income Tax Purposes

Learning Objective

LO 6 Understand the difference between accounting depreciation and tax depreciation.

Depreciation benefits under the income tax law are frequently confused with the depreciation charge in the financial statements. Financial statements must be prepared in conformity with accounting principles and standards. In contrast, income tax returns and related statements must comply with income tax regulations. While financial accounting and tax accounting are similar in some respects, they differ significantly in other areas. Depreciation is an example.

Income-tax rules permit tax payers to claim depreciation benefits at the prescribed rates using the WDV method.[2] The government seeks to encourage investment in new assets by allowing the rapid write-off of assets. So, in many countries including India, the tax law permits accelerated write-off of asset costs by prescribing recovery periods that are shorter than the estimated useful lives for accounting purposes as well as permitting recovery of a large portion of the cost of the investments in the early years. Also, the tax law requires legal ownership and use of an asset, but accounting depreciation is based on economic ownership. The stipulations for accounting and tax depreciation are different, simply because the objectives of financial reporting differ from those of taxation. Table 6.3 gives a sample of the tax depreciation rates.

TABLE 6.3

Depreciation Allowance Rates for Tax

Tax depreciation rates differ from accounting depreciation because financial reporting and tax reporting have different objectives.

Class of Assets	Depreciation Allowance Rate (Percentage of written-down-value)
Buildings	
• General	5
• Wooden structures	100
Furniture and fittings	
• Furniture	10
Machinery and Plant	
• General	15
• Motor cars	15
• Aeroplanes, aeroengines	40
• Motor buses, lorries	30
• Air pollution control equipment (e.g. electrostatic precipitator)	100
• Life-saving medical equipment (e.g. heart lung machine)	40
• Computer software	60
• Renewable energy devices (e.g. solar heater)	80
• Books, annual publications	100
Ships	
• Ocean-going vessels	20
Intangible Assets	
• Know-how, patents, copyrights, trademarks, licences, franchises and other business or commercial rights	25

Note: The above rates are effective from April 1, 2006. Depreciation rates change from time to time. The rates currently applicable can be obtained from the latest Income Tax Rules. The rate applicable to a particular asset will depend on the more detailed classification given in Appendix I of the Income Tax Rules.

---

[2] The straight-line method is prescribed for companies engaged in generation and distribution of power.

To illustrate the calculation of tax depreciation, let us revert to our bus example and apply a tax depreciation rate of 30 per cent.

Depreciation Schedule: Income Tax Reporting

Year	Calculation	Depreciation Allowance	Accumulated Depreciation	Carrying Amount
1	₹800,000 × 30%	₹240,000	₹240,000	₹560,000
2	560,000 × 30%	168,000	408,000	392,000
3	392,000 × 30%	117,600	525,600	274,400
4	274,400 × 30%	82,320	607,920	192,080
5	192,080 × 30%	57,624	665,544	134,456
6	134,456 × 30%	40,337	705,881	94,119

For tax purposes the business claims nearly two-thirds of the asset cost in the first three years, although the asset has an estimated useful life of six years. Different methods of depreciation may be used for reporting to shareholders and income tax authorities. In this sense, there is nothing devious about businesses maintaining "two sets of accounting records": one for shareholders and the other for tax authorities. Most large enterprises use straight-line depreciation in their financial statements, because it is convenient to apply and makes it possible to show higher earnings in the early years. But they use the WDV method for tax purposes, postponing payment of income taxes. Thus, they have the best of both worlds. Tax depreciation rates are not usually acceptable for shareholder reporting.

Derecognition of Property, Plant and Equipment

When an asset wears out or becomes obsolete, it is no longer useful. An enterprise scraps or sells it, or exchanges it for another asset. Seldom is the disposal value of an asset equal to its carrying amount. So it is usually necessary to recognize a gain or a loss on disposal.

Learning Objective

LO 7 Record derecognition of property, plant and equipment.

Accounting entries differ depending on the manner of disposal of a used asset: (a) discarding; (b) holding for disposal; (c) selling; or (d) exchanging for another asset. Depending on the manner of disposal, the entries must do the following:

1. Record depreciation for the part of the period ending with the date of disposal;
2. Remove the cost of the asset and the accumulated depreciation from the books;
3. Show any receipt or payment of cash;
4. Recognize any gain or loss on disposal; and
5. Recognize any new asset acquired.

Suppose Amit Company acquired a photocopier on April 1, 20X1, for ₹170,000 with an estimated useful life of eight years and residual value of ₹10,000. It charges straight-line depreciation. The financial year end is March 31. The company disposes of the photocopier on June 30, 20X6, i.e. after five years and three months. At March 31, 20X6, the asset and accumulated depreciation appear in the books as follows:

Photocopier

Balance	170,000		

Accumulated Depreciation

		Balance	100,000

The following entry records depreciation for the period April 1 to June 30, 20X6:

Depreciation Expense	5,000	
Accumulated Depreciation, Photocopier		5,000

The Accumulated Depreciation has a balance of ₹105,000, as shown below:

Accumulated Depreciation

	Balance	100,000
	Depreciation, April 1 to June 30, 20X6	5,000
	Balance	105,000

The carrying amount of the asset is now ₹65,000. We will now see the procedure for recording the disposal of the asset in different ways.

Discarding Asset

Suppose Amit Company abandons the photocopier without realizing any amount. It will remove the asset and accumulated depreciation accounts and recognize the asset's carrying amount as a loss. The following entry will record the disposal:

Accumulated Depreciation, Photocopier	105,000	
Loss on Disposal of Photocopier...	65,000	
Photocopier..		170,000
Discarding of photocopier at a loss of ₹65,000		

Holding Asset for Sale

Suppose the company withdraws the asset for intended sale. As before, it will remove the asset and accumulated depreciation accounts, and recognize the lower of the asset's carrying amount and estimated net realizable value (i.e. fair value *less* costs to sell) as a non-current asset held for sale. It will recognize the carrying amount of the asset *less* estimated net realizable value as loss. Assume that the photocopier is estimated to sell for ₹10,000 after deducting estimated selling costs. The following entry records the disposal:

Photocopier Held for Sale	10,000	
Accumulated Depreciation, Photocopier	105,000	
Loss on Disposal of Photocopier...	55,000	
Photocopier..		170,000
Holding photocopier for sale		

Selling Asset

Suppose Amit Company sells the photocopier for ₹50,000 after meeting the selling costs. It will remove the asset and accumulated depreciation accounts, record the net sale proceeds, and recognize the difference between the carrying amount of the asset *less* net sale proceeds as gain or loss. It will record the transaction as follows:

Cash..	50,000	
Accumulated Depreciation, Photocopier	105,000	
Loss on Disposal of Photocopier...	15,000	
Photocopier..		170,000
Sale of photocopier at a loss of ₹15,000 (₹65,000 – ₹50,000)		

If the asset is sold for an amount greater than its carrying amount, a gain will result. Assume that the net sale proceeds are ₹90,000. The following entry records the gain:

Cash..	90,000	
Accumulated Depreciation, Photocopier	105,000	
Photocopier..		170,000
Gain on Disposal of Photocopier...		25,000
Sale of photocopier at a gain of ₹25,000 (₹90,000 – ₹65,000)		

If the net sale proceeds equal the carrying amount of the asset, there is no gain or loss. In that case, Amit removes the asset and accumulated depreciation accounts and records the net sale proceeds, as follows:

Cash..	65,000	
Accumulated Depreciation, Photocopier	105,000	
Photocopier...		170,000
Sale of photocopier at carrying amount		

Exchanging Assets

Suppose Amit Company exchanges the existing photocopier for another asset or a combination of another asset and a cash payment. At what amount should it record the asset received? Should it recognize a gain or loss on the exchange?

The principle is that an asset acquired in an exchange should be measured at fair value if (i) the exchange transaction has "commercial substance"; and (ii) the fair value of either the asset received or the asset given up can be reliably measured. An acquired asset not measured at fair value is recorded at the carrying amount of the asset given up. If both the fair value of the asset received and the fair value of the asset given up can be estimated with equal reliability, the asset received should be measured at the fair value of the asset given up. If the fair value of the asset received can be measured with more reliability, that value is used. The fair value or carrying amount is adjusted for any cash paid or received.

An exchange transaction has commercial substance if the cash flow configuration (risk, timing, and amount) of the two assets differs or the net present value of the post-tax cash flows of the operations of the enterprise changes as a result of the exchange.[3] In either case, the difference should be significant relative to the fair value of the assets exchanged.

Suppose Amit Company exchanges the photocopier with a fair value of ₹75,000 and a cash amount of ₹25,000 for a scanner with a fair value of ₹100,000. Since the two assets are different, the transaction has commercial substance. The company will record the scanner at its fair value of ₹100,000 and the gain on the exchange of ₹10,000, the difference between fair value and the carrying amount of the photocopier:

Scanner...	100,000	
Accumulated Depreciation, Photocopier	105,000	
Cash		25,000
Photocopier..		170,000
Gain on Disposal of Photocopier...		10,000
Exchange of photocopier for scanner at a gain of ₹10,000		

Suppose the fair value of the photocopier is ₹60,000. Prepare the journal entry to record the exchange.

TEST YOUR UNDERSTANDING 6.7
Exchange of Asset

Now let us Suppose Amit Company exchanges the photocopier with a fair value of ₹75,000 and cash of ₹25,000 for a new photocopier with a fair value of ₹100,000. On the face of it, there is a gain of ₹10,000. But the transaction lacks commercial substance because the assets are similar. In effect, the company is in the same position as it was before the transaction, and there is no gain, really. So it recognizes the asset received at the carrying amount of the asset given up, adjusting for the cash paid:

Photocopier..	90,000	
Accumulated Depreciation, Photocopier....................................	105,000	
Cash		25,000
Photocopier...		170,000
Exchange of photocopier for a new photocopier at a gain of ₹10,000		

In other words, the cost of the asset received is reduced by the amount of notional gain.

Gains and Losses under Tax Laws

For tax purposes, gains and losses on disposal of depreciable assets are calculated in respect of a "block of assets", a group of assets that have the same depreciation rates within the asset classes of buildings, furniture, machinery and plant, ships, and intangible assets.

---

[3] *Net present value* is the difference between the present value of the cash inflows from an asset and the cash outflow for acquisition of the asset. Appendix C on time value of money explains present value calculation.

Under the tax laws, there is no need to maintain item-wise records. The block increases with the addition of assets and decreases with disposals. So long as the proceeds from the sale of an asset (or the fair value of the asset obtained in exchange) are less than the depreciable amount of the block to which the asset pertains, no gain arises for tax purposes. A gain will arise for tax purposes only if the carrying amount of the block at the time of the disposal is less than the value of the asset being disposed of. A loss will arise only if all the assets in a block have been disposed of and a balance remains in the block after deducting the disposal value of the asset already being disposed.

Myths About Depreciation

Learning Objective

LO 8 **Dispel the myths about depreciation.**

To accountants, depreciation is the allocation of an asset's cost to the periods over which it is expected to be useful. Many users of financial statements seem to have fanciful notions of depreciation. Here are three such notions:

Myth 1: Depreciation is a source of cash.

Myth 2: Depreciation is intended to provide funds for replacement.

Myth 3: Depreciation is a valuation process.

Let's now dispel them.

Myth 1: Depreciation is a source of cash.

Many users of financial statements believe that depreciation is a source of cash. The greater the provision for depreciation, they figure, the higher the firm's cash generation. They could be imagining that accumulated depreciation represents wads of currency notes waiting to be used when aged manufacturing plant is to be replaced.

Depreciation expense is similar to any other expense in that it reduces net profit. But it does not entail a cash outflow, unlike other expenses, e.g. salaries. This is not the same thing as a cash inflow. Depreciation expense is just the result of an accounting entry to allocate the cost of an asset to different reporting periods. The accumulated depreciation account is a contra asset account in that it represents the amount of the cost an asset already written off. Note that the cash account has a *debit* balance, whereas the accumulated depreciation account has a *credit* balance. Consider a sample journal entry for recording depreciation expense.

Depreciation Expense	2,500	
Accumulated Depreciation..		2,500

This entry does not affect cash. We can appreciate this better with the help of a statement of cash flows. Suppose you start a business with cash of ₹10,000. You pay cash and buy equipment costing ₹6,000 with an estimated useful life of four years and zero residual value. You charge straight-line depreciation. In the first year, your business makes cash sales for ₹8,000 and cash purchases for ₹5,000. The statement of cash flows for the first year would be as follows:

Cash flows from operating activities		
Cash received from customers..	₹ 8,000	
Cash paid to suppliers and employees...	(5,000)	
Net cash provided by operating activities......................................		₹ 3,000
Cash flows from investing activities		
Purchase of equipment	(6,000)	
Net cash used in investing activities...		(6,000)
Cash flows from financing activities		
Capital invested by owner..	10,000	
Net cash provided by financing activities......................................		10,000
Net increase in cash and cash equivalents		7,000
Beginning balance...		0
Ending balance..		7,000

Note that depreciation does *not* appear as an inflow in the statement. The ending cash balance will be ₹7,000, whether the depreciation rate is 0, 25, or 100 per cent. It is thus clear that depreciation accounting has nothing to do with the generation of cash. Smart businessmen have always known that there is only one source of cash from operations, and that is the cash provided by sales to customers.

FINANCIAL VIEW

Funding Capex with "Depreciation"?

Consider the following extract from a press release issued by Maruti Suzuki on March 15, 2014: "The Board of Directors of Maruti Suzuki India Limited today reviewed the Gujarat project in the context of the views and opinions expressed and took the following decisions: The entire capex for the Gujarat Sub would be funded by depreciation and equity brought in by Suzuki Motor Corporation..." Equity brings funds; you can check the bank balance to see if it went up after a share issue. Thinking that depreciation can fund capex arises from a fundamental misconception of the nature of depreciation. The statement in the press release implies *adding back* depreciation to accrual profit to arrive at cash flow. It's astonishing that even some board members and senior managers think that depreciation brings cash.

Myth 2: Depreciation is intended to provide funds for replacement.

As we have seen, accumulated depreciation does not exist in the form of cash. Very few businesses earmark a part of their cash balance for asset replacement, since investment in plant and equipment is much more profitable. Occasionally, we may come across a company that has a *depreciation fund*, a reserve represented by cash or investment in securities earmarked for financing asset replacement.

In addition, there is the problem of inflation. Asset prices rise in times of inflation; so, the cost of a new asset that will replace an existing asset will be greater than the amount of profit retained based on the historical cost of the asset. Recall that the purpose of depreciation is to spread out the cost of an asset. The depreciation charge is related to the historical cost of an asset, *not* its replacement cost. As a result, dividends and other payments are made based on 'illusory' profits, leaving insufficient funds for replacement of property, plant and equipment. In fact, this is one of the major weaknesses of the historical cost system.

Businesses can handle the problem of finding cash in several ways:

1. *Revalue property, plant and equipment and relate the depreciation charge to the replacement cost of the assets.* This is the **modified historical cost system**, described in the next section. While many companies have revalued their property, plant and equipment, unfortunately, they continue to provide depreciation based on the historical costs of the assets to avoid reporting lower profit to shareholders.

2. *Set aside in a reserve a supplementary depreciation equal to the excess of current value depreciation over the historical cost-based charge.* This may be done with or without a revaluation of assets. The supplementary depreciation would form part of a company's distributable reserves. This is a 'below the line' item, i.e. not an expense.

3. *Prepare comprehensive inflation-adjusted statements and pay dividend on the basis of the revised profit.*

These approaches reduce the amount of cash available for distribution and thus reduce the cash outflow. In India, hardly any company does any of these things.

Myth 3: Depreciation is a valuation process.

Financial statements do not purport to show the fluctuating market values of property, plant and equipment. Therefore, we depreciate an asset even if its market value has increased. For example, buildings have gone up in value in many parts of the world. Yet the accountant depreciates buildings because they have a finite useful life over which their cost must be expensed. Accounting depreciation does not mean a decline in the market value of an asset. Consequently, the balance sheet values of property, plant and equipment seldom reflect their current market values.

Revaluation of Property, Plant and Equipment

Learning Objective

LO 9 Explain revaluation of property, plant and equipment.

Traditionally, property, plant and equipment have been shown in the financial statements at their cost of acquisition. Persistent and high inflation leads to substantial differences between the historical costs and current market values of assets. Some argue that the information on asset values given in the balance sheet is irrelevant to the needs of managers, investors, and other users because the balance sheet does not reflect the current worth of a business. Responding to this criticism, many businesses recognize the current replacement values of their property, plant and equipment assets.

The disconnect between historical costs and current values is particularly evident in the case of land and buildings, since property values have appreciated significantly. Revaluation enables a company to present a healthier balance sheet by lowering the *debt-to-equity ratio*, a measure of the extent of a firm's reliance on borrowings and an indicator of its long-term solvency. Also, a company may revalue its assets with the aim of lifting its stock price by informing investors of its current value. A rise in the stock price would make the company a less attractive takeover target.

Enterprises can choose either the historical cost model or the revaluation model for property, plant and equipment. Under the historical cost model, the asset appears at its cost *less* accumulated depreciation and impairment losses. Under the revaluation model, the asset appears at its fair value at the date of the revaluation *less* accumulated depreciation and impairment losses. Regular revaluations are necessary to ensure that the asset's carrying amount does not differ materially from its fair value. Selective revaluation of assets can lead to a confusing mixture of costs and values on different dates. Therefore, when a firm revalues an item of property, plant and equipment, it should revalue the entire class of assets to which the item belongs. Examples of classes are land, land and buildings, machinery, ships, aircraft, motor vehicles, furniture and fixtures, and office equipment. Usually, enterprises obtain periodic appraisals of assets from valuers. A look at published reports over the years would show that the number of Indian companies revaluing their assets has been increasing.[4]

Revaluation Reserve

An increase in an asset's carrying amount arising from revaluation goes directly to equity as revaluation reserve. As a matter of prudence, a decrease in the carrying amount is charged to the statement of profit and loss. An increase will go to the statement of profit and loss to the extent it reverses a past charge, and a decrease will go to revaluation reserve to the extent it reverses a past surplus. Revaluation surplus is an unrealized gain. Based on legal and accounting principles, it is a *capital reserve*, a reserve that is not available for distribution as dividends or for the issue of bonus shares. (You will learn more about reserves in Chapter 11.)

Accounting for Revaluation

Assume that Victor Company bought a plant on January 1, 20X0 for ₹15,000 with an estimated useful life of five years and depreciated it using the straight-line method. On December 31, 20X2, the plant would appear in the balance sheet as follows:

Cost..	₹15,000
Deduct Accumulated depreciation: ₹15,000 × 3/5..	9,000
Carrying amount	6,000

---

[4] Revaluations are also common in many British Commonwealth countries including the United Kingdom, Australia, and New Zealand. Revaluations are *prohibited* in the United States.

Assume further that the current purchase price of a new plant is ₹25,000. If the existing plant is revalued, the above numbers would be revised as follows:

Current purchase price.. ₹25,000
Deduct Accumulated depreciation: ₹25,000 × 3/5....................................... 15,000
Carrying amount 10,000

The journal entry to record the revaluation is as follows:

Plant 10,000
    Accumulated Depreciation, Plant 6,000
    Revaluation Reserve... 4,000

The credit of ₹6,000 to Accumulated Depreciation is the "backlog" depreciation for three years for the difference between depreciation based on the revalued amount and on cost.

Depreciation on Revalued Assets

Business opts for revaluation because they want to present the current value of their assets. It follows that the charge for consumption of assets should also be in current value terms. From the time of revaluation, the depreciation charge should be based on the revalued amount. In the above example, the depreciation expense for 20X3 would be ₹5,000, as compared to ₹3,000 under the cost model.

Shree Textiles bought a building on January 1, 20X2, for ₹100,000. The estimated useful life of the building was 20 years. Straight-line depreciation was charged. In 20X9, the company engaged a valuer to determine the current value of the building. The valuer estimated the net increase in the value of the building, as at January 1, 20X9, at ₹97,500, the difference between the increase in cost, ₹150,000, and in accumulated depreciation, ₹52,500. The company follows the calendar year. Prepare a journal entry to record the revaluation.

TEST YOUR UNDERSTANDING 6.8
Revaluation

Why do firms revalue property, plant and equipment?

DISCUSSION QUESTION 6.4

. . . .

. . . .

. . . .

Which of the following statements about the revaluation model followed for an asset is correct?
  (a) All property, plant and equipment, not just the asset, must be revalued.
  (b) The entire class of property, plant and equipment to which the asset belongs must be revalued.
  (c) Selected assets within a class of property, plant and equipment to which the asset belongs must be revalued.
  (d) Revaluation of property, plant and equipment must be made at least every three years.

ONE-MINUTE QUIZ 6.4
Revaluation

Intangible Assets

An **intangible asset** is a separately identifiable, non-financial asset without physical substance. Intangible assets represent legal rights with associated economic benefits. Intangible assets are long-term assets that can generate future earnings. The value of an intangible asset arises from the long-term rights, privileges, or advantages it confers on its owner.

    Identifiability, control, and future benefits are necessary in order to recognize an item as an intangible asset. An intangible asset meets the identifiability criterion when it (a) can be separated or divided from the enterprise and sold or transferred, and

Learning Objective
LO 10 Describe and account for intangible assets.

(b) arises from contractual or other legal rights. A copyright is an intangible asset because it is identifiable separately from other assets, it arises from a legal right, and the owner has exclusive control over its use, and expects future benefits from it. Other examples of intangible assets are aircraft landing rights, brand names, trademarks, customer lists, computer software, patents, movies, mobile phone licences, website domain names, carbon credits, import quotas, and franchises. Business enterprises certainly benefit from supplier relationships, customer loyalty, employee skills, and market share. Unfortunately, these do not meet the definition of an intangible asset (particularly, identifiability and control) and hence enterprises can't recognize them in the financial statements.

- Rising Pune Supergiants paid ₹145 million ($2.16 million) for the England all-rounder, Ben Stokes at the 2017 Indian Premier League auctions. The contract with IPL players provides for playing for the team that owns the player. IPL franchise rights are intangible assets.

Intangible Assets and Competitive Advantage

It is easy for a business to acquire tangible assets such as buildings and equipment. Hence, having such assets cannot give a business an edge over its rivals. Intangible assets, such as the reputation of a brand, strength of research and development, and highly trained and motivated employees, are much more difficult to develop, acquire or copy. The competitive advantage that gives a firm higher profitability relative to its industry peers comes mainly from intangible assets.

QUICK QUESTION
Intangible assets

List what you think are the intangible assets of Amazon, Apple, Facebook, Goldman General Electric, Sachs, Google, HDFC Bank, Hindustan Unilever, Infosys, Larsen & Toubro, Microsoft, Reliance Industries, and Zynga.

Today, much of a firm's worth is represented by intangible assets. As the role of service industries with a large number of intangible assets continues to rise, the question of recognizing these assets is becoming important for a large number of companies and the users of their financial statements. Efforts are on to develop more objective methods of valuing intangible assets. Accounting for intangibles is likely to occupy the agenda of accounting regulators in the coming decades.

Recording Acquisition of Intangible Assets

The first step in accounting for an intangible asset is to arrive at its cost of acquisition. Similar to tangible assets, the cost of an intangible asset comprises its purchase price, duties and taxes, after deducting trade discounts, and any directly attributable costs of bringing the asset to working condition for its intended use. Directly attributable costs include costs of employee benefits, e.g. salaries, pensions and other benefits, professional fees, such as lawyers' fees, and costs of testing whether the asset is functioning properly. Trade discounts, rebates, and refundable or adjustable taxes are deducted in arriving at the purchase price.

Suppose a publisher buys the copyright for a book titled *How to Live Happily Forever* for ₹100,000. The company pays ₹5,000 for its lawyer's services and ₹2,000 for copyright filing and registration. We record the purchase of the copyright as follows:

Copyright	107,000	
Cash		107,000

Amortization of Intangible Assets

Amortization is the term used for depreciation of intangible assets. Many intangible assets have finite useful lives. A number of factors, such as likely obsolescence, competitors' actions, and contractual and legal terms on the use of the asset, determine the useful life of an intangible asset. For example, the useful life of a patent for a CT scanner will depend on its typical product life cycle (introduction, growth, maturity, decline, and exit), likely technological developments, competitors' products, regulatory requirements, and so on. The method used for amortization is usually straight-line, though other methods such as the WDV method and the production-units method may be appropriate in some cases.

Suppose the publisher expects *How to Live Happily Forever* to be sold over the next five years, although the copyright has a legal life of sixty years. The following entry records the yearly amortization charge:

```
Amortization Expense .................................................................... 21,400
    Accumulated Amortization, Copyright ....................................        21,400
        Yearly amortization of copyright: ₹107,000/5 years = ₹21,400
```

Table 6.4 outlines the accounting for selected intangible assets. The Income Tax Rules provide that for tax purposes the following intangible assets can be amortized at the rate of 25 per cent on a WDV basis: know-how, patents; copyrights; trademarks; licences; franchises; or any other business or commercial rights of similar nature.

TABLE 6.4
Accounting for
Intangible Assetss

The owner's legal rights over, and commercial value of, the assets determine the accounting.		
Asset	**Description**	**Accounting**
Patent	▪ A monopoly right granted by the government to an inventor to make, use, exercise, sell or distribute exclusively an invention consisting of a new product or employing a new process for a period of 20 years.	▪ Record at cost of acquisition. ▪ If the patent is the result of in-house research, capitalize the direct costs of development. ▪ Amortize over the lower of the estimated useful life and the legal life.
Copyright	▪ An exclusive right granted by the government in relation to a literary, dramatic, artistic, musical or other expression ordinarily for the lifetime of the author and a period 60 years following the death of the author (50 years in India).	▪ Record at cost of acquisition. ▪ Amortize over the lower of the estimated useful life and the legal life.
Trademark, Brand Name	▪ Marks or other signs that are capable of identifying products/services as those of a particular producer and distinguishing them from those of its competitors. ▪ The registration is initially for 10 years, but renewable indefinitely for successive periods of 10 years each.	▪ Record at cost of acquisition. ▪ Amortize over the estimated useful life. ▪ Do not recognize internally generated brands.
Franchise, Licence	▪ A contractual right to trade in an exclusive area or to manufacture using a special process.	▪ Record any lump sum payment to the franchiser. ▪ Amortize over the period of franchise or licence.

Internally Generated Intangible Assets

Brands Names such as *Airtel, Amul, Apple, Bournvita, Coke, Colgate, CNBC, Dettol, Horlicks, Lux, Maggi, Nescafe, Nike, Nirma, Samsung, Sony, Surf, Van Heusen,* and *Visa* are among the scores of brands that dominate the daily lives of millions of consumers. Brands command enormous loyalty from consumers who frequently remain largely indifferent to the brand's ultimate ownership. (Do you know who owns the Bournvita brand?) Brands are increasingly recognized as the most important of all marketing tools, and that's why businesses are investing heavily in acquiring and developing brands. Yet, in India, as in most other countries, brands do not appear on the balance sheet.

Accounting principles permit recording acquired brands, but not "home-grown" or internally generated brands and other intangible assets. The cost of developing home-grown brands is indistinguishable from the cost of developing a business as a whole. Whether acquired or home-grown, brands require considerable expenditure, generate substantial income, and are valuable to their owner. Businesses argue that disallowing recognition of home-grown brands results in balance sheets that reflect only the value of acquired brands, and companies that have generated brands internally do not have the benefit of showing the strength of their brands in their balance sheets. Excluding brands from the financial statements understates the value of companies and potentially exposes them to the risk of hostile takeover.

Goodwill Goodwill means many things to many people. Businessmen use the term goodwill to refer to a company's advantages, such as excellent reputation, an enviable location, and superior personnel. While few will doubt the contribution of these factors to a company's well-being, placing a monetary value on them is extremely difficult. Since personal opinions play an important part in measuring these items, it is not possible to value goodwill objectively. The inclusion in financial statements of subjective amounts as goodwill may give a misleading view of the worth of a business and undermine the reliability of these statements. Internally generated goodwill does not have the essential characteristics of an intangible asset because it is neither separable from the enterprise nor does it arise from contractual or other legal rights. Therefore, it is not possible to recognize any internally generated goodwill. However, "purchased" goodwill is recognized[5].

Research and Development (R & D) Companies in hi-tech industries spend considerable sums of money on pure research as well as the development of new and improved products, processes, and materials. In most cases, there is little, if any, a direct relationship between the amount of current R & D costs and future benefits, because the amount and timing of such benefits are usually uncertain. Accountants distinguish between *research* and *development* phases:

- *Research* involves gaining new knowledge and understanding (e.g. searching for a new drug molecule).
- *Development* involves the application of research findings for the production of better materials, products or processes (e.g. designing and testing a new drug).

An enterprise should expense any amounts spent on research as incurred because it is not possible to demonstrate the existence of any future economic benefits at the research phase. The development phase of a project is further advanced than the research phase. If it is not possible to distinguish between these two phases of a project, the amounts spent on the project should be expensed as incurred. An intangible asset arising from development should be recognized only if a number of conditions (e.g. technical feasibility, market, and profitability) are satisfied. It is not possible to reinstate past amounts expensed as part of the cost of an intangible asset at a later date.

The financial statements should disclose the aggregate amount of R & D expenditure recognized as an expense during the period. Companies are required to report the expenditure on R & D. It appears that many Indian companies do not view reporting on R & D matters as an opportunity to communicate their long-term growth prospects to their shareholders and others. Comprehensive reporting on R & D activities will enable users of financial statements to take a long-term view of companies instead of unduly focusing on earnings per share. While managers constantly fault the "short-termism" of analysts and institutional investors, they disclose too little about expenditure on R & D to help users make informed judgments. Increasingly, large institutional shareholders are seeking to bring about greater disclosure of R & D efforts. Companies are concerned about the fallout of the additional information becoming available to their competitors and must balance the benefits of improved disclosure to their investors and the competitive costs of such disclosure.

Software Expenditure on the development of software for internal purposes is treated similar to R & D costs. Costs incurred until technological feasibility is established are

---

[5] We will see this in Chapter 8.

similar to research costs and are expensed. Costs incurred thereafter may be capitalized, similar to development costs, if certain conditions are met.

FINANCIAL VIEW
Drug Side Effects

On August 5, 2016, the shareholders of Bristol-Myers Squibb lost $21 billion after its trial on a cancer drug failed. The Big Pharma company was trying to broaden the use of Opdivo (generic name nivolumab), the immunotherapy blockbuster. Immunotherapy releases the body's immune system to fight cancer, unlike chemotherapy which uses drugs to kills cancer cells. In the second quarter of 2016, Bristol sold $840 million of Opdivo – roughly seven times the sale in the year-ago quarter. The drug was also outselling Merck's Keytruda, its rival. Both Opdivo and Keytruda are effective in treating lung, skin, kidney and other cancers. The clinical trial failed in patients who have just 5 per cent or more of the protein, PD-L1. In contrast, Merck's Keytruda has greater precision because it targets tumours that have 50 per cent or more of the protein. Bristol went for the big bucks because a successful trial would have brought more patients and vastly expanded the market for Opdivo. Unfortunately, things didn't work out. This example illustrates the high degree of uncertainty associated with drug trials. Bristol spent $5.92 billion on research and development in 2015 that was nearly 36 per cent of its revenue. Capitalizing R & D would be a nice idea for management, but extremely risky for investors.

"Expensing R & D hinders the development of new drugs." What do you think?

DISCUSSION QUESTION 6.5

....

....

....

Natural Resources

Learning Objective
LO 11 Account for natural resources.

Natural resources may be either non-renewable or renewable. Accounting for extracting non-renewable resources (e.g. mines and oil wells) and for developing renewable resources (e.g. forests and plantations) involve different kinds of complexities. We now examine accounting for non-renewable resources.

Non-renewable assets are in essence stockpiles of inventories that are exploited over a number of reporting periods. **Depletion** is the act of recovering the natural resources available, such as mining coal or pumping out oil. The term also means the allocation of the cost of a natural resource to the units extracted in a period. Depletion, unlike depreciation, focuses on the narrow physical phenomenon of exhaustion of a resource. The accounting procedure for depletion is similar to the production-units method of depreciation.

Enterprises in extractive industries look for and take out natural resources that lie underneath the earth. To illustrate, the oil and gas industry has seven broad phases:

1. *Prospecting* involves analyzing historical geological data and carrying out topographical, geological and geophysical studies. Since the information generated from prospecting activities do not give rise to enforceable rights, the associated costs would not be recognized as an asset. Prospecting costs are expensed as incurred.

2. *Acquisition of mineral rights* entails acquiring a licence from a government to explore a defined area for oil and gas. The legal rights may take several forms, such as property titles conferring outright ownership of the oil and gas property, lease or concession arrangements that are granted by the owner of the rights (usually a government), or production sharing contracts with governments. These rights meet the definition of an asset because the enterprise that owns them alone can engage in exploration in the defined area and the rights have a positive value. A common process for selling exploration rights is to auction new exploration blocks to the highest bidder. The amount paid by the winning bidder would represent a legal rights asset.

3. *Exploration* involves searching for oil and gas. Exploration costs in the oil and gas industry include the costs of seismographic shooting, core drilling, and drilling of an exploratory well.

4. *Evaluation* refers to determining the technical feasibility and commercial viability of extracting oil and gas. The evaluation takes place only if oil and gas have been found. Evaluation costs include the costs of drilling appraisal wells and costs of detailed engineering studies to determine how best the reservoir can be developed to obtain maximum recovery.

5. *Development* refers to gaining access to the oil and gas deposit. Development costs include the costs of constructing platforms or preparing drill sites from which to drill wells to gain access to and produce oil and gas and installing equipment and facilities necessary for bringing oil and gas to the surface. Development costs should be recognized as part of the legal rights asset to the extent they have future economic benefits.

6. *Production* involves extracting oil and gas from the earth and making the produce marketable or transportable. Production costs include lifting the extracted oil and gas and removal of impurities, transportation, and storage. Besides, the costs accumulated as an asset until the development phase should be depreciated/amortized over the quantity of reserves to reflect the consumption. Property, plant and equipment used in production should be depreciated similarly. Some assets may have a shorter life, while others can be redeployed in other locations. In that case, the component approach should be followed and the assets depreciated separately.

7. *Closure and decommissioning* involve dismantling and removing the assets and restoring the site on which it is located. The exploration licence usually imposes an obligation for closure and decommissioning. The related liability should be dealt with similar to other operating liabilities discussed in Chapter 9.

Oil and gas companies face significant uncertainties. To begin with, there is no direct relationship between the amount of exploration costs and the prospects of finding oil and gas. For example, a small expenditure may lead to a major find, while a large expenditure may yield nothing. Even if an exploration is successful, the quantity of oil and gas that can be extracted would depend on geological, technical, and economic conditions. The uncertainties persist during the development and production phases. The political and regulatory environment often exacerbates the uncertainties. It would seem that the oil and gas industry has a lot in common with research and development.

Currently, there are two methods of accounting followed in the oil and gas industry: (a) the successful efforts method (SEM), and (b) the full cost method (FCM). Table 6.5 summarizes the essential differences between them. As you can see, SEM is more prudent.

TABLE 6.5
Successful Efforts Method and Full Cost Method

The success efforts method expenses costs and losses earlier than the full cost method.		
	Successful Efforts Method	**Full Cost Method**
Costs	■ Costs that lead directly to the discovery, acquisition, or development of mineral resources are capitalized. ■ Other costs are expensed as incurred.	All exploration and evaluation costs are capitalized.
Unit of accounting	Each property, licence, concession or production sharing contract is treated as a cost centre for determining success.	The cost centre is much larger than a licence area. It is often a country but may even be a group of countries.
Loss recognition	Exploration costs of a dry well are immediately expensed.	The costs of a dry well are retained as part of a larger cost centre that would have both successful and unsuccessful wells.

To illustrate oil and gas accounting, assume that BigOil is interested in bidding for three licence areas in the Krishna-Godavari basin.

Prospecting BigOil incurs the following costs in 20X1 (all amounts in this illustration are in million):

Cost Item	Licence Area 1	Licence Area 2	Licence Area 3	Total
Geological survey....................................	₹11,000	₹10,000	₹23,000	₹44,000
Topographical survey	9,000	2,000	4,000	15,000
Total...	20,000	12,000	27,000	59,000

Under both methods, BigOil expenses geological survey and topographical survey cost as incurred, since these occur prior to the acquisition of licences (in practice, there will be separate entries on many dates):

Geological Survey Expense..	44,000	
Topographical Survey Expense...	15,000	
Cash		59,000
Prospecting costs expensed		

Mineral Rights and Exploration BigOil bids for all three licence areas, but wins Licence Areas 1 and 2. It incurs the following further costs in 20X1:

Cost Item	Licence Area 1	Licence Area 2	Total
Licence acquisition	₹124,000	₹190,000	₹314,000
Exploratory well	3,000	3,500	6,500
Total..	127,000	193,500	320,500

Under both SEM and FCM, the company will record these expenditures as follows:

Exploration and Evaluation Expenditure	320,500	
Cash		320,500
Licence acquisition and exploratory well drilling costs		

Exploration and evaluation expenditure of ₹320,500 will be carried as an intangible item in the 20X1 balance sheet.

Evaluation and Development In 20X2, the company incurs the following expenditures:

Cost Item	Licence Area 1	Licence Area 2	Total
Appraisal well..	₹ 11,000	₹ 3,000	₹ 14,000
Development well..	140,000	0	140,000
Platforms and pipelines	310,000	0	310,000
Total..	461,000	3,000	464,000

In late 20X2, the company finds oil in Area 1, but determines that Area 2 is not commercially feasible and so abandons further efforts. The company estimates the reserves in Area 1 to be 100 million tonnes. Both SEM and FCM will record the expenditures initially as follows:

Exploration and Evaluation Expenditure	14,000	
Development Expenditure	450,000	
Cash		464,000
Cost of appraisal well, development well and platforms and pipelines		

From now on, the two methods will differ. We will describe the successful efforts method first.

Successful Efforts Method

BigOil defines each licence area as a cost centre. At the time of deciding to abandon Area 2, BigOil records the following:

Exploration and Evaluation Expenditure Written Off 196,500
    Exploration and Evaluation Expenditure   196,500
        Licence acquisition, exploratory well and appraisal well costs
        for Licence Area 2

The Exploration and Evaluation Expenditure account now has a balance of ₹138,000, representing only the expenditure on Area 1 so far (recall that we expensed prospecting expense). BigOil transfers that amount and the balance in Development Expenditure to an oil asset, as follows:

Oil and Gas Properties 588,000
    Exploration and Evaluation Expenditure   138,000
    Development Expenditure   450,000
        Accumulated exploration and evaluation expenditure for
        Area 1, determined successful, transferred to asset

Suppose BigOil produces 5 million tonnes in 20X3. It records the depletion of the well as follows:

Depletion Expense 29,400
    Accumulated Depletion, Oil and Gas Properties   29,400
        Depletion expense: 5 million tonnes × ₹5,880 per tonne
        (i.e. ₹588,000/100 million tonnes)

Full Cost Method

Suppose BigOil defines the entire Krishna-Godavari basin as a cost centre. Here BigOil does not write off the expenditure on the unsuccessful licence area. Instead, it carries it as an asset along with the costs incurred on the successful licence area. At the time of the decision to continue with Area 1 and abandon further activities in Area 2, BigOil transfers the balance of ₹334,500 in Exploration and Evaluation Expenditure (i.e. the entire amount spent so far except prospecting expense) and the development expenditure, as follows:

Oil and Gas Properties 784,500
    Exploration and Evaluation Expenditure   334,500
    Development Expenditure   450,000
        Accumulated exploration and evaluation expenditure
        transferred to asset

BigOil records the depletion cost in 20X3 as follows:

Depletion Expense 39,225
    Accumulated Depletion, Oil and Gas Properties   39,225
        Depletion expense: 5 million tonnes × ₹7,845 per tonne
        (i.e. ₹784,500/100 million tonnes)

A comparison of the two methods shows that BigOil would report a lower profit under SEM by recognizing the cost of the dry well in 20X2, but recognizes lower depletion expense in future. But FCM defers the loss from the dry well to the future, hence it recognizes a higher depletion expense.

Oil and gas reserves are notoriously difficult to estimate. In February 2017, ExxonMobil cut its proved oil and gas reserves from 24.8 billion barrels of oil equivalent to 20 billion. As a result of very low prices during 2016, certain quantities of oil and natural gas that qualified as proved reserves in prior years did not qualify as proved reserves at year-end 2016. Low prices could make some oil and gas fields economically unviable. Estimating oil reserves involves technical, economic, political and other considerations. The depletion expense would go up as a result of downgrading reserves. There could also be an impairment charge for a write-down in the carrying amount of the assets.

FINANCIAL VIEW

Oil Shock

Impairment of Long-lived Assets

Depreciation accounting aims at planned expensing of an asset's carrying amount over its useful life. It assumes that an enterprise will be able to recover the carrying amount from its future revenue. However, unanticipated events, such as physical damage, changes in product markets, technological progress, new government regulations, and economic and political developments, often diminish an asset's value.

Learning Objective

LO 12 Explain impairment of long-lived assets.

- Audio and video cassettes are not in demand after CDs and DVDs came, and facilities that once churned out millions of metres of those tapes are not worth much now.

The balance sheet value of an asset should stand for its expected future economic benefits. If the benefits are expected to be less valuable, the asset has been impaired and accountants require the asset to be written down to the amount it is worth now.

Impairment loss is the amount by which an asset's carrying amount exceeds its *recoverable amount*. **Recoverable amount** is the higher of (a) its fair value less costs to sell, and (b) its value in use. "Fair value less costs to sell" is the amount obtainable from an asset's sale in an arm's-length transaction between knowledgeable, willing parties, *less* disposal costs. *Value in use* is the present value of the future cash flows expected to be derived from an asset. Appendix C presents the idea of present value. Where groups of assets, rather than individual assets, generate cash inflows, we determine impairment at the group level referred to as a **cash-generating unit** (CGU).

- The output of the coke oven battery in a steel plant does not have a market. The steel plant is the CGU.

The following discussion applies to both asset and CGU, though for convenience we refer to asset. Evidence of impairment may be available from:

(a) *external indicators* such as a decline in an asset's market value, adverse developments in an enterprise's product market, technological, economic or legal environment, increase in interest rates, the carrying amount of an enterprise's assets *less* liabilities exceeding its market capitalization, and

(b) *internal indicators* such as an asset's obsolescence or physical damage, asset becoming idle, and plans for disposal of an asset or for restructuring the operation to which an asset belongs.

Note the following points on how an enterprise should account for impairment:

1. Assess at the end of each reporting period whether there is any indication that an asset (tangible or intangible) may be impaired. If any such indication is available, the enterprise should estimate the recoverable amount of the asset. If it is not possible to estimate the recoverable amount of an individual asset, the firm should estimate the recoverable amount of the CGU to which the asset belongs.

2. Recognize an impairment loss.

3. Depreciate/amortize the asset's revised carrying amount *less* any residual value on a systematic basis over its remaining useful life.

4. Assess at the end of each reporting period whether there is any indication that an impairment loss recognized in prior periods may no longer exist or may

have decreased. If any such indication is available, the firm should estimate the recoverable amount of the asset and recognize a reversal of impairment loss immediately in the statement of profit and loss. After the reversal, it should depreciate/amortize the revised carrying amount of the asset *less* any residual value on a systematic basis over its remaining useful life.

In practice, companies set up a contra-asset account similar to accumulated depreciation/ amortization, to recognize impairment loss rather than reduce the cost of the asset.

HANDHOLD 6.10
Impairment Loss

Satya Company, a graphic design service, purchased a laptop for ₹50,000 on April 1, 20X1. The laptop had a four-year life, a ₹1,000 residual value, and was depreciated using the straight-line method. At September 30, 20X3, a test for impairment indicates that the present value of future cash flows from the laptop is ₹15,000. The fair value less costs to sell of the laptop on that date is ₹12,000. We calculate Satya Company's loss on impairment on September 30, 20X3 as follows:

Cost of laptop	₹50,000
Deduct Residual value	1,000
Depreciable amount	49,000
Yearly depreciation expense: ₹49,000 ÷ 4	12,250
Accumulated depreciation: ₹12,250 × 2.5 years	30,625
Carrying amount on September 30, 20X3	19,375
Fair value less cost to sell (a)	15,000
Value in use (b)	12,000
Recoverable amount: Higher of (a) fair value less cost to sell and (b) value in use	15,000
Impairment loss: Carrying amount − Recoverable amount, i.e., ₹19,375 − ₹15,000 = ₹4,375	

The following entry records the impairment loss:

Impairment Loss	4,375	
Accumulated Depreciation and Impairment		4,375

> ## Financial Analysis of Property, Plant and Equipment

Learning Objective

LO 13 Analyze the utilization of property, plant and equipment.

Effective utilization of property, plant and equipment increases operating revenue. **Property, plant and equipment turnover,** or **fixed-asset turnover,** measures a firm's efficiency in utilizing property, plant and equipment. It indicates how many times a firm turned over the assets in a period and thereby generated sales. If the property, plant and equipment turnover is high, the firm is able to get more sales out of its property, plant and equipment. On the other hand, if the turnover is low, the firm has idle or under-utilized property, plant and equipment. Averages rather than year-end amounts of assets are often a better measure of the level of assets held during the year. The PPE turnover measure is computed as follows:

$$\text{PPE turnover} = \frac{\text{Sales}}{(\text{Beginning PPE} + \text{Ending PPE})/2}$$

To illustrate, assume the following data for Varun Company:

Annual sales	₹50,000
Beginning property, plant and equipment	15,000
Ending property, plant and equipment	25,000
Average property, plant and equipment: (₹15,000 + ₹25,000)/2	20,000
Property, plant and equipment turnover: ₹50,000/₹20,000 = 2.5 times	

Whether the PPE turnover of 2.5 times is good or not depends on the company's business. A capital-intensive business, such as steel or cement, requires huge initial investment in property, plant and equipment and a PPE turnover of 2.5 times would appear to be impressive. However, businesses such as consulting or travel agency do not need much property, plant and equipment. Therefore, we should compare the PPE turnover for enterprises in the same business to find out where an enterprise stands in relation to its competitors. Also, we can study the movement of an enterprise's ratio over time to see if there are any trends.

Investment Property

Investment property is land or building held to earn rentals or for capital appreciation. It excludes items that would be classified as property, plant and equipment. For example, an enterprise may buy an apartment for several reasons. If it is for use in its own business, it should be classified as property, plant and equipment. If it intends to sell it as part of its business (e.g. a real estate dealer), it is a part of its inventories. If it invests in the apartment with a view to benefiting from an anticipated increase in its market value rather, it is an investment property.

Learning Objective

LO 14 Explain and account for investment property.

Investment property is recognized as an asset only when it satisfies the usual conditions to be considered an asset: future economic benefits and reliable measurement of cost. It is measured initially at its cost. Transaction costs are included in the initial measurement. Professional fees for legal services and property transfer taxes, such as stamp duty and registration fee, are examples of transaction costs. After recognition, investment property is measured at cost. However, it should measure the fair value of the investment property for the purpose of disclosure, unless the fair value is not reliably measurable or the investment property is classified as held for sale.

On April 1, 20X1, Sudhir Company acquires an investment property for ₹100,000. In addition, it incurs lawyer's fees of ₹2,000 and stamp duty and registration charges of ₹8,000. The investment property should be initially recorded at ₹110,000. Sudhir Company applies the cost model. Suppose at March 31, 20X2, the fiscal year end, the property has a fair value of (a) ₹112,000 or (b) ₹105,000. Sudhir Company will not recognize any gain in case (a) or loss in case (b) but will disclose the fair value in its financial statements for the year ended March 31, 20X2 in either case. In case (b), the asset has to be tested for impairment.

HANDHOLD 6.11
Investment Property

Property, plant and equipment, intangible assets and natural resources figure often in accounting fraud. The techniques include the following:

FORENSIC CORNER
Long-lived Asset Fraud

- Capitalizing repair and maintenance and R & D expenses.
- Expensing capital expenditure.
- Not recognizing impairment losses in a timely manner.
- Recognizing assets the company does not have title to.
- Purchase of an asset at an inflated price from a related party.
- Incorrect depreciation calculations.
- Inflated amounts in revaluation.
- Overstatement or understatement of oil and gas reserves.
- Removing an asset without authorization (also known as stealing).

Red flags signalling long-lived assets fraud:

- Unusual increase or decrease in the ratio of depreciation to property, plant and equipment.
- Unusual increase or decrease in repair and maintenance expense.
- Persistent excess of actual capital expenditure over budget.
- Frequent disposals of property, plant and equipment.
- Frequent changes in depreciation methods and useful life estimates.
- Discrepancies in physical verification of assets.

APPLICATION
Long-lived Assets

Here are some examples of how companies account for long-lived assets.

Long-lived Assets	Explanation
▪ Oil and natural gas properties, including related pipelines, are depreciated using a unit-of-production method. The cost of producing wells is amortized over proved developed reserves. Licence acquisition, common facilities and future decommissioning costs are amortized over total proved reserves. (*BP*)	▪ Estimating oil and natural gas reserves requires significant management judgment. If proved reserves estimates are revised downwards, earnings would be affected by higher depreciation expense and/or an immediate write-down of the property's carrying amount.
▪ Depreciation is provided as per the useful life prescribed in Schedule II of the Companies Act 2013, for captive power plant-related assets based on the WDV method and for other assets based on SLM. (*Ambuja Cements*)	▪ Most companies use a single method, e.g. straight-line, for all their assets. A few follow a combination of straight-line and written-down-value methods. This is because straight-line depreciation may not represent the pattern of consumption of some assets.
▪ During the six months ended 30 September 2016, an impairment charge of €6.3 billion was recorded in respect of the Group's investment in India... The impairment charge relates to goodwill, other intangible assets and property, plant and equipment. The impairment charge was driven by lower projected cash flows within the business plans resulting from our reassessment of expected future business performance following the recent change in competitive dynamics. (*Vodafone*)	▪ The impairment charge was caused by Reliance Jio's offer of free trial services and a significant discount on price plans. For calculation of value in use, Vodafone used a pre-tax risk adjusted discount rate of 13.3 per cent and long-term growth rate of 4.9 per cent, among others. Sensitivity analysis provided by the company indicated that a 2 percentage point increase in the discount rate would increase the impairment loss by €2.6 billion, while a 2 percentage point decrease would decrease the loss by €4.3 billion.

About 80 per cent of the S&P Nifty 100 companies follow SLM. The rest follow WDV or both SLM and WDV. What do you think could be the reasons for the overwhelming preference for SLM?

IFRS, IND AS AND INDIAN GAAP
Long-lived Assets

Here are the key differences between these systems.

IFRS	Ind AS	Indian GAAP
IAS 16, IAS 40	Ind AS 16, Ind AS 40	AS 6, AS 10
▪ Estimated dismantling, removing and site restoration costs capitalized.		▪ No specific requirement.
▪ Cost of major inspections recognized in the carrying amount if conditions are met.		▪ Cost of major inspections expensed when incurred.
▪ Revaluations, if done, to be made regularly.		▪ No specific requirement.
▪ Components of assets to be depreciated separately.		▪ No specific requirement.
▪ No minimum depreciation.		▪ Schedule II sets out the useful lives of classes of assets.
▪ Transfer from revaluation reserve to statement of profit and loss not allowed.		▪ Transfer from revaluation reserve to statement of profit and loss allowed.
▪ A variety of depreciation methods can be used.		▪ SLM, WDV and production-units methods allowed.
▪ Change in depreciation method to be applied prospectively.		▪ Change in depreciation method to be applied retrospectively.
▪ Excludes investment property, since it is covered in IAS 10/Ind AS 40		▪ Covers investment property.
▪ Investment property to be measured at its cost or current value.	▪ Investment property to be measured at its cost.	▪ Investment property to be measured at its cost.

RECAP

- *Long-lived assets* are held for own use and not for resale.
- Long-lived assets may be *property, plant and equipment, intangible assets* or *natural resources.*
- The cost of property, plant and equipment comprises purchase price, import duties and taxes on the purchase, directly attributable costs and estimated dismantling, removing and site restoration costs.
- *Depreciation* or *amortization* is the allocation of the cost of an asset over its *useful life.* Straight-line and *written-down-value* methods are the most commonly used methods.
- Expenditure on purchase, expansion or improvement of assets is *capital expenditure.* Expenditure on operation or maintenance of assets is *revenue expenditure.*
- Tax depreciation is more generous than accounting depreciation. It can't be used for financial reporting.
- The cost and accumulated depreciation of an item of property, plant and equipment are derecognized on its disposal. Any gain or loss on disposal is recognized.
- Depreciation is not a source of cash.
- Revaluation of property, plant and equipment brings carrying amount closer to current replacement cost.
- Accounting principles for *intangible assets* are similar to those for property, plant and equipment.
- Depletion of a natural resource is recognized over the estimated quantity of the resource.
- An impairment loss should be recognized by writing down the carrying amount of the impaired asset to *recoverable amount.*
- *Property, plant and equipment turnover* measures a firm's efficiency in utilizing its long-lived assets.
- *Investment property* is held to earn rentals or for capital appreciation. It is measured at its cost.

Review Problem

Ganesh Construction Company bought an earth moving machine for ₹200,000. The equipment was expected to be useful for six years, or 15,000 hours, with an estimated residual value of ₹20,000 at the end of that time. The equipment logged 2,000 hours in the first year.

Required

Compute the depreciation expense for the first year under each of the following methods: (1) Straight-line (SLM), (2) Written-down-value (WDV), (3) Sum-of-the-years'-digits (SYD), and (4) Production-units (PU).

Solution to the Review Problem

Depreciation	SLM	WDV	SYD	PU
Rate	—	$1 - \sqrt[6]{\dfrac{20,000}{200,000}}$ $= 31.87\%$	—	$\dfrac{₹200,000 - ₹20,000}{15,000 \text{ hours}}$ $= ₹12 \text{ per hour}$
Calculation	$\dfrac{₹200,000 - ₹20,000}{6 \text{ years}}$	₹200,000 × 31.87%	$(₹200,000 -$ $₹20,000) \times \dfrac{6}{21}$	₹12 × 2,000
Expense	₹30,000	₹63,740	₹51,429	₹24,000

ASSIGNMENT MATERIAL

Questions

1. What are the chief characteristics of *property, plant and equipment*?
2. How is accounting for property, plant and equipment useful to a business?
3. "Interest costs on debt incurred for financing an asset can be capitalized." Do you agree?
4. What does *depreciation* mean?
5. Is land depreciated? Why or why not?
6. Is it necessary to depreciate a building when its market value exceeds the cost of acquisition? Why or why not?
7. Why is the *useful life* of an asset often less than its physical life?
8. How is the *straight-line method* different from an *accelerated method*?
9. When can a business justify the use of an accelerated method?
10. When is the production-units method more appropriate than other depreciation methods?
11. Why is the straight-line method popular?
12. What non-accounting considerations could influence the selection of a depreciation method?
13. Explain the relevance of Schedule II depreciation rates to financial reporting.
14. Is it necessary or possible to follow the same depreciation method for accounting and tax purposes?
15. "There is nothing devious about companies maintaining one set of accounting records for shareholders and another set for tax authorities." Explain.
16. How is depreciation for partial periods recorded?
17. How does a revision in the remaining useful life of an asset affect the past and future depreciation expense?
18. How are assets of low value accounted for?
19. When can a company change the depreciation method? How is it reported in Ind AS?
20. When can assets be grouped for depreciation purposes?
21. What would be the effect on reported profit of charging routine maintenance to an asset account?
22. A rental car company recently replaced the petrol engines in its cars with diesel engines. How should it account for the expenditure?
23. Evaluate the following statement: "It's not necessary to show a fully depreciated asset on the balance sheet because the omission does not affect its carrying amount."
24. Sudhir Enterprises exchanges its old computer for a new one by paying a small amount. At what cost is the new computer to be recorded?
25. How are gains and losses on disposal treated for tax purposes?
26. Does accumulated depreciation represent cash? Explain why or why not.
27. In highly inflationary periods, how can a company ensure that adequate funds are available for replacement of assets?
28. Why do companies revalue property, plant and equipment?
29. Can brands be shown on the balance sheet? When? At what amount?
30. How is the amortization period for intangible assets determined? What pattern of amortization is generally followed?
31. Why is testing for asset impairment necessary when an asset is depreciated?
32. "Natural resources are long-term inventories." Do you agree?
33. Renu Company intends to sell its surplus land. Is this investment property?

Problems

Problem 6.1
Determining Asset Classification *

State whether each of the following is an item of property, plant and equipment.

Item	Yes	No	Explanation
(a) Bus used for staff pick-up			
(b) Computer used in marketing manager's office			
(c) Building that houses the warehouse and the manufacturing facility			
(d) Office building constructed on land taken on a 25-year lease			
(e) Furniture used in branch offices			
(f) A fully depreciated car			
(g) A hypertension drug formula acquired by a pharmaceutical firm			

Mehra Polymer Company bought a new machine. The company incurred the following expenditures in connection with the purchase:

(a) Purchase price (net of discount, ₹60,000), ₹540,000
(b) GST (not adjustable), ₹40,000
(c) Freight, ₹12,000
(d) Unloading and loading due to truck breakdown, ₹1,000
(e) Transit insurance, ₹3,000
(f) Special bedding to be changed twice during the life of the machine, ₹6,000
(g) Cost of trial production runs, ₹4,000
(h) Compensation to a worker for injury while unloading the machine, ₹2,000.

Problem 6.2
Determining Cost of Acquisition *

Required

Compute the cost of acquisition of the machine.

Shyam Rubber Company bought a machine on July 1, 20X7, at a cost of ₹34,000. It is expected to be useful life for five years and has a residual value of ₹2,000. The company's year end is March 31.

Problem 6.3
Depreciation for Partial Periods *

Required

Compute the depreciation expense for the year ended March 31, 20X8, using the straight-line method.

Leo Consultants bought a screen projector on April 1, 20X4 for ₹40,000. It was expected to last for nine years and have a residual value of ₹4,000. Straight-line depreciation was charged. The equipment was disposed of on September 30, 20X9. The company follows the calendar year.

Problem 6.4
Disposal of Property, Plant and Equipment *

Required

Prepare journal entries to record the disposal under each of the following independent cases, making sure to update depreciation. The equipment was:
1. Scrapped as having no sale value.
2. Sold for ₹18,000.
3. Sold for ₹21,200.

(a) Vinay Shah paid ₹200,000 to be the exclusive franchisee of Computerland for a training school in three districts in Gujarat. The franchise is valid for four years and may be renewed by mutual consent.
(b) In 20X4, Chopra Company spent ₹200,000 in developing a new software, *Big Bull*, to be used by stockbrokers and financial analysts. The technological feasibility of the software was established in 20X5, during which the company spent a further ₹1,000,000. The product was successfully completed in 20X5. The company expects the product to yield ₹5,000,000 in revenues over five years beginning 20X6.

Problem 6.5
Amortization of Intangible Assets *

Required

Compute the annual amortization of the franchise and the software.

Rayalaseema Granite Company bought a granite quarry for ₹6 million. The quarry was estimated to contain one million tonnes of granite. It incurred an expenditure of ₹1 million in developing the quarry site. The company extracted and sold 300,000 tonnes in the first year.

Problem 6.6
Depletion Charge *

Required

1. Prepare a journal entry to record the depletion expense for the first year.
2. Present the quarry on the balance sheet of Rayalaseema Granite Company at the end of the first year.

Hamid Builders bought construction machinery on January 1, 20X3, at a cost of ₹800,000, with an estimated useful life of nine years and an estimated residual value of ₹80,000. The management decides to change the depreciation method from WDV to straight-line from the year ended December 31, 20X8.

Problem 6.7
Change in Depreciation Method **

Required

Prepare a journal entry to record the depreciation expense for 20X8.

Problem 6.8

Depreciation, Income Tax, and Cash Flow ✳✳

Shree Sugar Mills installed a new plant costing ₹600,000 with an estimated useful life of seven years and an estimated residual value of ₹40,000. In the first year, the company's cash revenues were ₹3,000,000 and cash expenses were ₹2,000,000. For tax purposes, the plant is eligible for depreciation at the rate of 25 per cent. The income tax rate is 30 per cent.

Required

Compute for the first year the profit after tax (assuming straight-line depreciation) and the cash flow from operations after tax.

Problem 6.9

Determining Cost of Acquisition ✳✳✳

Image Processing Products developed a research laboratory in 20X3. The costs incurred in connection with this project and collected in the Laboratory Project account are as follows:

Land	₹ 500,000
Architects' fees	19,000
Fences	15,000
Demolishing an old building	3,500
Parking lots and driveways	20,000
Levelling the land	3,500
Commission paid to estate agents	10,000
Laboratory equipment	530,000
Installing equipment	70,000
Construction of building	656,000
	1,827,000

The laboratory was commissioned on October 1, 20X3. The company follows the calendar year.

Required

1. Prepare a statement classifying the items into these categories: Land, Land Improvements, Building, and Equipment.
2. Prepare a journal entry on October 1, 20X3 to record the costs associated with the project.
3. Prepare a journal entry to record the depreciation expense for 20X3 using the straight-line method. The estimated useful life of building and land improvements is 25 years, while that of equipment is 10 years.

Problem 6.10

Determining Cost of Acquisition ✳✳✳ Alternative to Problem 6.9

Joshi Company took up the expansion of its plant in 20X7. The costs incurred in connection with this project and collected in the Plant Expansion Project account are as follows:

Land	₹1,500,000
Parking lots and driveways	60,000
Commission paid to estate agents	30,000
Clearing and levelling the land	10,500
Construction of building	1,968,000
Fences	45,000
Architects' fees for building and land improvements (90 per cent for building).	57,000
Purchase price of machinery	1,590,000
Installing machinery	210,000
Freight inward on machinery	12,000
Trial production runs	17,000
Lawyers' fees for title search and other services	20,000
Registering transfer of title to land	150,000
Repairing a wall that was damaged in handling the machinery	6,000
Additional electrification work in building	40,000
Development charges payable to the city corporation	25,000
	5,740,500

The expansion was financed partly by borrowings of ₹3.5 million, on which interest is payable at 15 per cent per year. The principal amount will be repaid in equal annual instalments over the next six years. Interest for 20X7 was debited to Interest Expense. Work on the project commenced on February 1, 20X7. The new plant was commissioned on December 1, 20X7. It is to be assumed that the borrowings were applied equally to the building and the plant.

A production supervisor was posted to assist in the project. He spent one month on the preparation of the land, one month on improvements, four months on the construction of the building, and another four months on the installation of the machinery. The supervisor's annual salary of ₹60,000 was charged to Salaries Expense.

Required

1. Prepare a statement classifying the items into these categories: Land, Land Improvements, Building, and Equipment.
2. Prepare a journal entry on December 1, 20X7 to record the costs associated with the project.
3. Prepare a journal entry to record the depreciation expense for 20X7 using the straight-line method. The estimated useful life of building and land improvements is 25 years, while that of equipment is 10 years.

Kiran Computers bought a machine for making printed circuit boards (PCBs) for ₹800,000. The machine was expected to be useful for five years and an estimated residual value of ₹40,000. The machine is expected to produce 50,000 PCBs. It produced 15,000 PCBs in Year 1; 12,000 PCB's in Year 2; 3,000 PCBs in Year 3; 16,000 PCBs in Year 4; and 4,000 PCBs in Year 5.

Problem 6.11
Comparison of Depreciation Methods
***

Required

1. Compute the depreciation expense for each year under each of the following methods: (a) straight-line, (b) written-down-value, (c) sum-of-the-years'-digits, and (d) production-units.
2. Comment on the trend of yearly depreciation expense and carrying amount.

Bond Company bought for ₹600,000 a device to detect defective bottles. The equipment has an estimated useful life of six years and an estimated residual value of ₹60,000. It is expected to last 50,000 hours. The machine worked 10,000 hours in Year 1; 18,000 hours in Year 2; 2,000 hours in Year 3; 11,000 hours in Year 4; 6,000 hours in Year 5; and 3,000 hours in Year 6.

Problem 6.12
Comparison of Depreciation Methods
*** Alternative to Problem 6.11

Required

1. Compute the yearly depreciation expense for each year under each of the following methods: (a) straight-line, (b) written-down-value, (c) sum-of-the-years'-digits, and (d) production-units.
2. Comment on the trend of yearly depreciation expense and book value.

Kamadhenu Dairy has four assets, data on which are as follows:

Problem 6.13
Comprehensive Depreciation Calculations
***

Asset	Date of Purchase	Cost	Residual Value	Useful Life	Depreciation Method
Freezer	November 1, 20X5	₹90,000	₹4,000	5 years	SYD
Delivery van	March 1, 20X6	60,000	5,000	50,000 km	Production-units
Refrigerator	October 1, 20X4	12,000	800	6 years	WDV
Display shelves	December 1, 20X3	8,000	600	10 years	Straight-line

The delivery van logged 6,000 km in the year ended March 31, 20X6.

Required

1. Compute the depreciation expense for the period ended March 31 in 20X4, 20X5, and 20X6. Round the amounts to the nearest rupee.
2. Present these assets on the balance sheet on March 31 each year.

Milan Saree Centre has four assets, data on which are as follows:

Problem 6.14
Comprehensive Depreciation Calculations
*** Alternative to Problem 6.13

Asset	Date of Purchase	Cost	Residual Value	Useful Life	Depreciation Method
Van	January 1, 20X8	₹40,000	₹5,000	40,000 km	Production-units
Counters	August 1, 20X7	25,000	2,000	8 years	SYD
Name board	April 1, 20X6	6,000	300	5 years	WDV
Cash box	December 1, 20X6	2,000	400	10 years	Straight-line

Required

1. Compute the depreciation expense for the year ended June 30 in 20X6, 20X7, and 20X8. Round the amounts to the nearest rupee.
2. Present these assets on the balance sheet on June 30 each year.

Problem 6.15

Revision of Depreciation Rates ✳✳✳✳

KBU Corporation provides air transport services for short distances. It acquired an aircraft costing ₹100 million. The aircraft was expected to last 50,000 flying-hours with an estimated residual value of ₹4 million. At the beginning of Year 4, the company carried out a modification to the aircraft engine at a cost of ₹8 million. At the time, the aircraft had completed 30,000 flying-hours. After the modification, the aircraft will have a remaining estimated useful life of 30,000 flying-hours and an estimated residual value of ₹7.5 million. In Year 4, the aircraft flew 8,000 hours.

Required

1. Prepare journal entries to record the cost of the modification and the depreciation expense for Year 4.
2. Repeat Requirement 1, assuming that the modification was not carried out. In the beginning of Year 4, the aircraft was estimated to have a remaining useful life of 10,000 flying-hours and a residual value of ₹4 million. In Year 4, the aircraft flew 8,000 hours.

Problem 6.16

Revision of Depreciation Rates ✳✳✳✳ Alternative to Problem 6.15

Goa Tourism Company offers local sight-seeing trips. It acquired an air-conditioned coach costing ₹1.5 million. The coach was expected to last for six years and have an estimated residual value of ₹45,000. At the beginning of Year 4, the company carried out an overhaul of the coach at a cost of ₹150,000. As a result, it is expected that the coach will have a remaining useful life of five years and a residual value of ₹100,000. Straight-line depreciation is provided.

Required

1. Prepare journal entries to record the cost of the overhaul and the depreciation expense for Year 4.
2. Repeat Requirement 1, assuming that the overhaul was not carried out. In the beginning of Year 4, the coach was estimated to have a remaining useful life of five years and a residual value of ₹45,000.

Problem 6.17

Depreciation, Income Tax, Cash Flow and Managerial Behaviour ✳✳✳✳

Mary Industries Limited started a business with equity capital of ₹2.5 million in cash. Soon after, it bought machinery costing ₹2 million for cash. The machinery had an estimated useful life of 10 years and an estimated residual value of ₹100,000. In the first year, the company's revenues (in cash) were ₹7 million and cash operating expenses were ₹4.5 million. The machinery was depreciated on the straight-line basis. For tax purposes, the machinery was eligible for depreciation at the rate of 25 per cent. Income tax rate was 35 per cent.

Required

1. Prepare the statement of profit and loss and the statement of cash flows for Year 1. Using a reconciliation statement, explain the difference between the profit after tax and the cash flow from operations.
2. Repeat Requirement 1, assuming that the machinery has an estimated useful life of eight years and residual value of ₹100,000. Does the cash flow from operations differ from that in Requirement 1? Explain.
3. Repeat Requirement 1, assuming that the company uses the income tax depreciation for accounting purposes as well. How do the results differ from your answer to Requirement 1?
4. Comment on the implications of your analysis for managerial behaviour.

Problem 6.18

Depreciation, Income Tax, Cash Flow and Managerial Behaviour ✳✳✳✳ Alternative to Problem 6.17

Amit Textiles started a business with a capital of ₹4 million in cash. Soon after, it purchased machinery costing ₹3.7 million for cash. The machinery had an estimated useful life of seven years and residual value of ₹200,000. In the first year, the company's revenues (in cash) were ₹10 million and cash operating expenses were ₹6.5 million. The machinery was depreciated on a straight-line basis. For tax purposes, the machinery was eligible for depreciation at the rate of 25 per cent. Income tax rate was 30 per cent.

Required

1. Prepare the statement of profit and loss and the statement of cash flows for Year 1. Using a reconciliation statement, explain the difference between the profit after tax and the cash flow from operations.
2. Repeat Requirement 1, assuming that the machinery has an estimated useful life of five years and an estimated residual value of ₹200,000. Does the cash flow from operations differ from that in Requirement 1? Explain.
3. Repeat Requirement 1, assuming that the company uses the income tax depreciation for accounting purposes as well. How do the results differ from your answer to Requirement 1.
4. Comment on the implications of your analysis for managerial behaviour.

Azad Company bought the following assets:

Problem 6.19
Depreciation – Change in Method and Revision of Rates ✱✱✱✱✱

Asset	Cost	Residual Value	Useful Life	Depreciation Method
Machinery	₹500,000	₹ 25,000	5 years	WDV
Building	700,000	100,000	25 years	Straight-line

After using these assets for three years, the company decided to change its depreciation policy as follows:

(a) Change the method of depreciation for machinery to the straight-line method;
(b) Revise the remaining useful life of building to 30 years, keeping its residual value at ₹100,000.

These changes are to be implemented in the financial statements for Year 4.

Required

1. Prepare a journal entry to record the depreciation expense for Year 4.
2. Compute the depreciation expense for Year 4 without giving effect to the change in depreciation policy. What is the effect of the change on the profit before tax for Year 4?
3. What disclosures should the company make in its financial statements for Year 4?

Republic Company purchased the following assets:

Problem 6.20
Depreciation – Change in Method and Revision of Rates ✱✱✱✱✱ Alternative to Problem 6.19

Asset	Cost	Residual Value	Useful Life	Depreciation Method
Machinery	₹1,200,000	₹80,000	7 years	SYD
Building	1,500,000	90,000	30 years	Straight-line

After using these assets for four years, the company decided to change its depreciation policy as follows:

(a) Change the method of depreciation for machinery to the straight-line method;
(b) Revise the remaining useful life of building to 40 years, keeping its residual value at ₹90,000.

These changes are to be implemented in the financial statements for Year 5.

Required

1. Prepare a journal entry to record the depreciation expense for Year 5.
2. Compute the depreciation expense for Year 5 without giving effect to the change in depreciation policy. What is the effect of the change on the profit before tax for Year 5?
3. What disclosures should the company make in its financial statements for Year 5?

Sharief Company purchased a diesel generator for ₹1 million. The generator had an estimated useful life of eight years with an estimated residual value of ₹40,000.

Problem 6.21
Accounting for Disposals ✱✱✱✱✱

Required

Prepare journal entries to record the disposal of the generator at the end of the third year in each of the following independent situations. Straight-line depreciation was charged.

1. It was sold for ₹390,000.
2. It was sold for ₹700,000.
3. It was exchanged for a different generator costing ₹1.1 million. It was allowed ₹720,000, and the balance was paid in cash.

4. It was exchanged for a similar generator costing ₹1.1 million. It was allowed ₹720,000, and the balance was paid in cash.
5. Same as Requirement 3 except that it was allowed ₹580,000.
6. Same as Requirement 4 except that it was allowed ₹580,000.
7. It was totally damaged in an accident. The insurer paid ₹700,000 in full settlement.

Problem 6.22
Accounting for Disposals
✶✶✶✶✶ Alternative to Problem 6.21

Standard Manufacturing Company purchased a robot for its assembly operations. The cost of the robot was ₹1.4 million. It had an estimated useful life of four years. It could be sold for an estimated ₹100,000 at the end of four years.

Required

Prepare journal entries to record the disposal of the robot at the end of the second year in each of the following independent situations. Straight-line depreciation was charged.

1. It was sold for ₹660,000.
2. It was sold for ₹810,000.
3. It was exchanged for a different robot costing ₹1.7 million. It was allowed ₹910,000, and the balance was paid in cash.
4. It was exchanged for a similar robot costing ₹1.7 million. It was allowed ₹910,000 and the balance was paid in cash.
5. Same as Requirement 3 except it was allowed ₹690,000.
6. Same as Requirement 4 except it was allowed ₹690,000.
7. It was totally damaged in an accident. The insurer paid ₹470,000 in full settlement.

Problem 6.23
Revaluation of Property, Plant and Equipment
✶✶✶✶✶

Ahuja Dyestuff Company bought machinery on April 1, 20X1 for ₹600,000. The machinery was expected to have a useful life of ten years. The company followed the straight-line depreciation method. In 20X6, the company engaged a valuer to determine the current value of the machinery. The valuer reported that at April 1, 20X6 similar machinery with an estimated useful life of 10 years would cost ₹1 million. The company's year end is March 31.

Required

1. Prepare a journal entry to record the revaluation.
2. Prepare a journal entry to record the depreciation expense for the year ended March 31, 20X7.

Problem 6.24
Revaluation of Property, Plant and Equipment
✶✶✶✶✶ Alternative to Problem 6.23

Premium Automobile Ltd. purchased a building on January 1, 20X3 for ₹900,000. The building was expected to have a useful life of 25 years. The company charged straight-line depreciation. In 20X8, the company commissioned a valuer to determine the current value of the building. The valuer reported that at January 1, 20X8, a similar building with an estimated useful life of 25 years would cost ₹1.4 million. The company's reporting period corresponds to the calendar year.

Required

1. Prepare a journal entry to record the revaluation.
2. Prepare a journal entry to record the depreciation expense for 20X8.

Business Decision Cases

BDC 6.1
Benefice Limited

Benefice Limited, a pharmaceutical firm, has grown by the acquisition of companies engaged in drug discovery and development. Oncocure, another pharmaceutical firm, owns the rights to several product candidates. It is only engaged in R & D in immunotherapy, a new field that offers great promise in the treatment of cancer with fewer side effects. Recently Benefice acquired Oncocure Limited, including the rights to all of its product candidates and testing and development equipment, and hires all of the scientists formerly employed by Oncocure who were working on the development of the acquired product candidates.

Rupali Agarwal, Benefice's controller, is pondering the company's accounting for acquisitions. The management of Benefice has considerable experience in making acquisitions. It has a robust system of identifying potential targets, performing due diligence, valuing the target, negotiating deals, complying with securities, tax and accounting requirements and integrating the acquiree successfully. While there have been some problem cases, most acquisitions have worked well.

Of particular relevance to this case is the valuation of the acquiree's business. Inventories and trade receivables are valued at realizable amounts. Property, plant and equipment items are valued based on current or recent transaction prices. Patents and in-process research and development (IPR & D) are the most contentious assets. The target company's owners often build their case for a high valuation based on these assets.

Also, there is a great deal of unease within Benefice on how to allocate the purchase price among the various assets. Spot-on, Benefice's valuers for many years, uses standard methods based on income and cash flows. Even then, Rupali feels that there is much scope for discretion in distributing the purchase price. Since the acquirees often do not have established products, the numbers available are less consistent than for established businesses. Rupali recalled her professor's comment in a financial statement analysis course that valuation was ultimately a matter of opinion.

The auditors had raised concerns about the valuation methodology on Benefice's last acquisition. They felt that the company was pushing the envelope too far in valuing IPR & D. Some in the management were in favour of assigning as much of the purchase price to IPR & D. Others preferred a more conservative approach of expensing as much of IPR & D as possible as part of the acquisition-related costs.

Rupali is beginning to wonder if Benefice's accounting requires rethinking. The trigger is the aggressive action being taken by the Securities and Exchange Board of India (SEBI) and the Ministry of Corporate Affairs on acquisition-related accounting including allocation of the purchase price to intangible assets. A major worry is the effect of any changes in the current accounting practice on earnings. Benefice's investor relations manager has cautioned her against a negative surprise in earnings because of the fallout on stock prices. Rupali plans to meet with Benefice's chief financial officer, Srikant Kelkar, to discuss her concerns. Before the meeting she has asked for data from the research staff.

Required

1. What issues should Rupali consider in her decision?
2. How will a decision affect Benefice's current and future earnings?
3. What can we learn from the accounting for IPR & D about Benefice's business prospects?

Ashwin Rao is the chief financial officer of Vista Microchips, a rapidly growing manufacturer of advanced chips. The moment he reached his office on January 3, his secretary told him that the managing director, Mahima Jain, wanted to see him urgently. He rushed to the MD's office, suspecting that something must have gone wrong.

BDC 6.2
Vista Microchips Limited

His conversation with Mahima went as follows:

Mahima: We are going to be in serious trouble in Q3.

Ashwin: What happened?

Mahima: You know that in the Q2 earnings call we told the analysts that we were on track to meet the earnings target. It looks like we will miss the target. We may be short of ₹1.9 million in profit, or about ₹1.25 per share.

Ashwin: Well, I don't think so. I checked the preliminary sales reports yesterday and we have met the quarterly revenue target. Everything else is in control.

Mahima: That's all right. Two unexpected things have happened. One, the new plant is getting ready for commissioning ahead of schedule. In fact, it was nearly ready in late December. I have told the engineering department to hold on.

Ashwin: Isn't that a good thing? We can start the sales sooner than expected, so it should help us. And what's the second thing?

Mahima: It's the opposite situation. The R & D project is delayed. By now, the prototype should have been ready and tested. But it's still giving problems.

Ashwin: Now I see what you are coming to. The depreciation on the plant would be about ₹400,000. The R & D project cost should be around ₹1.4 million. I agree these two items will make a hole in our profit projection.

Mahima: But we can't let that happen. Investors are getting restive. You know we have been working on a new strategy. Now everyone will question us. Tell me how to get out of this situation.

Ashwin: According to accounting principles....

Mahima: The last thing I need now is a lecture on accounting. I need your ideas on how to meet the target.

Ashwin: We can look at the plant to see if it needs further work. There's usually some testing or calibration left. If the plant hasn't started producing, we can think of delaying capitalizing it for sometime. But I doubt if the auditors will agree.

Mahima: You should be able to handle the auditors. After all, you know them well.

Ashwin: On the R & D project, there seems to be little option. It has to be expensed.

Mahima: Does it have to be *either* capital *or* expense? In the real world, we can't be that rigid. There should be options. Can you come back with some ideas?

Ashwin sees himself as being under pressure to meet an earnings target that appears to have been almost missed.

Required

1. Explain the two issues mentioned by the managing director.
2. What options are available to the chief financial officer on the two issues?
3. What would be your advice to the chief financial officer?

Interpreting Financial Reports

IFR 6.1
Lanco Infratech Limited (1)

Lanco Infratech, a power and construction business, reported a net profit of ₹705 million for the quarter ended September 30, 2010 (Q2FY11), a decline of 43 per cent over the quarter ended September 30, 2009 (Q2FY10). The company's revenue increased 6 per cent over the same period. The depreciation charge increased four times, because of a change in the method. The charge for Q2FY11 was nearly one-half of that for FY10. This was despite a smaller growth in the fixed assets. Under the new method, the depreciation charge was ₹1,370 million, compared with ₹498 million under the old method. The company's advertisement and press release highlighted that the cash profit went up by 60 per cent year on year and EBITDA by 48 per cent.

Required

1. What was the justification for the change in the depreciation method?
2. In your view, why did the company change the depreciation method?
3. What was the effect of the change in the depreciation method on the profit for Q2FY11 and for the year ended March 31, 2011?
4. Comment on the quality of disclosure of the effect of the change on the profit.
5. The company's spokesperson said that the company opted for higher depreciation in order "to conserve cash." What was that supposed to mean?

IFR 6.2
Lanco Infratech Limited (2)

Lanco Infratech's consolidated financial statements for the year ended March 31, 2015 contained the following note:

53. In case of LKPL,

(b) During the financial year 2014-15, Lanco Kondapalli Power Limited (LKPL) has capitalized ₹2,722 million (March 31, 2014: ₹1,695 million from 1 July, 2013 to March 31, 2014) of borrowing costs incurred on loans pertaining to Phase III project which is yet to complete the commissioning activities due to non-availability of required resources and fuel which are beyond the control of the LKPL. The LKPL is of the view that as the plant is not ready for commissioning, it is eligible to capitalize the borrowing cost till the completion of required commissioning activities. The lenders of the project approved the above interest during construction as a part of the project cost. Besides this, the LKPL has also re-approached Ministry of Corporate Affairs (MCA) seeking relaxation from the applicability of provisions of Accounting Standard (AS) 16 to continue the capitalisation of borrowing costs.

The company's auditors, P. Brahmayya & Co. made the following comment on the financial statements:

Attention is invited to

(c) Note 53(b) to the Consolidated Financial Statements, where Lanco Kondapalli Power Limited (LKPL), a step-down subsidiary of the Company has capitalised borrowing costs amounting to ₹2,722 million and ₹4,417 million for the year ended and cumulatively up to March 31, 2015 (July 1, 2013 to March 31, 2015) respectively incurred on a plant which is substantially complete, notwithstanding the management's view, pending commissioning in respect of which, LKPL has to secure the supply of requisite natural gas. However, in our opinion, the capitalization of such expenses is not in accordance with the relevant Accounting Standard. Had the aforesaid expenditure not been capitalised, loss of the Group (net of minority interest) for the year ended March 31, 2015 and cumulatively up to March 31, 2015 would have been higher by ₹1,606 million and ₹2,606 million respectively.

The company's board of directors responded to the auditors' comment as follows:

> The step-down subsidiary is implementing gas based power project expansion which is yet to complete commissioning activities due to non-availability of required resources and fuel which are beyond the control of Lanco Kondapalli Power Limited (LKPL). The activities are still not completed to test for capability and suitability of its intended use of the plant. Therefore the asset is eligible to capitalise its borrowing costs till the completion of required commissioning activities. The lenders of the project approved the above interest during construction as a part of the project cost. LKPL has re-approached Ministry of Corporate Affairs (MCA) to seek clarification on the applicability of provisions of Accounting Standard 16 to continue the capitalisation of borrowing costs. The management is of the view that the interest capitalization is as per Accounting Standard 16.

Lanco Infratech reported a loss of ₹20,367 million in FY 2015 and ₹22,739 million in FY 2014. Equity decreased to – ₹4,478 million in FY 2015 from ₹14,575 million in FY 2014.

Required

1. Why was LKPL's accounting for borrowing costs referred to in Lanco Infratech's financial statements?
2. Was LKPL justified in capitalizing borrowing costs? Why or why not?
3. What was the auditors' point about capitalization of borrowing costs? Was the audit qualification justified?

Financial Analysis

Study a sample of company annual reports for five years.

FA 6.1
Depreciation Methods

Required

1. Prepare an analysis of the depreciation methods followed by the companies.
2. Explain the results of your analysis.
3. Comment on possible managerial considerations for depreciation method changes by the sample companies. Your comments should be based on the information available in the financial statements and other portions of the annual report.
4. How is your study useful for analyzing financial statements?

Study a sample of company annual reports for five years.

FA 6.2
Revaluing Fixed Assets

Required

1. Locate companies that present fixed assets at revalued amounts.
2. Comment on possible managerial considerations for revaluation in the case of the sample companies. Your comments should be based on the information available in the financial statements and other portions of the annual report.
3. How important is revaluation to the sample companies? To assess this, calculate the percentage of revaluation reserve to total reserves and surplus.
4. How would the adoption of Ind AS affect the sample companies?

Study a sample of company annual reports.

FA 6.3
Understanding Intangible Assets

Required

1. Prepare a list of intangible assets in the financial statements.
2. How significant are intangible assets to the companies? To assess this, calculate the percentage of intangible assets to total fixed assets.
3. Prepare a list of intangible assets that do not appear in the financial statements.
4. Comment on the accounting policies for intangible assets.
5. How is your study useful for analyzing and interpreting financial statements?

Study a sample of company annual reports for five years.

FA 6.4
Analyzing Asset Impairment

Required

1. Analyze instances of asset impairment. How did impairment affect the reported profit?
2. How is this study useful for analyzing and interpreting financial statements?

FA 6.5 Accounting for R & D	Study a sample of company annual reports for five years. **Required** 1. Analyze accounting policies for R & D. Do you see any patterns? 2. Explain why this study is important for analyzing and interpreting financial statements.
FA 6.6 Analyzing Fixed Asset Utilization	Study a sample of annual reports of companies in any one industry for five years. **Required** 1. Prepare an analysis of the companies' property, plant and equipment turnover. 2. Explain the results of your analysis. 3. Why is your study important for analyzing and interpreting financial statements?

Answers to One-minute Quiz

6.1 a, b, c.
6.2 d.
6.3 d.
6.4 b.

Answers to Test Your Understanding

6.1 Capitalize items (b), (d), (e), (g), (h) and (i). Normal spoilage during trial run, item (h), is often an unavoidable cost of putting a machine to use. Expense items (c) and (f), because demurrage and repair charges are avoidable and do not increase the value or the productive capacity of the asset. Item (a) is a receivable.

6.2

Asset	Fair Value	Proportion of Purchase Price	Allocated Cost
Land	₹180,000	180,000/400,000 × 300,000	₹135,000
Building	150,000	150,000/400,000 × 300,000	112,500
Equipment	50,000	50,000/400,000 × 300,000	37,500
Furniture	20,000	20,000/400,000 × 300,000	15,000
	400,000		300,000

6.3 Depreciation Expense 60,000
      Accumulated Depreciation, Van.. 60,000

6.4 (a) Straight-line, ₹112,000; (b) Written-down-value, ₹250,920; (c) Sum-of-the-years'-digits, ₹186,667.

6.5 Cost .... ₹120,000
Deduct Estimated residual value 5,000
Original depreciable amount.. 115,000
Original estimated useful life (years)... 10
Yearly depreciation expense: ₹115,000 ÷ 10 11,500
Accumulated depreciation: ₹11,500 × 3.. 34,500
Carrying amount: ₹120,000 – ₹34,500... 85,500
Revised estimated residual value.. 1,000
Revised depreciable amount: ₹85,500 – ₹1,000..................................... 84,500
Revised estimated useful life (years).. 5
Depreciation expense for Year 4: ₹84,500 ÷ 5.. 16,900

6.6 Cost .... ₹700,000
Deduct Estimated residual value 60,000
Original depreciable amount.. 640,000
Original estimated useful life (years 8
Yearly depreciation expense: ₹640,000 ÷ 8 80,000
Accumulated depreciation: ₹80,000 × 5.. 400,000
Carrying amount: ₹700,000 – ₹400,000... 300,000

	Add Cost of major repair capitalized		150,000
	Revised estimated residual value..		60,000
	Revised depreciable amount: ₹300,000 + ₹150,000 – ₹60,000....................		390,000
	Revised estimated useful life (years)...		5
	Depreciation expense for Year 4: ₹390,000 ÷ 5..		78,000
6.7	Scanner..	100,000	
	Accumulated Depreciation, Photocopier	105,000	
	Loss on Disposal of Photocopier..	5,000	
	Cash		40,000
	Photocopier..		170,000
6.8	Building	150,000	
	Accumulated Depreciation, Building.......................................		52,500
	Revaluation Reserve...		97,500

CHAPTER

7

Financial Assets

LEARNING OBJECTIVES

After studying this chapter, you should be able to:

1. Describe financial instruments.
2. Describe financial assets.
3. Explain fair value.
4. Explain the significance of cash and cash equivalents.
5. Explain accounting for trade receivables.
6. Estimate credit losses on trade receivables.
7. Understand the effect of transfer of trade receivables.
8. Record transactions in bills receivable.
9. Analyze the quality of receivables.
10. Understand financial and operating investments.
11. Account for financial investments.
12. Understand derivative financial instruments.
13. Explain impairment of financial assets.

WHEN THE PARTY ENDS...

For a long time, life was simple: accountants recorded everything at historical cost. Then someone said that historical cost was irrelevant and assets must appear at their fair value in the financial statements. That divided the world neatly into two camps: those who stood by historical cost ("cost is a fact, value is an opinion") and those who embraced fair value ("cost is about the past, value is about the future"). Many reasons have been advanced for the financial crisis in 2008: Alan Greenspan, bankers' greed, Chinese savings, derivatives, easy liquidity, rating agencies, regulatory failure, southern Europeans.... Politicians held fair value responsible for first blowing the bubble and then bursting it. They contended: "When the markets were booming, the fair value went up and investors made paper profits. This led to further investments in those assets causing their prices to rise even further leading to a bubble. When the bubble burst, the markets fell and everyone rushed to sell the assets and this deepened the crisis."

The problem got complicated because there were many financial products for which there were no public markets and these had to be valued using some models. Warren Buffett, the investment superstar, said that many financial assets were "marked to myth". Did fair value accounting cause the financial crisis?

SPEED READ

Businesses keep cash for meeting payment needs, have receivables because of credit sales and invest in other entities in order to earn income. Financial assets are measured at fair value or at amortized cost, depending on the objective of holding them and their characteristics. Fair value and amortized cost are the two ways of measuring investments. The shift from incurred loss to expected loss for impairment of financial assets has profound implications particularly for banks and other financial firms.

Financial Instruments

A financial instrument is a contract that gives one party a right to receive cash from another party who has an obligation to pay. The right to receive is a *financial asset* and the obligation to pay is a *financial liability*. Consider these familiar examples of financial instruments and the rights and obligations attached to them.

Learning Objective

LO 1 Describe financial instruments.

Financial Instrument	Right	Obligation
▪ Bank deposit	▪ The customer is entitled to withdraw the deposit and interest.	▪ The bank must repay the deposit and interest.
▪ Trade receivable	▪ The seller is entitled to receive the invoice amount.	▪ The buyer is obliged to pay the seller.
▪ Bank guarantee	▪ The lender is entitled to payment if the borrower defaults.	▪ The guarantor must pay the lender if the borrower defaults.
▪ Bond	▪ The bondholder is entitled to payment of principal and interest.	▪ The bond issuer must pay the principal and interest.
▪ Share	▪ The shareholder is entitled to dividends declared and residual assets.	▪ The company must pay the dividends declared and residual assets.

In the above examples, cash changes hands. That's what the adjective *financial* implies. Therefore, a contract to provide goods or services is not a financial instrument. A contract to exchange financial instruments is also a financial instrument, even if it does not involve any cash payment (e.g. a contract to convert bonds into equity shares). Financial instruments can be *financial assets* (e.g. trade receivables), *financial liabilities* (e.g. bonds payable) or *equity instruments* (e.g. shares). We consider financial assets in this chapter, financial liabilities in Chapter 10 and equity instruments in Chapter 11.

Financial instruments are arguably the most difficult topic in accounting. This chapter presents the basics of financial instruments, so that you can make sense of the items in financial statements. A sound understanding of financial instruments is a must for anyone who fancies a career in banking, insurance or asset management.

Financial Assets

A financial asset is a contractual right to receive cash or an equity instrument. Financial assets are contractual rights to receive definite amounts. Accounting for financial assets is complex. Here is a 90-word synopsis of the issues.

Learning Objective

LO 2 Describe financial assets.

- *Initial recognition:* Recognize a financial asset when an entity becomes a party to the contractual provisions of the instrument.

- *Initial measurement:* Measure it at fair value.

- *Classification:* Classify it on the basis of the entity's business model and the cash flow characteristics of the financial asset.

- *Subsequent measurement:* Use amortized cost or fair value. If fair value, take gains and losses to the statement of profit and loss or other comprehensive income.

- *Impairment:* Recognize expected credit losses.

- *Derecognition:* Derecognize it when the contractual rights expire or the asset is transferred.

In this chapter, you will learn about cash, receivables and investments.

Which of the following is a financial asset? There may be more than one correct answer.
(a) Prepaid rent.
(b) Interest receivable.
(c) Investments in government securities.
(d) Route permit for a bus.

Fair Value

Learning Objective

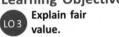 **Explain fair value.**

Fair value is the price of an asset in an orderly transaction between independent parties. It is an *exit price*, i.e. sale price, and not the purchase price, at the best market for the asset. The price should reflect the asset's condition and location on the reporting date. The fair value measurement process should try to 'imitate' the one that market participants are expected to follow to price the asset. Fair value is a market-based measurement. In contrast, the going-concern value is an entity-specific measurement. Fair value is the basis of valuation of financial assets.

The fair value hierarchy categorizes into three levels the inputs to valuation techniques used to measure fair value. It ranges from quoted prices in active markets for identical assets (*Level 1 inputs*) to unobservable inputs for specialized assets (*Level 3 inputs*). Table 7.1 presents the illustrates these inputs.

TABLE 7.1
Fair Value Hierarchy

Fair value inputs range from Level 1 to Level 3 depending on the quality of the information about asset prices.

Input	Definition	Explanation	Example
Level 1	Quoted prices in active markets for identical assets or liabilities	Prices are not adjusted.	Quoted prices in an active stock exchange
Level 2	Inputs other than quoted prices included within Level 1 that are observable for the asset, either directly or indirectly	Prices are adjusted for any differences.	Quoted prices for similar stocks in an active stock exchange
Level 3	Unobservable inputs	Prices are based on assumptions.	Entity-specific pricing model

QUICK QUESTION
Fair value

Give examples of Level 2 and Level 3 inputs.

DISCUSSION QUESTION 7.1

Did fair value accounting cause or aggravate the 2008 financial crisis?

....

....

....

Cash

Learning Objective

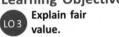 **Explain the significance of cash and cash equivalents.**

Business enterprises keep cash in several forms. **Cash** comprises cash on hand (i.e. notes and coins) and current accounts. Business organizations keep only an insignificant amount in notes and coins. Cash includes any item that banks will accept for immediate deposit. Thus, post-dated cheques are not cash.

Cash equivalents are short-term, highly liquid investments that can be quickly converted into definite amounts of cash. Generally, an investment is a cash equivalent only when it has a short maturity of, say, three months or less from the date of acquisition. Treasury bills, certificates of deposit, commercial paper, and money market deposits are examples of cash equivalents. Current account balances can be withdrawn without notice. Time deposits that can be withdrawn without prior notice or on payment of penalty may also be considered cash equivalents. All other bank deposits are classified as 'other financial assets'.

Liquidity refers to the ease with which an asset can be converted into other assets, or used to buy services or satisfy obligations. Clearly, cash is the most liquid asset. Every business needs some cash in order to pay bills for purchases and operating expenses on time and meet emergency needs.

- As at March 31, 2016, the Hindustan Unilever group had cash and bank balances of ₹30.28 billion. Cash on hand was ₹4 million and current account balance was ₹2.89 billion. The rest was in interest-earning deposits of maturities ranging from less than three months to 12 months. You can see how the company tries to balance liquidity and profitability: keep some money in current accounts and short-term deposits for paying employees, suppliers, and taxes but the bulk of the cash is in interest-yielding deposits.

Trade Receivables

Trade receivables arise from credit sales of goods and services. Manufacturers, wholesalers, and retailers allow their customers some time to pay after the sale. Economic growth depends, in part, on the availability of credit for purchases by individuals and businesses. Advanced and sophisticated economies are characterized by a high percentage of credit sales.

Learning Objective

LO5 Explain accounting for trade receivables.

Extending credit can be profitable. The profit from credit sales should exceed the costs of interest, credit investigation and credit rating, record-keeping, and credit losses. Inadequate control over receivables is often a major cause of business failure. Therefore, businesses are keen to ensure that they sell to customers who will pay on time. The credit department evaluates customers' ability and willingness to pay and recommends credit terms.

Trade receivables have a financing component if there is a difference between the price payable and the cash selling price. The difference between the two prices represents interest charge. Such receivables should be measured at fair value. Trade receivables that do not have a significant financing component should initially be measured at the selling price.

Credit Losses

Defaults occur despite meticulous credit appraisals. **Credit risk** is the risk of financial loss because of failure to discharge an obligation. In trade receivables, it is the risk of default by a customer who bought on credit. **Credit losses** (more commonly known as *bad debts*) are the difference between the amounts due to an entity and the amounts it expects to receive. Credit losses may arise due to several factors, such as low credit standards, unexpected financial problems of customers, and a general increase in business failures. Some amount of credit loss may be an inevitable cost of selling on credit.

Learning Objective

LO6 Estimate credit losses on trade receivables.

The matching principle requires expenses to be matched with revenue. Therefore, credit losses should be recognized in the period in which the revenue from credit sales is recognized. Credit losses differ from other expenses because it is hard to say when a receivable actually becomes unrecoverable. A default does not mean that the customer won't pay. The customer may be experiencing a temporary problem or may have forgotten to pay. Credit losses pertaining to a period may not be known until later. Since businesses must prepare periodic financial statements, they have to estimate credit losses.

Estimating Credit Losses

Business enterprises estimate credit losses on the basis of past experience, interest rates, economic growth, current payment trends and other factors. Since the estimation process involves considerable judgment, it is possible to produce estimates ranging from "highly pessimistic", or conservative, to "highly optimistic", or liberal. A credit loss is an impairment in the value of a receivable. A business should recognize a loss allowance for expected credit losses on receivables. **Expected credit loss** is the weighted average of credit losses with the risk of default as the weight. Exhibit 7.1 illustrates how to calculate the expected credit loss for a trade receivable of ₹10,000 with an assumed probability distribution of default.

EXHIBIT 7.1
Estimating Expected
Loss

Expected credit loss is the product of credit loss and its likelihood.

Credit Loss	Risk of Default	Expected Credit Loss
₹10,000	0.001	₹10
9,000	0.002	18
8,000	0.003	24
7,000	0.004	28
6,000	0.006	36
5,000	0.010	50
4,000	0.015	60
3,000	0.019	57
2,000	0.040	80
1,000	0.200	200
0	0.700	0
Total	1.000	563

The simplified model of estimating credit losses for trade receivables is as follows:

1. For trade receivables of one year or less or ones which do not contain a significant financing component, an entity should always recognize a loss allowance at an amount equal to lifetime expected credit losses.

2. For trade receivables which contain a significant financing component, entities are allowed the option of recognizing a loss allowance at an amount equal to lifetime expected credit losses.

Lifetime expected credit losses are the expected shortfalls in payments during the life of a financial asset. In practice, businesses use a *provision matrix*. The use of a provision matrix is known as the *percentage of receivables method*. Here, the enterprise estimates credit losses as a percentage of trade receivables on the reporting date. An **ageing schedule** classifies trade receivables by age of the invoices that remain unpaid after the expiry of the credit period. For example, an invoice that remains unpaid 26 days after the credit period would appear in the column titled *1–30 days*. Exhibit 7.2 presents a standard ageing analysis.

EXHIBIT 7.2
Ageing Schedule

The ageing schedule is useful for monitoring trade receivables and estimating credit losses.

			SANJAY COMPANY				
			Analysis of Trade Receivables by Age, March 31, 20X8				
		Not Yet			Past Due		
Account	Total	Due	1–30 days	31–60 days	61–90 days	91–120 days	>120 days
Abid	₹ 1,800	₹	₹1,800	₹	₹	₹	₹
Bala	480					480	
Chetan	2,200				2,200		
⋮	⋮	⋮	⋮	⋮	⋮	⋮	⋮
Wagle	1,700						1,700
Xavier	2,300			2,300			
Zainab	1,500	1,500					
	39,100[1]	4,500	8,200	6,300	5,600	11,300	3,200

Ageing analysis of trade receivables is also useful in other ways. For example, credit controllers find ageing analysis handy in identifying customers who have delayed payments and deciding on the line of action to be taken. Auditors use ageing analysis to see if the provision for credit losses is adequate.

---

[1] The column totals do not add up, because the list of accounts is not complete.

Older receivables have a higher probability of turning into credit losses ("out of sight, out of mind"). An analysis of past credit losses combined with expected future trends will generally provide a good estimate of expected losses. The enterprise reviews these rates periodically and revises them, as appropriate. Exhibit 7.3 gives the lifetime expected credit loss rates for the various age categories and applies these rates to the trade receivables in Exhibit 7.2. The last column of Exhibit 7.3 shows the lifetime expected credit loss for each age category and the column total equals the allowance for credit loss at March 31, 20X8.[2]

EXHIBIT 7.3

Estimating Credit Losses Using a Provision Matrix

The probability of default increases with the age of the receivables.			
SANJAY COMPANY Estimating Allowance for Credit Losses, March 31, 20X8			
Age Category	**Amount**	**Lifetime Expected Credit Loss Rate (%)**	**Allowance for Credit Losses**
Current	₹ 4,500	1	₹ 4,500
1–30 days	8,200	3	246
31–60 days	6,300	10	630
61–90 days	5,600	20	1,120
91–120 days	11,300	50	5,650
> 120 days	3,200	70	2,540
	39,100		10,231

The required allowance for credit losses at March 31, 20X8 is ₹10,231. Suppose the available allowance is ₹2,812. We must recognize bad debt expense of ₹7,419, as follows:

Bad Debt Expense 7,419
    Allowance for Credit Losses..   7,419
        To record estimated bad debt expense

Allowance for Credit Losses is a contra-asset account. After posting the adjusting entry, the general ledger accounts appear as follows:

Trade Receivables

Balance	39,100		

Allowance for Credit Losses

		Balance	2,812
		Bad debt expense	*7,419*
		Balance	*10,231*

Sanjay Company will recognize bad debt expense of ₹7,419 in the statement of profit and loss for the year ended March 31, 20X8. Trade receivables and allowance for credit losses appear on the balance sheet as follows:

Trade receivables .... ₹39,100
Less Allowance for credit losses 10,231
    Trade receivables, net ....   ₹28,869

There is a no-one-size-fits-all approach to developing a provision matrix. Each entity will need to consider its own circumstances, including the materiality of expected losses and the data available (without undue cost or effort). For example, receivables may be segregated into groups based on geographical region, product type, customer rating, collateral or trade credit insurance, type of customer and so on. In some cases, a single rate may be appropriate for all trade receivables.

---

[2] Other terms for allowance for credit losses include *provision for doubtful receivables, provision for doubtful debts,* and *provision for bad and doubtful debts.*

Under previous accounting rules, an *incurred loss* was recognized, but an *expected loss* was not to be recognized. In other words, the possibility of loss was to be estimated as at the reporting date. The shift from incurred loss to expected loss requires entities to provide for loss expected over the lifetime of a trade receivable. In many cases, the effect would be to *advance* the timing of recognition of loss and *decrease* current profits.

Accounting for bad debts can be bewildering. In the percentage of receivables method, the periodic bad debt expense is calculated as the difference between the required balance and the current balance of the allowance for credit losses account. The journal entry records the bad debt expense; it does not record the required ending balance. *Bad debt expense is a number derived from the two balances.* For example, suppose the amount of trade receivables on the balance sheet date is ₹10,000, 15 per cent of the trade receivables may not pay, and the existing allowance is ₹1,000. The required allowance is ₹1,500. The bad debt expense for the period would be ₹500: required balance, ₹1,500 – existing balance, ₹1,000.

On December 31, 20XX, Hiren Company's trade receivables has a balance ₹50,000. Prepare journal entries to adjust for expected losses assuming loss accounts are estimated at 2 per cent of trade receivables, if the Allowance for Credit Losses account has (i) a credit balance of ₹800; (ii) a debit balance of ₹950.

Writing off Loss Accounts

When it is clear that an account is unrecoverable, it is written off by debiting Allowance for Credit Losses and crediting Trade Receivables. For example, suppose Bala (one of the customers appearing in Exhibit 7.2) becomes insolvent on July 3, 20X8 and Sanjay Company determines that the receivable of ₹480 is a loss. The following entry records the write-off:

July 3   Allowance for Credit Losses 480
                Trade Receivables.. 480
                    To write off the balance due from Bala

Note that we record the write-off in Allowance for Credit Losses, and *not in Bad Debt Expense*. This is because we have already recognized an estimated bad debt expense. After posting the write-off entry, the general ledger accounts would appear as follows:

Trade Receivables

Balance	39,100	Write-off	480
Balance	*38,620*		

Allowance for Credit Losses

Write-off	480	Balance	10,231
		Balance	*9,751*

The entry reduces the balances in the trade receivables and the allowance accounts by equal amounts. As a result, the estimated realizable value of trade receivables before and after the write-off remains unchanged, as shown below:

	Before Write-off	After Write-off
Trade receivables	₹39,100	₹38,620
Deduct Allowance for credit losses	10,231	9,751
Estimated realizable value..................................	28,869	28,869

Anil Company has trade receivables of ₹45,000 and an allowance for credit losses of ₹4,500. It writes off a loss account of ₹1,200. Does the write-off affect the estimated realizable value of the trade receivables? Why or why not?

Recovery of Loss Accounts

A customer may pay after write-off. We record two entries. The first entry reverses the write-off to the extent of the payment, and the second entry is the usual entry to record collection. To illustrate, suppose on May 12, 20X9 Sanjay Company receives a cheque for ₹200 from Bala's insolvency administrator. The following pair of entries records this transaction:

20X9

May	12	Trade Receivables	200	
		Allowance for Credit Losses...		200
		To restore the part balance due from Bala		
	12	Cash...	200	
		Trade Receivables...		200
		To record the amount received from Bala		

A common practice is to credit bad debt recoveries to miscellaneous income. It is wrong for two reasons. First, income is earned by providing goods and services; recovery of a loss is not an income. Second, it omits information on subsequent payment by the customer. The information is useful for making future credit decisions.

TEST YOUR UNDERSTANDING 7.3
Accounting for Recovery of Loss Accounts

Prepare journal entries to record the following transactions of Kannan Company:

Mar. 31   Kannan Company estimates that 2 per cent of the trade receivables of ₹40,000 will become a loss.

June 18   An amount of ₹970 receivable from Ramesh Company was written off.

Oct. 25   Ramesh Company paid the amount.

Is the incurred loss approach a tool to manage earnings?

DISCUSSION QUESTION 7.2

••

••

••

In November 2016, newspapers reported that the State Bank of India had written off more than ₹70 billion in loans to 63 of its wilful defaulters. These included loans of ₹12 billion to Kingfisher Airlines. The issue assumed political overtones with the Opposition raising the issue in Parliament. The Government and the SBI clarified that write-off did not mean waiver. What exactly happened? Bad debts don't look pretty on a bank's balance sheet. Writing off bad debts cleans up the balance sheet. Write-off changes nothing. The borrower is still obliged to pay back the loan and the bank continues to pursue recovery. Banks write off loans to meet a technical accounting requirement that loss assets should not be carried in the books. The amounts have already been provided for in previous periods. Writing off bad loans enables banks to claim tax benefits for the losses. As you know, when a loan or receivable has been provided for, writing it off does not change its estimated realizable value: it was zero both before and after write-off.

FINANCIAL VIEW
Mistaken Bonanza

Transfer of Trade Receivables

Sometimes, the seller needs cash during the credit period. The seller can transfer a receivable to raise cash. Let's see how this affects the financial statements. Generally, a trade receivable is transferred if the entity transfers the rights to receive the amount. The entity derecognizes a financial asset if substantially all the risks and rewards of ownership of the financial asset have been transferred. If the entity retains substantially all the risks and rewards, it should continue to recognize the financial asset.

Learning Objective
LO 7 Understand the effect of transfer of trade receivables.

Factoring is a transfer of receivables without recourse. The *factor*, i.e. the party who buys the receivables, assumes the risk of credit loss and absorbs any bad debts. Factored receivables qualify for derecognition from the seller's balance sheet. The factor retains a portion of the value of the receivables, known as *holdback*, to cover unexpected sales returns. The difference between the amount of trade receivables and the amount realized is a loss (or finance charge). Usually, the seller informs the buyer of the transfer asking it to pay the factor directly.

Suppose Ganesh Company factors ₹100,000 of its receivable from Vipul Company with Standard Factors. The factor levies a finance charge of 2 per cent of the amount of trade receivables and retains an amount equal to 5 per cent of the trade receivables. Ganesh Company records the transaction as follows:

Cash...	93,000	
Due from Factor	5,000	
Loss on Sale of Trade Receivables...	2,000	
Trade Receivables..		100,000

Ganesh Company will include the amount of ₹5,000 due from Standard Factors in other financial assets. It will recognize the loss of ₹2,000 in its statement of profit and loss. Vipul Company will pay Standard Factors directly at the end of the credit period. If Vipul Company defaults, Standard Factors has to bear the loss. Ganesh Company removes the trade receivables, because it does not retain the risks and rewards of ownership of the receivables.

Hypothecation is an agreement for using receivables as security for a loan. Here the bank lends on the basis of its relationship with the borrower and the quality of the receivables. There is no formal transfer of the receivables. The buyer whose account has been hypothecated will pay the seller. The seller must repay the loan, whether or not the buyer pays the seller on the due date. Hypothecation has no effect on accounting for receivables. The loan and interest expense are recorded in the usual manner. The borrower presents the receivable as an asset and the loan as a liability in its financial statements and discloses the hypothecation.

Bills Receivable

Learning Objective

LO 8 Record transactions in bills receivable.

A **bill of exchange** is an instrument in writing containing an unconditional order signed by the maker directing a certain person to pay on demand, or at a fixed or determinable future time, a certain sum of money to, or to the order of, a certain person, or to the bearer of the instrument. Businesses use bills in credit sales to facilitate smooth flow of money. The Negotiable Instruments Act 1881 lays down the law on bills, cheques, and promissory notes.[3] Bills can be transferred with ease and the law provides simpler rules of evidence for bills. Consequently, it is easier to realize bills than trade receivables. Also, bills are self-liquidating in that, once a bill falls due for payment, the payment procedure is almost automatic and the buyer's bank pays the bill routinely. That is why businesses prefer bills to open-ended accounts. A bill involves the following transactions:

- *Drawing* The *drawer* (seller) draws up the bill, signs it, and addresses it to the *drawee* (buyer) for acceptance.[4] Interest may or may not be payable.

- *Acceptance* The drawee conveys his assent to the bill and becomes the *acceptor*. He should pay the holder of the bill.

- *Presentation for payment by drawer* The drawer can retain the bill. On the due date, he presents the bill to the acceptor for payment. If the acceptor pays, he *honours* the bill. If not, he *dishonours* the bill. In the latter case, the drawer gets a certificate from a notary public *noting and protesting* the dishonour. The acceptor is legally bound to pay the amount due, i.e. the amount of the bill, any interest, and noting and protesting fee.

---

[3] A *cheque* is a bill of exchange drawn on a specified banker and payable on demand. A *promissory note* is an instrument in writing (not being a bank-note or a currency-note) containing an unconditional undertaking signed by the maker, to pay on demand or at a fixed or determinable future time a certain sum of money only to, or to the order of a certain person, or to the bearer of the instrument. While bills, cheques, and promissory notes differ in several respects, the accounting procedure for them is similar.

[4] The drawer may make the bill payable either to himself or to another person. The person to whom the bill is payable is the *payee*. We assume the drawer to be the payee.

- *Discounting* Before the due date, the drawer (*endorser*) can transfer the bill to another person (*endorsee*). Before the due date, an endorsee can further endorse the bill.

- *Presentation for payment by endorsee* On the due date, the last endorsee – the holder – presents the bill to the acceptor for payment. If the acceptor does not pay, the holder gets a certificate from a notary public *noting and protesting* the dishonour. The endorsee collects the amount due from its endorser. In a similar fashion, every endorsee collects the amount due from its endorser and the bill traces its way back to the drawer who pays its endorsee and collects the amount due from the acceptor.

Figure 7.1 illustrates these transactions.

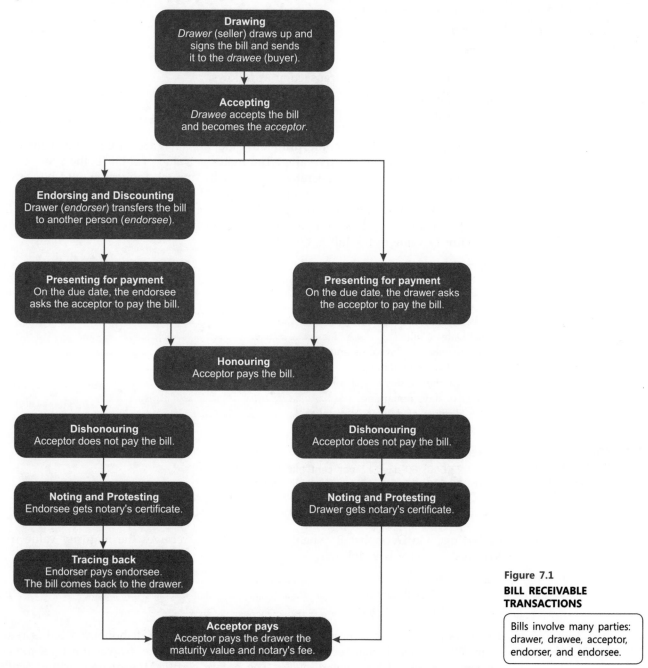

Figure 7.1
BILL RECEIVABLE TRANSACTIONS

Bills involve many parties: drawer, drawee, acceptor, endorser, and endorsee.

Drawing and Accepting Suppose on September 3, Vibha Company sells goods on credit to S. Krishna for ₹10,000 and draws a 12 per cent, 90-day bill on him for ₹10,000.

S. Krishna accepts and returns the bill the same day. Vibha Company is the drawer as well as the payee. S. Krishna is the acceptor. It is a **bill receivable** to Vibha Company and a **bill payable** to S. Krishna. Figure 7.2 shows the bill.

VIBHA COMPANY BILL RECEIVABLE

Figure 7.2
A BILL RECEIVABLE

The bill receivable is an order to pay a certain amount by a specific date.

Baroda
September 3, 20X6

₹10,000

Ninety days after date pay me or to my order the sum of ₹10,000 for value received with interest at 12 per cent per annum.

Accepted   Vibha Company

S. Krishna

Vibha company records the transaction as follows:

Sep. 3   Bills Receivable...   10,000
          Sales...   10,000

Computing interest   The amount printed on the bill is its **face value** or the **principal** and the amount due is the **maturity value**. The maturity value of a bill is the sum of its face value plus any interest. Interest rates are normally annual. Interest should be computed for the period stated in days or months in the bill. For convenience, we shall assume that a year has 360 days. Interest is computed using the formula, *Interest = Principal × Rate × Time*. The interest on Vibha Company's bill is ₹300, computed as: ₹10,000 × 12% × 90/360. The maturity value of the bill is ₹10,300.

Determining maturity date   The date on which a bill falls due for payment is the **maturity date**.[5] The maturity date of Vibha Company's bill is computed as follows:

Term of the bill in days		90
Number of days in September	30	
Deduct Date of bill...	3	
Deduct Number of days outstanding in September........................		27
Number of days remaining...		63
Deduct Number of days in October...		31
Number of days remaining...		32
Deduct Number of days in November..		30
Due date in December..		2

TEST YOUR UNDERSTANDING 7.4
Maturity Dates for Bills

Determine the maturity date and maturity value of each of the following bills receivable:

(a) ₹2,000, 60-day, 12 per cent bill dated March 15.
(b) ₹6,000, 90-day, 15 per cent bill dated June 5.
(c) ₹10,000, 30-day, 18 per cent bill dated January 18.
(d) ₹5,000, 90-day, 16 per cent bill dated August 31.

Collecting   On December 2, when Vibha Company receives the maturity value from S. Krishna, the entry is as follows:

Dec. 2   Cash...   10,300
             Bills Receivable   10,000
             Interest Income   300

Dishonouring   If the acceptor fails to pay at maturity, the dishonoured bill is removed from Bills Receivable and recorded in Trade Receivables. The drawer must get the fact of dishonour recorded by a *notary public*. The notary certifies the dishonour and sends the

---

[5] We do not consider the sometimes customary three-day grace period.

acceptor a *notice of protest*. The acceptor is legally obliged to pay the notary's *protest fee*, together with the maturity value of the bill. Suppose S. Krishna did not pay the bill on maturity. The following entry records the dishonour and a protest fee of ₹50:

Dec. 2	Trade Receivables..	10,350	
	Bills Receivable...		10,000
	Interest Income...		300
	Cash...		50

Should interest income be recognized on dishonoured bills?

QUICK QUESTION
Interest income on dishonoured bills

Discounting   A bill may be converted into cash before the due date. This happens because the holder (the drawer or an endorsee) needs cash and cannot wait until maturity. **Discounting** involves selling the bill to a bank with recourse to the holder. When a bill is discounted, the holder endorses and delivers the bill to the bank in exchange for cash. The bank deducts an interest charge called **discount** from the maturity value and pays the holder the balance. The discount is the bank's finance charge for the **discount period**, the period from the discounting date to the maturity date.

Assume that on October 3, Vibha Company discounted the bill at the bank at 15 per cent. We calculate the discount period as follows:

Term of the bill in days...		90
Number of days in September	30	
Deduct Date of bill...	3	
Number of days held in September..	27	
Add Number of days held in October	3	
Deduct Total days held by Vibha Company		30
Discount period in days..		60

We compute the proceeds as follows:

Face value of the bill	₹10,000
Interest at 12% for 90 days...	300
Maturity value..	10,300
Deduct Discount at 15% for 60 days: ₹10,300 × 15% × 60/360	258
Proceeds...	10,042

Vibha Company records the discounting as follows:

Oct. 3	Cash..	10,042	
	Bills Receivable...		10,000
	Interest Income...		42

If the proceeds are less than the face value, we debit the difference to interest expense. For example, suppose the bank discounts the bill at 18 per cent. The discount would be ₹309, calculated as follows: $₹10,300 \times 18\% \times \dfrac{60}{360}$.

The transaction is recorded as follows:

Oct. 3	Cash..	9,991	
	Interest Expense	9	
	Bills Receivable...		10,000

Dishonouring an endorsed bill   If the acceptor pays a discounted bill on the maturity date, the drawer or any subsequent endorser does not record any journal entries. If the acceptor defaults on the bill, the drawer or other endorser is required to pay. In the latter case, the bank should follow the procedure of noting and protesting. Every endorser is liable to pay his endorsee. The dishonoured bill will trace its way back to the drawer who can collect the amount from the acceptor. To illustrate, assume that S. Krishna dishonoured the bill and the bank sent Vibha Company a notice of protest and levied a protest fee of ₹50. Vibha Company will pay the bank ₹10,350 and record the following entry:

Dec. 2	Trade Receivables..	10,350	
	Cash...		10,350
	S. Krishna dishonoured bill discounted earlier		

HANDHOLD 7.1
Dishonouring an
Endorsed Bill

Manish draws a bill on Vishwesh who accepts and returns the bill to Manish. Manish endorses the bill to Raju who in turn endorses it to Vijay who further endorses it to Ashwin, as shown below:

Drawing and acceptance: Manish (Drawer) sends the bill → Vishwesh (Drawee) accepts (Acceptor from now on) and returns the bill → Manish (Drawer)

Endorsement: Manish (Drawer) → Raju (Endorsee 1) → Vijay (Endorsee 2) → Ashwin (Endorsee 3) On the due date Ashwin presents the bill to Vishwesh, who dishonours it. The bill travels back as follows:

Presentation, dishonour, and payment: Ashwin (Endorsee 3) presents the bill → Vishwesh (Acceptor) dishonours → Ashwin (Endorsee 3) claims from → Vijay (Endorsee 2) pays Ashwin and claims from → Raju (Endorsee 1) pays Vijay and claims from → Manish (Drawer) pays Raju and claims from → Vishwesh (Acceptor) pays → Manish (Drawer).

TEST YOUR UNDERSTANDING 7.5
Bills Receivable
Transactions

Vighnesh Company sold good to Pradeep Company for a ₹10,000, 60-day, 12 per cent bill dated March 11. Prepare journal entries in its records under the following independent cases:

Case 1: Pradeep Company paid the bill on the maturity date.

Case 2: On April 3, Vighnesh Company discounted the bill at 15 per cent. Pradeep Company paid the bill on the maturity date.

Case 3: On April 3, Vighnesh Company discounted the bill at 15 per cent. Pradeep Company dishonoured the bill on the maturity date and the bank had a notice of protest sent by a notary public. The protest fee was ₹25.

Accruing interest income Interest income accrues on a day-to-day basis, but usually is only recorded at the bill's maturity date. If a bill is outstanding at the end of a reporting period, interest income should be accrued. For example, assume that Vibha Company's reporting date is September 30. The following entry records accrued interest for 27 days (the number of days held in September as calculated in determining the maturity date) on the bill:[6]

| Sep. 30 | Interest Receivable.. | 90 | |
| | Interest Income.. | | 90 |

$$\text{Accrued interest on S. Krishna's bill: } ₹10,300 \times 12\% \times \frac{27}{360} = 90$$

The following entry records the collection of the bill on December 2:

Dec. 2	Cash..	10,300	
	Bills Receivable..		10,000
	Interest Receivable...		90
	Interest Income..		210

This entry eliminates the bill and interest receivable and recognizes interest income of ₹210 for the 63 days the bill was held in the current reporting period.[7]

Expected credit losses on bills are estimated and provided similar to trade receivables.

Financial Analysis of Receivables

Learning Objective
Analyze the quality of receivables.
LO 9

Managers, lenders and analysts are concerned with the age and realizability of a company's trade receivables and bills receivable. The **average collection period** (also known as **days sales outstanding** or *DSO*) is an overall measure of the quality of receivables. It is computed as follows:

---

[6] We are being consistent with the procedure for determining the maturity date. Alternatively, we can include the date of the bill. In this case, we will calculate accrued interest for 28 days, but interest income allocated to the next period will be for 62 days (instead of 63 days).

[7] As an exercise, you may try the reversing entry described in Chapter 4.

$$\text{Average collection period} = \frac{\text{Average receivables}}{\text{Average daily credit sales}}, \text{ where}$$

$$\text{Average receivabls} = \frac{\text{Beginning receivables} + \text{Ending receivables}}{2} \text{ and}$$

$$\text{Average daily credit sales} = \frac{\text{Annual credit sales}}{360}$$

To illustrate, assume the following data for Mega Company:

Beginning receivables..	₹11,500
Ending receivables..	14,000
Annual credit sales...	54,000
Average receivables: (₹11,500 + ₹14,000)/2..	12,750
Average daily credit sales: ₹54,000/360	150
Average collection period: ₹12,750/150 = 85 days	

It means that the customers of Mega Company took, on average, 85 days to pay their invoices. If the company's standard credit period is 60 days, it would appear that the customers paid late by 25 days. Possible reasons for delay may include poor credit rating of customers, laxity in the collection and economic slowdown.

We can compare the average collection period with past experience and industry norms. Ideally, the ratio should be computed using credit sales. Since financial statements do not report cash sales and credit sales separately, we have to use total sales. If the ratio of credit sales to total sales remains more or less unchanged over time, the comparison of average collection period from one period to another will not be affected much.

Win Company has the following information:

ONE-MINUTE QUIZ 7.2
Collection Period

	20X2	20X1
Total sales..	₹83,500	₹77,000
Cash sales..	10,000	9,000
Credit sales..	73,500	68,000
Sales returns and allowances on cash sales....................................	1,000	900
Sales returns and allowances on credit sales..................................	1,500	1,200
Trade receivables..	15,000	14,000
Allowance for credit losses..	2,000	1,800

The average collection period in 20X2 is:
(a) 56 days.
(b) 72.5 days.
(c) 63 days.
(d) 61.71 days.

Financial and Operating Investments

What sets apart an investment from other assets is that it is not intended to be available for the investor's production, selling or administrative activities. Investments are financial claims on other entities, such as equity shares or debt instruments. A business may want to invest its surplus cash in order to earn a return. Some businesses, such as banks and insurers, are in the business of lending and investing. Their intention is to earn a *financial return* in the form of interest, dividend and increase in the value of the investment. These investments are *financial investments*. Financial investments are financial assets. Investments held for the purpose of expanding or strengthening operations are *operating investments*. We consider and operating investments in Chapter 8.

Financial investments may be equity instruments or debt instruments. **Equity instruments** carry ownership rights. The investor in an equity instrument is entitled to (a) dividends declared by the company and (b) assets remaining after paying off liabilities.

Learning Objective

LO 10 Understand financial and operating investments.

The investor may receive repayment of capital in the event of a share buyback. The equity contract does not specify any amount payable to the investor. Shares and stock options are examples of equity instruments.

Debt instruments represent amounts owed to a lender (i.e. creditor or bondholder) by a borrower (i.e. debtor or issuer). The investor in a debt instrument is entitled to periodical interest payments and principal repayment on specified dates. Bonds, debentures, bank loans, home mortgages, and credit card receivables are examples of debt instruments. The debt contract specifies (a) the principal amount, or **face value**, (b) the interest rate, or **coupon**, and (c) the repayment date. The coupon is applied to the face value of the instrument to compute the amount of periodical interest.

Suppose a ₹1,000, 12 per cent, five-year bond is issued on January 1, 20X1. Interest is payable in arrears, i.e. after the period to which it relates (this is usual, so followed in this book). The face value is ₹1,000, the coupon is 12 per cent and the repayment date is December 31, 20X5. The holder of the bond is entitled to receive an interest payment of ₹120 (i.e. ₹1,000 × 12%) on December 31 for five years and principal repayment of ₹1,000 on December 31, 20X5.

You should review Appendix C to understand the idea of the time value of money.

Accounting for Financial Investments

Learning Objective

LO 11 Account for financial investments.

Accounting for financial assets depends on an entity's *business model* for managing the financial assets and the *contractual cash flow characteristics* of the financial assets.

Business model Business model means the objective of holding the financial assets. It determines how an entity manages its financial assets in order to generate cash flows. The business model may involve collecting contractual cash flows, selling financial assets or both. Consider the following business models:

1. *The hold to collect model:* An entity holds financial assets in order to collect contractual cash flows (e.g. trade receivables, originated loans[8] and debt securities held to maturity).

2. *The hold to collect and sell model:* An entity holds financial assets both to collect contractual cash flows and sell financial assets (e.g. liquidity portfolio and assets held by an insurer to back insurance liabilities).

Entities have different investment objectives in holding financial assets. These are influenced by industry needs, government policies and regulatory requirements.

- Retail banks and insurers hold some amount of government securities in order to earn interest income and receive principal on maturity. *This is the hold to collect model.*
- Manufacturing companies usually invest in financial assets as a way of parking their surplus cash and sell the assets when they need cash for supplier payments, capital expenditure or dividends. *This is the hold to collect and sell model.*
- Investment banks, mutual funds and brokerages buy and sell financial assets in order to make trading gains, i.e. *neither the hold to collect model nor the hold to sell model.* Examples are trading portfolios and assets managed on a fair value basis.

For the purpose determining the business model, instruments may be grouped in suitable portfolios reflecting management's intentions. For example, an entity may manage one portfolio in order to collect contractual cash flows and another portfolio in order to realize fair value changes. Similarly, in some circumstances, it may be appropriate to separate a portfolio of financial assets into subportfolios in order to reflect the level at which an entity manages those financial assets. For example, that may be the case if an

---

[8] An *originated loan* is a loan given by a lender after processing a borrower's application. A *purchased loan* is a loan bought by a lender from another lender.

entity originates or purchases a portfolio of mortgage loans and manages some of the loans with an objective of collecting contractual cash flows and manages the other loans with an objective of selling them. Assessing a business model requires judgment.

Indebted, a mutual fund, holds debt investments to collect interest and principal payments. It sells investments when investors request redemption or an investment falls below a specified credit rating. It regularly monitors fair values and credit ratings of the investments. The business of the entity is to hold the financial assets. Sales made to meet redemption needs or credit rating criteria or monitoring fair values as part of credit risk management would not change the position.

HANDHOLD 7.2
Business Model

Recon Company purchases troubled loans from banks. If payment is not made on the loans, it attempts to realize the contractual cash flows through various means, such as contacting the debtor by mail, telephone or other methods. Its objective is to collect the contractual cash flows and it does not manage any of the loans with an objective of realizing cash flows by selling them. The company is not certain whether it will receive the contractual cash flows because the assets are credit-impaired. What is the company's business model?

TEST YOUR UNDERSTANDING 7.6
Business Model

Contractual cash flow characteristics   Contractual cash flow characteristics are the contract terms for payment of principal and interest. In a basic lending arrangement, such as a standard loan, contractual cash flows are solely payments of principal and interest. In such arrangements, interest usually covers the time value of money, credit risk, administrative costs and a profit margin.[9] However, contractual terms that introduce exposure to risks or volatility in the contractual cash flows that is unrelated to a basic lending arrangement, such as exposure to changes in equity prices or commodity prices, do not give rise to contractual cash flows. Contractual terms that permit the issuer to prepay a debt instrument or the holder to put a debt instrument back to the debtor or permit the issuer or the holder to extend term of a debt instrument are solely payments of principal and interest.

On January 1, 20X0, Bond Fund buys a ₹1,000 bond with the following terms: (1) annual interest rate is 10 per cent; (2) payments of principal and interest are linked to the consumer price index; (3) the bond will mature on December 31, 20X9. The contractual cash flows are solely payments of principal and interest. Inflation-indexing of payments of principal and interest resets the time value of money to a current level. As a result, the interest rate on the bond reflects 'real' interest.

HANDHOLD 7.3
Contractual Cash Flows

On January 1, 20X3, Epsilon Fund buys a ₹1,000 bond with the following terms: (1) annual interest rate is 10 per cent; (2) payments of interest are indexed to the debtor's return on assets; (3) the bond will mature on December 31, 20X7. Are the contractual cash flows solely payments of principal and interest?

TEST YOUR UNDERSTANDING 7.7
Contractual Cash Flows

Which of the following terms of a bond would be inconsistent with a basic lending arrangement? There may be more than one correct answer.
   (a) The amount payable on the maturity of the bond is linked to an equity price index.
   (b) The bondholder can ask for payment of the principal before the maturity date.
   (c) Interest payments vary depending on dividend payments.
   (d) The maturity date may be extended by the consent of the issuer and the bondholder.

ONE-MINUTE QUIZ 7.3
Contractual Cash Flows

On the basis of the business model test and the cash flow characteristics test, we measure financial assets as follows:

   1. Amortized cost.
   2. Fair value through other comprehensive income.
   3. Fair value through profit or loss.

Figure 7.3 presents the classification of financial assets on the basis of the business model test and the contractual cash flow characteristics test.

---

[9] Interest rates are negative in some countries. In such cases, the deposit-holder pays the bank for holding its money.

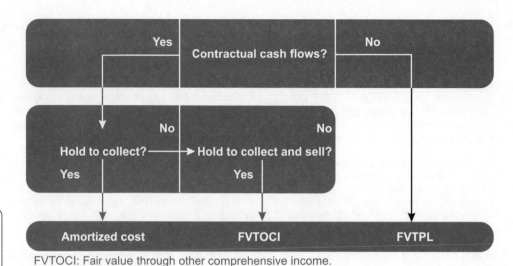

Figure 7.3

CLASSIFICATION OF FINANCIAL ASSETS

An entity classifies financial assets based on its business model and the cash flow characteristics of the assets.

FVTOCI: Fair value through other comprehensive income.
FVTPL: Fair value through profit or loss.

QUICK QUESTION
Contractual cash flows

Do equity investments have contractual cash flows?

Amortized Cost

Amortized cost is the amount at which a financial asset is measured at initial recognition minus principal repayments and adjusted for periodic amortization of the difference between the amount of initial recognition and the amount payable on maturity. The **effective interest method** calculates the amortized cost of a financial asset and allocates the interest income at the rate that exactly discounts estimated future interest receipts to the carrying amount of the financial asset. This rate is also known as the *internal rate of return* (IRR). Suppose F_0 is the fair value of an investment, $I_1, ..., I_n$ are interest, S the sum payable on maturity, n the investment period, and i the effective interest rate.[10] The following equation gives the relationship between these variables:

$$F_0 = \frac{I_1}{(1+i)^1} + \cdots + \frac{I_n}{(1+i)^n} + \frac{S}{(1+i)^n}$$

The value of i can be obtained by trial and error plugging in different values for i or by using the IRR function in a spreadsheet. The effective interest rate is also known as *market interest rate* or *yield*. To be consistent, we use yield.

LADDER
Coupon and Yield

Coupon applied to the face value gives the amount of periodical interest payment. The fair value of a loan is the present value of the principal and interest payments. Yield is the market interest rate for a loan with equivalent terms and credit quality. Coupon determines the interest payment and has no other use. Once we know the amount, we use the yield to discount the payments.

A financial asset should be measured at amortized cost if (a) the asset is held in order to collect contractual cash flows and (b) the terms of the asset provide for principal and interest payments on specified dates. This is the 'hold to collect' model. In this model, the business is not concerned with changes in fair value resulting from changes in the yield. Therefore, such changes are *not* recognized as gains or losses in the statement of profit and loss or other comprehensive income. The assets are debt instruments.

HANDHOLD 7.4
Amortized Cost

Harish Company bought a ₹1,000, 12 per cent, five-year debenture with a remaining maturity of four years at its current market price of ₹1,063. It invests in financial assets in order to collect principal and interest. The debenture carries contractual interest and principal payments. Harish Company records the investment at the fair value of ₹1,063, as follows:

Investments in Debentures 1,063
    Cash 1,063

---

[10] In other words, fair value is the present value of the cash flow stream. Chapter 10 explains this calculation.

The yield, *i*, is given by solving the following equation for *i*:

$$1,063 = \frac{120}{(1+i)} + \frac{120}{(1+i)^2} + \frac{120}{(1+i)^3} + \frac{120}{(1+i)^4} + \frac{1,000}{(1+i)^4}$$

The rate is approximately 10.01 per cent. Rounding it to 10 per cent, we apply the amortized cost method as follows:

Year	Amortized Cost: Start of Year	Interest Income	Interest Received	Principal Received	Amortized Cost: End of Year
	(A)	(B)	(C)	(D)	(E)
		10% of A			(A + B – C – D)
1	₹1,063	₹106	₹120	₹ 0	₹1,049
2	1,049	105	120	0	1,034
3	1,034	103	120	0	1,017
4	1,017	103	120	1,000	0

We adjust the rounding difference in Year 4 interest income.

Year 1 interest income is ₹106 (calculated as 10% of ₹1,063) is recorded as follows:

Cash	120	
Interest Income		106
Investments in Debentures		14

Note that over the life of the debenture the total interest income is ₹417 and the total interest received is ₹480. The difference of ₹63, the premium over the principal amount, is allocated to each period. The credit to the investment of ₹14 is the portion of the premium allocated to the first year and represents the recovery of the investment. The carrying amount on the balance sheet is the amortized cost. Thus, the investment will appear at ₹1,049 on the first year balance sheet. Just before redemption, the investment will have a carrying amount of ₹1,000.

This a continuation of Handhold 7.4. Prepare journal entries to record interest income over the remaining life of the debenture.

TEST YOUR UNDERSTANDING 7.8
Amortized Cost

On January 1, 20X0, Viraj Company bought Maya Company's ₹10,000, 12 per cent, 10-year debenture. Interest is payable semi-annually on June 30 and December 31. The yield is 16 per cent per annum. It invests in financial assets in order to collect interest on its investments. Prepare the amortization table from Year 1 to Year 5 and record the journal entry for Year 1 interest income.

TEST YOUR UNDERSTANDING 7.9
Amortized Cost

Fair value through Other Comprehensive Income

Other comprehensive income is a component of equity other than share capital, share premium and retained earnings. A financial asset should be measured at **fair value through other comprehensive income** (FVTOCI) if (a) the asset is held in order to collect (i) contractual cash flows and (ii) cash flows from selling it *and* (b) the terms of the asset provide for principal and interest payments on specified dates.

This is the *hold to collect and sell* model. In this model, the business is *partly* concerned with changes in fair value resulting from changes in the yield. Since the intention is both to collect *and* sell, such changes are recognized as gains or losses in other comprehensive income and not in the statement of profit and loss. The assets are debt instruments. Interest income is calculated using the effective interest method. At initial recognition, an entity may make an irrevocable election to follow FVTOCI for an investment in an *equity instrument* that is not *held for trading*. Dividends are recognized when they are declared.

Vikrant Company bought a ₹1,000, 12 per cent, five-year debenture with a remaining maturity of four years at its current market price of ₹1,063. It invests in financial assets in order to collect interest and principal and sell financial assets. The debenture carries solely contractual principal and interest payments. Therefore, the financial asset should be measured at FVTOCI. Vikrant Company will record the investment at the fair value of ₹1,063, as follows:

HANDHOLD 7.5
FVTOCI

Investments in Debentures	1,063	
Cash		1,063

Interest income is recognized by applying the effective interest method. We will use the table in Handhold 7.4, since the numbers are identical. At the end of Year 1, it records interest income of ₹106, as follows:

Cash	120	
Interest Income...		106
Investments in Debentures..		14

Suppose at the end of Year 1 the yield on the debenture becomes 9 per cent. The fair value of the debenture is given by the following calculation: $\dfrac{120}{1.09} + \dfrac{120}{1.09^2} + \dfrac{120}{1.09^3} + \dfrac{1,000}{1.09^3}$

Using Appendix C, Tables 3 and 4, we have: $120 \times 2.5313 + 1,000 \times 0.7722 = 1,076$. Thus, the fair value of the debenture at the end of Year 1 is ₹1,076. Since the amortized cost at the end of Year 1 is ₹1,049, there is a fair value gain of ₹27. The following entry records the gain:

Investments in Debentures...	27	
Other Comprehensive Income...		27

The fair value of ₹1,076 replaces the amortized cost. The amortization table for the remaining period is as follows:

Year	Amortized Cost Start of Year	Interest Income	Interest Received	Principal Received	Amortized Cost End of Year
	(A)	(B)	(C)	(D)	(E)
		9% of (A)			(A + B − C − D)
1	—	—	—	—	₹1,076
2	₹1,076	₹97	₹120	₹ 0	1,053
3	1,053	95	120	0	1,028
4	1,028	92	120	1,000	0

At the end of Year 2, it records interest income of ₹97 (i.e. 9 per cent on of ₹1,076), as follows:

Cash	120	
Interest Income...		97
Investments in Debentures..		23

The entries for the remaining periods are as follows:

Year 3:

Cash	120	
Interest Income...		95
Investments in Debentures..		25

Year 4:

Cash	120	
Interest Income...		92
Investments in Debentures..		28
Cash	1,000	
Investments in Debentures..		1,000

On derecognition of the debenture at the end of Year 4, the fair value gain of ₹27 is 'recycled' from other comprehensive income to statement of profit and loss as follows:

Other Comprehensive Income	27	
Statement of Profit and Loss		27

TEST YOUR UNDERSTANDING 7.10
FVTOCI

This is a continuation of Handhold 7.5. Suppose at the end of Year 2 the yield on the debenture becomes 8 per cent. Prepare journal entries to record the transactions in the debenture until maturity.

Fair Value through Profit or Loss

Fair value through profit or loss (FVTPL) is a residual category. This is for an entity that follows neither the 'hold to collect' model nor the 'hold to collect and sell' model. In other words, its business is to *buy and sell* financial assets. A financial asset should be measured at FVTPL unless it is measured at amortized cost or at fair value through other comprehensive income. Thus, debt instruments held for trading and all equity instruments should be measured at FVTPL. As mentioned earlier, if an equity instrument is *not held for trading,* an entity may make an irrevocable election at initial recognition to follow FVTOCI.

On June 12, 20X1, Gamma Company invested surplus cash of ₹10,000 in the shares of Delta Company at ₹80 per share intending to sell them any time. On September 17, 20X1, Delta Company paid a dividend of ₹5 per share. Gamma Company's fiscal year ended on March 31, 20X2, when Delta Company's share closed at ₹90 in the stock market. It records the transactions as follows:

HANDHOLD 7.6
FVTPL – Equity Investments

20X1

June 12	Investments in Shares		10,000	
	Cash			10,000
Sep. 17	Cash		625	
	Dividend Income			625

20X2

Mar. 31	Investments in Shares		1,250	
	Gain on Investments in Shares			1,250
Mar. 31	Gain on Investments in Shares		1,250	
	Statement of Profit and Loss			1,250

On October 6, 20X1, Smart Active Fund bought 500 shares of Navin Company at ₹50 per share. On November 12, Navin Company paid a dividend of ₹2 per share. On December 2, Smart Active Fund sold 250 shares at ₹49 per share. On December 31, the share was trading at ₹52. On March 31, 20X2, the share traded at ₹48. Prepare journal entries to record Smart Active Fund's transactions.

TEST YOUR UNDERSTANDING 7.11
FVTPL – Equity Investments

On July 1, 20X1, Alpha Company invested surplus cash in 1,000 of Omega Company's 12 per cent, ₹100 debentures at ₹98 per debenture, to be sold when it needed cash. Interest is payable on June 30 and December 31. Alpha Company's fiscal year ended on March 31, 20X2, when Omega Company's debenture traded at ₹90 plus accrued interest. Interest was received as stated. It records the transactions as follows:

HANDHOLD 7.7
FVTPL – Debt Investments

20X1

July 1	Investments in Debentures		98,000	
	Cash			98,000
Dec. 31	Cash		6,000	
	Interest Income			6,000

20X2

Mar. 31	Accrued Interest Receivable		3,000	
	Interest Income			3,000
	Accrued interest for three months			
Mar. 31	Loss on Investments in Debentures		8,000	
	Investments in Debentures			8,000
Mar. 31	Statement of Profit and Loss		8,000	
	Loss on Investments in Debentures			8,000

This is a continuation of Handhold 7.7. On April 1, 20X2, Alpha Company sold 300 debentures at ₹91 per debenture plus accrued interest. On March 31, 20X3, Omega Company's debenture traded at ₹102 plus accrued interest. Interest was received as stated. Prepare journal entries to record these transactions.

TEST YOUR UNDERSTANDING 7.12
FVTPL – Debt Investments

Why is the FVTOCI classification required?

QUICK QUESTION
FVTOCI

Which of the following events would give rise to a fair value gain or loss on a debt instrument after initial recognition? There may be more than one correct answer.

ONE-MINUTE QUIZ 7.4
Fair Value Gains and Losses

(a) Increase in yield.
(b) Decrease in yield.
(c) Increase in expected credit losses.
(d) Decrease in expected credit losses.

Derivative Financial Instruments

Derivative financial instruments, such as forward contracts, futures contracts, swaps and options are used extensively in risk management. Suppose that Indian Oil wants to protect itself against an increase in the price of crude oil in the international market. It can enter into a *forward contract* for the purchase of crude at a specified price on a certain date. In this manner, the company can ensure that it will be able to buy oil at the contracted price even if the price goes up. A *futures contract* is a standardized forward contract traded in a market. Both forwards and futures are binding on both parties. An *option* is a right but

Learning Objective
LO 12 Understand derivative financial instruments.

not an obligation to buy or sell shares, commodities or other items. Unlike forwards and futures, options are not binding on the holder.

In an *interest rate swap*, a party who wants to borrow at a fixed rate for protection but finds the borrowing too expensive swaps the interest payments with another borrower who has a fixed-rate loan but wants a floating rate. This is a convenient way to limit exposure to rising interest rates for a borrower with a substantial amount of variable debt. Further, companies with low credit ratings that can't borrow in the fixed-rate market can swap into it. Of course, a risk-taker can swap a fixed-rate borrowing for a floating rate. Banks, insurers, and large manufacturing and trading firms have huge exposures under derivative contracts.

Derivatives can be used for risk management or hedging purposes, as in the Indian Oil example. They are also traded as part of treasury activities. Since derivatives are financial instruments, fair value accounting applies to them. Derivatives do not meet the contractual cash flow characteristics test, since contractual cash flows are solely payments of principal and interest. Therefore, all derivatives are measured at FVTPL. If the entity has elected to apply hedge accounting by designating the derivative as a hedging instrument in an eligible hedging relationship, some or all gains or losses may be recognized in other comprehensive income.

Impairment of Financial Assets

Learning Objective

LO 13 Explain impairment of financial assets.

An allowance for expected credit losses is required for financial assets that are measured at amortized cost or at FVTOCI. There are two steps:

Step 1: Recognize a 12-month expected credit loss at initial recognition of a financial asset.

Step 2: Recognize a lifetime expected credit loss when there has been a significant increase in credit risk after the initial recognition.

HANDHOLD 7.8

Impairment of Financial Assets: Amortized Cost

Safe Bank gives a five-year term loan of ₹10,000. The bank's standard interest rate for AAA-rated loans is 8 per cent per annum. The borrower's credit rating is BBB, and Safe Bank's estimate of the expected credit losses is ₹200 per year over the five-year term. Accordingly, Safe Bank charges the borrower 10 per cent to reflect the yield on the instrument to include a return to cover those credit losses expected when the loan is first recognized. The present value of the lifetime expected credit losses of ₹200 per year for five years discounted at 10 per cent is ₹758: ₹200 × 3.7908 (Appendix C, Table 4). The present value of the 12-month expected credit losses of ₹200 for the first year discounted at 10 per cent is ₹182: ₹200 × 0.9091 (Appendix C, Table 3).

At initial recognition, Safe Bank records the following journal entries:

(a) Loans Receivable	10,000	
Cash		10,000
To recognize the loan at gross amount		
(b) Impairment Loss	182	
Allowance for Credit Losses		182
To recognize 12-moth expected credit losses		

The loan and the allowance would appear in the Year 1 balance sheet as follows:

Loan receivable	₹10,000	
Deduct Allowance for credit losses	182	
Loan receivables, net		₹9,818

If, at the end of Year 1, there is no significant deterioration of the credit quality, there would be no change to the recognition of the 12-month expected credit losses. Suppose, at the end of Year 1, there is a significant deterioration of the credit quality and Safe Bank re-estimates that the present value of the lifetime expected credit losses is ₹634. It recognizes the lifetime expected credit losses, as follows:

Impairment Loss	452	
Allowance for Credit Losses		452
To recognize lifetime expected credit losses: (₹634 − ₹182)		

In this case, the Year 1 balance sheet would be as follows:

Loan receivable	₹10,000	
Deduct Allowance for credit losses	634	
Loan receivables, net		₹9,336

Risk Bank gives a ten-year term loan of ₹100,000. The bank's standard interest rate for AAA-rated loans is 6 per cent per annum. The borrower's credit rating is B+ and Risk Bank estimates that there is a possibility the borrower might default on the payments and the expected credit losses are estimated at ₹3,000 per year over the ten-year term.

(a) What should be the yield on the instrument?
(b) Record the loan at initial recognition.
(c) At the end of Year 1, there is a significant deterioration of the credit quality. Risk Bank's estimate of the lifetime expected credit losses is ₹17,986. Record the impairment loss at the end of Year 1.

TEST YOUR UNDERSTANDING 7.13
Impairment of Financial Assets: Amortized Cost

Bucks Bank gives a five-year loan of ₹100,000 at 5 per cent interest. The yield, R_d, is 6 per cent consisting of MIBOR (Mumbai Inter Bank Offered Rate) of 5 per cent plus a credit spread of 1 per cent. Bucks Bank classifies the debt instrument as measured at FVTOCI. At initial recognition, the loan is not credit-impaired. Based on the credit rating, Bucks Bank recognizes an impairment loss in profit or loss at an amount equal to 12-month expected credit losses of ₹1,000 based on the credit spread.

HANDHOLD 7.9
Impairment of Financial Assets: Fair Value at Other Comprehensive Income

At initial recognition, Bucks Bank records the following journal entries:

(a) Loans Receivable.. 95,792
　　 Cash.. 95,792
　　　　 To recognize the loan at gross amount at fair value:
　　　　 ₹5,000 × 4.2124 + ₹100,000 × 0.7473 = ₹95,792

(b) Impairment Loss... 1,000
　　 Other Comprehensive Income... 1,000
　　　　 To recognize 12-moth expected credit losses

Impairment loss goes to the statement of profit and loss and other comprehensive income goes to the balance sheet as part of equity.

Suppose at the end of Year 1, MIBOR increases to 6 per cent and the credit spread of the issuer increases to 2 per cent. The issuer's yield at the end of Year 1 is 8 per cent and the market value of the loan declines to ₹90,061: 5,000 × 3.3121 + 100,000 × 0.7350. The analysis of the change in value under various scenarios of yield, R_d, is as follows:

Year	R_d did not change	Only MIBOR changed	Both MIBOR and credit risk changed
	(A)	(B)	(C)
2 to 5	5,000	5,000	5,000
5	100,000	100,000	100,000
Discount rate	6%	7%	8%
Present value calculation	5,000 × 3.4651 + 100,000 × 0.7921	5,000 × 3.3872 + 100,000 × 0.7629	5,000 × 3.3121 + 100,000 × 0.7350
Present value	**96,536**	**93,226**	**90,061**
Total change in fair value (95,792 – C)			(5,731)
Accretion due to time factor as interest income (95, 792 – A)			744
Decrease due to MIBOR change (A – B)			(3,310)
Decrease due to credit risk (B – C)			(3,165)

Suppose Bucks Bank determines that there has not been a significant increase in credit risk since initial recognition and that it is still appropriate to measure expected credit losses at an amount equal to 12-month expected credit losses. The expected credit losses have increased by ₹2,165 (i.e. ₹3,165 – ₹1,000). At the end of Year 1, Bucks Bank records the following entries to recognize interest income at effective interest based on gross carrying amount and to recognize additional impairment loss and fair value loss:

(a) Cash 5,000
　　 Loans Receivable.. 748*
　　　　 Interest Income... 5,748
　　　　 To recognize interest income: ₹95,792 × 6% (* 4 is rounding difference)

(b) Impairment Loss... 2,165
　　 Other Comprehensive Income 4,310
　　　　 Loans Receivable... 6,475
　　　　 To recognize impairment loss (₹3,165 – ₹1,000) and fair value loss (₹3,310 + ₹1,000)

**TEST YOUR
UNDERSTANDING 7.14**
Impairment of Financial
Assets: Fair Value at
Other Comprehensive
Income

Centum Company buys 1,000 of Decem Company's 4 per cent, ₹100 five-year debentures at fair value. The yield is 7 per cent consisting of MIBOR (Mumbai Inter Bank Offered Rate) of 5 per cent plus a credit spread of 2 per cent. Centum Company classifies the debt instrument as measured at FVTOCI. At initial recognition, the loan is not credit-impaired. The 12-month expected credit losses equal ₹2,500. At the end of Year 1, MIBOR increases to 6 per cent and the credit spread of the issuer increases to 3 per cent. There has not been a significant increase in credit risk since initial recognition and it is still appropriate to measure expected credit losses at an amount equal to 12-month expected credit losses. Record the transactions.

Table 7.2 summarizes the discussion on accounting for financial assets.

TABLE 7.2
Classification and
Measurement of
Financial Assets

Financial assets are classified and measured according to the business model of an entity and the cash flow characteristics of the asset.					
Classification and Measurement	**Business Model of Entity**	**Cash Flow Characteristics of Financial Asset**	**Financial Asset Type**	**Fair Value Gains and Losses**	**Impairment Loss**
Amortized cost	Hold to collect	Solely payments of principal and interest	Debt	None	Statement of profit and loss
Fair value through other comprehensive income (FVTOCI)	Hold to collect and sell	Solely payments of principal and interest	Debt; equity if entity makes an irrevocable election at initial ecognition	Recognized in other comprehensive income (balance sheet equity)	Statement of profit and loss
Fair value through profit or loss (FVTPL)	Other	Any payments (i.e. principal, interest, dividend, buyback)	Debt, equity	Recognized in statement of profit and loss	No impairment

QUICK QUESTION
Fair value

Recognition of impairment loss is not required for financial assets measured at FVTPL. Why?

FORENSIC CORNER
Financial Asset Fraud

Stealing cash and cash equivalents, receivables and financial investments is easier than carting away property, plant and equipment or inventories. Fraud includes money laundering, tax evasion, and terror funding. The following are the more common techniques of misappropriation and accounting fraud involving financial assets:

- Writing off receivables without proper authority.
- Opening accounts without complying with know-your-customer (KYC) guidelines.
- Depositing cheques received from customers into a fraudulent account (often in a government entity's name).
- Suppressing bad debts.
- Misclassifying investments or frequently changing their classification.

Red flags signalling financial assets fraud:

- Persistent differences between cash book balance and bank balance
- Letters sent to a large number of customers returned "addressee untraceable"
- Customers with unusual addresses (e.g. Rashtrapati Bhavan, Raj Bhavan, Police Commissioner's office), same customer's name from multiple addresses or multiple customers from the same address
- Employees not taking vacations
- Year-end credit (debit) to a customer's account followed by an identical debit (credit) early next year
- Old account balances
- Suspicious cash transactions involving large amounts
- Poor audit trail of transactions
- Absence of maker-checker control
- Absence of bank balance confirmation

Let's see how financial and non-financial businesses account for financial assets.

Financial Assets	Explanation
▪ The Group has made an irrevocable election to present in other comprehensive income subsequent changes in the fair value of equity investments not held for trading. *(TCS)*	▪ This will insulate the statement of profit and loss from changes in the fair value of such equity investments. As a result, profits will be less volatile.
▪ In determining the fair value of its financial instruments, the group uses a variety of methods and assumptions that are based on market conditions and risks existing at each reporting date. The methods used to determine fair value include discounted cash flow analysis, available quoted market prices and dealer quotes. All methods of assessing fair value result in a general approximation of value, and such value may never actually be realized. *(Infosys)*	▪ Fair value comes from a variety of sources, ranging from market prices (more reliable) to discounted cash flow models (significantly influenced by assumptions). It is important to understand the assumptions and the methods used in order to assess the risks associated with the valuation of particular financial assets.
▪ Securities sold under agreements to repurchase ("repos") and securities purchased under agreements to resell ("reverse repos") generally do not constitute a sale for accounting purposes of the underlying securities, and so are treated as collateralized transactions. *(HDFC Bank)*	▪ Agreements to repurchase or resell do not result in the transfer of title. The related gain or loss is not recognized. The assets are treated as security for the transaction.

Here are the key differences between these systems.

IFRS	Ind AS	Indian GAAP
IFRS 9	**Ind AS 109**	**AS 13**
▪ Initial measurement generally at fair value.	Same as IFRS	▪ No specific requirement.
▪ Classified as measured at amortized cost, FVTPL or FVTOCI.	Same as IFRS	▪ Classified as long-term or current.
▪ Expected credit loss.	Same as IFRS	▪ Incurred credit loss.

RECAP

- A financial instrument contains a right of one entity and an obligation of another entity. A financial asset is a cash, an equity instrument or a right to receive a financial asset from another entity.
- Fair value is the sale price of an asset in an orderly transaction. Fair value inputs range from quoted prices in active market prices to unobservable prices.
- Cash and cash equivalents are the most liquid assets.
- Expected credit losses on trade receivables should be recognized and reviewed. Provision matrix based on an ageing schedule is useful for estimating credit losses.
- Factoring results in the transfer of trade receivables.
- Bills receivable are transferable by endorsement and delivery.
- The average collection period indicates the quality of trade receivables.
- Financial investments are held for the purpose of earning interest, dividend or increase in value. Operating investments are held for business purposes.
- Financial assets are measured at amortized cost, at FVTOCI or at FVTPL. An entity's business model and cash flow characteristics determine the classification of financial assets.
- An impairment loss should be recognized for financial assets measured at amortized cost or at FVTOCI.
- Derivative financial instruments are measured at FVTPL unless the entity has elected to apply hedge accounting.

Review Problem

On August 1, 20X5, Pushpak Company bought Navin Company's ₹100,000, 15 per cent, 10-year debentures for ₹86,304. Its business model is to hold to collect. Interest is payable on June 30 and

December 31. The company's year end is March 31. Prepare journal entries to record the following:
1. Purchase of debentures on August 1, 20X5.
2. Receipt of semi-annual interest on December 31, 20X5 and amortization of discount.
3. Accrual of interest on March 31, 20X6 and amortization of discount.

Solution to the Review Problem

The implied yield is 9 per cent. The investment will be recorded initially at its fair value of ₹86,304, verified as follows: 7,500 × 9.1285 + 100,000 × 0.1784. We apply the amortized cost method as follows:

20X5

Aug. 1	Investments in Debentures		86,304	
	Cash			86,304
Dec. 31	Cash		6,250	
	Investments in Debentures		223	
	Cash			6,473

           Received interest for five months: ₹100,000 × 15/100 × 5/12 =
           ₹6,250 + Discount amortization: ₹267 × 5/6 = ₹223

20X6

Mar. 31	Accrued Interest Receivable		3,750	
	Investments in Debentures		141	
	Interest Income			3,891

           Accrued interest for three months: ₹100,000 × 15% × 3/12 = ₹3,750 +
           Discount amortization: (₹267 × 1/6 = ₹44 + ₹291 × 2/6 = ₹97)

ASSIGNMENT MATERIAL

Questions

1. What is a *financial instrument*?
2. What is a *financial asset*?
3. What is *fair value*?
4. Explain Level 1, Level 2 and Level 3 inputs.
5. Are certificates of deposit classified as cash? Why or why not?
6. What is *liquidity*?
7. Why do companies sell on credit though some customers don't pay?
8. What is *credit risk*?
9. What is an *ageing schedule*?
10. "Allowance for credit losses is a contra-asset." Explain.
11. How is providing for an expected credit loss different from writing off a loss account?
12. How is *expected loss* different from *incurred loss*?
13. "A factor is a financier-cum-insurer." Do you agree?
14. How is a bill receivable different from a trade receivable?
15. Can a bill be made payable to the drawer?
16. How is the average collection period useful for financial analysis?
17. Why is it important to treat equity shares

held as financial investments differently from equity shares held as operating investments?
18. Distinguish between *equity instruments* and *debt instruments*.
19. Which of these indicates the rate of return on a bond: coupon or yield?
20. Explain the *hold to collect* and the *hold to collect and sell* models.
21. How are financial assets classified for measurement?
22. Explain *amortized cost*.
23. Can an equity instrument be measured at *FVTOCI*?
24. "Fair value through profit or loss is only for equity instruments." Do you agree?
25. Distinguish between impairment loss and fair value loss of a debt instrument.
26. Are financial assets measured at amortized cost subject to impairment review?
27. In which statement is impairment loss on financial assets measured at *FVTOCI* recognized?
28. How are derivative financial instruments measured? Why?

Problems

Veena Trading Company had the following customer account balances on December 31, 20XX:

Problem 7.1

Ageing Analysis of Trade Receivables *

Account	Amount	Due Date	Account	Amount	Due Date
R. Anand	₹11,070	November 30	V. Hariharan	₹6,310	August 14
J. Bhowmick	3,570	June 12	B. Kamal	980	December 14
K. Chandra	9,250	January 10 (next year)	M. Lakshman	10,720	January 27 (next year)
E. Dawood	5,980	October 23	C. Pankaj	2,310	September 3
A. Eknath	7,190	November 15	S. Uday	3,210	October 7
N. Govind	1,480	December 8	D. Wilson	1,120	December 31

Required

Prepare an ageing analysis of the trade receivables under the following age categories: Not yet due; 1–30 days past due; 31–60 days past due; 61–90 days past due; 91–120 days past due; over 120 days past due.

On March 1, Thomas Company buys ₹1 million of 10%, 15-year debentures. Interest is payable semi-annually on August 31 and February 28 or 29.

Problem 7.2

Fair Value of Debenture *

Required

Compute the fair value of the debentures if the yield on March 1 is (a) 18 per cent, (b) 10 per cent, or (c) 8 per cent.

On October 17, 20X1, Suhrid Company bought 2,000 equity shares of Piyush Company at ₹24 per share as part of its cash management. On January 12, 20X2, Piyush Company paid an interim dividend of ₹2 per share. On March 31, 20X2, Suhrid Company's fiscal year end, Piyush Company's share traded at ₹27. On July 15, 20X2, Piyush Company paid a final dividend of ₹4 per share. On January 19, 20X3, Piyush Company paid an interim dividend of ₹3 per share. On March 31, 20X3, Piyush Company's share traded at ₹25.

Problem 7.3

FVTPL: Equity Investments **

Required

Prepare journal entries to record the transactions.

On January 1, 20X1, Dinesh Company invested surplus cash in 1,000 of Chand Company's 15 per cent, ₹100 debentures bought at ₹97 per debenture, ex-interest. Interest is payable on June 30 and December 31. On September 30, 20X1, Dinesh Company's fiscal year end, the debenture traded at ₹93 plus accrued interest. On September 30, 20X2, the debenture traded at ₹94 plus accrued interest. Interest was received as stated.

Problem 7.4

FVTPL: Debt Investments **

Required

Prepare journal entries to record the transactions.

On November 3, 20X1, Ashwin Company bought 1,000 equity shares of Vipul Company at ₹45 per share. Mohan Company makes an irrevocable election at initial recognition to present subsequent changes in the investment in Vipul Company at FVTOCI. On March 14, 20X2, it received an interim dividend of ₹3 per share. The share had a fair value of ₹49 on March 31, 20X2, Ashwin Company's fiscal year end. On September 12, 20X2, Vipul Company paid a final dividend of ₹5 per share. On March 9, 20X3, it paid an interim dividend of ₹2 per share. On March 31, 20X3, the share traded at ₹42.

Problem 7.5

FVTOCI: Equity Investments **

Required

Prepare journal entries to record the transactions.

The following information is taken from the accounting records of Jaykay Company on December 31, 20X1 (fiscal year end):

Problem 7.6

Using a Provision Matrix ***

Trade Receivables

Dec. 31	901,800

Allowance for Credit Losses

Dec. 31	12,482

The ageing analysis of the trade receivables at December 31 is as follows:

Age Category	Amount
Not yet due	₹395,900
1–30 days past due	160,500
31–60 days past due	120,400
61–90 days past due	110,200
91–120 days past due	79,500
Over 120 days past due	35,300
Total	901,800

To determine the expected credit losses for the portfolio, Jaykay Company uses a provision matrix. The provision matrix is based on its historical observed default rates over the expected life of the trade receivables and is adjusted for forward-looking estimates. The company uses the following provision matrix:

Age Category	Lifetime Expected Credit Loss Rate (%)
Not yet due	2
1–30 days past due	5
31–60 days past due	8
61–90 days past due	10
91–120 days past due	15
Over 120 days past due	25

Required

1. Calculate the amount of allowance for credit losses at December 31, 20X1.
2. Prepare the general journal entry to record the bad debt expense for the year.
3. Post the journal entry to the Allowance for Credit Losses account.
4. On February 16, 20X2, Jaykay Company decided to write off a receivable of ₹4,200. What effect will this have on: (a) the company's net profit for that year; and (b) estimated net realizable value of its trade receivables?

Problem 7.7
Using a Provision Matrix
✳✳✳ Alternative to
Problem 7.6

The following information is taken from the accounting records of Harinder Company on March 31, 20X1 (fiscal year end):

Trade Receivables

Mar. 31	582,000

Allowance for Credit Losses

	Mar. 31	9,380

The ageing analysis of the trade receivables at March 31 is as follows:

Age Category	Amount
Not yet due	₹275,400
1–30 days past due	110,900
31–60 days past due	87,500
61–90 days past due	65,100
91–120 days past due	27,800
Over 120 days past due	15,300
Total	582,000

To determine the expected credit losses for the portfolio, Harinder Company uses a provision matrix. The provision matrix is based on its historical observed default rates over the expected life of the trade receivables and is adjusted for forward-looking estimates. The company uses the following provision matrix:

Age Category	Lifetime Expected Credit Loss Rate (%)
Not yet due	3
1–30 days past due	6
31–60 days past due	10
61–90 days past due	15
91–120 days past due	25
Over 120 days past due	50

Required

1. Calculate the amount of allowance for credit losses at March 31, 20X1.
2. Prepare the general journal entry to record the bad debt expense for the year.
3. Post the journal entry to the Allowance for Credit Losses account.
4. On April 19, 20X2, Harinder Company decided to write off a receivable of ₹3,290. What effect will this have on: (a) the company's net profit for that year; and (b) estimated net realizable value of its trade receivables?

Mohan Company owned the following equity investments on December 31, 20XX, its fiscal year end:

Problem 7.8
FVTPL and FVTOCI: Equity Investments ✳✳✳

Investment	Cost	Fair Value
Abhijit Company	₹17,000	₹18,100
Victor Company...	19,300	17,400
Vincent Company..	10,100	10,800

Required

1. Prepare journal entries assuming that all are measured at FVTPL.
2. Prepare journal entries assuming that all are measured at FVTOCI.
3. Prepare journal entries assuming that Mohan Company makes an irrevocable election at initial recognition to present subsequent changes in the investment in Vincent Company at FVTOCI.

Pavan Company owned the following equity investments on December 31, 20XX, its fiscal year end:

Problem 7.9
FVTPL and FVTOCI: Equity Investments ✳✳✳
Alternative to Problem 7.8

Investment	Cost	Fair Value
Akash Company	₹27,000	₹29,100
Antariksh Company..	14,100	11,900
Surya Company	34,200	46,100

Required

1. Prepare journal entries assuming that all are measured at fair value through profit or loss.
2. Prepare journal entries assuming that all are measured at fair value through other comprehensive income.
3. Prepare journal entries assuming that Pavan Company makes an irrevocable election at initial recognition to present subsequent changes in the investment in Antariksh Company at FVTOCI.

Bhandari Company engaged in the following transactions in trade receivables and bills receivable during April 1, 20X1 to March 31, 20X2:

Problem 7.10
Comprehensive Problem on Receivables ✳✳✳✳

Apr. 12 Sold merchandise to Navin Gupta for a 12 per cent, 90-day bill for ₹10,000.
May 18 Ganesh Apte sent a 12 per cent, 90-day, ₹20,000 bill in settlement of the amount receivable from him.
    23 Wrote off the ₹2,100 account balance receivable from Jane Company.

June 17   Discounted at Country Bank the bill received from Ganesh Apte on May 18. The discount rate was 15 per cent.

July 11   Received payment from Navin Gupta on his bill of April 12.

Aug. 16   Paid the bank the maturity value plus protest fee of ₹50 on receiving notice that Ganesh Apte had dishonoured his bill.

Sep. 15   Received from Ganesh Apte payment of the maturity value of his dishonoured bill plus protest fee, and interest at 12 per cent for 30 days beyond the maturity date.

Oct. 8   Sold merchandise to Mahesh Jain and accepted a 14 per cent, 90-day bill for ₹15,000.

Nov. 7   Discounted at Country Bank the bill received from Mahesh Jain on October 8. The discount rate was 16 per cent.

      23   Received a 14 per cent, 90-day, ₹30,000 bill in settlement of the amount receivable from Vidya Mohan.

Jan. 6   Received intimation from Mahesh Jain that he has paid Country Bank the maturity value of the bill accepted by him on October 8.

Feb. 21   Vidya Mohan dishonoured her bill of November 23. The protest fee was ₹50.

      23   Received from Vidya Mohan payment of the maturity value of her dishonoured bill plus protest fee.

Required

Prepare general journal entries to record the above transactions. Round interest calculations to the nearest rupee.

Problem 7.11
Comprehensive
Problem on Receivables
* * * * Alternative to
Problem 7.10

Samyukt Company engaged in the following transactions involving trade receivables and bills receivable during July 1, 20X4 to June 30, 20X5:

July 13   Accepted a 15 per cent, 120-day, ₹30,000 bill in settlement of the account balance receivable of Hari.

      19   Wrote off the ₹1,700 account balance receivable from Naresh Chander.

Aug. 10   Sold merchandise to Srinivasan and accepted a 15 per cent, 120-day, ₹20,000 bill.

      12   Discounted at National Bank the bill received from Hari on July 13. The discount rate was 20 per cent.

Nov. 10   Received notice that Hari had dishonoured his bill and paid the bank the maturity value plus protest fee of ₹50.

Dec. 8   Received payment from Srinivasan on his bill of August 10.

      10   Received payment from Hari of the maturity value of his dishonoured bill plus protest fee, and interest at 15 per cent for 30 days beyond the maturity date.

Mar. 1   Sold merchandise to Mary Selvaraj and accepted a 15 per cent, 120-day, ₹25,000 bill.

      31   Discounted at National Bank the bill received from Mary Selvaraj on March 1. The discount rate was 20 per cent.

Apr. 10   Accepted a 15 per cent, 120-day, ₹10,000 bill in settlement of the past-due account receivable of Arun Kumar.

May 10   Discounted at National Bank the bill received from Arun Kumar on April 10. The discount rate was 20 per cent.

June 29   Received intimation from Mary Selvaraj that she has paid National Bank the maturity value of the bill accepted by her on March 1.

Required

Prepare general journal entries to record the above transactions. Round interest calculations to the nearest rupee.

Problem 7.12
Impairment of Financial
Assets: Amortized Cost
* * * * *

Fair Bank gives a five-year loan of ₹1 million. The bank's yield for AAA-rated loans is 4 per cent per annum. The borrower's credit rating is B and Fair Bank's estimate of expected credit losses is ₹10,000 per year over the five-year term.

Required

1. What should be the yield that would cover the credit losses expected when the loan is first recognized?
2. Record the loan at initial recognition.
3. Record the interest income at the end of Year 1.

4. At the end of Year 1, there is a significant deterioration of the credit quality of the loan. Fair Bank's estimate of the present value of lifetime expected credit losses is ₹17,986. Record the impairment loss.

5. At the end of Year 3, there is a further significant deterioration in the credit quality. Fair Bank's estimate of the present value of lifetime expected credit losses is ₹21,419. Record the impairment loss.

6. Record the repayment of the loan and reversal of lifetime expected credit losses at the end of Year 5.

Good Bank gives a ten-year loan of ₹500,000. The bank's yield for AAA-rated loans is 5 per cent per annum. The borrower's credit rating is BB and Good Bank's estimate of expected credit losses is ₹15,000 per year over the ten-year term.

Problem 7.13
Impairment of Financial Assets: Amortized Cost
✶✶✶✶✶ Alternative to Problem 7.12

Required

1. What should be the yield that would cover the credit losses expected when the loan is first recognized?
2. Record the loan at initial recognition.
3. Record the interest income at the end of Year 1.
4. At the end of Year 1, there is a significant deterioration of the credit quality of the loan. Good Bank's estimate of the present value of lifetime expected credit losses is ₹19,241. Record the impairment loss.
5. At the end of Year 4, there is a further significant deterioration in the credit quality. Good Bank's estimate of the present value of lifetime expected credit losses is ₹21,735. Record the impairment loss.
6. Record the repayment of the loan and reversal of lifetime expected credit losses at the end of Year 10.

Bonum Company buys 500 of Benefit Company's 5 per cent, ₹100 five-year debentures at fair value. The yield is 7 per cent consisting of MIBOR of 4 per cent plus a credit spread of 3 per cent. Bonum Company classifies the debt instrument as measured at FVTOCI. At initial recognition, the debenture is not credit-impaired. The 12-month expected credit losses are estimated at ₹900.

Problem 7.14
Impairment and Fair Value Changes: FVTOCI
✶✶✶✶✶

Required

1. Record the debentures at initial recognition.
2. Record the interest income for Year 1.
3. At the end of Year 1, MIBOR increases to 5 per cent and the credit spread of the issuer increases to 4 per cent. There has not been a significant increase in credit risk since initial recognition.

Gratis Company buys 200 of Free Company's 3 per cent, ₹100 five-year debentures at fair value. The yield is 6 per cent consisting of MIBOR of 4 per cent plus a credit spread of 2 per cent. Gratis Company classifies the debt instrument as measured at FVTOCI. At initial recognition, the debenture is not credit-impaired. The 12-month expected credit losses are estimated at ₹500.

Problem 7.15
Impairment and Fair Value Changes: FVTOCI
✶✶✶✶✶ Alternative to Problem 7.14

Required

1. Record the debentures at initial recognition.
2. Record the interest income for Year 1.
3. At the end of Year 1, MIBOR increases to 6 per cent and the credit spread of the issuer increases to 4 per cent. There has not been a significant increase in credit risk since initial recognition.

Business Decision Cases

Nova Bank invests a portion of its assets in long-term government securities and corporate debt securities. These instruments carry annual interest payments and principal repayment at maturity. The issuers follow a book-building arrangement for price discovery. Under this arrangement, bidding banks indicate their purchase prices and the issuer allots the instruments to the bidders at the median price.

BDC 7.1
Nova Bank

On January 1, 20X1, Nova Bank purchased debt securities for ₹300 billion and allocated them equally to three portfolios, as follows:

Portfolio	Intended Terms of Business	Classification and Measurement
A	To trade as part of the bank's treasury operations for liquidity	Fair value through profit or loss
B	To receive interest and principal payments and sell a part or whole of the investments when the prices are advantageous	Fair value through other comprehensive income
C	To receive interest and principal payments	Amortized cost

Required

1. How should the bank measure the investments at initial recognition? Do the bank's intentions for the three portfolios matter? Why or why not?
2. Subsequent to initial recognition, the bank engages in the following independent activities. How would they affect bank's initial classification and measurement?
   (a) It sells a portion of the investments in Portfolio C in order to rebalance its overall investment holdings. Would it make a difference if the amount of the investments is (say) ₹1 billion or ₹10 billion?
   (b) It shifts a portion of the investments in Portfolio B to Portfolio A. Would it make a difference if the amount of the investments is (say) ₹1 billion or ₹10 billion?
   (c) It shifts a portion of the investments in Portfolio A to Portfolio C. Would it make a difference if the amount of the investments is (say) ₹1 billion or ₹10 billion?
3. How would changes in the yield over the life of the instruments affect their balance sheet value?
4. How would an increase in the credit risk affect their balance sheet value?

BDC 7.2
Mumbai Mutual Fund

Mumbai Mutual Fund invests in various types of financial instruments, such as equity shares with voting rights, equity shares with no voting rights but higher dividend payments, preference shares, convertible preference shares, fixed-rate bonds, floating-rate bonds, inflation-indexed bonds, equity-linked bonds, bonds redeemable at a premium, convertible bonds, perpetual bonds, and contingent convertible bonds.

Required

1. Describe the cash flow characteristics of each of these financial instruments.
2. Which of these can be classified at initial recognition as measured at amortized cost? Explain.

BDC 7.3
Flexi Bank

You are the chief financial officer of Flexi Bank. Vikram Suri, the bank's chief executive, has worked in large banks in New York and London. Flexi Bank's loan and investment portfolio grew from ₹3 billion to ₹9 billion in the three years since he joined. Suri believes that the bank must take full advantage of India's rapid economic progress but thinks that it has been too conservative. He is pushing for aggressive corporate and consumer lending and active investing in the financial markets. He laments that the bank's "current accounting policies are unhelpful in presenting the bank's extraordinary growth story."

Required

1. What do you think could the chief executive have meant when he says that the bank's "current accounting policies are unhelpful in presenting the bank's extraordinary growth story"? Do you agree with his view?
2. Prepare a note setting out how institutional safeguards, including accounting principles, are necessary to protect the bank's investors, creditors, and employees – you and the chief executive, included.

Interpreting Financial Reports

IFR 7.1
ICICI Bank

On March 4, 2008, the shares of ICICI Bank, the largest non-government bank in India, ended 5 per cent lower than the previous close.[11] The trigger was an announcement in Parliament that as

---

[11] ICICI Bank takes $264-m hit on overseas credit exposure, *Business Line*, March 5, 2008.

at January 31, 2008 ICICI Bank had suffered mark-to-market losses of $264 million (about ₹15,560 million) on account of exposure to overseas credit derivatives and investments in fixed income assets. Read the related reports.

Required

1. Explain the following terms: *mark-to-market loss; credit derivative; fixed income asset.*
2. Prepare a note setting out the principles of valuation of credit derivatives and fixed income assets and the issues in applying the principles.

Unicredit, one of the largest banks in Europe, announced on April 23, 2008 that it would be recording write-downs of about €1 billion ($1.6 billion) in January and February because of the global financial crisis.[12] Read the related reports. The bank had already announced a loss of €1 billion in its asset-backed securities. Unicredit's largest holdings of these securities included interests in real estate and car loans and only a tiny exposure to the subprime sector. There will be a further write-down of €350 million as a result of adverse movements in spreads in bonds and credit default swaps.

**IFR 7.2
Unicredit**

Required

1. Explain the following terms: *asset-backed security; subprime sector; credit default swap.*
2. Prepare a note setting out the principles of valuation of asset-backed securities and the issues in applying the principles.

Elite Advisers was co-founded by Miriam Mascherin and Michel Tamisierin 2007. The company specializes "in the creation of niche and elitist products", according to its website. It invests in fine wine and collectable watches. Elite Advisers manages Nobles Crus, a Luxembourg-based specialized fund that invests in wine. The website states: "The wines in the portfolio are valued every month on the basis of four price lists, two of which come from wine merchants in Continental Europe and the United Kingdom, and two of which come from leading auction houses such as Sotheby's or Christie's. In total, around sixty wine merchants may be used as a basis for the valuation. This comprehensive valuation process also includes an annual review of our merchants to ensure their pricing policy is correct and their quality standards meet our criteria." Nobles Crus launched with €2 million in 2008 and had grown to €109 million by 2012. Interest in wine funds has grown as investors are looking at alternatives to a troubled equity market.

**IFR 7.3
Nobles Crus**

On September 30, 2012, the *Financial Times* questioned the valuation of the holdings of Nobles Crus. The fund reported a gain every month since the start of 2011, though the benchmark Liv-ex Fine Wine index declined to 260.08 in September 2012 from a peak of 364.69 in June 2011. For example, one of the wines, a Lafite Rothschild 1996, was valued by Nobles Crus at €1,718, more than double the Liv-ex price of €855. Elite Advisers said that Noble Crus valued its wines by taking the average of two prices from auction houses, without removing commission, and two from wine merchants. Live-ex valuations are based on actual transaction prices on its Fine Wine Exchange. Responding to the criticism of its valuation method, Nobles Crus stated that it had been working on an "automatic and scientific valuation system with two renowned finance professors and that this valuation method would be implemented next year. Also, it engaged Ernst & Young, a Big Four accounting firm, and a wine auction house to provide an independent third party review of the fund's portfolio, valuation, and valuation methodology.

Required

1. How should wine investment funds account for their holdings?
2. Comment on Nobles Crus' accounting policy.
3. Evaluate Nobles Crus' response to the criticism of its accounting?

Financial Analysis

In the wake of the financial crisis, there was a lot of criticism of fair value accounting. Commentators argued that fair value accounting was defective both in theory and in practice for valuing securities that had illiquid markets or when the market had seized up. A few went to the extent of saying that fair value accounting caused the financial crisis and its "pro-cyclicality" aggravated the crisis.

**FA 7.1
Fair Value Accounting**

Required

1. Prepare a report outlining the arguments for and against fair value accounting.

---

[12] Adrian Michaels, Unicredit to write down €1 billion, *Financial Times*, April 24, 2008.

2. What does "pro-cyclicality" mean in the context of fair value accounting?
3. Examine how the International Accounting Standards Board and the Financial Accounting Standards Board have responded to concerns about fair value accounting.

FA 7.2
Expected Loss and
Incurred Loss

Accounting for financial assets is changing from incurred loss and expected loss. This is expected to have a significant impact on the financial statements of banks and other financial enterprises. The shift to expected loss is intended to address some of the problems that surfaced in the financial crisis.

Required

1. Explain expected loss and incurred loss.
2. Why was accounting based on incurred loss followed (and expected loss prohibited) in the past?
3. Explain how the shift to expected loss is likely to affect the behaviour of lenders.

Answers to One-minute Quiz

7.1 b, c.
7.2 c.
7.3 a, c.
7.4 a, b.

Answers to Test Your Understanding

7.1 (i) Bad Debt Expense.. 200
          Allowance for Credit Losses 200
      (ii) Bad Debt Expense.. 1,950
          Allowance for Credit Losses 1,950

7.2 The write-off reduces both trade receivables and allowance for credit losses by a like amount. Since the estimated realizable value of trade receivables equals trade receivables less allowance, the write-off does not affect that amount.

7.3 Mar. 31 Bad Debt Expense... 800
            Allowance for Credit Losses 800
     June 18 Allowance for Credit Losses.. 970
            Trade Receivables 970
     Oct. 25 Trade Receivables.. 970
            Allowance for Credit Losses 970
         25 Cash... 970
            Trade Receivables 970

7.4 (a) May 14, ₹2,040; (b) September 3, ₹6,225; (c) February 17, ₹10,150; (d) November 29, ₹5,200.

7.5 Mar. 11 Bills Receivable.. 10,000
            Sales... 10,000

Case 1

     May 10 Cash... 10,200
            Bills Receivable 10,000
            Interest Income.. 200

Case 2

     Apr. 3 Cash... 10,043
            Bills Receivable 10,000
            Interest Income.. 43
     May 10 No entry

Case 3

     Apr. 3 Cash... 10,043
            Bills Receivable 10,000
            Interest Income.. 43
     May 10 Trade Receivables... 10,225
            Cash... 10,225

7.6 The business model is to hold the financial assets in order to collect the contractual cash flows.

7.7 The interest payments were indexed to the debtor's performance (i.e. return on assets). As a result, the contractual cash flows reflect a return that is inconsistent with a basic lending arrangement. Therefore, the contractual cash flows are not payments of interest.

7.8

Year 2	Cash	120	
	Interest Income		105
	Investments in Debentures		15
Year 3	Cash	120	
	Interest Income		103
	Investments in Debentures		17
Year 4	Cash	120	
	Interest Income		103
	Investments in Debentures		17

7.9 At the yield of 16 per cent per annum, or 8 per cent per semi-annual period, Viraj Company pays ₹8,036, the fair value of the debentures, calculated as follows: $600/1.08^1 + \ldots + 600/1.08^{20} + 10,000/1.08^{20}$. The relevant values are as follows: Amortized cost: Period 1, ₹8,079; Period 2, ₹8,125; Period 3, ₹8,175; Period 4, ₹8,229; Period 5, ₹8,287. Interest income: Period 1, ₹643; Period 2, ₹646; Period 3, ₹650; Period 4, ₹654; Period 5, ₹658.

Period 1: Cash	600	
Investment in Debentures	43	
Interest Income		643

7.10 Year 2 interest income is recorded as in Handhold 7.5.

Year 2 Investments in Debentures	18	
Other Comprehensive Income		18

Fair value, ₹1,071: 120 × 1.7833 + 1000 × 0.8573

Amortized cost: Year 2, ₹1,071; Year 3, ₹1037. Interest income: Year 3, ₹86; Year 4, ₹83.

Year 3 Cash	120	
Interest Income		86
Investment in Debentures		34
Year 4 Cash	120	
Interest Income		83
Investment in Debentures		40
Year 4 Cash	1,000	
Investment in Debentures		1,000
Year 4 Other Comprehensive Income	45	
Investment in Debentures		45

Fair value gain: Year 1, ₹27 + Year 2, ₹18 = ₹45

7.11 20X1

Oct.	6	Investments in Shares	25,000	
		Cash		25,000
Nov.	12	Cash	1,000	
		Dividend Income		1,000
Dec.	2	Cash	12,250	
		Loss on Sale of Investments in Shares	250	
		Investments in Shares		12,500
		250 × (₹49 − ₹50)		
Dec.	31	Investments in Shares	500	
		Gain on Investments in Shares		500
		250 × (₹52 − ₹50)		

20X2

Mar.	31	Loss on Investments in Shares	1,000	
		Investments in Shares		1,000
		250 × (₹48 − ₹52)		

7.12 20X2

Apr. 1 Cash.. 28,200

         Investments in Debentures... 27,000

         Accrued Interest Receivable 900

         Gain on Investments in Debentures... 300

             Sale proceeds, 300 × ₹91 + accrued interest, ₹900; total cash
received ₹28,200; gain 300 × (₹91 – ₹90)

June 30 Cash... 4,200

         Interest Income.. 2,100

         Accrued Interest Receivable 2,100

            700 × ₹100 × 12% × 6/12

Dec. 31 Cash... 4,200

         Interest Income.. 4,200

            700 × ₹100 × 12% × 6/12

20X3

Mar. 31 Accrued Interest Receivable.. 2,100

         Interest Income.. 2,100

            700 × ₹100 × 12/100 × 3/12

Mar. 31 Investments in Debentures 8,400

         Gain on Investments in Debentures... 8,400

            700 × (₹102 – ₹90)

7.13 (a) The bank's yield for loans rated AAA is 6 per cent per annum. The expected credit losses for the loan rated B+ are ₹3,000 per year over the ten-year term of the loan of ₹100,000. This works out to a risk premium of 3 per cent (i.e. 3,000/100,000) for the B+ rating over AAA. Accordingly, the required yield is 9 per cent.

    (b) At initial recognition:

      (i) Loans Receivable..100,000

         Cash 100,000

      (ii) Impairment Loss... 2,752

         Allowance for Credit Losses.. 2,752

           12-moth expected credit losses: ₹2,752: ₹3,000 × 0.9174

    (c) Year 1:

      Impairment Loss... 15,234

         Allowance for Credit Losses.. 15,234

           To recognize lifetime expected credit losses (₹17,986 – ₹2,752)

7.14 At initial recognition:

    (a) Investments in Debentures 87,701

        Cash.. 87,701

          To recognize the debenture at gross amount at fair value:
4,000 × 4.1002 + 100,000 × 0.7130 = 87,701

    (b) Impairment Loss... 2,500

        Other Comprehensive Income.. 2,500

          To recognize 12-moth expected credit losses

      Year 1:

      Value under various scenarios of R_d: 7%, ₹89,839; R_d: 8%, ₹86,748; R_d: 9%, ₹ 83,799.

    (a) Cash 4,000

        Loans Receivable... 2,139*

        Interest Income... 6,139

          To recognize interest income: ₹87,701 × 7% (*₹1 is rounding difference)

    (b) Impairment Loss... 449

        Other Comprehensive Income 5,591

         Loans Receivable... 6,040

          To recognize impairment loss (₹2,949 – ₹2,500) and fair value loss (₹3,091 + ₹2,500)

Operating Investments

LEARNING OBJECTIVES

After studying this chapter, you should be able to:

1. Explain equity investments held as operating investments.
2. Define a subsidiary and explain control.
3. Explain consolidated financial statements.
4. Explain business combination and goodwill.
5. Prepare consolidated financial statements.
6. Define a joint arrangement and explain joint control.
7. Explain accounting for joint arrangements.
8. Define an associate and explain significant influence.
9. Explain the equity method for joint ventures and associates.
10. Account for investments in separate financial statements.

SPEED READ

Operating investments are for business purposes. Subsidiaries, joint arrangements and associates enable businesses to expand their operations. An investor controls subsidiaries, has joint control in joint arrangements and exercises significant influence on associates. The investor's accounting for its investment depends on the nature of the relationship with the investee. Business combinations result from acquisitions and give rise to goodwill. Consolidated financial statements reflect the economic reality of a business group, disregarding the legal form of the entities in the group.

A LIMOUSINE CROWDS INTO A RUNABOUT

In 2008, Tata Motors acquired Jaguar Land Rover (JLR), the iconic British car maker. Announcing the acquisition, Ratan Tata, Chairman, Tata Group, said, "We are very pleased at the prospect of Jaguar and Land Rover being a significant part of our automotive business." Back then, Tata Motors was one of the major automobile companies in India in the passenger and transport segments and JLR was in financial troubles. The acquisition of JLR was part of Tata Motors' ambition to be an international car manufacturer.

Zip to 2016. The standalone statement of profit and loss of Tata Motors reported revenue of ₹445 billion and profit of about ₹2 billion. The consolidated statement of profit and loss of the Tata Motors Group consisting of Tata Motors and its 78 subsidiaries and 19 joint ventures posted revenue of ₹2,765 billion and profit of ₹110 billion. JLR is the main explanation for the difference between the two sets of numbers. Which statement should the analysts be looking at? It is obvious that there is no Tata Motors Group without JLR. Tata Motors, the parent, is rather a pale shadow of its subsidiary, JLR. Though JLR is a separate legal entity, it's part of the Tata Motors Group, the economic entity. Tata Motors received a dividend of ₹10 billion from its subsidiaries including JLR. This hardly captures the importance of JLR to the Tata Motors Group.

In 2016, the story was the reverse of what it was in 2008: the passenger car business of Tata Motors is not doing well but the subsidiary is in rude health. Actually, the subsidiary is helping the parent ride out its troubles. To ignore this reality would be absurd. In perfect irony, Tata Motors is now a significant part of the JLR family.

Equity Investments for Business Purposes

A company (investor) may buy another company (investee) in order to expand its business. This is no different from buying property, plant and equipment, intangible assets or inventories. A company may acquire another company for several reasons:

- Acquiring an existing company with readily available manufacturing facilities, distribution network, experienced employees, and long-standing suppliers and customers, rather than setting up a business from scratch, gives a head start.
- Starting a greenfield venture is considerably more risky, because of problems in land acquisition and getting government approvals, delays in project completion, developing brands, and so on.
- There may be legal and regulatory requirements to set up a separate entity or there may be tax considerations. For instance, banking regulators in many countries require foreign banks to set up local subsidiaries.

Equity investments such as these are *operating investments* and are different from *financial investments* discussed in Chapter 7. Though these investments are in equity instruments and hence are financial assets, they are made for business purposes (e.g. obtaining technology, expanding production, enlarging product markets, sourcing raw materials, and accessing distribution networks), rather than for getting dividend income or benefiting from capital appreciation. Accounting should reflect the investor's investment objective. The appropriate accounting for investments would depend on the investor's *intent*, i.e. whether the investor plans to sell the shares for a profit or intends to hold the shares for an unspecified time. In the latter case, it will gain or lose depending on the investee's long-term performance. A simple way to figure this out is to look at the investment time horizon.

FINANCIAL VIEW
Long-Term Equity Investments

Here are a few recent acquisitions for getting technology, products and customers.

Acquirer	Acquiree	Price
▪ AT&T	▪ Time Warner	▪ $85 billion
▪ Softbank	▪ Arm Holdings	▪ $32 billion
▪ Shire	▪ Baxalta	▪ $32 billion
▪ Microsoft	▪ LinkedIn	▪ $26 billion
▪ Infosys	▪ Panaya	▪ $200 million

The acquirers might have found it difficult to maintain or enhance growth without the acquisitions. For example, the huge risks in developing new drugs and obtaining regulatory approvals are the main reasons for acquisitions in the pharmaceutical industry.

Accounting for equity investments made for business purposes depends on the nature of the investor's interest in an investee. The principle of **substance over form** is the basis of accounting for such investments. Financial statements should reflect the substance and economic reality of transactions and not merely their legal form. Depending on the degree of the investor's say in running the investee's business, we classify the investee as a subsidiary, joint arrangement or associate.

Subsidiaries

Control

A **parent** is an entity that *controls* another entity, called a **subsidiary**. A **group** consists of a parent and all its subsidiaries. A subsidiary may be an incorporated entity such as a company or an unincorporated entity such as a partnership or a trust. An investor controls an investee when it has *rights* to returns from its investment and has the *ability* to influence those returns through its *power* over the investee. Figure 8.1 depicts the three elements of control.

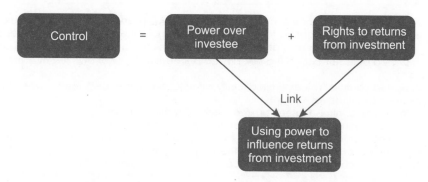

Figure 8.1
ELEMENTS OF CONTROL

Control is the combined effect of power, rights to returns and ability to use the power to influence the returns.

We will now consider the elements of control.

Power   An investor should have the authority to direct the investee's activities. The activities include buying and selling goods and services, financial assets and property, plant and equipment, introducing new products, hiring key employees and determining their remuneration, and raising capital. Power arises from contractual or statutory rights. For example, it may come from owning majority voting rights associated with equity shares or an agreement with a shareholder.

Returns   An investor's returns from its investment should vary as a result of the investee's performance. Dividends are variable returns. Interest from debt securities is also variable returns because the investor is exposed to the bond issuer's credit risk. Although only one investor can control an investee, more than one party can share in the returns of an investee. For example, holders of non-controlling interests can share in the dividends paid by an investee.

Link between Power and Returns   For an investor to have control it should be able to use its power to influence the returns. This will depend on whether the investor is a principal (i.e. it can act on its own) or an agent (i.e. it has to carry out the instructions of another party). For example, suppose a fund manager manages a fund for a fee of 2 per cent of assets but has to act within the strict investment rules set by the investors. The fund manager is an agent and does not control the fund. It could be different if the fund manager receives a fee related to the performance of the fund.

Habib Company owns more than one-half of the voting rights of Hanif Company. In practice, it seldom intervenes in Hanif Company's financial and operating policies. Does Habib Company's ownership constitute control? It does. Habib Company has the *ability to use its power* over Hanif Company's financial and operating policies. The actual exercise of that power doesn't matter. Therefore, Habib Company controls Hanif Company.

HANDHOLD 8.1
Control

Tanvi Company owns 40 per cent of Varun Company's voting rights and has an agreement with Abhay Company, another shareholder, that the latter holding 15 per cent of voting rights will always vote in support of Tanvi Company. Does Tanvi Company control Varun Company?

TEST YOUR UNDERSTANDING 8.1
Control

Manoj Company, Shankar Company, and Vishwesh Company form Anant Company to manufacture electric cars. Their shareholding in Anant Company is as follows: Manoj Company, 45%; Shankar Company, 30%; Vishwesh Company, 25%. They provide capital in proportion to their shareholding and will have representation on the board in proportion to their shareholding. They enter into an agreement specifying that Manoj Company shall provide the manufacturing technology and shall have the power to decide on the number of electric cars to be produced. Anant Company's board of directors must follow Manoj Company's instruction on this matter, but the board will decide on all other matters. Does Manoj Company control Anant Company?

TEST YOUR UNDERSTANDING 8.2
Control

QUICK QUESTION
Control

Vinod Company has guaranteed a significant portion of Raja Company's debts. Given Raja Company's credit rating, it would find it difficult to raise funds without the guarantee. Does Vinod Company control Raja Company?

ONE-MINUTE QUIZ 8.1
Control

Azim Limited owns 40 per cent of the voting rights of Prateek Limited. Of the remaining 60 per cent, Megha Limited owns 11 per cent and the rest is owned by thousands of shareholders spread across the country. Which of the following statements best describes the status of Prateek Limited?

(a) Azim Limited does not control Prateek Limited because it does not own the majority of voting rights.

(b) Azim Limited controls Prateek Limited jointly with Megha Limited because between them they have the majority of voting rights.

(c) Megha Limited controls Prateek Limited jointly with the shareholders other than Azim Limited because between them they have the majority of voting rights.

(d) Azim Limited controls Prateek Limited, though it does not own the majority of voting rights because there is a low likelihood of the remaining shareholders including Megha Limited cooperating to challenge its dominance.

Consolidated Financial Statements

Learning Objective

LO3 Explain consolidated financial statements.

Business enterprises often conduct their activities through several entities under the ultimate control of the group's parent for legal, tax, and other reasons. For example, the parent may be a *shell company* registered in a tax haven, such as St. Kitts, with investments in many subsidiaries. The parent would have no revenues or expenses of its own. In such cases, the parent's financial statements do not present a complete view of its activities.

Consolidated financial statements are the financial statements of a parent and its subsidiaries presented as those of a single economic entity. For example, the financial statements of Mahindra & Mahindra Limited pertain to that company. In contrast, its consolidated financial statements for 2016 cover not only that legal entity but also its 171 group companies, such as Mahindra & Mahindra Financial Services, Mahindra Holidays and Resorts, Tech Mahindra, and Ssangyong Motor Company. Consolidated financial statements are more useful than parent's statements, because they present information about the group as a whole. Note that the parent and its subsidiaries are separate legal entities that have their respective assets, liabilities and share capital and prepare their own financial statements.

The parent applies **consolidation** for its investments in subsidiaries in the consolidated financial statements. The consolidation procedure consists of three important steps:

1. *Combine line items:* Line items such as revenues, expenses, assets, liabilities, and equity of the parent are added with those of the subsidiaries in the group. For this reason, the consolidation method is also known as *line-by-line consolidation*.

2. *Eliminate intragroup items:* Financial statement items that represent transactions or claims within the group, such as the parent's investment in a subsidiary or a loan payable by a subsidiary to the parent, are eliminated in the consolidation.

3. *Identify non-controlling interests:* **Non-controlling interests** representing the share of a subsidiary's profit or loss and equity not attributable to the parent are determined and presented separately.

Recognizing income simply on the basis of dividends or even applying the equity method (discussed later in this chapter) may not be an adequate measure of the income earned by an investor from an enterprise it controls. Consolidated financial statements reflect the substance and economic reality of control over a subsidiary.

HANDHOLD 8.2
Applying the Consolidation Procedure

Rajeev Company controls 75 per cent of Mithun Company's voting shares. On the balance sheet date, the two companies have the following receivable and payable amounts:

	Rajeev Company	Mithun Company
Trade receivables	₹50,000	₹35,000
Trade payables	45,000	20,000

Mithun Company's trade receivables include an amount of ₹10,000 payable by Rajeev Company. Rajeev Company's trade payables include that amount. The consolidated financial statements will be prepared as follows:

	Rajeev Company	Mithun Company	Total	Eliminations	Consolidated Balance Sheet
Trade receivables............	₹50,000	₹35,000	₹85,000	₹−10,000	₹75,000
Trade payables................	45,000	20,000	65,000	−10,000	55,000

Ujjwal Company holds 70 per cent of Diya Company's voting shares and 55 per cent of Deep Company's voting shares. On the balance sheet date, the three have the following investments in bonds and bonds payable amounts:

TEST YOUR UNDERSTANDING 8.3
Applying the Consolidation Procedure

	Ujjwal Company	Diya Company	Deep Company
Investments in bonds........	₹100,000	₹25,000	₹ 5,000
Bonds payable..................	95,000	40,000	10,000

Ujjwal Company holds ₹10,000 of Diya Company's bonds and ₹2,000 of Deep Company's bonds. Diya Company holds ₹6,000 of Deep Company's bonds. Deep Company holds ₹1,000 of Ujjwal Company's bonds. How will the investments in bonds and bonds payable appear in the consolidated financial statements.

Using the information in the consolidated financial statements, we can understand better the performance of a group. If major subsidiaries incur losses, they will damage the group's performance. Those losses won't show up in the parent's financial statements. Consider these examples.

FINANCIAL VIEW
Are Consolidated Financial Statements Informative?

- Tata Motors Limited reported a profit of ₹2.34 billion for FY16. Its consolidated financial statements reported a profit of ₹11.02 billion. The boost to the group's performance came from the company's Jaguar Land Rover operations.

- Reliance Industries Limited posted an 18 per cent *increase* in profit at ₹77.04 billion for Q2FY16, compared to ₹65.34 billion in Q2FY15. The consolidated net profit for the quarter was ₹78.33 billion, a 24 per cent *drop* from ₹103.14 billion in the year-ago quarter.

Reporting for the economic entity is more meaningful because it tells the parent's shareholders a lot more. Consolidated financial statements provide information on the effect of investment decisions, whether the investments are made within the company or by the acquisition of other companies. Imagine what the investors of Tata Motors and Reliance Industries would have thought, if they did not have the consolidated numbers.

Source: Company annual reports.

Business Combination

A **business combination** is a transaction in which an entity (acquirer) obtains control over a business (acquiree). Several structures are possible for a business combination. The choice of a structure depends on the acquirer's business, legal, tax, and other objectives. Here are some possibilities:

Learning Objective
LO 4 Explain business combination and goodwill.

- *Parent and subsidiary continue as legal entities:* A parent-subsidiary relationship is a common form of business combination. The acquirer-parent and the acquiree-subsidiary continue to be separate legal entities. In this case, we consolidate the parent's and the subsidiary's financial statements.

- *Acquiree merges with the acquirer:* The acquiree's business legally merges into the acquirer's business and the acquiree ceases to exist as a legal entity. In this case, the acquiree's assets and liabilities come on the acquirer's financial statements.

- *Acquirer and acquiree merge with a new entity:* The combining entities transfer their net assets to a newly formed entity and cease to be legal entities.

A business combination requires a *business,* usually understood to mean applying processes to inputs to produce outputs (e.g. making steel by melting and purifying iron ore and manganese and adding carbon). The mere acquisition of an asset or a group of assets (e.g. acquiring a steel melting shop) does not constitute a business combination. The key element in a business combination is an *acquisition.* It means that one of the parties to a business combination can always be identified as the acquirer. Recall the idea of control from the earlier discussion on parent and subsidiary. Often, the parties engaged in a business combination describe the transaction as a "true merger" or "merger of equals", implying that there is no acquisition by either of them. Such talk may be intended to help the parties assure their shareholders that they continue to have control over the future of their companies, but it has no significance for accounting purposes. In accounting, every business combination is an acquisition and one party is the acquirer and the other, the acquired. There are no two ways about it.

Goodwill

The consideration for an acquisition may be a cash payment, an issue of shares or a mix of cash and shares. The consideration covers the value to the acquirer of the acquiree's *identified* assets less liabilities. Usually, it includes a premium, called goodwill, representing the future economic benefits from assets that are *not individually identified and separately recognized*. Suppose a business has highly satisfied customers, talented staff, and a good location. The acquirer has to pay not only for the acquiree's net assets, i.e. tangible assets and identifiable intangible assets less liabilities but also for the future benefits from superior customer relations, reliable suppliers, employee talent, and advantageous location. That extra is the goodwill component of the purchase price.

Irrespective of whether there is any indication, goodwill acquired in a business combination should be tested annually for impairment. For the purpose of testing, it should be allocated to each of the acquirer's *cash-generating units* (explained in Chapter 6) that are expected to benefit from the combination. *Unlike other intangible assets, goodwill is not amortized.*

Acquisition Method

A business combination must be accounted for by applying the acquisition method, also known as the purchase method, as of the acquisition date. The elements of this method are as follows:

1. The acquirer recognizes the identifiable assets acquired, the liabilities assumed, and any non-controlling interest in the acquiree.
2. The acquirer measures each identifiable asset acquired and liability assumed at its acquisition-date *fair value*.
3. The acquirer recognizes goodwill, measured as the *excess* of (a) over (b) below:
   (a) the sum of:
       (i) the fair value of the consideration;
       (ii) the amount of any non-controlling interest in the acquiree (this will be zero if it is a 100 per cent acquisition); and
       (iii) the fair value of the acquirer's previously held equity interest, if any (this will be zero if the acquirer gains control in a single investment, rather than investing in installments);
   (b) the net identifiable assets acquired.

There are two acceptable methods for measuring non-controlling interest in the acquiree. Both methods are based on fair value. The *full goodwill method* views the group as an economic entity and does not distinguish between the controlling and non-controlling interests. So it records the entire goodwill. The *partial goodwill method* views the group from the controlling shareholder's viewpoint and does not consider goodwill relating to the non-controlling interest. Neither method attributes control premium to the non-controlling interest.

HANDHOLD 8.3
Non-controlling Interest and Goodwill

Vikas Company pays cash for 90 per cent (900 shares) of Chandra Company's voting shares at ₹110 per share. On December 31, the acquisition date, Chandra Company's shares trade at ₹100 per share. On that date, the fair value of Chandra Company's net assets is ₹89,000. The consideration of ₹99,000 consists of three components:

(a) Acquirer's share of fair value of identifiable net assets: 90% of ₹89,000   ₹80,100
(b) Acquirer's share of 'normal' premium: ₹90,000 (i.e. 900 × ₹100) – ₹80,100   9,900
(c) Control premium: 900 × (₹110 – ₹100)   9,000

    99,000

Full goodwill method: Vikas Company will recognize the acquired business at ₹109,000, calculated as follows:

Fair value of the consideration... ₹99,000
Fair value of non-controlling interest: 100 × ₹100.............................. 10,000

109,000

The amount of ₹109,000 is that referred to in point 3 (a) in the discussion on the acquisition method. The fair value of the acquiree's net assets is ₹89,000. This is the amount referred to in point 3(b). The goodwill is ₹20,000, being the excess of the first amount over the second. On acquisition, Vikas Company records the following entry:

Dec. 31	Net Assets	89,000	
	Goodwill	20,000	
	Non-controlling Interest		10,000
	Cash		99,000

The goodwill of ₹20,000 consists of two components:

1. Acquirer's (or controlling) interest of ₹18,900, calculated as follows: Fair value of the consideration, ₹99,000 – Acquirer's share in the fair value of net assets, ₹80,100, i.e. 90% of ₹89,000.
2. Non-controlling interest of ₹1,100, calculated as follows: Fair value of non-controlling interest, ₹10,000 – Non-controlling interest's share in the fair value of net assets, ₹8,900, i.e. 10% of ₹89,000.

Since the acquirer's shareholding is nine times that of the non-controlling interest's, its share of the goodwill should have been ₹9,900, the "normal" premium. However, the acquirer paid, in addition, a "control" premium of ₹9,000, i.e. 900 × (₹110 – ₹100). So its share of goodwill is ₹18,900.

Partial goodwill method: In this method, Vikas Company will recognize the acquired business at ₹107,900, calculated as follows: Fair value of the consideration, ₹99,000 + Non-controlling interest's share of the fair value of net assets, ₹8,900, i.e. 10% of ₹89,000. The amount of ₹107,900 is that referred to in point 3 (a) in the discussion on the acquisition method. The fair value of the acquiree's net assets is ₹89,000. This is the amount referred to in point 3 (b). The goodwill is ₹18,900, being the excess of the first amount over the second. On acquisition, Vikas Company records the following entry:

Dec. 31	Net Assets	89,000	
	Goodwill	18,900	
	Non-controlling Interest		8,900
	Cash		99,000

The goodwill consists only of the acquirer's interest of ₹18,900. The non-controlling interest's share is not considered. Under both methods, non-controlling interest does not include any control premium because, by definition, non-controlling shareholders do not have control and they will not pay any control premium.

Wouldn't life be much simpler if control is defined in terms of majority share ownership?

DISCUSSION QUESTION 1.2

··

··

··

Consolidated Financial Statements and Business Combination Illustrated

On January 1, 20XX, Libra Company acquired for cash 75 per cent of the outstanding shares of Virgo Company at ₹32 per share. On that date, Virgo Company's share price was ₹30. Exhibit 8.1 presents the balance sheets of Libra Company and Virgo Company *just before* the acquisition.

Learning Objective

LO 5 **Prepare consolidated financial statements.**

EXHIBIT 8.1

Libra Company and
Virgo Company
Balance Sheet,
January 1, 20XX

Just Before Acquisition		
	Libra	**Virgo**
Assets		
Non-current assets		
Property, plant and equipment: Cost	₹160,000	₹70,000
Deduct Accumulated depreciation	95,000	25,000
Net	65,000	45,000
Current assets		
Inventories	18,000	7,000
Trade receivables	23,000	9,000
Cash	52,000	1,000
	158,000	62,000
Equity and Liabilities		
Equity		
Equity share capital	₹ 50,000	₹ 20,000
Other equity: Retained earnings	63,000	24,000
Liabilities		
Non-current liabilities		
Bonds payable	32,000	16,000
Current liabilities		
Trade payables	13,000	2,000
	158,000	62,000

The consideration for the acquisition is ₹48,000, i.e. 1,500 shares × ₹32 per share. Libra Company records the acquisition as follows:

Investment in Shares of Virgo Company 48,000
    Cash   48,000
         Acquired 75% in Virgo Company

We take that Libra Company obtains control of Virgo Company by means of owning more than half of the latter's voting rights. So Libra Company is the acquirer and Virgo Company is the acquiree. The acquisition date is January 1, 20XX, the date on which control is obtained.

Exhibit 8.2 presents the financial statements of the two companies *just after* the acquisition.

EXHIBIT 8.2

Libra Company and
Virgo Company
Balance Sheet,
January 1, 20XX

Just After Acquisition		
	Libra	**Virgo**
Assets		
Non-current assets		
Property, plant and equipment: Cost	₹160,000	₹70,000
Deduct Accumulated depreciation	95,000	25,000
Net	65,000	45,000
Investment in Virgo Company	48,000	—
Current assets		
Inventories	18,000	7,000
Trade receivables	23,000	9,000
Cash	4,000	1,000
	158,000	62,000
Equity and Liabilities		
Equity		
Equity share capital	₹ 50,000	₹ 20,000
Other equity: Retained earnings	63,000	24,000
Liabilities		
Non-current liabilities		
Bonds payable	32,000	16,000
Current liabilities		
Trade payables	13,000	2,000
	158,000	62,000

The appraisal report on Virgo Company as of the acquisition date indicated the following:

- Property, plant and equipment were worth 20 per cent higher.
- A patent worth ₹3,000 came to light.
- Inventories included obsolete items costing ₹1,000.
- Trade receivables included irrecoverable amounts of ₹2,000.
- A trade payable of ₹1,000 had been omitted.
- The fair values of the remaining assets and liabilities were equal to their carrying amounts.

Exhibit 8.3 presents the effect of the fair value adjustments in Virgo Company's balance sheet.

Acquisition Date Fair Value Adjustments			
	Carrying Amount	Fair Value Adjustment	Fair Value
Assets			
Property, plant and equipment: Cost	₹70,000	+₹14,000	₹84,000
Deduct Accumulated depreciation	25,000	+ 5,000	30,000
Net	45,000	+ 9,000	54,000
Patents	0	+ 3,000	3,000
Inventories	7,000	− 1,000	6,000
Trade receivables	9,000	− 2,000	7,000
Cash	1,000	0	1,000
	62,000	+ 9,000	71,000
Deduct			
Liabilities			
Bonds payable	16,000	0	16,000
Trade payables	2,000	+ 1,000	3,000
	18,000	+ 1,000	19,000
Identifiable net assets	44,000	+ 8,000	52,000

EXHIBIT 8.3
Virgo Company Balance Sheet, January 1, 20XX

Note the following in the fair value adjustments:

1. Both property, plant and equipment and accumulated depreciation increase by 20 per cent.
2. The patent is an identifiable asset with a fair value. So we include it in the fair value calculation, though the acquiree did not recognize it.

Libra Company pays ₹32 per share when the market price is ₹30 per share, implying a *control premium* of ₹3,000 on the 1,500 shares acquired. The consideration of ₹48,000 consists of three components:

(a)	Acquirer's share of fair value of identifiable net assets: 75% of ₹52,000	₹39,000
(b)	'Normal' goodwill: 1,500 × ₹30 – ₹39,000	6,000
(c)	Control premium: 1,500 × (₹32 – ₹30)	3,000
		48,000

The acquirer pays a goodwill of ₹9,000, the sum of 'normal' goodwill and control premium. The non-controlling interest's share of goodwill is ₹2,000, calculated as follows: fair value of non-controlling interest, ₹15,000 (i.e. 500 shares × ₹30 per share) – non-controlling interest's share of fair value of identifiable net assets, ₹13,000 (i.e. 25% of ₹52,000).

Under the full goodwill method, we consider goodwill paid by the acquirer and non-controlling interest's share of goodwill. Libra Company will record net assets of ₹52,000, *goodwill of ₹11,000* (= acquirer's goodwill, ₹9,000 + non-controlling interest's share, ₹2,000), non-controlling interest of ₹15,000, and consideration of ₹48,000. Exhibit 8.4 presents the worksheet on January 1, 20XX that Libra Company will prepare to consolidate the balance sheets of the two companies applying the fair value.

Under the partial goodwill method, we consider goodwill paid by the acquirer, but ignore non-controlling interest's share of goodwill. In other words, we recognize non-controlling interest's proportionate share of the acquiree's identifiable net assets. Applying this method, Libra Company will record net assets of ₹52,000, *goodwill of ₹9,000*, the non-controlling interest of ₹13,000, and consideration of ₹48,000. Exhibit 8.5 presents the worksheet according to this method.

EXHIBIT 8.4

Libra Company and Virgo Company Consolidation Worksheet, January 1, 20XX

Full Goodwill						
			Adjustments and Eliminations		Non-controlling Interest	Consolidated Balance Sheet
	Libra Company	Virgo Company	Debit	Credit		
Property, plant and equipment.....	160,000	70,000	14,000			244,000
Accumulated depreciation.............	(95,000)	(25,000)		5,000		(125,000)
Investment in Virgo Company......	48,000			48,000		
Patents		0	3,000			3,000
Inventories.................................	18,000	7,000		1,000		24,000
Trade receivables	23,000	9,000		2,000		30,000
Cash..	4,000	1,000				5,000
Goodwill.....................................			11,000			11,000
	158,000	62,000				192,000
Trade payables	13,000	2,000		1,000		16,000
Bonds payable	32,000	16,000				48,000
Share capital..............................	50,000	20,000	15,000		5,000	50,000
Retained earnings.......................	63,000	24,000	18,000		6,000	63,000
Share of fair value adjustment.....				2,000	2,000	
Share of goodwill........................				2,000	2,000	
			61,000	61,000		
Non-controlling interest................					15,000	15,000
	158,000	62,000				192,000

EXHIBIT 8.5

Libra Company and Virgo Company Consolidation Worksheet January 1, 20XX

Partial Goodwill						
			Adjustments and Eliminations		Non-controlling Interest	Consolidated Balance Sheet
	Libra Company	Virgo Company	Debit	Credit		
Property, plant and equipment.....	160,000	70,000	14,000			244,000
Accumulated depreciation.............	(95,000)	(25,000)		5,000		(125,000)
Investment in Virgo Company......	48,000			48,000		
Patents		0	3,000			3,000
Inventories.................................	18,000	7,000		1,000		24,000
Trade receivables	23,000	9,000		2,000		30,000
Cash..	4,000	1,000				5,000
Goodwill.....................................			9,000			9,000
	158,000	62,000				190,000
Trade payables	13,000	2,000		1,000		16,000
Bonds payable	32,000	16,000				48,000
Share capital..............................	50,000	20,000	15,000		5,000	50,000
Retained earnings.......................	63,000	24,000	18,000		6,000	63,000
Share of fair value adjustment.....				2,000	2,000	
			59,000	59,000		
Non-controlling interest................					13,000	13,000
	158,000	62,000				190,000

Exhibit 8.6 presents the consolidated balance sheet of Libra Company and Virgo Company after the business combination on January 1, 20XX according to the two methods. The difference between the two methods is in the treatment of goodwill. The full goodwill method allocates goodwill to both controlling and non-controlling interests. The partial goodwill method allocates goodwill only to controlling interest; non-controlling interest is calculated based on its share of the fair value of net identifiable assets, i.e. excluding goodwill. There is a consequent difference in the amount of non-controlling interest.

EXHIBIT 8.6
Libra Company and Virgo Company Balance Sheet, January 1, 20XX On Combination

Libra Company and Virgo Company Consolidated Balance Sheet, January 1, 20XX Immediately after Combination	Full Goodwill	Partial Goodwill
Assets		
Non-current assets		
Property, plant and equipment: Cost	₹244,000	₹244,000
Deduct Accumulated depreciation	125,000	125,000
Net	119,000	119,000
Goodwill	11,000	9,000
Patents	3,000	3,000
Current assets		
Inventories	24,000	24,000
Trade receivables	30,000	30,000
Cash	5,000	5,000
	192,000	190,000
Equity and Liabilities		
Equity		
Equity share capital	₹ 50,000	₹ 50,000
Other equity: Retained earnings	63,000	63,000
Owners of parent	113,000	113,000
Non-controlling interest	15,000	13,000
Liabilities		
Non-current liabilities		
Bonds payable	48,000	48,000
Current liabilities		
Trade payables	16,000	1 6,000
	192,000	190,000

FINANCIAL VIEW
Lost Goodwill

Goodwill is not amortized but tested for impairment at the reporting date. So any drop in the value of goodwill resulting from impairment is often large. Take the case of Vedanta Limited (formerly Sesa Sterlite), a natural resources company. Vedanta acquired Cairn India in 2011, when oil and gas prices were very high. Prices softened later and the value of Cairn India dropped. The company announced a goodwill impairment charge of ₹191.8 billion for the loss of value of Cairn India. Overpayment for goodwill is fairly common in many acquisitions. Tata Steel is another recent example of a large goodwill write-down. In 2013 and 2015, it took a goodwill write-down of ₹153 billion for its overseas acquisitions, mainly Corus in the UK.

Consolidation Requirements

Scope and exemptions A parent should present consolidated financial statements. The following are exempted:

1. An unlisted subsidiary that meets certain conditions.
2. An employment benefit plan.
3. An investment entity that is required to measure all of its subsidiaries at fair value through profit or loss.

Reporting dates Ideally, the parent and its subsidiaries should have the same reporting date. In any case, the difference between the reporting dates should not be more than three months.

HANDHOLD 8.4
Reporting Dates

Pi Company is the parent of Sigma Company. Consider the following cases.

Case A: Pi has prepared financial statements for the year ended March 31, 20X2. Sigma has prepared financial statements for the year ended December 31, 20X1. The difference is three months. The companies should proceed as follows:

1. Ideally, Sigma should change its reporting period to March 31, 20X2. This will be a one-time change. Thereafter, both companies will report for the year ended March 31.
2. Alternatively, Sigma should prepare additional financial statements for consolidation purposes as of March 31, 20X2.
3. Suppose it is impracticable to prepare additional financial statements for consolidation purposes as of March 31, 20X2. Pi should prepare consolidated financial statements for the year ended March 31, 20X2 using Sigma's financial statements for the year ended December 31, 20X1 adjusted for the effects of significant transactions or events that occurred during the period January 1, 20X2 to March 31, 20X2.

Case B: Pi's reporting date is March 31 and Sigma's reporting date is September 30. The difference is more than three months. Sigma should change its reporting date to March 31.

Accounting policies If a subsidiary uses accounting policies different from those adopted in the consolidated financial statements, appropriate adjustments should be made to its financial statements for consolidation purposes.

HANDHOLD 8.5
Accounting Policies

Pi Company is the parent of Sigma Company. Pi follows the straight-line method of depreciation for a certain class of assets, while Sigma follows the written-down-value method for the same class of assets. Appropriate adjustments should be made to Sigma's financial statements, so that the depreciation for that class of assets is based on the straight-line method.

Non-controlling interests Non-controlling interests are presented in the consolidated balance sheet within equity, separately from the equity of the parent's shareholders.

Intragroup balances and transactions In the consolidated financial statements, the parent's investment in a subsidiary and the subsidiary's equity are eliminated. Intragroup balances shall be eliminated fully. While the reason for this is obvious in the case a wholly-owned subsidiary, it may not be intuitive in a partially-owned subsidiary. Remember that consolidated financial statements seek to present the group as an economic entity. Transactions and balances within the group have no place in them.

HANDHOLD 8.6
Eliminations

Pi Company is the parent of Sigma Company owning 70 per cent of the latter's voting rights. Consider the following cases.

Case A: Pi holds an investment of ₹10,000 out of Sigma's bonds payable of ₹100,000. In its consolidated balance sheet, Pi will eliminate *both* (a) its investment of ₹10,000 in the bonds appearing as an asset in its balance sheet and (b) an amount of ₹10,000 from the bonds payable appearing in Sigma's balance sheet. Thus, the consolidated balance sheet will show a liability of ₹90,000 for bonds payable by the group to outsiders.

Case B: Pi sold inventory costing ₹10,000 to Sigma at ₹12,000 and the inventory is with Sigma at the year end. In its consolidated financial statements, Pi will eliminate the revenue of ₹12,000, the cost of goods sold of ₹10,000, and the unrealized profit (unrealized from the group's standpoint) of ₹2,000. The inventory will appear at ₹10,000 after deducting the unrealized gain.

ONE-MINUTE QUIZ 8.2
Business Combination

Which of the following intangibles should not be recognized as an asset in a business combination? There may be more than one correct answer.

(a) Copyrights.
(b) In-process R&D.
(c) Employee loyalty.
(d) Customer contracts.

Building a business successfully from scratch requires hard work, skill and luck. Firms unable to grow are more likely to acquire other firms. It is often difficult to separate the effect of the acquisition on reported performance. So after an acquisition, the acquirer could appear to have done better but it is impossible to tell if this is the true position. Further, most acquisitions are overvalued and involve substantial goodwill. Since goodwill is not amortized but only tested for impairment, there are questions about its worth. Nearly in every acquisition, huge goodwill write-downs happen soon. Finally, when an acquisition fails and the acquired entity is sold, there is often a substantial loss. One-time charges and losses create earnings quality problems.

EARNINGS QUALITY ANALYSIS
Do Acquisitions Affect Earnings Quality?

Joint Arrangements

Learning Objective
LO 6 Define a joint arrangement and explain joint control.

A **joint arrangement** is a contractual arrangement in which the parties have joint control. *Contractual arrangement* and *joint control* are essential for a joint arrangement. A contractual arrangement is usually evidenced by a document. The contractual arrangement sets out the purpose of the joint arrangement, appointment of the board of directors, voting rights of the parties, capital contributions required, and sharing of assets, liabilities, revenues, expenses or profit or loss. The existence of a contractual arrangement distinguishes a joint venture from an associate, i.e. an entity in which an investor has significant influence. Simply stated, "no contractual arrangement, no joint venture".

Joint control is the contractually agreed sharing of control of an arrangement. No party can have its way disregarding the views of the others because no single party controls the arrangement on its own. A party who has joint control can prevent other parties from controlling the arrangement. Joint arrangements may be set up to enable the parties to share costs and risks, provide them access to new technology or new markets, or comply with local laws and regulatory requirements. Some arrangements require a *separate vehicle*, a separate legal entity with its own equity and debt capital, while others don't.

Aman and Shant each hold 50 per cent of the voting rights of Pax. They have always voted together on Pax's operating and financial matters. Is Pax a joint arrangement? On the face of it, Pax may appear to be a joint arrangement. However, we need to ask whether there is a binding agreement between Aman and Shant for unanimous decision-making on operating and financial matters. If there is no such agreement, Pax is not a joint arrangement even though the two always voted together in the past. Their voting in unison *every time* is not a substitute for a contractual arrangement. *Question:* Can they vote differently in future? *Answer:* Nothing prevents them from doing so, since there is no contractual requirement of unanimity.

HANDHOLD 8.7
Joint Arrangement

Vijay Company, Vikram Company, and Vir Company form Dare Company with the following ownership distribution: Vijay Company, 38 per cent; Vikram Company, 13 per cent; Vir Company, 49 per cent. Vijay Company and Vikram Company contract that they shall vote together on Dare Company's financial and operating matters. Dare Company is an entity formed under the Companies Act, so its decisions require a simple majority. Is Dare Company a joint arrangement?

TEST YOUR UNDERSTANDING 8.4
Joint Arrangement

A joint arrangement is either a joint operation or a joint venture depending on the rights and obligations of the parties to the arrangement. In a joint operation, the joint operators have rights to the assets, and obligations for the liabilities, relating to the arrangement. In a joint venture, the joint venturers have rights to the net assets of the arrangement. The classification of joint arrangements depends on the parties' contractual rights and obligations. Figure 8.2 presents an illustrative classification of joint arrangements.

Joint Operation

A joint operation is not set up as a separate vehicle. Typically, each party pays its own expenses and takes a share of the revenue from the operations. For the parties, it is business as usual. For example, suppose some automobile manufacturers form a joint arrangement. One makes engines, another makes transmission, yet another makes chassis, and so on. One of them assembles the parts and sells the car. The party who makes engines uses its own manufacturing facilities, pays its own production costs, and gets a share of the revenue from the sale of the car that represents the agreed value of the engine. It does not pay any of the costs of the other manufacturers.

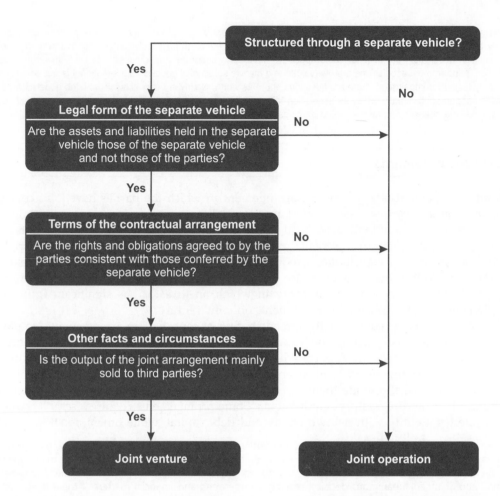

Figure 8.2

CLASSIFICATION OF A JOINT ARRANGEMENT

The classification of a joint arrangement depends on the parties' rights and obligations.

In other cases, the parties to a joint arrangement might agree, for example, to share and operate an asset together. A joint asset may be an asset contributed by a party or acquired for the purpose of the venture. The asset may belong to one of the parties or there may be joint ownership of the asset. The parties agree to take a share of the output from the asset and each bears an agreed share of the expenses incurred. There is no separate entity that owns the asset. Joint assets are common in the oil and gas industry, e.g. oil and gas pipelines. Each party uses the pipeline to transport its own products and bears an agreed share of the operating expenses.

Joint Venture

A joint venture requires a separate vehicle. However, the mere existence of a separate vehicle is not enough to make it a joint venture. The substance of the arrangement determines whether it is a joint operation or a joint venture. If the arrangement gives the parties rights to the assets, and obligations for the liabilities, it is a joint operation. If it gives them rights to the net assets of the arrangement, it is a joint venture. In other words, if the parties are concerned with using assets and paying liabilities, they are joint operators. If they are concerned with benefiting from the arrangement as a whole, they are joint venturers.

Accounting for Joint Arrangements

Learning Objective

LO 7   Explain accounting for joint arrangements.

A joint operator should recognize in relation to its interest in a joint operation its assets, liabilities, revenue and expenses. For example, a joint operator in an oil refinery recognizes the following in its financial statements:

1. Share of the refinery's cost;
2. Share of the refinery's trade payables;
3. Revenue from the sale of its share of the output from the refinery's sales of oil;
4. Share of the revenue of the refinery's output; and
5. Share of the refinery's operating and maintenance expenses.

A joint venturer or a participant to a joint arrangement that has significant influence should account for its interest in a joint venture using the equity method. If it has neither joint control nor significant influence, it should account for its interest as a financial asset.

Associates

An **associate** is an enterprise over which an investor has **significant influence**: the power to *participate* in an entity's financial and operating policy decisions but without control or joint control of those policies. An associate may be an incorporated entity such as a company, or may be an unincorporated entity such as a partnership. If an entity holds 20 per cent or more of an investee's voting rights, there is a rebuttable presumption that it has significant influence. If an entity holds less than 20 per cent of an investee's voting rights, there is a rebuttable presumption that it does not have significant influence. Thus, the 20 per cent of voting rights test is a fuzzy line, not a bright line.

An investor can have significant influence even when another investor has majority ownership in the investee. For determining whether an investor has significant influence, we should consider the investor's direct and indirect ownership. Evidence of significant influence would include the investor's representation in the investee's board and purchases and sales between the investor and the investee.

Learning Objective

LO 8 Define an associate and explain significant influence.

Vinay Limited owns 25 per cent of the voting rights of Karuna Limited. Callous Limited holds the rest. It had two directors out of 12 in Karuna's board of directors. Until last year, it accounted for the investment using the equity method. At a recent meeting of the shareholders of Karuna, Vinay's two directors were removed without any reason and it was unlikely to get board representation in the near future. How should Vinay account for the investment in Karuna?

(a) As a financial asset.
(b) As investment held for sale.
(c) As investment in associate.
(d) Write down the investment to a nil value.

ONE-MINUTE QUIZ 8.3
Significant Influence

The Equity Method: One-line Consolidation

An entity with joint control of, or significant influence over, an investee shall account for its investment in an associate or a joint venture using the **equity method**. For convenience, we will use associate. In this method, the investor recognizes the investment at cost at the time of acquisition and adjusts it for subsequent changes in the investor's share of the associate's net assets. When the investee earns a profit, its net assets increase; when it incurs a loss, its net assets decrease. Reflecting these changes, the carrying amount of the investment increases by the amount of the investor's share of the associate's profit and decreases by the amount of its share of the associate's loss. Concurrently, the investor recognizes in its statement of profit and loss its share of the associate's profit or loss. Dividends received from the associate reduce the carrying amount of the investment. Recognizing a dividend income would result in double counting because the investor would have already recorded as income its share of the associate's profit or loss.

Accountants think that recognizing income simply on the basis of dividends may not be an adequate measure of the income earned by an investor on an investment in an associate, because the dividends received may bear little relation to the associate's performance. The investor has an interest in the associate's performance that goes beyond passively receiving

Learning Objective

LO 9 Explain the equity method for joint ventures and associates.

dividends. The associate's performance as measured by its earnings is a better indicator of its performance and the investor's share of those earnings provides a superior measure of the return on the investment in the associate. Thus, the equity method reflects the economic substance of the investment, rather than its mere legal form of receiving dividends. The equity method is also known as *one-line consolidation* because it shows the investor's interest in the associate in a single line rather than in the manner of line-by-line consolidation followed for subsidiaries.

HANDHOLD 8.8
Equity Method

On September 30, 20X1, Suresh Company acquired 25 per cent of the equity share capital of Raj Company for ₹25,000. On that date, Raj Company had the following balance sheet: share capital, ₹40,000; retained earnings, ₹60,000; property, plant and equipment (net), ₹100,000. On December 11, 20X1, Raj Company paid its shareholders an equity dividend of ₹4,000. It records the transactions as follows:

```
20X1
Sep.  30   Investments in Associates...........................................  25,000
                  Cash.................................................................                25,000
                        Invested in Raj Company's shares
Dec.  11   Cash ....................................................................   1,000
                  Investments in Associates ................................                 1,000
                        Received dividend from Raj Company: 25% of ₹4,000
```

Suresh Company paid ₹25,000 for 25 per cent of Raj equity of ₹100,000, consisting of share capital, ₹40,000 and retained earnings, ₹60,000. Its carrying amount of the investment on December 31, 20X1, its reporting date, is ₹24,000, calculated as follows:

Share in book value of Raj Company's net assets....................	₹25,000
Deduct Dividend received from Raj Company..........................	1,000
Carrying amount, December 31, 20X1....................................	24,000

The dividend reduces the carrying amount of the investment; it is not an income.

On September 30, 20X2, Raj Company reported a net profit of ₹10,000 for the year ended that date. Suresh Company records the following entry:

```
20X2
Sep.  30   Investments in Associates...........................................  2,500
                  Share of Earnings in Associates ........................                 2,500
                        Share in Raj Company's earnings: 25% of ₹10,000
```

The carrying amount of the investment on December 31, 20X2 is ₹26,500, calculated as follows:

Carrying amount, December 31, 20X1...	₹24,000
Add Share of Raj Company's earnings......................................	2,500
Carrying amount, December 31, 20X2...	26,500

Suresh Company takes its share of earnings in associates of ₹2,500 as an income to its consolidated statement of profit and loss for the year ended December 31, 20X2.

The investor ascertains the fair value of the associate's assets and liabilities at the time of acquisition. Note that the investor also considers assets and liabilities not recognized by the associate. The excess of the cost of acquisition over the investor's share of the fair value is goodwill. To illustrate, suppose Ajay Company acquires a 30 per cent interest in Deepak Company for ₹200,000. At that date, the carrying amount of Deepak's net assets was ₹500,000. The fair value of Deepak's net assets was equal to their carrying amount except for a piece of land that had a book value of ₹40,000 and a fair value of ₹50,000. Ajay calculates a goodwill of ₹47,000, as follows:

Cost of the investment..		₹200,000
Carrying amount of net assets..	₹500,000	
Add Difference between fair value and book value of land ...	10,000	
Fair value of net assets	510,000	
Ajay's share of fair value: 30% of ₹510,000................................		153,000
Goodwill...		47,000

Ajay records the acquisition as follows:

Investments in Associates...	200,000	
Cash..		200,000

Acquired 30% in Deepak Company at ₹200,000 for the following:

Share in book value of net assets: 30% of ₹500,000..................	₹150,000
Share in fair value of adjustment for land: 30% of ₹10,000....	3,000
Goodwill: ₹200,000 – ₹150,000 – ₹3,000.....................................	47,000
Cost of the investment..	200,000

TEST YOUR UNDERSTANDING 8.5
Equity Method

On December 31, 20X1, Jyoti Company acquired 20 per cent of the equity share capital of Pradeep Company for ₹40,000. On that date, Pradeep Company had the following balance sheet: share capital, ₹25,000; retained earnings, ₹120,000; property, plant and equipment, ₹145,000. The property, plant and equipment had a remaining estimated useful life of four years and a fair value of ₹170,000. On February 18, 20X2, Pradeep Company paid its shareholders an equity dividend of ₹6,000. On December 31, 20X2, the company reported a net profit of ₹15,000 for the year ended that date. How would Jyoti Company record these transactions? Calculate the carrying amount of the investment in Jyoti Company's balance sheet on March 31, 20X2 and 20X3.

The fair value adjustment in the above illustration relates to land, a non-depreciable asset. So the investor does not depreciate the amount of ₹3,000. Fair value adjustment relating to a depreciable asset should be charged over the asset's remaining useful life. For example, suppose the fair value adjustment related to equipment with a remaining useful life of 10 years. Ajay should recognize a yearly charge of ₹300 for 10 years in its consolidated statement of profit and loss and reduce the carrying amount of the investment. Furthermore, the investor should adjust the carrying amount for his share of any changes in the associate's other comprehensive income arising from the revaluation of property, plant and equipment, foreign exchange translation differences and marking to market securities held under the hold to collect and sell model.

Note that the investor includes goodwill in the carrying amount of the investment and does not record it separately. For this reason, goodwill is not tested for impairment in the equity method, unlike goodwill acquired in a business combination. Instead, the entire carrying amount of the investment is tested for impairment as a single asset.

Equity Method Requirements

Scope and exemptions An entity should use the equity method to account for its investment in an associate or a joint venture. The following are exempted:

1. An entity that is a parent if it is exempt from preparing consolidated financial statements or if it is a wholly-owned subsidiary that meets certain conditions.
2. An investment in an associate held by an investment entity, if the entity elects to measure the investment at fair value through profit or loss.
3. An investment that is classified as held for sale.

Reporting dates The difference between the reporting dates should not exceed three months.

Accounting policies If an associate or a joint venture uses accounting policies different from those of the entity, appropriate adjustments should be made.

Figure 8.3 presents the classification and accounting for subsidiaries, joint arrangements and associates.

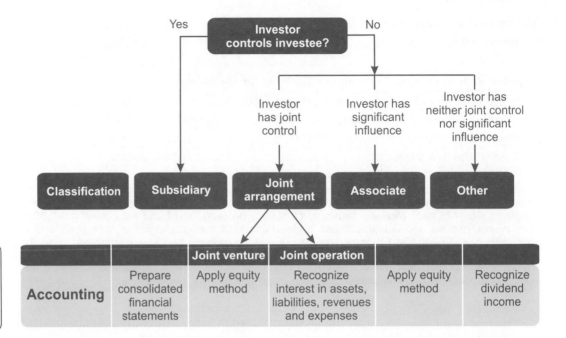

Figure 8.3

OPERATING INVESTMENTS: CLASSIFICATION AND ACCOUNTING

Operating investments are classified and accounted for depending on the investor's influence over the investee.

REAL WORLD
Tata Group

Family-owned and family-controlled companies in India and in many Asian countries have complex crossholdings and common directors. Consider the Tata Group, India's largest conglomerate. Tata Sons Limited is the promoter of the major operating Tata companies and has significant shareholdings in these companies. Tata Sons is also the owner of the Tata name and several Tata trademarks, which are registered in India and around the world. The directors of Tata Sons include N Chandrasekaran (chairman), Ratan N Tata, Venu Srinivasan, and Ralf Speth.

About 66 percent of the equity capital of Tata Sons is held by philanthropic trusts endowed by members of the Tata family. The largest of these trusts are the Sir Dorabji Tata Trust and the Sir Ratan Tata Trust. The trustees of The Sir Dorabji Tata Trust included Ratan N Tata (chairman), N A Soonawala, R K Krishna Kumar, Venu Srinivasan, R Venkataramanan. The trustees of the Sir Ratan Tata Trust include Ratan Tata (chairman), N A Soonawala, K B Dadiseth, R K Krishna Kumar, and R Venkataramanan.

Tata Sons and the trusts hold shares in Tata companies. For instance, in Tata Motors the Tata entities own 34.13 per cent of the company's voting rights. Of these, Tata Sons holds 28.21 per cent, Tata Steel 2.85 per cent and Tata Industries 2.46 per cent. The board of directors of Tata Motors includes N Chandrasekaran (chairman) and Ralf Speth. The directors of Tata Steel include N Chandrasekaran (chairman) and Ishaat Hussain. The board of directors of Indian Hotels includes N Chandrasekaran (chairman). The board of directors of Tata Consultancy Services includes Ishaat Hussain N Chandrasekaran (chairman) and Ishaat Hussain.

As you can see, the Tata Group controls the companies through a web of common share ownership and common directors and trustees. Intra-group transactions further complicate our understanding of the activities of the companies.

Sources: Tata Group companies' websites. Information about share ownership is as of December 31, 2016 and board membership is as of March 31, 2017.

Separate Financial Statements

Learning Objective

LO 10 Account for investments in separate financial statements.

Separate financial statements are financial statements in which an entity accounts for its investments in subsidiaries, joint ventures or associates at cost or as financial assets. Dividends from these entities are recognized when they are declared. In India, companies are required to prepare separate financial statements, in addition to consolidated financial statements. These are known as *standalone financial statements*.

Does the requirement to prepare consolidated financial statements reduce the scope for earnings management?

....

....

....

Group entities are commonly used as tools for perpetrating financial reporting fraud, money laundering and tax evasion. Here are some examples:

- Omitting consolidation of loss-making group entities.
- Transferring a major liability to a subsidiary and omitting it from consolidation, so that the liability becomes off-balance sheet.
- Over invoicing imports from and under invoicing exports to group entities in order to take foreign exchange out of the country.
- Transferring profits from a subsidiary in a high-tax country to a subsidiary in a low-tax country or in a tax haven through transfer pricing.
- Overcharging a joint venture for common expenses or services provided.

Red flags signalling group entity fraud:

- A complex of web of interconnected entities through cross-holdings.
- Subsidiaries operating in tax havens and in countries with weak enforcement of laws, high incidence of bribery and corruption, and low standards of accounting, auditing and securities regulation.
- Extensive movement of goods and services through domestic and foreign subsidiaries.
- Disproportionately large cash balances held by subsidiaries.
- Repeated acquisitions and disposals of operating investments.
- Large amounts of goodwill carried for a long time.

The 2016 annual report of Biocon Limited explains the purpose and process of preparing consolidated financial statements.

The consolidated financial statements ... reflect the financial position and the results of operations of Biocon together with its subsidiaries, joint venture company, and associate company. The Group has accounted for its investments in associate under the equity method as per which the share of profit/ loss of the associate company has been added to/reduced from the cost of investment. The accounting policies have been consistently applied by the Group and are consistent with those used in the previous year. The financial statements of subsidiaries and associate company have been drawn up to the same reporting date as that of the Company. All material inter-company transactions and balances between the entities included in the consolidated financial statements have been eliminated. The excess of the purchase price over the proportionate share of the book value of the net assets of the acquired subsidiary company/increase in shareholding in the subsidiary company on the date of investment is recognized in the consolidated financial statements as goodwill and disclosed under Intangible Assets. In case the cost of investment in subsidiary companies is less than the proportionate share of the book value of the net assets of the acquired subsidiary company on the date of investment, the difference is treated as a capital reserve and shown under Reserves and surplus.

Note the following points.

- The consolidated financial statements encompass the activities of the Biocon Group consisting of Biocon Limited – the parent – and its subsidiaries, joint venture and associate.
- Investment in associate is accounted for under the equity method.
- Accounting policies are similar across entities in the Group and are consistent.
- The parent and the other entities in the Group have the same reporting date.
- Intra-group transactions and balances have been eliminated.

IFRS, IND AS AND INDIAN GAAP
Operating Investments

Here are the key differences between these systems.

- *Separate financial statements:* IFRS requires investments in associates and joint ventures to be measured at cost or as financial assets or using the equity method. Ind AS does not allow the equity method. Indian GAAP requires them to be measured at cost less any impairment loss in the separate financial statements.

- *Joint arrangements:* Both IFRS and Ind AS require a joint operation to recognize assets it controls and expenses liabilities and expenses it incurs and its share of income earned and joint venture to apply the equity method. Indian GAAP requires proportionate consolidation for joint ventures.

- *Control:* Both IFRS and Ind AS define control based on power and rights to returns. In Indian GAAP, it is based on majority voting rights and control of the board of a directors.

- *Business combinations:* Both IFRS and Ind AS deal with business combinations. In Indian GAAP, there is no standard on business combination. IFRS allows only the purchase method. Ind AS allows pooling of interests in some cases. Indian GAAP allows both. IFRS and Ind AS don't allow negative goodwill (or capital reserve), while Indian GAAP does. Both IFRS and Ind AS require assets to be measured at fair value. Indian GAAP allows either fair value or carrying amount (book value). Under both IFRS and Ind AS, goodwill is not amortized but tested for impairment at least annually. Indian GAAP requires goodwill to be amortized over not more than five years.

RECAP

- Equity instruments may be held as long-term investments.
- A *subsidiary* is an enterprise over which an investor – *parent* – has *control*.
- *Consolidated financial statements* are the financial statements of a *group* consisting of a parent and all its subsidiaries presented *as if* they were a single economic entity.
- The *consolidation* procedure combines line items of the individual companies, eliminates intragroup items, and identifies and presents *non-controlling interests*.
- A *business combination* is a transaction in which an entity obtains control over a business.
- The key element in a business combination is an *acquisition*.
- *Goodwill* is the premium paid over the fair value of the net assets.
- *Non-controlling interest* is presented separately from the parent's equity.
- A *joint arrangement* is a contractual arrangement whereby two or more parties have *joint control*. It may be a *joint operation* or a *joint venture*.
- An *associate* is an entity over which an investor has *significant influence*.
- Under the *equity method*, the investor recognizes the investment at cost at the time of acquisition and adjusts it for subsequent changes in its share of the associate's net assets.
- The equity method is used to account for joint ventures and associates.
- *Separate financial statements* are those in which investments in subsidiaries, joint ventures and associates are accounted for at cost or as financial assets.

Review Problem

On March 31, 20X1, Alpha Company invests ₹100,000 in return for 25 per cent of the equity shares with proportionate voting rights in Beta Company. On October 9, 20X1, Beta Company pays dividends of ₹4,000. During the year ended March 31, 20X2, it earns ₹10,000. On September 15, 20X2, it pays dividends of ₹6,000. During the year ended March 31, 20X3, it earns ₹15,000.

Required

1. Record the transactions.
2. At what amounts will the investment appear in Alpha Company's balance sheet at March 31, 20X1, 20X2 and 20X3.

Solution to the Review Problem

(a) Transactions

20X1

Mar. 31	Investments in Associates			100,000	
	Cash				100,000
Oct. 9	Cash			1,000	
	Investments in Associates				1,000

20X2

Mar. 31	Investments in Associates			2,500	
	Share of Earnings in Associates				2,500
Sep. 15	Cash			1,500	
	Investments in Associates				1,500

20X3

Mar. 31	Investments in Associates			3,750	
	Share of Earnings in Associates				3,750

(b) Balance sheet, March 31

	20X3	20X2	20X1
Investments in Associates	103,750	101,500	100,000

ASSIGNMENT MATERIAL

Questions

1. How are *operating investments* different from *financial investments*?

2. How are consolidated financial statements more useful than a parent's financial statements?

3. What is the criterion for an *acquisition*?

4. Suppose the consideration for an acquisition is equal to the fair value of the net assets acquired. Would it be correct to say that there is no goodwill in this acquisition?

5. Explain the two methods of measuring *non-controlling interest*.

6. Distinguish between *control* and *joint control*.

7. When is a parent exempted from preparing consolidated financial statements?

8. What elements constitute a *joint arrangement*?

9. How does a participant in a joint arrangement who does not have joint control account for its investment?

10. How is *significant influence* different from *joint control*?

11. Why is the equity method known as *one-line consolidation*?

12. What are *separate financial statements*?

13. How is the treatment of dividend income in separate financial statements different from that in consolidated financial statements?

Problems

On January 1, 20XX, Francis D 'Costa paid ₹200,000 for a senior solicitor's practice with the following assets and liabilities: equipment, ₹20,000; furniture, ₹15,000; prepaid rent, ₹8,000; electricity expense payable, ₹700; salaries payable, ₹3,000.

Problem 8.1
Recording Business
Acquisition *

Required

Prepare the journal entry to record the acquisition.

On April 1, 20XX, All Metal Company, a commodity trader, acquired FerroWorld, an iron ore trading business for a cash consideration of ₹1,000,000. FerroWorld had the following assets and liabilities: building, ₹400,000; equipment, ₹100,000; furniture, ₹50,000; trade receivables, ₹60,000;

Problem 8.2
Recording Business
Acquisition * *

prepaid insurance, ₹5,000; trade payables, ₹12,000; income tax payable, ₹10,000; pensions payable, ₹35,000. FerroWorld had an online auction house valued at ₹300,000.

Required

Prepare the journal entry to record the acquisition.

Problem 8.3
Calculating Non-controlling Interest and Goodwill ✳✳✳

On October 1, 20XX, Far Company acquired 80 per cent (8,000 shares) of Near Company's voting rights for ₹960,000. On the acquisition date, Near Company's shares traded at ₹115 per share. On that date, the fair value of Near Company's net assets was ₹800,000.

Required

1. Calculate non-controlling interest and goodwill based on the full goodwill method.
2. Calculate non-controlling interest and goodwill based on the partial goodwill method.

Problem 8.4
Calculating Non-controlling Interest and Goodwill ✳✳✳
Alternative to Problem 8.3

On May 1, 20XX, Proximate Company acquired 60 per cent (6,000 shares) of Distant Company's voting rights for ₹1,200,000. On the acquisition date, Distant Company's shares traded at ₹150 per share. On that date, the fair value of Distant Company's net assets was ₹930,000.

Required

1. Calculate non-controlling interest and goodwill based on the full goodwill method.
2. Calculate non-controlling interest and goodwill based on the partial goodwill method.

Problem 8.5
Joint Arrangement ✳✳✳

On January 1, 20XX, Abhik Company and Uday Company jointly established Abhyuday Company as an incorporated entity to produce plastic goods. The assets and liabilities held in Abhuday Company are those of Abhuday Company. Abhik Company and Uday Company each own 50 per cent of the equity shares in Abhuday Company. The contractual terms of the joint arrangement state that Abhik Company has the rights to all of the injection moulding machine and the obligation to pay the bank loan payable in Abhuday Company. Abhik Company and Uday Company have rights to all other assets in Abhyuday Company, and obligations for all other liabilities in Abhyuday Company, in proportion to their equity interests.

Abhyuday Company's first balance sheet is as follows:

ABHUDAY COMPANY Balance Sheet, December 31, 20XX	
Assets	
Non-current assets	
Property, plant and equipment:* Cost	₹50,000
Deduct Accumulated depreciation	10,000
Net	40,000
Current assets	
Inventories	62,000
Trade receivables	25,000
Cash	10,000
	137,000
Equity and Liabilities	
Equity	
Equity share capital	₹100,000
Other equity: Retained earnings	5,000
Liabilities	
Non-current liabilities	
Bank loan payable	24,000
Current liabilities	
Trade payables	8,000
	137,000

* Injection moulding machine costing ₹20,000 with a useful life of five years and compression moulding machine costing ₹30,000 with a useful life of five years. Both are depreciated on the straight-line method.

Required

1. Is the joint arrangement a joint operation or a joint venture? Explain.
2. How should Abhik Company and Uday Company account for their investment in Abhyuday Company?

On April 1, 20X1, Surya Company and Rashmi Company jointly established Helios Company as an incorporated entity to produce solar power systems. The assets and liabilities held in Helios Company are those of Helios Company. Surya Company and Rashmi Company each own 50 per cent of the equity shares in Helios Company. The contractual terms of the joint arrangement state that Surya Company has the rights to all of the solar panel manufacturing plant and the obligation to pay the bonds payable in Helios Company. Surya Company and Rashmi Company have rights to all other assets in Helios Company, and obligations for all other liabilities in Helios Company, in proportion to their equity interests.

Problem 8.6
Joint Arrangement ✳✳✳
Alternative to Problem 8.5

Helios Company's first balance sheet is as follows:

HELIOS COMPANY
Balance Sheet, March 31, 20X2

Assets

Non-current assets

Property, plant and equipment:* Cost....................................	₹80,000
Deduct Accumulated depreciation..	20,000
Net..	60,000

Current assets

Inventories..	10,000
Trade receivables	15,000
Cash..	6,000
	91,000

Equity and Liabilities

Equity

Equity share capital	₹40,000
Other equity: Retained earnings.................................	6,000

Liabilities

Non-current liabilities

Bonds payable..	40,000

Current liabilities

Trade payables	5,000
	91,000

* Solar panel manufacturing plant costing ₹60,000 with a useful life of four years and storage battery manufacturing plant costing ₹20,000 with a useful life of four years. Both are depreciated on the straight-line method.

Required

1. Is the joint arrangement a joint operation or a joint venture? Explain.
2. How should Surya Company and Rashmi Company for their investment in Helios Company?

Shalom Company acquired for cash all the equity shares of Kiran Company on March 31, 20XX for ₹60,000. The balance sheets of the two companies just before the acquisition were as follows:

Problem 8.7
Consolidated Financial Statements, Wholly-owned Subsidiary ✳✳✳

	March 31, 20XX	
	Shalom Company	Kiran Company
Assets		
Non-current assets		
Property, plant and equipment: Cost...	₹100,000	₹60,000
Deduct Accumulated depreciation..	70,000	45,000
Net..	30,000	15,000
Current assets		
Inventories...	12,000	9,000
Trade receivables..	14,000	10,000
Cash...	62,000	3,000
	118,000	37,000
Equity and Liabilities		
Equity		
Equity share capital	₹50,000	₹15,000
Other equity: Retained earnings.................................	27,000	3,000
Liabilities		
Non-current liabilities		
Bonds payable..	22,000	12,000
Current liabilities		
Trade payables..	19,000	7,000
	118,000	37,000

The appraisal report as of acquisition date indicated the following:

- Property, plant and equipment had a fair value of ₹20,000.
- Inventories included obsolete items costing ₹2,000.
- A trade payable of ₹1,000 was omitted.
- Fair values of the remaining assets and liabilities were equal to their carrying amounts.
- Kiran Company's payables included an amount of ₹2,000 due to Shalom Company.

Required

1. Prepare the balance sheets of the two companies just after the acquisition.
2. Prepare a statement showing fair value adjustments as of acquisition date.
3. Prepare a consolidation worksheet as of acquisition date.
4. Prepare a consolidated balance sheet as of acquisition date.

Problem 8.8
Consolidated Financial
Statements, Wholly-
owned Subsidiary ✶✶✶✶
Alternative to Problem 8.7

Hamid Company acquired for cash all the equity shares of Shabnam Company on July 31, 20XX for ₹80,000. The balance sheets of the two companies just before the acquisition were as follows:

	July 31, 20XX	
	Hamid Company	Shabanam Company
Assets		
Non-current assets		
Property, plant and equipment: Cost.................................	₹150,000	₹50,000
Deduct Accumulated depreciation......................................	90,000	32,000
Net..	60,000	18,000
Non-current investments..	8,000	3,000
Current assets		
Inventories...	15,000	12,000
Trade receivables	24,000	7,000
Cash...	95,000	4,000
	202,000	44,000

Equity and Liabilities
Equity

Equity share capital, paid-up ₹10 each.............................	₹100,000	₹25,000
Other equity: Retained earnings...	17,000	2,000

Liabilities
Non-current liabilities

Bonds payable..	42,000	8,000

Current liabilities

Trade payables	43,000	9,000
	202,000	44,000

The appraisal report as of acquisition date indicated the following:

- Property, plant and equipment was worth ₹27,000
- A licence worth ₹5,000 had not been recognized.
- Inventories included obsolete items costing ₹1,000.
- Trade receivables included a loss account of ₹2,000.
- Fair values of the remaining assets and liabilities were equal to their carrying amounts.
- Shabnam Company's investments included Hamid Company's bonds of ₹2,000.

Required

1. Prepare the balance sheets of the two companies just after the acquisition.
2. Prepare a statement showing fair value adjustments as of acquisition date.
3. Prepare a consolidation worksheet as of acquisition date.
4. Prepare a consolidated balance sheet as of acquisition date.

Abhinav Company acquired for cash 80 per cent of the outstanding shares of Prakriti Company on September 30, 20XX at ₹20 per share. On that date, Prakriti Company's share price was ₹18. The balance sheets of the two companies just before the acquisition were as follows:

Problem 8.9
Consolidated Financial Statements, Majority-owned Subsidiary
✴ ✴ ✴ ✴ ✴

	September 30, 20XX	
	Abhinav Company	**Prakriti Company**
Assets		
Non-current assets		
Property, plant and equipment: Cost	₹250,000	₹90,000
Deduct Accumulated depreciation.....................................	110,000	54,000
Net..	140,000	36,000
Non-current investments...	18,000	4,000
Current assets		
Inventories...	47,000	12,000
Trade receivables	29,000	31,000
Cash..	148,000	15,000
	382,000	98,000
Equity and Liabilities		
Equity		
Equity share capital, paid-up ₹10 each............................	₹100,000	₹30,000
Other equity: Retained earnings..	64,000	10,000
Liabilities		
Non-current liabilities		
Bonds payable..	150,000	40,000
Current liabilities		
Trade payables	68,000	18,000
	382,000	98,000

The appraisal report as of acquisition date indicated the following:

- Property, plant and equipment had a fair value of ₹45,000.
- Inventories included obsolete items costing ₹3,000.
- A trade payable of ₹2,000 was omitted.
- Fair values of the remaining assets and liabilities equalled their carrying amounts.
- Abhinav Company's investments included Prakriti Company's bonds of ₹8,000.

Required

1. Prepare the balance sheets of the two companies just after the acquisition.
2. Prepare a statement showing fair value adjustments as of the acquisition date.
3. Prepare a consolidation worksheet as of acquisition date applying (a) the full goodwill, and (b) the partial goodwill methods.
4. Prepare a consolidated balance sheet as of acquisition date applying (a) full goodwill, and (b) partial goodwill methods.

Problem 8.10
Consolidated Financial Statements, Majority-owned Subsidiary
✶✶✶✶✶ Alternative to Problem 8.9

Anupam Company acquired for cash 60 per cent of the outstanding shares of Uttam Company on April 1, 20XX for at ₹45 per share. On that date, Uttam Company's share price was ₹41. The balance sheets of the two companies just before the acquisition were as follows:

| | April 1, 20XX | |
	Anupam Company	Uttam Company
Assets		
Non-current assets		
Property, plant and equipment: Cost	₹400,000	₹250,000
Deduct Accumulated depreciation	230,000	130,000
Net	170,000	120,000
Non-current investments	10,000	12,000
Current assets		
Inventories	29,000	15,000
Trade receivables	53,000	26,000
Cash	290,000	12,000
	552,000	185,000
Equity and Liabilities		
Equity		
Equity share capital, paid-up ₹10 each	₹200,000	₹100,000
Other equity: Retained earnings	25,000	20,000
Liabilities		
Non-current liabilities		
Bonds payable	200,000	38,000
Current liabilities		
Trade payables	127,000	27,000
	552,000	185,000

The appraisal report as of acquisition date indicated the following:

- Property, plant and equipment were worth ₹156,000.
- Inventories included obsolete items costing ₹7,000.
- Trade receivables included a loss account of ₹4,000.
- A trade payable of ₹3,000 was omitted.
- The fair values of the remaining assets and liabilities were equal to their carrying amounts.
- Uttam Company's investments included Anupam Company's bonds of ₹8,000.

Required

1. Prepare the balance sheets of the two companies just after the acquisition.
2. Prepare a statement showing fair value adjustments as of the acquisition date.

3. Prepare a consolidation worksheet as of acquisition date applying (a) the full goodwill, and (b) the partial goodwill methods.
4. Prepare a consolidated balance sheet as of acquisition date applying (a) full goodwill, and (b) partial goodwill methods.

On March 31, 20X1, Amar Company acquired for cash 30 per cent of the equity shares of Lahar Company for ₹45,000. On that date, Lahar Company's balance sheet was as follows: equity share capital, ₹40,000; retained earnings, ₹60,000; property, plant and equipment, ₹100,000. The property, plant and equipment had a remaining useful life of five years and a fair value of ₹140,000. On June 11, 20X1, Lahar Company paid a dividend of ₹10,000. On March 31, 20X2, the company reported a net profit of ₹17,000 for the year ended that date. Amar Company's fiscal year end is June 30.

Problem 8.11
Equity Method for Associate ✶✶✶✶✶

Required

1. Prepare journal entries to record these transactions by Amar Company.
2. Prepare an analysis of the carrying amount of the investment in Amar Company's balance sheet on (a) June 30, 20X1, and (b) June 30, 20X2.

On September 30, 20X1, Vinod Company acquired for cash 25 per cent of the equity shares of Sachin Company for ₹51,000. On that date, Sachin Company's balance sheet was as follows: equity share capital, ₹20,000; retained earnings, ₹100,000; property, plant and equipment, ₹120,000. The property, plant and equipment had a remaining useful life of 10 years and a fair value of ₹180,000. On November 14, 20X1, Sachin Company paid a dividend of ₹12,000. On September 30, 20X2, Sachin Company reported a net profit of ₹32,000 for the year ended that date. Vinod Company's fiscal year end is December 31.

Problem 8.12
Equity Method for Associate ✶✶✶✶✶
Alternative to Problem 8.11

Required

1. Prepare journal entries to record these transactions by Vinod Company.
2. Prepare an analysis of the carrying amount of the investment in Vinod Company's balance sheet on (a) December 31, 20X1, and (b) December 31, 20X2.

Business Decision Cases

Dibrugarh Oil Limited and Gujarat Hydrocarbon Limited, two petroleum marketing companies, plan to set up an oil refinery to be called Vishakha Refinery Limited. The terms of the arrangement between the two parties are as follows:

BDC 8.1
Vishakha Refinery Limited

1. The refinery will be owned and managed by Vishakha Refinery, a company to be incorporated with a share capital of ₹1 million to be issued at par for cash. Dibrugarh Oil and Gujarat Hydrocarbon will hold the shares in the ratio of 3:2.
2. Significant decisions require unanimous approval of the two companies. All disagreements will be referred to an independent arbitrator, whose award will be final and binding on the parties.
3. The parties will contribute to the refinery's construction cost in the ratio of 2:1.
4. The refinery will come up on land owned by Dibrugarh Oil.
5. The parties will share the refinery's output and operating and maintenance expenses in the ratio of 3:1.
6. Gujarat Hydrocarbon will take an interest-bearing loan to pay for its share of the cost. Dibrugarh Oil will use its surplus cash.
7. Dibrugarh Oil and Gujarat Hydrocarbon will sell their share of the refinery's output through their respective petrol stations.
8. Vishakha Refinery will pay salaries on the last day of the month and other expenses on the first day of the following month.

Required

1. Is this a joint arrangement? Explain.
2. How should Dibrugarh Oil and Gujarat Hydrocarbon account for and present the assets, liabilities, revenues and expenses of, and their contribution to, Vishakha Refinery Limited?

Interpreting Financial Reports

IFR 8.1
Olympus Corporation

On October 14, 2011, Olympus Corporation, a Japanese camera maker, sacked its president, Michael Woodford following his questioning of the company's past acquisitions. Mr. Woodford accused the company's executives of paying too much for acquisitions. In one of the acquisitions, Olympus's 2008 purchase of the British medical equipment maker Gyrus, the Japanese group paid $687 million to a little-known financial adviser and a fund in the Cayman Islands. Olympus booked the payment as an intangible asset. In all, it was a $1.7 billion fraud that went all the way back to the 1990s.

In essence, the fraud involved hiding investment losses by selling the securities at cost to an entity in the Cayman Islands. The entity was not consolidated in the financial statements of Olympus. The entity was financed by some financial institutions. The amounts were repaid by inflating advisory fees for acquisitions.

Questions were raised about auditing and corporate governance in Olympus. Commentators observed that the company's board of directors and audit committee did not monitor the working of the company and were even possibly complicit in the fraud.

Required

1. Explain the fraud in Olympus. Use journal entries, where possible, to illustrate your explanation.
2. Why was the fraud not detected for well over a decade? How did it finally come to light?
3. Examine the role of the company's board and audit committee in the matter. What improvements would you recommend to the company's governance arrangements?
4. Did the company's external auditors fulfil their responsibilities to the shareholders?

Financial Analysis

FA 8.1
Impairment of Goodwill

Companies often pay large amounts of goodwill to acquire other entities in happy times. Unfortunately, they invariably find that they overpaid.

Required

1. Prepare a report using actual company data on the amount of goodwill paid for acquisitions. You can select a sample of companies across industries or a couple of industries for this study.
2. Track the performance of the acquisitions over the next few years. Does the post-acquisition performance of the companies indicate overvaluation?
3. Examine company practices for recognizing an impairment of goodwill.

Answers to One-minute Quiz

8.1 d.
8.2 c.
8.3 a.

Answers to Test Your Understanding

8.1 By virtue of the agreement, Tanvi Company has control over Abhay Company's shareholding. Therefore, Tanvi Company controls Varun Company.

8.2 Production decisions and technology affect profitability, capital investment and dividend distribution. Therefore, Manoj Company controls Anant Company.

8.3 Investment in bonds, ₹111,000. Bonds payable, ₹126,000.

8.4 Vijay Company and Vikram Company have joint control over Dare Company. Vir Company has neither control nor joint control, though it holds the largest voting block; it is an investor in the joint venture.

8.5 20X1

Dec. 31	Investments in Associates..	40,000	
	Cash		40,000

Cost = Share in book value of net assets: 20% of
₹145,000, i.e. ₹29,000 + Share in fair value adjustment
for property, plant and equipment: 20% of ₹25,000,
i.e. ₹5,000 + Goodwill, ₹6,000 = ₹40,000

20X2

Feb. 18	Cash..	1,200	
	Investment in Associates..		1,200
Dec. 31	Investment in Associates	1,750	
	Share of Earnings in Associates....................................		1,750

Share of earnings = 20% of reported earnings of
₹15,000, i.e. ₹3,000 – Depreciation on share of fair
value adjustment: ₹5,000/4 years, i.e. ₹1,250 = ₹1,750

Carrying amount: March 31, 20X3, ₹40,550; March 31, 20X2, ₹38,800.

CHAPTER

9

Operating Liabilities

LEARNING OBJECTIVES

After studying this chapter, you should be able to:

1. Define liabilities.
2. Distinguish between operating liabilities and financial liabilities.
3. Understand current liabilities.
4. Understand definite liabilities and estimated liabilities.
5. Explain accounting profit and taxable profit.
6. Account for current income tax.
7. Account for deferred income tax.
8. Account for employee benefits.
9. Explain contingent liabilities.

TAX WORKS FOR YOUR BUSINESS

Warren Buffett, the legendary investor thinks that the rich should pay more tax. However, his businesses don't seem to heed his view. At December 31, 2015, Berkshire Hathaway and its subsidiaries owed $63 billion in deferred taxes. The amount was less than $10 billion in 2008, and it has been rising steadily. Is there a contradiction? Deferred tax highlights the difference between accounting and tax rules. Berkshire is in capital-intensive businesses, such as BNSF Railway (BNSF) and Berkshire Hathaway Energy (BHE). BNSF and BHE are investing in capacity. They get tax credits and high depreciation when they invest. As a result, they pay less taxes. The tax benefits have the effect of delaying tax payment. Since the companies keep investing year after year, their tax is postponed further and further into the future. According to Berkshire's 2015 annual report, BNSF's physical facilities would be improved at the end of every year and BHE made major commitments to the future development of renewables. The amount of $63 billion sums up the tax postponed by utilizing tax benefits. To be sure, they don't imply that Mr. Buffett's words and actions differ. The delayed tax payment helps Berkshire finance its capital expenditure without having to borrow or raise equity. That's shrewd and legitimate.

SPEED READ

Liabilities are amounts payable now or later. They may arise from operations or borrowing funds. Current liabilities are payable as part of operating activities. Long-term liabilities are payable after the current period. Some liabilities are precise, while others must be estimated. Current income tax is payable now. The difference between accounting profit and taxable profit gives rise to deferred taxes. Employees are paid salaries and other benefits for work done in the current period. Employment contracts require payment of provident fund, gratuity, pensions and health care benefits after retirement. These costs should be recognized in the current period. Contingent liabilities may become payable depending on how things turn out in the future. They should be disclosed.

Liabilities in Perspective

A liability is an enterprise's present obligation resulting from a transaction or event to part with assets. Most obligations arise from *contracts*, e.g. an agreement to pay rent or salary. Some obligations result from *statutory* requirements, e.g. payment of income tax and contribution to provident fund. Obligations may also be *constructive*, i.e. regarded as payable even without a legally enforceable claim. For instance, a store may allow a full refund for goods returned even after the contractual period. An airline may voluntarily compensate its customers for flight delays.

Learning Objective

LO 1 Define liabilities.

Liabilities result from transactions or other events that have *already occurred*, not *expected to occur*. Buying goods on credit is a transaction and it creates an obligation to pay. Enterprises often enter into contracts for future transactions. For example, a contract for the purchase of materials is a *commitment* to purchase and pay. There is no obligation to pay if there is no purchase. Therefore, commitments are not liabilities.

The settlement of an obligation involves giving up something of value. Typically, obligations are settled by cash payment. Obligations may also be settled by other means, such as transferring goods or other assets or providing services. An obligation is also cleared when an entity's creditor waives its rights.

For an obligation to be recognized as a liability, it should exist independently of an enterprise's future actions, i.e. it should be *unavoidable* regardless of what the enterprise does. An action that an enterprise intends to take voluntarily does not give rise to a liability. For example, a leather-processing plant should recognize a liability for the cost of undoing the damage already caused to the surrounding paddy fields. However, if it plans to install cleaning equipment to eliminate or reduce future damage, it should not recognize a liability for the estimated cost of the equipment.

Let's take two illustrations to understand whether a liability exists.

1. The law requires a owner to replace its trucks not later than 15 years.
2. The licence for a nuclear power plant requires the operator to decommission the plant not later than 25 years.

HANDHOLD 9.1
Liability

We should ask: Is there a present obligation as a result of an event that has already occurred? A present obligation implies *inevitability*. In other words, it is not possible to avoid it regardless of what an enterprise may do in the future.

Applying this test, we find the following:

Replacement of trucks: The owner is not under a present obligation to replace its trucks. The decision on replacement will have to be made when a truck completes 15 years. That's a future obligation. Until then, it has several options such as selling, gifting, exchanging or scrapping the trucks. At the end of 15 years, it may decide to retire the trucks without replacing them. In such cases, there will be no need for replacement. Consequently, there is no liability.

Decommissioning of a nuclear power plant: When the nuclear power company executes the licensing agreement, it accepts a present obligation for decommissioning, clean-up and restoration. Its obligation will not change regardless of what it may do in the future. It must fulfil its obligation even if it decides to shut down the plant. It can't escape the liability by selling or abandoning the plant. Therefore, there is a liability. The company should capitalize the estimated cost of decommissioning, removal and restoration and set up a provision.

Operating Liabilities and Financial Liabilities

Operating liabilities result from a firm's operating activities, i.e. providing goods or services. They are settled by payment of cash or by providing goods or services. Trade payables, income taxes and pensions are settled by cash. Unearned revenue, mileage points, loyalty points, free product upgrades, and warranties are settled by providing goods or services. Financial liabilities are settled by paying cash, giving another financial asset or issuing equity shares. They are usually contracted for the acquisition of businesses and long-lived

Learning Objective

LO 2 Distinguish between operating liabilities and financial liabilities.

assets. Debentures, mortgages, and leases are financial liabilities. Financial liabilities are more commonly known as *debt*. Some items may have the characteristics of both. For example, trade payables and bills payable are related to operations and are, therefore, operating liabilities; since they are financial instruments, they are also financial liabilities. Chapter 10 discusses financial liabilities.

Current Liabilities

Learning Objective

LO 3 Understand current liabilities.

An enterprise should classify a liability as a **current liability** when it expects or intends to settle the liability in its normal operating cycle or within 12 months after the reporting period. Current liabilities are normally paid by using existing current assets, creating other current liabilities or fulfilling contractual obligations to provide goods or services. Trade payables, bills payable, bank overdraft, unearned revenue, and income tax payable are examples of current liabilities. A liability which is not a current liability is a **non-current liability** or **long-term liability**. Deferred taxes, post-retirement health care, and pensions are examples of non-current liabilities. Current portion of a non-current liability is classified as a current liability. Current liabilities are part of an enterprise's operating cycle and are routinely settled by cash received from customers. Classifying a current liability as non-current would understate an enterprise's short-term cash needs and mislead creditors. Inability to pay current liabilities on time is a sign of cash problems.

Definite Liabilities and Estimated Liabilities

Learning Objective

LO 4 Understand definite liabilities and estimated liabilities.

Current liabilities can be definite liabilities or estimated liabilities. We will discuss these now.

Definite Liabilities

Definite liabilities are current obligations that can be determined precisely. Examples are trade payables, salaries payable, interest payable, bills payable, GST payable, and current portions of long-term debt. In Part One, you have seen the first three items. We now consider the other items.

Bills payable   When a business buys goods on credit, it issues a bill payable to the seller. Sometimes, a bill payable may substitute a past-due account payable. The accounting procedure for bills payable is the mirror image of the procedure for bills receivable, discussed in Chapter 7. Figure 9.1 shows a bill payable for ₹10,000 drawn by Hindustan Finance (drawer) on Sapna Corporation (drawee and acceptor) for a credit purchase.

₹10,000   ***Mysore***
                                                                                                       May 1, 20XX

Figure 9.1
BILL PAYABLE

A firm that buys on credit or takes a loan issues a bill payable to its supplier.

Ninety days after date pay me or to my order the sum of ten thousand rupees for value received with interest at 12 per cent per annum.

Hindustan Finance

Accepted
Sapna Corporation

HANDHOLD 9.2
Bills Payable

Consider the bill payable in Figure 9.1. Sapna Corporation records the transaction as follows:

May 1   Purchases...   10,000
             Bills Payable...   10,000
                      To record 90-day, 12% bill payable of ₹10,000

When Sapna Corporation pays the bill on the maturity date, it records the following entry:

July 30   Bills Payable 10,000

          Interest Expense 300

             Cash 10,300

             Paid 90-day, 12% bill payable of ₹10,000 with interest

Suppose the company's financial year ends on June 30. The company must recognize 60 days' interest (consisting of 30 days in May excluding the date of the bill and 30 days in June) on the bill as an expense of the period. The accrued interest expense is recorded as follows:

June 30   Interest Expense 200

           Interest Payable.. 200

             To record accrued interest for 60 days: ₹10,000 × 12/100 × 60/360

Goods and services tax payable   The goods and services tax (GST), introduced by the Constitution (101st Amendment) Act 2016 is a tax on supply of goods and services. It replaces a number of Central, State and local levies, such as Central excise duty, service tax, Central sales tax, value added tax (VAT), purchase tax, entry tax, and luxury tax. Unlike excise duty, service tax and VAT, GST is a tax on supply of goods or services rather than on manufacture or sale of goods or provision of services. Central GST (CGST) and State GST (SGST) are levied on intra-state supply and Integrated GST (IGST) on inter-State supply.

GST allows input tax credit. The seller collects GST from the buyer and claims credit for the GST paid on the inputs, i.e. purchases of goods and services. To illustrate, suppose Hari in Dibrugarh sells a chair for ₹1,000 plus tax to Ganesh in Guwahati. Assume CGST of 5 per cent, SGST of 5 per cent and IGST of 10 per cent. Ganesh pays ₹1,100 consisting of product price ₹1,000 and GST ₹100 (i.e. CGST ₹50 and SGST ₹50) in Assam. Suppose Ganesh sells the chair to Joseph, a consumer, in Bengaluru for ₹1,600 plus tax, adding a profit of ₹600. Joseph pays Ganesh ₹1,760.

Hari and Ganesh record the following entries:

Hari's journal		
(a) *Hari sells to Ganesh*		
Trade Receivables (or Cash)	1,100	
Sales..		1,000
CGST Payable...		50
SGST Payable...		50
(b) *Hari pays GST*		
CGST Payable	50	
SGST Payable	50	
Cash...		100

Ganesh's journal		
(a) *Ganesh buys from Hari*		
Purchases..	1,000	
CGST Recoverable	50	
SGST Recoverable	50	
Trade Payables (or Cash)		1,100
(b) *Ganesh sells to Joseph*		
Trade Receivables (or Cash)	1,760	
Sales..		1,600
IGST Payable		160
(c) *Ganesh pays GST*		
IGST Payable...	160	
Cash...		60
CGST Recoverable		50
SGST Recoverable		50

The difference between Ganesh's sales and purchases is his profit of ₹600. GST receivable and GST payable are part of the operations and will be classified as current asset and current liability.

Current maturities of long-term debt   Debt is a financial liability. A portion of long-term debt may be payable in the course of next 12 months. Suppose a loan of ₹100,000 is to be paid in annual instalments of ₹10,000 in the next 10 years. The instalment of ₹10,000 payable in the next financial year is a current liability.

Estimated Liabilities

An **estimated liability** (or **provision**) is a known liability but the amount is uncertain. Estimated liabilities are definite obligations; only their precise timing or amount cannot be determined presently. The difficulty is in making a reasonable estimate of the amount of the liability. Product warranties, income tax, and employee benefits examples of estimated liabilities. We will consider product warranties now and income tax and employee benefits later.

Product warranties   A product warranty is a contract under which the seller or manufacturer is legally obliged during a certain period to bear the cost of replacement parts or repair costs, if the product fails to perform. Warranty cost is an expense in the period in which the product is sold, since the warranty helped the sale. However, the exact amount of warranty expense is not known at the time of sale, so the expense is estimated based on past experience.

HANDHOLD 9.3
Product Warranty
Liability

Chrono Company sells watches at an average price of ₹1,500 with a one-year warranty. Under the terms of the warranty, for one year from the date of sale the company will replace any defective parts free of charge and the labour charges are to be paid by the customer. During the year ended March 31, 20XX, the company sells 2,000 watches. Past experience shows that 5 per cent of the watches is defective and that the cost of warranty replacement parts is ₹50 per unit. The adjusting entry to estimated warranty expense and liability is as follows:

Mar. 31 Product Warranty Expense	5,000	
Estimated Warranty Liability		5,000
To record estimated product warranty expense and liability: 2,000 × 5% × ₹50		

When a watch is serviced under warranty, the cost of the repair is charged to the estimated warranty liability account. For example, assume that 13 watches are returned in April because of defects and the company carries out repairs at a cost of ₹45 per watch. The transaction is recorded as follows:

Apr. 30 Estimated Warranty Liability	585	
Cash (or Merchandise Inventory)		585
To record replacement of parts under warranty		

TEST YOUR UNDERSTANDING 9.1
Estimating Warranty Expense

Ghanshyam Company sells electric ovens at ₹4,500 each and provides a one-year warranty for free replacement of defective parts. In 20XX, the company sold 2,300 ovens. The estimated warranty cost is ₹200 per oven. Based on past experience, it is estimated that 3 per cent of the ovens sold requires replacement of parts. Record the estimated warranty liability.

ONE-MINUTE QUIZ 9.1
Liability

Himani Company sells mobile phones with a one-year warranty, limited to ₹1,000 per phone. It arranges for all repairs through Anytime Help, an agency which runs service stations for many phone manufacturers. What is Himani Company's estimated warranty liability per phone?
(a) ₹1,000 per phone.
(b) ₹500 per phone.
(c) Not more than ₹1,000.
(d) ₹0, because customers have to go to Anytime Help for service.

Income Taxes

A company is a separate taxable entity and must pay income tax. The Central government levies corporate income tax in accordance with the Income Tax Act 1961. Tax calculations are often complex because they must take into consideration the provisions of the Act and the numerous decisions of the courts and the instructions issued by the Central Board of Direct Taxes. Besides, disputes over the amount of tax payable involve time-consuming legal procedures. Consequently, the precise amount of income tax liability is seldom known when the financial statements are prepared. Since income tax is an expense in the year in which income is earned, it should be estimated and provided for.

Learning Objective

LO 5 Explain accounting profit and taxable profit.

Tax expense and tax payable are important items in the financial statements. While the tax law determines taxable profit, accounting principles and policies are the basis for measuring accounting profit. The objectives of the tax law and accounting are different. The objective of tax law is to raise revenue to meet government expenditure; the objective of accounting is to measure financial performance. Therefore, taxable profit and accounting profit differ frequently and sometimes significantly.

Accounting profit is profit or loss for a period before deducting income tax expense. It is the outcome of applying accounting principles, standards and policies to an enterprise's transactions. Revenue recognition, matching, accrual, going concern, and prudence are the key determinants of accounting profit. Consider the following standard accounting practices:

1. Revenue is recognized when goods or services are provided to customers.
2. The accrual system recognizes receivables, payables and non-cash expenses.
3. Allowance for expected credit losses is recognized.

The carrying amounts of assets and liabilities are the effect of applying accounting rules. For example, the carrying amount of a receivable is the amount expected to be realized net of estimated credit losses. The carrying amount of a plant signifies the amount expected to be recovered from the plant over its remaining useful life. Unearned revenue represents the amount for which an enterprise is liable to provide goods or services for payment already received.

Taxable profit (tax loss) is the profit (loss) for a period, determined in accordance with the rules established by the taxation authorities; income tax is payable (recoverable) on this income.[1] The tax system sometimes works differently from the accounting system. For example, tax laws mandate the WDV method, while the straight-line method is commonly used in accounting. Therefore, the carrying amount of a depreciable item for accounting purposes differs from that for tax purposes.

Current Tax

Current tax is the amount of income tax payable (recoverable) in respect of the taxable profit (tax loss) for a period. Think of current tax as the amount that a business needs to pay as income tax to avoid falling foul of the law. Usually, current tax is payable in instalments, called *advance tax*, during the period in which the taxable profit is earned. Any excess payment (short payment) is a current tax asset (current tax liability). To illustrate, suppose Vipul Company's accounting profit is ₹40,000 a year for three years. It buys a computer for ₹30,000 and depreciates it equally over three years. Assume that for tax purposes the asset is expensed equally over two years. The tax rate is 30 per cent. Exhibit 9.1 presents the calculation of Vipul Company's taxable profit and current tax expense.

Learning Objective

LO 6 Account for current income tax.

---

[1] It is also known as *taxable income* (*tax loss*). For convenience, we will use *taxable profit*.

EXHIBIT 9.1
Current Tax Expense

	Year 1	Year 2	Year 3
Accounting profit	₹40,000	₹40,000	₹40,000
Add Accounting depreciation	10,000	10,000	10,000
Deduct Tax depreciation	15,000	15,000	0
Taxable profit	35,000	35,000	50,000
Current tax expense: 30% of taxable profit	10,500	10,500	15,000

Vipul Company records the current tax expense as follows:

Year 1 and Year 2

| Income Tax Expense | 10,500 | |
| Income Tax Payable | | 10,500 |

Year 3

| Income Tax Expense | 15,000 | |
| Income Tax Payable | | 15,000 |

HANDHOLD 9.4
Calculating Current Tax Expense

Sriya Company buys a machine costing ₹10,000 with an estimated useful life of five years and no residual value. The company follows straight-line depreciation. Its profit before depreciation and tax expense is ₹8,000 a year from 20X1 to 20X5. For tax purposes, the machine is depreciated equally over four years. The tax rate is 30 per cent. We calculate the company's taxable profit and current tax expense, as follows:

	20X1	20X2	20X3	20X4	20X5
Profit before depreciation and tax	₹8,000	₹8,000	₹8,000	₹8,000	₹8,000
Deduct Tax depreciation	2,500	2,500	2,500	2,500	0
Taxable profit	5,500	5,500	5,500	5,500	8,000
Current tax: 30% of taxable profit	1,650	1,650	1,650	1,650	2,400

In 20X1, Sriya Company records the current tax expense as follows:

| Income Tax Expense | 1,650 | |
| Income Tax Payable | | 1,650 |

It recognizes a current tax liability of ₹1,650 in 20X1. In 20X2, it pays and records the following entry:

| Income Tax Payable | 1,650 | |
| Cash | | 1,650 |

If Sriya Company had paid an advance tax of ₹1,500 in 20X1 based on its estimate of taxable profit, it presents a current tax liability of ₹150 in 20X1. If it had paid an advance tax of ₹2,000, it presents an asset for a tax refund of ₹350.

TEST YOUR UNDERSTANDING 9.2
Calculating Current Tax Expense

Continuing with Handhold 9.4, calculate Sriya Company's current tax expense for 20X2 to 20X5 assuming the following tax rates: 35% in 20X2; 40% in 20X3; 25% in 20X4; and 20% in 20X5.

Minimum Alternative Tax

Tax payable on taxable profit is a *normal tax*. **Minimum alternative tax (MAT)** is a tax calculated on accounting profit. A company must pay the *higher* of normal tax and MAT. The effect of MAT is that companies with zero taxable profit pay tax and companies with a low taxable profit pay a tax larger than a *normal tax*. To illustrate, assume that Abhinav Company has to pay MAT at 15 per cent and normal tax at 30 per cent for three years. Let us look at four cases:

Case	Description	Taxable Profit	Normal Tax Rate	Normal Tax	Accounting Profit	MAT Rate	MAT	Tax Status	Tax Payment
1	MAT > Normal Tax	₹ 0	30%	₹ 0	₹20,000	15%	₹3,000	MAT	₹3,000
2	MAT > Normal Tax	8,000	30	2,400	20,000	15	3,000	MAT	3,000
3	MAT = Normal Tax	10,000	30	3,000	20,000	15	3,000	Normal	3,000
4	MAT < Normal Tax	12,000	30	3,600	20,000	15	3,000	Normal	3,600

Case 1: It has no taxable profit, but has an accounting profit. So it pays MAT of ₹3,000.

Case 2: It has a taxable profit, but normal tax is less than MAT. So it pays MAT of ₹3,000.

Case 3: Normal tax is equal to MAT. So it pays normal tax of ₹3,000.

Case 4: Normal tax is more than MAT. So it pays normal tax of ₹3,600.

MAT credit   MAT is current tax and is expensed as incurred. However, MAT paid can be carried forward and adjusted against normal tax payable in a specified number of future years. This is known as *MAT credit*, which is treated as a recoverable during that period. In Year 1, assume Case 1: Abhinav Company paid MAT of ₹3,000. It can claim credit for the amount from normal tax payable in the future. Suppose in Year 2, it has a taxable profit of ₹15,000 and an accounting profit of ₹14,000. Its normal tax is ₹4,500 and MAT is ₹2,100. So it pays normal tax, but can claim MAT credit. Since it must pay a *minimum* of ₹2,100, it claims MAT credit of ₹2,400 and pays a *normal tax* of ₹2,100. It carries forward the unutilized MAT credit of ₹600 (i.e. Year 1 MAT paid, ₹3,000 – Year 2 MAT credit utilized, ₹2,400). Suppose in Year 3, it has a taxable profit of ₹18,000 and an accounting profit of ₹15,000. Its normal tax is ₹5,400 and MAT is ₹2,250. It pays a normal tax of ₹4,800, after claiming the remaining MAT credit of ₹600.

Deferred Tax

Differences between accounting profit and taxable profit may be permanent or temporary. *Permanent differences* do not have future tax effects. For example, tax-free interest income is not taxable in current or future periods. In contrast, *temporary differences* have future tax effects. We will study them now.

Learning Objective

LO 7 Account for deferred income tax.

Temporary differences arise when revenues, expenses, gains or losses are included in taxable profit earlier or later than they are recognized in accounting profit. A temporary difference is the difference between the tax base and the carrying amount of an asset or liability. *Tax base* (or *tax basis*) is the amount of an asset or liability determined in accordance with the tax law. *Carrying amount* is the amount reported in the financial statements.

Let's take some items to understand whether they are permanent or temporary differences.

HANDHOLD 9.5
Permanent Differences and Temporary Differences

1. *A copyright depreciated equally over ten years for accounting and equally over five years for tax:* Since the tax depreciation is more than the accounting depreciation in Years 1 to 5, accounting profit will exceed taxable profit. There will be no tax depreciation in Years 6 to 10 but accounting depreciation will continue. As a result, taxable profit will exceed accounting profit. It is a temporary difference. Tax base is the cost of the copyright less cumulative depreciation allowed for tax. Carrying amount is the cost less accumulated depreciation in the financial statements.

2. *Product development cost amortized in accounting over five years but deductible when paid:* Since the tax law allows full deduction on payment, accounting profit will exceed taxable profit in Year 1. In Years 2 to 5, taxable profit will exceed accounting profit because of the amortization charge in accounting. It is a temporary difference. Tax base is zero, since the entire expenditure has been deducted for tax. Carrying amount is the unamortized product development cost in the financial statements.

3. *Capital gain on sale of house not taxable:* Capital gain increases accounting profit but has no effect on taxable profit now or later. It is a permanent difference.

4. *Fine paid for violation of factory safety regulations not deductible:* Fine paid decreases accounting profit but has no effect on taxable profit now or later. It is a permanent difference.

5. *Expected credit losses not deductible but loss accounts written off deductible:* Allowance for expected credit losses decreases accounting profit. Since it is not deductible, taxable profit will exceed accounting profit. In the year in which a receivable is written off accounting profit will exceed taxable profit. It is a temporary difference. Tax base is zero, since the allowance is not deductible. Carrying amount is the amount of expected credit loss.

TEST YOUR
UNDERSTANDING 9.3
Permanent Differences
and Temporary
Differences
Determine whether the items below result in a permanent or temporary difference.
  (a) Profit earned from a business in a special economic zone not taxable.
  (b) Contribution paid to a charitable hospital not deductible.
  (c) Revenue received in advance taxable.
  (d) Dividend received from a subsidiary not taxable.
  (e) Allowance for credit losses not deductible but actual losses written off are deductible.
  (f) Accrued interest expense deductible on payment.

QUICK QUESTION
Tax base

Suppose research costs are expensed as incurred for determining accounting profit but allowed for tax purposes in one or more future periods. What is the tax base of research costs?

ONE-MINUTE QUIZ 9.2
Temporary Differences

A temporary difference arises in which of the following cases? There may be more than one correct answer.
  (a) A revenue is recognized before it is taxable.
  (b) A revenue is recognized after it is taxable.
  (c) An expense is recognized before it is deductible.
  (d) An expense is recognized after is deductible.

Deferred Tax Liability

In Vipul's Company's illustration (Exhibit 9.1), the tax base of the computer in Year 1 is ₹15,000, i.e. cost ₹30,000 less cumulative tax depreciation ₹15,000. By Year 2, the asset is fully depreciated. As a result, the tax base is zero in Year 2 and Year 3. Exhibit 9.2 presents these calculations.

EXHIBIT 9.2
Tax Base

Year	Cost (A)	Tax Depreciation Allowance (B)	Cumulative Tax Depreciation (C)	Tax Base (D)
		50% of (A) in Year 1 and Year 2		(A – C)
1	₹30,000	₹15,000	₹15,000	₹15,000
2	30,000	15,000	30,000	0
3	30,000	0	30,000	0

Vipul Company depreciates the asset on a straight-line basis over three years. So the annual depreciation expense is ₹10,000. In Year 1, the carrying amount is ₹20,000 (cost, ₹30,000 – accumulated depreciation, ₹10,000). In Year 2, it is ₹10,000 (cost, ₹30,000 – accumulated depreciation, ₹20,000). By Year 3, the computer is fully depreciated and its carrying amount is zero. Exhibit 9.3 presents these calculations.

EXHIBIT 9.3
Carrying Amount

Year	Cost (A)	Depreciation Expense (B) 1/3 of (A)	Accumulated Depreciation (C)	Carrying Amount (D) (A – C)
1	₹30,000	₹10,000	₹10,000	₹20,000
2	30,000	10,000	20,000	10,000
3	30,000	10,000	30,000	0

In Year 1, the carrying amount is ₹20,000 and the tax base is ₹15,000. The temporary difference of ₹5,000 is taxable. Therefore, it is a **taxable temporary difference**. The tax on a taxable temporary difference is a **deferred tax liability**. At the tax rate of 30 per cent, the deferred tax liability on Vipul Company's computer is ₹1,500 at the end of Year 1. At the end of the asset's life, both the taxable temporary difference and deferred tax liability become zero. Exhibit 9.4 presents deferred tax liability calculations for Vipul Company's computer.

EXHIBIT 9.4
Calculating Deferred
Tax Liability

Year	Tax Base (A)	Carrying Amount (B)	Taxable Temporary Difference (C)	Deferred Tax Liability (D)
	From Exhibit 9.2	From Exhibit 9.3	(A) – (B)	30% of (C)
1	₹15,000	₹20,000	₹ 5,000	₹1,500
2	0	10,000	10,000	3,000
3	0	0	0	0

Note that the carrying amount and the tax base are equal both at the beginning and at the end of the asset's useful life. The difference between them *originates* in periods in which the tax depreciation allowance is more than the accounting depreciation expense – the position in the early part of the asset's life because of generous tax benefits for new assets. The position *reverses* in subsequent years.

A machine costs ₹10,000 and has an estimated useful life of 10 years and no residual value. Accounting follows straight-line depreciation. For tax purposes, the asset is depreciated equally over four years. The tax rate is 30 per cent. Calculate the deferred tax liability on the asset over its life.

Accumulated depreciation for an asset is as follows: 20X1, ₹30,000; 20X2, ₹90,000; 20X3, ₹180,000. Cumulative tax depreciation allowance for the asset is as follows: 20X1, ₹100,000; 20X2, ₹150,000; 20X3, ₹180,000.

(a) Calculate the deferred tax liability. The tax rate is 30 per cent.
(b) Rework your answer to (a) assuming that the tax rate is 30 per cent in 20X1 and 25 per cent in 20X2 and 20X3.

TEST YOUR UNDERSTANDING 9.4
Calculating Deferred Tax Liability

TEST YOUR UNDERSTANDING 9.5
Calculating Deferred Tax Liability

Deferred Tax Expense and Income Tax Expense

Income tax expense comprises current tax expense and deferred tax expense. **Deferred tax expense** is measured as the *change* in deferred tax liability over the period. Vipul Company's deferred tax expense is calculated as follows: Year 1, ₹1,500 (Year 1, ₹1,500 – Year 0, ₹0); Year 2, ₹1,500 (Year 2, ₹3,000 – Year 1, ₹1,500); Year 3, – ₹3,000 (Year 3, ₹0 – Year 2, ₹3,000). Exhibit 9.5 presents the calculation of Vipul Company's deferred tax expense and income tax expense.

Year	Deferred Tax Liability (A) From Exhibit 9.4	Deferred Tax Expense (B) Change in (A)	Current Tax Expense (C) From Exhibit 9.1	Income Tax Expense (D) (B) + (C)
1	₹1,500	₹1,500	₹10,500	₹12,000
2	3,000	1,500	10,500	12,000
3	0	– 3,000	15,000	12,000

EXHIBIT 9.5
Deferred Tax Expense and Income Tax Expense

The deferred tax expense of ₹1,500 of each in Year 1 and Year 2 results from *originating* temporary differences and the amount of – ₹3,000 in Year 3 is the effect of *reversing* of those differences. Exhibit 9.6 shows the presentation of income tax expense in Vipul Company's statement of profit and loss.

		Year 1		Year 2		Year 3	
Profit before depreciation and tax.............................			₹50,000		₹50,000		₹50,000
Depreciation expense			10,000		10,000		10,000
Profit before tax..			40,000		40,000		40,000
Income tax expense: Current tax	₹10,500			₹10,500		₹15,000	
Deferred tax	1,500	12,000		1,500	12,000	– 3,000	12,000
Profit after tax...			28,000		28,000		28,000

EXHIBIT 9.6
Presenting Income Tax Expense in Statement of Profit and Loss

Marginal Tax Rate, Effective Tax Rate, and Deferred Tax Accounting

An enterprise must pay tax on its taxable profit at the rate specified in the tax law. This is the **marginal tax rate**, or **statutory tax rate**. Vipul Company's marginal tax rate is 30 per cent. For example, in Year 1 the company has to pay a tax of ₹10,500 on its taxable profit of ₹35,000 at 30 per cent. The Finance Act enacted by Parliament every year specifies the marginal tax rate.

Effective tax rate is the rate at which an enterprise pays tax on its profit. It is measured as the ratio of income tax expense to accounting profit. It tells us about an enterprise's *tax burden*. If we take tax as only current tax, Vipul Company's effective tax rate for is 26.25 per cent (10,500/40,000) in both Year 1 and Year 2, and 37.5 per cent in Year 3 (15,000/40,000). This gives an incomplete idea of the effect of tax on the enterprise because it ignores the effect of temporary differences between accounting and tax, which are bound to even out over time. We have seen how this works in the case of depreciation. Considering only current tax expense distorts the tax burden and is likely to mislead the users of the financial statements on the true taxation cost. Therefore, we should learn to think of income tax expense as consisting of both current tax expense and deferred tax expense. Applying this concept, we get an effective tax rate of 30 per cent for each year (12,000/40,000). This is reasonable. If the profit from operations and the marginal tax rate are constant over time, the enterprise's tax burden should also be constant. Exhibit 9.7 sums up the position of taxable profit, accounting profit, deferred tax and tax rates. It also sums up the discussion so far on deferred tax.

EXHIBIT 9.7

Marginal Tax Rate and Effective Tax Rate: Deferred Tax Liability

	Tax			Accounting		
	20X1	20X2	20X3	20X1	20X2	20X3
Profit	₹35,000	₹35,000	₹50,000	₹40,000	₹40,000	₹40,000
Current tax expense	10,500	10,500	15,000	10,500	10,500	15,000
Income tax expense	10,500	10,500	15,000	12,000	12,000	12,000
Tax rate: Current tax expense/Profit	30%	30%	30%	26.25%	26.25%	37.5%
Tax rate: Income tax expense/Profit	30%	30%	30%	30%	30%	30%

Vipul Company records the income tax expense consisting of current and deferred components for each year as follows:

Year 1:

Year 1	Income Tax Expense	12,000	
	Income Tax Payable		10,500
	Deferred Tax Liability		1,500

As a result of this entry, the deferred tax liability of ₹1,500 *originates*. In Year 1, the Deferred Tax Liability account has a balance of ₹1,500, as shown below:

Deferred Tax Liability

	Year 1	*Originating*	*1,500*
		Ending Balance	*1,500*

Year 2:

Year 2	Income Tax Expense	12,000	
	Income Tax Payable		10,500
	Deferred Tax Liability		1,500

When we record the income tax expense for Year 2, a further deferred tax liability of ₹1,500 *originates*. As a result, the balance in the Deferred Tax Liability account increases by ₹1,500. In Year 2, the account has a balance of ₹3,000, as shown below:

Deferred Tax Liability

	Year 1	Originating	1,500
		Ending Balance	1,500
	Year 2	*Originating*	*1,500*
		Ending Balance	*3,000*

Year 3:

Year 3	Income Tax Expense	12,000	
	Deferred Tax Liability	3,000	
	Income Tax Payable		15,000

When we record the income tax expense for Year 3, the accumulated deferred tax liability *reverses* and the balance becomes zero, as shown below:

Deferred Tax Liability

			Year 1	Originating	1,500
				Ending Balance	1,500
			Year 2	Originating	1,500
				Ending Balance	3,000
Year 3	*Reversing*	*3,000*	*Year 3*	*Ending Balance*	*0*

Here are some more examples of taxable temporary differences.

- *Unrealized gains:* Accounting recognizes fair value gains on investments. But they may be taxed when they are realized.

- *Expenses allowed earlier when paid:* Prepaid expenses may be deductible for tax when paid but recognized in accounting later in the relevant period.

- *Revenues taxed later when received:* Revenue from instalment sales may be taxed when instalments are received after the revenue is recognized in accounting.

A taxable temporary difference may arise even when a gain is not recognized in the statement of profit and loss. Gain on revaluation is an example. Revaluation increases the carrying amount of an asset. However, the tax authorities do not allow higher depreciation because of revaluation. So the tax base of an asset is not increased by the difference between an asset's fair value and carrying amount. But this difference represents future benefits from either using or disposing of the asset and these benefits are taxable. As a result, revaluation gives rise to a deferred tax liability.

Deferred Tax Asset

Suppose Simran Company has an accounting profit of ₹60,000 per year for three years. It recognizes an allowance for credit losses of ₹12,000 in Year 1; the actual credit loss is ₹9,000 in Year 2 and ₹3,000 in Year 3. The tax authorities allow only actual losses written off. Assume a tax rate of 30 per cent. Exhibit 9.8 presents the calculation of the company's current tax expense.

	Year 1	Year 2	Year 3
Accounting profit	₹60,000	₹60,000	₹60,000
Add Allowance for credit losses	12,000	0	0
Deduct Actual loss written off	0	9,000	3,000
Taxable profit	72,000	51,000	57,000
Current tax expense: 30% of taxable profit	21,600	15,300	17,100

EXHIBIT 9.8
Current Tax Expense

The sum of the accounting profit for the three years is ₹180,000. It is the same as the sum of the taxable profit for the three years. The difference between the accounting profit and the taxable profit for Year 1 is a temporary difference. The right to deduct actual losses in determining taxable profit in future periods results in a lower taxable profit in those periods. It is a **deductible temporary difference**. It gives rise to a **deferred tax asset**: the amount of income tax recoverable in future periods in respect of deductible temporary differences. We will now see how to account for it.

Year 1: The carrying amount of the allowance for credit losses is ₹12,000 and its tax base is zero. The temporary difference is ₹12,000. Since the tax authorities will allow the actual loss in future periods, this is a deductible temporary difference. Since the related income tax is recoverable, a deferred tax asset of ₹3,600 (30 per cent of ₹12,000) originates in Year 1. The following entry records the income tax expense consisting of current tax expense and deferred tax income (i.e. future tax benefit) and recognizes the deferred tax asset:

Year 1	Income Tax Expense	18,000	
	Deferred Tax Asset	3,600	
	Income Tax Payable		21,600

Deferred tax asset of ₹3,600 *originates*. In Year 1, the Deferred Tax Asset account has a balance of ₹3,600, as shown below:

Deferred Tax Asset

| Year 1 | *Originating* | 3,600 | |
| | *Ending Balance* | 3,600 | |

Year 2: The tax authorities allow the actual loss of ₹9,000. As a result, deferred tax asset reverses to the extent of ₹2,700 (30 per cent of ₹9,000). Simran Company records the following entry to recognize the income tax expense and the reversal:

Year 2	Income Tax Expense	18,000	
	Income Tax Payable		15,300
	Deferred Tax Asset		2,700

The balance in the Deferred Tax Asset account would be reduced by ₹2,700 and, in Year 2, the account would show a balance of ₹900, as shown below:

Deferred Tax Asset

Year 1	Originating	3,600			
	Ending Balance	3,600			
Year 2	Ending Balance	900	Year 2	Reversing	2,700

Year 3: The tax authorities allow the remaining loss of ₹3,000. The balance of the deferred tax asset of ₹900 (30 per cent of ₹3,000) reverses. The following entry records the income tax expense and the reversal:

Year 3	Income Tax Expense	18,000	
	Income Tax Payable		17,100
	Deferred Tax Asset		900

We can now summarize the Deferred Tax Asset account:

Deferred Tax Asset

Year 1	Originating	3,600			
	Ending Balance	3,600			
Year 2	Ending Balance	900	Year 2	Reversing	2,700
Year 3	Ending Balance	0	Year 3	Reversing	900

Exhibit 9.9 sums up the position of taxable profit, accounting profit, deferred tax and tax rates. Here again, we note that defining income tax expense as consisting of both current and deferred tax measures the tax burden accurately.

EXHIBIT 9.9

Marginal Tax Rate and Effective Tax Rate: Deferred Tax Asset

	Tax			Accounting		
	Year 1	Year 2	Year 3	Year 1	Year 2	Year 3
Profit	₹72,000	₹51,000	₹57,000	₹60,000	₹60,000	₹60,000
Current tax expense	21,600	15,300	17,100	21,600	15,300	17,100
Income tax expense	21,600	15,300	17,100	18,000	18,000	18,000
Tax rate: Current tax expense/Profit	30%	30%	30%	36%	25.5%	28.5%
Tax rate: Income tax expense/Profit	30%	30%	30%	30%	30%	30%

Here are some more examples of deductible temporary differences.

- *Estimated liabilities:* Accounting recognizes estimated warranty liability in order to match warranty expense with sales revenue. However, the tax authorities do not allow provisions for estimated expenses. They allow warranty expense only on payment or when a definite liability exists.

- *Unrealized losses:* Accounting recognizes asset impairment losses, fair value losses on investments and inventory write-downs. But the tax authorities allow only actual losses.

- *Expenses allowed later on payment:* The tax law allows deduction of certain items for computing taxable profit in the year in which they are paid. Examples are payables for tax, duty or cess, employer's contribution to provident fund, pension fund or gratuity fund, interest on bank loan and compensated absence. But accounting recognizes these items on accrual.

- *Revenue taxed earlier on receipt:* Receipts (e.g. subscriptions received in advance) may be taxed before they are recognized as revenue in accounting later.

An enterprise should recognize deferred tax assets only when it is probable that taxable profits will be available against which the deductible temporary differences can be utilized.

Karuna Company's taxable profit is ₹100,000 for 20X1 and ₹85,000 for 20X2. The 20X1 taxable profit includes interest receipt of ₹15,000 that will be recognized in accounting in 20X2. The tax rate is 30 per cent. The current tax expense is ₹30,000 in 20X1 and ₹25,500 in 20X2. Since the interest receipt was taxed prior to its recognition, it will not be taxed again when recognized. In 20X1, the carrying amount of the item is ₹15,000 and its tax base is nil. The temporary difference is ₹15,000. This is a deductible temporary difference because the amount will not be taxed again in 20X2. It gives rise to a deferred tax asset of ₹4,500 (30 per cent of ₹15,000) in 20X1 which will reverse in 20X2. The following entry records the income tax expense, deferred tax asset and tax payable in 20X1:

HANDHOLD 9.6
Deferred Tax Asset: Deductible Temporary Differences

20X1	Income Tax Expense	25,500	
	Deferred Tax Asset	4,500	
	Income Tax Payable		30,000

As a result of this entry, the income tax expense for 20X1 is reduced by ₹4,500. This reduction in income tax expense can be thought of as deferred tax income, i.e. a lower charge to income tax expense because of deferred tax asset. The following entry records the income tax expense, reversal of deferred tax asset and tax payable in 20X2:

20X2	Income Tax Expense	30,000	
	Income Tax Payable		25,500
	Deferred Tax Asset		4,500

In 20X1, Shashank Company reported an accounting profit of ₹50,000 after recognizing estimated warranty expense of ₹3,000. The tax authorities disallowed the expense in that year but would allow it later on actual payment. The tax rate was 30 per cent. Prepare the journal entry to record the income tax expense.

TEST YOUR UNDERSTANDING 9.6
Calculating Deferred Tax Asset from Deductible Temporary Differences

Deferred tax assets can also arise from carryforward unused tax losses and unused tax credits. We will discuss these now.

Unused Tax Loss Carryforward

The tax authorities allow current period tax losses to be carried forward to future periods and deducted from future taxable profits, subject to conditions. Tax loss carryforwards would represent future economic benefits, provided an enterprise can make profits in the future and deduct the losses from future taxable profits. In India, tax loss can be carried forward for eight years, after which it lapses. The tax depreciation component of tax loss (commonly known as *unabsorbed depreciation* in India) can be carried forward for an indefinite number of years. To illustrate, suppose Maria Company has a tax loss of ₹30,000 in Year 1 and there are no taxable temporary differences. Assume that it is probable sufficient taxable profit will be available in Year 2 against which the tax loss can be utilized. The tax rate is 30 per cent. The company records the following entry in Year 1:

Year 1	Deferred Tax Asset..	9,000	
	Income Tax Expense		9,000

The tax recoverable of ₹9,000 (30 per cent of ₹30,000) is an asset.

Suppose Maria Company's taxable profit in Year 2 is ₹50,000, equal to its accounting profit. The company's current tax expense is ₹15,000 (30 per cent of ₹50,000). The following entry records the income tax expense for Year 2:

Year 2	Income Tax Expense..	15,000	
	Income Tax Payable		15,000

To the extent of the deferred tax asset of ₹9,000 from past taxable loss, it does not have to pay tax. Therefore, the net tax payable is ₹6,000. The following entry records this payment:

Year 2	Income Tax Payable..	15,000	
	Deferred Tax Asset..		9,000
	Cash		6,000

Exhibit 9.10 shows the statement of profit and loss for the two years.

EXHIBIT 9.10

Presenting Deferred Tax Asset from Tax Loss Carryforward in Statement of Profit and Loss

	Year 1	Year 2
Profit before tax	− ₹30,000	₹50,000
Income tax expense: Current tax..	− 9,000	15,000
Profit after tax	− 21,000	35,000

Unused Tax Credit Carryforward

In India, the tax authorities allow MAT paid in a year to be adjusted against normal tax payable within 10 years. This is an example of tax credit forward. Unused tax credits would represent future economic benefits if an enterprise can make sufficient taxable profit in future periods and avail of the credits.

Suppose in Year 1 Vaibhav Company has an accounting profit of ₹20,000 and has no taxable profit or taxable temporary differences. Assume a MAT rate of 15 per cent, a normal tax rate of 30 per cent and unused MAT credit carryforward period of 10 years. So it pays a MAT of ₹3,000 that can be adjusted against normal tax in future periods. The following entries record this transaction:

Income Tax Expense..	3,000	
Income Tax Payable		3,000
Recognized MAT payable		
Income Tax Payable..	3,000	
Cash		3,000
Paid MAT		
Deferred Tax Asset...	3,000	
Income Tax Expense		3,000
Recognized deferred tax for MAT credit		

Suppose in Year 2 it has a taxable profit of ₹25,000, equal to its accounting profit. Its normal tax is ₹7,500. After adjusting the MAT credit of ₹3,000 from Year 1, it pays ₹4,500. The following entries record this transaction:

Income Tax Expense..	7,500	
Income Tax Payable		7,500
Recognized income tax payable		
Income Tax Payable...	7,500	
Deferred Tax Asset..		3,000
Cash		4,500
Paid income tax after adjusting MAT credit		

Exhibit 9.11 shows the statement of profit and loss for the two years.

	Year 1	Year 2
Profit before tax..	₹20,000	₹25,000
Income tax expense: Current tax..	3,000	7,500
MAT credit	– 3,000	0
	0	7,500
Profit after tax..	20,000	17,500

EXHIBIT 9.11
Presenting Deferred Tax Asset from Unused Tax Credit Carryforward in Statement of Profit and Loss

Deferred tax asset arising from tax loss carryforward or unused tax credit carryforward is similar to a receivable from the tax department and is realized by paying a lower tax in the future. Note that it does not reverse, but adjusted at the time of paying tax.

When an enterprise has been incurring losses lately, it may be optimistic to think that it can turn profitable in future. In such cases, deferred tax asset from tax loss or tax credit should be recognized only to the extent that it has sufficient taxable temporary differences or there is strong evidence that sufficient taxable profit will be available against the tax loss or tax credit can be utilized. In practice, such evidence is hard to come by.

ONE-MINUTE QUIZ 9.3
Deferred Tax Accounting

Joy Company buys for the use of its chief executive a watch costing ₹1 million with an estimated useful life of five years and no residual value. The tax rate is 30 per cent. Depreciation on the asset is not allowed for tax purposes, and any gain or loss on disposal would not be taxable or deductible. How much deferred tax asset should Joy Company recognize for the item?
(a) ₹300,000.
(b) ₹240,000.
(c) ₹60,000.
(d) ₹0.

Presenting Income Taxes in the Financial Statements

The periodic income tax expense related to profit or loss from ordinary activities should be presented in the statement of profit and loss. Tax effects on items recognized in other comprehensive income should be recognized in other comprehensive income. Current tax assets can be offset against current tax liabilities only if an entity has a legally enforceable right to set off the amounts. The right of set-off is normally available within a tax jurisdiction but not across tax jurisdictions. Even within a tax jurisdiction, there may be restrictions. For example, advance income tax paid for a year can be deducted while paying the final tax; so the two can be offset. However, tax refund receivable for a year can't be deducted from tax payable for another year.

FINANCIAL VIEW
Understanding Deferred Tax Information

The 2016 annual report of Reliance Industries Limited illustrates accounting and presentation of deferred tax liability and deferred tax asset. The deferred tax liability as on March 31 comprises the following:

			In billions	
		2016		**2015**
Deferred tax liability (net)				
(a) Deferred tax liability:				
Related to fixed assets..		₹220		₹200
(b) Deferred tax assets:				
Related to fixed assets..	₹2		₹1	
Disallowance under the Income Tax Act 1961	4		3	
Carried forward losses of subsidiaries...........................	76	82	66	70
		138		130

The item *Related to fixed assets* under deferred tax liability refers to assets that have higher tax depreciation than accounting depreciation. Most of the fixed assets would be of this type. The item *Related to fixed assets* under deferred tax assets refers to assets that have higher accounting depreciation than tax depreciation. The item *Disallowance under the Income Tax Act 1961* relates to expenses that have been accrued but will be allowed when paid under Sec. 43B of the Act. These three items will reverse in the normal course and don't pose any difficulty to analysts. The item *Carried forward losses of subsidiaries* refers to the tax loss carryforward of subsidiaries. This is a big amount, so it requires closer examination. How likely is it that the subsidiaries will become profitable and be able to claim the tax losses in the future? The analyst should look at the recent performance of the subsidiaries, industry conditions and other relevant factors before treating them as assets.

Employee Benefits

Learning Objective

LO 8 **Account for employee benefits.**

Many organizations provide a variety of benefits to their employees. **Employee benefits** are salaries, wages, bonus, paid leave, employer's contribution to provident fund and state insurance, retrenchment compensation, gratuity, pension, health care and other kinds of reward given to employees for their services to an entity. Employee benefits can be of the following types:

(a) *In-service benefits* are provided during employees' service. Salaries, wages, bonus, paid leave, cash for unused leave, health care, cars, housing, club membership, employer's contribution to provident fund and state insurance, and loyalty rewards are in-service benefits.

(b) *Post-employment benefits* are provided after employees' separation, i.e. retirement, resignation, dismissal, or death. Provident fund, gratuity, commuted pension, monthly pension, health care, and retrenchment compensation are examples of such benefits.

We will now illustrate how to recognize the benefits.

In-service benefits   Most in-service benefits, such as salaries, wages and bonus are paid in the normal course of operations and expensed. Some benefits may be paid in subsequent periods. Paid leave is an example. There are many types of paid leave such as study leave, sick leave, maternity or paternity leave, casual leave, and earned leave (vacation pay). Most types of paid leave (e.g. such as study leave, sick leave, maternity or paternity leave and casual leave) should be used in the reporting period in which the employees get the entitlement. The related expense is usually a part of the payroll expense.

Earned leave may be carried forward to and used in future periods. The expected cost of such leave should be recognized when the employees render service. Earned leave may be either *vesting* (cash payment for unused leave, or leave encashment) or *non-vesting* (no cash payment for unused leave). In either case, an obligation exists which the enterprise must recognize. The obligation would equal the additional amount that the enterprise expects to pay for the unused entitlement.

HANDHOLD 9.7
Paid Leave

Ganesh Company allows its employees 10 days of paid leave every year. Employees can carry forward unused leave to the next year, at the end of which it will lapse. The company has 20 employees. Suppose in Year 1 the average unused leave is three days per employee. The leave is taken first out of the current year's entitlement and then out of any balance brought forward from the previous year (LIFO basis). From past experience, the company expects 15 employees to take not more than 10 days of leave on average in Year 2, and the remaining five employees to take 12 days on average. In Year 1, the company has no obligation to the 15 employees because they will take all or some of their leave entitlement for Year 2 and there is no further need to draw on their Year 1 unused leave. Any unused leave from Year 1 will lapse at the end of Year 2. However, the other five employees will use up all the entitlement for Year 2 and will, in addition draw on their Year 1 unused leave to the extent of two days. (They cannot carry forward the remaining one day of leave not taken because it will lapse in Year 2.) Therefore, at the end of Year 1, the company has an obligation for 10 days of leave: 5 employees × 2 days per employee. If the average daily wage is ₹1,000, the estimated obligation will be ₹10,000.

Post-employment benefits   These benefits are of two types:
1. Defined contribution plans; and
2. Defined benefit plans.

Defined contribution plans   In a defined contribution plan (DCP), the enterprise often agrees to contribute to a separate trust fund to provide for the payment of post-employment benefits to its employees. The amount of annual contribution is determined by agreement between the enterprise and its employees. The employee may also contribute to the fund. The benefits depend solely on the amounts contributed to, and income accumulated in the fund.

In India, provident fund (PF) is a common DCP required for most of the enterprises. The National Pension System (NPS) is a DCP for government employees who joined service on or after January 1, 2004. It has been extended to non-government employees. In addition, some enterprises may have their own DCPs such as employee welfare fund and savings plans. The key point is that a DCP does not promise a specified amount to its beneficiaries.

Accounting for the cost of benefits under a DCP is fairly straightforward. The enterprise should recognize its contribution as an expense as part of the payroll and a corresponding payment, or liability if the contribution has not been paid.

Defined benefit plans   In a defined benefit plan (DBP), the enterprise is required to provide post-employment benefits to its employees, determined by reference to a formula normally based on employees' remuneration and years of service. Pension and gratuity are common examples of DBP. The enterprise should estimate the amount of annual contribution necessary to meet the retirement obligations that will arise in the future. Assurance of a minimum interest rate on the balance in the PF account could make it a DBP.

When a DBP is funded, the annual contributions are paid into a separate trust fund which disburses the benefits. When a DBP is not funded, the enterprise pays the benefits as they fall due. In a DBP, the employer is obliged to provide the promised retirement benefits regardless of the funding arrangements made. For example, if the trust fund does not have sufficient assets, the employer must make up the shortfall. Sometimes the employer may appoint a fund manager to administer the assets. The fund manager, usually an insurer or a pension fund, is not responsible for paying the defined benefits. The employer should make good any deficiency in the fund assets by periodic top-ups.

Determining liability under DBPs is complex. An *actuary* – an expert on insurance risk assessment – is engaged to prepare a valuation of the company's liability for pension and other benefits. Primarily designed to calculate funding requirements, actuarial valuations are also used to determine the expense to be recognized. The annual expense includes the following items:

- Current service cost;
- Interest cost; and
- Expected return on plan assets.

Other items are actuarial gains and losses, past service costs, and the effects of any curtailments or settlements.

Suppose that an employee of Abhiman Company is entitled to a pension of ₹1,000 per year of service. Currently, he is 30 years of age and will retire at 60. The actuary estimates that the company's employees will have a life expectancy of 80 years. Thus, the employee will receive ₹1,000 per year for each year of service for 20 years after his retirement. He will receive the first pension at the age of 61. The following time-line shows the position:		**HANDHOLD 9.8** Pensions

Employee earns pension of ₹1,000 each year for 30 years	Employee gets pension of ₹1,000 each year for each year of service for 20 years
Now employee is 30 years old	Employee will retire at 60, i.e. 30 years from now

Employee is expected to live up to 80 years, i.e. for 20 years after retirement

Assuming a discount rate of 10 per cent, at the time of his retirement this annuity of ₹1,000 per year will be worth ₹8,514: ₹1,000 × 8.5136 (Appendix C, Table 4). This sum is receivable 30 years from now. The present value of this sum is ₹488: ₹8,514 × 0.0573 (Appendix C, Table 3). This is the *current service cost* for Year 1 of the employee's service. The current service cost for Year 2 will be ₹536: 8514 × 0.0630. Note that we now discount for 29 years. Besides, the obligation of ₹488 for Year 1 has grown by ₹48 by the end of Year 2. This is the effect of compounding and is the *interest cost*. (This is known as 'unwinding'.) We will assume that the company funds its pension liability and deposits the amount of liability with a trust which will invest the funds in specified assets. Assume further that the plan administrator expects to earn a return of 8 per cent over the long-term on plan assets. The expected return on plan assets in Year 2 will be ₹39. (Since we invested only at the end of Year 1, there was no return in that year.) With these numbers we can set up the pension expense schedule:

	Year 1	Year 2
Current service cost	₹488	₹536
Interest cost	0	48
Expected return on plan assets	(0)	(39)
Pension cost	488	545

TEST YOUR UNDERSTANDING 9.7
Pensions

Continuing with Handhold 9.8, calculate the pension expense for Year 3.

ONE-MINUTE QUIZ 9.4
Employment Benefits

Which of the following would increase pension cost?

	Discount rate	Return on plan assets
(a)	Increase	Increase
(b)	Increase	Decrease
(c)	Decrease	Increase
(d)	Decrease	Decrease

FINANCIAL VIEW
Pension Funds and Interest Rates

A lot of people enjoy low-interest rates, but pension funds don't. Pension liabilities and interest rates have a hostile relationship. The discount rate is an important part of the calculation of pension liability. The lower the discount rate, the higher the present value of pension liability. In recent years, interest rates have come down worldwide. Some countries even have negative interest rates, i.e. you pay the bank to keep your money.

Pension funds invest in government securities and corporate bonds. Low-interest rates reduce the interest income from their investments and exacerbate the increase in pension liability caused by low discount rate. This double whammy of low return on pension fund assets and low discount rate leads to a "black hole" in the funds. Pension fund regulators often require companies to increase contributions to reduce the deficit. The increase in cash outflow leaves companies with less cash for investment and dividends. If pension funds may hold equity investments, they would have less dividend income to meet their pension payment obligations. They face the risk of defaulting on their obligations. Pension fund managers have no option but to pray for an increase in the market interest rate and/or their pensioners' death rate.

The following examples illustrate the effect of low-interest rates on pension funds.

- *BHS*: This example appears in Introduction. The company was sold for the ridiculously low price of £1. If you consider that the company's DBP had a deficit, the deal looks much less sweet. The company was reported to have a £571-million deficit and it went into administration in April 2016.

- *Tata Steel UK*: When Tata Steel acquired Corus (formerly British Steel), the employees of Corus were covered by the British Steel Pension Scheme, a DBP. As Tata Steel's UK operation became unprofitable and was beginning to drown in debt, it wanted to convert the DBP into a DCP. The company had to engage in difficult negotiations to persuade the unions to agree to the change for its plant in Talbot, Wales. At one time, the hole in the pension fund was said to be £700 million but subsequent estimates were lower.

Contingent Liabilities

Learning Objective
LO 9 Explain Contingent Liabilities

A contingent liability is a potential liability. Whether it will be payable or not will depend on the outcome of an uncertain future event. Suppose Caring Bank gives a guarantee for the benefit of its customer, Just Dealer, to Best Wholesaler for the purchase of goods. If Just Dealer pays Best Wholesaler as agreed, Caring Bank has no obligation. However, if Just Dealer defaults, the bank will be required pay up. A contingent liability is "iffy". Contingent liabilities are disclosed unless the chances of loss are remote. For example, most frivolous lawsuits are dismissed (though some curious lawsuits have been won). However, if there is a reasonable chance of an event taking place and causing a liability, the likely loss should be estimated and provided for. For example, if a firm contests an income tax demand, it should estimate and provide for the probable liability. Evaluating contingent liabilities requires judgment based on business practices and legal position. It may be necessary to take legal advice in appropriate cases. Bills discounted, disputed taxes, product liability suits, and wage demands are common items of contingent liabilities.

HANDHOLD 9.9
Contingent Liability

Rex Company has received a legal notice demanding damages of ₹1 million for injury caused to a customer using the company's shampoo. What factors must the company consider in determining whether to record a liability?

Whether a liability is to be recorded would depend on the degree of likelihood of the company having to pay the damages. The factors that would aid the company in making the decision include the facts of the case (e.g. whether the customer actually bought the company's shampoo, used it, and suffered injury), past experience of the company in similar cases, past experience of other companies in the industry, relevant case law, opinion of the company's lawyer, reasonableness of the amount, and the company's policy on litigation (does it want to fight the case or settle the matter out of court?). The company should set up an estimated liability for an amount which it admits or believes is likely to become a liability eventually and disclose the balance of the claim as a contingent liability.

EARNINGS QUALITY ANALYSIS
Lawsuit against Tata Consultancy Services

According to the 2016 annual report of Tata Consultancy Services, in October 2014, Epic Systems Corporation filed a legal claim against the company for alleged unauthorized download and misuse of Epic's confidential information and trade secrets. In April 2016, the company received an unfavourable jury verdict awarding damages totalling ₹62.27 billion ($940 million) to Epic which the trial judge had indicated his intent to reduce. On the basis of legal opinion and legal precedence, the company expected to defend itself against the claim and believed that the claim would not sustain. Meanwhile, the uncertainty persists for the investor. The amount of claim was about 25 per cent of the profit for the year. However, parties sometimes settle cases outside court and some cases are dismissed. It is impossible to say how this case would proceed. Contingent liabilities are not in the financial statements but are buried in some footnote in small font. But that is no reason to ignore them altogether without analyzing the facts and the chances of a successful defence. As a matter of caution, analysts should assess the probability of contingent liabilities becoming liabilities.

FORENSIC CORNER
Operating Liabilities

Estimating pensions, warranties and taxes involve significant assumptions and judgment. It is not surprising that these are used to smooth earnings. Here are some tools used:

- Continuing to use high discount rates when interest rates have fallen.
- Assuming low life expectancy based on outdated mortality tables.
- Assuming high expected return on plan assets, sometimes so high that pension expense is negative.
- Sales staff using "side letters" to give extended warranty cover.
- Using past data to estimate warranty ignoring the recent experience of higher claims.
- Carrying deferred tax assets in the face of continuing losses.

Red flags signalling operating liabilities fraud:

- High levels of borrowing.
- An ageing workforce.
- High rates of product recalls and returns.
- Persistent, wide difference between effective and marginal tax rates.

APPLICATION
Provisions and Contingent Liabilities

Provisions, contingent liabilities and commitments reported by companies tell us about the risks in particular industries. Let's take some examples.

Provisions:

- Bharat Heavy Electricals Limited (BHEL) manufactures power plant equipment. The company's contracts with power-generating companies stipulate periodic maintenance and repairs when equipment breaks down. BHEL provides 2.5 per cent of contract revenue to meet warrant obligations.

- Steel Authority of India Limited (SAIL) has a large workforce (88,655 employees at April 1, 2016). SAIL's defined benefit plans are gratuity, cash payment for unused leave, provident fund, post-retirement health care benefits, post-retirement settlement benefits, family benefits, and long-term service award. At March 31, 2016, the company's assumptions included a discount rate of 8 per cent, expected return on plan assets of 8 per cent and a salary increase of 7 per cent. Life expectancy was based on the Indian Assured Lives Mortality (2006-08) table.

Contingent liabilities: Contingent liabilities relate to a variety of matters. Here is a sample:

- Claims from contractors for enhancement of the contract price, revision of work schedule with price escalation, compensation for the extended period of work and idle charges contested by the company, ₹95 billion (NTPC, March 2016).
- Disputed demand for one-time spectrum charge, ₹51 billion (Bharti Airtel, March 2016).
- Disputed demand for retrospective income tax on capital gains, ₹142 billion (Vodafone, December 2015).
- Guarantees given on behalf of constituents, ₹2,186 billion (State Bank of India, March 2016).

IFRS, IND AS AND INDIAN GAAP
Provisions, Income Taxes and Employee Benefits

Here are the key differences between these systems.

- *Provisions:* Both IFRS and Ind AS require provisions for legal and constructive obligations. Indian GAAP does not require provisions constructive obligations. Both IFRS and Ind AS require discounting of provisions when the effect of time value of money is material. Indian GAAP doesn't allow discounting. Both IFRS and Ind AS don't allow recognition of contingent assets but require disclosure if the benefits are probable. Indian GAAP allows neither recognition nor disclosure of contingent assets.
- *Income taxes:* Both IFRS and Ind AS require deferred taxes to be computed based on temporary differences between the carrying amounts of assets and liabilities and their tax base. Indian GAAP is based on timing differences in the statement of profit and loss. Both IFRS and Ind AS allow recognition of deferred tax asset for unused tax losses and tax credits to the extent it is probable that future taxable will be available. Indian GAAP requires virtual certainty that sufficient future taxable income will be available.
- *Employee benefits:* Both IFRS and Ind AS require actuarial gains and losses to be recognized in other comprehensive income. Indian GAAP requires recognition of such items in the statement of profit and loss.

RECAP

- *Liabilities* are amounts payable. *Current liabilities* are payable in the course of operations.
- Liabilities may be definite or estimated. *Definite liabilities* are known precisely. *Estimated liabilities* require assumptions and judgment.
- *Accounting profit* differs from *taxable profit*. Current income tax is payable on taxable profit.
- The difference between accounting profit and taxable profit may be permanent or temporary. *Permanent differences* don't require recognition in accounting.
- *Temporary differences* give rise to a future tax payable or a future tax benefit. Future tax payable results in *deferred tax liability*; future tax benefit results in *deferred tax asset*.
- Minimum alternative tax is payable on accounting profit, if it is less than taxable profit. MAT credit is an asset.
- Post-employment benefits, such as pensions and health care, should be recognized in the current period based on estimates.
- *Contingent liabilities* may be payable depending on the occurrence or non-occurrence of events in the future. They should be disclosed.

Review Problem

Vishesh Company reported profit before tax of ₹100,000 each year from 20X1 to 20X4. In 20X1, it bought equipment costing ₹100,000. For accounting purposes, the equipment was depreciated over four years using the straight-line method. For tax purposes, it is depreciated at 50 per cent using the WDV method. The equipment was scrapped in 20X4. In 20X1, it received rent income of ₹10,000 per year in advance for three years. The entire income was taxed on receipt. The tax rate is 30 per cent.

Required

Calculate the company's current income tax and income tax expense for 20X1, 20X2, 20X3 and 20X4.

Solution to the Review Problem

	20X1	20X2	20X3	20X4
Accounting profit (profit before tax)	₹100,000	₹100,000	₹100,000	₹100,000
Add Accounting depreciation on straight-line method	25,000	25,000	25,000	25,000
Deduct Tax depreciation on WDV method	50,000	25,000	12,500	12,500
Add Rent income for tax on receipt	30,000	0	0	0
Deduct Rent income for accounting on accrual	10,000	10,000	10,000	0
Taxable profit	95,000	90,000	102,500	112,500
Current income tax: 30% of taxable profit	28,500	27,000	30,750	33,750
Add Deferred tax expense	7,500	0	– 3,750	– 3,750
Deduct Deferred tax income	6,000	– 3,000	– 3,000	0
Income tax expense	30,000	30,000	30,000	30,000

Notes:

1. Deferred tax expense related to depreciation:

	Carrying Amount	Tax base	Taxable Temporary Difference	Deferred Tax Liability	Change in Deferred Tax Liability
20X1	₹75,000	₹50,000	₹25,000	₹7,500	₹7,500
20X2	50,000	25,000	25,000	7,500	0
20X3	25,000	12,500	12,500	3,750	– 3,750
20X4	0	0	0	0	– 3,750

Change in deferred tax liability is deferred tax expense. Minus denotes reversal.

2. Deferred tax income related to rent income:

	Received	Recognized	Carrying Amount	Tax Base	Deductible Temporary Difference	Deferred Tax Asset	Change in Deferred Tax Asset
20X1	₹30,000	₹10,000	₹20,000	₹0	₹20,000	₹6,000	₹ 6,000
20X2	0	10,000	10,000	0	10,000	3,000	–3,000
20X3	0	10,000	0	0	0	0	–3,000

Change in deferred tax asset is deferred tax income. Minus denotes reversal.

ASSIGNMENT MATERIAL

Questions

1. "All liabilities involve obligations but all obligations are not liabilities." Do you agree?
2. Are liabilities always settled by cash payment?
3. Why is it important to distinguish between *current liabilities* and *non-current liabilities*?
4. How does an *estimated liability* differ from a *definite liability*? Give three examples each.
5. How should *contingent liabilities* be reported?
6. "Pensions are deferred wages." Do you agree?
7. What is *current service cost*? Why should it be accrued?
8. Why is it necessary to accrue interest cost on pension liability?
9. Distinguish between *accounting profit* and *taxable profit*.
10. Explain *tax base*.
11. Can a *temporary taxable difference* or *temporary deductible difference* result from a transaction that does not affect the statement of profit and loss? Give an example.
12. Does tax-free interest income give rise to a *deferred tax liability*?
13. When can *minimum alternative tax* paid be recognized as an asset?
14. Distinguish between *unused tax loss carryforward* and *unused tax credit carryforward*.

Problems

Problem 9.1

Classification of liabilities ✶

Marissa Company's balance sheet has the following items.
  (a) Unearned revenue.
  (b) Deferred tax liability.
  (c) Gratuity payable.
  (d) Salaries payable.
  (e) GST payable.
  (f) Liability for product warranties.
  (g) Liability for frequent flyer points.

Required

Classify the items as (a) current or non-current liabilities, (b) definite or estimated liabilities and (c) operating or financial liabilities.

Problem 9.2

Classification of liabilities ✶ Alternative to Problem 9.1

Farida Company's balance sheet has the following items.
  (a) Current tax liability.
  (b) Debentures payable.
  (c) Mortgages payable.
  (d) Current portion of debentures payable.
  (e) Interest payable.
  (f) Trade payables.
  (g) Pensions payable.

Required

Classify the items as (a) current or non-current liabilities (b) definite or estimated liabilities, and (c) operating or financial liabilities.

Problem 9.3

Bills Payable Transactions ✶✶

On March 1, 20XX, Mahati Company bought goods for ₹20,000 and accepted a 60-day, 15 per cent bill. It paid the bill on the maturity date. The company's fiscal year ends on March 31.

Required

Record the transactions.

Problem 9.4

Income Tax ✶✶

Ritu Company reported an accounting profit of ₹50,000 and tax loss of ₹20,000 for the year ended March 31, 20XX. The income tax rate is 35 per cent and the MAT rate is 10 per cent.

Required

Prepare the journal entry to record the income tax expense for the year.

Problem 9.5

Bills Payable Transactions ✶✶✶

Lucky Traders had the following bills payable transactions:

Mar. 11   Purchased merchandise from Khan Company on a 90-day, 18 per cent bill for ₹20,000.
Apr. 24   Borrowed from Vijaya Bank on a 60-day, 16 per cent bill for ₹30,000.
May   4   Purchased merchandise on account from Khan Company, ₹8,000.
June   9   Paid the 90-day bill payable to Khan Company.
      10   Issued a 90-day, 18 per cent bill in settlement of the amount due to Khan Company.
June 23   Paid Vijaya Bank.
Sep.   8   Paid Khan Company.
      17   Purchased merchandise from Khan Company on a 90-day bill for ₹10,400.

Required

  1. Prepare journal entries to record the transactions.
  2. Prepare the adjusting entry on May 31, the company's year-end, to record the accrued interest payable on the two bills.

Problem 9.6

Bills Payable Transactions ✶✶✶ Alternative to Problem 9.5

Satnam Company had the following bills payable transactions:

July   28   Borrowed from Union Bank on a 90-day, 20% bill, ₹50,000.
Aug. 10   Purchased merchandise on account from Mithun Company, ₹10,000.
      31   Borrowed from Times Bank ₹30,000 on a 90-day bill, ₹31,250.
Sep. 17   Issued a 60-day, 22% bill in settlement of the amount due to Mithun Company.

Oct. 26 Paid Union Bank.
Nov. 16 Paid Mithun Company.
 22 Purchased merchandise from Mithun Company on a 60-day, 20% bill, ₹25,000.
 29 Paid Times Bank.

Required

1. Prepare journal entries to record the transactions.
2. Prepare the adjusting entry on September 30, the company's year-end, to record the accrued interest payable on the two bills.

On September 14, 20XX, Asif Brassware in Moradabad sold on credit a vase for ₹5,000 plus tax to Veena Traders in Lucknow. On October 19, 20XX, Veena Traders sold the vase for cash to Praveen Kumar, a consumer, in Patna for ₹7,000 plus tax. CGST is 5 per cent, SGST is 5 per cent and IGST is 10 per cent. GST was paid to the government on the first day of the following month.

Problem 9.7
Goods and Services Tax
Transactions ✳✳✳

Required

Record the transactions in the journals of Asif Brassware and Veena Traders.

On March 8, 20XX, Jain Granites in Chittorgarh sold for cash a stone block for ₹25,000 plus tax to Arihant Homes in Udaipur. On May 25, 20XX, Arihant Traders sold the stone block on credit to Vishal, a consumer, in Mumbai for ₹32,000 plus tax. CGST is 5 per cent, SGST is 5 per cent and IGST is 10 per cent. GST was paid to the government on the first day of the following month.

Problem 9.8
Goods and Services
Tax Transactions ✳✳✳
Alternative to Problem 9.7

Required

Record the transactions in the journals of Jain Granites and Arihant Traders.

Siraj Company sells geysers under a warranty contract that requires the company to replace defective parts free of charge, but the customer must pay the labour charges. In the past, 5 per cent of the sales required warranty replacement costing ₹150 per piece. During March, the company sold 700 pieces at an average price of ₹4,300. During the month, the company received 60 pieces under the warranty and these were returned after repairs costing ₹7,430. The company collected labour charges of ₹600.

Problem 9.9
Product Warranty Liability
✳✳✳

Required

1. Prepare journal entries to record (a) the cost of warranty repairs completed during the month, assuming that the company follows the cash system of accounting for warranty; and (b) receipt of service revenue.
2. Prepare journal entries to record (a) the cost of warranty repairs completed during the month; (b) the estimated liability for warranty for sales during the month, assuming that the company follows the accrual system of accounting for warranty; and (c) receipt of service revenue.
3. Assume that the company follows the accrual system and at the beginning of the month, the estimated warranty liability account had a credit balance of ₹71,230. Compute the balance of the account at the end of the month. How would it appear on the balance sheet on March 31?
4. Describe the circumstances in which the cash system of accounting for the warranty can be followed.

Jaya Company sells toasters under a warranty contract that requires the company to replace defective parts free of charge, but the customer must pay the labour charges. In the past, 3 per cent of the sales required replacement under warranty, costing ₹200 per piece. During July, the company sold 1,200 pieces at an average price of ₹6,000. During the month, the company received 20 pieces under warranty and these were returned after repairs costing ₹3,190. The company collected labour charges of ₹400 from customers under the terms of the warranty.

Problem 9.10
Product Warranty Liability
✳✳✳ Alternative to
Problem 9.9

Required

1. Prepare journal entries to record (a) the cost of warranty system repairs completed during the month, assuming that the company follows the cash system of accounting for warranty; and (b) receipt of service revenue.
2. Prepare journal entries to record (a) the cost of warranty repairs completed during the month; (b) the estimated liability for warranty for sales during the month, assuming that the company follows the accrual system of accounting for warranty; and (c) receipt of service revenue.

3. Assume that the company follows the accrual method and at the beginning of the month, the estimated warranty liability account had a credit balance of ₹47,160. Compute the balance of the account at the end of the month. How would it appear on the balance sheet on July 31?
4. Describe the circumstances in which the cash system of accounting for the warranty can be followed.

Problem 9.11
Accounting for Income
Tax ✴✴✴✴

After one year of operations, Mayank Company has the following financial statements.

MAYANK COMPANY
Balance Sheet, March 31, 20X1

Assets

Non-current assets

Equipment	₹9,000
Deduct Accumulated depreciation	900
	8,100

Current assets

Inventories	3,400
Trade receivables (net of allowance for credit losses, ₹450)	5,360
Cash	5,080
Other current assets	1,360
	23,300

Equity and Liabilities

Equity

Equity share capital	₹10,000
Other equity	2,290

Liabilities

Non-current liabilities

Bonds payable	1,000

Current liabilities

Trade payables	2,750
Other current liabilities	7,260
	23,300

MAYANK COMPANY
Statement of Profit and Loss
For the year ended March 31, 20X1

Revenues

Sales	₹9,010

Expenses

Salaries expense	2,690
Office supplies expense	600
Telephone expense	630
Rent expense	800
Depreciation expense	900
Other expenses	1,100
	6,720
Profit before tax	2,290

The financial statements are complete except for income tax.

Additional information:

(a) Other current liabilities include (i) unearned sales revenue, ₹1,000 and (ii) sales tax payable, ₹400. Sales revenue and sales tax are taxable when received; sales tax is deductible when paid.

(b) Other current assets include advance tax, ₹800.

(c) Other expenses include (i) fine, ₹150 and (ii) estimated credit loss, ₹500. Both are non-deductible. Actual credit loss of ₹50 is deductible.

(d) Tax depreciation on equipment is ₹3,000.

(e) Income tax rate is 30 per cent; MAT rate is 10 per cent.

Required

1. Calculate the company's (a) current tax expense, (b) temporary differences, and (c) deferred tax assets and liabilities, if any.

2. Prepare the journal entry to record the income tax expense as of March 31, 20XX.

3. Prepare the company's revised balance sheet and statement of profit and loss for 20X1.

4. On June 12, 20X1, the Income Tax Department accepted Mayank Company's calculation of taxable income and income tax payable. On the same day, the company paid or received the balance. Prepare the journal entry to record the transaction.

After one year of operations, Partha Company has the following financial statements.

Problem 9.12
Accounting for Income Tax ✴✴✴✴ Alternative to Problem 9.11

PARTHA COMPANY	
Balance Sheet, March 31, 20X1	

Assets

Non-current assets

Equipment	₹3,000
Deduct Accumulated depreciation	600
	2,400
Investments	1,000

Current assets

Inventories	270
Trade receivables (net of allowance for credit losses, ₹260)	3,180
Cash	1,870
Other current assets	960
	9,680

Equity and Liabilities

Equity

Equity share capital	₹5,000
Other equity	1,340

Liabilities

Non-current liabilities

Loan payable	500

Current liabilities

Trade payables	1,810
Other current liabilities	1,030
	9,680

PARTHA COMPANY	
Statement of Profit and Loss	
For the year ended March 31, 20X1	

Revenues

Sales	₹5,260
Other income	460
	5,720

Expenses

Salaries expense	1,250
Raw materials consumed	1,070
Electricity expense	210
Insurance expense	400
Depreciation expense	600
Other expenses	850
	4,380
Profit before tax	1,340

The financial statements are complete except for income tax.

Additional information:

(a) Other current liabilities include (i) unearned interest income, ₹120 and (ii) employer's provident fund contribution payable, ₹160. Interest income is taxable when received; employer's provident fund contribution is deductible when paid.

(b) Other current assets include advance tax, ₹350.

(c) Other income includes interest on tax-free bonds, ₹100.

(d) Other expenses include (i) donation, ₹180 and (ii) estimated credit loss, ₹300. Both are non-deductible. Actual credit loss of ₹40 is deductible.

(e) Tax depreciation on equipment is ₹1,000.

(f) Income tax rate is 30 per cent; MAT rate is 10 per cent.

Required

1. Calculate the company's (a) current tax expense, (b) temporary differences, and (c) deferred tax assets and liabilities, if any.
2. Prepare the journal entry to record the income tax expense as of March 31, 20XX.
3. Prepare the company's revised balance sheet and statement of profit and loss for 20X1.
4. On May 28, 20X1, the Income Tax Department accepted Partha Company's calculation of taxable income and income tax payable. On the same day, the company paid or received the balance. Prepare the journal entry to record the transaction.

Problem 9.13
Employee Benefits
★★★★

An employee of Vidyut Company is entitled to a pension of ₹5,000 per year of service. Currently, she is 25 years of age and will retire at 62. The company funds its pension liability and deposits the amount of liability with a pension plan which will invest the funds. The actuary's assumptions are as follows:

(a) The discount rate is 8 per cent.
(b) The pension plan assets are expected to earn a return of 6 per cent over the long-term.
(c) The company's employees will have a life expectancy of 75 years.

Required

1. Prepare a schedule showing current service cost, interest cost and expected return on plan assets for the first five years of the employee's service. Use the tables in Appendix C.
2. Prepare the journal entry to record the pension expense for the first five years of the employee's service.

Problem 9.14
Employee Benefits
★★★★ Alternative to
Problem 9.13

An employee of Mrutyunjay Company is entitled to a pension of ₹3,000 per year of service. Currently, he is 22 years of age and will retire at 60. The company funds its pension liability and deposits the amount of liability with a trust which will invest the funds. The actuary's assumptions are as follows:

(a) The discount rate is 7 per cent.
(b) The pension plan assets are expected to earn a return of 5 per cent over the long-term.
(c) The company's employees will have a life expectancy of 79 years.

Required

1. Prepare a schedule showing current service cost, interest cost and expected return on plan assets for the first five years of the employee's service. Use the tables in Appendix C.
2. Prepare the journal entry to record the pension expense for the first five years of the employee's service.

Business Decision Cases

BDC 9.1
Chandra Rubber
Company

Chandra Rubber Company manufactures a range of rubber products with industrial and domestic applications. The company's corporate head office is in Kochi. A significant part of the revenues is earned from exports to the United States and to several countries in Europe. On May 15, 20X6, Suresh Nair, chief financial officer of the company, was reviewing the company's financial statements for the year ended March 31, 20X6. In the course of his review, he noticed the following items:

1. The company has received a notice from Rai & Co., lawyers, claiming damages of ₹250,000 under the Consumer Protection Act. The notice stated that a seven-year-old child in Mumbai

was injured while riding a toy car made from rubber produced by the company. This is the first time Chandra Rubber has received a product liability claim. The company has decided to accept the claim to avoid adverse publicity, although its legal advisers feel that the amount of damages can be reduced to about ₹150,000 in a legal proceeding.

2. The assessment order for the year ended March 31, 20X4 issued by the Assistant Commissioner of Income Tax disallowed expenses of ₹180,000 incurred by the company for the visit of the managing director to Switzerland in November 20X3 on the ground that "it was not incurred wholly and exclusively for business purposes". As a result, the company is required to pay income tax of ₹72,000 and penalty of ₹36,000. The company's accountants advised the company to appeal the assessment order to the Commissioner of Income Tax and were reasonably certain that the Commissioner would allow half of the travel and completely waive the penalty since there was no intention to avoid payment of tax. Accordingly, the company has filed an appeal to the Commissioner of Income Tax. If the company were to lose the appeal, it can go on further appeal to the Income Tax Appellate Tribunal and, if necessary, to the High Court. Similarly, the Income Tax Department can go on appeal to these authorities, should it lose the appeal.

3. Walt Disney Company has sued the company in a Delhi court claiming exemplary damages of ₹10 million for infringement of its intellectual property rights since the characters portrayed in the company's recent promotion campaign closely resembled Aladdin, a Walt Disney copyright. The company's legal advisers expect the case to be settled at an amount ranging from ₹100,000 to ₹500,000 and estimate the probable amount at ₹200,000. The company does not want to publicize the case since it could lead to sanctions against the company in the United States, a major destination for its exports.

4. A past employee of the company has filed an appeal in the Calcutta High Court against the company for wrongful dismissal and has claimed back wages of ₹40,000 and damages of ₹100,000. The company's legal department believes that it has an iron-clad case since the employee was caught red-handed while removing the company's materials outside the factory. The company won the case in the labour court in October 20X4 and again in the district court in January 20X6.

5. The residents of a village near the company's main plant in Howrah have written to the West Bengal State Pollution Control Board demanding the closure of the plant alleging air and water pollution. The company feels that the case is not sustainable since it complies with relevant pollution control standards and the effluents are treated as required by law. However, the company may have to close down operations in the plant if the Board determines that there has been a violation by the company; alternatively, the company can continue operations after installing pollution control equipment costing ₹150 million. Either way, the company will face significant financial problems. The Board is under enormous pressure from environmental activists to close down the plant. On May 10, 20X6, the Board has informed the company that it was deputing a team of officers for an on-the-spot study in the next two weeks. At the moment, there is no clue as to which way the matter will go. Information from several sources indicates that the Pollution Control Boards in many States have taken a fairly stringent view of similar cases on orders from the Supreme Court.

Required

1. How should the chief financial officer report each of the above items in the company's financial statements for the year ended March 31, 20X6? Explain.
2. The chief executive of the company is apprehensive about the negative effect of reporting items 1, 2, 3 and 5 on the company's stock prices. He asks the chief financial officer to come up with a solution without violating the law or any accounting principle. What considerations are involved?

Interpreting Financial Reports

Essar Oil Limited is one of the largest oil refining companies in India. The company opted to defer payment of sales tax collected by it for sales from its refinery on the basis of a scheme of the Government of Gujarat. This meant that the company could retain the sales tax collected for some

IFR 9.1
Essar Oil Limited

years before remitting it to the government. Sales tax is normally payable in the month following the month in which it is collected. The deferred sales tax liability was effectively an interest-free loan that was intended to encourage companies to set up business in Gujarat. However, the refinery could not start operations by August 15, 2003, the specified time-limit for availing of the deferral benefit, because of a cyclonic storm in 1998 and a High Court stay in 1999. As a result, the company would not be eligible for sales tax deferral. In January 2004, the Supreme Court lifted the stay and the company could resume work on the project. The company requested the government to extend the time-limit, but the government did not grant an extension. In response to the company's petition, on April 22, 2008 the High Court directed the government to consider the company's application for deferral. From May 1, 2008, the company started deferring sales tax payment. On July 14, 2008, the government challenged the High Court's order in the Supreme Court. On January 17, 2012, the Supreme Court set aside the High Court's order.

Since May 1, 2008, the company transferred its liability to pay deferred sales tax to a related party at its present value. As a result, the company did not show any deferred sales tax liability and recognize the difference between the deferred sales tax payable and its present value as a gain in its statement of profit and loss for each year. The following table gives these amounts:

	2011	2010	2009
			(in millions)
Deferred sales tax payable	₹18,114	₹14,741	₹15,165
Present value	5,915	4,412	3,318
Contingent liability for deferred sales tax payable	49,019	29,905	15,165

Required

1. What could be possible managerial considerations for removing the deferred sales tax liability from Essar Oil's financial statements?
2. What are the accounting requirements for derecognizing a liability? Do you think Essar Oil met those requirements?

**IFR 9.2
Kingfisher Airlines
Limited**

Kingfisher Airlines Ltd. was one of the largest aviation companies in India. The company's jaunty slogan "Welcome to a world without passengers" was meant to say that the passenger is "made to feel like a guest and not just a passenger". Unfortunately for the company, the slogan soon acquired its literal meaning.

The company's financial statements for the year ended March 31, 2012 contained the following information on deferred taxes:

Note 8: Deferred tax

	March 31	
	2012	2011
		(in millions)
Particulars		
Deferred tax liability		
On account of depreciation on fixed assets	₹2,121	₹3,183
On account of timing differences in recognition of expenditure	202	408
	2,323	3,591
Deferred tax asset		
On account of timing differences in recognition of expenditure	84	94
On account of disallowance under section 40 (ia)	7,917	6,612
On account of unabsorbed losses and depreciation under the Income Tax Act 1961	34,781	26,164
	42,782	32,869
Net deferred tax asset	40,459	29,278

Note 39:

Deferred tax asset on unabsorbed depreciation and business losses has been recognized on the basis of a business plan prepared by the management which takes into account certain future receivables arising out of contractual obligations. The management is of the opinion that there is virtual certainty supported by convincing evidence that sufficient future taxable income will be available against which the deferred tax asset can be realized.

The auditors' report (paragraph 10) contained the following observation (italics in original):

Attention of the members is invited to note 39 regarding recognition of deferred tax credit on account of unabsorbed losses and allowances during the year aggregating to ₹11,181 million (year ended March 31, 2011 ₹4,934 million) (Total amount recognized up to March 31, 2012 ₹40,458 million). This does not satisfy the virtual certainty test for recognition of deferred tax credit as laid down in AS 22.

A note to the company's financial statements for the year ended March 31, 2013 stated:

Note 39:

Deferred tax credit earlier recognized up to March 31, 2012 aggregating to ₹40,459 lacs has been derecognized during the year by debit to surplus account (reserves and surplus) in the balance sheet.

Required

1. Do you agree with the company's position on deferred taxes? Explain.
2. Identify possible management considerations for the position adopted. Examine to what extent they might apply in this case.

Financial Analysis

Study the disclosures of post-employment benefits, such as pensions and health care, appearing in the financial statements of a sample of companies. You will find them in schedules, statement of accounting policies, and notes.

FA 9.1
Understanding Post-Employment Benefits

Required

1. Prepare a comparative analysis of the discount rates, expected return on plan assets and salary increase assumptions. Why might these assumptions differ for your sample companies?
2. Prepare a sensitivity analysis of changes in these assumptions. What do you learn from this analysis?
3. Explain how this study is useful in analyzing and interpreting financial statements.
4. Study the income tax expense (current and deferred) in the statement of profit and loss and the items appearing in the schedule of deferred tax assets and deferred tax liabilities in the balance sheet of a sample of companies.

Study the income tax expense (current and deferred) in the statement of profit and loss and the items appearing in the schedule of deferred tax assets and deferred tax liabilities in the balance sheet of a sample of companies.

FA 9.2
Deferred Tax Accounting

Required

1. Prepare a list of items for which companies recognize deferred tax assets and deferred tax liabilities. Explain why each of the items in your list qualifies for deferred tax accounting.
2. Analyze the composition of income tax expense in the statement of profit and loss. Calculate current tax, deferred tax liability, and deferred tax asset for each of the items.
3. Explain how this study is useful in analyzing and interpreting financial statements.

Answers to One-minute Quiz

9.1 c.
9.2 a, b, c, d.
9.3 d.
9.4 d.

Answers to Test Your Understanding

9.1 Product Warranty Expense... 13,800

Estimated Warranty Liability... 13,800

2,300 units × 3% × ₹200 = ₹13,800

9.2 20X2, ₹1,925; 20X3, ₹2,200; 20X4, ₹1,375; 20X5, ₹1,600.

9.3 Permanent differences: a, b and d. Temporary differences: c, e and f.

9.4 Year 1, ₹1,450 ; Year 2, ₹900; Year 3, ₹1,350; Year 4, ₹1,800; Year 5, ₹1,500; Year 6, ₹1,200; Year 7, ₹900; Year 8, ₹600; Year 9, ₹300; Year 10, ₹0.

9.5 (a) 20X1, ₹21,000; 20X2, ₹18,000; 20X3, ₹0. (b) 20X1, ₹21,000; 20X2, ₹15,000; 20X3, ₹0.

9.6 Income Tax Expense.. 15,000

Deferred Tax Asset... 900

Income Tax Payable 15,900

9.7 Pension cost = Current service cost, ₹590 + Interest cost, ₹107 – Expected return on plan assets ₹86 = ₹611.

CHAPTER

10

Financial Liabilities

LEARNING OBJECTIVES

After studying this chapter, you should be able to:

1. Explain financial liabilities.
2. Understand measurement of financial liabilities.
3. Describe the principal features of debentures.
4. Record the issue of debentures and account for interest expense.
5. Understand the presentation of redeemable preference shares.
6. Account for debenture redemption and retirement.
7. Explain the operation of a debenture redemption fund.
8. Account for compound financial instruments.
9. Account for mortgages.
10. Account for leases.
11. Explain off-balance sheet financing arrangements.

SPEED READ

Financial liabilities result from borrowings. A debenture is a written promise to pay a principal amount and interest. The interest rate depends on the credit rating of the debenture. Debentures are recorded at amortized cost. Redeemable preference shares are classified and presented as debt. Debentures are derecognized on redemption, retirement or conversion. Compound financial instruments are a hybrid of equity and debt instruments. Debenture redemption fund is intended to provide funds for repayment of debentures. Mortgages are secured by immovable property and are usually repaid in equal instalments consisting of principal and interest. A finance lease is in-substance borrowing. Operating lease rentals are expensed. Off-balance sheet financing results in a future commitment but it does not appear on the balance sheet.

OOPS! MY BOND PRICES HAVE GONE UP

In October 2012, JP Morgan reported that it lost $211 million because the yield on its bonds *decreased*. This may sound absurd, but it's true. How did this happen? Yield is the interest rate at which the market discounts the future interest and principal payments to determine the value of a bond. When the bond yield declines, the bond value goes up. Unfortunately, this has an adverse effect. Banks had to mark their financial liabilities to market. So when the value of its bonds goes up, the bank must recognize the increase as a mark-to-market loss. In 2012, bond yields were falling because investors were clamouring for the extra yield that was available from banks' bonds, pushing up prices and lowering bond yields. In 2008, when liquidity was scarce, bond prices plummeted and, applying fair value accounting, banks recognized impressive gains from the decrease in their liabilities. When a bank's credit rating falls, its yield goes up and the fair value of its debt falls. The difference is a gain. Benefiting from one's own credit problems would seem bizarre. As a result, changes in the fair value of a financial liability attributable to own credit risk are now to be taken to the statement of profit and loss only if the liability is intended to be repaid in the near future.

Financial Liabilities in Perspective

Learning Objective

LO 1 Explain financial liabilities.

Business enterprises often borrow large sums to pay for capital expenditure and acquisitions. Financial liabilities are contractual obligations to pay definite amounts often over long periods. Debentures, loans, mortgages and leases are examples of financial liabilities. Financial liabilities usually involve interest payments.

Financial liabilities may be secured or unsecured. A secured liability is backed by a legal interest in the borrower's assets in the form of a mortgage, pledge or hypothecation. In a mortgage, the lender has a hold on the borrower's immovable assets such as land or building, e.g. home loan. In a pledge, the lender has physical possession of the borrower's asset, e.g. gold loan. In a hypothecation, the borrower uses the asset but can't sell it without the lender's permission, e.g. car loan. If the borrower defaults, the creditor can sell the asset and use the proceeds to settle the dues. An unsecured liability is backed by the borrower's credit standing, and not by any specific assets.

ONE-MINUTE QUIZ 10.1
Secured and Unsecured
Liabilities

Which of the following loans would be classified as secured? There may be more than one correct answer.
(a) A loan backed by an irrevocable bank guarantee from the borrower.
(b) A loan backed by hypothecation of the borrower's inventories.
(c) A loan backed by hypothecation of the borrower's receivables.
(d) A loan backed by a mortgage on the borrower's land and building.

Measurement of Financial Liabilities

Learning Objective

LO 2 Understand measurement of financial liabilities.

Financial liabilities are measured at amortized cost or at fair value through profit or loss (FVTPL). Most financial liabilities are measured at amortized cost using the effective interest method, explained in Chapter 7. Financial liabilities are accounted for at FVTPL are (a) held for trading or (b) designated as measured at FVTPL on inception.

A financial liability is held for trading (HFT) if it is intended to be repaid in the near future. At initial recognition, an entity has an option to designate a financial liability as measured at FVTPL if it provides more relevant information. The decision to measure at FVTPL once made is *permanent*.

The fair value of a financial liability would change depending on how the yield changes after initial recognition, resulting in a gain or loss. An increase in the yield reduces the value of a financial liability and results in a gain; a decrease raises the value of a financial liability and results in a loss.[1] For example, if an entity's credit rating is downgraded, the borrowing cost goes up pushing up the yield and the fair value of the debt goes down. As a result, there is a gain. An upgrade pushes down the yield and the fair value of the goes up. As a result, there is a loss.

FINANCIAL VIEW
Fair Value Accounting for
Liabilities

Fair value accounting can produce unexpected outcomes. Barclays PLC is a large UK-based bank with operations in many countries. In 2008, the year of the financial crisis, the bank reported a group profit before tax of £6,077 million, down 14% on 2007. Profit included a number of one-time and unusual items including "gains on own credit" of £1,663 million. Thereby hangs a tale.[2] "Gains on own credit" refers to the decrease in the fair value of financial liabilities in 2008. This means that when Barclays' creditworthiness falls, the market value of its own debt will decrease. The resulting "gain" goes to the statement of profit and loss. The results announcement said: "Barclays Capital was affected by very challenging market conditions in 2008, with income falling by £1,888 million (27%) on 2007, reflecting gross losses of £6,290 million relating to credit market assets, partially offset by *gains of £1,663 million on the fair valuation of notes issued by Barclays Capital due to widening of credit spreads* and £1,433 million in related income and hedges." (italics not in original). The accounting treatment followed IAS 39 that requires fair value accounting for both financial assets and financial liabilities. The outcome in the case of liabilities looks perverse, but it was in line with IAS 39. This was viewed as a case of "mark-to-market gone mad".

---

[1] Recall from Chapter 7 that the present value of future cash flows from a financial asset is inversely related to the discount rate. The same reasoning holds here.

[2] The Barclays example is only to illustrate the point. All entities that followed IAS 39 would have had such items.

Debentures Payable

Learning Objective

LO 3 Describe the principal features of debentures.

A debenture, or bond, consists of a written promise to pay a principal amount at a specified time and interest at a specified rate. The parties to a debenture are the issuer (borrower) and the debentureholder (lender). A debenture issue consists of a large number of debentures of small denominations rather than one large bond. For example, a borrowing of ₹10 million could consist of 10,000 debentures of ₹1,000, thus enabling many investors to participate in the issue. The debenture certificate is evidence of the issuer's obligation to the debentureholder. The *debenture trust deed* (also known as *bond indenture*) is a legal document that sets out the rights and obligations of the parties. It contains do's and don'ts for the protection of the debentureholders. These may include dividend payment restrictions, borrowing limits and security value.

An issuer may sell debentures directly to the public or to an *underwriter*, an investment firm which will sell the debentures to the public later. Even in a public issue of debentures, the issuer often engages an underwriter who is paid a commission in return for a promise to buy the debentures not taken up by the public. The issuer appoints a *debenture trustee* to represent the debentureholders. The trustee should ensure that the issuer complies with the terms of the trust deed.

The terms of a debenture are a matter of contract between the borrower and the lender. They reflect the borrower's financing needs and the lender's expectations. Debentures with a wide variety of features are in use. *Secured debentures* are backed by specific assets. *Unsecured debentures* are backed only by the issuer' creditworthiness. *Term debentures*, or *bullet bonds*, fall due for payment on the same date. *Serial debentures* mature in instalments on specified dates. For example, a ₹10 million issue of serial debentures may mature at the rate of ₹1 million per year for 10 years. *Convertible debentures* are converted into the issuer's shares at a stipulated rate. *Callable bonds* give the issuer the right to prepay them. The *call price* the issuer must pay is specified in advance. If the yield falls, the issuer can pay back costly debt and substitute it with cheaper debt. *Zero-coupon bonds*, or *deep discount bonds*, do not carry any periodic interest payment, or *coupon*. Zero-coupon bonds have a low issue price, a high maturity value and a long repayment term.

Credit Quality	Rating Symbol
Highest Safety	AAA
High Safety	AA
Adequate Safety	A
Moderate Safety	BBB
Moderate Risk	BB
High Risk	B
Very High Risk	C
Default	D

Credit rating agencies assign rating symbols indicating their view of the safety of principal and interest payments on debt securities. Ratings help investors understand the degree of risk associated with investment in debt instruments. A rating is not a recommendation to purchase, sell, or hold a debenture nor is it an evaluation of the issuer. It is the professional judgment of a group of independent experts relating to a specific instrument. Ratings influence borrowing costs. An AA-rated bond will have a lower interest rate than a BBB-rated bond. A bond rated BB or lower by Standard & Poor's (or equivalent by other rating agencies) is a *high-yield bond* or *junk bond*. A bond rated BBB or above is an *investment grade bond*.

FINANCIAL VIEW
Credit Rating

Debentures that are repayable in instalments over their term are
(a) Serial debentures.
(b) Term debentures.
(c) Convertible debentures.
(d) Unsecured debentures.

ONE-MINUTE QUIZ 10.2
Debentures

Issuing Debentures

Learning Objective

LO 4 Record the issue of debentures and account for interest expense.

Debentures have a face value (or par value), the principal amount that must be repaid on the maturity date. Face value is not entered in the accounting records. Debentures are financial liabilities and are recorded initially at their fair value.

Debenture prices and interest rates The debenture certificate specifies the coupon. Suppose on January 1, 20X0, Maya Company issues ₹100,000 of 12 per cent, 10-year debentures. Interest is payable semi-annually on June 30 and December 31 in arrears. Maya Company will pay interest of ₹6,000 on those dates until maturity. Yield is the investors' required interest rate for debentures of a particular risk category. It is the investor's opportunity cost. The greater the default risk, the higher the yield. Yield is affected by, among others, the Reserve Bank of India's benchmark rates, inflation expectations, liquidity conditions, and the size of government borrowing.

If a bond's coupon equals its yield, the investor will get a fair return and the bond will be priced at par. Here, the fair value would equal the face value. However, if coupon and yield differ, the bond has to be issued at a discount or premium. For example, if the yield is 16 per cent, Maya Company won't be able to issue its debentures at par. A potential investor can earn ₹8,000 per period by lending at the yield, as against ₹6,000 on Maya Company's debentures. So Maya Company has to issue the debentures at a **discount**, i.e. below par. If the yield is 10 per cent, Maya Company will be able to issue the debentures at a **premium**, i.e. above par. Debenture prices are often stated as *x* percent of par. For example, if a debenture is issued at 104, it means that a debenture is sold at a premium of 4 per cent. An issue price of 98 would mean that the debenture is sold at a discount of 2 per cent.

HANDHOLD 10.1
Debenture Pricing

In the Maya Company example, suppose the yield is 16 per cent, or 8 per cent per semi-annual period. This is more than the coupon. The present value calculations using a discount rate of 8 per cent and 20 periods are as follows:

(a) Present value of 20 interest payments at 8%: ₹6,000 x 9.8181 (Appendix C, Table 4) .... ₹58,909
(b) Present value of ₹100,000 payable after 20 periods at 8%: ₹100,000 x 0.2145 (Appendix C, Table 3) 21,450
Present value of the debenture issue 80,359

Since the yield is higher than the coupon, the company will issue the debentures *at a discount*. Thus, the maximum price that investors will offer for the issue is ₹80,359. The price of a ₹100 face value debenture will be ₹80.359.

Suppose in the above example the yield is 10 per cent or 5 per cent per semi-annual period. This is *below* the coupon. The present value calculations using a discount rate of 5 per cent and 20 periods are as follows:

(a) Present value of 20 interest payments at 5%: ₹6,000 x 12.4622 (Appendix C, Table 4) .... ₹74,773
(b) Present value of ₹100,000 payable after 20 periods at 5%: ₹100,000 x 0.3769 (Appendix C, Table 3) 37,690
Present value of the debenture issue 112,463

Since the yield is less than the coupon, the debentures will be issued *at a premium*. The price of a ₹100 face value debenture will be ₹112.463.

We will now see how to record the issue of debentures.

Debentures issued at par Assume that on January 1, 20X0, Maya Company issues ₹100,000 of 12 per cent, 10-year secured debentures at par. Interest is payable semi-annually on June 30 and December 31. The entry to record the issue is as follows:

20X0			
Jan. 1	Cash	100,000	
	Debentures Payable		100,000

Interest of ₹6,000 (₹100,000 × 12% × 6/12) is due each June 30 and December 31 until the debentures mature. The entry to record the first interest payment is as follows:

20X0			
June 30	Debenture Interest Expense	6,000	
	Cash		6,000

Debentures issued at a discount or premium Assume that Maya Company issues debentures for ₹80,359 when the yield is 16 per cent. We record the issue of the debentures as follows:

20X0
Jan. 1 Cash.. 80,359
        Debentures Payable.. 80,359

If Maya Company issues the debentures for ₹112,463 when the yield is 10 per cent, the following entry records the issue:

20X0
Jan. 1 Cash.. 112,463
        Debentures Payable.. 112,463

Effective interest method for amortization of debenture discount and premium The effective interest method discussed in Chapter 7 calculates the amortized cost of a financial asset and allocates the interest income at the rate that exactly discounts estimated future interest receipts to the carrying amount of the financial asset. Applying the semi-annual yield of 8 per cent to the proceeds of ₹80,359, we get the interest expense of ₹6,429 for the period ended June 30, 20X0. The interest payment is ₹6,000. The difference of ₹429 is the discount amortization for the period. The following entry records the interest payment and amortization:

20X0
June 30 Debenture Interest Expense... 6,429
        Cash... 6,000
        Debentures Payable.. 429

Exhibit 10.1 presents the debenture discount amortization schedule. Note that the periodic interest expense (Column B) is a constant 8 per cent of the start-of-period carrying amount (Column A). The amortization in an interest period equals the difference between the interest expense and the interest paid in the period. The procedure for amortizing premium is similar to that illustrated in Exhibit 10.1.

We adjust the rounding difference in the last period's interest expense.					**EXHIBIT 10.1**
Period	Amortized Cost: Start of Period (A)	Interest Expense (B) 8% of (A)	Interest Paid (C)	Principal Paid (D)	Amortized Cost: End of Period (E) (A) + (B) − (C) − (D)
1	₹80,359	₹6,429	₹6,000	—	₹80,788
2	80,788	6,463	6,000	—	81,251
3	81,251	6,500	6,000	—	81,751
4	81,751	6,540	6,000	—	82,291
5	82,291	6,583	6,000	—	82,874
6	82,874	6,630	6,000	—	83,504
7	83,504	6,680	6,000	—	84,184
8	84,184	6,735	6,000	—	84,919
9	84,919	6,794	6,000	—	85,713
10	85,713	6,857	6,000	—	86,570
11	86,570	6,926	6,000	—	87,496
12	87,496	7,000	6,000	—	88,496
13	88,496	7,080	6,000	—	89,576
14	89,576	7,166	6,000	—	90,742
15	90,742	7,259	6,000	—	92,001
16	92,001	7,360	6,000	—	93,361
17	93,361	7,469	6,000	—	94,830
18	94,830	7,586	6,000	—	96,416
19	96,416	7,713	6,000	—	98,129
20	98,129	7,871	6,000	₹100,000	0

Accounting for Debentures − Effective Interest Method

Year-end accrual of debenture interest expense   Suppose Maya Company's reporting date is March 31. The following entry records interest accrued for three months:

20X0			
Mar. 31	Debenture Interest Expense..	3,215	
	Accrued Interest Payable..		3,000
	Debentures Payable..		215
	Accrued interest on 12% debentures: ₹100,000 × 12% × 3/12 = ₹3,000		
	+ Discount amortization: ₹429 × 3/6 = ₹215		

Debentures issued between interest dates   Assume that Maya Company issued the debentures on April 1, 20X0 and interest is payable semi-annually on June 30 and December 31. The issue occurs between interest payment dates. In this case, the issuer pays interest for the partial period for which the debentures were held. The entry to record the interest payment for the first semi-annual interest period for three months is as follows:

20X0			
June 30	Debenture Interest Expense..	3,215	
	Cash		3,000
	Debentures Payable..		215
	Paid semi-annual interest on 12% debentures: ₹100,000 × 12% × 3/12		
	= ₹3,000 + Discount amortization: ₹429 × 3/6 = ₹215		

Debenture issue expenses   Debenture issue involves transaction costs, such as expenses of printing debenture certificates and offer documents, accountants' and lawyers' fees, advisers' fees, brokers' and underwriters' commissions, regulators' filing fees, and marketing expenses. These are incremental costs directly attributable to the issue. At the time of initial recognition, transaction costs are deducted from the amount originally recognized for liabilities. The effective interest method is applied to the amount *net* of transaction costs.

TEST YOUR UNDERSTANDING 10.1
Effective Interest Method

Suppose Maya Company incurs transaction costs of ₹1,000 for issuing the 12 per cent, 10-year debentures. The yield is 16 per cent per annum. Interest is payable on June 30 and December 31 in arrears. Rework Exhibit 10.1.

ONE-MINUTE QUIZ 10.3
Debenture Pricing

When a debenture is issued at less than its face value, the yield is:
(a) Negative.
(b) Equal to the coupon.
(c) More than the coupon.
(d) Less than the coupon.

Redeemable Preference Shares

Learning Objective

LO 5 Understand the presentation of redeemable preference shares.

Preference shares are explained in Chapter 11. Redeemable preference shares are repayable after the period of holding stated in the share certificate. There may be a redemption premium. In addition, the dividend at a fixed rate is payable periodically. The Companies Act 2013 prohibits the issue of irredeemable preference shares or preference shares redeemable after 20 years from the date of issue.

     Assume that a ₹10 par value preference share is redeemable with a premium of ₹2 per share. On redemption, a preference shareholder will receive the following: (a) the par value of the share; (b) the redemption premium; (c) any dividends in arrears if the shares are cumulative; and (d) the proportionate dividend for the current year. The redemption feature is useful to the issuer because it can pay back the preference share capital when it has surplus cash or it can substitute the preference capital by debt with a lower interest rate.

     Contractual payment obligation is a characteristic feature of debt. Redeemable preference shares must be repaid and a fixed dividend must be paid on them. Therefore, in substance, they are debt instruments. Applying the principle of substance over form, they should be considered debt. Schedule III to the Companies Act 2013 requires them to be classified and presented as borrowings under non-current liabilities. Dividends and redemption premium should be presented as finance costs (interest expense) in the statement of profit and loss.

Derecognition of Debentures

Derecognition involves the removal of a financial liability from an entity's balance sheet. A financial liability is derecognized when it is extinguished. Extinguishment can happen in several ways, such as the following: (a) the borrower pays the obligation; (b) the lender waives its rights; or (c) the obligation expires. In each case, the borrower is *legally released* from its obligation to pay the creditor. We examine three cases of derecognition of debentures: redemption, retirement, and conversion. The first two are discussed below, and the last in the next section.

Learning Objective

LO 6 Account for debenture redemption and retirement.

Redemption is the payment of debentures at maturity. When Maya Company redeems its debentures, it derecognizes the liability:

20X9
Dec. 31   Debentures Payable 100,000
         Cash 100,000

Retirement is the early payment of debentures. An issuer may retire its debentures in order to reduce its debt or issue new debt at a lower interest rate. Debentures may contain a *call option* that enables the issuer to retire them before maturity. Even without a call option, the issuer may purchase its debentures on the open market and cancel them. In either case, the issuer recognizes a gain or loss for the difference between the consideration paid and the carrying amount. A gain arises if the purchase price of the debentures is less than the carrying amount, and a loss occurs if the purchase price is more than the carrying amount. Any transaction costs incurred in connection with retirement should be adjusted in calculating the gain or loss.

As an example, assume that on January 1, 20X4 Maya Company retired at 82 the 12 per cent debentures it had issued for ₹80,359 on January 1, 20X0. On this date, the carrying amount of the debentures was ₹84,919 (Exhibit 10.1, Period 8, column E). The transaction is recorded as follows:

20X4
Jan. 31   Debentures Payable 84,919
         Cash 82,000
         Gain on Redemption of Debentures 2,919

Debenture Redemption Fund

Companies should have cash to pay back its debentures at maturity. Some debenture trust deeds require companies to make periodic cash deposits to a *debenture redemption fund*, or *sinking fund*. The debenture trustees invest the cash in high-quality income-earning securities. The periodic deposits *plus* the earnings on the investments accumulate in the fund. When the debentures mature, the trustees sell the investments and use the proceeds to pay the debentureholders, and return any excess cash to the issuer; the company must make up any shortfall. Sinking fund investments are non-current assets.

Learning Objective

LO 7 Explain the operation of a debenture redemption fund.

To illustrate the operation of a debenture redemption fund, assume that Kiran Company issues ₹100,000 of five-year debentures on January 1. The trustee expects to earn a return of 10 per cent on the investments, *net* of expenses of administering the fund. Referring to Appendix C, Table 2, we find that if ₹1 is invested at the end of every year for five years at 10 per cent, it will cumulate to ₹6.1051 in Year 5. The amount of sinking fund deposit is ₹16,380, calculated as 100,000/6.1051. At the end of five years, the value of the sinking fund investments will be equal to the maturity value of the debentures, as shown in Exhibit 10.2.

EXHIBIT 10.2
Sinking Fund
Investments

> We adjust the rounding difference in the last period's interest expense.

Year	Beginning Balance (A)	Interest Income (B) 10% of (A)	Annual Deposit (C)	Ending Balance (D) (A) + (B) + (C)
1	—	—	₹16,380	₹16,380
2	₹16,380	₹1,638	16,380	34,398
3	34,398	3,440	16,380	54,218
4	54,218	5,422	16,380	76,020
5	76,020	7,600	16,380	100,000

The entry to record the amount deposited every year are as follows:[3]

Dec. 31	Sinking Fund Investments...	16,380	
	Cash		16,380

At the end of every year, the trustees will report the earnings on the investments to the issuer. The issuer then records the sinking fund earnings in its accounts and reports them on its statement of profit and loss. For example, if the investments yielded 10 per cent in the second year, Kiran Company records the income in Year 1 as follows:

Year 1

Dec. 31	Cash...	1,638	
	Income from Sinking Fund Investments.....................................		1,638
	Received income from sinking fund investments		
Dec. 31	Sinking Fund Investments...	1,638	
	Cash		1,638
	Invested interest received		

Income from investments goes to the statement of profit and loss.

In Year 5, the investments will be sold and the proceeds utilized to repay the debentures. Any gain or loss will be recognized at this time. Suppose the investments are sold for ₹102,500. The sale is recorded as follows:

Year 1

Dec. 31	Cash...	102,500	
	Sinking Fund Investments...		100,000
	Gain on Sale of Investments..		2,500
	Sold sinking fund investments		
Dec. 31	Debentures Payable..	100,000	
	Cash		100,000
	Redeemed debentures on maturity		

Gain on sale of investments goes to the statement of profit and loss.

Compound Financial Instruments

Learning Objective

LO 8 Account for compound financial instruments.

Compound financial instruments contain both a liability and an equity component. A common form of a compound financial instrument is a **convertible debenture**. It is a debenture with an embedded conversion option. It can be converted into the issuing company's equity shares. The conversion feature gives the debentureholder an opportunity to benefit from a rise in the price of the issuer's equity shares. Further, the debentureholder receives interest at the specified rate until conversion and is, therefore, subject to less risk relative to a shareholder. The advantage to the issuer is that convertible debentures carry a lower yield than non-convertible debentures.

---

[3] The Companies Act 2013 requires transfer of an amount equal to the amount of deposit from Retained Earnings to Debenture Redemption Reserve. At the time of repayment of the debentures, the balance in Debenture Redemption Reserve is transferred back to Retained Earnings.

Convertible debentures come with many variations. The terms may compel the holder to convert the debenture or leave it to the holder's option. The interest rate may be variable or fixed. The holder may have a *call option* (i.e. right to buy) to convert the debentures into a specified number of shares. Here again, the holder may be able to convert at maturity (*European call option*) or before maturity (*American call option*). We will now examine the accounting issues in convertible debentures with relatively simple features.

Issue of Convertible Debentures

The basic requirement here is to measure and recognize the liability and equity components separately. The components are as follows:

- *Financial liability:* The issuer's obligation to pay interest and redeem the debenture; and
- *Equity instrument:* The holder's right to call for the issuer's shares.

The issuer has to record the two components separately. This is 'split accounting'. The issuer determines the fair value of the liability component and determines the equity component as the residual amount.

HANDHOLD 10.2
Split Accounting for
Convertible Debentures

On January 1, 20X0, Sukhdev Company issues 1,000 debentures. The 10 per cent, 6-year debentures are issued at par with a face value of 100 each. So the proceeds are ₹100,000. Interest is payable on June 30 and December 31 in arrears. So the interest payment will be ₹5,000 on each date. Each debenture can be converted at any time up to maturity into 10 equity shares of ₹10, but the holder is under no compulsion to do so. If the holder opts not to exercise, she will get the principal amount of the debenture. The yield for similar debentures without conversion options is 12 per cent per annum. First, we measure the liability component based on the payments that the issuer is required to make. The present value calculations using a discount rate of 6 per cent and a period of 12 are as follows:

(a) Present value of 12 interest payments at 6%: ₹5,000 x 8.3838 (Appendix C, Table 4) .... ₹41,919
(b) Present value of ₹100,000 payable after 12 periods at 6%: ₹100,000 x 0.4970
  (Appendix C, Table 3) 49,700
  Present value of the liability component 91,619

Next, we calculate the value of the equity component as the balance of the proceeds, i.e. ₹8,381. We record the transaction as follows:

20X0
Jan. 1 Cash 100,000
        Debentures Payable 91,619
        Written Equity Call Option 8,381

Continuing with Handhold 10.2, suppose Sukhdev Company incurs issue costs of ₹1,000 for the convertible debentures. Recalculate the amounts to be allocated to the liability and the equity components.

TEST YOUR
UNDERSTANDING 10.2
Convertible Debentures

Conversion at Maturity

On conversion of a convertible debenture at maturity, the entity derecognizes the liability component and recognizes it as equity. Both the original equity component and the new equity component are allocated to other line items such as share capital, securities premium, and so on in accordance with legal requirements. There is no gain or loss on conversion at maturity.

Continuing with Handhold 10.2, on December 31, 20X5, Sukhdev Company's debentures were converted into 10,000 equity shares. We record the conversion as follows:

HANDHOLD 10.3
Conversion at Maturity

20X5
Dec. 31 Debentures Payable 100,000
         Equity Share Capital 100,000

Note that in this case, we do not recognize any gain or loss on conversion. The balance in Written Equity Call Option, ₹8,381 may be retained in that account or transferred within equity to another line item. The holders have the option not to convert, in which case they will get back the principal amount of ₹100,000. They are likely to convert if the share is trading at more than ₹10 on December 31, 20X5.

Conversion before Maturity

The holders may exercise the conversion option before maturity if the equity share is trading above the conversion price. There is no specific guidance on the accounting treatment if the holder opts to convert the debenture early. We can take the view that since the instrument 'matures' on the date that the holder converts in accordance with the contractual terms of the instrument, the position is essentially the same as that for conversion at maturity. The amount recognized in equity should be the carrying amount of the liability for the debt with adjustment for cash received or paid.

HANDHOLD 10.4
Conversion Before Maturity

Continuing with Handhold 10.2, suppose Sukhdev Company's debentures were converted into 10,000 equity shares of ₹10 at par on December 31, 20X3. First, we calculate the amortized cost at that date:

Period	Amortized Cost: Start of Period (A)	Interest Expense (B) 8% of (A)	Interest Paid (C)	Principal Paid (D)	Amortized Cost: End of Period (E) (A) + (B) − (C) − (D)
1	₹91,619	₹5,497	₹5,000		₹92,116
2	92,116	5,527	5,000		92,643
3	92,643	5,559	5,000		93,202
4	93,202	6,540	5,000		93,794
5	93,794	6,583	5,000		94,422
6	94,422	6,630	5,000		95,087
7	95,087	6,680	5,000		95,792
8	95,792	6,735	5,000		96,540

At the time of conversion, the amortized cost is ₹96,540. The conversion is recorded as follows:

20X5
Dec. 31   Debentures Payable.. 96,540
        Cash... 3,460
            Equity Share Capital.. 100,000
            Retired 12% debentures at 82

The holders need to pay the difference between, the amount of share capital and the amortized cost of the debentures (representing the value of the liability).

Mortgages Payable

Learning Objective

LO 9 Account for mortgages.

A **mortgage** is a legal arrangement in which a borrowing is secured by specific immovable assets such as land or building. If the borrower does not pay, the lender has the legal right to have the specific assets sold and pay itself out of the proceeds. A home loan is a common example of mortgage in which the borrower gives his house as security for repayment of the loan in monthly instalments over a fairly long period.

Mortgages can be of different types. At one extreme is **conditional mortgage** in which the borrower's legal title to the property is transferred to the lender and is re-transferred to the borrower when the loan is repaid. At the other end, **equitable mortgage** is a relatively simple arrangement in which the borrower deposits the title deed for the property with the lender and takes them back when the loan is repaid.

Mortgage payments are generally made in equal instalments that comprise both interest and principal components (e.g. equated monthly instalment, or EMI). Each payment is applied first to the accrued interest and the remainder reduces the principal. In the early years of repayment, the principal is high. Therefore, a major portion of the instalment goes towards interest. As the repayment period progresses, the principal gradually decreases until the balance payable reaches zero.

To illustrate, assume that on January 1 a mortgage debt of ₹100,000 was obtained. The mortgage carries interest at 18 per cent per annum and is repayable in 48 monthly instalments of ₹2,937.[4] Exhibit 10.3 shows the repayment schedule for the first three months split into principal and interest.

Payment Date	Beginning Principal (A)	Borrowing (B)	Instalment (C)	Interest (D) 1.5% of (A)	Reduction in Principal (E) (C) – (D)	Ending Principal (F) (A) + (B) – (E)
Jan. 1	—	₹100,000	—	—	—	₹100,000
Feb. 1	₹100,000	—	₹2,937	₹1,500	₹1,437	98,563
Mar. 1	98,563	—	2,937	1,478	1,459	97,104
Apr. 1	97,104	—	2,937	1,457	1,480	95,624

EXHIBIT 10.3
Mortgage Repayment Schedule

The entry to record the first monthly payment on February 1 is as follows:

Feb. 1	Interest Expense	1,500	
	Mortgage Payable	1,437	
	Cash		2,937

Leases

As you learnt in Chapter 4, a **lease** is an agreement that allows the use of an asset for a certain period of time. The owner of the asset is the **lessor** and the user of the asset is the **lessee**. Leasing makes it possible to use an asset without having to invest own or borrowed funds. There are two types of lease: *finance lease* and *operating lease*. Table 10.1 illustrates the key features of finance lease and operating lease.

Learning Objective
LO10 **Account for leases.**

A finance lease is effectively a borrowing, whereas an operating lease is a rental arrangement.

TABLE 10.1
Finance and Operating Leases

Feature	Finance Lease	Operating Lease
Economic substance	▪ Effective transfer of ownership	▪ Rental arrangement
Lease term	▪ Long	▪ Short
Accounting	▪ Recognize leased asset and obligation	▪ Expense lease rental when incurred

Finance Lease

Finance lease transfers substantially *economic* ownership of an asset. Economic ownership entails risks (upside) and rewards (downside). The decrease in the price of the asset, decrease in the price of the asset's output and unexpected obsolescence are examples of ownership risks. The increase in the price of the asset and increase in the price of the asset's output are examples of ownership rewards. In a finance lease, the lessor (a leasing company) transfers the risks and rewards of ownership of an asset to the lessee for a series of rental payments under a non-cancellable lease contract. Acquisition of assets on finance lease is equivalent to obtaining a secured loan. The principle of **substance over form** requires entities to account for and present transactions and events in accordance with their economic substance and reality, and not merely their legal form.

---

[4] We calculate the monthly instalment with the help of the formula, $P_{i,n} = \{(1 + i)n - 1\}/i(1 + i)n$. $i = 0.015$ and $n = 48$.

While the legal form of a finance lease agreement is that the lessee does not acquire legal ownership of the leased asset, the substance is that the lessee acquires the economic benefits of the use of the asset for a major part of its useful life. Examples of situations in which a lease is normally classified as a finance lease include the following:

1. The lease transfers ownership of the asset to the lessee by the end of the lease term;
2. The lease has a "bargain purchase" option, i.e. the lessee has the right to buy the asset at a price much lower than its fair value;
3. The lease term covers the major part of the economic life of the asset;
4. At the inception of the lease the present value of the minimum lease payments amounts to at least substantially all of the fair value of the leased asset; and
5. The leased assets are of such a specialized nature that only the lessee can use them without major modifications.

In practice, "major part of the economic life of the asset" is taken to be 75 per cent and "at least substantially all of the fair value of the leased asset" is taken to be 90 per cent. The classification of a lease as an operating lease or a finance lease will depend on the substance of the transaction rather than on the form of the contract. A finance lease must be recognized in the lessee's balance sheet as an asset and an obligation, a practice known as **lease capitalization**. Table 10.2 presents the definitions of key terms in lease accounting.

TABLE 10.2
Key Terms Used in
Lease Accounting

Finance lease   A lease that transfers the economic ownership of an asset.

Operating lease   A lease other than a finance lease.

Lease term   The non-cancellable period of a lease contract.

Minimum lease payments for a lessee   The payments the lessee is required to make and any amounts guaranteed by the lessee or by a party related to the lessee.

Minimum lease payments for a lessor   The payments the lessee is required to make and any residual value guaranteed by the lessee, a party related to the lessee, or an unrelated third party.

Fair value   The price of an asset, liability or equity in an arm's-length transaction.

Interest rate implicit in the lease   The discount rate at which the present value of (a) the minimum lease payments and (b) the unguaranteed residual value is equal to the fair value of a leased asset.

Lessee's incremental borrowing rate of interest   The interest rate the lessee would have to pay on a similar lease or on a borrowing on similar terms.

To illustrate lease capitalization, assume that Abdullah Company signs an agreement with a leasing company to lease equipment from that date. The information about the lease is as follows:

1. The lease is for four years and the agreement is non-cancellable. The equipment reverts to the lessor at the end of the period.
2. Lease rental of ₹28,679 must be paid at the beginning of each year. The first rental is payable on signing the agreement.
3. The equipment has a fair value of ₹102,000 at the inception of the lease, an estimated useful life of four years, and no residual value.
4. The lessee's incremental borrowing rate is 12 per cent.
5. The lessor is known to charge an interest rate of 10 per cent on the lease.
6. The lessee uses straight-line depreciation of similar equipment.

The procedure for lease capitalization is as follows:

1. *Determine whether the agreement is a finance lease.* The agreement is clearly a finance lease because it is non-cancellable for the entire useful life of the equipment. Therefore, it passes the test of substantial transfer of risks and rewards incident to ownership of the asset.
2. *Compute the present value of the minimum lease payment.* The minimum lease payments consist of the annual lease rentals payable by the lessee at the beginning of each year. Since the lessor's interest rate is known (10 per cent), it is used as the discount rate disregarding the lessee's incremental borrowing rate. The present value calculation is as follows:

Present value of four payments of ₹28,679: ₹28,679 × 3.4869 (Appendix C, Table 5) ₹100,000

Note that Table 5 shows the present value of *annuity due*, i.e. payable at the *beginning* of the period. Table 4 is for *ordinary annuity*, i.e. payable at the *end* of the period.

3. *Take the lower of fair value and the present value of minimum lease payments.* Since the present value of minimum lease payments of ₹100,000 is less than the fair value of ₹102,000, the lease will be recorded by the lessee as an asset and a liability at ₹100,000.

The following entry records the transaction:

Leased Equipment.. 100,000
   Finance Lease Obligation... 100,000

Abdullah Company presents leased equipment as part of property, plant and equipment and finance lease obligation as a borrowing in non-current liabilities. It depreciates the asset and records the following entry for each period:

Depreciation, Expense, Leased Equipment 25,000
   Accumulated Depreciation, Leased Equipment...................................... 25,000

The first lease rental is paid immediately on signing the agreement and is therefore fully offset against the lease obligation. The second, third and fourth lease rentals consist of principal and interest. Exhibit 10.4 shows the computation of interest expense in each period. Using this information, the entry to record the first lease payment is as follows:

Finance Lease Obligation.. 28,679
   Cash 28,679
     Paid the first lease rental

Payment of the second lease rental is recorded as follows:

Interest Expense... 7,132
Finance Lease Obligation.. 21,547
   Cash 28,679
     Paid the first lease rental

Year	Beginning Obligation (A)	Lease Payment (B)	Interest (C) 10% of (A)*	Reduction in Obligation (D) (B) – (C)	Ending Obligation (E) (A) – (D)
1	₹100,000	₹28,679	—	₹28,679	₹71,321
2	71,321	28,679	₹7,132	21,547	49,774
3	49,774	28,679	4,977	23,702	26,072
4	26,072	28,679	2,607	26,072	0

*Since lease payment for Year 1 occurs at the inception of the lease, it is entirely towards reduction of the obligation.

EXHIBIT 10.4
Lease Payment Schedule

Accounting for leases is one of the most controversial topics. Lessees have resisted lease capitalization in order to keep the debt-to-equity ratio low. They found clever ways to circumvent the capitalization rules, such as setting the lease term at marginally less than 75 per cent. The IASB has proposed a radical overhaul of lease accounting that would require capitalization of a "right-of-use asset" for all leases of more than 12 months.

Operating Lease

Operating lease is a short-term rental arrangement such as renting office space, car or photocopier. The lessee expenses operating lease payments. Normally, the lessee recognizes the expense on a straight-line basis over the lease period unless another systematic basis is more representative of the time pattern of the user's benefits. The lessee does not capitalize assets under operating lease.

TEST YOUR UNDERSTANDING 10.3
Operating Lease

Mihir Company takes a car on lease for two years on a monthly rental of ₹30,000 per month. The rental is ₹40,000 per month for the first year and ₹20,000 per month for the second year of the lease. How should Mihir Company account for the lease payments?

FINANCIAL VIEW
Leases

What difference does it make whether leases are off or on balance sheet? For capitalized leases, the statement of profit and loss recognizes depreciation and interest charges. For non-capitalized leases, the lease rental expense (that includes depreciation and interest) is spread out over the lease term. As a result, earnings and other numbers can differ widely depending on the accounting treatment of leases. Those who depend heavily on leased assets, such as retailers, airlines and ship operators, would have to show more liabilities if large numbers of leases are capitalized. Further, some companies that are on the edge of compliance with their loan covenants could breach them. Bondholders and credit rating agencies are already including in debt a substantial portion of lease rentals payable, regardless of how companies account for their leases. Ordinary investors' perception of how indebted their companies are could change drastically, when leases are capitalized.

ONE-MINUTE QUIZ 10.4
Lease Payments

The date of inception of a five-year finance lease is March 31, 20X1. The agreement specifies equal annual lease payments on March 31 of each year. For the lessee, the payment on March 31, 20X1 includes:

	Interest Expense	*Reduction of the Lease Obligation*
(a)	Yes	Yes
(b)	Yes	No
(c)	No	Yes
(d)	No	No

Off-balance Sheet Financing

Learning Objective
LO 11 Explain off-balance sheet financing arrangements.

Off-balance sheet financing refers to the availing of a source of finance which is not required to be recognized as a liability. So the financing is not apparent from the balance sheet. Possible motivations for off-balance sheet financing include:

- An increase in the borrowing capacity of the enterprise as the debt-equity ratio is kept low;
- Better view of the liquidity position of the enterprise; and
- Improved return on assets.

In a world characterized by intense competition for funds and better terms for raising capital, these motivations can be significant. As one business writer commented, "The basic drives of man are a few: to get enough food, to find shelter, and to keep debt off the balance sheet."

Enterprises recognize assets owned and liabilities owed. The question is whether the balance sheet should list the enterprise's legal assets and liabilities or show its economic resources and obligations. Accounting regulators have eliminated many forms of off-balance sheet financing, but some variations of these keep surfacing from time to time. We will now see some transactions with potential for off-balance sheet financing.

Transfer of Receivables with Recourse

As discussed in Chapter 7, a transfer of receivables with recourse in the form of pledging or assignment should be treated as a borrowing, and not as a sale, by the transferor. This is because the 'sale' of receivables is nothing more than a financing transaction, the receivables merely serving as a security for the borrowing. The difference between the proceeds and the receivables is an interest cost. It cannot derecognize the receivables. An entity can derecognize a financial asset (such as a receivable) only when it transfers the asset.

TEST YOUR UNDERSTANDING 10.4
Transfer of Receivables with Recourse

On February 1, Javed Company transfers its receivables of ₹25,000 to National Factor for an equal amount of cash with the understanding that they would be transferred back on May 1 for ₹26,500. How should it report this transaction in its financial statements?

Product Financing Arrangement

This is a transaction in which an enterprise (the sponsor) sells and agrees to repurchase inventory at a later date. The repurchase price equals the original sale price plus holding and financing costs. The substance of a product financing arrangement, regardless of its legal form, is that of a financing arrangement rather than a sale or purchase by the sponsor. As a result, the sponsor finances its inventory without reporting either the liability or the inventory. Product financing arrangements are often referred to as *parking transactions* because the seller simply "parks" the inventory on the balance sheet of another enterprise.

To illustrate, assume that Kapil Company sells inventory costing ₹8,000 to Saif Company for ₹10,000 and agrees to repurchase the same inventory for ₹10,500 in 30 days. Kapil Company should enter the transaction as follows:

(a)	Cash..	10,000	
	Due to Saif Company under Product Financing Arrangement...........		10,000
(b)	Inventory under Product Financing Arrangement	8,000	
	Inventory		8,000

The difference of ₹500 between the sale price and the purchase price is interest expense.

Unconditional Purchase Obligation

An **unconditional purchase obligation** results when one party is required to transfer funds to another party in return for future delivery of specified quantities of goods or services at specified prices. Accounting principles do not require the recording of *executory transactions*, i.e. transactions in which the parties to the contract have not completed the performance. Exchanges are recorded when the transfer of resources or obligations occurs. However, if significant purchase commitments are not disclosed, the financial statements may be misleading.

- In a *take-or-pay contract*, the buyer agrees to pay specified periodic amounts for certain products or services. The buyer must make the payments, even if it does not take delivery of the products or services.
- In a *throughput contract*, one party agrees to pay specified periodic amounts to another party for the transportation or processing of a product. The payments must be made, even if the minimum quantities specified in the agreement have not been sent to the other party transporting or processing the product.

The characteristic feature of take-or-pay and throughput contracts is that the periodic payments do not depend on the occurrence of a specified event or the fulfilment of a condition. So they are different from contingent liabilities. The Companies Act requires disclosure of the following commitments: (a) estimated amount of contracts remaining to be executed on capital account and not provided for; (b) uncalled liability on shares and other investments partly paid; and (c) other commitments.

Can off-balance sheet financing be eliminated?

DISCUSSION QUESTION 10.1

....

....

....

FORENSIC CORNER
Enron's Invisible Debt

Enron, the byword for accounting fraud, used special purpose entities (SPEs) to keep debt off its balance sheet. The SPEs, owned by the company's chief financial officer Andrew Fastow, borrowed large amounts. Enron had no ownership interest in the SPEs. As a result, such entities were not required to be consolidated. Since the debt was not reported in Enron's financial statements, the company kept debt of over $30 billion away from the eyes of its investors, keeping the debt-to-equity ratio within an acceptable limit. This was done to satisfy credit rating agencies Moody's and Standard & Poor's. Another benefit was to increase the return on assets. Such transactions were disclosed in notes to the financial statements that were so obscure that even analysts had difficulty understanding them. Enron collapsed in November 2001. Andrew Fastow was convicted and sentenced to six years' imprisonment. In 2003, the FASB widened the scope for consolidation of "variable interest entities", i.e. special purpose entities.

APPLICATION
Financial Liabilities

Here are some typical examples of financial liabilities.

- *Tata Motors:* Accounts payable, acceptances, borrowings and interest on them and derivative financial instruments. Financial liabilities are classified into financial liabilities at fair value through profit or loss and other financial liabilities. The latter are measured at amortized cost using the effective interest method.
- *HDFC Bank:* Interest-bearing and non-interest-bearing deposits, short-term borrowings, and long-term debt.

IFRS, IND AS AND INDIAN GAAP
Financial Liabilities

IFRS and Ind AS have two measurement categories for financial liabilities: amortized cost and FVTPL. Indian GAAP has no specific guidance. IFRS and Ind AS require a financial liability to be derecognized when it is extinguished. Indian GAAP has no specific guidance.

RECAP

- *Financial liabilities* are contractual obligations to pay definite amounts. Financial liabilities fund long-term needs.
- Financial liabilities are measured at amortized cost or at FVTPL.
- Debentures may be *secured* or *unsecured, term* or *serial, convertible* or *non-convertible, callable* or *non-callable, coupon* or *zero-coupon*.
- Debentures are recorded at a *fair value* obtained by discounting the principal and interest payments. Interest expense is calculated using the *effective interest method*.
- *Redeemable preference shares* are classified as debt and the dividend on them is classified as interest.
- *Redemption* is the payment of debentures at maturity. *Retirement* is early payment. A gain or loss is recognized for the difference between the price paid and the carrying amount of the debentures.
- *Debenture redemption fund*, or *sinking fund*, ensures sufficient cash to pay back the debentures.
- A *compound financial instrument*, such as a convertible debenture, is part equity and part debt. The liability and equity components should be measured and recognized separately.
- Mortgage payments are separated into interest and principal components.
- A lessee recognizes a *finance lease* as an asset and an obligation.
- *Off-balance sheet financing* items are disclosed.

Review Problem

On August 1, 20X5, Navin Company issued ₹500,000, 15%, 10-year debentures. Interest is payable on June 30 and December 31 in arrears. The company's year end is March 31. The yield was 18 per cent.

Required
Prepare journal entries to record the following:

1. Issue of debentures on August 1, 20X5.
2. Payment of semi-annual interest on December 31, 20X5 and amortization of discount.
3. Accrual of interest on March 31, 20X6 and amortization of discount.

Solution to the Review Problem

The issue proceeds are ₹431,519, calculated as follows: 37,500 × 9.1285 + 500,000 × 0.1784. We discount the cash flows at 9 per cent for 20 periods.

20X5

Aug. 1	Cash...	431,519	
	Debentures Payable..		431,519
	Issued 15%, 10-year debentures at a discount		
Dec. 31	Debenture Interest Expense..	32,364	
	Cash		31,250
	Debentures Payable..		1,114
	Paid semi-annual interest on 15% debentures for five months: 500,000 × 15% × 5/12 = 31,250 + Discount amortization: 1,337 × 5/6 = 1,114		

20X6

Mar. 31	Debenture Interest Expense..	19,459	
	Accrued Interest Payable		18,750
	Debentures Payable..		709
	Accrued interest on 15% debentures for three months: 500,000 × 15% × 3/12 = 18,750 + Discount amortization: 1,337 × 1/6 = 223 + 1,457 × 2/6 = 486		

ASSIGNMENT MATERIAL

Questions

1. What are the common forms of providing security for a debt?

2. When are financial liabilities measured at FVTPL?

3. Why is the *debenture trust deed* important?

4. How does the call option of a debenture help the issuer?

5. How is yield determined?

6. For a debenture issued at a discount, why does the interest expense increase over the life of the debenture?

7. Are *redeemable preference shares* debt or equity? Explain.

8. How should debenture redemption premium be accounted for?

9. How does a debenture redemption fund protect the debentureholders' interest?

10. What is a *compound financial instrument*? Give two examples.

11. Is *operating lease* a source of off-balance sheet financing? Explain.

12. What is a *product financing arrangement*?

13. Are unfulfilled purchase orders liabilities? Why or why not?

14. Does signing a *take-or-pay contract* result in a liability?

Problems

On April 1, 20X1, Vani Company issues ₹1 million of 10%, 15-year debentures. Interest is payable semi-annually on March 31 and September 30 in arrears. Compute the issue price of the debentures if the yield on April 1 equals (a) 18 per cent, (b) 10 per cent, or (c) 8 per cent.

Problem 10.1
Computing Issue Price of Debentures∗

On January 1, 20X3, Easy Ways Company issued ₹300,000, 18%, 10-year debentures. Interest is payable on June 30 and December 31 in arrears. The company's financial year ends on December 31.

Problem 10.2
Recording Debenture Issue∗

Required

1. Prepare journal entries to record the issue if the proceeds were (a) ₹280,000, and (b) ₹310,000.

2. Prepare journal entries in 20X3 to record interest expense.

Problem 10.3
Debenture Conversion *

On January 1, 20XX, Veer Company issued ₹500,000 of 15 per cent, 5-year, ₹1,000 debentures convertible into 30 equity shares of face value of ₹10 at par. Interest is payable on June 30 and December 31 in arrears. On June 30, 20XX, after paying interest and amortizing discount, unamortized discount was ₹20,000. On that date, ₹200,000 of the debentures were converted.

Required

Prepare the journal entry to record the conversion of the debentures.

Problem 10.4
Accrual of Debenture Interest *

On February 1, 20X5, Vivian Company issued ₹100,000 of 18 per cent, 10-year debentures for ₹88,000. Interest is payable on January 31 and July 31. The company's financial year end is March 31.

Required

Prepare journal entries to record the accrual of interest and amortization of discount on March 31, 20X5 and payment of interest and amortization of discount on August 1, 20X5.

Problem 10.5
Sinking Fund **

On January 1, 20X7, Kamal Company issued ₹200,000 of 12 per cent, 20-year debentures. The debenture trust deed requires the company to create a sinking fund and invest the assets in investment grade securities that yield an annual return of 10 per cent. Investments and interest receipts will take place on December 31.

Required

Prepare journal entries to record payment of the deposit on December 31, 20X7 and receipt of the earnings from the deposit on December 31, 20X8.

Problem 10.6
Operating Lease **

On January 1, 20X1, Jeet Company took furniture on lease for 18 months. The lease rental is ₹10,000 per month in the first year and ₹4,000 per month in the second year. All payments are made at the end of the quarter, beginning March 31, 20X1. The furniture had an estimated useful life of five years.

Required

Prepare journal entries to record payment of the lease rental expense.

Problem 10.7
Debenture Transactions ***

On July 1, 20X0, Arjun Company issued ₹300,000 of 12 per cent, 8-year secured debentures at ₹246,895. The debentures yield 16 per cent. Interest is payable on June 30 and December 31 in arrears. The debentures are due for redemption on July 1, 20X8. The company's year end is December 31.

Required

1. Prepare a discount amortization schedule.
2. Prepare journal entries to record the following: (a) issue of debentures; (b) interest expense on December 31, 20X0; (c) interest expense on June 30, 20X1; and (c) redemption of debentures.

Problem 10.8
Debenture Transactions *** Alternative to Problem 10.7

On January 1, 20X4, Barnali Company issued ₹500,000 of 16 per cent, 5-year secured debentures at ₹438,534. The debentures yield 20 per cent. Interest is payable on June 30 and December 31. The debentures are due for redemption on January 1, 20X9. The company's year end is December 31.

Required

1. Prepare a debenture discount amortization schedule.
2. Prepare journal entries to record the following: (a) issue of the debentures on January 1, 20X4, (b) payment of interest and amortization of the discount on July 1, 20X4; (c) payment of the interest and amortization of the discount on January 1, 20X5; and (d) redemption of debentures on January 1, 20X9.
3. What would have been the balance in the discount on debentures payable account on December 31, 20X6 if the company had followed the straight-line method amortization? Assume that the interest payment due on January 1, 20X7 is accrued on December 31, 20X6.

Problem 10.9
Sinking Fund ****

On August 1, 20X0, De Silva Company issued ₹200,000 of 16 per cent, 9-year debentures for ₹182,490, callable at the market price on or after July 31, 20X7. The yield at the time was 18 per cent per annum. The debenture trust deed requires the company to deposit ₹14,728 with the trustee at the end of every reporting period during the life of the debentures. The company's year end is July 31. Interest is paid on January 31 and July 31. The sinking fund investments are expected to earn a return of 10 per cent per year. All deposits were made and the amounts were invested as stipulated in the trust deed. After payment of interest on July 31, 20X8, the company called the debentures at the market price of 95.6, sold the investments for ₹165,110, and paid the debentureholders.

Required

1. Prepare a schedule showing accumulation of sinking fund investments up to July 31, 20X8.
2. Prepare a debenture discount amortization schedule up to July 31, 20X8.
3. Prepare journal entries to record the following transactions: (a) issue of debentures; (b) sinking fund investment on July 31, 20X1; (c) sale of sinking fund investments; and (d) retirement of debentures.

On January 1, 20X2, Christina Company issued ₹500,000 of 14 per cent, 7-year debentures for ₹458,797, callable at the market price on or after December 31, 20X7. The yield at the time was 16 per cent per annum. The debenture trust deed requires the company to deposit ₹49,559 with the trustee at the end of every reporting period during the life of the debentures. The company's fiscal year ends on December 31. Interest is paid on June 30 and December 31. The sinking fund investments are expected to earn a return of 12 per cent per year. All deposits were made and the amounts were invested as stipulated in the trust deed. On December 31, 20X7, the company called the debentures at the market price of 96.4, sold the investments for ₹404,310, and paid the debentureholders.

Problem 10.10
Sinking Fund ✶✶✶✶
Alternative to
Problem 10.9

Required

1. Prepare a schedule showing accumulation of sinking fund investments up to December 31, 20X7.
2. Prepare a debenture discount amortization schedule up to December 31, 20X7.
3. Prepare journal entries to record the following transactions: (a) issue of debentures; (b) sinking fund investment on December 31, 20X2; (c) sale of sinking fund investments; and (d) retirement of debentures.

On August 15, 20X1, the board of directors of Mahendra Company approved the issue of ₹150,000 of 10 per cent, 10-year convertible debentures and of ₹100,000 of 16 per cent, 8-year callable debentures. Each 10 per cent debenture of ₹100 is convertible into six shares of ₹10 face value. The company's year end is March 31. The company completed the following transactions pertaining to the debentures:

Problem 10.11
Comprehensive Debenture
Transactions ✶✶✶✶

20X1
Sep. 1 Issued 16% debentures for cash at face value. The debentures are callable at 98. Interest is payable on June 30 and December 31.
Nov. 1 Issued 10% debentures for cash so as to yield 14%. Interest is payable on April 30 and October 31.
Dec. 31 Paid interest on 16% debentures.
20X2
Mar. 31 Recorded accrued interest on all debentures.
Apr. 30 Paid interest on 10% debentures.
June 30 Paid interest on 16% debentures.
Oct. 31 Paid interest on 10% debentures.
Nov. 30 Called and retired 16% debentures and paid accrued interest.
20X3
Mar. 31 Recorded accrued interest on 10% debentures.
Apr. 30 Converted all 10% debentures into equity after paying interest.

Required

Prepare journal entries to record the transactions.

On March 22, 20X4, the board of directors of Ranatunga Company approved the issue of ₹200,000 of 12 per cent, 15-year convertible debentures and of ₹300,000 of 18 per cent, 10-year callable debentures. Each 12 per cent debenture of ₹100 is convertible into four shares of ₹10 face value. The company's financial year end is November 30. The company completed the following transactions pertaining to the debentures:

Problem 10.12
Comprehensive Debenture
Transactions ✶✶✶✶
Alternative to
Problem 10.11

20X4

Apr. 1 Issued 12% debentures for cash to yield 10%. Interest is payable on March 31 and September 30.

July 1 Issued 18% debentures for cash at face value. The debentures are callable at 99. Interest is payable on January 31 and July 31.

July 31 Paid interest on 18% debentures.

Sep. 30 Paid interest on 12% debentures.

Nov. 30 Recorded accrued interest on all debentures.

20X5

Jan. 31 Paid interest on 18% debentures.

May 30 Paid interest on 12% debentures.

July 31 Paid interest on 18% debentures.

Sep. 30 Paid interest on 12% debentures.

Nov. 30 Recorded accrued interest on all debentures.

Dec. 1 Called and retired 18% debentures and paid accrued interest.

20X6

Mar. 31 Paid interest on 12% debentures.

Sep. 30 Converted all 12% debentures into equity after paying interest.

Required

Prepare journal entries to record the transactions.

Problem 10.13
Accounting for Leases
✶✶✶✶✶

Part I

An equipment lease agreement has the following features:

  (a) The term of the lease is four years and the lease agreement is non-cancellable. The equipment reverts to the lessor at the end of the period.
  (b) Lease rental of ₹28,679 must be paid at the beginning of each year. The first rental is payable on signing the agreement.
  (c) The equipment has a fair value of ₹100,000 at the inception of the lease, an estimated useful life of eight years, and no residual value.
  (d) The lessee's incremental borrowing rate is 12 per cent.
  (e) The lessor is known to charge an interest rate of 10 per cent on the lease.
  (f) The lessee uses the straight-line method for depreciation of similar equipment.

Part II

Same facts as in Part I, except that the equipment has (a) a fair value of ₹106,830 and (b) an unguaranteed residual value of ₹10,000.

Part III

Same facts as in Part I, except that the equipment has (a) a fair value of ₹103,415 and (b) a residual value of ₹5,000, guaranteed by the lessee.

Part IV

Same facts as in Part I, except that the equipment has (a) a fair value of ₹103,415 and (b) a residual value of ₹5,000, guaranteed by an independent third party financially capable meeting the obligation.

Part V

Same facts as in Part I, except that the equipment has (a) a fair value of ₹113,660 and (b) an unguaranteed residual value of ₹20,000.

Part VI

Same facts as in Part I, except that the equipment has (a) a fair value of ₹113,660, (b) an unguaranteed residual value of ₹20,000, and (c) a useful life of five years.

Required

Answer the following questions separately for each Part.

  1. What are the minimum lease payments from the standpoint of (a) the lessee? (b) the lessor?
  2. Is this a finance lease? Why or why not?
  3. What is the interest rate implicit in the lease?
  4. How should the lessee record the lease?

Part I

An equipment lease agreement has the following features:

Problem 10.14
Accounting for Leases
✱✱✱✱✱ Alternative to
Problem 10.13

(a) The term of the lease is six years and the lease agreement is non-cancellable. The equipment reverts to the lessor at the end of the period.

(b) Lease rental of ₹30,044 must be paid at the beginning of each year. The first rental is payable on signing the agreement.

(c) The equipment has a fair value of ₹150,000 at the inception of the lease, an estimated useful life of ten years, and no residual value.

(d) The lessee's incremental borrowing rate is 9 per cent.

(e) The lessor is known to charge an interest rate of 8 per cent on the lease.

(f) The lessee uses the straight-line method for depreciation of similar equipment.

Part II

Same facts as in Part I, except that the equipment has (i) a fair value of ₹159,453 and (ii) an unguaranteed residual value of ₹15,000.

Part III

Same facts as in Part I, except that the equipment has (i) a fair value of ₹155,042 and (ii) a residual value of ₹8,000, guaranteed by the lessee.

Part IV

Same facts as in Part I, except that the equipment has (i) a fair value of ₹155,042 and (ii) a residual value of ₹8,000, guaranteed by an independent third party financially capable of meeting the obligation.

Part V

Same facts as in Part I, except that the equipment has (i) a fair value of ₹168,906 and (ii) an unguaranteed residual value of ₹30,000.

Part VI

Same facts as in Part I, except that the equipment has (i) a fair value of ₹170,166, (ii) an unguaranteed residual value of ₹32,000, and (iii) a useful life of eight years.

Required

Answer the following questions separately for each Part.

1. What are the minimum lease payments from the standpoint of (i) the lessee? (ii) the lessor?
2. Is this a finance lease? Why or why not?
3. What is the interest rate implicit in the lease?
4. How should the lessee record the lease?

Business Decision Cases

The chief financial officer of Softscape Corporation is considering two alternatives for financing the company's proposed acquisition of computers costing ₹1,000,000. The computers have an estimated useful life of three years and a residual value of ₹100,000. The company can borrow at 20 per cent per annum from its bank and pay for the assets. The loan is repayable in six equal semi-annual instalments that include principal and interest. Expro Finance, a leasing company, has given a proposal for leasing the equipment at a semi-annual lease rental of ₹229,605 over the lease term. The equipment reverts to the lessor at the end of the lease period. Loan instalments and lease rentals are paid at the end of each semi-annual period. Softscape Corporation follows straight-line depreciation.

BDC 10.1
Softscape Corporation

Required

1. Compute the amount of expense that must be recognized in each of the three years under the borrowing and leasing alternatives, assuming (a) capitalization and (b) no capitalization.
2. Prepare the journal entry to record the lease at the time of inception of the contract.
3. Evaluate the leasing and borrowing alternatives.
4. The marketing manager of Expro Finance informed Softscape that the proposed lease would be "off-balance sheet". What does it mean? In your view, should Softscape capitalize the lease?

Interpreting Financial Reports

IFR 10.1
Lehman Brothers[5]

On January 29, 2008, Lehman Brothers reported record revenues of nearly $60 billion and record earnings in excess of $4 billion for the fiscal year ending November 30, 2007. During January 2008, Lehman's stock traded as high as $65.73 per share and averaged in the high to mid-fifties, implying a market capitalization of over $30 billion. Less than eight months later, on September 12, 2008, Lehman's stock closed under $4. On September 15, 2008, Lehman filed for bankruptcy, the largest ever. The examiner's report referred to "balance sheet manipulation" by Lehman executives.

Lehman employed off-balance sheet devices, known as "Repo 105" and "Repo 108" transactions, to temporarily remove securities inventory from its balance sheet, usually for a period of seven to ten days, and to create a materially misleading picture of the firm's condition in late 2007 and 2008. Repo 105 transactions utilized fixed income securities and required a minimum of $105 worth of securities in exchange for $100 cash borrowed; Repo 108 transactions utilized fixed income securities and required a minimum of $108 worth of securities in exchange for $100 cash borrowed. Repo 105 (we use this term to refer to both Repo 105 and Repo 108) transactions were nearly identical to standard repurchase and resale ("repo") transactions that Lehman and other investment banks used to secure short-term financing with a critical difference: Lehman accounted for Repo 105 transactions as sales.

Lehman regularly increased its use of Repo 105 transactions in the days prior to reporting periods to reduce its publicly reported net leverage. It did not disclose the cash borrowing from the Repo 105 transactions. It used the cash from Repo 105 transactions to pay other liabilities, thereby reducing both the total liabilities and the total assets reported on its balance sheet and lowering its leverage ratios.

Required

1. How is a standard repo transaction accounted? How is Repo 105 transaction accounted? Why does the accounting differ?
2. According to the examiner's report, "Lehman's auditors, Ernst & Young, were aware of but did not question Lehman's use and nondisclosure of the Repo 105 accounting transactions." What would your response be as the auditor?
3. What safeguards would be useful in dealing with Repo 105 and similar practices?

Financial Analysis

FA 10.1
Financial Liabilities

Study a sample of company annual reports for five years.

Required

1. Identify items of financial liabilities, such as debentures, loans and lease obligations.
2. Summarize the terms of borrowing, such as period of repayment, interest rate, and security offered.

FA 10.2
Leases

Study a sample of the annual reports of retail, airline and shipping companies.

Required

1. Identify finance leases and operating leases.
2. Explain how the IASB's proposal on leases is likely to affect them.

Answers to One-minute Quiz

10.1 b, c, d.
10.2 a.
10.3 c.
10.4 c.

---

[5] This case is based on newspaper reports and draws substantially on the report of Anton R. Valukas, Examiner.

Answers to Test Your Understanding

10.1 After adjusting for the transactions costs, the effective interest is 8.1214%, rounded to 8%. The reworked schedule is as follows:

Period	Amortized Cost: Start of Period (A)	Interest Expense (B) 8% of (A)	Interest Paid (C)	Principal Paid (D)	Amortized Cost: End of Period (E) (A) + (B) − (C) − (D)
1	₹79,359	₹6,445	₹6,000	₹ 0	₹79,804
2	79,804	6,481	6,000	0	80,285
3	80,285	6,520	6,000	0	80,806
4	80,806	6,563	6,000	0	81,368
5	81,368	6,608	6,000	0	81,976

10.2 We allocate the issue costs between the liability and the equity components in proportion to the allocation of the proceeds. The net proceeds will be as follows:

	Equity Component	Debt Component	Total
Gross proceeds...	₹8,381	₹91,619	₹100,000
Issue costs	(84)	(916)	(1,000)
Net proceeds..	8,297	90,703	99,000

10.3 Every quarter it will expense lease rental of ₹90,000. Applying the straight-line method, the quarterly rental is ₹90,000, calculated as follows: (₹40,000 × 12 + ₹20,000 × 12)/8 quarters. Mihir Company will expense operating lease rental of ₹90,000 every quarter, though the pattern of the rental payments differs over the lease period. It actually pays ₹120,000 over a quarter in the first year as compared to ₹60,000 in the second year. The difference is treated as a prepayment and adjusted later.

10.4 The transaction is a financing arrangement using the receivables as security. Javed Company retains the risks and rewards of ownership of the receivables. This transaction is similar to the transfer of receivables with recourse. Therefore, the receivables will appear on Javed Company's balance sheet.

LEARNING OBJECTIVES

After studying this chapter, you should be able to:

1. Describe the features of a corporate organization.
2. Explain the components of capital stock.
3. Record transactions involving share capital.
4. Describe the features of preference shares.
5. Describe the different kinds of reserves.
6. Account for activities in foreign currency.
7. Explain buyback of shares and treasury stock operation.
8. Account for the issue of bonus shares.
9. Account for payment of dividends.
10. Explain share-based compensation.
11. Understand the statement of changes in equity.
12. Present non-controlling interest in the financial statements.
13. Compute earnings per share.

SPEED READ

Equity is residual interest in a business and consists of share capital and reserves. Corporations are creatures of law with a separate legal identity. Equity shareholders have ownership rights. Equity shares may be issued at par or at a premium. Preference shareholders have prior rights to dividend and return of capital. Reserves may come from retained earnings or from capital transactions. They may be voluntary or mandatory. Some reserves can be distributed as dividends, and some can be used for bonus issue. Foreign currency transactions and translations result in exchange differences. Buyback reduces equity. Bonus issue increases capital. Dividend is a distribution of cash to the shareholders. Share-based compensation is recorded at the fair value of stock options or other equity instruments issued. The statement of changes in equity explains the changes in the share capital, reserves and other comprehensive income. In consolidated financial statements, non-controlling interest is presented separately from the interest of the parent's owners. Earnings per share is an important summary measure of a company's financial performance.

LETTER FROM A FAILED BUSINESS TYCOON

Dear Shareholders, Lenders and Staff, I hope you are doing well. Most probably, not. Your company Underwater Shipping which I started with a lot of ballyhoo has collapsed. You must be wondering where I am and what I am doing. I am criticized for living an opulent life when your company has foundered. It's sad you didn't get paid. We can only blame it on our collective bad luck or, more appropriately, limited liability: the idea that a company's shareholders are not bound to pay the company's debts beyond their agreed contribution. Limited liability applies to the founder as much as it does to the other shareholders. Though some of you may disagree, this is the law of the land. I am simply following the law. I don't understand why the law is following me.

Yours

The Corporate Organization

A **corporation** is an artificial legal person created by a charter. It comprises many members. The word 'corporation' is derived from the Latin word *corpus*, meaning 'body'. It refers to a body of people that acts on behalf of all of them. Corporations, in the sense of shareholders forming a private business enterprise for profit, existed in the Mauryan empire in ancient India.[1]

Corporations come into existence in different ways. A **chartered corporation** is constituted by a royal charter issued by the Crown. The British East India Company chartered by Queen Elizabeth I of England in 1600 is an early example of a chartered corporation. A **statutory corporation** is established by legislation. For example, the Reserve Bank of India was set up under the Reserve Bank of India Act 1934. A **company** is a typical corporate business organization. In India, companies are registered under the Companies Act 2013 or the earlier Acts. Tata Motors Limited, Wipro Limited, and Bharat Electronics Limited are examples of companies.

The Companies Act is a comprehensive code covering the formation, management, and liquidation of companies. A company is registered by filing the memorandum of association and the articles of association with the Registrar of Companies. We will now see the key features of a corporate organization.

Separate legal existence   A company is a separate legal entity distinct from its members. It has most of the rights and obligations of a natural person. It can buy, sell or own assets, borrow money, and employ people; it is liable to pay taxes; it can even be declared bankrupt. Since a company has a distinct legal entity, it can have multiple contractual relationships with its members. For example, a company's shareholder can also be its employee, customer, supplier or lender. Companies don't have certain rights that only natural persons can have; for example, they cannot vote at, or contest, elections.

Limited liability of shareholders   Since a company is a separate legal entity, it is obliged to pay its debts from *its* assets. The liability of the members is limited to the amount they have agreed to invest in the company, *less* any amount already invested by them. Limited liability enables individuals to participate in risky ventures by limiting their risk to predetermined amounts.

Free transferability of ownership rights   The shares of a company can be freely transferred by one shareholder to another. Transfer of shares does not affect the company's business operations. Free transferability of shares, coupled with the existence of an active stock market, enables individuals and financial institutions to buy and sell shares at will and makes it easy for companies to raise capital. Private companies restrict share transfers.

Perpetual existence   A company continues to exist until it is dissolved by a legal process. The death or incapacity of any, some or even all of its members does not affect the continued existence of the company.

In a case decided by an Australian court, a man and his wife were the sole shareholders and directors of two companies. Both of them died in a road accident. The court held that their deaths did not terminate the legal existence of the companies. The companies continued to own the properties and had to fulfil the unfinished contracts. The shares would go to the shareholders' legal heirs.

Common seal   A company's actions are authenticated by affixing its common seal to a document. It is made of metal and embossed on important documents, such as share certificates and contracts.

Professional management   A company's shareholders elect a board of directors but do not take part in its day-to-day activities. The board appoints a chief executive and other

Learning Objective

LO 1 Describe the features of a corporate organization.

HANDHOLD 11.1
Perpetual Existence

---

[1]   Vikramaditya S. Khanna, *The Economic History of the Corporate Form in Ancient India.* University of Michigan, Ann Arbor, Michigan, 2005.

officers to manage the business. The separation of ownership from management enables the company to entrust the business to individuals who have the necessary qualifications and experience.

Government regulation The privilege of limited liability has its costs. Companies are subject to detailed regulation by the government and regulatory agencies. They must file the financial statements and numerous reports and documents.

FINANCIAL VIEW
Class Action, Activist Shareholders, and Proxy Advisory Firms

The separation of ownership from management creates an agency problem, i.e. the interests of the managers may not be aligned with those of the shareholders. The problem becomes serious when share ownership is widely dispersed among individuals. It is difficult for shareholders from different parts of a large country, such as India, to come together and question improper managerial decisions. *Class action* enables the shareholders to act as a group. The Companies Act 2013 allows class action by shareholders and depositors if "the affairs of the company are being conducted in a manner prejudicial to the interests of the company or its members or depositors". A class action is also possible against a company's auditors. If used properly, a class action can be an effective safeguard. *Activist shareholders* monitor the management's actions. They are not passive recipients of dividends. They analyze the company's proposals, financial statements, and documents. *Proxy advisory firms* give advice to institutional investors on how to vote at shareholders' meetings on matters such as managerial remuneration, share buyback, mergers and acquisitions, and related party transactions. In the US, Institutional Shareholder Services and Glass, Lewis & Co. are well-known proxy advisory firms. In India, InGovern, Institutional Investors Advisory Services, and Stakeholders Empowerment Services are the major proxy firms.

Share Capital

Learning Objective

LO 2 **Explain the components of capital stock.**

The shareholders' equity of a company consists of two parts:

- Share capital
- Reserves and surplus.

Share capital represents the initial and later issues of capital. Exhibit 11.1 illustrates the presentation of share capital using the September 2016 quarter statement of Tata Consultancy Services Limited (TCS).

EXHIBIT 11.1
TATA STEEL LIMITED: Presentation of Share Capital

The authorised, issued, subscribed and fully paid-up share capital comprises of equity shares and redeemable preference shares having a par value of ₹1 each as follows:

Note 15: Share Capital	As at September 30, 2016
Authorized	*(In millions)*
(a) 4,600,500,000 equity shares of ₹1 each	₹ 4,600
(b) 1,050,250,000 redeemable preference shares of ₹1 each	1,050
	5,650
Issued, Subscribed and Fully paid-up	
1,970,427,941 equity shares of ₹1 each	1,970

We will now consider some of the terms related to share capital.

Capital stock The capital stock of a company is divided into a number of units called **shares of stock** or **shares**. Each share has a distinctive number. The **share certificate** indicates the kind and number of shares as well as their distinctive serial numbers. It is signed by the company secretary and bears the company's common seal. Initially, it is sent to the individual who applied for the shares. When a shareholder transfers her shares, she must complete a share transfer form and send along with it the share certificate to the company for recording the change in share ownership. Large companies appoint registrars and transfer agents to handle the numerous ownership changes in their shares. Many companies keep their shares in electronic form, known as dematerialized or *demat* shares, to avoid the paperwork associated with share transfers.

A company may be authorized to issue either only equity share capital or both equity share capital and preference share capital. Equity share capital represents the **residual equity** in the company since equity shareholders can be paid only after all other claims have been paid. As the real owners of the company, equity shareholders appoint the company's directors and declare dividends. Preference shareholders enjoy certain privileges over equity shareholders. You may have noticed that TCS has both equity and preference share capital.

Authorized capital The memorandum of association specifies the maximum number of shares that may be issued and the par value of each share. This is the **authorized capital**. Generally, a company obtains authorization for more shares than it plans to issue initially, so that it can issue additional shares later. A company can increase its authorized capital with its shareholders' approval. TCS's authorized capital has 4,600 million equity shares and 1,050 million preference shares.

Issued, subscribed, and paid-up capital Issued capital is the number of shares issued by a company. **Subscribed capital** is the number of shares taken up by the public. **Paid-up capital** is the amount of share capital that has been received by the company. For example, a company may have an authorized capital of 100,000 equity shares of ₹10 each. Of these, it may have issued 40,000 shares and the public may have taken up 25,000 shares. If the company has called up and received ₹6 on each share, its paid-up capital will be ₹150,000 (25,000 shares × ₹6 per share). TCS has issued 1,970,427,941 equity shares, all of which are subscribed and fully paid up. It has not issued any preference shares.

Par value It represents the minimum amount that a shareholder must pay on a share. The par value (or **face value**) of a company's stock constitutes the company's legal minimum capital. Each shareholder can be compelled to pay the par value of the shares held by him. TCS's equity shares have a par value of ₹1. Companies are prohibited from returning any part of the minimum capital except by following a special procedure. This is intended to protect the company's creditors from the possibility of the shareholders withdrawing assets from the company and leaving behind an empty shell.

> The following information relates to Shree Company's share capital: authorized capital, 10,000 equity shares of ₹10 each and 3,000 redeemable preference shares of ₹10 each; issued capital, 6,000 equity shares; subscribed and fully paid-up capital, 3,500 equity shares. Compute Shree Company's minimum legal capital.

TEST YOUR UNDERSTANDING 11.1
Minimum Capital

Accounting for Share Capital

A company may issue capital stock with or without a par value. **Par value** specifies an amount that must be recorded as share capital. Any amount received in excess of par value is **securities premium** or **share premium**, which is part of shareholders' equity. **No-par stock** is a capital stock that does not have a par value. In the latter case, a company may assign a **stated value** which becomes its legal capital. If there is no stated value, the entire proceeds are taken as share capital. Indian law does not permit no-par stock. A company may issue share capital for cash or other assets or for services.

Learning Objective
LO3 Record transactions involving share capital.

Issue of Share Capital

Issue of share capital with par value When a company issues shares for cash, it credits the par value to Share Capital and the rest of the proceeds to Securities Premium. For example, assume that Deepak Company issues 1,000 equity shares of ₹10 per equity shares at ₹15 (including premium ₹5) requiring full payment. The following entry records this transaction:

Cash	15,000	
Equity Share Capital		10,000
Securities Premium		5,000
To record issue of equity shares at a premium		

> Kabir Company issued 2,000 equity shares of ₹10 par value (a) at par (b) at a premium of ₹2 per share. Prepare journal entries to record the issue of capital.

TEST YOUR UNDERSTANDING 11.2
Share Capital

Issue of share capital without par value When a company issues no-par stock, it credits the entire proceeds from the issue to Share Capital. For example, assume that Deepak Company issued 1,000 shares of no-par value at ₹15 per share. The following entry records this transaction:

Cash	15,000	
Equity Share Capital		15,000
To record issue of no-par value equity shares		

The law may require a company to designate a part of the proceeds as "stated value" which is not allowed to be withdrawn. Assume that the no-par stock in the above example has a stated value of ₹7. In this case, it will record the above transaction as follows:

Cash	15,000	
Equity Share Capital		7,000
Securities Premium		8,000
To record issue of no-par value equity shares at a stated value		

Issue of share capital for non-cash assets and services A company may issue share capital in exchange for non-cash assets such as land, buildings, and plant or for services. If fair value can be estimated reliably, the company should record the exchange at the fair value of the assets or services received. If not, the assets or services should be recorded by reference to the fair value of the shares issued. To illustrate, assume that Deepak Company's lawyers agree to accept 500 shares of ₹10 par value for the preparation of legal documents and other services rendered in connection with the formation of the company. The fair value of the services is ₹8,000. The following entry records this transaction:

Preliminary Expenses	8,000	
Equity Share Capital		5,000
Securities Premium		3,000
To record issue of shares to lawyers in exchange for services		

If the fair value of the goods or services can't be estimated reliably, the market price of the shares may be used. Suppose the company issues 10,000 equity shares of ₹10 each to acquire a piece of land but the fair value of the land is not evident. If the company's shares trade at ₹18, we record the exchange as follows:

Land	180,000	
Equity Share Capital		100,000
Securities Premium		80,000
To record issue of shares in exchange for land		

Sweat equity refers to equity shares issued by a company to its directors or employees for providing intangible assets such as know-how. The accounting for issuing such shares is similar to the above. Sweat equity can be issued at less than par.

Rights issue of share capital When a company intends to make an additional issue of share capital, the law gives the company's existing shareholders the pre-emptive right to subscribe for the new shares. This right enables them to maintain their proportion of the company's share capital. The offer of shares to the existing shareholders in pursuance of the right of pre-emption is known as a **rights issue**, or "rights". Generally, the price of rights is lower than the current market price of the shares. An existing shareholder who receives a rights offer may (a) take up all the shares offered to him, (b) take up less than the number of shares offered to him, (c) renounce his rights in favour of another person (who need not be a current shareholder of the company), or (d) ignore the rights offer. The procedure for recording proceeds from rights issues is the same as that for the first issue of share capital.

Receipt of Share Capital in Instalments

The offer document specifies terms of the issue, i.e. how much is to be paid with the share application, on the allotment and on calls made by the board of directors. To illustrate, assume that Deepak Company issued 10,000 shares of ₹10 each at par payable as follows:

₹3 with the application, ₹2 on the allotment, and the balance when called. On April 3, the company received applications for 15,000 shares. On May 20, the company's board allotted 10,000 shares and refunded the application money for the remaining shares. The amounts payable on allotment were received on June 25. On August 7, the board made the first call for ₹3 per share and the amounts were received on September 16. The second and final call was made on November 22 and the amounts were received on December 29. Entries to record these transactions are as follows:

Apr. 3	Cash...	45,000	
	Share Application and Allotment		45,000
May 20	Share Application and Allotment...	65,000	
	Equity Share Capital...		50,000
	Cash		15,000
June 25	Cash...	20,000	
	Share Application and Allotment		20,000
Aug. 7	Share First Call	30,000	
	Equity Share Capital...		30,000
Sep. 16	Cash...	30,000	
	Share First Call		30,000
Nov. 22	Share Second and Final Call...	20,000	
	Equity Share Capital...		20,000
Dec. 29	Cash...	20,000	
	Share Second and Final Call....................................		20,000

Forfeiture of Shares

A shareholder may not pay allotment or call amounts. In that event, the board of directors can decide to take back the shares and retain the amounts already paid and the shareholder forfeits his shares. The shares are called **forfeited shares**. The company debits the total amount due on allotment or calls on the forfeited shares to Share Capital and credits Share Allotment or Share Call. The amount already paid goes to Shares Forfeited. Assume that, in the above example, Deepak Company did not receive the amount of second call on 100 shares and the shares were forfeited on January 17. The following entry records the forfeiture:

Jan. 17	Equity Share Capital..	1,000	
	Share Second and Final Call....................................		200
	Shares Forfeited		800
	To record forfeiture of shares		

The balance in Shares Forfeited is regarded as a part of share capital. It is not available for dividends. TCS has no forfeited shares.

Ace Company Limited was set up on April 1, 20XX with an authorized capital of 10,000 shares of ₹5 par value. On April 17, 20XX, it issued 3,000 shares for cash at ₹12. On September 26, 20XX, it issued 3,000 shares in exchange for the founder's patent with a fair value of ₹25,000. Securities premium would increase on:

ONE-MINUTE QUIZ 11.1
Share Issue

	April 17, 20XX	September 26, 20XX
(a)	Yes	Yes
(b)	Yes	No
(c)	No	Yes
(d)	No	No

Preference Share Capital

Companies can issue two classes of share capital: (a) equity, and (b) preference. Preference shareholders enjoy preference over equity shareholders in two aspects:

- Payment of periodic dividends; and
- Distribution of assets on liquidation of the company.

Learning Objective

LO 4 Describe the features of preference shares.

Preference shares usually carry a fixed rate of dividend which is payable when the company has earned adequate profits and preference dividend is declared in the company's annual general meeting. Preference shareholders get the dividend before equity shareholders. On liquidation, they are paid after the creditors but before the equity shareholders. There are many types of preference shares depending on the rights attached to them. We will now see some of them.

Cumulative and non-cumulative preference shares The holders of cumulative preference shares receive dividends for one or more year(s) in which no dividend was paid. The preference dividends not declared in a period are called **dividends in arrears**. To illustrate, assume that Pratibha Company has 10,000 of 10 per cent, ₹10 par value cumulative preference shares. The annual dividend is ₹10,000. If dividends are in arrears for three years, preference shareholders are entitled to receive a total dividend of ₹40,000 in Year 4 before any payment is made to equity shareholders, as shown below:

Arrears of preference dividends (₹10,000 × 3)	₹30,000
Current year dividend	10,000
Total preference dividends	40,000

Dividends in arrears are not a liability because no obligation exists until the dividend is declared by the company. However, the amount of the arrears must be disclosed in the notes to the financial statements. Arrears of past dividends are not payable in non-cumulative preference shares.

Participating and non-participating preference shares Participating preference shares carry the right to share in the profits of the company after the equity shareholders are paid a certain rate of dividend. These shares can also carry the right to share in the assets of the company over and above their face value. The holders of non-participating preference shares can only receive the fixed dividend and can't share in the surplus left after paying equity dividend.

To illustrate, assume that Khalid Company has ₹100,000 of 12 per cent par value participating preference shares and ₹1,000,000 of par value equity shares. It must pay ₹12,000 of preference dividends (₹100,000 × 12%) and ₹120,000 of equity dividends (₹1,000,000 × 12%) before the participating right takes effect. Additional dividends are distributed between the preference and the equity shareholders on the basis of their respective par values. The total share capital is ₹1,100,000 (₹100,000 + ₹1,000,000). The ratio of distribution is 1/11 (₹100,000/₹1,100,000) for preference shareholders and 10/11 (₹1,000,000/₹1,100,000) for equity shareholders. If the company pays ₹110,000 of additional dividends, preference shareholders will receive ₹10,000 (1/11 of ₹110,000) and equity shareholders will receive ₹100,000 (10/11 of ₹110,000).

Redeemable and irredeemable preference shares Recall the discussion in Chapter 10. Redeemable preference shares are repayable after the period of holding stated in the share certificate. The Companies Act 2013 prohibits the issue of irredeemable preference shares or preference shares redeemable after 20 years from the date of issue. Schedule III to the Companies Act 2013 requires redeemable preference shares to be classified and presented as borrowings under non-current liabilities. There may be a redemption premium. Irredeemable preference shares can't be repaid except at the time of liquidation. The law requires the transfer of an amount equal to the par value of the preference share capital redeemed to capital redemption reserve except when the redemption is made out of the proceeds of a fresh issue of share capital. Capital redemption reserve is, for most purposes, like share capital.

Convertible and non-convertible preference shares Convertible preference shares can be converted into equity at a predetermined ratio. Non-convertible preference shares always remain preference shares. Suppose Parag Company issued ₹200,000 of 10 per cent, ₹10 par value preference shares with two preference shares convertible into one equity share of ₹10 five years later. In Year 5, the company's 20,000 preference shares will stand converted into 10,000 equity shares of ₹10 par value and the balance of ₹100,000 becomes securities premium.

Reserves and Surplus

Reserves are the other component of the shareholders' equity of a company. In the balance sheet, reserves appear under Other equity. There are several kinds of reserves. **Capital reserves** are not available for distribution to shareholders as dividends (e.g. securities premium). **Revenue reserves**, or **free reserves**, arise from business operations and are available for payment of dividends (e.g. retained earnings). **Statutory reserves** are set up to comply with the requirements of a law such as the Income Tax Act in order to avail of certain tax benefits. They are not available for distribution to shareholders during the period specified in the law (e.g. investment allowance reserve). **Realized reserves** arise from receiving cash or other assets received in an exchange transaction (e.g. gain on disposal of equipment). **Unrealized reserves** are the result of accounting entries without any underlying exchange transaction (e.g. revaluation reserve). Let's now discuss some of the reserves.

Learning Objective

LO5 Describe the different kinds of reserves.

Securities premium Securities premium, similar to share capital, can't be returned to the shareholders. However, Section 52 of the Companies Act 2013 provides that the balance in the securities premium account can be utilized for the following purposes:

1. Issuing fully paid bonus shares.
2. Writing off the preliminary expenses of the company.
3. Writing off the expenses of, or commission paid or discount allowed on, an issue of shares or debentures of the company.
4. Providing for the premium payable on the redemption of redeemable preference shares or debentures of the company.

Daman Company issues 1,000 shares of ₹10 par value at ₹13 per share. Can the company treat the excess over par value as income? Why or why not?

TEST YOUR UNDERSTANDING 11.3
Proceeds in Excess of Share Capital

Capital redemption reserve The amount required for redemption of redeemable preference shares must come out of the proceeds of a fresh issue of shares. Otherwise, the company must transfer from retained earnings an amount equal to the par value of the shares redeemed to capital redemption reserve. Also, when a company buys back its own equity shares, it must transfer an amount equal to the nominal value of the shares to capital redemption reserve. It is similar to share capital in that the amount can't be returned to the shareholders. However, a company can issue fully paid bonus shares out of capital redemption reserve.

Debenture redemption reserve The debenture trust deed may require the issuer to transfer an amount to debenture redemption reserve. The purpose of the transfer is to prevent the company from distributing the amount as dividends, so that the company's assets are not reduced to the detriment of its creditors. The balance in debenture redemption reserve is not available for issue of bonus shares until the debentures are repaid and is transferred to retained earnings at the time of repayment of the debentures.

Investment allowance reserve The Income Tax Act has a special allowance, known as *investment allowance*, for investment in plant and machinery. A condition for the allowance is that the company must transfer a specified percentage of the amount of the allowance to an *investment allowance reserve*. The balance in the account is not available for dividends or bonus shares for eight years from the year of investment.

Ram, a director in your company's board, thinks that retained earnings should equal cash available with the company. Is he right?

DISCUSSION QUESTION 11.1

....

....

....

Transfer to a reserve is known as **appropriation**. Note that this process does not affect dividend distribution since a company can pay dividends out of its current or past profits regardless of how these are designated. Transfers to certain reserves such as investment allowance reserve and export profit reserve are required by law. As already stated, such reserves are not distributable. Appropriations and dividends appear in the retained earnings column of the statement of changes in equity, and are known as 'below the line' items.

TEST YOUR UNDERSTANDING 11.4
Recording Appropriations

On March 31, 20X5, Salman Company had a balance of ₹12,000 in the Retained Earnings account. During the year ended March 31, 20X6, the company earned a profit after tax of ₹73,200. The board of directors proposed a dividend of ₹10,000 for the year. The following appropriations are to be made at the year end: ₹13,000 to Investment Allowance Reserve; ₹19,800 to Export Profit Reserve; ₹25,000 to Dividend Equalization Reserve; and ₹10,000 to Contingency Reserve. Prepare journal entries to record the appropriations and compute the ending balance in the Retained Earnings account.

Accumulated other comprehensive income As you learnt in Chapter 7, gains and losses relating to financial assets measured at FVTOCI are taken to **other comprehensive income**, a component of equity. Translation gains and losses resulting from foreign operations and gains and losses on certain derivative financial instruments too are part of other comprehensive income. Accumulated other comprehensive income may have a debit balance or credit balance.

QUICK QUESTION
Reserves

Why can't unrealized reserves be distributed as dividends?

Foreign Currency Transactions and Translations

Learning Objective
LO 6 Account for activities in foreign currency.

Many businesses have foreign currency transactions and foreign operations. The amounts in foreign currency have to be expressed in the currency in which the financial statements are presented. **Functional currency** is the currency in which an entity does business. For example, the functional currency of Infosys India is the Indian rupee. The functional currencies for Infosys America, Infosys Australia, Infosys China and Infosys Mexico are the respective local currencies. **Foreign currency** is a currency other than the functional currency. Thus, for Infosys India the US dollar is a foreign currency, and for Infosys America, the Indian rupee is a foreign currency. **Reporting currency** (or **presentation currency**) is the currency in which an entity's financial statements are presented. The reporting currency for the consolidated financial statements of the Infosys group (Infosys and its subsidiaries) is the Indian rupee.

Foreign Currency Transactions

Foreign currency transaction involves buying or selling foreign currency by paying or receiving functional currency. Exports of goods and services and overseas borrowings result in foreign currency receipts that are converted into functional currency. For example, when Infosys India receives dollars from its US customers, it sells them and buys Indian rupees. Imports of equipment, goods and services and investment in overseas subsidiaries result in foreign currency payments. For example, when Infosys India acquires a US company, it buys dollars and sells Indian rupees. Foreign currency transactions are recorded in the functional currency at the *spot exchange rates*, i.e. exchange rates prevalent in the market.

Foreign Currency Translations

Foreign currency translation is the expression of an amount in a foreign currency in terms of the functional currency. It does not involve receipt or payment in a foreign currency. Translation is required when:

1. An entity's foreign currency-denominated assets and liabilities have to be expressed in its functional currency; and

2. An entity's financial statements in its functional currency have to be expressed in a different reporting currency.

Foreign currency assets and liabilities The principles for translating an entity's foreign currency-denominated assets and liabilities into its functional currency are as follows:

- Translate monetary items at the closing rate.[2]
- Translate non-monetary items measured at historical cost at the transaction date rate.
- Translate non-monetary items measured at fair value at the valuation date rate.
- Take exchange differences to the statement of profit and loss.

Foreign entity's financial statements The principles for translating a foreign entity's financial statements into a different reporting currency are as follows:

- Translate assets and liabilities at the closing rate.
- Translate revenues and expenses at the transaction rates.
- Take exchange differences to other comprehensive income.

Example 1

This example explains how to record foreign currency transactions and translate related foreign currency balances. Let's first take a monetary item. Suppose Ananya Exports in Ahmedabad sells T-shirts to High Fashion in Chicago on credit on February 1 for $1,000, payable on June 10. The firm's functional currency is the Indian rupee and its fiscal year end is March 31. Assume the following exchange rates:

Date	Exchange Rate
February 1	$1 = ₹66
March 31	$1 = ₹67
June 10	$1 = ₹70

It records the sale at the exchange rate on the transaction date as follows:

Feb. 1 Trade Receivables 66,000
     Sales 66,000
        Sale of goods for $1,000 at the exchange rate $1 = ₹66

On March 31, the firm's fiscal year end, the rupee depreciates by ₹1. The gain of ₹1,000 is recorded as follows:

Mar. 31 Trade Receivables 1,000
     Foreign Currency Gain.. 1,000
        To record foreign currency gain: $1,000 × (₹67 − ₹66)

The gain goes to the statement of profit and loss. Trade Receivables will appear at ₹67,000. On June 10, the firm receives $1,000 and converted it to ₹70,000. The transaction is recorded as follows:

June 10 Cash.. 70,000
     Trade Receivables.. 67,000
     Foreign Currency Gain 3,000
        To record foreign currency gain: $1,000 × (₹70 − ₹67)

The gain goes to the statement of profit and loss.

Let's now take a non-monetary item. Suppose Ananya Exports buys a machine from Tech Frontier in Cincinnati on July 7 for a bill payable for $2,000, payable on November 12. The reporting date is September 30. Assume the following exchange rates:

---

[2] Monetary items are receivable or payable in stated amounts of money, e.g. trade receivables and trade payables.

Date	Exchange Rate
July 7	$1 = ₹69
September 30	$1 = ₹71
November 12	$1 = ₹72

It records the equipment at the exchange rate on the transaction date as follows:

July 7   Equipment... 138,000
                Bills Payable   138,000
                    Purchase of machine for $2,000 at the exchange rate $1 = ₹69

On September 30, the rupee depreciates by ₹2. The loss of ₹4,000 is recorded as follows:

Sep. 30   Foreign Currency Transaction Loss.   4,000
                Bills Payable   4,000
                    To record foreign currency loss: $2,000 × (₹71 – ₹69)

The loss goes to the statement of profit and loss. Bills Payable will appear at ₹142,000. On November 12, the firm pays ₹144,000 to buy $2,000. The transaction is recorded as follows:

Nov. 12   Bills Payable... 142,000
                Foreign Currency Transaction Loss   2,000
                    Cash   144,000
                    To record foreign currency gain: $2,000 × (₹72 – ₹71)

The loss goes to the statement of profit and loss.

Example 2

This example explains how to translate financial statements from functional currency to reporting currency. Ultramarine Bank is an Indian bank. On January 1, 20X1, it sets up a US subsidiary, Ultramarine Bank US, Inc. with a share capital of $800. The functional currency of the bank in India is the Indian rupee. The functional currency of its US subsidiary is the US dollar. The subsidiary's 20X1 financial statements are presented in Exhibit 11.2.

EXHIBIT 11.2
Foreign Entity's
Financial Statements
in Functional Currency

Financial statements are prepared in an entity's functional currency.

Ultramarine Bank US, Inc.
Statement of Financial Position, December 31, 20X1

Assets	
Cash..	$1,000
Loans..	9,000
Total assets...	10,000
Liabilities	
Deposits..	8,000
Borrowings..	1,000
Total liabilities..	9,000
Equity	
Share capital...	800
Retained earnings..	200
Total equity	1,000
Total liabilities and equity..	10,000

Income Statement, For the year ended December 31, 20X1

Revenue	$1,000
Expenses..	800
Net profit	200

The exchange rates in 20X1 are as follows:

Date	Exchange Rate
January 1	$1 = ₹45
December 31	$1 = ₹50
Average for the year	$1 = ₹48

Exhibit 11.3 illustrates how to translate the items in the financial statements of Ultramarine Bank US, Inc. into the Indian rupee, the parent's reporting currency.

EXHIBIT 11.3
Foreign Entity's Financial Statements Translated into the Parent's Reporting Currency

Financial statements in a functional currency are translated into a reporting currency at the appropriate rates.

Ultramarine Bank US, Inc.
Statement of Financial Position, December 31, 20X1

	In Functional Currency	Exchange Rate	In Reporting Currency
Assets			
Cash	$1,000	$1 = ₹50[1]	₹50,000
Loans	9,000	$1 = ₹50	450,000
Total assets	10,000		500,000
Liabilities			
Deposits	8,000	$1 = ₹50	400,000
Borrowings	1,000	$1 = ₹50	50,000
Total liabilities	9,000		450,000
Equity			
Share capital	800	$1 = ₹45[2]	36,000
Retained earnings	200		9,600[3]
Currency translation reserve		Difference	4,400
Total equity	1,000	$1 = ₹50	50,000
Total liabilities and equity	10,000		500,000

Income Statement, For the year ended December 31, 20X1

	In Functional Currency	Exchange Rate[4]	In Reporting Currency
Revenue	1,000	$1 = ₹48	48,000
Expenses	800	$1 = ₹48	38,400
Net profit	200	$1 = ₹48	9,600

Notes:
1. Exchange rate on the reporting date.
2. Exchange rate on the date of investment.
3. Transferred from the translated income statement.
4. Average rate for the year.

TEST YOUR UNDERSTANDING 11.5
Foreign Operation

Kangaroo Australia Pty. Ltd., Peacock India Limited's Australian subsidiary, has the following expenses incurred in Australian dollar (A$) for the year ended December 31, 20X4: Depreciation on equipment (purchased on January 1, 20X1), A$10,000; Bad debt expense, A$300; Rent expense, A$5,000. The exchange rates are as follows (rupee per Australian dollar): January 1, 20X1, ₹49.94; December 31, 20X4, ₹51.24; Average for the year ended December 31, 20X4, ₹50.63. The Australian dollar is the subsidiary's functional currency. The expenses occurred approximately evenly during the year. What is the total amount of expenses to be included in Peacock India's consolidated statement of profit and loss?

ONE-MINUTE QUIZ 11.2
Foreign Currency Transaction and Translation

Suchi Company in India bought car parts on credit from a supplier in Japan on February 12, 20X1 for ¥100,000, when the spot rate was ¥100 = ₹58.33. At Suchi Company's March 31, 20X1 year end, the spot rate was ¥100 = ₹59.91. On June 28, 20X1, the invoice was paid when the spot rate was ¥100 = ₹56.15. How much foreign currency gain or loss should Suchi Company report for 20X1 and 20X2?

	20X1	20X2
(a)	Gain ₹1,580	Loss ₹3,760
(b)	Loss ₹1,580	Gain ₹3,760
(c)	Gain ₹0	Loss ₹1,580
(d)	Loss ₹1,580	Gain ₹0

Buyback of Shares and Treasury Stock Operation

Learning Objective

LO 7 Explain buyback of shares and treasury stock operation.

A company may reacquire its shares for a number of reasons, such as the following:

1. It has surplus cash, but does not have any plans for capital expenditure or acquisitions. So it wants to return a part of the cash to its shareholders.
2. It faces a hostile takeover. By buying its shares, it can reduce the number of shares available to the bidder in the market and thus hopes to thwart the takeover.
3. It wants to signal that the stock is undervalued.
4. It is overcapitalized and the dividend outgo is large.

Reacquiring own shares may be by means of a buyback or treasury stock operation.

Buyback

Buyback reduces the number of shares and the paid-up capital. The Companies Act 2013 permits a company to buyback its own shares for cancellation. Section 68 of the Act lays down the following conditions, among others:

1. A company can buyback its shares to the extent of its free reserves and securities premium or out of the proceeds of a fresh issue of shares, or other specified securities.
2. Buyback should not be less than 10 per cent or more than 25 per cent of the company's paid-up capital and free reserves.
3. Buyback should be authorized by the company's articles of association and a resolution of the shareholders.
4. The excess of the buyback price over the paid-up capital is debited to free reserves.[3]

Suppose Samir Company has 2,000 fully paid shares of ₹10 each and ₹50,000 in securities premium. It decides to buyback 500 shares at ₹25. It records the buyback as follows:

Equity Share Capital..	5,000	
Securities Premium	7,500	
Cash		12,500
To record buyback of 500 equity shares of the company at ₹25 per share		

The Companies Act requires transfer to the capital redemption reserve account of a sum equal to the paid-up capital of the shares bought back. The following entry records this transfer:

Retained Earnings...	5,000	
Capital Redemption Reserve...		5,000
To transfer an amount equal to the paid-up share capital bought back		

Treasury Stock Operation

Treasury stock is a company's own share capital that was issued and reacquired by the company as an investment. As the term suggests, *treasury stock operation* is part of a company's cash management activities. Treasury stock is often a temporary investment until the company identifies long-term investment opportunities. It may be either preference shares or equity shares and may be held for any period of time, reissued or retired. Dividends are not paid on treasury stock and these shares do not carry voting rights in the meetings of shareholders. Treasury stock is not part of outstanding shares. *Currently, treasury stock is not allowed in India.*

---

[3] For the purpose of buyback, "free reserves" includes securities premium account (Explanation II to Section 68 of the Companies Act 2013).

Purchase   When a company purchases its own shares, it reduces both assets and equity by equal amounts. To illustrate, assume that Shweta Company purchases 1,000 of its fully paid equity shares at ₹22 per share. The transaction is recorded as follows:

Treasury Stock...	22,000	
Cash		22,000
To record purchase of 1,000 own shares at ₹22 per share		

Treasury stock is deducted from equity. Note that the purchase does not change the amount of issued share capital. However, it reduces the amount of *outstanding* share capital representing the number of shares available for trading.

Reissue Treasury stock may be reissued at, above, or below cost. If reissued at cost, the entry to record the transaction is the reverse of the entry to record the purchase. If sold at above cost, the amount received in excess of the cost goes to the Securities Premium, Treasury Stock account. For example, if Shweta Company sells 500 of the treasury shares purchased at ₹22 per share for ₹25 per share, the transaction would be recorded as follows:

Cash..	12,500	
Treasury Stock...		11,000
Securities Premium, Treasury Stock...		1,500
To record sale of 500 own shares at ₹25 per share		

If treasury stock is reissued at below cost, the excess of cost over the sale price is debited to Securities Premium, Treasury Stock to the extent of the balance available. Any remaining excess is debited to Retained Earnings. For example, if Shweta Company sells its remaining treasury stock at ₹15 per share, the entry to record the sale is as follows:

Cash..	7,500	
Securities Premium, Treasury Stock	1,500	
Retained Earnings..	2,000	
Treasury Stock...		11,000
To record sale of 500 own shares at ₹15 per share		

Retirement   A company may acquire its own shares to retire the share capital rather than holding it as treasury stock. When shares are retired, they are removed from share capital. If the purchase price of the treasury stock is more than the original issue price, the difference is debited to Retained Earnings. If the purchase price is less than the original issue price, the difference is credited to Securities Premium, Treasury Stock. For example, assume that Shweta Company decides to cancel the entire treasury stock purchased for ₹22,000. Assuming that the ₹10 equity shares were originally issued at a premium of ₹4 each, the entry to record the retirement is as follows:

Equity Share Capital..	10,000	
Securities Premium, Equity	4,000	
Retained Earnings..	8,000	
Treasury Stock...		22,000
To record retirement of 1,000 own shares at ₹22 per share		

If the company paid ₹12 per share for the treasury stock, the entry would be as follows:

Equity Share Capital..	10,000	
Securities Premium, Equity	4,000	
Treasury Stock...		12,000
Securities Premium, Treasury Stock...		2,000
To record retirement of 1,000 own shares at ₹12 per share		

ONE-MINUTE QUIZ 11.3
Treasury Stock

In 20X1, Win Company purchased 2,000 its ₹10 par value equity shares for ₹45,000. In 20X2, it reissued 500 of these shares for ₹35,000. Which of the following entries correctly records the reissue?
(a) Debit Cash 35,000; Credit Treasury Stock 5,000; Credit Securities Premium, Treasury Stock 30,000.
(b) Debit Cash 35,000; Credit Treasury Stock 11,250; Credit Securities Premium, Treasury Stock 23,750.
(c) Debit Cash 35,000; Credit Treasury Stock 11,250; Credit Retained Earnings 23,750.
(d) Debit Cash 35,000; Credit Equity Share Capital 5,000; Credit Securities Premium, Treasury Stock 30,000.

Bonus Shares

Learning Objective
LO 8 Account for the issue of bonus shares.

Bonus shares are additional shares of a company's share capital distributed to its shareholders without payment. The board of directors proposes the terms of distribution of bonus shares to the shareholders, who approve the distribution. The issue of bonus shares does not affect the company's assets or shareholders' equity. Its effect is to transfer retained earnings or other items in reserves and surplus to share capital. For this reason, the issue of bonus shares is also known as *capitalization of reserves*. Reasons for the issue of bonus shares include the following:

1. Profitable companies that are engaged in a major capital expenditure programme prefer to issue bonus shares rather than pay current dividends in order to avoid payment of cash.
2. Companies issue bonus shares in order to reduce the market price per share by increasing the number of shares in circulation.
3. Managers use bonus issues to signal to the shareholders their confidence in the company's prospects. In theory, a bonus issue should not have any effect on a company's stock price. However, evidence suggests that it is not always so, indicating the *signalling effect* of bonus issue.

Bonus shares can be issued out of retained earnings or other reserves permitted by the company law. The credit balances in the following accounts, among others, can be capitalized:

- Statement of profit and loss or retained earnings;
- General reserve;
- Securities premium; and
- Capital redemption reserve.

Unrealised reserves such as revaluation reserve and foreign currency translation reserve are not available for bonus issues. To illustrate the accounting procedure for a bonus issue, assume that Xavier Company has the following equity components on March 31:

Share capital		
20,000 shares authorized; 10,000 shares of ₹10 each fully paid up...................		₹100,000
Other equity		
Securities premium	₹40,000	
Revaluation reserve...	23,000	
Retained earnings...	25,000	88,000
		188,000

Assume further that the board of directors declares a 50 per cent bonus issue (meaning one bonus share for two existing shares) on August 10, distributable on September 30 to shareholders of the company's record on September 15. The bonus shares are to be issued by capitalizing securities premium, and, if needed, retained earnings. The entry to record the transaction is as follows:

Sep. 30	Securities Premium, Equity	40,000	
	Retained Earnings..	10,000	
	Equity Share Capital...		50,000
	To record the issue of 5,000 bonus shares		

After the bonus issue, the company has 15,000 equity shares.

A **stock split**, similar to a bonus issue, results in an increase in the number of shares available in the market and does not affect the total shareholders' equity. However, after a stock split, the par value of the share is reduced and the reserves remain unchanged. If Xavier Company makes a stock split of two for one, it will have 20,000 shares of ₹5 par value after the split. Bonus shares and stock splits are applicable to all shares including treasury stock.

Securities premium can be used for bonus issues but can't be distributed as dividends. Why?

QUICK QUESTION
Bonus shares

Dividends

A **dividend** is a distribution of cash to shareholders. A company's board of directors recommends payment of dividend and the shareholders approve the payment by a declaration at the company's annual general meeting. This is also known as the **final dividend**. The board can declare **interim dividends** during the year. The amount of dividend can't ordinarily exceed the total of the current and past profits of the company. Any dividend in excess of profit is a return of the legal minimum capital and is prohibited except in such as liquidation or capital reduction.

Learning Objective

LO 9 **Account for payment of dividends.**

In addition to profits, the company must have sufficient cash or other liquid assets, so that the dividend outgo does not affect its normal operations. Tax considerations may also be important. Dividends are stated as x percent of paid-up capital or x rupees per share. For instance, a company may declare a dividend of 25 per cent or ₹2.50 per share, and a shareholder who has 100 fully paid shares of ₹10 each will receive a dividend of ₹250. Dividends are paid by means of a special cheque known as **dividend warrant** or by bank transfer. Dividends can't be paid in kind.

The shares of a listed company are traded in the market. After declaring a dividend, the company fixes a date known as the **date of record** for the purpose of determining the right of shareholders to receive the dividend. On this date, the company will temporarily stop recording share transfers in order to prepare the list of shareholders eligible for the dividend. Dividends are paid to those who hold the shares on the date of record. All purchases of shares up to this date are **cum-dividend**, i.e. the buyer will receive the dividend. After this date, the purchases are **ex-dividend**, i.e. the seller will receive the dividend.

To sum up, the following four steps are important in connection with dividends:

Step	Dividend-related Activity	Accounting Action
1	Board of directors recommends dividend.	None.
2	Shareholders approve the dividend.	Set up a dividend payable account.
3	Recording share transfers is suspended.	None.
4	Dividend is paid.	Clear the dividend payable account.

Proposed dividend is disclosed in the notes to the financial statements.

QUICK QUESTION
Proposed dividend

Is proposed dividend a liability?

On June 10, 20XX, the board of directors of Sawan Company recommended to the shareholders a final dividend of 10 per cent on 40,000 fully paid shares of ₹10 each. Accepting the board's recommendation, the shareholders declared the dividend at the annual general meeting on July 18. August 1 was the date of record. The company issued dividend warrants on August 10. On declaration by the shareholders, we record the following entries (ignoring dividend distribution tax):

HANDHOLD 11.2
Dividends

July 18	Dividends..	40,000	
	Dividend Payable		40,000
Aug. 10	Dividend Payable..	40,000	
	Cash		40,000

DISCUSSION QUESTION 11.2

Both dividend and share buyback return cash to a company's shareholders. Your company has cash for which it has no use in the near future. Should it pay a special dividend or buyback some of the shares?

....

....

....

LADDER
Face Value Has No Meaning

Suppose a company issues shares for cash at ₹100 each, made up of the share capital of ₹10 and securities premium of ₹90. Would it have mattered if the issue price was split as the capital of ₹1 and premium of ₹99, or any other arbitrary split of ₹100? The short answer is "No". The share issue increases cash (and equity) by ₹600. This is because both share capital and securities premium are part of shareholders' equity. Therefore, the transaction has the same effect on the accounting equation, regardless of how the company breaks up the issue price between capital and premium. How does a company decide on the break-up? First, it decides on the face value. A company is free to choose its face value. Tata Steel has a face value of ₹10, RPG Life Sciences ₹8, Infosys ₹5, Wipro ₹2 and TCS ₹1. Next, it determines the issue price based on the valuation of the shares. Last, the company arrives at the premium as the excess of the issue price over the face value. Whatever may be the break-up of the issue price, the shareholder is obliged to pay the amount when demanded by the company. Also, when a company is liquidated, its assets are sold and liabilities are paid off. Any remaining amount is paid to the shareholders without distinguishing between share capital and securities premium. When a dividend is stated as a percentage of share capital, the dividend amount will depend on the paid-up value. When a dividend is stated as a per-share amount, the face value does not matter.

ONE-MINUTE QUIZ 11.4
Dividends

Panera Company's paid-up capital at March 31, 20XX consisted of the following:
- Preference share capital: 10,000 shares of 10 per cent ₹100 par value each, fully participating.
- Equity share capital: 4,000,000 shares of ₹1 par value each.

The company declared dividends of ₹800,000. How much dividend did the equity shareholders receive?
  (a) ₹160,000.
  (b) ₹400,000.
  (c) ₹640,000.
  (d) ₹700,000.

Share-based Compensation

Learning Objective

LO 10 Explain share-based compensation.

Share-based compensation is a benefit an employee receives in the employer's shares or stock options or in amounts based on the price of the employer's stock. Share-based compensation is often an important part of the total compensation in technology companies and investment banks. A **stock option plan** gives employees the right to acquire shares in the future. Stock options became popular in the 1990s with start-up companies choosing to give their employees options instead of cash salaries.[4]

Let's begin with the case for stock options. A company is owned by its shareholders, but managed by the chief executive and other officers under the supervision of the board of directors. Separation of ownership and management is the essence of the corporate form. In theory, this arrangement is beneficial to the shareholders, since the company is run by professionals.

---

[4] Wayne Guay, S.P. Kothari, and Richard Sloan provide an economic analysis of the issues in accounting for share-based payment in "Accounting for employee stock options", *American Economic Review*, May 2003, pp. 405–409.

A major drawback of the corporate form is the *moral hazard problem*, i.e. the risk that managers may not act in the best interests of shareholders. For example, managers may not feel any need to improve the company's performance, if they don't get to participate in the benefits of better performance. A manager who holds stock options has the right to buy a company's shares in the future at a fixed price even if the share price goes up. Since stock price usually has a positive relationship to company performance, a manager who holds stock options has an incentive to perform better. Therefore, stock options are useful in aligning managerial behaviour with shareholders' interests.

Many types of stock option plans are in vogue. An employer selects a plan based on several considerations such as the plan's effect on employee motivation, tax, and industry practices. The plan that is best for a steel company may not be suitable for a software company. Share-based payment plans, including stock option plans, are thought of as a means of compensating, attracting, motivating, and retaining good employees. Fast-growing, knowledge-based start-up companies that normally can't afford large salaries find them particularly useful. Most stock option plans require employees to put in a minimum service period to be eligible for the options and specify a period thereafter within which the options must be exercised. Table 11.1 presents the definitions of key terms used in stock options.

Exercise price The price payable by an employee to subscribe to shares under a stock option.

Fair value The price of a stock option in an arm's-length transaction.

Grant date The date at which an employer and an employee agree to a stock option.

Intrinsic value The excess of the fair value of a stock option over its exercise price.

Measurement date The date a stock option is granted. The fair value of the option is fixed as of this date.

Stock option A contract that gives a holder the right, but not the obligation, to subscribe to the employer's shares stock.

Vesting conditions The conditions that entitle an employee to receive a stock option.

Vesting period The period during which the vesting conditions of a stock option are to be satisfied.

TABLE 11.1
Key Terms Used in Stock Options

The **fair value method** measures the cost of share-based compensation at the fair value of the stock options on the grant date. Fair value is determined using an option-pricing model that considers factors such as the current price of the stock, exercise price, expected life of the option, risk-free interest rate, expected volatility, and expected dividend yield. The **Black-Scholes model** and the **binomial model** are among the most widely used methods for pricing options. If the fair value can't be estimated reliably, the *intrinsic value* should be used. Intrinsic value is the excess of the market price at the grant date over the exercise price.

To illustrate, let us assume that on January 1, 20X4 Abhay Company grants its managers 1,000 stock options. Each option entitles the holder to buy one share of ₹10 par value at ₹100, the market price on the grant date. The options will vest on January 1, 20X8 and may be exercised until December 31, 20X8 that year. On the basis of an option-pricing model, the options have a fair value of ₹55 each on the grant date. The company follows the calendar year. The following discussion illustrates how to apply the fair value method.

Recognizing compensation expense The fair value of the options is ₹55,000, i.e. 1,000 × ₹55. Compensation expense is recognized on a straight-line basis over the vesting period of four years. The yearly compensation expense is ₹13,750 [i.e. ₹55,000/4 years]. From 20X4 to 20X7, the company records the following entry to recognize the compensation expense:

20X4 to 20X7
Dec. 31   Compensation Expense 13,750
          Outstanding Stock Options... 13,750

Compensation expenses is a part of employee benefits expense. Outstanding stock options is a part of equity.

Exercise of the options Assume that 900 options are exercised on November 1, 20X8. The company receives the exercise price of ₹100 and removes the outstanding stock option of ₹55:

20X8

Nov. 1	Cash..	90,000	
	Outstanding Stock Options	49,500	
	Equity Share Capital..		9,000
	Securities Premium...		130,500

Expiry of the options Suppose the remaining options are not exercised and hence they lapse. Abhay Company should not reverse the amount recognized for services received from the employees. It should transfer the balance in Outstanding Stock Options to another equity account, such as general reserve.

Share-based arrangements are also used to pay for goods, services, intellectual property rights and property, plant and equipment. You have seen earlier in this chapter issue of share capital for professional services and other non-cash consideration.

TEST YOUR UNDERSTANDING 11.6
Stock Options

On January 1, 20X1, Mukul Company granted its president an option to purchase 1,000 shares of ₹10 par value at the current market price of ₹40 per share between January 1, 20X5 and December 31, 20X6. Each option has a fair value of ₹25. Record the exercise of the options under the fair value method.

Statement of Changes in Equity

Learning Objective

LO 11 Understand the statement of changes in equity.

The **statement of changes in equity** explains the changes in a company's share capital and reserves and surplus. The statement of changes in equity presents the following information:

- Number of shares and amount of share capital for each type or class of shares, e.g. preference, equity, Class A, and Class B;
- Securities premium;
- Reserves, e.g. revaluation reserve and general reserve;
- Other comprehensive income, e.g. gains and losses from fair value changes and currency translations; and
- Retained earnings.

The statement of changes in equity presents in one place all owner and non-owner changes in equity. *Owner changes* result from a company's transactions with its shareholders such as (a) share issue and on conversion of bonds or preference shares into equity, (b) buyback, (c) dividends, and (d) bonus shares. *Non-owner changes* result from transactions with non-shareholders recognized either in the statement of profit and loss or directly in equity.

Non-controlling Interest

Learning Objective

LO 12 Present non-controlling interest in the financial statements.

In the consolidated statement of profit and loss and statement of changes in equity, non-controlling interest's share of profit and total comprehensive income for the period should be presented separately from that attributable to the owners of the parent. In the consolidated balance sheet, non-controlling interest should be presented within equity separately from that attributable to the owners of the parent.

Vodafone Group Plc's 2016 financial statements contain the following items relating to owners of the parent and non-controlling interests:

REAL WORLD
Vodafone Group Plc

	March 31		
	2016	2015	2014
			(In millions)
Consolidated statement of profit and loss			
(Loss)/profit for the financial year	£(3,818)	£5,917	£59,420
Attributable to: Owners of the parent	(4,024)	(5,761)	(59,254)
Non-controlling interests	206	156	166
Consolidated statement of comprehensive income			
Total comprehensive expense/(income) for the year	(50)	(810)	56,702
Attributable to: Owners of the parent	(123)	(1,076)	56,711
Non-controlling interests	73	266	(9)
Consolidated statement of financial position			
Equity			
Total attributable to owners of the parent	65,885	66,145	
Total non-controlling interests	1,432	1,588	
Total equity	67,317	67,733	

Earnings Per Share

Earnings per share (EPS) is an important measure of corporate performance for shareholders and potential investors. EPS numbers are the focus of prospectuses, media discussions, and analyst reports. EPS is reported only for equity share capital. The computation of EPS depends on a company's capital structure. A *simple capital structure* has equity share capital and non-convertible preference share capital. A *complex capital structure* has convertible debentures, convertible preference share capital, and stock options – instruments that can increase the number of equity shares. Companies that have a simple capital structure calculate basic EPS. Companies that have a complex capital structure calculate diluted EPS in addition.

Learning Objective
LO 13 Compute earnings per share.

Basic Earnings Per Share

Basic earnings per share are computed by dividing the net profit or loss for the period attributable to equity shareholders by the weighted average number of equity shares outstanding during the period. Basic EPS provides a measure of the interest of each equity share in the performance of the entity in a period. In consolidated financial statements, we consider the profit or loss attributable to the parent company's equity shareholders (i.e. excluding the portion attributable to non-controlling interests). For example, assume that Trishul Company has 100,000 equity shares and has reported a profit after tax of ₹500,000 for the year ended March 31, 20X1. We now compute the company's basic earnings per share as: $\dfrac{₹500,000}{₹100,000} = ₹5$ per share.

If Trishul Company has non-convertible preference shares, we must deduct the preference dividend before computing earnings per share on equity shares. Assume that Trishul Company has ₹50,000 of ₹10 par value, 10 per cent cumulative preference shares. We now recompute the company's basic earnings per share as: $\dfrac{₹500,000 - ₹5,000}{₹100,000} = ₹4.95$ per share.

Issue and buyback of shares If a company issues or buys back equity shares during the year, the amount of resources available during the period is not constant. So we compute EPS based on the weighted-average number of shares. Assume that Trishul Company had

100,000 shares on April 1, 20X1 and issued 50,000 additional shares on July 1, 20X1. The company bought back 30,000 shares on January 1, 20X2. The weighted-average number of shares and EPS for the year ended March 31, 20X2 are computed as follows:

Number of Shares		Weight		Product
100,000	×	3/12	=	25,000
150,000	×	6/12	=	75,000
120,000	×	3/12	=	30,000
Weighted number of shares				130,000

$$\text{Basic earnings per share} = \frac{₹500,000}{130,000 \text{ shares}} = ₹3.85 \text{ per share}$$

Bonus issue and stock split   When a company issues bonus shares, the number of shares and the amount of share capital increase, but the amount of shareholders' equity remains unchanged. There is no change in the resources available to the company as bonus shares are issued without payment. In the event of an issue of bonus shares during a period, we calculate the EPS *as if* the issue had occurred prior to the beginning of the period.

Continuing with the above example, assume that on October 1, 20X2 Trishul Company issued two equity shares for every equity share outstanding on that date. The number of shares after the bonus issue is 360,000, consisting of 120,000 original shares and 240,000 bonus shares. Suppose the company has a profit after tax (PAT) of ₹522,000 for the year ended March 31, 20X3. We calculate the EPS for the year as follows:

$$\frac{₹522,000}{360,000 \text{ shares}} = ₹1.45 \text{ per share}$$

In order to make the figures comparable over time, we adjust the EPS for the previous period using the same denominator. So we recalculate the EPS for 20X2 as ₹1.39 (₹500,000/360,000 shares).

Rights issue   As with any issue of shares, the number of outstanding shares changes when there is a rights issue. Therefore, the weighted-average number of shares during the period should be used to calculate the EPS. However, a rights issue is different because the issue price is generally lower than the current market price of the share. Therefore, it has a bonus element. The denominator number of equity shares for calculating the EPS for all periods prior to the rights issue is the number of equity shares outstanding prior to the issue, multiplied by the following adjustment factor:

$$\frac{\text{Fair value per share immediately prior to the exercise of rights}}{\text{Theoretical ex-rights fair value per share}}$$

We first calculate the theoretical ex-rights fair value per share by adding the aggregate fair value of the shares immediately prior to the exercise of the rights to the proceeds from the exercise of the rights, and dividing it by the number of shares outstanding after the exercise of the rights.

Continuing with the above example, assume that on September 1, 20X3 Trishul Company made a rights issue of one share for every four shares outstanding (i.e. it issued 90,000 shares) at a price of ₹20 per share. The rights were to be exercised not later than November 1, 20X3, and the market price on that date was ₹30. The theoretical ex-rights fair value per share is ₹28, calculated as follows:

$$\frac{(360,000 \times ₹30) + (90,000 \times ₹20)}{(360,000 + 90,000) \text{ shares}} = \frac{₹12,600,000}{450,000 \text{ shares}} = ₹28 \text{ per share}$$

We now calculate the adjustment factor:

$$\frac{\text{Fair value per share immediately prior to the exercise of rights}}{\text{Theoretical ex-rights fair value per share}} = \frac{₹30}{₹28} = 1.07 \text{ (approx.)}$$

Suppose the profit after tax for the year ended March 31, 20X4 is ₹545,000. The EPS is calculated as follows:

Earnings per share	20X4	20X3
As originally reported: ₹522,000/360,000		₹1.45
Restated for rights issue: ₹522,000/(360,000 × 1.07)		₹1.36
Including effect of rights issue: ₹545,000/[(360,000 × 1.07 × 7/12) + (₹450,000 × 5/12)]	₹1.32	

The factors 7/12 and 5/12 are the weights for the periods before and after November 1, 20X3.

Diluted Earnings Per Share

Many companies have a *complex capital structure* which includes securities that may be converted into equity share capital. The conversion, if effected, has the potential of reducing or *diluting* the EPS by increasing the number of equity shares. **Dilution** is a reduction in EPS under the assumption that convertible instruments are converted, options or warrants are exercised, or equity shares are issued.

Diluted earnings per share are computed *as if* all potentially dilutive securities would be converted into equity shares. The objective of diluted EPS is to provide a measure of the interests of each equity share in the performance of the entity in a period, while giving effect to all dilutive potential equity shares outstanding. In consolidated financial statements, we consider the profit or loss attributable to the parent company's equity shareholders (i.e. excluding the portion attributable to non-controlling interests). The net profit for the period is recomputed by adding back preference dividend, interest on convertible debentures, and any other changes that would result from the conversion of the potentially dilutive securities. This is because, after the conversion of these securities, the company will not have to pay preference dividend and convertible debenture interest. We will now illustrate the calculation of diluted earnings per share using convertible debentures and stock options.

Convertible debentures   To illustrate the dilutive effect of convertible debentures, assume that Trident Company has 100,000 equity shares and 1,000 of 10 per cent debentures of ₹100 convertible into 10 equity shares each. For the year ended March 31, 20X1, the company has a profit after tax of ₹500,000 and the income tax rate is 35 per cent. We calculate the company's basic earnings per share as follows:

$$\text{Basic earnings per share} = \frac{₹500,000}{100,000 \text{ shares}} = ₹5 \text{ per share}$$

We calculate the diluted earnings per share as follows:

(a) Number of equity shares (given)	100,000
(b) Equivalent number of equity shares of convertible debentures: 1,000 × 10 (given)	10,000
(c) Number of equity shares for calculating diluted earnings per share: (a) + (b)	110,000
(d) Profit after tax (given)	₹500,000
(e) *Add* Debenture interest after tax: (b) × 65%[5]	6,500
(f) Adjusted profit diluted earnings per share: (d) + (e)	506,500
(g) Diluted earnings per share: (f) ÷ (c)	₹4.61

---

[5] The after-tax cost of interest is the pre-tax rate multiplied by (1 − tax rate), i.e. 10% × (1 − 0.35).

Stock options To illustrate the dilutive effect of stock options, assume that Trident Company has 100,000 equity shares and 10,000 equity shares under stock options. The fair value of an equity share is ₹50, and the exercise price is ₹40. The company has a profit after tax of ₹500,000. The excess of the fair value over the exercise price is expressed in terms of equity shares and added to the number of equity shares outstanding. As before, the basic earnings per share works out to ₹5. We calculate the diluted earnings per share as follows:

(a)	Number of equity shares (given)	100,000
(b)	Number of equity shares under option (given)	10,000
(c)	Number of equity shares that would have been issued at fair value: 10,000 × 40/50	8,000
(d)	Effect of dilution in equivalent number of equity shares: (b) – (c)	2,000
(e)	Number of equity shares for calculating diluted earnings per share: (a) + (d)	102,000
(f)	Profit after tax (given)	₹500,000
(g)	Diluted earnings per share: (f) ÷ (e)	₹4.90

The drop of ₹0.10 in the earnings per share is the measure of the 'free' element implicit in the stock option. The option holders can buy 10,000 shares at ₹10 per share lower than the market price. The 'loss' to the existing shareholders would be ₹100,000. At the current market price of ₹50, this is equivalent to the company issuing 2,000 shares for free (₹100,000/50). So the denominator becomes 102,000 shares. Since there will be no additional earnings to the company from the 2,000 'free' shares, the profit after tax is unchanged at ₹500,000.

ONE-MINUTE QUIZ 11.5
Shares Issued and Outstanding

On January 1, 20X1, Asif Company issued 200,000 equity shares. On October 11, 20X1, it acquired 15,000 shares as treasury stock. On June 4, 20X2, it sold 2,000 shares of treasury stock. On November 29, 20X2, it issued a further 30,000 shares. On December 23, 20X2, it made a split of 2:1. At March 31, 20X2, how many shares of Asif Company were issued and outstanding?

	Shares Issued	Shares Outstanding
(a)	400,000	370,000
(b)	460,000	445,000
(c)	460,000	447,000
(d)	460,000	434,000

FORENSIC CORNER
Equity

Most cases of frauds affect equity. For example, overstatement of revenue results in overstatement of retained earnings. Here are a few examples of fraud that affect equity:

- Embezzlement of dividends by diverting them to fraudulent accounts.
- Exaggerated, fraudulent or misleading statements or promises in offer documents.
- Diverting funds raised from shareholders to the controlling group's entities.
- Classifying loans as equity or equity as loans.

Red flags signalling equity fraud:

- Persistent losses.
- High debt-to-equity ratio.
- Negative equity.

APPLICATION
Equity

Let's see examples of equity items from the financial statements of companies.

- On February 14, 2017, Berkshire Hathaway's A shares hit a record close of $250,412. Mr. Warren Buffett has said that a high share price is a form of "shareholder eugenics" that ensures that only long-term investors ("partners" in his words) invest in the company. Other companies would have done numerous stock splits to keep the price low. In India, MRF traded at ₹60,145 on March 27, 2017.
- Founders use dual structures to keep their control. Facebook has a dual-class structure with Class A shares having one vote per share and Class B shares, which its founder Mark Zuckerberg and other company insiders own, conferring 10 votes per share. In February 2017, the messaging company Snap issued Class A shares with zero voting rights. Class B shares owned by Evan Spiegel and Booby Murphy have all the voting rights.

- IFRS and Ind AS classify redeemable preference shares as debt and treat preference dividend as interest expense. Indian GAAP treats them as share capital and dividend. **IFRS, IND AS AND INDIAN GAAP** Equity
- IFRS and Ind AS don't treat proposed dividend as a liability. Schedule III requires them to be disclosed in the notes to the financial statements. Indian GAAP treats it as a provision.
- Under IFRS and Ind AS, treasury shares are to be deducted from equity and resales of treasury shares are equity shares. Under Indian GAAP, there are no treasury shares because shares purchased must be cancelled immediately.
- IFRS and Ind AS require stock options to be measured at fair value. Indian GAAP allows either fair value or intrinsic value to be used.

RECAP

- The key features of a corporation are separate legal entity, limited liability, free transferability of shares, perpetual existence, common seal, professional management, and government regulation.
- The share capital is divided into a number of *shares*. *Authorized capital* is the maximum number of shares that may be issued. *Issued capital* is the number of shares issued so far. *Subscribed capital* is the number of shares taken. *Paid-up capital* is the amount received for share capital.
- Capital stock has a *par value*. Share capital may be issued at par or at a premium for cash, non-cash assets or services.
- *Preference shares* enjoy preference over equity shares in periodic dividends and liquidation. Preference shares usually carry a fixed rate of dividend.
- *Revenue reserves* can be distributed as dividends, but not *capital reserves*. *Unrealized reserves* result from accounting entries without any exchange transaction.
- *Foreign currency transactions* and *foreign currency translations* result in exchange differences.
- *Buyback* reduces the number of shares and the paid-up share capital. *Treasury stock* is a temporary investment by a company in its own share capital.
- *Bonus shares* are additional shares of a company's share capital given to its shareholders without payment.
- *Dividend* is a distribution of cash to shareholders.
- The *fair value* of stock options is expensed over the vesting period.
- The *statement of changes in equity* presents owner and non-owner changes in a reporting period.
- The share of *non-controlling interest* should be presented separately from the share of the owners of the parent.
- *Basic earnings per share* equals the profit after tax divided by the number of equity shares. *Diluted earnings per share* considers all potentially *dilutive securities*.

Review Problem

On January 1, Inder Ltd. was incorporated with an authorized capital of 50,000 shares. On January 5, the company issued 20,000 shares of ₹10 each at par payable as follows: ₹2 with the application, ₹2 on the allotment, and the balance when called. On January 10, the company received applications for 25,000 shares. On January 18, the company's board allotted 25,000 shares. The amounts payable on allotment were received on February 15. On March 20, the board made the first call for ₹4 per share and the amounts were received on April 22. The second and final call was made on June 10 and the amounts were received on July 27.

Required

Prepare journal entries to record the transactions.

Solution to the Review Problem

Jan.	10	Cash..	50,000	
		Share Application and Allotment		50,000
		To record receipt of share application money		
	18	Share Application and Allotment..	100,000	
		Equity Share Capital..		100,000
		To record allotment of shares and refund		

Feb. 15	Cash..	50,000	
	Share Application and Allotment		50,000
	To record receipt of allotment amounts		
Mar. 20	Share First Call	100,000	
	Equity Share Capital..		100,000
	To record first call on shares		
Apr. 22	Cash..	100,000	
	Share First Call		100,000
	To record receipt of first call amounts		
June 10	Share Second and Final Call	50,000	
	Equity Share Capital..		50,000
	To record second and final call on shares		
July 27	Cash..	50,000	
	Share Second and Final Call..		50,000
	To record receipt of second and final call amounts		

ASSIGNMENT MATERIAL

Questions

1. Why are companies subject to more government regulation than proprietorships and partnerships?
2. What is the significance of the shareholders' pre-emptive right?
3. Whom does *legal capital* help?
4. How does dividend differ from bonus share?
5. "Securities premium is a waste of shareholders' money because dividend is payable only on the share capital component." Do you agree?
6. What is the basis for recording issue of share capital for services or non-cash assets?
7. How are currency exchange differences treated?
8. Why are stock option plans more popular with technology companies?
9. Why do the book value and market value of a company's shares differ?
10. What is a *stock split*? How is it different from a bonus issue?
11. How is treasury stock similar to and different from a company's other investments?
12. What is *appropriation*? Why do companies make appropriations?
13. Why does a company with a *complex capital structure* have to report two EPS amounts?

Problems

Problem 11.1
Payment of Equity and Preference Dividends *

The share capital of Veer Company consists of 10,000 equity shares of ₹10 par value and 2,000 10 per cent, preference shares of ₹10 par value. The company declared and paid total dividends in the first four years of operation as follows: Year 1, ₹800; Year 2, ₹1,200; Year 3, ₹14,000; Year 4, ₹17,000.

Required

1. Determine the rate of dividend on each class of share capital in Years 1 to 4, assuming that the preference share capital is cumulative.
2. Determine the rate of dividend on each class of share capital in Years 1 to 4, assuming that the preference share capital is non-cumulative.

Problem 11.2
Issue of Bonus Shares *

On September 1, 20X1, Guna Company issued one bonus share for every share held by its shareholders by capitalizing all of its securities premium and retained earnings, to the extent required. On that date, the company had 100,000 equity shares of ₹10 par value, all fully paid-up, held by 1,230 shareholders. The company had a balance of ₹710,000 in the securities premium account and ₹491,200 in the statement of profit and loss.

Required

Prepare the journal entry to record the issue of bonus shares.

Sahib Company entered into the following treasury stock transactions during 20XX:

Jan. 4 Purchased 500 of its own ₹10 par value shares at ₹35 per share.

Mar. 15 Sold 300 of the treasury stock purchased on January 4 for ₹45 per share.

Aug. 7 Sold 100 of the treasury stock purchased on January 4 for ₹30 per share.

Problem 11.3
Treasury Stock Transactions
**

Required

Prepare journal entries to record the transactions.

Shamsher Company earned a profit after tax of ₹210,000 for the year ended December 31, 20XX. The company had 20,000 equity shares at the beginning of the year. On October 1, 20XX, it issued 40,000 shares.

Problem 11.4
Earnings Per Share **

Required

Compute the company's weighted-average earnings per share for the year.

Benoy Company was incorporated on January 1, 20XX with an authorized capital of 100,000 equity shares of ₹10 par value. The following transactions took place in the first year:

Problem 11.5
Share Capital and Dividend Transactions ***

Jan. 1 Issued 20,000 equity shares at ₹18 for cash.

Apr. 15 Issued 400 equity shares in exchange for services rendered by the company's lawyer. The services were valued at ₹5,000.

July 20 Issued 10,000 equity shares in exchange for the following assets with fair market values as indicated: land, ₹25,000; building, ₹40,000; plant and machinery, ₹75,000.

Nov. 12 The board of directors declared an interim dividend of 10 per cent to be paid on December 15 to shareholders of record on December 1.

Dec. 15 Paid the interim dividend.

Dec. 31 Closed the revenue and expense accounts for the year. Revenues were ₹410,000 and expenses ₹230,000.

Required

1. Prepare journal entries to record the transactions.
2. Prepare the shareholders' equity section of the company's balance sheet as at December 31, 20XX.

Durai Company was incorporated on April 1, 20X5 with an authorized capital of 200,000 equity shares of ₹10 par value. The following transactions took place in the first year:

Problem 11.6
Share Capital and Dividend Transactions *** Alternative to Problem 11.5

20X5

Apr. 1 Issued 50,000 equity shares at ₹25 for cash.

June 23 Issued 1,000 equity shares in exchange for the services of the founders in connection with the formation of the company. The services were valued at ₹25,000.

Aug. 5 Issued 15,000 equity shares in exchange for the following assets with fair market values as indicated: land, ₹35,000; building, ₹70,000; plant and machinery, ₹110,000.

20X6

Feb. 19 The board of directors declared an interim dividend of 15 per cent to be paid on March 20 to shareholders of record on March 1.

Mar. 20 Paid the interim dividend.

31 Closed the revenue and expense accounts for the year. Revenues were ₹782,000 and expenses ₹458,000.

Required

1. Prepare journal entries to record the transactions.
2. Prepare the shareholders' equity section of the balance sheet as at March 31, 20X6.

On February 1, 20XX, Pranav Company issued 500,000 shares of ₹10 par value at ₹15 with the option to retain up to an additional 20 per cent of the shares in the event of oversubscription. Payment was due as follows: with application ₹5, including premium of ₹2; on allotment ₹5, including premium of ₹3; the balance when called in at least two instalments. The following transactions took place in connection with the issue:

Problem 11.7
Share Capital Transactions
***

Feb. 1 Collected ₹3,500,000 on applications for 700,000 shares.

Mar. 10 Allotted 600,000 shares, retained ₹200,000 of application money for adjustment against amounts due on the allotment, and refunded the balance application money.

May 17 Received the amount due on the allotment and adjusted the application money retained.

July 12 Issued the first call for ₹2 per share.

Aug. 9 Received the first call amounts on all except 2,000 shares held by Madan.

Oct. 16 Issued the second and final call for ₹3 per share.

Nov. 28 Received the second and final call on all except 2,000 shares held by Madan and 1,000 shares held by Umesh.

Dec. 10 Forfeited the shares held by Madan and Umesh.

Required

1. Prepare journal entries to record the transactions.
2. Prepare the shareholders' equity section of the balance sheet as at December 31, 20XX.

Problem 11.8

Share Capital Transactions
∗∗∗ Alternative to
Problem 11.7

On January 1, 20XX, Amal Company issued 100,000 shares of ₹10 par value at ₹12 with the option to retain up to an additional 10 per cent of the shares in the event of oversubscription. Payment was due as follows: with application ₹5, including premium of ₹2; on allotment ₹3; the balance when called in at least two instalments. The following transactions took place in connection with the issue:

Jan. 8 Collected ₹750,000 on applications for 150,000 shares.

Feb. 15 Allotted 110,000 shares, retained ₹100,000 of application money for adjustment against amounts due on the allotment, and refunded the balance application money.

Apr. 21 Received the amount due on the allotment and adjusted the application money retained.

June 15 Issued the first call for ₹2 per share.

Sep. 9 Received the first call amounts on all except 1,000 shares held by Hitesh.

Nov. 10 Issued the second and final call for ₹2 per share.

Dec. 13 Received the second and final call on all except 1,000 shares held by Hitesh and 500 shares held by Sanjay.

Dec. 23 Forfeited the shares held by Hitesh and Sanjay.

Required

1. Prepare journal entries to record the transactions.
2. Prepare the shareholders' equity section of the balance sheet on December 31, 20XX.

Problem 11.9

Payment of Dividend
∗∗∗∗

Sharad Company has 1,000 of 10 per cent, ₹100 par value convertible preference shares and 50,000 equity shares of ₹10 par value. During the last five years, the company paid out the following amounts in dividends:

20X1	₹ 2,000
20X2	15,000
20X3	0
20X4	35,000
20X5	47,000

No dividends were in arrears for the years prior to 20X1.

Required

1. Compute the amount of dividend on preference shares and equity shares separately under each of the following assumptions: (a) The preference shares are non-cumulative and non-participating; (b) The preference shares are cumulative and non-participating; and (c) The preference shares are cumulative and fully participating.
2. At the option of the company, the preference share capital can be converted into equity after 20X5 at the rate of one equity share for one preference share. Will the existing equity shareholders benefit from the conversion assuming that the company expects to earn and distribute a profit after tax of ₹96,000 for 20X6? Assume that the preference shares are cumulative and fully participating.

Problem 11.10

Payment of Dividend
∗∗∗∗ Alternative to
Problem 11.9

Siddhartha Company has 1,500 of 15 per cent, ₹100 par value convertible preference shares and 100,000 equity shares of ₹10 par value. During the last five years, the company paid out the following amounts in dividends:

20X4	₹30,000
20X5	0
20X6	48,000
20X7	122,500
20X8	264,500

No dividends were in arrears for the years prior to 20X4.

Required

1. Compute the amount of dividend on preference shares and equity shares separately under each of the following assumptions: (a) The preference shares are non-cumulative and non-participating; (b) The preference shares are cumulative and non-participating; (c) The preference shares are cumulative and fully participating.
2. At the option of the company, the preference share capital can be converted into equity after 20X8 at the rate of two equity shares for one preference share. Will the existing equity shareholders benefit from the conversion assuming that the company expects to earn and distribute a profit after tax of ₹287,500 for 20X9? Assume that the preference shares are cumulative and fully participating.

Mohan Company reported an after-tax net profit of ₹317,000 for 20XX. On January 1, 20XX, the company had 96,000 equity shares of ₹10 par value and 1,000 of 12%, ₹100 non-convertible, cumulative preference shares. Information about transactions that affected the share capital account follows:

Problem 11.11
Earnings Per Share ✳✳✳✳

Mar. 1   Declared a 1:4 bonus.
May   1   Issued 60,000 shares at a premium of ₹25.
July   1   Purchased 12,000 shares to be held as treasury stock.
Aug. 1   Reissued 6,000 shares of treasury stock.
Oct.   1   Cancelled 2,000 shares of treasury stock.

On December 31, the company declared preference dividends of ₹12,000.

Required

1. Compute the basic earnings per share for 20XX.
2. Suppose Mohan Company did not declare preference dividends because it did not have cash. How would this affect the computation of earnings per share assuming that the preference shares were non-convertible, non-cumulative?
3. Suppose Mohan Company had dilutive securities throughout 20XX. Assuming that all dilutive securities had been converted at the beginning of the year, the weighted number of equity shares would have been 250,000. Compute the diluted earnings per share.

Avik Company reported an after-tax net profit of ₹362,500. On January 1, 20X3, the company had 240,000 equity shares of ₹10 par value and 1,500 of 10 per cent, ₹100 non-convertible, cumulative preference shares. Information about transactions that affected the share capital account follows:

Problem 11.12
Earnings Per Share
✳✳✳✳ Alternative to Problem 11.11

Feb.   1   Issued 120,000 shares at a premium of ₹25.
Apr.   1   Purchased 30,000 shares to be held as treasury stock.
June 1   Declared a 1:3 bonus.
Sept. 1   Purchased a further 30,000 shares for treasury.

On December 31, the company declared preference dividends of ₹15,000.

Required

1. Compute the basic earnings per share for 20X3.
2. Suppose Avik Company did not declare preference dividends because it did not have cash. How would this affect the computation of earnings per share, assuming that the preference shares were non-convertible, non-cumulative?
3. Suppose Avik Company had dilutive securities throughout 20X3. Assuming that all dilutive securities had been converted at the beginning of the year, the weighted number of equity shares would have been 450,000. Compute the diluted earnings per share.

Problem 11.13
Comprehensive Equity
Transactions ✶✶✶✶✶

Raja Company's shareholders' equity section on March 31, 20X4 was as follows:

Equity share capital

10% Preference shares, ₹100 par value, 10,000 shares fully paid up .... ₹1,000,000
Equity shares, ₹10 par value, 2,000,000 shares authorized, and
   300,000 shares issued and fully paid up.. 3,000,000

Other equity

Capital redemption reserve... 500,000
Securities premium 2,500,000
Revaluation reserve.. 3,400,000
General reserve 6,000,000
Retained earnings... 2,600,000

During the year ended March 31, 20X5, Raja Company was engaged in the following transactions:

20X4

Apr. 15 Purchased 10,000 equity shares for treasury at ₹18 per share.

May 23 Declared and paid a dividend of 10 per cent on preference shares and 25 per cent on equity shares. Both were shown as a liability on March 31, 20X4.

July 10 Declared a bonus of 2 for 1 on the outstanding equity shares by capitalization of capital redemption reserve, securities premium, and general reserve.

Aug. 26 Issued 50,000 equity shares at ₹25 per share.

Oct. 1 Issued 10,000 stock options to senior managers entitling them to buy 10,000 shares at the current market price of ₹30. The fair value of each option is ₹70 under the Black-Scholes model. The options are to be exercised on January 1, 20X8.

Nov. 3 Reissued at ₹25 per share 3,000 of the treasury stock purchased on April 15.

20X5

Jan. 18 Declared and paid an interim dividend of 15 per cent on equity shares.

Mar. 31 Recorded compensation expense on a stock option on the basis of a service period of two years.

31 Proposed a final dividend of 10 per cent on preference shares and 20 per cent on outstanding equity shares.

31 Closed the Statement of Profit and Loss, and Interim Dividend and Dividend accounts. Net profit for the year was ₹1,596,700.

Required

1. Prepare journal entries to record the transactions.
2. Prepare a statement of changes in equity for the year ended March 31, 20X5.
3. Prepare a schedule of equity on March 31, 20X5.

Problem 11.14
Comprehensive
Equity Transactions
✶✶✶✶✶ Alternative to
Problem 11.13

Prabhakar Company's shareholders' equity section on December 31, 20X1 was as follows:

Equity share capital

8% preference shares, ₹100 par value, 20,000 shares fully paid up .... ₹2,000,000
Equity Shares, ₹10 par value, 1,000,000 shares authorized, and
   600,000 shares issued and fully paid up.. 6,000,000

Other equity

Capital redemption reserve... 1,000,000
Securities premium 800,000
Revaluation reserve.. 1,400,000
General reserve 4,000,000
Retained earnings... 2,900,000

During the year ended December 31, 20X2, Prabhakar Company engaged in the following transactions:

20X2

Jan. 21 Declared and paid a dividend of 8 per cent on preference shares and 25 per cent on equity shares. Both were shown as a liability on December 31, 20X1.

Feb. 3 Purchased 10,000 equity shares for treasury at ₹50 per share.

Apr. 17   Issued 5,000 stock options for senior managers entitling them to buy 5,000 shares at the current market price of ₹40. The fair value of each option is ₹25 under the Black-Scholes model. The options are to be exercised on January 1, 20X4.

June 10   Declared a 1:1 bonus on the outstanding equity shares by capitalization of capital redemption reserve, securities premium, general reserve, and retained earnings.

July 11   Issued 100,000 equity shares at ₹30 per share.

Oct. 5   Reissued at ₹25 per share 3,000 of the treasury stock purchased on February 3.

Nov. 11   Declared and paid an interim dividend of 10 per cent on equity shares.

Dec. 31   Recorded compensation expense on a stock option on the basis of a service period of two years.

    31   Proposed a final dividend of 8 per cent on preference shares and 20 per cent on outstanding equity shares.

    31   Closed the Statement of Profit and Loss, and Interim Dividend and Dividend accounts. Net profit for the year was ₹44,530,000.

Required

1. Prepare journal entries to record the transactions.
2. Prepare a statement of changes in equity for the year ended December 31, 20X2.
3. Prepare a schedule of equity on December 31, 20X2.

Business Decision Cases

The board of directors of Infrastructure Finance Corporation is discussing payment of final dividend for the year just ended. This is how the discussion went:

BDC 11.1
Infrastructure Finance Corporation Limited

> *Managing Director:* This year we have done quite well; in fact, much better than last year. The management is looking at several investment opportunities. I suggest that we maintain the dividend at last year's level.
>
> *Major Investor (Mutual Fund):* I expect a fair return on my investment. The company should pay a larger dividend. If I have to retain the confidence of my investors, I have to show growth in my profit.
>
> *Finance Director:* Paying dividend entails cash outflow. Since we have plans for investing in projects that would yield much higher returns than some of our current projects, a larger dividend outflow would not be prudent. Besides, we have to pay the dividend distribution tax. So the total cash outflow will be even larger.
>
> *Independent Director:* Lenders are important stakeholders too. We have domestic and international lenders. As a finance company, we are far more dependent on debt than on equity. The RBI's guidelines on finance companies allow us to borrow about ten times of equity. We are close to that limit. Also, paying higher dividends could compromise lenders' interests and it will have adverse consequences for us. We have to comply with a number of bond covenants.
>
> *Major Investor:* My fund members are mainly pensioners. They expect growth in dividend every year.
>
> *Finance Director:* Besides, we have to transfer profits to the bond redemption reserve. That won't leave us with much cash to distribute.

Required

1. What should be the objectives of the company' dividend policy?
2. Examine the constraints on dividend payment that were pointed out in the discussion.
3. Do you see a conflict between the investors' interests and the lenders' interests in this case?
4. What is the bond redemption reserve? How does the transfer of profit to the reserve affect distributable profits?

Dynamic Bank is headquartered in New Delhi and has operations in New York and London. The bank's equity at March 31, 20X8 is as follows:

BDC 11.2
Dynamic Bank Limited

Equity share capital

Equity shares, 10 par value, 800,000 shares authorized, issued, subscribed and
    fully paid up .... ₹800,000

Other equity

Securities premium	400,000
Capital redemption reserve	900,000
Revaluation reserve	300,000
Foreign currency translation reserve	700,000
Statutory reserve	700,000
General reserve	50,000
Retained earnings	600,000
Total	4,450,000

On September 8, the bank's chief executive officer sent the following agenda note to the bank's board of directors:

> The bank has ₹700,000 in the foreign currency translation reserve. Of this, ₹500,000 relates to the bank's US subsidiary. It is proposed to repatriate the profit to India by transferring an equivalent amount of US dollars to the bank's central office in India on September 28, 20X8. An identical amount will be transferred back to the US subsidiary on October 3, 20X8 in order to meet the capital requirements in the US. As a result of this transaction, the bank can take an amount of ₹210,000 in the reserve to the statement of profit and loss. The Board may approve the proposal.

Soon after receiving the note, the board's audit committee chair sent the following response to the bank's chairman:

> The balance in the currency translation reserve is an unrealized gain. It cannot be recognized in the statement of profit and loss until the disposal of the foreign operation. The round-tripping of money between the bank's US subsidiary and head office is not a transaction at all. Since there is no disposal of the US operation or any part of it, it does not result in the realization of the amount. In view of this, I am unable to agree with the proposed accounting.

The chairman replied as follows:

> I am not an accountant. While I understand that there may be technical issues, we should not lose sight of the larger point. The bank is faced with mountains of bad loans and has to provide for them this fiscal year. That could very well wipe out the profit and even push the bank into a loss. Those consequences also need to be kept in mind, as we take a view of this matter. However, I fully appreciate your concerns as the audit committee chair. I suggest that the CEO and you discuss the matter.

The telephone conversation between the CEO and the audit committee chair (ACC) went as follows:

CEO: I hope you have read the proposal. There is a strong case for repatriating the profit to India. At the moment, the currency translation reserve is a dormant account and the amount is of no use to us.

ACC: The idea looks like round-tripping of money. I can't see how it can produce a gain.

CEO: Look, the money coming in represents the repatriated profit.

ACC: Assuming for a moment that the money coming in is repatriated profit, why is the money going back to the US operation?

CEO: The money going out is altogether different. It is our further investment in the US subsidiary. It is an entirely different transaction. It is just a coincidence that the amounts are equal. We have to transfer the money back to maintain the capital of the US subsidiary.

ACC: I have a simple question on this transaction. If the bank receives an amount from someone and pays back the same amount to that person, can the bank make a profit?

CEO: That is what I am trying to explain. You should not confuse the two transactions. The money that is coming in is with us for good. It is not going back at all. The money that is going back is our new investment.

ACC: If the bank intends to invest more in the subsidiary, why should it withdraw its investment in the first place?

CEO: The further investment is because of the capital adequacy requirements of US regulators. If we don't do this, they will not let us take the profit out of the US.

ACC: I am beginning to get a sense of the transaction, though I still don't understand why it is being done. Accounting standards do not allow the currency translation reserve to be taken to the statement of profit and loss, unless the foreign operation is disposed of. So what is being disposed of here?

CEO: We are not disposing of the operation. But I understand that even a part disposal of the operation would suffice.

ACC: Yes. A part of the operation can be disposed of and to the extent of the disposal, the balance in the currency translation reserve can be taken to the statement of profit and loss. Which part of the operation is being disposed of? I don't remember to have seen anything on this in board meetings.

CEO: We are looking at our international operations and will come to the board with a proposal. Quite apart from that, this is not simply a matter of accounting standards. It is a larger institutional issue. But you don't seem to be getting it. I will take it up in the next board meeting. (Cuts the call.)

The audit committee chair called the chairman and briefed him on the discussion. The chairman suggested a meeting of the three of them. This is what happened in that meeting.

Chairman: The reason why we are here is because the audit committee chair has concerns about the repatriation of profit from our US subsidiary. The CEO can explain the background to the transaction.

CEO: First, I want to say that we are not proposing anything wrong. The transaction is completely within the accounting standards. In fact, any other way of treating the transaction would be wrong. Second, some other banks have done similar transactions and I see no reason we can't do the same thing.

ACC: I have gone through the financial statements of a few banks that have done similar transactions. There is not enough information to explain what actually happened. In fact, the information is buried in some footnote. Unless I understand the exact details of the transactions, I will not be able to comment.

CEO: I have those details with me. They are no different from what we are planning to do. They have been audited by reputable firms and I would have done nothing wrong. Also, they have taken the RBI's approval for the transactions. Investing and withdrawing capital is an ongoing activity for banks.

ACC: I don't see any economic substance in the transaction. I can't convince myself that some money comes in, the money goes back and the money that came in is a profit. This is similar to a sale-and-repurchase transaction and there is no revenue at all. Some others may have done it but that is no reason why I should agree when I am clear that the accounting standard does not allow it. As you know, the audit committee is responsible for ensuring the credibility of the financial reporting process under the listing regulations. I don't see how the RBI comes in this except for approval of remittance of foreign currency.

Chairman: I have a meeting with another director. The two of you can carry on. I will be back in five minutes.

CEO: I am not recommending any manipulation, in case that is your concern. The situation is very serious. We are faced with a huge backlog of bad debts that my predecessor let pile up without provision. I am taking a number of measures to improve the bank's profitability. I am working on recovering bad debts but there are legal hurdles to quick recovery. I am planning to sell our surplus land and buildings. I am going to sell our non-core investments. I am cutting costs. I am thinking of raising more capital. The profit to be repatriated will not be the biggest of the measures. Please understand my situation. I need your support.

ACC: In my view, the position is clear: there has to be disposal of the foreign operation for the currency translation reserve to be taken to the statement of profit and loss. There is no disposal here. As I mentioned before, this is just round-tripping of money with no gain at all. The currency translation reserve is an unrealized reserve and the transaction does not result in the realization of the reserve.

Chairman: So what have you decided?

CEO: I have not been able to convince the audit committee chair. He is taking a narrow technical view. I can get an opinion from a reputable firm. I hope that will convince him. I have talked to a partner of a leading firm and he is willing to give an opinion.

ACC: I am simply going by what I believe to be my mandate. I am open to taking independent professional advice, if necessary. But in this case, I don't think I need to consult with anyone. I believe accounting should reflect operations. To me, this looks like opportunistic accounting. I will not be able to support accounting subterfuge.

Chairman: It looks like there is no convergence of views. We will meet again to discuss this matter.

Required

1. What does the foreign currency translation reserve mean? How does it arise? What can be done with it?
2. Explain the transaction the CEO is proposing. What is its economic effect?
3. Is the audit committee chair justified in rejecting the proposal to recognize a portion of the foreign currency translation reserve in the statement of profit and loss? Why or why not?
4. List the reasons given by the chairman and the CEO for the proposal. Do you agree with them? Explain.
5. Suppose the audit committee and the board overrule the audit committee chair and proceed with the proposal and the bank's external auditors agree with the practice. What are the audit committee chair's options?

Interpreting Financial Reports

IFR 11.1
Housing Development Finance Corporation Limited

Housing Development Finance Corporation Limited (HDFC) is the largest home mortgage lender in India. The financial statements for the year ended March 31, 2013 had the following note:

Note 5.2

During the year, ₹5,015.6 million (previous year ₹5,488.3 million) has been utilized out of the Securities Premium account in accordance with Section 78 of the Companies Act 1956. Out of the above, ₹nil (previous year ₹1.7 million) has been utilized by one of the subsidiary companies towards debenture issue expenses, ₹163.9 million (previous year ₹165.7 million) has been utilized by one of the subsidiary companies towards buyback of equity shares, ₹1.0 (previous year ₹nil) has been utilized by one of the subsidiary companies towards share issue expenses and ₹4,850.7 million (net of tax ₹2,232.5 million) [(previous year ₹5,320.9 million) (net of tax ₹nil)] has been utilized by HDFC Ltd. towards the proportionate premium payable on the redemption of zero-coupon secured redeemable non-convertible debentures. HDFC Ltd. has also written back ₹nil (₹937.6 million) on conversion of FCCBs to the Securities Premium account.

In a report titled "The last bastion falls", two analysts from Macquarie Equities Research downgraded their rating on HDFC's stock to "underperform" from "outperform" citing a likely structural de-rating of the lender as its earnings quality and return on equity were being driven by its corporate customers and aggressive accounting practices. The analysts stated:

> Over the past two years, HDFC Ltd. has been adopting aggressive accounting practices by passing provisioning through reserves and also making the adjustments for zero-coupon bonds (ZCBs) through reserves. We believe FY11 and FY12 earnings are overstated by 38% and 24% respectively and reported return on equity [ROE] would have been 600 and 400 bps (basis points) lower at 16% and 18% respectively, if the adjustments had been made through the P&L. In other words, earnings growth has been managed, in our view.

HDFC responded that the ZCBs were used to raise funds for investment in subsidiaries' businesses. Since under Indian accounting principles, the income from subsidiaries (barring dividends) was not taken into account, HDFC was charging the interest costs on ZCBs to the securities premium account. On provisions, HDFC said that it was a one-time requirement pertaining to past assets and was transitory in nature.

Required

1. Explain the transaction described in the note.
2. Comment on the company's accounting for interest on ZCBs and provisions for standard assets.
3. Examine the possible reasons for a company engaging in the transaction and the related accounting.

Financial Analysis

FA 11.1
Accounting for Stock Options

Identify a sample of companies that have stock options and study their annual reports.

Required

1. Explain why the companies may have stock option plans. Provide any references to relevant information in the financial statements and other parts of the annual report.
2. How do the companies account for stock options? Summarize the methods and their features.
3. Comment on the quality of disclosure on stock option plans.
4. Restate the net profit of the companies in accordance with the fair value method. Some companies provide information in the footnotes that would enable you to do this exercise. How would the adoption of the fair value method affect the profit of these companies?

FA 11.2
Understanding Reserves

Collect annual reports of a sample of companies.

Required

1. Prepare a list of reserves that appear on the balance sheet of these companies. Classify them according to the categories described in this chapter.
2. How much of the reserves is available for (a) dividend payment and (b) bonus issue?
3. Most companies have a general reserve. Explain why they keep this reserve rather than keep the amount in the statement of profit and loss.

Identify companies that have had a share buyback in the last five years.

FA 11.3
Analyzing Share Buyback

Required

1. Explain on the basis of the information provided in the offer document why each company bought back its shares. Do you agree with the reasons given?
2. Analyze the cash position of the companies before and after the buyback.
3. The dividend payment is an alternative to buyback. Explain why the companies preferred buyback to the dividend.

Identify a sample of companies that have had a bonus issue in the last five years.

FA 11.4
Analyzing Bonus Issues

Required

1. What do you think are the reasons for bonus issue in each of the sample companies?
2. Identify the reserves that the companies capitalized.

Answers to One-minute Quiz

11.1 b.
11.2 b.
11.3 b.
11.4 c.
11.5 d.

Answers to Test Your Understanding

11.1 ₹35,000, its paid-up capital.

11.2 (a) Cash.. 20,000

Equity Share Capital... 20,000

(b) Cash.. 22,000

Equity Share Capital... 20,000

Securities Premium 2,000

11.3 The excess over par value is securities premium and is part of shareholders' equity. Since it is a capital transaction, it is not an item of income.

11.4 20X6

Mar. 31 Retained Earnings.. 67,800

Investment Allowance Reserve.............................. 13,000

Export Profit Reserve 19,800

Dividend Equalization Reserve 25,000

Contingency Reserve 10,000

Retained Earnings:

Balance, March 31, 20X5 12,000

Profit for the period.. 73,200

Amount available for appropriation....................................... 85,200

Appropriations (see journal entry) 67,800

Balance, March 31, 20X6 17,400

Note: Dividend will be paid out of retained earnings.

11.5 The Australian currency is the functional currency of the subsidiary. Expenses have to be translated at the rates on the transaction dates. Since the expense transactions occurred approximately evenly through the year, the expenses can be translated at the average rate. Thus, the amount to be recognized in Peacock's statement of profit and loss is ₹774,639, calculated as follows: (A\$10,000 + A\$300 + A\$5,000) × ₹50.63.

11.6 Jan. 1 Cash.. 40,000

Outstanding Stock Options 25,000

Equity Share Capital... 10,000

Securities Premium 55,000

Securities Premium: 1,000 × (₹65 – ₹10) = ₹55,000

Interview with Mr. P. R. Ramesh, Deloitte India

Mr. P. R. Ramesh is Chairman of the Board of Deloitte India and Partner, Deloitte Haskins & Sells LLP.

"Auditors' lives would no longer be the same and without doubt be extremely challenging."

Question: What are the major challenges for accountants and auditors today?

Answer: The accountants of today face many challenges. The CFO is generally perceived to be the second most important person in the organization after the CEO and is the face of the organization to regulators. This imposes upon him the onerous task of compliance with ever increasing regulations and dealing with regulators. The explosion of on-line information sources, competing real-time news feeds in the form of TV channels devoted exclusively to business, the rapid developments in technology, the advent of "information on the move", access to information on hand-held mobile devices, and globally inter-connected markets – in sum the thirst for real-time and relevant information – have significantly impacted the quality and timeliness of financial reporting by accountants. Accounting standards which have not kept pace with newer business arrangements and emerging financial products pose additional challenges to accountants. After all, standards are akin to a house we raise over our heads. They define the perimeter within which a person, family, business or society can function. We live by the standards we set and it is to our peril that we dismantle them or lower the bar.

Given the tendency to flood the financial statements with endless disclosures, it is important for the accountant to pay attention to the quality and the relevance of disclosures. It has often been noted that the lengthier a disclosure, the more it obfuscates the underlying facts. Samuel Johnson once said: "Where secrecy or mystery begins, vice or roguery is not far off". Possibly he had disclosures accompanying financial statements in mind! The challenges an auditor of today faces are no less than that of an accountant but on a different canvas – the ever increasing expectation from investors and regulators, the oft-misconstrued role that an auditor lends insurance rather than assurance, the need to keep abreast of the sophisticated and rapid changes in the technological environment and, therefore, the need to retool, stakeholder activism and increased independent oversight, just to cite a few.

Question: How has Satyam changed reporting and auditing in India?

Answer: In my view, Satyam has had a limited and temporary impact on reporting and auditing in India. This is evident from the frauds which have surfaced in the last two years. The absence of a robust system of internal control over financial reporting (equivalent to the Sarbanes-Oxley Act requirement), compliance with independent director and audit committee requirements in form rather than substance by a large umber of companies, and the limited regulatory oversight on financial reporting and the attest function has resulted in companies and auditors being complacent. The slow and time-consuming systems of enforcement and punishment have not instilled the necessary fear or concern for the quality of financial reporting or attestation. The auditing profession enjoys the unique mandate of "independence" which stems from statute and bears the burden of not only being objective and independent at all times but also having to appear at all times to be objective and independent. This is a very strong public expectation and is only expected to grow in days to come.

Question: How can the National Financial Reporting Authority (NFRA) make the auditors more accountable?

Answer: The pre-requisites for achieving quality in any service or function are formulating standards, compliance of which will ensure high quality and a monitoring mechanism to oversee such compliance. Increasingly there is an expectation that the monitoring of compliance has to be carried out by persons independent of those responsible for compliance with the standards. The International Forum of Independent Audit Regulators (IFIAR) was formed for this very purpose. Unfortunately, India is not a member of IFIAR as there is no independent body which regulates the audit function which is presently regulated by The Institute of Chartered Accountants of India (ICAI). This is not a reflection of the quality of oversight by ICAI but the perception of lack of independence or a feeling of a 'shepherd protecting his flock'. NFRA, being independent, and if staffed by trained professionals like in the PCAOB in the US would significantly impose oversight and enhance auditor accountability.

Question: How is auditor rotation working?

Answer: The transition period for implementation of the provisions of the Companies Act, 2013 relating to rotation and the final phase of auditor appointments is coming to an end. There does not seem to have been an adverse shift in audit concentration of the big firms. Certain firms who have been impacted by the rotation have represented for mandatory implementation of joint audits. If mandatory joint audit is introduced it would have a retrograde collateral impact of audit rotation. The last two years of implementation of audit rotation have not seen any qualitative improvement in financial reporting or any revelations of auditors having compromised with their clients leading to misleading financial reporting. Whilst no published analysis is available, the general experience has been a reduction in audit fees due to competitive bidding.

Question: What have been the major challenges in Ind AS implementation?

Answer: This is the first year of implementation of Ind AS. There were requests from certain listed companies for relaxation in reporting comparative information which was accepted by SEBI. There have been no major challenges except in determining expected credit losses in the infrastructure sector. There have also been some challenges in roll-out of Ind AS in the banking and insurance sectors but it is expected to be resolved by the implementation. There have also been some challenges in maintaining dual set of books by entities where some of the consolidating entities are not under Ind AS, e.g. subsidiaries which are NBFCs. Taxation too, particularly book profits tax, is a challenge.

Question: Are Indian companies and banks ready for fair value accounting?

Answer: In my understanding, a large part of the Indian corporate sector including the banking sector is not fully ready for fair value accounting. There is an imperative need for more guidance and training, accreditation and oversight of valuers. It is also necessary for corporates and banks to prepare for the significant effect of transition to fair value accounting. Even a simple mark-to-market effect of foreign currency assets and liabilities has seen Indian corporate sector seeking relief.

Question: What do Indian accountants have to do to come up with a global accounting firm similar to the Big Four?

Answer: The Big Four have grown to their size by a series of mergers, acquisitions, and alliances. Indian accountants have to first change their mind-set and transition from being family-run firms to become fully professionally managed firms. The next steps would possibly involve merging with other like-minded firms or acquisitions or alliances. This would necessarily mean a willingness to re-align existing management control or seniority, change in the way of working and ability to handle the challenges large firms face, etc. It would mean transforming the existing firms to multi-disciplinary firms by partnering with non-CAs and also widening the geographical presence and changing from being pure local firms to firms with national or international operations.

PART THREE

ANALYZING AND INTERPRETING FINANCIAL STATEMENTS

This Part presents the common tools and techniques used to analyze financial statements. Strengthened by your understanding of the basics of financial statements and the recognition and measurement principles, you will be able to develop a method of analysis of financial statements.

Chapter 12 describes a number of techniques that investors, creditors, and analysts use to analyze and interpret the information contained in the balance sheet and the statement of profit and loss of a non-financial enterprise.

Chapter 13 discusses the statement of cash flows, a financial statement that discards accrual. You will learn how to prepare, present, and interpret the statement of cash flows of a non-financial enterprise.

Chapter 14 describes the financial statements of banks and explains how to analyze and interpret them.

Chapter 15 presents earnings analysis, non-traditional measures and analysis of qualitative information in annual reports.

CHAPTER
12

Balance Sheet and Statement of Profit and Loss

LEARNING OBJECTIVES

After studying this chapter, you should be able to:

1. Describe the objectives of financial statement analysis.
2. Describe the public sources of financial information.
3. Explain the standards of comparison for financial statement analysis.
4. Explain horizontal analysis, trend analysis, vertical analysis, and ratio analysis.
5. Analyze profitability.
6. Analyze liquidity.
7. Analyze solvency.
8. Evaluate capital market standing.

THE HOUSE OF DEBT

The GVK group built India's first six-lane expressway, the shining airports in Bengaluru, Mumbai and Bali, and power plants. It bought coal mines in Australia. These are just a few of the group's assorted businesses. It turns out that the house of GVK was built on debt. Unlike equity, debt entails unfailing interest and principal payment obligations. By 2015, the group's debt was 10.7 times its equity, leaping from 1.3 times in 2010. Interest cover – profit as a multiple of interest expense – dropped from 2.3 times in 2007 to 0.6 times in 2015, meaning that the profit was not even sufficient to pay the interest. In the boom years after 2008, Indian companies borrowed heavily. Unfortunately, their growth expectations were over-optimistic. Without the anticipated revenues, many companies including some in the GVK group defaulted on bond payments. In a speech in Kolkata in December 2015, the then Governor of the Reserve Bank of India, Raghuram Rajan, cautioned: "Debt is very much like a dynamite. It is an instrument which is very useful in right places and explosive in others."

SPEED READ

Financial statement analysis involves applying techniques to condense the mass of numbers in the financial statements into a set of incisive measures. It is an aid to informed investment and credit decisions. Financial information is available from many sources. Comparisons with rule-of-thumb indicators, a firm's past, internal standards and industry standards are useful. Horizontal, vertical and trend analyses give an overview of performance. The DuPont profitability analysis separates the effect of margin, turnover and leverage on return. Liquidity is the ability to pay short-term obligations. Solvency analysis looks at threats to long-term stability from debt. The price-earnings ratio and the price-to-book ratio are useful in understanding whether a stock is overvalued or undervalued.

Objectives of Financial Statement Analysis

Learning Objective

LO 1 Describe the objectives of financial statement analysis.

Financial statement analysis is the collective name for the tools and techniques intended to provide relevant information to decision-makers. Financial statement analysis helps us understand how a business enterprise fared in the past and find out where it was successful and where it veered off course. With the benefit of these insights, we can use financial statement analysis to develop expectations for the future.

Evaluating Past Performance

The starting point is to look at the record and evaluate the management's performance of its stewardship function. An assessment of current status will show where the company stands at present in property, plant and equipment, inventories, receivables, payables, borrowings, and cash. To a large extent, the expectations of investors and creditors about future performance are shaped by their evaluation of past performance and current position.

Individual investors have neither time nor expertise to understand the complexities of financial statements and business. They are happy with regular dividends. Dissatisfied investors sell their shares and take their money elsewhere. In contrast, institutional investors closely monitor the companies in which they have invested. They are more active and at times they insist on major business and management changes when the company does not fare well. They question related party transactions and vote out proposals for appointment of directors. Consider these examples of shareholder activism in India.

- In July 2014, minority shareholders of Tata Motors defeated resolutions proposed by the company relating to remuneration of three of its top executives. The company had sought approval for minimum remuneration in case of inadequacy of profits and ratification of the excess remuneration paid to executive directors.
- In November 2016, Elliott Management Corp., an activist investor, advised Cognizant Technology Solutions Corp. to get rid of an "antiquated, growth-at-all-costs" business model and focus instead on shareholder returns.
- In November 2014, minority shareholders of Siemens India rejected the offer price for its metals technologies business to its German parent as too little. Siemens Germany raised the offer price by about 20 per cent.

Predicting Future Performance

Information about the past is useful in assessing future prospects. For example, trends in past sales, earnings, cash flow, profit margin, asset utilization, debt, and return on investment aid in assessing a firm's prospects. Investors and creditors use information about the past to assess a company's prospects. They look ahead by looking back, so to speak. Investors expect an adequate return from the company in the form of dividends and stock price appreciation. Creditors expect the company to pay interest and principal according to the loan contract. Therefore, they are interested in predicting the earning power and debt-paying ability of the company.

Investors and creditors earn returns in the form of interest, dividend and stock price growth. Volatile returns are riskier than stable returns. A highly profitable business yields high returns but it also involves high risk. Investors and creditors expect to be compensated for risks. They will put their money in high-risk ventures only if they can get adequately high returns. For instance, we can predict the sales of electricity next year more accurately than the box-office collections of a movie due for release next week.

Therefore, investors would demand higher returns from movie producers than from electricity distributors.

Public Sources of Information

Individual investors and creditors must often depend on publicly available information about companies. The most common sources of information about listed companies are annual and quarterly reports, stock exchanges, and government reports.

Annual reports contain valuable financial and other information. They are the beginning and ending points in obtaining information about individual companies. As a starter, they provide an overview of the company's business, current status, and past performance. At the end of the information gathering process, they are used to corroborate the vast array of company-specific data assembled from various sources. An annual report includes directors' report, management discussion and analysis, financial statements, schedules and notes to the financial statements, and auditor's report.

Some annual reports provide tables and charts showing current period highlights and track record, chairman's letter to the shareholders, and a lot of other information that is difficult to audit, such as brand valuation, human assets valuation, corporate social responsibility initiatives and, of course, impressive photographs of products, people, and facilities.

The annual report is sent to the shareholders of the company free of charge and is usually available on the company's website. Listed companies are required to publish, in addition, quarterly financial results in leading newspapers. Quarterly results are not audited but are subjected to a "limited review" by the auditors.

Listed companies must file financial statements and other documents with the stock exchanges. The National Stock Exchange of India (NSE) is the leading stock exchange in India. The Bombay Stock Exchange (BSE) is the oldest stock exchange in Asia. Company filings are available on their websites. The listing agreement requires companies to inform the stock exchange promptly of major developments affecting them, including management and auditor changes, director resignations, board meetings, bonus and dividend decisions, strikes, accidents, and plant closures.

The Government of India and the Reserve Bank of India issue reports on the performance of the economy. These include past data and forecasts on GDP (gross domestic product), agricultural and industrial production, rainfall, inflation and foreign exchange reserves. Industry and trade associations provide industry-specific data.

Learning Objective

(LO 2) Describe the public sources of financial information.

Standards of Comparison

In order to judge whether the results of the financial statement analysis are favourable or unfavourable, we can compare them with rule-of-thumb indicators, past performance, internal standards and industry standards. We will now discuss them.

Learning Objective

(LO 3) Explain the standards of comparison for financial statement analysis.

Rule-of-thumb Indicators

Bankers use *rule-of-thumb* or benchmark financial ratios. For example, it is generally thought that a current ratio of 2:1 or above is satisfactory. Rule-of-thumb measures are useful in making broad comparisons of firms. Nevertheless, they should be used with great caution since individual circumstances often differ. For example, a firm with a current ratio of 2.2:1 may have slow-moving inventories and past-due receivables, while another firm having a current ratio of 1.6:1 may have fast-moving inventories and not-yet-due receivables.

Past Performance

Comparing a company's current performance with its past performance will show whether the company is improving or declining. Also, a study of past ratios and percentages may assist in extrapolating them.

However, there are problems with historical comparisons:

1. Fundamental changes in a company's environment, such as government regulation, competition, and technology, can make it difficult to project past trends into the future.
2. Accounting policy changes (e.g. change in depreciation method) will affect the comparability of the past figures.
3. Non-operating items (e.g. gains and losses on sales of investments) are not predictable.
4. Comparisons with the company's own past can, at times, create an illusion of growth. For instance, an annual rise of 10 per cent in a company's sales may in itself sound good, but would not be considered adequate if the market is growing at 30 per cent. The success of a business, in the long run, depends on whether it outperforms its competitors rather than its own past.

REAL WORLD
The Kodak Moment, Passed

The Kodak camera was the iPhone of its day. Eastman Kodak was among the first to invent the instant camera and the digital camera. Kodak's sales peaked at $16 billion in 1996 and profits at $2.5 billion in 1999. Digital cameras and smartphones gutted Kodak. The company filed for bankruptcy in January 2012. In boardrooms and classrooms, Kodak is cited as an example of how a company can become a victim of its own success and complacency.

Internal Standards

Companies follow internal standards for monitoring and rewarding performance. There are broad corporate goals for profit, return on assets, sales growth, market share, new product launches and so on. Budgets specify detailed targets for profit centres, business units and departments. Standard costs are predetermined costs of making a product and are based on the standards for material consumption and prices, labour efficiency and wage rates, and the expected level of operations laid down by the management. These are used primarily for control of operational costs.

Internal standards are greatly useful in evaluating an enterprise's performance. They are directly relevant to the enterprise's circumstances and are, therefore, likely to be more meaningful as a basis for comparison. They are regularly revised in light of changes in the enterprise's economic and business environment. Unfortunately, they are not generally available to outsiders. Nevertheless, analysts question the management about internal expectations specified in budgets and other internal documents.

Industry Standards

The performance of a company can be compared with that of other companies in the industry. Comparisons with industry standards help overcome the limitations of historical comparisons. For example, if a company has a gross margin of 7 per cent, while the industry average is 12 per cent, its operations are not as profitable as some of its peers.

Industry comparisons can be problematic for the following reasons:

1. *Size and products:* Comparisons are difficult for companies that operate in many lines of business. For example, Hindustan Unilever makes soaps, detergents, toothpaste, and food. Procter & Gamble is in detergents, but it is also in other products that HUL does not sell. ITC is in food, but it is also in hotels and tobacco. Colgate makes toothpaste but not any of HUL's other products. Comparing HUL with these companies is not much useful.

2. *Accounting policies:* Companies often follow different accounting policies. Inventory valuation methods, useful life estimates for assets, and revenue recognition practices differ across companies.

3. *Fiscal year:* Most companies follow the March 31 year end, but a few don't. For instance, Ambuja Cement follows the calendar year, while India Cements follows March 31. The Companies Act 2013 requires companies to use the March 31 fiscal year unless they qualify for the exemption.

Techniques of Financial Statement Analysis

Few numbers in financial statements are significant in themselves. But we can draw meaningful inferences from their relationship to others or their change from one period to another. The tools of financial statement analysis help in establishing significant relationships and changes. The most commonly used analytical techniques are horizontal analysis, trend analysis, vertical analysis, and ratio analysis.

Learning Objective

LO 4 — Explain horizontal analysis, trend analysis, vertical analysis, and ratio analysis.

In this section, we illustrate the application of these techniques using the 2016 consolidated financial statements of Dr. Reddy's Laboratories Limited (DRL). DRL is a leading pharmaceutical company. Its business includes generics, biologics, active pharmaceutical ingredients, pharmaceutical services, and proprietary products. The financial statements are in Appendix B. They have both Ind AS and Indian GAAP numbers for 2016. We use Indian GAAP numbers, since Ind AS numbers are not available for earlier years.

Horizontal Analysis

Financial statements present comparative information for at least two years. **Horizontal analysis** calculates the amount and percentage changes from the previous year to the current year. It is simple but useful. While an amount change in itself may mean something, converting it to percentage is more useful in appreciating the magnitude of the change. Exhibits 12.1 and 12.2 present the horizontal analysis of DRL's financial statements.

DR. REDDY'S LABORATORIES LIMITED Condensed Statement of Profit and Loss For the year ended March 31, 2016			
	2016	2015 *(in millions)*	Change (%)
Revenue from operations	₹156,978	₹150,233	4.49
Other income	2,693	2,741	(1.75)
Total revenue	159,671	152,974	4.38
Total expenses	(128,299)	(123,978)	3.49
Profit before exceptional items and tax	31,372	28,996	8.19
Exceptional items	(4,621)	0	—
Profit before tax	26,751	28,996	(7.74)
Tax	(5,237)	(5,632)	(7.01)
Profit for the year	21,514	23,364	(7.92)

EXHIBIT 12.1

Horizontal Analysis: Statement of Profit and Loss

In 2016, revenue from operations was up 4.49 per cent, while expenses rose only by 3.49 per cent or at less than half the revenue growth rate. Further, tax expense declined by 7.01 per cent. So profit should have increased but it was down 7.92 per cent. Foreign exchange losses took away 14.73 per cent of the profit before exceptional items and tax. Other income declined but not significantly. Excluding exceptional items and other income for both years profit increased by 10.43 per cent, better than sales growth. Earnings quality analysis helps us get the real picture.

EXHIBIT 12.2

Horizontal Analysis: Balance Sheet

DR. REDDY'S LABORATORIES LIMITED Condensed Balance Sheet, March 31	2016	2015 *(in millions)*	Change (%)
Assets			
Property, plant and equipment	₹46,296	₹41,837	10.67
Capital work-in-progress	6,631	5,290	25.35
Intangible assets	19,338	11,933	62.05
Non-current investments	1,456	1,456	0.00
Long-term loans	5,194	4,181	24.23
Deferred tax assets, net	2,853	2,450	16.45
Other non-current assets	135	64	110.94
Non-current assets	81,903	67,211	21.86
Inventories	25,799	25,699	0.39
Current investments	21,122	21,022	0.48
Trade receivables	41,667	41,012	1.60
Cash and cash equivalents	18,358	18,724	(1.95)
Short-term loans	10,058	10,747	6.41
Other current assets	1,197	1,563	23.42
Current assets	118,201	118,767	(0.48)
Total assets	200,104	185,978	7.60
Equity and Liabilities			
Equity	₹117,009	₹98,531	18.92
Borrowings	10,690	14,315	(25.32)
Other long-term liabilities	2,498	2,733	8.60
Long-term provisions	947	779	21.57
Deferred tax liabilities	592	1,407	(57.92)
Non-current liabilities	14,727	19,234	(23.43)
Short-term borrowings	22,718	21,857	3.94
Trade payables	9,309	8,673	7.33
Other current liabilities	24,395	26,244	(7.05)
Short-term provisions	11,946	11,439	4.43
Current liabilities	68,368	68,213	0.23
Total equity and liabilities	200,104	185,978	7.60

Another way to look at performance is to compare the company's revenue growth with asset growth. From Exhibit 12.2, we see that assets were up 7.60 per cent, more than the revenue growth rate. While non-current assets increased by 21.86 per cent, property, plant and equipment grew much lower at 10.67 per cent. Capital work-in-progress increased by 25.35 per cent, indicating that the company is expanding capacity. The increase of 62.05 per cent in intangible assets is because of products acquired. Non-current investments were flat. Most current assets didn't change much. Inventories were up 0.39 per cent, less than the sales growth rate. The smaller rise in inventories could be because of better inventory management. But it also raises a question whether DRL's inventories are sufficient. It may also be a sign of less optimistic sales growth expectation. Trade receivables lagged revenue growth. This could be because of tightening of credit standards, reduction of credit period, or better collection efforts. All these are conjectures that need to be tested with more data. Equity funding increased because of retained earnings. Long-term borrowings declined significantly, but short-term borrowings increased. The increase in trade payables is in step with sales growth. Another way to analyze the percentage changes is to compare them with the inflation rate.

Percentage changes can mislead. For example, property, plant and equipment increased by 10.67 per cent, while capital work-in-progress grew at 25.35 per cent but did so on significantly different base amounts.

Trend Analysis

Trend analysis involves studying changes in financial statement items for many years. It is an extension of horizontal analysis. We first assign a value of 100 to the financial statement items in a past financial year used as the base year and then express the amounts in the following years as a percentage of the base-year value. Exhibit 12.3 illustrates trend analysis with revenue from operations, net profit and property, plant and equipment for DRL from 2012 to 2016.

DR. REDDY'S LABORATORIES LIMITED Selected Financial Data					
	2016	2015	2014	2013	2012 *(in millions)*
Item					
Revenue from operations	₹156,978	₹150,233	₹134,153	₹118,956	₹98,145
Net profit	21,514	23,364	19,632	15,268	13,009
Property, plant and equipment	46,296	41,837	37,496	31,416	25,732
Trend					
Revenue from operations	160	153	137	121	100
Net profit	165	180	151	117	100
Property, plant and equipment	180	163	146	122	100

EXHIBIT 12.3
Five-Year Trend Analysis

For instance, using 2012 as the base year, the sales value in 2013 becomes 121 as shown below:

$$\text{Index in 2013} = \frac{2013 \text{ sales}}{2012 \text{ sales}} \times 100 = \frac{118,596}{98,145} \times 100 = 121$$

From 2012 to 2016, sales, net profit and property, plant and equipment grew. Over this period, revenue grew 60 per cent, yielding a compound annual growth rate (CAGR) of 12.47 per cent.[1] Net profit went up 65 per cent at a CAGR of 13.34 per cent. In contrast, property, plant and equipment jumped 80 per cent at a CAGR of 15.83 per cent. Net profit was moving nicely ahead of sales except in 2016, when it was hit by foreign exchange losses. The higher growth in property, plant and equipment relative to sales indicates the company's ambitious investment plans through in-house growth and acquisitions. These numbers imply that profit margin and asset utilization generally improved over the period. Trend analysis helps in identifying basic changes in the nature of the business. Since many large corporations publish performance summaries and selected financial indicators for five or more years, it is possible to perform trend analysis.

Zee Company has a net profit of ₹300,000, ₹425,000 and ₹640,000, respectively for 20X1, 20X2, and 20X3. Using 20X1 as the base year, the trend values for net profit are as follows:

$$\text{Index in 20X2} = \frac{20X2 \text{ profit}}{20X1 \text{ profit}} \times 100 = \frac{425,000}{300,000} \times 100 = 142$$

$$\text{Index in 20X3} = \frac{20X3 \text{ profit}}{20X1 \text{ profit}} \times 100 = \frac{640,000}{300,000} \times 100 = 213$$

HANDHOLD 12.1
Trend Analysis

Vertical Analysis

Vertical analysis is the expression of the amounts of financial statement items as percentages of the statement total. The results of vertical analysis are presented in the form of **common-size statements** in which the items within each statement are expressed in percentages of some common number and always add up to 100. It is conventional to express items in the

---

[1] The CAGR of 12.47 per cent is obtained by solving for x in the equation: $160 = 100 \times (1 + x)^4$. Note that the index in 2016 is rounded to 160.

statement of profit and loss as percentages of sales, and balance sheet items as percentages of the total equity and liabilities (or total assets). Vertical analysis helps in comparing companies that differ in size since the financial statements are expressed in comparable common-size format. Further, a study of common-size statements for several years may reveal important changes in the components over time.

Exhibits 12.4 and 12.5 show DRL's common-size statement of profit and loss and balance sheet for 2016 and 2015. The company made savings in expenses and taxes to the extent of 2 per cent. The foreign currency loss of 3 per cent wiped out these savings. As a result, it ended up with a drop of 1 per cent in profit. The increase in property, plant and equipment and intangible assets indicate expansion and acquisitions. The decrease in inventories and receivables suggest better management of working capital. On the financing side, there appears to be a move away from borrowings to equity. Common-size statements are especially useful in presentations to highlight key changes.

EXHIBIT 12.4

Vertical Analysis: Statement of Profit and Loss

DR. REDDY'S LABORATORIES LIMITED Common-size Statement of Profit and Loss For the year ended March 31, 2016		
	2016	2015
Total revenue	100	100
Total expenses	(80)	(81)
Profit before exceptional items and tax	20	19
Exceptional items	(3)	0
Profit before tax	17	19
Tax	(3)	(4)
Profit for the year	14	15

EXHIBIT 12.5

Vertical Analysis: Balance Sheet

DR. REDDY'S LABORATORIES LIMITED Common-size Balance Sheet, March 31, 2016		
	2016	2015
Assets		
Property, plant and equipment	23	23
Capital work-in-progress	3	3
Intangible assets	10	6
Non-current investments	1	1
Long-term loans	3	2
Deferred tax assets, net	1	1
Other non-current assets	0	0
Inventories	13	14
Current investments	11	11
Trade receivables	21	22
Cash and cash equivalents	9	10
Short-term loans	5	6
Other current assets	0	1
Total assets	100	100
Equity and Liabilities		
Equity	59	53
Long-term borrowings	5	8
Other long-term liabilities	1	1
Long-term provisions	1	0
Deferred tax liabilities	0	1
Short-term borrowings	11	12
Trade payables	5	5
Other current liabilities	12	14
Short-term provisions	6	6
Total equity and liabilities	100	100

Ratio Analysis

Ratio analysis involves establishing a relevant financial relationship between components of financial statements. For instance, two companies may have the same amount of profit in a year but unless the profit is related to sales, we can't say which of them is more profitable. Ratio analysis helps in identifying significant relationships between financial statement items for further investigation. Combined with a good knowledge of the business, it can be a powerful tool for recognizing a company's strengths and its potential trouble spots.

Financial ratios are used to evaluate profitability, liquidity, solvency, and capital market strength. You have seen some ratios in earlier chapters. In this chapter, we put together the major ratios. Our evaluation is based on the information available in DRL's published reports. You should use additional information, such as internal benchmarks, where available.

Profitability Analysis

Profitability ratios measure the degree of operating success of a business. Investors finance a firm in the hope of getting a reasonable return in the form of capital gain and dividends. Therefore, they are keen to learn about the firm's ability to earn revenues in excess of expenses. They will not be interested in a company that does not earn a sufficient profit. Failure to earn an adequate profit over a period will drain the company's cash and impair its liquidity. The commonly used ratios to evaluate profitability are:

Learning Objective

LO 5 Analyze profitability.

- Profit margin;
- Asset turnover;
- Return on assets;
- Return on equity; and
- Earnings per share.

We discuss these ratios below.

Profit Margin

This ratio, also known as **return on sales (ROS)**, measures the amount of net profit earned from each rupee of revenue.[2] Using the revenue and profit amounts in Exhibit 12.1, we compute DRL's profit margin as follows:

Profit margin	2016	2015
$\dfrac{\text{Profit}}{\text{Sales}}$	$\dfrac{21,514}{156,978} = 13.71\%$	$\dfrac{23,364}{150,233} = 15.55\%$

Profit margin declined to 13.71 per cent in 2016 from 15.55 per cent in 2015. From the horizontal analysis, we know that regular expenses increased slower than revenues and other income didn't change much. Net profit is a "noisy" measure, because of the inclusion of other income and exceptional items.

Profit margin provides some indication of the cushion available in the event of an unexpected increase in costs or a drop in selling prices, because of recession or greater competition. The margin was 14.63 per cent in 2014. The pressure on margin in 2016 should be analyzed by looking at major categories of expenses, such as materials, employee benefits, R & D, and advertising. For example, employee benefits went up from 19.60 per cent of revenue in 2015 to 20.30 per cent in 2016. Spending on clinical trials and R & D and

---

[2] To be consistent, we use revenue from operations as the measure of sales throughout this chapter.

advertising *decreased* in 2016. Since a significant portion of DRL's revenue is from exports, exchange rate changes too affect the margin.

Recall the discussion on gross profit ratio in Chapter 4. Using DRL's IFRS statements, we compute the company's gross profit margin as follows:

Gross profit margin	2016	2015	2014
$\dfrac{\text{Profit}}{\text{Sales}}$	$\dfrac{92,281}{154,708} = 59.65\%$	$\dfrac{85,403}{148,189} = 57.63\%$	$\dfrac{75,801}{132,170} = 57.35\%$

Gross profit margin has been improving steadily over the three-year period. We need to examine operating expenses to find out why the profit margin declined despite a higher gross margin.

Asset Turnover

Asset turnover (ATO) is a measure of a firm's efficiency in utilizing its assets. It indicates how many times the assets were turned over in a period in order to generate sales. If the asset turnover is high, we can infer that the enterprise is managing its assets efficiently. A low asset turnover implies idle assets. Averages rather than year-end amounts of assets are a better measure of the level of assets held during the year. The difference between average and year-end amounts will be more pronounced for companies that are engaged in expanding or reducing capacity.

From Exhibit 12.2 and Appendix B, DRL's assets are as follows: 200,104 in 2016; 185,978 in 2015; and 160,296 in 2014. Average assets are: 193,041 in 2016 and 173,137 in 2015. Using the revenue amount in Exhibit 12.1 and the average assets, we can now compute DRL's asset turnover:

Asset turnover	2016	2015
$\dfrac{\text{Sales}}{\text{Assets}}$	$\dfrac{156,978}{193,041} = 0.81 \text{ times}$	$\dfrac{150,233}{173,137} = 0.87 \text{ times}$

In 2016, DRL had sales of ₹81 per ₹100 of investment in assets as compared to ₹87 in 2015. The decrease of ₹6 indicates a significant deterioration in asset utilization in 2016. This is in line with our observation from the horizontal analysis that assets grew much faster than sales. The decrease in asset turnover could be because of lower demand, poor equipment maintenance, delay in availability of raw materials and power, ineffective management of inventories, receivables and cash, poor industrial relations, and so on. Asset turnover rates differ from one industry to another. A fast-food restaurant operating from rented premises may have an asset turnover of 20, while a refinery's asset turnover could be even less than one.

Return on Assets

Return on assets (ROA), also known as **return on investment** (ROI), is a measure of profitability from a given level of investment. It is an excellent indicator of a company's overall performance. We compute DRL's ROA as follows:

Return on assets	2016	2015
$\dfrac{\text{Profit}}{\text{Assets}}$	$\dfrac{21,514}{193,041} = 11.14\%$	$\dfrac{23,364}{173,137} = 13.49\%$

The fall of 2.35 per cent in the ROA indicates a significant deterioration in the company's overall profitability. The ROA decreased because of the worsening of both margin and turnover, as we saw earlier. We note that the lower ROA came from a larger investment, suggesting that the additional investment was probably less profitable.

DuPont financial analysis clearly brings out the effect of these two drivers on the ROA. Figure 12.1 presents the DuPont chart. It shows how profit margin and asset turnover interact to produce ROA. Level 1 is the return on equity, which we will consider shortly. Look at Level 2 – return on assets, and Level 3 – its drivers. It is possible to produce a certain ROA by varying margin and turnover. For example, a 20 per cent ROA can come from a margin of 10 per cent and a turnover of two times or a margin of 4 per cent and a turnover of five times. Level 4 describes the calculation of margin and turnover.

A firm selects a combination that reflects how it intends to do business, or "strategy" in the jargon. Does it want to sell upmarket, differentiated products or cheap, mass market products? To achieve a certain ROA, businesses can choose between various combinations of margin and turnover. Companies that target the mass market, such as supermarkets, typically have low profit margins, but keep high asset turnover – "low margin, high volume" strategy. Companies that sell premium products such as designer dresses or operate in a *niche* market enjoy high profit margins, but have low asset turnover – "high margin, low volume" strategy.

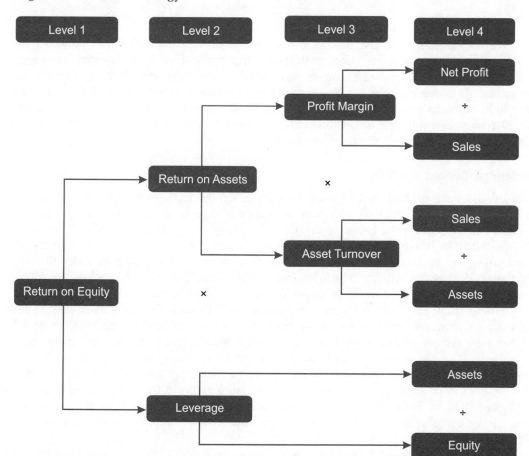

Figure 12.1
THE DUPONT FINANCIAL ANALYSIS CHART

Return on equity is the product of margin, turnover and leverage.

Using the DuPont chart, we can analyze DRL's ROA as follows:

Year	Profit margin $\dfrac{\text{Profit}}{\text{Sales}}$	Asset turnover $\dfrac{\text{Sales}}{\text{Assets}}$	Return on assets $\dfrac{\text{Profit}}{\text{Assets}}$
2016	13.71%	0.81 times	11.14%
2015	15.55%	0.87 times	13.49%

This analysis shows that the company earned a lower ROA in 2016, because of *both* lower margin *and* lower turnover. As a result, the ROA was down 2.35 per cent.

Are the following products as "low margin, high volume" or "high margin, low volume"? (a) Aston Martin, (b) Chloé, (c) Ginger Hotel, (d) Lifebuoy, (e) Lux, (f) Taj Vivanta, (g) Ulysse Nardin, (h) Xiaomi.

Return on Equity

Return on equity (ROE) is a measure of profitability from the shareholders' standpoint. It measures the efficiency in the use of shareholders' funds. In order to moderate the influence of share issue and buyback and change in retained earnings, analysts generally use the average of beginning and ending amounts for the year. From Exhibit 12.2 and Appendix B, DRL's equity is as follows: 117,009 in 2016; 98,531 in 2015; and 78,652 in 2014. Average equity is 107,770 in 2016 and 88,592 in 2015. Using the profit amount in Exhibit 12.1 and the average equity, we can now compute DRL's ROE:

Return on equity	2016	2015
$\dfrac{\text{Profit}}{\text{Equity}}$	$\dfrac{21,514}{107,770} = 19.96\%$	$\dfrac{23,364}{88,952} = 26.37\%$

We are not surprised that the ROE follows the downward movement noticed in the other profitability measures. Competitors try and replicate a firm's special advantages in product offerings, cost efficiencies, innovation, technology, distribution network, and brands. This adversely affects a firm's ability to maintain a supernormal ROE. As a result, the ROE tends to revert towards the industry mean over time. The decrease in the ROE in 2016 was caused by the lower ROA. Shareholders expect the ROE to be higher than the *cost of equity*, their expected rate of return.

Extended DuPont Analysis

You would have noticed that in both 2015 and 2016 the ROE was higher than the ROA, implying that the company earned more per rupee of shareholders' funds than per rupee of assets. One reason for the better return to DRL's shareholders is the use of debt financing. When the ROA is more than the interest rate on debt, shareholders benefit. **Leveraging,** or **trading on the equity,** is the use of debt finance to acquire assets in order to earn a higher ROE. The flip side of debt financing is that, when the ROA falls below the interest rate, shareholders lose. We will consider the risk of debt financing later in this chapter.

From Exhibit 12.5, borrowings are 16 per cent of DRL's financing. However, the company also gets significant interest-free credit from its suppliers of goods and services and by deferring payment of its obligations. Shareholders benefit from interest-free financing.

Figure 12.1 helps us to understand the effect of leverage on return on assets. From Levels 1 and 2, we note that ROE is the product of leverage and ROA, which in turn is the product of profit margin and asset turnover. For a given ROA, it is possible to produce a higher ROE by financing a part of the assets with debt. This is how the use of debt can "lever up" the ROA for the shareholders. The **assets-to-equity ratio** is a measure of leverage.

We can now see how Figure 12.1, Level 1 works. In 2016, DRL's ROA was 11.14 per cent. Its leverage was 1.71, calculated as follows: Average assets, 193,041/ Average equity, 107,770. The ROE of 19.96 per cent is the product of ROA of 11.14 per cent and leverage of 1.71.

Earnings Per Share

Financial analysts regard the **earnings per share (EPS)** as an important measure of profitability. DRL's basic EPS for 2016 was ₹126.15, down 8 per cent from 2015. EPS is useful in comparing performance over time. The decrease in DRL's EPS in 2016 means that the company did worse on the whole. But the EPS is not of much help in making comparisons across firms because the number of equity shares can differ (even if all of them happen to have the same amount of equity). It is useful as an input into the price-earnings ratio, which we shall see later in this chapter.

For 20X1, Mohan Company's profit margin and return on assets were 10 per cent and 18 per cent, respectively.

1. Compute the company's asset turnover for 20X1.

   For 2 and 3 below assume that the company's profit after tax for 20X1 was ₹2,700 and its total assets in 20X0 were ₹14,000.
2. Compute the company's total assets at the end of 20X1.
3. Suppose in 20X2 the company plans to increase sales by 15 per cent over 20X1. Compute its asset turnover for 20X2 assuming no increase in assets over 20X1.

Leonard Lauder, the chairman of Estée Lauder, a cosmetics firm coined the term 'lipstick index' when, during the 2001 recession, lipstick sales went up 11 per cent. In the past, lipstick sales recorded an increase during the Great Depression (the late 1920s to early 1930s) and the Second World War (1939–1945). It appears that demand for cosmetics increases when consumer confidence is low. However, in the aftermath of the 2008 financial crisis, L'Oréal, the world's largest beauty company, found that in the UK foundation edged out lipstick as the *must-have* product for women, with more than one-third of 18 and 19-year-olds citing it as their most essential beauty product against 8 per cent opting for lipstick. The sales of anti-depressants are also likely to be countercyclical. Then there may be services, such as those of cosmetic surgeons, psychiatrists and priests, that are in demand in both good and bad times. The point is that the sales of some products and services may be countercyclical or cycle-proof because people would flock to them in times of trouble. The analyst should look for links between a firm's sales and the wider social and economic conditions.

Trouble Company's gross margin decreased from 21 per cent in 20X1 to 15 per cent in 20X2. Which of the following events in 20X2 explains the change? There may be more than one correct answer.
(a) Credit period increased.
(b) Interest expense increased.
(c) Cost of raw materials increased but selling prices did not change.
(d) Sales growth rate decreased.

Liquidity Analysis

Liquidity is the ability of a business to meet its short-term obligations when they fall due. An enterprise should have enough current assets, which can be converted into cash so that it can pay its suppliers and lenders on time. For evaluating DRL's liquidity, we examine the following four ratios:
1. Current ratio;
2. Quick ratio;
3. Receivable turnover; and
4. Inventory turnover.

Current Ratio

The **current ratio** is the ratio of current assets to current liabilities. It is a widely used indicator of a company's ability to pay its obligations in the short-term. It shows the amount of current assets a company has per rupee of current liabilities. Current assets and current liabilities are those that are receivable or payable in the normal operating cycle or within 12 months after the reporting period.

From Exhibit 12.2, DRL's current assets are as follows: 118,201 in 2016 and 118,767 in 2015. Current liabilities are as follows: 68,368 in 2016 and 68,213 in 2015. We calculate the current ratio as follows:

Current ratio	2016	2015
$\dfrac{\text{Current assets}}{\text{Current liabilities}}$	$\dfrac{118,201}{68,368} = 1.73$	$\dfrac{118,767}{68,213} = 1.74$

A current ratio of more than one means that a business has more current assets per rupee of current liabilities, implying that it can pay its current liabilities using its current assets. In other words, its operations will not be disrupted. This assumes that the current assets will fetch at least the stated amounts. DRL's current ratio hardly changed in 2016. On the face of it, a ratio of less than one may look unfavourable for the company's short-term creditors. From another perspective, current assets have carrying costs in the form of profit foregone on the investment and actual costs, such as interest, insurance, storage, and bad debts. Next, we examine the quality of current assets.

Quick Ratio

Current assets range from cash to sticky inventories. Cash is readily available to make payments to suppliers. Receivables can be converted into cash with some effort. Inventories are two steps away from cash: sale and collection. Therefore, a large current ratio by itself is not a satisfactory measure of liquidity when inventories constitute a major part of the current assets. The **quick ratio**, or **acid test ratio**, is computed as a supplement to the current ratio. This ratio considers relatively more liquid current assets, usually current assets *less* inventories, to current liabilities.

From Exhibit 12.2, DRL's quick assets are as follows: 92,402 in 2016 and 93,068 in 2015. We calculate the current ratio as follows:

Quick ratio	2016	2015
$\dfrac{\text{Quick assets}}{\text{Current liabilities}}$	$\dfrac{92,402}{68,368} = 1.35$	$\dfrac{93,068}{68,213} = 1.36$

The decrease in the quick ratio is in line with the slight drop in the current ratio. As a rule of thumb, the current ratio is expected to be at least 2:1 and the quick ratio at least 1:1. The latter means that a firm must have at least as much liquid assets as its current obligations so that it will have no difficulty in paying those obligations. As you can appreciate, across-the-board measures are not much realistic, but they provide a broad basis for comparison. In practice, analysts further refine these liquidity measures by excluding prepaid expenses, non-trade receivables, and employee loans since these can't be converted into cash or realized at short notice.

Receivable Turnover

We should measure the liquidity of specific current assets in order to understand the quality of current assets. A company's ability to collect promptly from its customers enhances its liquidity. **Receivable turnover (RTO)** measures the efficacy of a firm's credit policy and collection mechanism and shows the number of times each year the receivables are turned into cash.[3] It provides some indication of the quality of a firm's receivables and the effectiveness of its collection efforts. A high RTO indicates that receivables are being converted rapidly into cash and the quality of the company's receivables is good.

Receivable turnover is the ratio of net sales to average receivables. Ideally, the numerator should include only net credit sales, but this information is not available in published reports. Therefore, the analyst has no option but to use net sales, though it would include cash sales. Average receivables are computed as the simple average of beginning and ending receivables. From Exhibit 12.2 and Appendix B, DRL's trade receivables are as follows: 41,667 in 2016; 41,012 in 2015; and 33,253 in 2014. Average trade receivables are 41,340 in 2016 and 37,133 in 2015. Using the sales data in Exhibit 12.1 and the average trade receivables, we can now compute DRL's RTO:

---

[3] Receivables consist of trade receivables and bills receivable.

Receivable turnover	2016	2015
$\dfrac{\text{Sales}}{\text{Receivables}}$	$\dfrac{159{,}671}{41{,}340} = 3.80$ times	$\dfrac{152{,}974}{37{,}133} = 4.05$ times

The significantly lower RTO in 2016 indicates relatively weaker management of receivables. It is common to express RTO in **average collection period**, or **days sales outstanding (DSO)**. We do this by a two-step procedure:

1. *Calculate average daily sales:* Net sales/360, assumed 360 days in a year. Average daily sales are 436 for 2016 and 417 for 2015.
2. *Calculate the average collection period:* It is average receivables divided by average daily sales.

Average collection period	2016	2015
$\dfrac{\text{Receivables}}{\text{Daily sales}}$	$\dfrac{41{,}340}{436} = 94.80$ days	$\dfrac{37{,}133}{417} = 88.98$ days

We can also compute the average collection period by dividing the number of days in a year by receivable turnover:

Average collection period	2016	2015
$\dfrac{360}{\text{Receivable turnover}}$	$\dfrac{360}{3.80} = 94.80$ days	$\dfrac{37{,}133}{4.05} = 88.98$ days

DRL's receivables remained outstanding, on average, for 95 days in 2016 as compared to 89 days in 2015, indicating slower collection. To assess whether this is satisfactory, we need information on the company's credit terms. For instance, if the terms are $n/120$, the company is doing well in collection, but not if the terms are $n/90$.

> Shree Company's average collection period is 35 days and Lakshmi Company's is 45 days. Both companies are travel agents. Can we say that Shree Company manages receivables better? What additional information about receivables do we need?

TEST YOUR UNDERSTANDING 12.2
Evaluating Receivable Management

Inventory Turnover

Inventory turnover (ITO) is the number of times a company's inventories are turned into sales. Investment in inventory represents idle cash. The lower the inventory level, the greater the cash available for meeting day-to-day operating needs and for investment in productive assets. Besides, lean, fast-moving inventory runs a lower risk of obsolescence and reduces interest, insurance, and storage charges. A high ITO is a sign of efficient inventory management. In recent years, many companies have started following just-in-time inventory practices whereby they make purchases at the time they are required for production or sales. DRL's IFRS consolidated income statement reports cost of goods sold (called *cost of revenue*) of 62,427 in 2016 and 62,786 in 2015.

From Exhibit 12.2, inventories are as follows: 25,799 in 2016; 25,699 in 2015; and 24,188 in 2014. Average inventories are 25,749 in 2016 and 24,944 in 2015. Using cost of goods sold and average inventories, we calculate inventory turnover:

Inventory turnover	2016	2015
$\dfrac{\text{Cost of goods sold}}{\text{Inventories}}$	$\dfrac{62{,}427}{25{,}749} = 2.42$ times	$\dfrac{62{,}786}{24{,}944} = 2.52$ times

The lower inventory turnover in 2016 points to less efficient inventory management. DRL's inventory turnover numbers imply an **average holding period** of 148.49 days in 2016, representing a deterioration from 143.02 days in 2015. The procedure for calculating the average holding period is similar to that for calculating the average collection period.

If the cost of goods sold is not available, we can use sales. But the ratio would be affected by changes in product prices. The calculations are as follows:

Inventory turnover	2016	2015
$\dfrac{\text{Sales}}{\text{Inventories}}$	$\dfrac{156,978}{25,749} = 6.10$ times	$\dfrac{150,233}{24,944} = 6.02$ times

These values imply a lower inventory holding period of 59.05 days in 2016, compared to 59.77 days in 2015.[4]

QUICK QUESTION
Current ratio and quick ratio

What is the effect of paying a trade payable on current ratio and quick ratio?

Operating Cycle

Operating cycle is the time between the acquisition of assets for processing and their realization in cash. It is the time taken to convert inventories into cash. It consists of two parts:

1. The time taken to turn inventories into receivables; and
2. The time taken to turn receivables into cash.

We calculate DRL's operating cycle (in days) as follows:

	2016	2015	Change
Average collection period	94.80	88.98	5.82
Average holding period	148.49	143.02	5.53
Operating cycle	243.29	232.00	11.35

The operating cycle time is longer by 11 days in 2016. This means that the company's funds were held up in receivables and inventories longer, resulting in additional interest, storage, and other expenses.

TEST YOUR UNDERSTANDING 12.3
Operating Cycle

Bansidhar Company has an inventory turnover of 4 and a receivable turnover of 8. Calculate its operating cycle.

ONE-MINUTE QUIZ 12.2
Current Ratio

Slow Company's current ratio decreased from 3.54 in 20X1 to 2.17 per cent in 20X2. Sales and credit terms remained unchanged. Which of the following events in 20X2 explains the change? There may be more than one correct answer.
(a) The statutory tax rate decreased.
(b) A loan taken in 20X1 was payable in 20X3.
(c) Dividend payment decreased.
(d) The risk of default in trade receivables increased.

Solvency Analysis

Learning Objective
LO 7 Analyze solvency.

A company's long-term stability is affected by the extent of debt used to finance its assets. Since debt finance is riskier than equity, heavy reliance on debt is a potential threaten to solvency. The debt-to-equity ratio and the interest cover ratio are important indicators of solvency.

---

[4] We are consistent in using revenue from operations for sales. Revenue from operations consists of sales, service income, licence fees, and other operating income. Inventories are unlikely for items other than sales. So we could use sales instead for this ratio.

Debt-to-equity Ratio

A wise mix of debt and equity can increase the return on equity for two reasons:

1. Debt is generally cheaper than equity.
2. Interest expense is tax-deductible, whereas dividends are paid from after-tax profits. In addition, dividend payment attracts dividend distribution tax.

However, excessive use of debt financing is risky. The borrower has a legal obligation to make periodical interest and principal payments. If it is unable to pay them on time, creditors may force liquidation of the firm. The **debt-to-equity ratio** measures the relationship of the capital provided by creditors to the amount provided by shareholders. Debt includes interest-bearing liabilities, both short-term and long-term, but excludes operating liabilities. As you have seen earlier, redeemable preference shares are treated as debt.

The ratio indicates the extent of use of **financial leverage**. A high debt-to-equity ratio indicates the aggressive use of leverage, and a highly leveraged company is more risky for creditors. A low ratio, on the other hand, suggests that the company has a small degree of leverage and is conservative. DRL's debt consists of long-term and short-term borrowings. The debt-to-equity ratio is computed as follows:

Debt-to-equity ratio	2016	2015
$\dfrac{\text{Debt}}{\text{Equity}}$	$\dfrac{33,408}{117,009} = 0.29$	$\dfrac{36,172}{98,531} = 0.37$

Note: These are year-end amounts.

In 2016, DRL's debt-to-equity ratio declined due a combination of lower debt because of repayment of borrowings and higher equity resulting from retained earnings. Most Indian companies have debt and some have significant amounts of debt. Financial leverage differs from industry to industry. Firms that have relatively stable demand for their products (e.g. electricity) tend to have high leverage. In contrast, firms that are subject to wide fluctuations in demand (e.g. consumer goods) prefer low leverage. The unpredictability of the outcome of R&D activities and of the drug approval process implies a high business risk for DRL. So low financial leverage is preferable.

Liabilities-to-equity Ratio

A variant of the debt-to-equity ratio is the **liabilities-to-equity ratio**. Here, the numerator has all liabilities, not only borrowings. The ratio is computed as follows:

Liabilities-to-equity ratio	2016	2015
$\dfrac{\text{All liabilities}}{\text{Equity}}$	$\dfrac{83,095}{117,009} = 0.71$	$\dfrac{87,447}{98,531} = 0.89$

The fall in the liabilities-to-equity ratio indicates DRL's decreasing dependence on liabilities, much of which is interest-free. This measure is especially useful in the case of firms that keep rolling over short-term obligations. In effect, some of the current liabilities take a long-term character and are not essentially different from interest-free debt. Since these are available for the firm's use for a long period of time, they may have been invested in long-term assets such as property, plant and equipment. You may have noted that the liabilities-to-equity ratio is related to the assets-to-equity ratio that you saw in the discussion on return on equity.

Operating Leverage

Operating leverage indicates the extent of fixed costs in the operations. Fixed costs are incurred regardless of the amount of sales or production. Salaries, rent, insurance, and building maintenance are examples of fixed costs. Having a large proportion of fixed costs is risky, because even when the business is not doing well, the firm will be required to pay them. Combining high financial leverage with high operating leverage jacks up the overall risk of a business. Since we don't have information about fixed costs in the financial statements, we are unable to calculate the degree of operating leverage.

FINANCIAL VIEW
Debt, Music, and
Skyscraper

"When you're highly leveraged, getting ugly doesn't take a lot", says Professor Carmen Reinhart, co-author with Professor Kenneth Rogoff of *This Time is Different*, an analysis of debt crises. "One failed deal, one disaster in a placement of a bond, what would seem like a short-run shortfall in rollover problems – anything can trigger that stampede scenario." What Professor Reinhart said about sovereign debt applies equally, perhaps even more, to corporate debt. Debt can be a dangerous attraction. The advice that Polonius gave his son comes to mind: "Neither a borrower nor a lender be/ For loan oft loses both itself and friend/ And borrowing dulls the edge of husbandry" (Hamlet I.iii. 75–77).

Combining high financial leverage with high operating leverage is a recipe for disaster. Worldspace, a popular satellite radio service, had to fold up, because of its debt of $2.1 billion and large upfront programme acquisition and production costs and heavy satellite rentals. This was a case of debt stopping music from reaching the company's customers. Also, when a company uses debt to fund projects that have long gestation, there is a high chance of default. This was the case with Dubai World, the flagship company of the Government of Dubai, that announced a "debt standstill" (a brilliant euphemism for default) in November 2009. The company had developed some of the world's most extravagant real estate projects, such as Burj Khalifa the world's tallest tower, the skyscraper-and-villa-crammed Palm Jumeirah island, and the artificial Arabian Canal. In deciding on the level of debt, it is useful to remember Warren Buffett's famous quote about risky behaviour: "Only when the tide goes do you discover who's been swimming naked."

Interest Cover

Interest cover is a measure of the protection available to the creditors for payment of interest charges by the company. The ratio shows whether the company has sufficient income to cover its interest requirements by a wide margin. Interest cover is computed by dividing profit before interest and tax by interest expense. A high ratio implies adequate safety for payment of interest even if there were to be a drop in the company's earnings. DRL's interest cover is calculated as follows:

Interest cover	2016	2015
$\dfrac{\text{Profit before interest and tax}}{\text{Interest expense}}$	$\dfrac{32,196}{824} = 39.07$	$\dfrac{30,078}{1,082} = 27.80$

The extent of interest cover depends on profit, debt level, and interest rate. As we have seen, DRL doesn't have much interest-bearing debt; so a high-interest cover should come as no surprise.

**TEST YOUR
UNDERSTANDING 12.4**
Leverage and
Profitability

Selected information from the 20X6 financial statements of Company A and Company B is given below:

	Company A	Company B
Profit before interest and tax...	₹18,000	₹20,000
Interest expense..	3,000	14,400
Income tax	7,000	2,500
Debt...	20,000	60,000
Assets..	70,000	90,000
Equity...	35,000	20,000

Which company is more successful in using leverage? Why?

Is it possible to borrow wisely? Suzlon Energy manufactures wind turbines. Suzlon literally means 'smart debt': *suz* from the Gujarati *suz-buz* (intelligence or smartness) and *lon*, the Gujarati way of saying loan. In the early 2000s, the company was cited in the international media as an example of a successful emerging market giant. The company's chairman and managing director, Tulsi Tanti, pushed aggressively for growth. Suzlon set up manufacturing facilities around the world and acquired Hansen Transmissions International, Belgium and REpower Systems, Germany. The expansion was financed by debt of about ₹130 billion in foreign currency convertible bonds (FCCBs). In its enthusiasm to acquire Repower, Suzlon seemed to have overpaid for it and ended up with 94 per cent of the stake. The economic crisis following the collapse of Lehman Brothers in September 2008 adversely affected the company's wind power markets in the US and Europe. Nearly 60 per cent of the company's order book came from REpower. All of these contributed to Suzlon defaulting on the redemption of an instalment of FCCBs. Possibly, wind energy was (and still is) a good business, but it was brought down by debt. Too much debt would appear to be not such a smart idea.

Source: Company annual reports.

Borrower Company's long-term debt increased by 20 per cent in 20X2 over 20X1, but interest expense increased by 25 per cent over the same period. The debt-to-equity ratio was 2.2:1 in both years. Which of the following events in 20X2 explains the change? There may be more than one correct answer.

(a) Sales growth decreased.
(b) Some current debt was rolled over on a long-term basis at lower interest rates.
(c) Some current debt was rolled over on a long-term basis at the same interest rates.
(d) Some current debt was rolled over on a long-term basis at higher interest rates.

ONE-MINUTE QUIZ 12.3
Debt and Interest Rate

Capital Market Standing

Capital market ratios relate the market price of a company's share to the company's earnings and dividends. Price-earnings (PE) ratio, dividend yield, and price-to-book ratio are the most commonly used ratios that aid investors and analysts in understanding the strength of a company in the capital market.

Learning Objective
LO 8 Evaluate capital market standing.

Price-earnings Ratio

Price-earnings ratio, or PE ratio, is a popular measure extensively used in investment analysis. The PE ratio is often the only measure in discussions. It is the ratio of the market price of a share to the annual EPS. Many view the PE multiple as an indicator of a firm's growth prospects. Analysts use it as a screen to detect mispriced stocks. A high PE ratio indicates the stock market's confidence in the company's future earnings growth.

DRL's stock prices in the National Stock Exchange were as follows:

	March 2016	March 2015
High	₹3,283.00	₹3,575.00
Low	2,887.15	3,300.15
Average	3,085.08	3,437.58
Closing	3,035.20	3,488.75

We take the average of the high and low prices.[5] Using the basic EPS of ₹126.15 for 2016 and ₹137.18 for 2015, the computation of the price-earnings ratio is as follows:

Price-earnings ratio	2016	2015
$\dfrac{\text{Market price per share}}{\text{Earnings per share}}$	$\dfrac{3,085.08}{126.15} = 24.46$ times	$\dfrac{3,437.58}{137.18} = 25.06$ times

---

[5] We could also use the year-end closing price of the stock.

The decrease in the PE ratio could indicate that in 2016 the market has slightly less faith in DRL's growth prospects relative to 2015. The company's stock price is also affected by movement in the whole market.

Interpreting the price-earnings ratio The PE ratio tells us how much an investor is willing to pay per rupee of earnings. For example, a PE of 15 implies that an investor is ready to pay ₹15 for ₹1 of earnings. Is a PE of 15 high, low or reasonable? The PE ratio is deceptively simple and easy to calculate, and is therefore widely misused. To be able to use the PE ratio you don't need knowledge of accounting, finance or the company's business. So the lay investor is tempted to use the PE ratio. Many investors imagine that low PE stocks will generate high returns when the prices go up. In fact, some investment advisers tell their clients to buy single-digit PE stocks. At the other end, some investors feel that high PE stocks ought to be valuable because they are expensive.

Unfortunately, being a simple measure, the PE ratio is misunderstood. It should be interpreted with great care, precisely because it is simple. The PE ratio tells us about the earning power of a business based on its future growth. A low PE ratio might imply weak growth prospects, or the stock might be genuinely underpriced. Similarly, a high PE stock might have strong growth prospects, or it might be overpriced. We need to analyze the financial statements to decide which of these explanations to accept. Further, the EPS measure is affected by accounting method differences, one-time items and other earnings quality issues. Therefore, investing in a stock should be based on a detailed analysis of the company's business, earnings quality, competition, and industry and economic trends. The PE can, at best, be a good place to start. It would be naïve to think that a single number can capture the complexities of investment decisions.

Alternative price-earnings measures The PE ratio that we calculated is the *historical PE* or *trailing PE* and it is based on past earnings. The *rolling PE* uses the earnings per share from the latest four quarters. The *forward PE* or *leading PE* uses earnings forecast by analysts. Often, the *consensus forecast*, which is the average of individual analyst forecasts, is used for calculating the forward PE. One measure that has become widely popular is the *cyclically adjusted PE ratio* (CAPE) that uses 10 years of earnings. It was developed by Professor Robert Shiller, a professor of economics at Yale University, who was awarded the Nobel Prize in 2013. The intuition that underlies this measure is that the business cycle lasts ten years.

Earnings yield is the reciprocal of the PE ratio, i.e. EPS divided by market price per share. Using DRL's EPS and stock price, we calculate the earnings yield as follows:

Earnings yield	2016	2015
$\dfrac{\text{Earnings per share}}{\text{Market price per share}}$	$\dfrac{126.18}{3,085.08} = 4.09\%$	$\dfrac{137.18}{3,437.58} = 3.99\%$

Earnings yield is the investor's return on the stock based on earnings. Since earnings is an accrual measure, earnings yield indicates the return to the investor over the long term.

Dividend Yield

Dividend yield represents the current cash return to shareholders. It is the ratio of dividend per share to market price per share. The dividend yield for DRL is shown below:

Dividend yield	2016	2015
$\dfrac{\text{Dividend per share}}{\text{Market price per share}}$	$\dfrac{5}{3,085.08} = 0.16\%$	$\dfrac{5}{3,437.58} = 0.15\%$

We note that in 2016 dividend yield was a tad higher. The dividend is important to investors, such as retired persons and pension funds, who depend on it to meet their cash needs.

Stock Return

Stock return consists of dividend and change in stock price. The stock return in a period is, thus,

$$\frac{\text{Change in stock price over the period + Dividend for the period}}{\text{Beginning stock price}}$$

The calculation of stock return for 2016 is as follows:

$$\frac{(3,085.08 - 3,437.58) + 5}{3,437.58} = -10.11\%$$

Thus, DRL's shareholders earned a negative return of over 10 per cent on their investment. By any standards, this is poor performance. The shareholders did not receive a return commensurate with the risk assumed by them. Another way to look at this is to compare with the market trend. From April 2015 to March 2016, the NSE Nifty 100 stocks recorded a decline of 8.07 per cent. DRL's stock performed a little worse than the index.

Price-to-book Ratio

The **price-to-book ratio (PB ratio)** compares a company's stock price with the book value (or accounting value). Book value per share is the amount of shareholders' equity divided by the number of shares. We calculate DRL's price-to-book ratio as follows:

Price-to-book ratio	2016	2015
$\dfrac{\text{Market price per share}}{\text{Book value per share}}$	$\dfrac{3,085.08}{686.08} = 4.50$ times	$\dfrac{3,437.58}{578.52} = 5.94$ times

A low PB ratio is often seen as an indication of underpricing of the stock. A PB ratio of more than one means that the market expects the company to earn higher than the required rate of return on equity. The PB ratio too is affected by the choice of accounting methods, since the denominator is an accounting variable.

As you would know, the face value of a share does not matter for most purposes. However, investors are sometimes obsessed with par. Face value is irrelevant in calculating PE and PB ratios. Also, face value and stock price need not be related. For example, suppose two companies, Slice and Whole, that are identical have a market capitalization (the sum of the prices of their respective equity shares) of ₹1,000,000. Slice has 20,000 shares of face value of ₹1 and Whole has 10,000 shares of face value of ₹2. Both have the same paid-up capital, ₹20,000, but that amount is split into twice the number of shares in Slice as that in Whole. The price of a share of Slice is ₹50, i.e. ₹1,000,000 ÷ 20,000, while that of Whole is ₹100, i.e. ₹1,000,000 ÷ 10,000. The investor pays the market price, not the face value. To understand this better, suppose Slice performs well and its stock price rises to ₹75. There is no change in the face value of Slice's shares. Whole continues to perform as before, so its stock price does not change. Stock prices reflect expected performance.

LADDER
Face Value and Stock Price

Beta

Besides financial statement information, investors assess a number of factors such as management and governance quality, industry conditions, and general economic environment. The final results are expressed in the form of a rate of return required for a specified level of risk. The risk associated with the return on an equity share consists of two components:

- Systematic risk
- Unsystematic risk.

Systematic risk is the change in the price of a share for a change in the return on the market as a whole. **Beta** is a measure of systematic risk. For example, if a share has a beta of 1.5, a 10 per cent increase (decrease) in the market would likely result in a 15 per cent increase (decrease) in the price of the share. An equity share with a beta of 0.75 is a less risky investment because it is less swayed by market price movements. A beta of one means that the stock is just as risky as the market. The market is usually taken to be represented by an index of share prices such as the CNX S&P 500 Index. According to Reuters, DRL's beta was 0.15 in early April 2017.

Unsystematic risk is specific to a share and is not correlated with any other factor. Since the unsystematic risks of several shares will cancel out, this risk can be diversified away completely by investing in a portfolio of shares. The computation of beta for a portfolio enables investors to determine the risk level desired and the return required.

TEST YOUR UNDERSTANDING 12.5
Selecting Stocks

Information about two companies, both in the electrical appliances industry, is as follows:

	Company X	Company Y
Earnings per share	₹3.50	₹6.75
Dividend per share	₹2.00	₹3.00
Market price per share	₹60.00	₹95.00
Beta	1.30	1.50

Comment on the capital market standing of the two companies. Which share would you recommend?

ONE-MINUTE QUIZ 12.4
Price-earnings Ratio

Value Company forecasts the following for 20X2: operating profit, ₹100 million; interest expense, ₹10 million; preference dividends, ₹6 million; effective tax rate, 30 per cent; equity dividend payout ratio, 20 per cent; the number of equity shares, 3 million. The company's equity shares are expected to trade at a price-earnings ratio of 10. What would be the market price per equity share?
(a) ₹39.2.
(b) ₹190.
(c) ₹180.
(d) ₹196.

FORENSIC CORNER
Financial Statement
Analysis

Analysts and investigators look for tell-tale signs of financial statement fraud. But fraudsters are clever and cover their tracks well. Even so, some indicators of fraud may be available. For example, Benford's law says that in the real world in the first digit the number 1 is more likely to appear than the number 2, the number 2 is more likely to appear than the number 3, and so on. Benford's law predicts that the number 1 will appear about 30 per cent of the time in the first digit. If in an actual case it appears only 10 per cent of the time, it might suggest the possibility of fraud. Unfortunately, Benford's law is not a silver bullet. In fact, there is no silver bullet. Increasingly, data analytics are used to identify patterns and deviations. It is a rapidly evolving field with great potential for use in detection and investigation of accounting fraud.

Red flags signalling accounting fraud:
- Significantly higher or lower margin than competitors.
- Sales growth out of tune with changes in inventories and receivables.
- Always meeting or narrowly beating earnings estimates.
- A lower price-earnings ratio than the peers.
- Delay in announcement of financial results.
- Changing the fiscal year frequently.

RECAP

- *Financial statement analysis* helps investors to understand a company's earning power and make investments that would yield returns commensurate with the risks involved. Creditors use financial statement analysis to judge a company's debt-paying ability.
- The most common sources of information about listed companies are annual reports, quarterly statements, stock exchanges, and government reports.
- Analysts make comparisons with rule-of-thumb indicators, past performance, internal standards, and industry standards.

- *Horizontal analysis* looks at the year-on-year amount and percentage changes in financial statement items. *Trend analysis* considers percentage changes for a number of years. *Vertical analysis* is the proportional expression of each item on a financial statement to the statement total in common-size statements. *Ratio analysis* involves establishing a relevant financial relationship between components of financial statements.
- *Profitability ratios* tell us about a company's operating success. The major profitability ratios are *profit margin, asset turnover, return on assets, return on equity,* and *earnings per share.*
- *Liquidity ratios* tell us about the ability of a business to meet its short-term obligations. The common liquidity measures are *current ratio, quick ratio, receivable turnover, inventory turnover,* and *operating cycle.*
- *Solvency ratios* indicate the extent of dependence on debt. *Debt-to-equity ratio, liabilities-to-equity ratio,* and *interest cover* are the main solvency measures.
- *Price-earnings ratio* indicates a company's growth potential. *Dividend yield* is a measure of cash return on a stock. *Price-to-book ratio* tells us about a company's ability to earn abnormal profits. *Beta* measures the volatility of a stock in relation to the market.

Review Problem

In 2016, the following parties have to act based on their evaluation of DRL's financial statements:

- Maharashtra Bank is examining a request from DRL for long-term financing.
- Bharat Chemical Company is considering the supply of raw materials on credit to DRL.
- Arvind Shah is thinking whether to invest his retirement benefits in DRL's shares.

Industry averages for illustrative purposes for selected ratios are given below:

Profit margin	4.2%
Asset turnover	1.7 times
Return on assets	7.4%
Return on equity	21%
Earnings per share	₹4.21
Current ratio	1.46
Quick ratio	1.12
Debt-to-equity	2.3
Interest cover	4.13
Price-earnings ratio	27 times

Required

1. Select two or three indicators that would be most relevant to the three decision makers.
2. Based on your analysis of the indicators, what would you recommend?

Solution to the Review Problem

1. The bank should look at the debt-to-equity ratio and interest cover. The debt-to-equity ratio measures the company's dependence on borrowed funds. DRL is relatively low on debt. So the company has a low chance of defaulting on the proposed borrowing. Interest cover is high and the company's ability to pay interest on time is not in doubt. Also, debt-to-equity ratio and interest cover are reasonable relative to the industry average. The ratios should be reworked after including the effect of the proposed borrowing, based on information about the intended use of the funds.

2. The supplier should examine current ratio and quick ratio. The current ratio is an indicator of the company's ability to pay its liabilities in the short-term. It is above the industry average, and it did not change in the last two years. The quick ratio excludes inventories. DRL's quick ratio is has remained nearly constant over two years and is above the industry average.

3. The investor should study ROE and PE ratio. ROE measures the profitability on shareholders' funds. It fell sharply over the two-year period and is below the industry. PE ratio indicates investor confidence in growth. PE ratio has gone down and is below the industry average. The dividend yield is low, suggesting that the low cash return is a matter of concern to a retired person living off dividend income.

Note: The above discussion is only illustrative and is not intended to be a complete solution.

ASSIGNMENT MATERIAL

Questions

1. What are the objectives of *financial statement analysis*?
2. How are risks and returns related?
3. How is financial statement analysis useful to investors and creditors?
4. What are the main contents of a company annual report?
5. Which is better: comparison with industry standards or comparison with a company's past? Explain.
6. What is *horizontal analysis*? How is it useful?
7. How are *common-size statements* useful?
8. How is *trend analysis* different from *horizontal analysis*?

9. When will the *return on equity* exceed the *return on assets*?
10. What are the four levels of DuPont analysis?
11. Should *leverage* be high or low for a garment export firm?
12. What is the difference between *liquidity* and *solvency*?
13. What is the difference between the *current ratio* and the *quick ratio*?
14. Identify three critical ratios on which the management of a retail store should focus.
15. "Like many other things in life, debt is good when used in moderation." Explain.

Problems

Problem 12.1
Horizontal Analysis ✶

The statement of profit and loss of Manisha Company for the years ended March 31, 20X2, and 20X1 are as follows:

MANISHA COMPANY Statement of Profit and Loss For the year ended March 31		
	20X2	**20X1**
Net sales	₹97,000	₹85,000
Cost of goods sold	52,000	49,000
Gross profit	45,000	36,000
Operating expenses	12,000	9,000
Net profit	33,000	27,000

Required

Compute percentage changes from 20X1 to 20X2 and comment on them.

Problem 12.2
Vertical Analysis ✶

The comparative balance sheet of Milan Company as at December 31, 20X2, and 20X1 is as follows:

MILAN COMPANY Balance Sheet, December 31		
	20X2	**20X1**
Assets		
Non-current assets		
Property, plant and equipment	₹28,400	₹21,500
Non-current investments	300	200
Current assets		
Inventories	21,300	10,800
Trade receivables	16,500	7,000
Cash and cash equivalents	4,500	3,500
Total assets	71,000	43,000

Equity and Liabilities
Equity

Equity share capital	₹13,700	₹13,700
Other equity	7,600	3,500

Liabilities
Non-current liabilities

Long-term borrowings	34,800	21,900

Current liabilities

Trade payables	14,900	3,900
Total equity and liabilities	71,000	43,000

Required

1. Prepare Milan Company's common-size balance sheet for 20X1 and 20X2.
2. Comment on the changes from 20X1 to 20X2.

The following items are taken from the financial statements of Karim Company for a five-year period using 20X1 as the base year.

Problem 12.3
Trend Analysis ✳✳

	20X5	20X4	20X3	20X2	20X1
					(in thousands)
Sales	₹8,433	₹7,680	₹6,471	₹5,137	₹3,939
Total operating expenses	7,342	7,060	5,489	4,553	3,704
Income from operations	1,091	620	982	584	235
Interest expense	206	192	205	198	169
Net profit	551	299	603	356	78
Total assets	8,834	8,249	6,484	5,954	5,380
Long-term borrowings	3,104	3,147	2,241	2,677	2,633
Equity	2,959	2,340	1,955	1,359	1,279

Required

Compute trend percentage for these items and comment on the trends.

Information related to Nazrul Islam Company from its financial statements is presented below:

Problem 12.4
Profitability Analysis ✳✳

	20X6	20X5
Net sales	₹86,000	₹71,000
Profit after tax	12,000	11,000
Assets	49,000	41,000
Equity	27,000	21,000

In 20X4, the company had assets of ₹35,000 and equity of ₹18,000.

Required

1. Compute the profit margin, asset turnover, return on assets, and return on equity for 20X5 and 20X6.
2. Comment on the company's profitability in 20X5 and 20X6.

Selected financial information about Vijay Merchant Company is given below:

Problem 12.5
Liquidity Analysis ✳✳

	20X2	20X1
Sales	₹69,000	₹43,000
Cost of goods sold	57,000	32,500
Inventories	11,400	5,500
Trade receivables	7,200	3,000
Cash and cash equivalents	1,500	800
Other current assets	4,000	2,700
Current liabilities	16,000	11,000

In 20X1, the company had receivables of ₹2,500 and inventories of ₹3,000.

Required

1. Compute the current ratio, quick ratio, average collection period, and inventory turnover for 20X1 and 20X2.
2. State whether there is a favourable or unfavourable change in liquidity from 20X1 to 20X2.

Problem 12.6
Effect of Transaction on Ratio ✱✱✱

Taqdir Company entered into the following transactions:

Item	Transaction	Ratio	Effect
(a)	Paid suppliers for past purchases.	Inventory turnover	
(b)	Issued equity shares for cash.	Return on equity	
(c)	Repaid a loan.	Receivable turnover	
(d)	Purchased machinery for cash.	Debt-to-equity	
(e)	Issued debentures for cash.	Return on assets	
(f)	Converted long-term loans into equity shares.	Quick ratio	
(g)	Collected from customers for past sales.	Profit margin	
(h)	Accrued festival bonus to employees.	Earnings per share	
(i)	Sold goods for cash.	Quick ratio	
(j)	Accrued interest expense.	Operating profit margin	
(k)	Issued bonus shares.	Return on equity	
(l)	Wrote off a bad debt.	Receivable turnover	
(m)	Issued debentures in exchange for equipment.	Debt-to-equity	
(n)	Entered into a finance lease for a new plant.	Interest cover	
(o)	Purchased goods on credit.	Asset turnover	
(p)	Accrued interest on investment in Treasury bill.	Return on equity	
(q)	Sold a plant at book value in exchange for shares.	Return on assets	
(r)	Transferred cash to a six-month deposit account.	Quick ratio	
(s)	Paid principal amount for instalment purchase of the plant.	Profit margin	

Required

State whether each transaction resulted in increase or decrease in the specified ratio or had no effect on it. Consider each transaction independently.

Problem 12.7
Effect of Transaction on Ratio ✱✱✱ Alternative to Problem 12.6

Balan Company entered into the following transactions:

Item	Transaction	Ratio	Effect
(a)	Received dividend from an associate.	Current ratio	
(b)	Made a down payment for the purchase of the plant.	Receivable turnover	
(c)	Sold investments for cash.	Interest cover	
(d)	Purchased copyrights with cash.	Asset turnover	
(e)	Retired a fully depreciated plant from use.	Return on assets	
(f)	Sold machinery at a loss.	Return on equity	
(g)	Received payment of invoices from customers.	Receivable turnover	
(h)	Purchased investments with cash.	Interest cover	
(i)	Paid advance to a supplier of equipment.	Receivable turnover	
(j)	Collected instalment payments for the sale of a plant.	Inventory turnover	
(k)	Accrued rent expense.	Profit margin	
(l)	Exchanged a building for a plant.	Debt-to-equity	
(m)	Sold patents at a gain.	Profit margin	
(n)	Sold machinery at a gain for cash.	Current ratio	
(o)	Sold a plant at book value on credit.	Asset turnover	
(p)	Issued convertible debentures for cash.	Debt-to-equity	
(q)	Paid instalments for the purchase of goods.	Quick ratio	
(r)	Collected instalment payments for the sale of goods.	Receivable turn	
(s)	Accrued income tax.	Interest cover	

Required

State whether each transaction resulted in increase or decrease in the specified ratio or had no effect on it. Consider each transaction independently.

The financial statements of Grace Corporation are as follows:

Problem 12.8
Horizontal and Vertical
Analysis ✳✳✳

GRACE CORPORATION
Balance Sheet, March 31

Assets		
Non-current assets		
Property, plant and equipment	₹32,200	₹26,500
Non-current investments	2,800	4,300
Current assets		
Inventories	10,600	4,900
Trade receivables	20,900	15,600
Cash and cash equivalents	4,400	7,000
Other current assets	1,200	1,400
Total assets	72,100	59,700
Equity and Liabilities		
Equity		
Equity share capital	₹25,000	₹25,000
Other equity	11,800	8,600
Liabilities		
Non-current liabilities		
Long-term borrowings	12,000	9,000
Current liabilities		
Trade payables	23,300	17,100
Total equity and liabilities	72,100	59,700

GRACE CORPORATION
Statement of Profit and Loss
For the year ended March 31

	20X2	20X1
Net sales	₹97,300	₹88,400
Cost of goods sold	68,500	57,600
Gross profit	28,800	30,800
Selling and administrative expenses	5,300	4,500
Profit before interest and tax	23,500	26,300
Interest expense	1,800	1,400
Profit before tax	21,700	24,900
Income tax	10,500	12,000
Profit after tax	11,200	12,900

Required

1. Prepare a horizontal analysis of the statement of profit and loss and balance sheet showing amount and percentage changes from 20X1 to 20X2.
2. Prepare a common-size statement of profit and loss and balance sheet.
3. Comment on the results obtained from Requirements 1 and 2.

Refer to Problem 12.8. The following additional information for Grace Corporation is available:

Problem 12.9
Ratio Analysis ✳✳✳

Market price per share	₹30.00	₹40.00
Dividend per share	3.20	2.80
Earnings per share	4.48	5.16

At the end of 20X0, the company had inventories of ₹3,700, receivables of ₹12,000, total assets of ₹41,000, and equity of ₹22,700.

Required

1. Compute profitability, liquidity, solvency, and capital standing market ratios.
2. Using the ratios computed in Requirement 1, evaluate Grace Corporation's profitability, liquidity, solvency and capital market standing.

Problem 12.10
Horizontal and Vertical Analysis ✳✳✳ Alternative to Problem 12.8

The financial statements of Navin Company are as follows:

NAVIN COMPANY Balance Sheet, September 30		
Assets		
Non-current assets		
Property, plant and equipment	₹27,000	₹26,000
Non-current investments	1,000	1,000
Current Assets		
Inventories	1,700	1,400
Trade receivables	3,000	2,700
Cash and cash equivalents	2,500	2,000
Other current assets	1,500	300
Total assets	36,700	33,400
Equity and Liabilities		
Equity		
Equity share capital	₹20,000	₹20,000
Reserves and surplus	7,500	5,100
Non-current liabilities		
Long-term borrowings	5,700	5,000
Current liabilities		
Trade payables	3,500	3,300
Total equity and liabilities	36,700	33,400

NAVIN COMPANY Statement of Profit and Loss For the year ended September 30		
	20X6	**20X5**
Net sales	₹60,000	₹51,000
Cost of goods sold	42,000	41,000
Gross profit	18,000	10,000
Selling and administrative expenses	7,800	7,000
Profit before interest and tax	10,200	3,000
Interest expense	1,800	900
Profit before tax	8,400	2,100
Income tax	4,000	900
Profit after tax	4,400	1,200

Required

1. Prepare a horizontal analysis of the statement of profit and loss and balance sheet showing amount and percentage changes from 20X5 to 20X6.
2. Prepare a common-size statement of profit and loss and balance sheet.
3. Comment on the results found in Requirements 1 and 2.

Refer to Problem 12.10. The following additional information for Navin Company is available:

Problem 12.11
Ratio Analysis ✱✱✱
Alternative to
Problem 12.9

	20X6	20X5
Market price per share	₹88.00	₹12.00
Dividend per share	1.00	0.50
Earnings per share	2.20	0.60

In 20X4, the company had inventories of ₹1,300, receivables of ₹2,000, total assets of ₹27,000, and equity of ₹24,900.

Required

1. Compute profitability, liquidity, solvency, and capital market standing ratios.
2. Using the ratios computed in Requirement 1 above, evaluate Navin Company's profitability, liquidity, solvency and capital market standing.

The National Bank has been approached by two customers for a short-term loan of ₹5,000. The following information is taken available from the latest financial statements:

Problem 12.12
Using Ratio Analysis ✱✱✱✱

	Granny Foods	Home Foods
Net sales	₹91,000	₹75,000
Gross profit	38,220	29,250
Interest expense	2,000	820
Income tax	7,500	5,000
Profit after tax	8,200	5,625
Inventories	9,000	6,520
Trade receivables	7,000	5,600
Cash and cash equivalents	600	1,800
Current liabilities	18,260	11,600
Non-current liabilities	16,000	13,000
Equity	18,000	14,000

The bank intends to accept one of the two loan requests.

Required

Which customer's loan request should be accepted and why? What additional information is required in making a decision? Assume that the year-end account balances are representative of the whole year.

Standard Bank has been approached by two customers for a short-term loan of ₹3,000. The following information is taken from the latest financial statements:

Problem 12.13
Using Ratio Analysis
✱✱✱✱ Alternative to
Problem 12.12

	Cute Shoes	Smart Shoes
Net sales	₹72,800	₹65,000
Gross profit	24,020	19,500
Interest expense	1,200	700
Income tax	6,500	5,000
Profit after tax	7,000	4,500
Inventories	9,000	3,500
Trade receivables	4,000	2,200
Cash and cash equivalents	900	1,200
Current liabilities	16,680	7,200
Non-current liabilities	19,000	11,000
Equity	21,000	22,000

The bank intends to accept one of the two loan requests.

Required

Which customer's loan request should be accepted and why? What additional information is required in making a decision? Assume that the year-end account balances are representative of the whole year.

Problem 12.14
Preparation of Statements from Incomplete Information ✱✱✱✱✱

The following information is available for Arogya Company:

AROGYA COMPANY Balance Sheet, August 31, 20X1		
Assets		
Property, plant and equipment	₹	?
Non-current investments		2,400
Inventories		?
Trade receivables		?
Cash and cash equivalents		1,500
Other current assets		600
Total assets		?
Equity and Liabilities		
Equity		
Equity share capital		₹28,000
Other equity		?
Liabilities		
Non-current liabilities		
Long-term borrowings		21,000
Other long-term liabilities		17,000
Current liabilities		
Trade payables		?
Total equity and liabilities		?

AROGYA COMPANY Statement of Profit and Loss For the year ended August 31, 20X1		
Net sales	₹	?
Cost of goods sold		33,000
Gross profit		?
Selling and administrative expenses		9,000
Profit before interest and tax		?
Interest expense		?
Profit before tax		?
Income tax		?
Profit after tax		3,500

Additional information: (a) Profit margin, 7 per cent; (b) Current ratio, 1.3; (c) Debt-to-equity, 1.5; (d) Inventory turnover, 2; (e) Average collection period, 72 days; (f) Interest cover, 8 times; and (g) Return on assets, 3.5 per cent.

Required

Complete the financial statements of Arogya Company for 20X1. Show supporting calculations. Assume that the year-end account balances are representative of the whole year.

The following information is available for Surat Company:

Problem 12.15
Preparation of Statements
from Incomplete
Information ✳✳✳✳✳
Alternative to
Problem 12.14

SURAT COMPANY
Balance Sheet, December 31, 20X4

Assets

Non-current assets

Property, plant and equipment	₹13,000
Non-current investments	?

Current assets

Inventories	?
Trade receivables	?
Cash and cash equivalents	1,000
Total assets	40,000

Equity and Liabilities

Equity

Equity share capital	₹9,500
Other equity	?

Liabilities

Non-current liabilities

Long-term borrowings	3,000

Current liabilities

Short-term borrowings	?
Trade payables	?
Total equity and liabilities	?

SURAT COMPANY
Statement of Profit and Loss
For the year ended December 31, 20X4

Net sales	₹ ?
Cost of goods sold	?
Gross profit	?
Selling and administrative expenses	1,300
Profit before interest and tax	?
Interest expense	?
Profit before tax	1,350
Income tax	?
Profit after tax	?

Additional information: (a) Asset turnover, 2.3; (b) Total liabilities to equity, 1.5; (c) Current ratio, 1.8; (d) Average collection period, 36 days; (e) Gross profit ratio, 15 per cent; (f) Interest expense consists of interest on long-term loans at 10 per cent per annum and on short-term loans at 15 per cent per annum; (g) Income tax, 50 per cent of profit before tax.

Required

Complete the financial statements of Surat Company for 20X4. Show supporting calculations. Assume that the year-end account balances are representative of the whole year.

Business Decision Cases

The statement of profit and loss of Sandra Corporation for the latest period are as follows:

BDC 12.1
Sandra Corporation

SANDRA CORPORATION
Statement of Profit and Loss
For the year ended March 31, 20X1

Net sales	₹730,000
Cost of goods sold	495,700
Selling and administrative expenses	87,200
Interest expense	22,100
Profit before tax	125,000
Income tax (40%)	50,000
Profit after tax	75,000

The company management is considering expansion of operations at a cost of ₹200,000. The expansion will result in additional sales of ₹450,000 on which the profit before interest and tax is estimated to be ₹93,000. The expansion can be financed by the sale of 10,000 equity shares at the current market price of ₹20 or by debentures carrying interest at 12 per cent per annum. Currently, the company has 7,500 equity shares of ₹10.

Required

1. Compute the earnings per share of the company after expansion for the equity financing and debt financing alternatives. Compare the results with the company's current earnings per share.
2. Compute the level of profit before interest and tax at which the earnings per share under the equity financing plan will be equal to that under the debt financing plan.
3. What are the factors to be considered by the company for deciding on the appropriate financing alternative?

**BDC 12.2
Tumkur Watch
Company**

Tumkur Watch Company was set up in 20X1 to manufacture quartz watches. The latest balance sheet of the company is as follows:

TUMKUR WATCH COMPANY
Balance Sheet, September 30, 20X4

(in thousands)

Assets	
Non-current assets	
Property, plant and equipment	₹47,200
Non-current investments	1,700
Current Assets	
Inventories	10,200
Trade receivables	9,600
Cash and cash equivalents	1,300
Total assets	70,000
Equity and Liabilities	
Equity	
Equity share capital	₹17,000
Other equity	12,000
Liabilities	
Non-current liabilities	
Long-term borrowings	25,000
Current liabilities	
Trade payables	16,000
Total equity and liabilities	70,000

The non-current liabilities appearing on the balance sheet include a loan of ₹14,000 taken by the company in 20X2 from National Industrial Bank. The company has been paying the bank interest at 12 per cent per annum regularly. The loan agreement with the bank stipulates that the company shall, at all times, maintain the following ratios:

Total liabilities to shareholders' equity .... 1.60 (maximum)
Non-current liabilities to shareholders' equity .... 1.00 (maximum)
Current assets to current liabilities .... 1.20 (minimum)

The company is currently negotiating with an equipment manufacturer and a finance company for obtaining equipment costing ₹20 million on lease. Under the terms of the lease, Tumkur Watch Company will have the right to use the equipment for a period of six years and must pay a lease rental of ₹4.5 million per annum. The equipment has a useful life of about 10 years. During the period of six years, the lease cannot be cancelled by any of the parties to the lease agreement.

In 20X4, the IASB is considering a proposal to amend the lease accounting standard to require recognition of leased assets, whether acquired on operating or finance lease terms, and the related future obligations.

Required

1. Compute the three ratios specified in Tumkur Watch Company's loan agreement with National Industrial Bank. Recompute these ratios if the proposal for lease capitalization is accepted by the government. Comment on the results.
2. What are the likely consequences of the company violating the stipulations in the loan agreement? How can the company avoid violation of these stipulations?
3. How can National Industrial Bank protect itself from similar violations of the loan agreement by Tumkur Watch Company as well as by other borrowers?

Interpreting Financial Reports

Amazon.com, the online retail giant, announces something new everyday except a big profit, so went the joke about the company's seemingly never-ending losses. The company sprang a pleasant surprise when it announced a net income of $2.37 billion for the year ended December 31, 2016. The company's consolidated statement of operations for 2016, 2015 and 2014 are given below (amounts in millions).

IFR 12.1
Amazon.com, Inc.

Amazon.com, Inc. Consolidated Statement of Operations For the year ended December 31			
	2016	2015	2014
New product sales	$94,665	$79,268	$70,080
Net service sales	41,322	27,738	18,908
Total net sales	135,987	107,006	88,988
Operating expenses:			
Cost of sales	88,265	71,651	62,752
Fulfillment	17,619	13,410	10,766
Marketing	7,233	5,254	4,332
Technology and content	16,085	12,540	9,275
General and administrative	2,432	1,747	1,552
Other operating expense, net	167	171	133
Total operating expenses	131,801	104,773	88,810
Operating income	4,186	2,233	178
Interest income	100	50	39
Interest expense	(484)	(459)	(210)
Other income (expense), net	90	(256)	(118)
Total non-operating income (expense)	(294)	(665)	(289)
Income (loss) before income taxes	3,892	1,568	(111)
Provision for income taxes	(1,425)	(950)	(167)
Equity-method investment activity, net of tax	(96)	(22)	37
Net income (loss)	2,371	596	(241)

Required

Explain how Amazon.com turned in a big increase in net income in 2016.

IFR 12.2
Kingfisher Airlines
Limited

Kingfisher Airlines Limited, set up by Vijay Mallya's United Breweries Group in 2003, started operations in 2005. Soon it became the second largest airline in India. It won a number of awards and was voted the best airline in many surveys. Its food and in-flight entertainment were considered the best in class. The crew was courteous to a fault. In 2007, it acquired Air Deccan, the low-cost carrier. Regrettably, Kingfisher Airlines was never a financial success, and its losses and debt snowballed. In October 2012, the Director-General of Civil Aviation cancelled its operating licence. The company kept defaulting on payment of salaries, airport charges, lease rentals, and principal and interest on bank loans. On December 6, 2013, the Karnataka High Court admitted a petition filed by a consortium of 14 banks for winding up of the company.

Year	Net loss
	(in millions)
2014Q1	₹11,569
2013	43,011
2012	34,461
2011	14,137
2010	20,100

For additional information, you should refer to the company's annual reports from the time it was set up.

Required

Analyze the financial performance of Kingfisher Airlines. In your view, what went wrong?

Financial Analysis

FA 12.1
Comparative Financial
Statement Analysis

Obtain the annual reports of two companies in the same industry for five years.

Required

1. Analyze the financial statements and other information using the techniques used in this chapter and prepare a report setting out your findings.
2. Recommend a buy, sell or hold the stocks.

FA 12.2
Revisiting Investment
Advice

Revisit FA 1.2 *Investment Advice*. Hopefully, you can analyze and interpret financial statements better now. Meanwhile, the stock market has recorded stratospheric growth. Your friend did not act on your earlier advice, but she regularly follows economic and business news. She feels that a high PE ratio implies good growth prospects for a stock. She wants you to tell her how to analyze a company's financial statements and how to interpret the PE ratio as part of analyzing and interpreting the statements. You should come up with a list of ten key ideas that you would like to highlight. Unlike you, your friend is not an accounting expert. But since she has a lot more money than you have, you have an opportunity to test out your newly acquired financial analysis skills.

Keep in mind that this is your last chance to make a favourable impression on someone who could be your future client.

Required

1. Prepare a report setting out the information an individual should have in order to decide on investing in stocks and where the information will be available.
2. List the advantages and disadvantages of alternative investment opportunities and how studying the information in the financial statements would be useful in making an informed decision.

Answers to One-minute Quiz

12.1 c.
12.2 b, d.
12.3 d.
12.4 b.

Answers to Test Your Understanding

12.1 1. ATO = ROA/PM = 0.18/0.10 = 1.8 times
2. Assets = Profit/ROA. Let x be total assets, 20X1. $(x + 14,000)/2 = 2,700/0.18 = 15,000$. $x + 14,000 = 30,000$. Total assets, 20X1 = 16,000.
3. Sales, 20X1 = 2,700/0.10 = 27,000. Sales, 20X2 = 27,000 × 1.15 = 31,050. ATO, 20X2 = 31,050/16,000 = 1.94 times.

12.2 Shree Company appears to manage its receivables better. Additional information about the companies, such as the companies' credit period, ageing analysis, and industry norm would be useful.

12.3 Average holding period (360 days/4), 90 days. Average collection period (360 days/8), 45 days. Operating cycle, 135 days.

12.4 The pre-tax operating ROA for Company A is 25.7 per cent, while Company B's ROA is lower at 22.2 per cent. However, Company B's interest rate is much higher at 24 per cent as compared to Company A's 15 per cent. Besides, Company B is much more leveraged than Company A. As a result, Company B's interest cover is 1.39 times, whereas Company A's cover is 6 times. Company A's ROE is 22.9 per cent as compared to Company B's 15.5 per cent. Clearly, Company B's excessive leverage is unhelpful, because its interest rate is greater than its ROA.

12.5 Company X has a higher PE ratio, a higher dividend yield and a lower beta. This means that it has better growth prospects, a better cash return and a lower risk relative to the market.

CHAPTER

13

Statement of Cash Flows

LEARNING OBJECTIVES

After studying this chapter, you should be able to:

1. Explain the need for the statement of cash flows.
2. Explain the purpose of the statement of cash flows and understand its structure.
3. Compute net cash flow from operating activities and distinguish between the direct and indirect methods.
4. Compute net cash flow from investing activities.
5. Compute net cash flow from financing activities.
6. Present the statement of cash flows.
7. Interpret the statement of cash flows.
8. Compute cash flow ratios.

GIVE IT BACK

Usually, having a lot of cash should be a cause for celebration. It need not be, as Infosys found out. At December 31, 2016, the company had cash of ₹305 billion. In February 2017, the company's founder questioned the board's governance record, including the high remuneration given to the CEO and the severance pay given to the former chief financial officer and the former chief compliance officer. One thing led to another. A former director demanded a share buyback, since the company had no need for so much of cash. Some institutional investors, even while affirming their faith in the management, wondered whether Infosys was in software or in financial services. They too wanted it to announce a large one-time buyback and periodical buybacks whenever it had surplus cash. To be fair, Infosys was not alone in this sea of cash. Its peer Cognizant agreed to return $3.5 billion in response to demands from the activist investor Elliott Management Corp. Industry leader TCS announced a buyback of ₹160 billion in order to reduce its cash pile.

SPEED READ

The statement of cash flows is an important financial statement, along with the balance sheet and the statement of profit and loss. Questions about the quality of accrual accounting have increased the value of cash flow information. Unlike accrual, cash flow presents few measurement problems. Cash receipts and payments result from operating, investing and financing activities. Cash flow information is useful in assessing an enterprise's liquidity, financial flexibility, profitability, and risk. Cash flows from operating activities can be computed directly by taking cash receipts from customers and cash paid to suppliers, employees and government, or indirectly by undoing the effect of accrual and removing non-operating items. Cash flows from investing activities consist of purchases and sales of property, plant and equipment and investments and interest and dividend income. Cash flows from financing activities arise from raising and repaying debt and equity capital and paying interest and dividend. Non-cash investing and financing activities are reported outside the statement of cash flows. A study of the statement of cash flows helps us to understand the reasons for the difference between profit and cash flow and the generation and distribution of cash.

Statement of Cash Flows in Perspective

Consider the following questions:

- Some profitable firms are unable to pay their suppliers promptly. Why?
- Why did Infosys hold cash of ₹305 billion (38 per cent of assets) at December 31, 2016?
- Despite recurring losses, how does Tesla stay afloat and expand?
- How does the Vedanta group pay for its big-ticket acquisitions?

Learning Objective

LO 1 Explain the need for the statement of cash flows.

Investors, analysts, bankers, suppliers, managers, and government authorities look for answers to such questions, but they will not find them in an enterprise's balance sheet or statement of profit and loss. The balance sheet provides information about an enterprise's assets and how those assets have been financed. But it does not explain the changes during a period in assets, liabilities, and equity resulting from the enterprise's activities. The statement of profit and loss provides information about an enterprise's financial performance. However, since earnings are measured by accrual accounting, they don't show the cash generated through the enterprise's operations.

In order to answer the kind of questions posed earlier, we need a statement that provides information on the major sources of cash receipts and cash payments. The **statement of cash flows** is now a standard feature of financial reporting along with the time-honoured balance sheet and statement of profit and loss.

There is a world of difference between a company's earnings and the cash generated from its operations. Accountants like to say: "Sales are vanity, profits are sanity and only cash is reality." Accrual-based statements consider items which have no effect on an enterprise's cash flows, such as depreciation and amortization, revenues earned but not received, and expenses incurred but not paid. Then, earnings suffer from measurement error and bias resulting from management's ability to choose from a range of methods and estimates. In contrast, reporting cash flows involves no allocations and estimates, and presents few recognition problems, because all cash receipts and payments are recognized when they occur. It is a tell-it-like-it-is system. Dramatic corporate failures have significantly heightened concerns about management's application of GAAP. Further, the downturn in the economies of many countries in recent years has led to higher company failures. In times of recession, the ability of an enterprise to meet its obligations, especially in the short term, is of paramount importance. As the saying goes, "Cash is king".

Purpose and Structure of the Statement of Cash Flows

The main purpose of the statement of cash flows is to provide relevant information about an enterprise's cash receipts and cash payments. The information will help users of financial statements assess the amounts, timing, and uncertainty of an enterprise's prospective cash flows. You may recall from Chapter 1 that investors, lenders, suppliers, employees and others regard an enterprise as a cash machine. They are directly concerned with the enterprise's ability to generate cash. The statement of cash flows provides information that enables them to evaluate the enterprise's liquidity, financial flexibility, profitability, and risk. It also provides a feedback about previous assessments of these factors.

Learning Objective

LO 2 Explain the purpose of the statement of cash flows and understand its structure.

Users of financial statements will find the information in the statement of cash flows useful in assessing the enterprise's ability to generate positive future net cash flows, meet its obligations, pay dividends and identify its needs for external financing. Understanding why net profit and cash flow differ is insightful.

The main purpose of the statement of cash flows is to provide relevant information about
   (a) An enterprise's ability to generate positive future net cash flows.
   (b) An enterprise's ability to meet its principal and interest obligations.
   (c) An enterprise's ability to pay dividends.
   (d) The cash receipts and cash payments of an enterprise during a period.

As part of their cash management activities, enterprises generally keep cash in excess of immediate needs in short-term, highly liquid investments that can be quickly converted into definite amounts of cash. You may recall from Chapter 7 that these are *cash equivalents*. Whether cash is on hand, on deposit, or invested in short-term financial instruments that are readily convertible into cash is largely irrelevant to users' assessments of liquidity and future cash flows. Therefore, the statement of cash flows focuses on the aggregate of cash and cash equivalents.

The statement of cash flows classifies cash flows into operating, investing and financing categories. Such a classification enables significant relationships within and among the three kinds of activities to be evaluated. The classification will depend on the nature of the business. For example, lending and borrowing are financing activities for manufacturing firms but are the core of the operations of banks. In this chapter, we discuss firms engaged in providing goods and services. Activities that don't result in cash receipts or payments are classified as non-cash activities. Table 13.1 gives examples of cash inflows and outflows and non-cash activities.

TABLE 13.1
Cash Flow Classification

Category	Inflows	Outflows
Operating activities: Producing and delivering goods and services.	▪ Cash sales. ▪ Unearned revenue. ▪ Collection of trade receivables.	▪ Purchase of materials and services. ▪ Payment of salaries and benefits. ▪ Payment of taxes and duties.
Investing activities: Acquiring and disposing of property, plant and equipment and investments.	▪ Sale of property, plant and equipment. ▪ Sale of investments. ▪ Sale of businesses. ▪ Receipt of interest and dividend.	▪ Purchase of property, plant and equipment. ▪ Purchase of investments. ▪ Acquisition of businesses.
Financing activities: Obtaining and returning funds.	▪ Issue of shares. ▪ Issue of bonds. ▪ Proceeds from loans.	▪ Buyback of shares. ▪ Repayment of bonds. ▪ Repayment of loans. ▪ Payment of interest and dividend.

Non-cash investing and financing activities: Transactions that affect assets or liabilities but do not result in cash inflows or outflows.

Examples:
   ▪ Converting debt into equity.
   ▪ Converting preference shares into equity.
   ▪ Purchasing a building by incurring a mortgage to the seller.
   ▪ Obtaining an asset on a finance lease.
   ▪ Exchanging a non-cash asset for another non-cash asset.

Figure 13.1 illustrates the statement of cash flows.

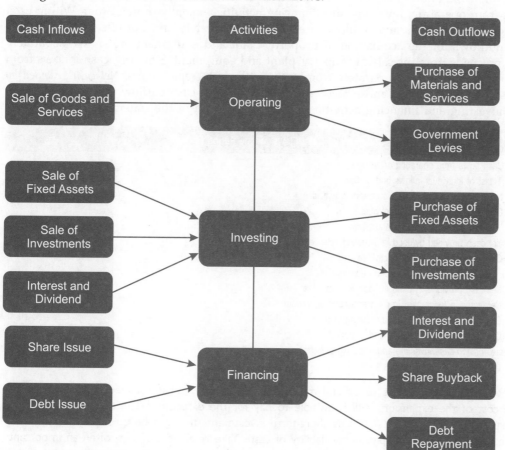

Figure 13.1
STRUCTURE OF CASH FLOWS

Cash flows arise from operating activities, investing activities, and financing activities.

Although non-cash transactions do not result in cash inflows or outflows in the period in which they occur, they generally have a significant effect on prospective cash flows. For example, conversion of debt into equity will eliminate payment of interest on the debt. Again, entering into a finance lease requires future lease payments. Therefore, information about all non-cash investing and financing activities should be disclosed in a note or schedule to the statement of cash flows.

At March 31, 20XX, Sanjay Company had the following balances in its accounts with State Bank of India: Current account #1, ₹10,000; Current account #2, overdraft ₹2,000; Money market account, ₹50,000; 90-day certificate of deposit, ₹125,000; 180-day certificate of deposit, ₹300,000. What amount should Sanjay Company report as cash and cash equivalents in its balance sheet on that date?

ONE-MINUTE QUIZ 13.2
Cash Equivalents

(a) ₹60,000.
(b) ₹183,000.
(c) ₹185,000.
(d) ₹483,000.

If a transaction is part cash and part non-cash, only the cash portion is reported in the statement of cash flows.

Sangeeta Company entered into the following transactions. Classify each as (i) operating activity, (ii) investing activity, (iii) financing activity, (iv) non-cash activity, or (v) cash management activity.

TEST YOUR UNDERSTANDING 13.1
Classifying Activities

(a) Purchased a 90-day Treasury bill.
(b) Redeemed debentures.
(c) Sold manufacturing plant.
(d) Purchased building.
(e) Issued equity in exchanged for land.
(f) Issued equity shares at a premium.
(g) Received interest on deposits.
(h) Paid dividend.
(i) Received dividend on equity investments.
(j) Collected bills receivable from customers.
(k) Paid suppliers.
(l) Obtained a computer on finance lease.

Exhibit 13.1 shows the format of the statement of cash flows. The statement reports cash flows from operating, investing and financing activities, usually in that order. Within each category, cash inflows and outflows are reported separately and not offset. For example, cash outflows for the acquisition of property, plant and equipment are shown separately from proceeds from the sale of property, plant and equipment. Similarly, cash inflows from borrowings are shown separately from cash outflows to repay loans. *Net cash provided by* refers to net cash inflow, and *net cash used in* refers to net cash outflow. A schedule of non-cash investing and financing activities appears at the end of the statement.

EXHIBIT 13.1
Format of Statement of Cash Flows

Statement of Cash Flows for the Period Ended ...		
(a) Cash flows from operating activities		
List of individual inflows and outflows	....	
Net cash provided by/used in operating activities		....
(b) Cash flows from investing activities		
List of individual inflows and outflows	....	
Net cash provided by/used in investing activities		....
(c) Cash flows from financing activities		
List of individual inflows and outflows	....	
Net cash provided by/used in financing activities		....
Net increase (decrease) in cash and cash equivalents		....
Cash and cash equivalents, beginning of period		....
Cash and cash equivalents, end of period		....
Schedule of non-cash investing and financing activities		
List of individual transactions		

LADDER
Depreciation, Reserves and Cash

Suppose a company plans to expand manufacturing capacity. It has retained earnings of twice the cost of the expansion. Will it be able to pay for the expansion? The company can pay if it has cash or other assets such as short-term investments that can be quickly converted into cash. Reserves do not imply the availability of cash. Take retained earnings, often an important part of reserves. They represent undistributed profits, but they are not necessarily stored in the cash chest. First, profit is the outcome of applying accrual accounting. Revenue includes both cash and credit sales. While credit sales contribute to profit, they do not bring in cash until the receivables are collected. Depreciation reduces profit, but leaves cash unaffected. Second, even if the profit is entirely in cash (as would be the case if all sales, purchases, and expenses are paid for immediately, there are no inventories and there is property, plant and equipment), there is no guarantee that cash will be available. For example, cash may have been used to repay loans, make acquisitions, or pay dividends. In that case, there would be retained earnings but no cash. Third, unrealized gains and losses from applying fair value accounting affect profit, but not cash. Similarly, revaluation increases reserves, but has no effect on cash. Therefore, cash and reserves are not the same thing. If you go shopping for a manufacturing plant thinking that your reserves will pay for the purchase, you should be aware that your cheque could bounce if the bank balance is insufficient, no matter how much your reserves are.

DISCUSSION QUESTION 13.1

Are the statement of profit and loss and the statement of cash flows substitutes or complements?

....

....

....

Preparing the Statement of Cash Flows

We shall now see an illustration on how to prepare the statement of cash flows. The data for this illustration consist of Compass Company's financial statements and additional information: two years' balance sheets (Exhibit 13.2), statement of profit and loss (Exhibit 13.3), notes to the financial statements (Exhibit 13.4), and transaction information (Exhibit 13.5).

COMPASS COMPANY: Balance Sheet, March 31					
	Note	20X5	20X4	Change	Increase or Decrease
Assets					
Non-current assets					
Property, plant and equipment....................................	1	₹421,000	₹313,000	108,000	Increase
Current assets					
Inventories..		176,000	118,000	58,000	Increase
Financial assets					
Investments..		117,000	142,000	(25,000)	Decrease
Trade receivables	2	125,000	93,000	32,000	Increase
Cash and cash equivalents.............................		20,000	51,000	(31,000)	Decrease
Other current assets...	3	3,000	5,000	(2,000)	Decrease
Total assets...		862,000	722,000	140,000	Increase
Equity and Liabilities					
Equity					
Equity share capital...		₹350,000	₹200,000	150,000	Increase
Other equity	4	71,000	53,000	18,000	Increase
Liabilities					
Non-current liabilities					
Financial liabilities					
Borrowings		60,000	137,000	(77,000)	Decrease
Bills payable...		111,000	62,000	49,000	Increase
Current liabilities					
Financial liabilities					
Borrowings		56,000	57,000	(1,000)	Decrease
Trade payables...		179,000	193,000	(14,000)	Decrease
Current tax liabilities		35,000	20,000	15,000	Increase
Total equity and liabilities...................................		862,000	722,000	140,000	Increase

EXHIBIT 13.2
Compass Company:
Balance Sheet

COMPASS COMPANY Statement of Profit and Loss For the year ended March 31, 20X5		
	Note	
Sales...		₹925,000
Other income	5	13,000
		938,000
Expenses		
Cost of goods sold[1]...		669,000
Finance costs...		22,000
Depreciation expense		98,000
Other expenses and losses	6	79,000
Total expenses...		868,000
Profit before tax		70,000
Tax expense		27,000
Profit for the period		43,000

EXHIBIT 13.3
Compass Company:
Balance Sheet

---

[1] *Cost of goods sold* is used here a shorthand for the sum of the cost of materials consumed, employee benefits expense, purchases, change in inventories, and manufacturing expenses.

EXHIBIT 13.4
Compass Company:
Notes to the Financial
Statements

1. Property, plant and equipment	20X5	20X4
Gross block	973,000	818,000
Deduct Accumulated depreciation	552,000	505,000
Net block	421,000	313,000

2. Trade receivables	20X5	20X4
Gross	134,000	100,000
Deduct Allowance for credit losses	9,000	7,000
Net	125,000	93,000

3. Other current assets	20X5	20X4
Prepaid expenses	3,000	5,000

4. Other equity	20X5	20X4
Retained earnings	71,000	53,000

5. Other income	20X5
Interest income	7,000
Gain on sale of equipment	6,000
	13,000

6. Other expenses and losses	20X5
Selling and administrative expenses	58,000
Bad debt expense	12,000
Loss on sale of investments	9,000
	79,000

EXHIBIT 13.5
Compass Company:
Transaction Information

Item	Transaction
1.	Purchased equipment for cash, ₹173,000.
2.	Sold equipment for cash, ₹22,000 (cost, ₹67,000; accumulated depreciation, ₹51,000).
3.	Purchased equipment on credit, ₹49,000.
4.	Purchased investments for cash, ₹26,000.
5.	Sold investments for cash, ₹42,000 (cost, ₹51,000).
6.	Issued shares at par for cash, ₹100,000.
7.	Converted debentures into equity shares of ₹10 at par, ₹50,000.
8.	Paid dividends, ₹25,000.
9.	Redeemed debentures, ₹27,000.
10.	Repaid a current loan, ₹1,000.
11.	Wrote off a trade receivable, ₹10,000.

We will now see how to compute net cash flow from operating activities, investing activities, and financing activities.

Computing Net Cash Flow from Operating Activities

Learning Objective

LO 3 Compute net cash flow from operating activities and distinguish between the direct and indirect methods.

Net profit is based on accrual: we record revenues and expenses when earned or incurred, although we may not have received or paid all of them. Further, depreciation, amortization, and allowance for credit losses do not reflect cash outflows in current or future periods. In order to arrive at net cash flow from operating activities, we have to restate revenues and expenses on a cash basis. We do this by undoing the accrual accounting adjustments. Figure 13.2 shows this process of going back from net profit to cash flow. In effect, we cancel out what we did in Chapter 4.

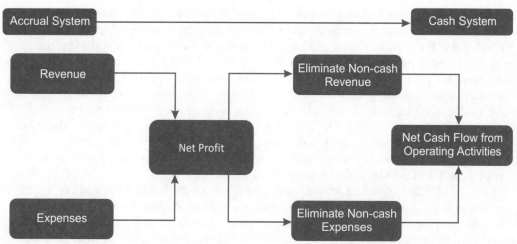

Figure 13.2

FROM NET PROFIT TO NET CASH FLOW FROM OPERATING ACTIVITIES

Starting with net profit, we eliminate the effect of revenues not received and expenses not paid in order to arrive at net cash flow from operating activities.

There are two ways of computing and reporting net cash flow from operating activities:

- The direct method
- The indirect method.

The **direct method** shows major classes of operating cash receipts and payments, such as cash received from customers, cash paid to suppliers and employees, and income tax paid, the sum of which is the net cash flow from operating activities. The **indirect method** starts with net profit and adjusts it for revenue and expense items that did not involve operating cash receipts or cash payments in the current period to arrive at net cash flow from operating activities.

Both methods result in the same figure of net cash flow from operating activities. We will first see the direct method. Then we reconcile the net profit to net cash flow from operating activities, so as to focus on the differences between these two amounts.

Cash received from customers Cash received from customers consists of cash sales and collections from customers. Cash sales result in cash inflows in the current period. However, collections require additional calculations. Sales from an earlier period may be collected in the current period, sales from the current period may be collected in a future period, and some receivables may not be collected at all. As a result, collections are seldom equal to credit sales.

The following equation states the relationship between credit sales, change in trade receivables, and collections:

Ending balance = Beginning balance + Credit sales – Cash received from customers – Write-offs

We can rewrite the above equation as follows:

Cash received from customers = Credit sales + Decrease (– Increase) in trade receivables – Write-offs

Changes in unearned revenue and unbilled revenue will be included. From Exhibits 13.2 and 13.3 for Compass Company, sales are ₹925,000, and trade receivables increased by ₹34,000 in 20X5. From Item 11 of Exhibit 13.5, Compass Company wrote off a trade receivable of ₹10,000. Thus, cash received from customers is ₹881,000, calculated as follows: ₹925,000 – ₹34,000 – ₹10,000.

The T-account explaining this relationship is as follows:

Trade Receivables			
Beginning balance	100,000[a]	*Cash collections*	*881,000*
Sales	925,000	Write-off	10,000
Ending balance	134,000[b]		

[a] Net receivables, 93,000 + Allowance for credit losses, 7,000 = Gross receivables, 100,000.
[b] Net receivables, 125,000 + Allowance for credit losses, 9,000 = Gross receivables, 134,000.

Cash paid to suppliers and employees The next step is to calculate cash paid to suppliers for the purchase of materials and services (such as insurance, advertising and the like) and to employees. We calculate cash paid to suppliers and employees by adjusting the cost of goods sold and expenses on the statement of profit and loss for (a) changes in inventories, trade payables (including bills payable), prepaid expenses, and (b) non-cash expenses. We must adjust the cost of goods sold for the change in inventories to arrive at purchases. If the cost of goods sold in the current period is more than purchases, there will be a decrease in inventories, and if the cost of goods sold is less than purchases, there will be an increase in inventories. Further, if credit purchases are more than cash paid to suppliers, there will be an increase in trade payables, and if credit purchases are less than cash paid to suppliers, there will be a decrease in trade payables.

Cash paid differs from expenses. Adjustments must be made for a change in prepaid expenses and for non-cash expenses. If expenses are more than cash payments, there will be a decrease in prepaid expenses, and if expenses are less than cash payments, there will be an increase in prepaid expenses. Finally, certain expenses do not entail cash payment and must not be considered for calculating expenses paid in cash. Depreciation, amortization, and depletion do not involve cash outflows, but are allocations of past expenditures for purchases of long-term assets. For example, Compass Company records depreciation for the year ended March 31, 20X5 as follows:

Depreciation Expense 98,000
    Accumulated Depreciation..   98,000

Again, Note 6 in Exhibit 13.4 states that Compass Company's bad debt expense was ₹12,000. There is no cash payment for depreciation or bad debt expense. Thus, to arrive at cash paid for expenses, we must deduct non-cash expenses if they have been included in the cost of goods sold, operating expenses or other expenses. If non-cash items are not included in any of these categories but are shown separately in the statement of profit and loss, there is no need to deduct them.

The following equation shows how cash paid to suppliers and employees is related to expenses and losses and changes in inventories, prepaid expenses, and trade payables:

Cash paid to suppliers and employees = Cost of goods sold + Selling and administrative expenses
                                              – Depreciation expense[a]
                                              – Bad debt expense[b]
                                              + Increase (– Decrease) in inventories
                                              + Increase (– Decrease) in prepaid expenses
                                              + Decrease (– Increase) in trade payables

[a] if included in cost of goods sold.
[b] if included in selling and administrative expenses.

From Exhibits 13.2, 13.3 and 13.4, the cost of goods sold is ₹669,000, selling and administrative expenses are ₹58,000, inventories increased by ₹58,000, prepaid expenses decreased by ₹2,000, and trade payables decreased by ₹14,000. Since depreciation expense and bad debt expense appear as separate items on the statement of profit and loss, there is no need to deduct them from expenses. Thus, cash paid to employees and suppliers is ₹797,000, calculated as follows: ₹669,000 + ₹58,000 + ₹58,000 + ₹14,000 – ₹2,000.

Income tax paid The amount of income tax paid usually differs from the income tax expense. The difference between tax payment and tax expense is the tax payable or refundable. Besides, deferred tax does not affect cash. If the tax expense is more than the tax paid, there is an increase in the tax payable during the current period. If the tax expense is less than the tax paid, there is a decrease in the tax payable. The following equation shows this relationship:

Income tax paid = Income tax expense + Decrease (– Increase) in tax payable

From Exhibits 13.2 and 13.3, we note that tax expense is ₹27,000 and tax payable increased by ₹15,000. Thus, income tax paid is ₹12,000.

Cash flows from operating activities — Direct method Exhibit 13.6 presents the cash flows from operating activities following the direct method. Recall from the foregoing discussion that Compass Company has the following operating items: cash received from customers, ₹881,000; cash paid to suppliers and employees, ₹797,000; and income tax paid, ₹12,000. The result is net cash flow from operating activities of ₹72,000.

COMPASS COMPANY Cash Flows from Operating Activities – Direct Method For the year ended March 31, 20X5		
Cash flows from operating activities		
Cash received from customers	₹881,000	
Cash paid to suppliers and employees	(797,000)	
Cash generated from operations	84,000	
Income tax paid	(12,000)	
Net cash provided by operating activities		₹72,000

EXHIBIT 13.6
Cash Flows From Operating Activities – Direct Method

Praveen Company had the following information available relating to the year ended December 31, 20X5:

(a) Cash sales were ₹25,000 and credit sales were ₹436,000. Trade receivables (gross) were ₹78,000 and ₹49,000 at the beginning and end of 20X5, respectively. Trade receivables of ₹16,000 were written off during 20X5.

(b) Cost of goods sold was ₹269,000 and selling and administrative expenses were ₹61,000. At the beginning of 20X5, inventories, prepaid expenses, and trade payables were ₹43,000, ₹7,000, and ₹62,000, respectively. At the end of 20X5, these were ₹51,000, ₹3,000, and ₹67,000, respectively. The cost of goods sold included depreciation expense of ₹39,000 and selling and administrative expenses included bad debt expense of ₹19,000.

(c) Income tax expense for 20X5 was ₹53,000. Income tax payable at the beginning and end of 20X5 was ₹14,000 and ₹11,000, respectively. Calculate net cash flow from operating activities.

TEST YOUR UNDERSTANDING 13.2
Computing Net Cash Flow from Operating Activities – Direct Method

Cash flows from operating activities – Indirect method Exhibit 13.7 shows net cash flow from operating activities using the indirect method. Under this method, a number of adjustments are made to profit to arrive at net cash provided by operating activities of ₹72,000, which is the same as computed under the direct method (Exhibit 13.6).

COMPASS COMPANY Cash Flows from Operating Activities – Indirect Method For the year ended March 31, 20X5		
Cash flows from operating activities		
Profit before tax	₹70,000	
Adjustments:		
Depreciation	98,000	
Bad debt expense	12,000	
Gain on sale of equipment	(6,000)	
Loss on sale of investments	9,000	
Interest expense	22,000	
Interest income	(7,000)	
Operating profit before working capital changes	198,000	
Increase in inventories	(58,000)	
Increase in trade receivables[2]	(44,000)	
Decrease in prepaid expenses	2,000	
Decrease in trade payables	(14,000)	
Cash generated from operations	84,000	
Income tax paid	(12,000)	
Net cash provided by operating activities		₹72,000

EXHIBIT 13.7
Cash Flows from Operating Activities – Indirect Method

---

[2] The amount includes bad debts written off. Excluding them would imply that we collected those amounts, and that would be incorrect.

We make the following three types of adjustments in order to convert net profit into net cash flow from operating activities:

1. *Non-cash items:* Depreciation and bad debt expense do not require cash outflows. Hence, we add them back.

2. *Non-operating items:* We move non-operating items, such as (a) gains and losses on disposal of property, plant and equipment, intangible assets and investments, (b) interest income, (c) dividend income and (d) interest expense from the operating activities section to the investing or the financing activities section, as appropriate.

3. *Changes in working capital items:* We adjust net profit for changes in working capital items, such as inventories, trade receivables, prepaid expenses, and trade payables. For example, if inventories increased during the current period, purchases will be more than the cost of goods sold. Similarly, if trade receivables increased during the current period, cash received from customers will be less than sales. Thus, to convert net profit into net cash flow from operating activities, we deduct increase (add decrease) in inventories, trade receivables, and prepaid expenses from (to) the net profit. Further, we add increase (deduct decrease) in trade payables to (from) the net profit. We should consider a change in income tax payable if the starting point of the computation is profit after tax.

Exhibit 13.8 summarizes these adjustments.

EXHIBIT 13.8
Adjustments to Convert Net Profit into Net Cash Flow from Operating Activities – Indirect Method

> Converting net profit into operating cash flow requires three kinds of adjustments.

Non-cash Items	Non-operating Items	Working Capital Items
+ Depreciation	+ Interest expense	+ Decrease in inventories
+ Amortization	+ Loss on disposal of PPE*	+ Decrease in trade receivables
+ Depletion	+ Loss on disposal of investments	+ Decrease in prepaid expenses
+ Bad debt expense	– Interest income	+ Increase in trade payables
– Excess provision written back	– Gain on disposal of PPE*	– Increase in inventories
	– Gain on disposal of investments	– Increase in trade receivables
		– Increase in prepaid expenses
		– Decrease in trade payables

* PPE is property, plant and equipment.

The reconciliation of profit to net cash flow from operating activities is also provided in the statement of cash flows under the direct method.

HANDHOLD 13.1
Cash Flow and Profit

During 20X3, Mahesh Furniture Company earned a net profit of ₹60,000 and net cash used in operating activities of ₹45,000. Possible reasons (illustrative, not exhaustive) for the difference are:

- Increase in trade receivables and/or inventories
- Decrease in trade payables
- Gain on sale of property, plant and equipment and/or investments
- Interest income.

LADDER
Depreciation and Cash

The relationship between depreciation and cash seems to be one of the eternal mysteries of accounting. You may recall from the discussion in Chapter 6 that depreciation is *not* a source of cash. Depreciation is an allocation of the cost of an asset over its useful life. In the indirect method, depreciation is added to profit to calculate net cash flow from operating activities. To some, this means depreciation brings in cash. When we move from cash to accrual, we deduct depreciation from cash profit to arrive at accrual profit. In the statement of cash flows, we move back from accrual to cash, so we add back depreciation to the accrual profit to arrive at cash profit. Suppose a business earns a revenue of ₹10,000 and pays expenses of ₹7,000, all of them in cash. Its cash profit is ₹3,000. Suppose depreciation is ₹1,000. In the statement of profit and loss, we deduct the depreciation from the cash profit to arrive at an accrual profit of ₹2,000. In the statement of cash flows, we start with the accrual profit of ₹2,000 and trace our way back to the cash profit of ₹3,000. For this, we *add back* the depreciation of ₹1,000 to the accrual profit. In short, in the statement of profit and loss we charge depreciation and in the statement of cash flows we undo that charge. This is what happened: ₹3,000 − ₹1,000 + ₹1,000. So how does depreciation bring in cash? Think of it also this way: If depreciation does result in an inflow of cash, why doesn't it appear in the statement of cash flows in the direct method?

Ajay Company reported a profit before tax of ₹432,000 for the year ended March 31, 20X7. Relevant balance sheet account balances at March 31 are as follows:

TEST YOUR UNDERSTANDING 13.3
Computing Net Cash Flow from Operating Activities – Indirect Method

	20X7	20X6
Inventories..	₹59,000	₹72,000
Trade receivables..	94,000	61,000
Prepaid expenses	14,000	3,000
Trade payables..	82,000	78,000
Income tax payable	13,000	19,000

The statement of profit and loss for the year ended March 31, 20X7 reported depreciation expense of ₹49,000, income tax expense of ₹92,000, and gain on sale of investments of ₹8,000.
Calculate the net cash flow from operating activities using the indirect method.

Which of the following information does not appear in the statement of cash flows prepared under the direct method?
   (a) Cash paid to suppliers.
   (b) Cash receipts from customers.
   (c) Depreciation and amortization expense.
   (d) Income tax paid.

ONE-MINUTE QUIZ 13.3
Disclosure in the Statement of Cash Flows

Computing Net Cash Flow from Investing Activities

The second step in preparing the statement of cash flows is computing net cash flow from investing activities. Investing activities involve purchases and sales of property, plant and equipment and investments. Receipts from the disposal of property, plant and equipment include directly related proceeds of insurance settlements. Cash receipts and cash payments from investing activities are computed by analyzing changes in the balance sheet amounts for property, plant and equipment and investments and considering the cash effects of the related transactions that took place during the period. Interest and dividends received are also part of cash inflows from investing activities.

Learning Objective
LO 4 Compute net cash flow from investing activities.

From Exhibit 13.5, Compass Company's investing activities during the year ended March 31, 20X5 are as follows:

1. Purchased equipment for cash, ₹173,000.
2. Sold equipment for cash, ₹22,000 (cost, ₹67,000; accumulated depreciation, ₹51,000).
3. Purchased equipment on credit, ₹49,000.
4. Purchased investments for cash, ₹26,000.
5. Sold investments for cash, ₹42,000 (cost, ₹51,000).

We examine these transactions.

Property, plant and equipment   From the balance sheet in Exhibit 13.2, there is an increase of ₹108,000 in property, plant and equipment. The increase represents the net effect of purchase and sale of property, plant and equipment and accumulated depreciation. Reviewing the entries for transactions relating to property, plant and equipment will assist us in understanding their effects on cash flows.

Item 1 says Compass Company purchased equipment costing ₹173,000. It would have recorded the transaction as follows:

Equipment... 173,000
   Cash *173,000*

This transaction resulted in a cash outflow of ₹173,000. Advance payments, down payments, or other amounts paid in connection with the purchase of property, plant and equipment are investing cash outflows.

Item 2 indicates that Compass Company sold equipment with a cost of ₹67,000 and accumulated depreciation of ₹51,000 for ₹22,000 at a gain of ₹6,000. The gain appears on the statement of profit and loss. The cash inflow from the sale of the equipment equals the sale price of ₹22,000. This is also clear from the entry to record this transaction:

Cash.. 22,000
Accumulated Depreciation 51,000
   Gain on Disposal of Equipment 6,000
   Equipment 67,000

The gain on sale of equipment is a part of the cash flows from investing activities, although it appears as a part of the profit in Exhibit 13.3.

Item 3 states that Compass Company purchased equipment for ₹49,000 on credit. This is a non-cash transaction, recorded as follows:

Equipment... 49,000
   Bills Payable 49,000

This transaction involved purchase of equipment (investing activity) and issuing a bill payable (financing activity) but did not result in either a cash inflow or a cash outflow. Nevertheless, considering the significance of the transaction, it will be shown in a schedule to the statement of cash flows.

The Equipment account and the Accumulated Depreciation account are as follows:

Equipment			
Beginning balance	818,000	Sale	67,000
Cash purchase	*173,000*		
Non-cash purchase	49,000		
Ending balance	973,000		

Accumulated Depreciation			
Sale	51,000	Beginning balance	505,000
		Depreciation expense	98,000
		Ending balance	552,000

Similar analyses must be made for other property, plant and equipment items and intangible assets, when such assets appear on the balance sheet.

TEST YOUR UNDERSTANDING 13.4
Computing Net Cash Flow from Investing Activities

A machine costing ₹70,000 with an accumulated depreciation of ₹49,000 is sold for ₹29,000. How will this transaction appear in the investing activities section of the statement of cash flows?

Investments The decrease of ₹25,000 in investments must be explained. As is the case with property, plant and equipment, the decrease is the net effect of both purchase and sale of investments.

From Item 4, Compass Company purchased investments for ₹26,000. This was recorded as follows:

Investments... 26,000
   Cash *26,000*

This transaction led to a cash outflow of ₹26,000.

Item 5 states that Compass Company sold investments costing ₹51,000 for ₹42,000, recorded as follows:

Cash... 42,000
Loss on Sale of Investments.. 9,000
   Investments... 51,000

This transaction resulted in a cash inflow of ₹42,000. The Investments account summarizes these changes:

Investments			
Beginning balance	142,000	Sale	51,000
Purchase	26,000		
Ending balance	117,000		

Interest and dividend received Interest and dividend received are classified as cash flows from investing activities, because they represent returns on the investments made by the enterprise. If we assume that Compass Company received the entire interest income, interest received is ₹7,000. If the company had accrued interest or dividend income, an adjustment would have to be made to arrive at interest or dividend received.

Exhibit 13.9 presents the above transactions.

COMPASS COMPANY Cash Flows from Investing Activities For the year ended March 31, 20X5	
Cash flows from investing activities	
Purchase of property, plant and equipment	₹(173,000)
Sale of property, plant and equipment	22,000
Purchase of investments	(26,000)
Sale of investments	42,000
Interest received	7,000
Net cash used in investing activities	₹(128,000)

EXHIBIT 13.9
Cash Flows from Investing Activities

All assets and current liabilities have been analyzed in the operating and investing activities sections. Equity and non-current liabilities are next.

ONE-MINUTE QUIZ 13.4
Investing Activities

In 20XX, Hosakere Company's manufacturing plant was destroyed in an explosion. The plant cost ₹100,000 and had accumulated depreciation of ₹25,000 at the time of the loss. The statement of profit and loss for 20XX reported a loss of ₹16,000. What was the increase or decrease in cash flows from investing activities in the company's 20XX statement of cash flows?

(a) ₹50,000 decrease.
(b) ₹59,000 increase.
(c) ₹75,000 decrease.
(d) ₹91,000 increase.

Computing Net Cash Flow from Financing Activities

The final step in the preparation of the statement of cash flows is computing net cash flow from financing activities. These involve raising and repayment of capital and loans. Cash inflows and cash outflows from financing activities are calculated by analyzing changes in the balance sheet amounts for equity and financial liabilities and considering the cash effects of transactions during the period. Interest and dividends paid are part of cash outflows from financing activities.

Learning Objective
LO 5 Compute net cash flow from financing activities.

From Exhibit 13.5, Compass Company's financing activities during the year ended March 31, 20X5 are as follows:

6. Issued shares at par, ₹100,000.
7. Converted debentures into equity shares of ₹10 at par, ₹50,000.

8. Paid dividends, ₹25,000.
9. Redeemed debentures, ₹27,000.
10. Repaid a current loan, ₹1,000.

The changes in the accounts affected by these transactions are explained below:

Share capital   Compass Company's share capital increased by ₹150,000, which is explained by Items 6 and 7. Item 6 states that Compass Company issued shares at par for ₹100,000. This transaction was recorded as follows:

Cash.. *100,000*
   Share Capital..   100,000

As a result, there was a cash inflow of ₹100,000.

The other transaction affecting share capital is Item 7, conversion of debentures of ₹50,000 into equity shares of ₹10 at par. It was recorded as follows:

Debentures Payable...   50,000
   Share Capital..   50,000

This is a non-cash transaction and is shown in the schedule of non-cash investing and financing activities.

The Share Capital account is as follows:

Share Capital	
Beginning balance	200,000
Cash	100,000
Conversion of debentures	50,000
Ending balance	350,000

Dividends   Item 8 states that Compass Company paid dividends of ₹25,000. The transaction will be recorded as follows:

Dividends...   25,000
   Cash *25,000*

The transaction resulted in a cash outflow of ₹25,000.[3]

Other equity Compass Company retained ₹18,000 out of the profit before tax of ₹70,000, after tax expense of ₹27,000 and dividends of ₹25,000. Profit before tax and tax expense have been considered for computing net cash flow from operating activities and the cash effect of paying the dividends has been discussed above. Thus, the increase of ₹18,000 in retained earnings has been fully analyzed and dealt with.

Non-current borrowings   Item 9 states that Compass Company redeemed debentures of ₹27,000 at par. The transaction is recorded as follows:

Debentures Payable...   27,000
   Cash *27,000*

There is a cash outflow of ₹27,000 as a result of this transaction.

Item 7, conversion of debentures into equity shares, has been analyzed in share capital. Together, Items 7 and 9 explain the decrease of ₹77,000 in non-current borrowings.

Other non-current liabilities Item 3, purchase of equipment on credit, is a non-cash item and has been discussed in the investing activities section.

---

[3] Ind AS requires dividend paid to be classified as part of financing actives. IFRS allows dividend paid to be classified as either operating or financing cash flow.

Current borrowings Item 10 indicates that a current loan of ₹1,000 was repaid. The entry for the transaction is as follows:

Loan Payable 1,000
  Cash *1,000*

Thus, the transaction resulted in a cash outflow of ₹1,000.

Interest paid It is a direct consequence of a financing decision and should, therefore, be classified as a cash outflow from financing activities.[4] If we assume that Compass Company paid the entire interest expense, interest paid is ₹22,000, the same as the amount of interest expense shown in Exhibit 13.3. If the company had accrued interest expense, an adjustment must be made to compute interest paid. Note that the statement of cash flows discloses the total amount of interest paid including any interest capitalized.

Exhibit 13.10 presents the financing activities section of the statement of cash flows.

COMPASS COMPANY Cash Flows from Financing Activities For the year ended March 31, 20X5	
Cash flows from financing activities	
Proceeds from issue of share...	₹100,000
Dividend paid	(25,000)
Redemption of debentures...	(27,000)
Repayment of short-term loan..	(1,000)
Interest paid	(22,000)
Net cash provided by financing activities	₹25,000

EXHIBIT 13.10
Cash Flows from Financing Activities

How will the following transactions appear on the statement of cash flows: (a) Acquisition of the assets of another company by issue of shares for ₹160,000; (b) conversion of 10,000 preference shares of ₹100 each into 50,000 equity shares of ₹10 at a premium of ₹10 per share; and (c) entering into a finance lease for a new plant with a fair value of ₹230,000?

TEST YOUR UNDERSTANDING 13.5
Computing Net Cash Flow from Financing Activities

"Is there such a thing as too much cash?" What a question to ask, you might say. "Don't you know the saying, 'Cash is king'?" There is no other asset like cash. It is real. A cash-rich firm can splurge on acquisitions, pay suppliers promptly, and shell out dividends. Cash is the quintessential asset. Isn't it *the* asset? Think about it this way. Cash is like a rescue boat on a ship. It has its use. But a rescue boat is for safety, not for travel. A large cash balance could mean that managers are unable to come up with good investment projects. It can be a sign of slowing down, not an index of strength. The market does not like companies that are sitting on cash, and marks down their stock prices. A surfeit of cash has other risks too. Managers may be tempted to go for boondoggles, travel by company jet, or hold meetings in exotic locales. A lot of cash may not be such a good thing, after all.

FINANCIAL VIEW
Cash: Boon or Bane?

Reporting Cash Flows

We now put together the results of the preceding steps for computing cash flows from operating, investing, and financing activities and the beginning and ending cash and cash equivalents in the form of a statement of cash flows. Exhibit 13.11 presents the statement of cash flows for Compass Company using the direct method. The statement reports the individual items of cash inflows and cash outflows from operating activities, as shown in Exhibit 13.6. When the direct method is used, a schedule explaining the difference between profit and cash from operating activities is provided in a format similar to that in Exhibit 13.7.

Learning Objective
LO 6 Present the statement of cash flows.

---

[4] Ind AS requires interest paid to be classified as part of financing actives. IFRS allows interest paid to be classified as either operating or financing cash flow.

EXHIBIT 13.11
Cash Flows from
Financing Activities –
Direct Method

COMPASS COMPANY Cash Flows from Operating Activities – Direct Method For the year ended March 31, 20X5		
Cash flows from operating activities		
Cash received from customers	₹881,000	
Cash paid to suppliers and employees	(797,000)	
Cash generated from operations	84,000	
Income tax paid	(12,000)	
Net cash provided by operating activities		₹72,000
Cash flows from investing activities		
Purchase of property, plant and equipment	(173,000)	
Sale of property, plant and equipment	22,000	
Purchase of investments	(26,000)	
Sale of investments	42,000	
Interest received	7,000	
Net cash used in investing activities		(128,000)
Cash flows from financing activities		
Proceeds from issue of share	100,000	
Dividend paid	(25,000)	
Redemption of debentures	(27,000)	
Repayment of short-term loan	(1,000)	
Interest paid	(22,000)	
Net cash provided by financing activities		25,000
Net decrease in cash and cash equivalents		(31,000)
Cash and cash equivalents at beginning of period		51,000
Cash and cash equivalents at end of period		20,000

Schedule of non-cash investing and financing activities
1. The company purchased equipment for ₹49,000 on credit.
2. The company converted debentures of ₹50,000 into equity shares of ₹10 at par.

Accounting Policy
The company considers all highly liquid debt instruments purchased with a maturity of three months or less from the date of acquisition to be cash equivalents.

Exhibit 13.12 presents the statement of cash flows using the indirect method. The statement reports the differences between profit and net cash provided by operating activities, as shown in Exhibit 13.7. The statement of cash flows also contains the schedule of non-cash investing and financing activities.

EXHIBIT 13.12
Cash Flows from
Financing Activities –
Indirect Method

COMPASS COMPANY Cash Flows from Operating Activities – Indirect Method For the year ended March 31, 20X5		
Cash flows from operating activities		
Profit before tax	₹70,000	
Adjustments		
Depreciation	98,000	
Bad debt expense	12,000	
Gain on sale of equipment	(6,000)	
Loss on sale of investments	9,000	
Interest expense	22,000	
Interest income	(7,000)	
Operating profit before working capital changes	198,000	
Increase in inventories	(58,000)	
Increase in trade receivables	(44,000)	
Decrease in prepaid expenses	2,000	
Decrease in trade payables	(14,000)	
Cash generated from operations	84,000	
Income tax paid	(12,000)	
Net cash provided by operating activities		₹72,000

Cash flows from investing activities

Purchase of property, plant and equipment	(173,000)	
Sale of property, plant and equipment	22,000	
Purchase of investments	(26,000)	
Sale of investments	42,000	
Interest received	7,000	
Net cash used in investing activities		(128,000)

Cash flows from financing activities

Proceeds from issue of share	100,000	
Dividend paid	(25,000)	
Redemption of debentures	(27,000)	
Repayment of short-term loan	(1,000)	
Interest paid	(22,000)	
Net cash provided by financing activities		25,000
Net decrease in cash and cash equivalents		(31,000)
Cash and cash equivalents at beginning of period		51,000
Cash and cash equivalents at end of period		20,000

Schedule of non-cash investing and financing activities

1. The company purchased equipment for ₹49,000 on credit.
2. The company converted debentures of ₹50,000 into equity shares of ₹10 at par.

Accounting Policy

The company considers all highly liquid debt instruments purchased with a maturity of three months or less from the date of acquisition to be cash equivalents.

The difference between the two approaches is limited only to presenting the cash flows from operating activities. For both methods, cash flows from investing and financing activities are taken from Exhibits 13.9 and 13.10.

FINANCIAL VIEW
Direct Method or Indirect Method?

Which is better: the direct method or the indirect method? The direct method shows operating cash receipts and cash payments. Equity analysts and loan officers point out that it is more consistent with the main purpose of the statement of cash flows: to provide relevant information about cash receipts and payments of an enterprise. The indirect method focuses on the difference between profit and net cash flow from operating activities. The lesser the gap between net profit and net cash flow from operations, the better the earnings quality. The presentation of cash flows under the direct method is more straightforward. The indirect method is less intuitive and interpreting the adjustments to net profit is more difficult. Evidence suggests that managers prefer the indirect method, while users prefer the direct method. Companies claim that a change to the direct method would impose excessive implementation costs. It is not clear what these costs are. The information required for the direct method is readily available from the accounting system. In any case, businesses use the direct method for internal reporting. So the argument is unconvincing. For the present, standard-setters in many countries, including the US, the UK, and Canada, have allowed the use of the indirect method, but have recommended the use of the direct method. Hardly anyone in these countries has opted for the direct method. Australia is one of the very few countries that *requires* the direct method.

Interpreting the Statement of Cash Flows

What can we learn from the statement of cash flows about Compass Company? Our questions include the following:

Learning Objective

LO 7   Interpret the statement of cash flows.

1. Why did the cash balance decrease when the company made a net profit for the period?
2. How did the company finance the acquisition of plant and machinery?
3. How did the company utilize the proceeds of the equity issue?
4. Is the capacity expansion straining the company's cash?
5. Does the company enjoy a fair degree of financial flexibility?
6. What inferences can we draw from the statement about the company's ability to generate future cash flows, repay its borrowings, and pay dividends?

We will now try to answer these questions using the information in Exhibit 13.11 and Exhibit 13.12.

Why did the cash balance decrease despite a net profit?   Compass Company's net cash flow from operations of ₹72,000 is less than the sum of net profit and depreciation that equals ₹141,000. It shows that the profit was not fully realized in cash because of accruals. Therefore, the company's earnings can't be said to be of high quality. However, the company converted receivables into cash rapidly, as indicated by cash received from customers of ₹881,000 compared to sales of ₹925,000 (cash to sales ratio of 95 per cent). The increase in inventories of ₹58,000 and trade receivables of ₹44,000 drained the cash generated from operations. We need to find out the reasons. Further, the company drew on its cash and cash equivalents to pay for capital expenditure.

How did the company finance the acquisition of equipment?   Compass Company paid for capital expenditure of ₹173,000. The expenditure was financed partly from three sources totalling ₹45,000:

1. Proceeds from the sale of old equipment, ₹22,000;
2. Proceeds from the sale of investments, net of purchase, ₹16,000; and
3. Interest receipts, ₹7,000.

The gap of ₹128,000 was financed as follows:

1. Net cash from operating activities, ₹72,000;
2. Net cash from financing activities, ₹25,000 (effectively from share issue);
3. Drawdown of cash and cash equivalents, ₹31,000.

Besides, the schedule shows that the company purchased machinery for ₹49,000 on credit, which did not involve any cash outflow during the current period. The *total* capital expenditure is, thus, ₹222,000.

How did the company utilize the proceeds of the equity issue?   We see from the financing activities section that Compass Company raised ₹100,000 from the issue of share capital and repaid loans totalling ₹28,000. Thus, the net realization from long-term sources was ₹72,000. The company paid dividends of ₹25,000 and interest of ₹22,000, and has been left with net cash of ₹25,000 from financing activities. Conversion of debentures into equity does not result in cash inflow.

Is the capacity expansion straining the company's cash?   It is clear that Compass Company expansion in manufacturing capacity during the period was a major drain on cash. The net cash outflow from investing activities of ₹128,000 was met from three sources: net cash flow from operating activities, ₹72,000; proceeds from the issue of share capital, ₹25,000 (after repaying loans and paying interest and dividends); and withdrawal from cash balance, ₹31,000. In other words, just about one-third of the financing for the expansion has come from long-term sources (share capital). As a result, the cash balance dipped. Inexplicably, at a time when cash requirements were increasing, payments to suppliers were accelerated and controls on inventories and trade receivables were loosened, leading to a further squeeze on cash.

Does the company enjoy a fair degree of financial flexibility?   Every cloud has a silver lining. Compass Company can do many things to survive a crisis, including the following:

1. Raise cash by selling its current investments without disrupting operations.
2. Issue additional debt or equity since its debt-to-equity ratio of 0.54:1 seems low.
3. Avail additional credit from suppliers.
4. Tap a bank line of credit or other sources given its strong financial position.

Besides, it has a large net cash flow from operating activities, which reduces its vulnerability to adverse changes in operating conditions. Thus, the company's overall risk is quite low. This means that it will almost certainly survive during a time of unexpected fall in demand resulting in a low net cash flow from operations. The company can even take advantage of a profitable and unexpected investment opportunity in the event of exit by any of its competitors.

What can we infer about the prospects for the company's creditors and shareholders? From the standpoint of Compass Company's creditors, net cash flow from operating activities covered interest payments well over three times (72,000/22,000). So the company is unlikely to default on interest payments, even under relatively adverse operating conditions. The position of the shareholders seems to be somewhat different. In a way, the company appears to be balancing the shareholders' need for dividend with its hunger for cash to pay for the expansion by paying a dividend of ₹25,000 as compared to net cash flow from operations of ₹50,000 (after deducting interest paid). Thus, it retained one-half of the net cash flow from operations *less* interest paid. During 20X5, the company paid a dividend of 12.5 per cent on the beginning share capital (25,000/200,000). If the company is keen to maintain the rate of dividend in the future, it will have to pay ₹43,750 (because of the increase in share capital). If the current level of cash flows is any guide, the company is unlikely to be able to maintain the rate of dividend in the future without further straining its liquidity.

The Big Picture

Compass Company financed large capital expenditure during the period by raising additional share capital, selling investments, diverting cash from operations, and drawing on cash balance. As a result, its liquidity has been strained. The company's strength in responding to unexpected needs or opportunities comes mainly from two sources: the ability to sell its investments without hampering operations and the ability to issue additional debt or equity at short notice. Profit was realized in cash. The company's management of working capital is a matter of serious concern and must be addressed immediately.

Cash Flow Ratios

The statement of cash flows provides information about cash generated from and used in operating, investing, and financing activities. Together with the balance sheet and statement of profit and loss ratios, cash flows ratios are useful in understanding the financial condition and performance of a business. In particular, they can provide a better view of liquidity. In addition, they are also a useful check on the reliability of the financial statements. Cash flow ratios are used in forensic auditing and criminal investigation. Here are some useful cash flow ratios.

Learning Objective
LO8 **Compute cash flows ratios.**

Operating cash margin   This is the cash equivalent of the profit margin ratio. It excludes profit stuck in receivables. It is defined as follows:

$$\frac{\text{Net cash provided by operating activities}}{\text{Net sales}}$$

The ratio would undo the effect of channel stuffing, sale and repurchase transactions and the like to boost revenue and profit. A ratio close to the accrual-based profit margin ratio would be an assurance that sales and profits are not the results of earnings management. Compass Company's cash return on sales ratio is 7.8 per cent (i.e. 72,000/925,000). This is less than 60 per cent of the accrual-based margin ratio (i.e. 43,000/925,000). When combined with the large percentage increase in trade receivables, it is a red flag.

Current liability cover   This is a measure of a firm's ability to meet its current liabilities out of cash flow from operating activities. It is defined as follows:

$$\frac{\text{Net cash generated by operating activities}}{\text{Current liabilities}}$$

A ratio of at least 2:1 indicates comfort, since a firm should be able to pay its current liabilities from regular cash flows. That would mean no disruption of its activities. Compass

Company has an operating cash flow ratio of 0.27:1 (i.e. 72,000/average current liabilities, 270,000). The ratio is too low and the company could default on its current obligations, unless it dips into its financial assets. The operating cash flow further confirms the company's liquidity strain. A variant of this ratio excludes dividends paid.

Capital expenditure cover This is a measure of a firm's ability to pay for its capital expenditure out of cash flow from operating activities. It is defined as follows:

$$\frac{\text{Net cash provided by operating activities}}{\text{Capital expenditure}}$$

The ratio tells us about the adequacy internal cash generation to meet capital expenditure and reinvest in the business. A ratio of 2:1 or above would mean that a firm can finance its expansion without depending on external support. A high ratio would be a matter of comfort to the lenders that the firm can pay back its debt from its current cash flows alongside the on-going expansion. Compass Company has a capital expenditure cover of 0.48:1 (i.e. 72,000/net capex of 151,000). The ratio indicates that the company is unable to finance its on-going expansion entirely from internal cash generation. Timely completion of the expansion depends crucially on its ability to raise additional debt or equity. This means low financial flexibility.

Long-term debt cover This is a measure of a firm's ability to repay its debt out of cash flow from operating activities. The idea is similar to current liability cover. It is defined as follows:

$$\frac{\text{Net cash provided by operating activities}}{\text{Non-current financial liabilities}}$$

It tells us about a firm's ability to pay its debt without having sell assets. Compass Company's long-term debt cover is 0.39:1 (i.e. 72,000/average non-current financial liabilities, 185,000). This suggests that the company generates sufficient cash in relation to its debt. Note that this ratio has been helped by the redemption of debentures.

Cash interest cover This is a measure of a firm's ability to interest out of cash flow from operating activities. The idea is similar to the interest cover. It is defined as follows:

$$\frac{\text{Net cash provided by operating activities}}{\text{Interest paid}}$$

Compass Company's cash interest cover is 3.27 times (72,000/22,000). It comfortably covers the interest payment.

DISCUSSION QUESTION 13.2

Would you expect the cash flows from operating, investing and financing activities to be positive or negative for (a) a growing business, (b) a mature business, and (c) a declining business?

....

....

....

FORENSIC CORNER
"I have cash." "Really?"

Conventional wisdom has it that companies can falsify sales, expenses, profits, inventories, and trade receivables but not cash. That was before Satyam happened. The Satyam scandal involved non-existent cash of ₹53.61 billion. Since cash has to be real, how can anyone fake it? After all, cash can be counted. Bank balance can be confirmed directly with the bank. According to reports, the Satyam fraud involved raising fictitious invoices, showing fictitious collections and forging evidence of bank deposits. In the wake of the Satyam scandal, some companies disclosed the names of their banks and the cash held with them in order to address potential investor concerns.

RECAP

- The *statement of cash flows* complements these statements by providing information on the major sources of cash receipts and cash payments.
- Investors and others can use the statement of cash flows to assess an enterprise's ability to generate future cash flows. Cash flows are classified into *operating*, *investing*, and *financing* categories.
- The *direct method* shows major classes of operating cash receipts and payments, whereas the *indirect method* starts with the net profit and adjusts it for revenue and expense items which did not involve operating cash receipts or cash payments. The presentation of cash flows under the direct method is more straightforward.
- *Investing activities* involve purchases and sales of property, plant and equipment and investments. Interest and dividend received are investing items.
- *Financing activities* involve raising and returning of capital and loans. Interest and dividends paid are financing items.
- The statement of cash flows puts together the cash flows from operating, investing, and financing activities and the beginning and ending cash and cash equivalents.
- Using the statement of cash flows, we can understand a firm's profitability, liquidity and financial flexibility.
- *Cash flow ratios* help us understand liquidity and are a check on the accrual numbers.

Review Problem

Western Telecommunication Company's balance sheet as at March 31, 20X7 and 20X8 and statement of profit and loss for the year ended March 31, 20X8 are as follows:

WESTERN TELECOMMUNICATION COMPANY Balance Sheet, March 31		
	20X8	**20X7**
Assets		
Non-current assets		
Property, plant and equipment	₹720,000	₹540,000
Deduct Accumulated depreciation	362,000	305,000
Property, plant and equipment, net	358,000	235,000
Current assets		
Inventories	151,000	119,000
Financial assets		
Investments	18,000	66,000
Trade receivables (net of allowance for credit losses ₹8,000; ₹12,000)	29,000	166,000
Cash and cash equivalents	12,000	69,000
Other current assets: Prepaid expenses	6,000	2,000
Total assets	574,000	657,000
Equity and Liabilities		
Equity		
Equity share capital	₹155,000	₹85,000
Other equity	102,000	120,000
Liabilities		
Non-current liabilities		
Financial liabilities		
Borrowings	87,000	57,000
Other non-current liabilities	191,000	191,000
Current liabilities		
Financial liabilities		
Trade payables	30,000	187,000
Current tax liabilities	9,000	17,000
Total equity and liabilities	574,000	657,000

WESTERN TELECOMMUNICATION COMPANY Statement of Profit and Loss For the year ended March 31, 20X8	
Sales	₹570,000
Interest income	2,000
Gain on sale of investments	7,000
Total income	579,000
Expenses	
Cost of goods sold	445,000
Depreciation expense	89,000
Selling and administrative expenses	46,000
Finance costs	14,000
Loss on sale of equipment	3,000
Total expenses	597,000
Profit before tax	(18,000)
Tax expense	0
Profit for the period	(18,000)

Additional information:
1. Purchased equipment for cash, ₹150,000.
2. Sold equipment for cash, ₹10,000 (cost, ₹45,000; accumulated depreciation, ₹32,000).
3. Purchased investments for cash, ₹30,000.
4. Sold investments for cash, ₹85,000 (cost, ₹78,000).
5. Purchased equipment in exchange for debentures, ₹75,000.
6. Issued shares for cash, ₹50,000.
7. Converted debentures into equity shares, ₹20,000.
8. Redeemed debentures, ₹25,000.
9. Wrote off ₹14,000 of trade receivables and recognized bad debt expense of ₹10,000, included in selling and administrative expenses.

Required
1. Prepare the statement of cash flows using the direct method.
2. Prepare the statement of cash flows using the indirect method.

Solution to the Review Problem
     1. **Statement of cash flows – Direct method**

WESTERN TELECOMMUNICATION COMPANY Statement of Cash Flows For the year ended March 31, 20X8		
Cash flows from operating activities		
Cash received from customers (i)	₹697,000	
Cash paid to suppliers and employees (ii)	(674,000)	
Cash generated from operations	23,000	
Income tax paid (iii)	(8,000)	
Net cash provided by operating activities		₹15,000
Cash flows from investing activities		
Purchase of property, plant and equipment	(150,000)	
Sale of property, plant and equipment	10,000	
Purchase of investments	(30,000)	
Sale of investments	85,000	
Interest received	2,000	
Net cash used in investing activities		(83,000)
Cash flows from financing activities		
Proceeds from issue of shares	50,000	
Redemption of debentures	(25,000)	
Interest paid	(14,000)	
Net cash provided by financing activities		11,000
Net decrease in cash and cash equivalents		(57,000)
Cash and cash equivalents at beginning of period		69,000
Cash and cash equivalents at end of period		12,000

Schedule of non-cash investing and financing activities
1. The company purchased machinery for ₹75,000 in exchange for debentures.
2. The company converted debentures of ₹20,000 to equity shares of ₹10 at par.

Accounting Policy

For purposes of the statement of cash flows, the company considers all highly liquid debt instruments purchased with a maturity of three months or less from the date of acquisition to be cash equivalents.

Notes:
(i)   (570,000 + 178,000 – 37,000 – 14,000)
(ii) (445,000 + 46,000 – 119,000 – 2,000 + 187,000 + 151,000 + 6,000 – 30,000 – 10,000)
(iii) (17,000 – 9,000)

2. **Statement of cash flows – Indirect method**

WESTERN TELECOMMUNICATION COMPANY		
Statement of Cash Flows		
For the year ended March 31, 20X8		

Cash flows from operating activities		
Net profit before income tax	₹(18,000)	
Adjustments		
Depreciation	89,000	
Bad debt expense	10,000	
Loss on sale of equipment	3,000	
Gain on sale of investments	(7,000)	
Interest expense	14,000	
Interest income	(2,000)	
Operating profit before working capital changes	89,000	
Decrease in trade receivables	127,000	
Increase in inventories	(32,000)	
Increase in prepaid expenses	(4,000)	
Decrease in trade payables	(157,000)	
Cash generated from operations	23,000	
Income tax paid	(8,000)	
Net cash provided by operating activities		₹15,000
Cash flows from investing activities		
Purchase of plant and machinery	(150,000)	
Proceeds from sale of plant and machinery	10,000	
Purchase of investments	(30,000)	
Proceeds from sale of investments	85,000	
Interest received	2,000	
Net cash provided by investing activities		(83,000)
Cash flows from financing activities		
Proceeds from issue of share capital	50,000	
Redemption of debentures	(25,000)	
Interest paid	(14,000)	
Net cash provided by financing activities		11,000
Net decrease in cash and cash equivalents		(57,000)
Cash and cash equivalents at beginning of period		69,000
Cash and cash equivalents at end of period		12,000

Schedule of non-cash investing and financing activities
1. The company purchased machinery for ₹75,000 in exchange for debentures.
2. The company converted debentures of ₹20,000 to equity shares of ₹10 at par.

Accounting Policy

For purposes of the cash flow statement, the company considers all highly liquid debt instruments purchased with a maturity of three months or less from the date of acquisition to be cash equivalents.

ASSIGNMENT MATERIAL

Questions

1. Why do we need the *statement of cash flows* apart from the statement of profit and loss and balance sheet?
2. Why do we consider *cash and cash equivalents* together in the statement of cash flows?
3. What is the purpose of the statement of cash flows?
4. How is the statement of cash flows useful to investors, analysts, suppliers and managers?
5. How are cash flows classified in the statement of cash flows? Give two examples for each category.
6. Why should information about non-cash transactions be disclosed?
7. How does the *direct method* differ from the indirect method?
8. How are the following items treated in computing net cash flow from operating activities: (a) Interest paid; (b) interest received; (c) dividend paid; (d) dividend received; (e) gain on sale of investments; (f) loss on exchange of a plant; and (g) gain on redemption of debentures?
9. How will the net profit be adjusted, if at all, for the following items in the statement of profit and loss to arrive at net cash flow from operating activities: (a) Decrease in bills receivable; (b) increase in inventories; (c) decrease in income tax payable; (d) amortization expense; (e) decrease in prepaid expenses; and (f) bad debt expense?
10. How can a company have a decrease in cash during a period in spite of earning a net profit?
11. From the statement of cash flows, how can we find out whether short-term funds have been used for long-term purposes?

Problems

Problem 13.1
Classification of Activities ✳

Hospet Company entered into the following transactions:
 (a) Deposited cash in the current account.
 (b) Paid bonus to employees.
 (c) Acquired equipment on credit.
 (d) Paid cash on maturity of bills payable for purchases of goods.
 (e) Paid income tax.
 (f) Paid cash to settle a suit for trademark infringement.
 (g) Purchased a 60-day certificate of deposit.
 (h) Issued equity shares on conversion of debentures.
 (i) Acquired a machine on hire purchase.
 (j) Issued equity shares at par.
 (k) Wrote off a receivable when a customer became insolvent.
 (l) Issued equity shares in exchange for preference shares.
 (m) Received cash on the maturity of bills receivable.

Required
Classify each as an operating activity, investing activity, financing activity, non-cash activity, or cash management activity.

Problem 13.2
Computing Cash Receipts and Payments from Revenue and Expenses ✳✳

	20X2	20X1
Unbilled revenue	₹2,100	₹1,800
Interest receivable	570	680
Unearned revenue	1,100	1,600
Prepaid rent	5,900	7,900
Salaries payable	1,200	850
Interest payable	730	810

The statement of profit and loss for 20X2 has the following information:

Fee revenue	₹22,510
Interest income	1,920
Rent expense	13,600
Salaries expense	7,170
Interest expense	1,760

Compute the following for 20X2:

(a) Fees received;
(b) Interest received;
(c) Rent paid;
(d) Salaries paid; and
(e) Interest paid.

Abhijit Company's statement of profit and loss for the year ended December 31, 20X5 is as follows:

Problem 13.3
Computing Net Cash Flow from Operating Activities – Direct Method ✶✶

ABHIJIT COMPANY Statement of Profit and Loss For the year ended December 31, 20X5	
Sales	₹72,900
Cost of goods sold	48,500
Depreciation expense	3,100
Selling and administrative expenses	5,600
Interest expense	2,700
Total expenses	59,900
Profit before tax	13,000
Tax expense	6,700
Profit for the period	6,300

Relevant balance sheet accounts on December 31 are as follows:

	20X5	20X4
Inventories	₹7,400	₹4,500
Trade receivables (net of allowance for credit losses: ₹1,400; ₹300)	8,300	8,900
Prepaid expenses	2,100	2,900
Trade payables	9,800	14,900
Income tax payable	4,800	3,300

Selling and administrative expenses include bad debt expense of ₹1,500. During the year ended December 31, 20X5, trade receivables totalling ₹400 were written off.

Required

Compute net cash flow from operating activities using the direct method.

Dutt Company's statement of profit and loss for the year ended June 30, 20X2 is as follows:

Problem 13.4
Computing Net Cash Flow from Operating Activities – Indirect Method ✶✶

DUTT COMPANY Statement of Profit and Loss For the year ended June 30, 20X2	
Sales	₹75,800
Gain on sale of investments	1,200
Interest income	900
Dividend income	300
Total income	78,200
Expenses	
Cost of goods sold	43,900
Depreciation expense	6,700
Selling and administrative expenses	8,500
Interest expense	1,100
Loss on sale of plant and machinery	800
Total expenses	61,000
Profit before tax	17,200
Tax expense	8,300
Profit for the period	8,900

Relevant balance sheet accounts on June 30 are as follows:

	20X2	20X1
Inventories...	₹9,300	₹7,900
Trade receivables (net of allowance for credit losses: ₹1,600 and ₹800)...........	6,600	5,300
Prepaid expenses...	1,100	800
Trade payables...	12,600	19,300
Income tax payable...	2,100	2,800

Selling and administrative expenses include bad debt expense of ₹1,500. During the year ended June 30, 20X2, trade receivables totalling ₹700 were written off.

Required

Compute net cash flow from operating activities using the indirect method.

Problem 13.5
Computing Net Cash Flow from Investing Activities **

Haveli Company had the following investing activities during the year ended March 31, 20X7:
(a) Purchased investments, ₹6,500.
(b) Sold investments, ₹3,800 (loss, ₹400).
(c) Purchased a plant, ₹15,800.
(d) Constructed a building for own use, ₹7,800 (including capitalized interest, ₹150).
(e) Sold a plant, ₹5,200 (cost, ₹9,500; carrying amount, ₹4,300).

Required

Compute net cash flow from investing activities.

Problem 13.6
Computing Net Cash Flow from Financing Activities **

Supra Corporation had the following financing activities during the year ended November 30, 20X9:
(a) Paid dividends, ₹1,200.
(b) Redeemed debentures, ₹4,700.
(c) Repaid bank overdraft, ₹2,100.
(d) Converted debentures into equity shares, ₹11,000.
(e) Issued convertible debentures, ₹17,000.

Required

Compute net cash flow from financing activities.

Problem 13.7
Preparing the Statement of Cash Flows ***

Given below are Sikandar Company's balance sheet as at March 31, 20X3 and 20X4 and statement of profit and loss for the year ended March 31, 20X4:

SIKANDAR COMPANY Balance Sheet, March 31		
	20X4	**20X3**
Assets		
Non-current assets		
Property, plant and equipment..	₹41,600	₹32,700
Deduct Accumulated depreciation....................................	9,400	7,500
Property, plant and equipment, net	32,200	25,200
Intangible assets: Patents	0	1,300
Current assets		
Inventories..	10,600	4,900
Financial assets		
Investments..	2,800	4,300
Trade receivables (net of allowance for credit losses ₹8,000; ₹12,000)......	20,900	15,600
Cash and cash equivalents...	4,400	7,000
Other current assets: Prepaid expenses...............................	1,200	1,400
Total assets...	72,100	59,700
Equity and Liabilities		
Equity		
Equity share capital	₹25,000	₹17,500

Other equity..	11,800	8,600
Liabilities		
Non-current liabilities		
Financial liabilities		
Borrowings	12,000	12,000
Current liabilities		
Financial liabilities		
Trade payables..	22,700	20,900
Current tax liabilities..	600	700
Total equity and liabilities...	72,100	59,700

SIKANDAR COMPANY
Statement of Profit and Loss
For the year ended March 31, 20X4

Sales...	₹97,300
Interest income..	800
Gain on sale of investments...	400
Total income...	98,500
Cost of goods sold	68,500
Depreciation expense..	7,600
Finance costs...	1,800
Selling and administrative expenses	5,300
Loss on disposal of patents..	900
Total expenses..	84,100
Profit before tax	14,400
Tax expense...	6,700
Profit for the period..	7,700

Additional information:
1. Paid dividends, ₹4,500.
2. Sold investments costing ₹3,800 (gain, ₹400).
3. Disposed of equipment, ₹4,100 (cost, ₹9,800; accumulated depreciation, ₹5,700).
4. Purchased equipment, ₹18,700.
5. Purchased investments, ₹2,300.
6. Disposed of patents, ₹400.
7. Issued at par shares, ₹7,500.

Required
Prepare the statement of cash flows using the direct method.

Sohan Company entered into the following transactions.

Problem 13.8
Classification of Activities
✳✳✳

    (a) Paid suppliers.
    (b) Received dividend from an associate.
    (c) Sold investments at a gain.
    (d) Purchased copyrights for cash.
    (e) Issued debentures in exchange for equipment.
    (f) Paid interest on bank overdraft.
    (g) Converted debentures into equity shares.
    (h) Received payments from customers.
    (i) Purchased investments for cash.
    (j) Purchased a 60-day certificate of deposit for cash.
    (k) Paid advance to a supplier of equipment.
    (l) Sold a 90-day Treasury bill.
    (m) Collected instalment payments for the sale of an old plant.
    (n) Earned a net profit.
    (o) Disposed of equipment at a gain.
    (p) Entered into a finance lease for a new machine.

(q) Sold equipment for cash at carrying amount.
(r) Issued convertible debentures for cash.
(s) Paid festival bonus to employees.
(t) Collected insurance proceeds from a patent infringement suit.
(u) Paid instalments for the purchase of inventories.

Required

1. Classify each as an operating activity, investing activity, financing activity, non-cash activity, or cash management activity.
2. State whether the transaction results in an increase in cash, a decrease in cash, or no effect on cash.

Problem 13.9
Classification of Activities
✱✱✱ Alternative to
Problem 13.8

Manu Company entered into the following transactions.
(a) Collected instalment payments for the sale of inventories.
(b) Paid income tax.
(c) Entered into a hire purchase for a new plant.
(d) Purchased goods for cash.
(e) Issued debentures.
(f) Paid a dividend.
(g) Issued commercial paper with a maturity of 60 days.
(h) Received interest on investment in Treasury bill.
(i) Exchanged equipment for shares.
(j) Made a two-year loan to a subsidiary.
(k) Paid principal amounts of price for instalment purchase of the plant.
(l) Converted non-current loan into equity shares.
(m) Transferred cash to a six-month deposit account.
(n) Disposed of equipment at a loss.
(o) Exchanged a building for a plant.
(p) Repaid bank overdraft.
(q) Retired equipment from use.
(r) Sold goods for cash.
(s) Issued shares at par.
(t) Disposed of patents at a gain.
(u) Made a down payment for the purchase of equipment.

Required

1. Classify each as an operating activity, investing activity, financing activity, non-cash activity, or cash management activity.
2. State whether the transaction results in an increase in cash, a decrease in cash, or no effect on cash.

Problem 13.10
Cash Flows from Operating
Activities ✱✱✱

Gopal Dairy Company's statement of profit and loss for the year ended September 30, 20X7 is as follows:

GOPAL DAIRY COMPANY Statement of Profit and Loss For the year ended September 30, 20X7	
Sales..	₹27,100
Interest income...	400
Gain on sale of investments...	100
Total income..	27,600
Expenses	
Cost of goods sold..	18,600
Depreciation expense..	4,800
Finance costs...	600
Selling and administrative expenses	1,900
Loss on sale of equipment..	200
Total expenses...	26,100
Profit before tax	1,500
Tax expenses...	800
Profit for the period..	700

During the period, inventories decreased by ₹900, trade receivables (gross) increased by ₹1,200, trade payables decreased by ₹700, and income tax payable increased by ₹300. Selling and administrative expenses include bad debt expense of ₹400. Trade receivables in the amount of ₹200 were written off during the period.

Required

1. Present the cash flows from operating activities using the direct method.
2. Present the cash flows from operating activities using the indirect method.

The statement of profit and loss of Shamsher Leather Company for the year ended March 31, 20X8 is as follows:

Problem 13.11
Cash Flows from Operating Activities ✱✱✱ Alternative to Problem 13.10

SHAMSHER LEATHER COMPANY Statement of Profit and Loss For the year ended March 31, 20X8	
Sales	₹76,900
Dividend income	300
Interest income	200
Gain on disposal of plant	800
Total income	78,200
Cost of goods sold	58,300
Depreciation expense	9,500
Finance costs	900
Selling and administrative expenses	2,700
Loss on sale of investments	300
Total expenses	71,700
Profit before tax	6,500
Tax expense	2,800
Profit for the period	3,700

During the period, inventories increased by ₹1,500, trade receivables (gross) decreased by ₹2,300, trade payables decreased by ₹1,600, and income tax payable decreased by ₹500. Selling and administrative expenses include bad debt expense of ₹700. Trade receivables in the amount of ₹300 were written off during the period.

Required

1. Present the cash flows from operating activities using the direct method.
2. Present the cash flows from operating activities using the indirect method.

Pioma Plastics Company's balance sheet as at April 30, 20X3 and 20X2 and statement of profit and loss for the year ended April 30, 20X3 are as follows:

Problem 13.12
Preparing and Interpreting the Statement of Cash Flows ✱✱✱✱

PIOMA PLASTICS COMPANY Balance Sheet, April 30		
	20X3	**20X2**
Assets		
Non-current assets		
Property, plant and equipment, at cost	₹59,800	₹60,500
Deduct Accumulated depreciation	19,000	16,300
Property, plant and equipment, net	40,800	44,200
Non-current investments	13,900	13,900
Current assets		
Inventories	16,500	9,300
Financial assets		
Investments	2,800	4,300
Trade receivables (net of allowance for credit losses ₹1,700; ₹1,100)	19,900	10,700
Cash and cash equivalents	8,300	13,300
Other current assets: Prepaid expenses	800	1,100
Total assets	100,200	92,500

Equity and Liabilities		
Equity		
Equity share capital	₹23,000	₹14,000
Other equity	12,800	7,500
Liabilities		
Non-current liabilities		
Financial liabilities		
Borrowings	59,100	45,900
Current liabilities		
Financial liabilities		
Trade payables	3,000	21,000
Current tax liabilities	2,300	4,100
Total equity and liabilities	100,200	92,500

PIOMA PLASTICS COMPANY
Statement of Profit and Loss
For the year ended April 30, 20X3

Sales	₹75,800
Dividend income	2,000
Interest income	5,400
Gain on sale of land	6,300
Total income	89,500
Expenses	
Cost of goods sold	53,700
Interest expense	5,700
Selling and administrative expenses	12,300
Loss on sale of plant	3,800
Total expenses	75,500
Profit before tax	14,000
Tax expense	2,200
Profit for the period	11,800

Additional information:

1. Property, plant and equipment include land, ₹4,000 in 20X3 and ₹11,000 in 20X2. The land is not depreciated.
2. Purchased machinery for cash, ₹5,300.
3. Sold a plant, ₹1,900 (cost, ₹6,800; accumulated depreciation, ₹1,100).
4. Purchased machinery in exchange for debentures, ₹7,800.
5. Paid dividends, ₹6,500.
6. Sold land, ₹13,300 (cost, ₹7,000).
7. Issued debentures, ₹5,400.
8. Issued at par equity shares, ₹9,000.
9. Wrote off ₹1,400 of trade receivables and recognized bad debt expense of ₹2,000, included in selling and administrative expenses.
10. Cost of goods sold includes depreciation of ₹3,800.

Required

1. Prepare the statement of cash flows using the direct method.
2. Present the statement of cash flows using the indirect method.
3. Explain why there was a decrease in cash in spite of Pioma Plastics Company earning a net profit of ₹11,800.

Problem 13.13
Preparing and Interpreting the Statement of Cash Flows ∗∗∗∗ Alternative to Problem 13.12

Vinay Electronics Company's balance sheet on July 31, 20X7 and 20X6 and statement of profit and loss for the year ended July 31, 20X7 are as follows:

VINAY ELECTRONICS COMPANY
Balance Sheet, July 31

	20X7	20X6
Assets		
Non-current assets		
Property, plant and equipment, at cost	₹59,900	₹39,700
Deduct Accumulated depreciation..	13,000	10,900
Property, plant and equipment, net	46,900	28,800
Intangible assets: Patents	0	2,900
Current assets		
Inventories...	7,900	13,700
Financial assets		
Investments..	5,700	9,300
Trade receivables (net of allowance for credit losses ₹2,400; ₹1,800)........	13,000	8,600
Cash and cash equivalents	16,100	3,300
Other current assets: Prepaid expenses	1,900	1,600
Total assets...	91,500	68,200
Equity and Liabilities		
Equity		
Equity share capital	₹23,000	₹21,000
Other equity..	2,700	7,500
Liabilities		
Non-current liabilities		
Financial liabilities		
Borrowings	37,200	15,000
Bills payable	6,300	0
Other non-current liabilities	16,300	10,000
Current liabilities		
Financial liabilities		
Trade payables...	11,800	12,700
Current tax liabilities...	500	2,000
Total equity and liabilities..	91,500	68,200

VINAY ELECTRONICS COMPANY
Statement of Profit and Loss
For the year ended July 31, 20X7

Sales...	₹43,900
Dividend income	1,200
Interest income..	1,400
Gain on sale of investments..	1,900
Total income...	48,400
Expenses	
Cost of goods sold	38,400
Finance costs...	6,400
Selling and administrative expenses	7,500
Loss on sale of patent	2,600
Total income...	54,900
Profit before tax..	(6,500)
Tax expense...	0
Profit for the period..	(6,500)

Additional information:

1. Purchased machinery for cash, ₹13,900.
2. Purchased machinery on long-term credit, ₹6,300.

3. Redeemed debentures, ₹2,400.
4. Repaid long-term loans, ₹1,400.
5. Sold patents for cash, ₹300.
6. Sold investments, ₹6,800 (cost, ₹4,900).
7. Issued debentures, ₹26,000.
8. Purchased investments, ₹1,300.
9. Issued at par equity shares, ₹2,000.
10. Wrote off ₹1,600 of trade receivables and recognized bad debt expense of ₹2,200, included in selling and administrative expenses.
11. Cost of goods sold includes depreciation of ₹2,100.

Required

1. Prepare the statement of cash flows using the direct method.
2. Present the statement of cash flows using the indirect method.
3. Explain why there was an increase in cash in spite of Vinay Electronics Company incurring a net loss of ₹6,500.

Problem 13.14
Preparing and Interpreting the Statement of Cash Flows ✶✶✶✶✶

Arun Music Company's its balance sheet as at October 31, 20X5 and 20X4 statement of profit and loss for the year ended October 31, 20X5 are as follows:

ARUN MUSIC COMPANY Balance Sheet, October 31		
	20X5	**20X4**
Assets		
Non-current assets		
Property, plant and equipment, at cost	₹89,500	₹68,600
Deduct Accumulated depreciation	41,900	37,600
Property, plant and equipment, net	47,600	31,000
Non-current investments	5,500	14,600
Current assets		
Inventories	21,300	16,400
Financial assets		
Trade receivables (net of allowance for credit losses ₹2,900; ₹1,800)	9,800	4,300
Cash and cash equivalents	1,200	3,800
Other current assets: Prepaid expenses	2,400	1,500
Total assets	87,800	71,600
Equity and Liabilities		
Equity		
Equity share capital	₹49,000	₹41,000
Other equity	12,600	9,700
Liabilities		
Non-current liabilities		
Financial liabilities		
Borrowings	9,500	14,200
Bills payable	5,500	0
Current liabilities		
Financial liabilities		
Trade payables	10,300	4,800
Current tax liabilities	900	1,900
Total equity and liabilities	87,800	71,600

ARUN MUSIC COMPANY
Statement of Profit and Loss
For the year ended October 31, 20X5

Sales	₹92,700
Dividend income	1,800
Interest income	1,200
Gain on sale of plant	2,300
Total income	98,000
Expenses	
Cost of goods sold	75,100
Finance costs	2,200
Selling and administrative expenses	14,500
Loss on sale of investments	1,400
Total expenses	93,200
Profit before tax	4,800
Tax expense	1,900
Profit for the period	2,900

Additional information:

1. Property, plant and equipment include land, ₹7,500 in 20X5 and 20X4. Land is not depreciated.
2. Purchased machinery for cash, ₹19,900.
3. Sold a plant, ₹5,000 (cost, ₹4,500; accumulated depreciation, ₹1,800).
4. Purchased machinery on long-term credit, ₹5,500.
5. Purchased investments, ₹1,900.
6. Sold investments, ₹9,600 (cost, ₹11,000).
7. Redeemed debentures, ₹4,700.
8. Issued at par equity shares, ₹8,000.
9. Wrote off ₹2,100 of trade receivables and recognized bad debt expense of ₹3,200, included in selling and administrative expenses.
10. Cost of goods sold includes depreciation of ₹6,100.

Required

1. Prepare the statement of cash flows using the direct method.
2. Present the statement of cash flows using the indirect method.
3. Explain why there was a decrease in cash in spite of Arun Music Company earning a net profit of ₹2,900.

Cochin Marine Foods Company's balance sheet as at November 30, 20X7 and 20X6 and statement of profit and loss for the year ended November 30, 20X7 are as follows:

Problem 13.15
Preparing and Interpreting the Statement of Cash Flows ✶✶✶✶✶
Alternative to Problem 13.14

COCHIN MARINE FOODS COMPANY
Balance Sheet, November 30

	20X7	20X6
Assets		
Non-current assets		
Property, plant and equipment, at cost	₹60,700	₹60,900
Deduct Accumulated depreciation	20,300	17,900
Property, plant and equipment, net	40,400	43,000
Non-current investments	1,800	6,900
Current assets		
Inventories	7,600	7,100
Financial assets		
Trade receivables (net of allowance for credit losses ₹0; ₹0)	9,300	6,500
Cash and cash equivalents	14,700	6,900
Other current assets: Prepaid expenses	500	1,200
Total assets	74,300	71,600

Equity and Liabilities

Equity

Equity share capital	₹21,500	₹19,500
Other equity	1,900	17,500

Liabilities

Non-current liabilities

Financial liabilities

Borrowings	39,000	25,200

Current liabilities

Financial liabilities

Trade payables	11,800	8,600
Current tax liabilities	100	800
Total equity and liabilities	74,300	71,600

COCHIN MARINE FOODS COMPANY
Statement of Profit and Loss
For the year ended November 30, 20X7

Sales	₹85,800
Gain on sale of investments	300
Dividend income	900
Interest income	100
Total income	87,100
Expenses	
Cost of goods sold	86,100
Selling and administrative expenses	11,200
Interest expense	4,300
Loss on sale of plant	1,100
Total expenses	102,700
Profit before tax	(15,600)
Tax expense	0
Profit for the period	(15,600)

Additional information:

1. Purchased machinery for cash, ₹3,300.
2. Sold a plant, ₹300 (cost, ₹3,500; accumulated depreciation, ₹2,100).
3. Issued loans, ₹9,000.
4. Issued equity shares at par, ₹2,000.
5. Sold investments, ₹5,400 (cost, ₹5,100).
6. Issued debentures, ₹5,200.
7. Redeemed debentures, ₹400.
8. Cost of goods sold includes depreciation, ₹4,500.

Required

1. Prepare the statement of cash flows using the direct method.
2. Present the statement of cash flows using the indirect method.
3. Explain why there was an increase in cash in spite of the Cochin Marine Foods Company incurring a net loss of ₹15,600.

Business Decision Cases

BDC 13.1
Reliance Stationary Company

On April 1, 20X3, Uday Ahuja started a store for selling high-quality stationery. His accountant has prepared the statement of cash flows for the first year, as shown in the following table:

RELIANCE STATIONERY COMPANY
Statement of Cash Flows
For the year ended November 30, 20X3

Cash receipts

Sale of inventories	₹28,960
Sale of investments	6,400
Sale of share of capital	35,200
Depreciation	5,600
Long-term credit for the purchase of van	2,400
Interest on investments	640
Total receipts	79,200

Cash payments

Purchase of fixtures and office equipment	₹27,200
Purchase of inventories	20,240
Operating expenses	12,800
Purchase of investments	6,800
Purchase on long-term credit	2,400
Repayment of loans	800
Interest on bill payable	240
Total payments	79,200
Net increase in cash	8720

Uday thinks that he has had a successful year with cash increasing by ₹8,720. You notice that the statement of cash flows is incorrectly prepared.

Required

1. Prepare a proper statement of cash flows using the direct method.
2. Prepare an evaluation of the Reliance Stationery Company's first year of working. Do you agree with Uday's assessment about the company?

Raghavendra Rao set up the Antariksh Materials Company in 20X3. The company supplies specialized materials to the Indian Space Research Organisation (ISRO) for use in the latter's space programme. Rao is considering proposals for investment totalling ₹100 million during 20X9. He hopes to meet the financing need by a combination of internal cash generation and bank loans. The balance sheet as at June 30, 20X8 and 20X7 and the statement of profit and loss for the year ended June 30, 20X8, are as follows:

BDC 13.2
Antariksh Materials
Company

ANTARIKSH MATERIALS COMPANY
Balance Sheet, June 30

	20X8	20X7
	(in thousands)	
Assets		
Non-current assets		
Property, plant and equipment, cost	₹191,000	₹174,000
Deduct Accumulated depreciation	44,300	36,000
	146,700	138,000
Intangible assets: Patents, net	8,000	9,000
Non-current investments	10,000	10,000
Current assets		
Inventories	153,000	85,000
Financial assets		
Trade receivables	95,425	54,000
Cash and cash equivalents	7,000	29,000
Other current assets: Prepaid expenses	1,100	8,000
Total assets	421,225	333,000

Equity and Liabilities

Equity

Equity share capital	₹125,100	₹103,100
Other equity	140,125	113,900

Liabilities

Non-current liabilities

Long-term borrowings	140,000	93,000

Current liabilities

Financial assets

Trade payables	12,000	18,000
Current tax liabilities	4,000	5,000
Total equity and liabilities	421,225	333,000

ANTARIKSH MATERIALS COMPANY
Statement of Profit and Loss
For the year ended June 30, 20X8

Sales	₹290,000
Gain on sale of plant	800
	290,800
Cost of goods sold	167,800
Selling and administrative expenses	20,500
Finance costs	2,000
Amortization of patents	1,000
	291,300
Profit before tax	99,500
Tax expense	42,000
Profit for the period	57,500

Additional information:

1. During the period, loans of ₹2,000,000 were repaid.
2. Cost of goods sold included depreciation of ₹9,000,000.
3. Plant costing ₹2,000,000 and having an accumulated depreciation of ₹700,000 was sold for ₹2,100,000.
4. Equity shares of ₹3,000,000 were issued at par for cash during the period.
5. Dividends of ₹31,275,000 were paid.
6. Debentures of ₹49,000,000 were issued for cash.
7. Plant costing ₹19,000,000 was acquired in exchange for equity shares.
8. Investments are in the form of equity shares in an associate.

Required

1. Prepare a statement of cash flows for the Antariksh Materials Company for the year ended June 30, 20X8.
2. How much cash did the company generate internally during the year ended June 30, 20X8?
3. Antariksh Materials Company approaches your bank for a loan of ₹60 million. As a lending officer in the bank, will you recommend the loan?

Interpreting Financial Reports

IFR 13.1
Suzlon Energy Limited

Suzlon Energy is a leading renewable energy business with international operations and markets. The global recession affected the company's performance adversely. In the year ended March 31, 2015, the company reported a net loss of ₹91.58 billion and cash generated from operations of ₹11.19 billion. The situation reversed in fiscal year 2016 with a net profit of ₹4.83 billion and cash used in operations of ₹8.05 billion. The consolidated statement of cash flows, suitably modified for this case, for the two years appears below.

SUZLON ENERGY LIMITED Statement of Cash Flows For the year ended March 31		
	2016	**2015** *in millions*
Cash flows from operating activities		
Loss before tax and exceptional items..	₹(5,952.6)	₹(25,044.2)
Adjustments for:		
Depreciation/amortization...	4,032.6	8,087.7
Loss on assets sold/discarded..	16.4	75.1
Loss on sale of investments, net		4.4
Interest income..	(290.9)	(398.2)
Interest expense	9,965.9	17,462.5
Profit on sale of mutual funds	(364.5)	0
Dividend income	0	(134.8)
Compensation in lieu of bank sacrifice	228.3	520.2
Amortization of ancillary borrowing costs	963.6	1,143.6
Operation, maintenance and warranty expenditure	731.1	1,590.9
Liquidated damages expenditure..	766.4	1,725.1
Performance guarantee expenditure...	1,580.5	1,463.8
Bad debts written off..	251.0	14.0
Provision for doubtful debts and advances...	74.6	1,637.9
Provision for diminution of investment	9.5	0
Adjustments for consolidation...	(362.4)	(6,554.6)
Exchange differences, net..	2,140.3	1,244.0
Employee stock option scheme	38.0	77.6
Operating profit before working capital changes...............................	13,827.8	2,915.0
Movements in working capital		
(Increase) decrease in trade receivables and unbilled revenue..................	(12,483.5)	15,750.2
Decrease (increase) in inventories..	(8,688.0)	6,721.3
Decrease (increase) in loans and advances and other assets	(824.6)	1,920.7
Decrease in trade payables, current liabilities and provisions	(120.1)	(14,022.0)
Cash generated from operating activities...	(8,288.4)	13,285.2
Direct taxes paid..	238.2	(2,093.2)
Net cash (used in) generated from operating activities (A)	(8,050.2)	11,192.0
Cash flows from investing activities		
Payment for purchase of property, plant and equipment	(3,969.6)	(7,363.3)
Investments in subsidiaries	(1,001.8)	0
Proceeds from sale of property, plant and equipment.............................	315.4	465.2
Proceeds from sale of stake in subsidiary	69398.0	0
Purchase of current investments	(47,742.2)	(2,500.0)
Proceeds from sale/maturity of current investments.............................	47,968.1	384.7
Inter-corporate deposits repaid (granted)..	(1.6)	720.8
Interest received..	249.3	397.6
Dividend received	0	21.0
Net cash (used in) generated from investing activities (B)...................	65,215.6	(7,874.0)
Cash flows from financing activities		
Proceeds from issuance of share capital including premium	18,000.0	81.8
Share issue expenses...	(173.7)	0
Proceeds from long-term borrowings	1,116.1	66.2
Repayment of long-term borrowings	(36,156.1)	(3,082.6)
Proceeds from (repayment of) short term borrowings, net	(26,660.9)	11,051.7
Dividend paid	(1.0)	(0.6)
Interest paid...	(11,756.7)	(10,104.9)
Net cash (used in) generated from financing activities (C).................	(55,632.3)	(1,988.4)
Net decrease in cash and cash equivalents (A + B + C)	1,533.1	1,329.6
Deduct Cash and bank balances adjusted on stake sale of subsidiary.....	(20,669.0)	
Add (deduct) Effect of exchange difference on cash and cash equivalents	0	(380.9)
Total	(19,135.9)	948.7
Cash and cash equivalents at beginning of period...................................	25,428.8	24,480.1
Cash and cash equivalents at end of period...................................	6,292.9	25,428.8

Required

In 2015, Suzlon Energy was making losses but reported net cash inflow from operations. In 2016, the company became profitable but reported a cash drain. Do you think the company has turned the corner?

Financial Analysis

FA 13.1
Which Measure is Better: Earnings or Cash Flow?

Plot the following for a sample of companies: stock returns on the *Y*-axis; and earnings (net profit) and cash flow on the *X*-axis. In order to improve the quality of your research, you should select companies from many industries and do this study over many years.

Required

1. Prepare a report explaining the results of your study.
2. Bring out the limitations of this research.

Answers to One-minute Quiz

13.1 d.
13.2 b.
13.3 c.
13.4 b.

Answers to Test Your Understanding

13.1 Operating: (j), (k). Investing: (c), (d), (g), (i). Financing: (b), (f), (h), (m). Non-cash: (e), (l). Cash management: (a).

13.2

(a) Cash received from customers (1)	₹474,000
(b) Cash paid to suppliers and employees (2)	(271,000)
(c) Income tax paid (3)	(56,000)
Net cash provided by operating activities	147,000

(1) 25,000 + 436,000 + 78,000 − 49,000 − 16,000
(2) 269,000 + 61,000 − 43,000 − 7,000 + 62,000 + 51,000 + 3,000 − 67,000 − 39,000 − 19,000
(3) 53,000 + 14,000 − 11,000

13.3

Profit before income tax	₹432,000
Adjustments	
Depreciation expense	49,000
Gain on sale of investments	(8,000)
Operating profit before working capital changes	473,000
Decrease in inventories	13,000
Increase in trade receivables	(33,000)
Increase in prepaid expenses	(11,000)
Increase in trade payables	4,000
Cash generated from operations	446,000
Income tax paid	(98,000)
Net cash provided by operating activities	348,000

13.4 The sale proceeds of ₹29,000 will appear as a cash inflow in the investing activities section of the statement of cash flows.

13.5 All three transactions will appear in the schedule of non-cash activities.

Financial Statements of Banks

LEARNING OBJECTIVES

After studying this chapter, you should be able to:

1. Explain the importance of banks.
2. Explain why banks are regulated more than other businesses.
3. Understand the legal framework for the financial statements of banks.
4. Explain the items on a bank's balance sheet.
5. Explain the items on a bank's statement of profit and loss.
6. Explain the drivers of a bank's financial performance.
7. Understand a bank's need for long-term capital.
8. Explain Basel III capital and liquidity regulations.
9. Explain the importance of off-balance activities for understanding the financial condition of banks.

REVERSING THE DECLINE

In January 2017, State Bank of India (SBI), India's largest bank, was reported to be working on a '2 by 20' plan: return on assets (ROA) of 2 per cent and return on equity (ROE) of 20 per cent. By implication, the bank would have a leverage of 10 times. This would be inconceivable for a non-financial firm. But banks are different. They are like inverted pyramids with a lot of debt at the top precariously balanced on a small base of capital. They are in the business of borrowing to lend. The more they can borrow, the more they can lend. But debt is inherently risky. For example, what if many depositors want their money back at the same time? Improbable, still not impossible. So banks should be prepared for such contingencies. Equity acts as the backstop when things don't go according to plan. SBI seems to think that it can increase its equity by becoming more profitable. So how good are the chances of the bank hitting its ROA and ROE targets? Recent numbers are not encouraging. In the September 2016 quarter, ROA was 0.44 per cent falling from 0.73 in the year-ago quarter. Over that period, ROE fell from 12.61 per cent to 7.68 per cent. In comparison, HDFC Bank – the best in class – clocked ROE of 17.97 per cent. So SBI's plan would seem too ambitious. Also, SBI is sitting on mountains of bad loans. Therefore, the bank has little option but to raise equity in order to have adequate capital to support its growth aspirations. Who said running a bank is easy?

SPEED READ

Banks bring together savers and borrowers. Protecting depositors is the main aim of strict government regulation of banks. Disclosure of relevant information and restrictions on risky activities improve the stability of banks. The Banking Regulation Act prescribes the form and content of the financial statements of banks. Debt jacks up the return on equity, but excessive dependence on debt is dangerous. Bank profitability depends on earning a higher return on its loans and investments than the interest cost and keeping tight control on bad debts and administrative costs. Banks need long-term capital in order to maintain liquidity and solvency. The Basel Accords lay down minimum capital standards for banks. Off-balance sheet activities, such as issuing guarantees and letters of credit and trading in derivatives and foreign exchange, increase profitability, but carry significant risks.

Understanding Banks

Banks receive deposits from the public and give loans for business and other purposes. They seek to channel savings into activities that benefit individuals, businesses, and governments. In a world without banks, savers can invest only in unproductive assets, such as gold and real estate. The main function of banks is to intermediate between savers and borrowers. Banks help in the smooth and cost-effective movement of resources to those who can utilize them profitably. By directing savings to those who can use them profitably, they encourage firms to become efficient and contribute to making the economy productive and competitive. Strong banks are a sign of a healthy economy, while struggling banks are a symptom of a faltering economy.

Banks specialize in different kinds of business. The following are some common types of banks:

- **Commercial banks** We are all familiar with commercial banks. You are sure to have a bank account and may have probably taken a loan. Commercial banks take deposits and give loans. They also provide other services such as transferring money and collecting phone bills.

  Examples: State Bank of India, Bank of Baroda, ICICI Bank, HDFC Bank.

- **Investment banks** Investment banks help business organizations raise capital from the financial markets. They facilitate issuing shares and bonds and advise on mergers and acquisitions. They design and trade in financial instruments. Investment banks do not have retail customers.

  Examples: Goldman Sachs, JPMorgan Chase, Credit Suisse, UBS.

- **Central banks** Central banks manage the financial system and regulate banks. They deal with governments and other banks, but do not have transactions with individuals and business organizations. They manage the money supply, set benchmark interest rates, buy and sell government securities, intervene in foreign exchange markets, lay down broad norms for lending, and supervise the working of banks and other financial entities.

  Examples: Reserve Bank of India, The Federal Reserve, Bank of England.

Many banks provide a range of services through separate business units or subsidiaries. For example, SBI provides investment banking services through its subsidiary, SBI Capital Markets. Banks are sometimes grouped into categories, such as the State Bank of India, nationalized banks (e.g. Bank of Baroda, Punjab National Bank), old private banks (e.g. the Federal Bank, City Union Bank), new private banks (e.g. ICICI Bank, HDFC Bank) and foreign banks (e.g. Standard Chartered Bank, BNP, HSBC). Besides, there are other classifications such as co-operative banks and regional rural banks. In this chapter, we look at commercial banks, though the discussion is also relevant to most other types of banks.

Bank Regulation

Learning Objective

LO 2 Explain why banks are regulated more than other businesses.

Banks are the backbone of the entire financial system. The objectives of bank regulation are to protect depositors, prevent serial bank failures, and ensure economic stability.

Protecting depositors Banks take deposits from the public and lend to individuals and businesses. Depositors are spread far and wide and many of them don't know much about banking. Banks should be careful about to whom, and how much, to lend and the associated risks. They need to be prevented from taking unreasonable risks that could lead to their failure causing loss to their depositors. Therefore, protecting depositors is an important objective of bank regulation.

Preventing serial bank failures   If there is an actual or anticipated bank failure, many depositors will try to withdraw their money all at once (known as a 'run on the bank'). Since a bank would have lent its funds for various periods, it will not have enough cash to pay the depositors immediately, and it will collapse. But unlike the collapse of most non-banking enterprises, bank failures have a systemic effect in that the failure of one bank will lead to a run on other banks. Like dominoes, they will fall one after another.

Ensuring economic stability   Terrified by the unexpected demand for cash from depositors, banks may suddenly stop lending, sell their assets or call back their loans. Since banks' clients are dependent on credit and can't pay back at short notice, they will fail. Thus, a bank failure will have a ripple effect on the whole economy and could even spread to other countries. Bank failures may also lead to social and political instability. The 1997 Asian financial crisis and the 2008 financial crisis are recent examples of bank failures setting off worldwide economic collapse.

In order to avoid such catastrophes, governments have extensive regulations for banks covering every area of their operations with the intention of maintaining public confidence in the financial system. For example, banks need a licence to do business, must keep a certain minimum percentage of their deposits in the form of cash, must have a minimum percentage of their capital from equity, have maximum limits on how much deposits they can accept, must avoid concentrated exposure to a few individuals, businesses or industries, have to hedge their foreign currency borrowings quickly, must file documents periodically with the regulator, and must provide detailed disclosures of their financial condition.

The on-going global economic crisis stemmed from a banking crisis in the mid-2000s. A number of well-known banks collapsed, went on a fire sale of their assets, or came under government ownership and control. These include Bear Stearns, Citigroup, Countrywide Financial, Fannie Mae, Freddie Mac, Lehman Brothers, Merrill Lynch, Northern Rock, Royal Bank of Scotland, Washington Mutual, and Wachovia. These banks' financial problems arose from subprime lending and excessive leverage.

HANDHOLD 14.1
The Subprime Crisis

A subprime borrower is one banks consider not highly creditworthy and is, therefore, charged a higher interest rate. The subprime crisis began in the US in 2007 and later spread to many other countries. Low interest rates in the US in the 1990s and 2000s encouraged many individuals to take home mortgage loans. The acronym NINJA described many of these borrowers: *no income, no job, and no assets*. House prices kept appreciating during those years leading to a huge speculative bubble. Low interest rates also induced banks to borrow heavily resulting in unprecedented leverage ratios. Lehman Brothers reported a net leverage of 16.1 in Q4 2007 and it would have been 17.8 without Repo 105 (See IFR 10.1 Lehman Brothers). The bubble came to an end in 2006 – 2007 when house prices began to fall. Many subprime customers started defaulting on their mortgages. Banks that had lent to these customers tried to recover their loans by foreclosing the mortgaged houses. Their attempts to sell the houses increased supply in a market that was already in a housing glut. This led to a downward spiral in house prices. Many international banks lost billions of dollars and two major banks, Bear Sterns and Lehman Brothers, collapsed. Some banks were taken over by others. The subprime crisis rapidly became a banking crisis and then it spread to other financial institutions such as insurance companies. Eventually, it became an economic crisis and threatened nations. Iceland and Ireland were among the countries that were hit hard. The fiscal stability of many countries in Europe, such as Portugal, Greece, Italy, and Spain, came under strain. The world is yet to recover from the aftermath of the subprime crisis.

Laws that Affect Banks

The principal law that regulates the working of banks in India is the Banking Regulation Act 1949. Section 5 (b) of the Act defines *banking* as "the accepting, for the purpose of lending or investment, of deposits of money from the public, repayable on demand or otherwise, and withdrawable by cheque, draft, order or otherwise". Section 5 (c) defines a *banking company* as "any company which transacts the business of banking in India". A *scheduled bank* is a bank included in the Second Schedule to the RBI Act. Scheduled banks can purchase, sell and discount certain bills of exchange and promissory notes, purchase and sell foreign exchange, and take loans from the RBI. In return for these privileges, scheduled banks are subject to more stringent regulation than other banks.

Besides the Banking Regulation Act, banks must comply with specific laws relating to them. For example, the State Bank of India is governed by the State Bank of India Act 1955. Nationalized banks are governed by the Banking Companies (Acquisition and Transfer of Undertakings) Act 1970. Besides, banks must comply with other applicable laws including the Companies Act 2013, Negotiable Instruments Act 1881, Information Technology Act 2000, Prevention of Money Laundering Act 2002, Securitisation and Reconstruction of Financial Assets and Enforcement of Security Interest Act 2002, Credit Information Companies Regulation Act 2005, Payment and Settlement Systems Act 2007, and the Reserve Bank of India 1934.

Legal Framework for Financial Statements

Learning Objective

LO 3 Understand the legal framework for the financial statements of banks.

The Banking Regulation Act lays down the requirements for a bank's financial statements. Section 29 (1) of the Act requires every bank to prepare a balance sheet and a statement of profit and loss in the forms set out in the Third Schedule to the Act. Form A of the Third Schedule contains the form of the balance sheet and Form B contains the form of the statement of profit and loss. The fiscal year end for banks in India is March 31. A foreign bank (i.e. a bank incorporated outside India) has to prepare a balance sheet and a statement of profit and loss in respect of its business transacted through its branches in India.

The financial statements must also comply with the requirements of Schedule III to the Companies Act 2013 (previously Schedule VI to the Companies Act 1956), to the extent they are not inconsistent with the requirements of the Banking Regulation Act. The RBI has issued instructions for the compilation of balance sheet and statement of profit and loss providing an authoritative interpretation of the requirements of the Third Schedule. In addition, the financial statements must follow the government's accounting standards issued under the Companies Act, SEBI's listing regulations, and the ICAI's guidelines. We will now see the items in a bank's balance sheet and statement of profit and loss, starting with the balance sheet.

Balance Sheet

Learning Objective

LO 4 Explain the items on a bank's balance sheet.

Many assets, liability, and equity items that appear on the balance sheet of a bank are similar to the ones on the balance sheet of non-financial enterprises. However, there are important differences:

Composition of assets Property, plant and equipment, and inventories constitute a significant proportion of the assets of non-financial enterprises. Since banks are service organizations, they do not carry any inventories, and their office buildings, furniture, and computing equipment are relatively a trivial part of their total assets. Financial assets in the form of loans, investments, and cash are their main assets.

Sources of finance For most non-financial enterprises, equity would be a major source of finance and debt is at best a small multiple of equity. In contrast, banks depend heavily on deposits from customers and borrowings from other financial institutions for carrying on their operations.

The balance sheet of a bank has two sections: (a) capital and liabilities and (b) assets. We will now see the balance sheet classifications and selected individual items.

Capital and Liabilities

Capital and liabilities are presented in the following five groups:

1. Capital;
2. Reserves and surplus;

3. Deposits;
4. Borrowings; and
5. Other liabilities and provisions.

Capital

Share capital details include authorized, issued, subscribed, and paid-up number of shares and per share amount. Calls unpaid and forfeited shares are shown separately. The disclosure requirements are similar to those described in Chapter 11.

Reserves and Surplus

Chapter 11 explains the various types of reserves. Banks present the following items:

- Statutory reserves;
- Capital reserves;
- Share premium;
- Revenue and other reserves; and
- Balance in profit and loss account.

Statutory reserves   Section 17 (1) of the Banking Regulation Act 1949 requires every bank incorporated in India to transfer 20 per cent of its profits to the reserve fund each year before declaring dividends. All scheduled commercial banks have to transfer not less than 25 per cent of the net profit to the reserve fund. Since transfer to statutory reserves is an appropriation, it does not affect the calculation of net profit.

Capital reserves   Capital reserves do not include any amount that is free for distribution to the shareholders. For instance, the surplus on revaluation or sale of fixed assets is a capital reserve.

Share premium   Share premium (or securities premium) can't be distributed. A bank has to report to the RBI any appropriations from the share premium account. Appropriations can be made only for the purposes specified in the Companies Act or in accordance the provisions governing reduction of share capital of that Act.

Revenue and other reserves   Revenue reserves are reserves other than capital reserves. Reserves other than statutory reserves, capital reserves, and share premium appear under this classification. Examples include general reserve and investment reserve.

Balance in profit and loss account   This is the balance of profit for the period after appropriations and dividends. In other words, it is the retained earnings.

Deposits

Deposits are the most important source of funds for commercial banks. Banks collect small amounts of deposits from a large number of customers. Deposits are classified as follows:

- Demand deposits;
- Savings bank deposits; and
- Term deposits.

Demand deposits   Demand deposits are repayable on demand and the depositor is not required to give prior notice of his intention to withdraw the deposit. Current accounts are the most common form of demand deposits. There is no restriction on the number of transactions (deposits or withdrawals) in current accounts. Banks do not pay any interest on these accounts. Business organizations keep current accounts because they often need to deposit and withdraw amounts frequently and at short notice.

Savings bank deposits   All of us have savings accounts with banks. Savings accounts are kept by individuals. The depositor is required to give prior notice of his intention to withdraw an amount of deposit above a specified limit. Also, banks have restrictions on the number of withdrawals in savings accounts and can impose service charges, if the depositor exceeds the number. The primary purpose of these accounts is to encourage savings. Banks pay interest on savings accounts.

Term deposits   Term deposits are repayable after a specified period of time agreed between the bank and the depositor. Banks pay higher interest rates on term deposits than on savings accounts. There are many variants of term deposits, such as the following:

Fixed deposits: The customer deposits a specified amount once. The bank pays interest periodically or on maturity and the proceeds on maturity.

Recurring deposits: The customer deposits a specified sum at regular intervals for a predetermined period. The bank pays the proceeds on maturity.

Cash certificates: The customer deposits the discounted value for a specified sum payable on maturity.

Certificates of deposit: These are short-term money market instruments that have a maturity of not more than one year.

Fixed deposits, recurring deposits, and cash certificates are not transferable. Term deposits from banks and others are disclosed separately. Also, the total amount of deposits of branches in India and outside India are disclosed separately.

Borrowings

Unlike deposits, borrowings take place at the bank's head office. Borrowings are classified as follows:

- Borrowings in India
  (i)   Reserve Bank of India;
  (ii) Other banks; and
  (iii) Other institutions and agencies.
- Borrowings outside India

Borrowings from the RBI include refinance obtained by the bank for loans to specified sectors. Specialized institutions such as Export-Import Bank of India (EXIM Bank), National Bank for Agriculture and Rural Development (NABARD), and Small Industries Development Bank of India (SIDBI) provide refinance to banks for loans extended to those sectors. Borrowings from other banks include refinance obtained by the bank from commercial banks. Since inter-bank liabilities have implications for the financial stability of the entire system, the RBI imposes limits on such liabilities. Borrowings are further classified and disclosed as follows: innovative perpetual debt instruments; hybrid debt capital instruments issued as bonds/debentures; perpetual cumulative preference shares[1]; redeemable non-cumulative preference shares; redeemable cumulative preference shares; and subordinated debt.

Other Liabilities and Provisions

These consist of the following items:

- Bills payable;
- Inter-office adjustments;
- Interest accrued; and
- Others (including provisions).

---

[1] Recall from the discussion in Chapters 10 and 11 that the Companies Act 2013 prohibits the issue of irredeemable preference shares or preference shares redeemable after 20 years from the date of issue.

Bills payable   These include demand drafts, traveller's cheques, banker's cheques, and similar instruments issued by the bank against money received from customers, but not presented for payment.

Inter-office adjustments   Inter-office adjustments represent unreconciled items within a bank. For example, one branch of the bank may have transferred an amount from a customer's account to another branch, but the second branch may not have received the amount until the balance sheet date. The existence of inter-office adjustments indicates the failure of the bank's internal control and reconciliation procedures. For instance, fraudulent transactions may be swept under this item. With extensive computerization, there should be no unreconciled items, and this item should not appear on the balance sheet. Nevertheless, such items are not unusual, especially in government-owned banks.

- SBI has inter-office adjustments of ₹27 billion in assets and ₹374 billion in liabilities as at March 31, 2016.

Interest accrued   Interest accrued may be (a) interest due and payable or (b) interest accrued but not due. For example, suppose that on December 31, a bank accepts a six-month deposit of ₹10,000 carrying interest at 12 per cent per annum. On March 31, the *interest accrued but not due* will be ₹300. On June 30, if the bank does not pay as agreed, the *interest due and payable* will be ₹600.

Others (including provisions)   Examples of items to be included in this group are provision for income tax, proposed dividend, outstanding expenses, staff security deposits, margin deposits, foreign currency translation gains, tax deducted at source, income tax collected on behalf of the government, and provision for gratuity, pension, and other staff benefits.

Contingent Liabilities and Bills for Collection

Contingent liabilities include claims against the bank not acknowledged as debts, liability for partly paid investments, liability on account of outstanding forward exchange contracts, and guarantees on behalf of constituents. Bill for collection are bills of exchange held by a bank on behalf of its customers. Contingent liabilities and bills for collection are disclosed in a footnote.

Assets

Assets are presented under the following groups:

1. Cash and balances with Reserve Bank of India;
2. Balances with banks and money at call and short notice;
3. Investments;
4. Advances;
5. Fixed assets; and
6. Other assets.

Cash and Balances with Reserve Bank of India

The following are disclosed:

- Cash in hand
- Balances with Reserve Bank of India
    (i) Current account;
    (ii) Other accounts.

Banking companies are required to maintain a certain minimum *cash reserve ratio* (CRR). Section 18 of the Banking Regulation Act requires every banking company to maintain a cash reserve of at least 4 per cent of the total of its demand and time liabilities in India as on the last Friday of the second preceding fortnight. *Demand liabilities* must be paid on demand (e.g. demand deposits, demand portion of savings deposits, and balances in overdue fixed deposits); other liabilities are *time liabilities*. The cash reserve may be kept with the bank, in a current account with the RBI, in current accounts with the SBI or its subsidiaries or nationalized banks, or a combination of these accounts. Section 42 (1) of the RBI Act requires every scheduled bank to maintain with the RBI an average daily balance of a prescribed percentage of the total of its demand and time liabilities in India on a fortnightly basis. If the average daily balance falls below the above minimum, the scheduled bank will be required to pay a penal interest and a higher penal interest for persistent default.

Section 24 of the Banking Regulation Act requires every banking company to maintain in India in cash, gold or unencumbered approved securities, at the close of business on any day, a minimum percentage of its demand and time liabilities in India specified by the RBI as on the last Friday of the second preceding fortnight. This is known as the *statutory liquidity ratio* (SLR). CRR and SLR are instruments by which the RBI controls the money supply and ensures availability of cash or near-cash assets for meeting banks' obligations.[2] *Approved securities* are securities issued or guaranteed by the Central government or a State government, or any other securities expressly authorized by the Central government in the Official Gazette. *Unencumbered* means not pledged as security for a loan.

TEST YOUR UNDERSTANDING 14.1
Demand and Time Liabilities

Fab Bank has the following deposits: current accounts, ₹50,000; savings accounts, ₹10,000 (including demand portion of ₹8,000); fixed deposits, ₹20,000 (including overdue deposits of ₹1,000). Calculate the bank's demand and time liabilities.

Balances with Banks and Money at Call and Short Notice

Banks maintain accounts with other banks, in addition to accounts with the RBI. The following are disclosed in this classification:

- In India
    - (i) Balances with other banks
        - (a) in current accounts;
        - (b) in other deposit accounts.
    - (ii) Money at call and short notice
        - (a) with banks;
        - (b) with other institutions.
- Outside India
    - (i) in current accounts;
    - (ii) in other deposit accounts; and
    - (iii) money at call and short notice.

Money at call and short notice refers to short-term investment in the money market in order to earn a return on surplus funds. Money lent for one day is *money at call*; money lent for more than one day, but not more than 14 days is *money at short notice*. These amounts are unsecured. The participants in the call and short-term money markets are mainly scheduled banks. They borrow from this market to meet their CRR or SLR requirements.

Investments

Banks' investments are regulated in order to ensure a minimum level of liquidity and to avoid excessive exposure to specific industries or business enterprises. The classification is as follows:

- Investments in India in
    - (i) Government securities;

---

[2] As of January 1, 2017, the CRR was 4 per cent and the SLR was 20.75 per cent.

    (ii)   Other approved securities;
    (iii) Shares;
    (iv)   Debentures and bonds;
    (v)   Subsidiaries and/or joint ventures; and
    (vi)   Others (to be specified).
- Investments outside India
    (i)   Government securities;
    (ii)   Subsidiaries and/or joint ventures abroad; and
    (iii) Other investments (to be specified).

Advances

Advances comprise loans made by the bank and are generally the largest item of the bank's balance sheet. Interest earned on advances is the most important source of income for banks. Advances are classified in three ways:

    (a) Type of advance;
    (b) Type of security; and
    (c) Location and sectoral distribution of advance.

The following are disclosed:

    (a) Type of advance:
        (i)   Bills purchased and discounted;
        (ii)   Cash credits, overdrafts and loans repayable on demand; and
        (iii) Term loans.
    (b) Type of security:
        (i)   Secured by tangible assets;
        (ii)   Covered by bank/government guarantees; and
        (iii) Unsecured.
    (c) Location and sectoral distribution of advance:
        I.   Advances in India
            (i)   Priority sectors;
            (ii)   Public sector;
            (iii) Banks; and
            (iv)   Others.
        II. Advances outside India
            (i)   Due from banks;
            (ii)   Due from others;
            (iii) Bills purchased and discounted;
            (iv)   Syndicated loans; and
            (v)   Others.

Bills purchased are "demand bills", i.e. the acceptor must pay at sight; *bills discounted* are "time bills" (also known as "usance bills"), i.e. the acceptor must pay after a specified time. *Cash credit* is for a relatively longer period and is usually secured. *Overdraft* is a temporary arrangement by which the holder of a current account is allowed to withdraw more than the balance available and may either be secured or "clean" (i.e. without security). Both cash credit and overdraft are intended to meet the gap between current assets and current liabilities. *Demand loans* are fixed amounts of loan repayable on demand. A "working capital demand loan" must be repaid or renewed, unlike a running cash credit account. *Term loans* are repayable in instalments over a period of time, but can be called back if the borrower defaults. Loans with a repayment period of up to 36 months are "demand loans" and those with a longer repayment are "term loans". *Priority sector* advances include advances for agriculture, advances to micro/small/medium enterprises, education loans, housing loans, and micro-credit.

Fixed Assets

Fixed assets consist of premises and other fixed assets. *Premises* are business and residential premises and usually include land. *Other fixed assets* include items such as furniture and fixtures, motor vehicles, office equipment, and computers. Fixed assets are not a major item for banks, unlike manufacturing enterprises.

- HDFC Bank's fixed assets at March 31, 2016 were ₹35 billion, less than 0.5 per cent of the bank's total assets.

Other Assets

Other assets include interest accrued, advance tax and tax deducted at source, stationery and stamps, non-banking assets acquired in satisfaction of claims, and deferred tax asset.

Exhibit 14.1 presents HDFC Bank's balance sheet.

EXHIBIT 14.1
Balance Sheet

HDFC Bank Balance Sheet, March 31			
	2016	**2015**	**2014**	**% Change in 2016**
			(in millions)	
Capital and Liabilities				
Capital	₹ 5,056	₹ 5,013	₹ 4,798	0.86
Reserves and surplus	737,985	626,528	436,868	17.79
Minority interest	1,806	1,616	1,517	11.76
Deposits	5,458,733	4,502,837	3,670,803	21.13
Borrowings	717,635	594,782	495,967	20.66
Other liabilities and provisions	381,403	340,189	426,246	12.12
	7,302,618	6,070,965	5,036,199	20.29
Assets				
Cash and balances with Reserve Bank of India	₹ 300,766	₹ 275,223	₹ 253,572	9.28
Balances with banks and money at call and short notice	89,923	90,041	145,562	– 0.13
Investments	1,616,833	1,642,726	1,195,710	– 1.58
Advances	4,872,904	3,834,080	3,154,189	27.09
Fixed assets	34,797	32,249	30,263	7.90
Other assets	387,395	196,646	256,903	– 12.15
	7,302,618	6,070,965	5,036,199	20.29
Contingent liabilities	8,535,274	9,752,786	7,231,729	
Bills for collection	234,900	223,049	209,431	

Statement of Profit and Loss

Learning Objective

LO 5 Explain the items on a bank's statement of profit and loss.

The statement of profit and loss has four broad heads:

- Income;
- Expenditure;
- Profit (loss); and
- Appropriations.

Income

Interest earned   This includes interest and discount on advances and bills, income from investments (interest and dividend income), interest on balances with RBI and other inter-bank funds, and other interest income (e.g. interest on advances to the bank's employees).

Other income   This includes commission, exchange and brokerage, profit on sale of investments, profit on revaluation of investments, and profit on sale of land, buildings, and other assets.

Expenditure

Interest expended   This includes interest on deposits and interest on RBI and inter-bank borrowings.

Operating expenses   This includes employee emoluments and benefits, rent, taxes and lighting, printing and stationery, advertisement and publicity, depreciation on bank's property, directors' fees and allowances, auditors' fees and expenses, law charges, postage, telegrams and telephones, repairs and maintenance, and insurance.

Provisions and contingencies   This includes provisions for non-performing assets, taxation, diminution in the value of investments, and contingencies.

Net Profit (Loss)

This section has net profit or loss for the period and the balance of profit or loss brought forward from the previous year.

Appropriations

These include transfers to statutory reserves, other reserves and dividends and balance carried to balance sheet.

Exhibit 14.2 presents HDFC Bank's statement of profit and loss.

HDFC Bank Statement of Profit and Loss, March 31 For the year ended March 31			
	2016	2015	% Change in 2016
		(in millions)	
I Income			
Interest earned	₹631,616	₹506,665	24.66
Other income	112,116	95,457	17.45
Total	743,732	602,122	23.52
II Expenditure			
Interest expended	340,696	272,885	24.85
Operating expenses	178,319	145,775	22.32
Provisions and contingencies	96,544	76,462	26.27
Total	615,559	495,122	24.32
III Profit			
Net profit for the year	128,173	107,000	19.79
Less Minority interest	197	144	36.81
Add Share in profits of associates	37	33	12.12
Consolidated profit for the year attributable to the group	128,013	106,889	19.76
Balance of profit brought forward	195,509	152,075	28.56
Total	323,522	258,964	24.93
IV Appropriations			
Transfer to statutory reserve	31,809	26,239	
Proposed dividend	24,018	20,052	
Tax (including cess) on dividend	5,124	4,245	
Dividend (including tax/cess) pertaining to previous year	(117)	8	
Transfer to general reserve	12,296	10,386	
Transfer to capital reserve	2,221	2,249	
Transfer to (from) investment reserve account	(85)	276	
Balance carried over to balance sheet	248,256	195,509	
Total	323,522	258,964	

EXHIBIT 14.2
Statement of Profit and Loss

Which of the following is generally the largest item on a bank balance sheet?
  (a) Share capital.
  (b) Deposits.
  (c) Borrowings.
  (d) Advances.

The Drivers of a Bank's Performance

Learning Objective

LO 6 Explain the drivers of a bank's financial performance.

Figure 14.1 presents the DuPont analysis modified for banks. The return on equity (ROE) is the product of return on assets (ROA) and leverage (LEV). ROA is, in turn, the product of profit margin (PM) and asset turnover (ATO). We calculate a number of additional measures to understand the drivers of profitability. Shareholders are interested in their bank's profitability and the associated risks. We will illustrate the analysis of the financial statements of banks using the 2016 financial statements of HDFC Bank.

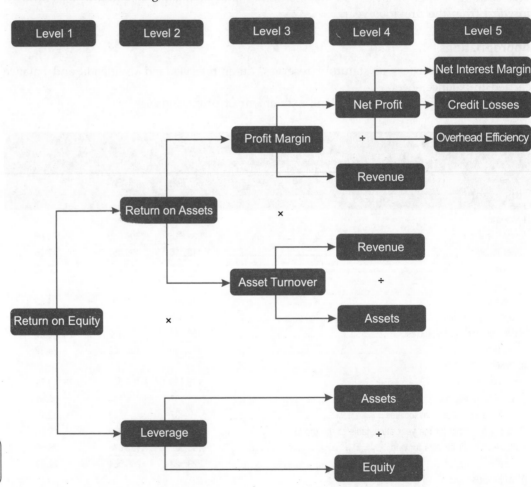

Figure 14.1

THE DUPONT FINANCIAL ANALYSIS CHART

Return on equity is the product of return on assets and leverage.

Return on Equity

The ROE measures the use of shareholders' funds. Analysts generally use the average of beginning and ending equity. Share capital, reserves and surplus, and non-controlling interest (minority interest) constitute equity. From Exhibit 14.1, HDFC Bank's equity is as follows: 744,847 in 2016; 633,157 in 2015; and 443,183 in 2014. Average equity is: 689,002 in 2016 and 538,170 in 2015. Using this information and net profit in Exhibit 14.2, we compute HDFC Bank's ROE as follows:

Return on equity	2016	2015
$\dfrac{\text{Profit}}{\text{Equity}}$	$\dfrac{128,173}{689,002} = 18.60\%$	$\dfrac{107,000}{538,170} = 19.88\%$

Shareholders expect an ROE higher than the cost of equity. Banks strive to improve performance by raising low-cost deposits and lending at high interest rates. The overall success of their efforts shows up in the ROE. HDFC Bank earned a lower ROE in 2016 than in 2015. We will now try to find out how this happened. For this, we look at the bank's ROA and LEV, the drivers of ROE.

Return on Assets

The ROA is a measure of profitability from a given level of investment. We use average assets. From Exhibit 14.1, HDFC Bank's assets are as follows: 7,302,618 in 2016; 6,070,965 in 2015; and 5,036,199 in 2014. Average assets are: 6,686,792 in 2016 and 5,553,582 in 2015. Using this information and net profit in Exhibit 14.2, we compute HDFC Bank's ROA as follows:

Return on assets	2016	2015
$\dfrac{\text{Profit}}{\text{Assets}}$	$\dfrac{128,173}{6,686,792} = 1.92\%$	$\dfrac{107,000}{5,553,582} = 1.93\%$

The bank's ROA decreased marginally in 2016. However, it is much lower than the ROE in both years. To understand why, we look at the bank's leverage.

Leverage

This is a measure of the extent to which a bank benefits from using borrowed funds, mainly deposits. Using the average assets and average equity from our earlier calculations, we compute LEV – the ratio of assets to equity – as follows:

Leverage	2016	2015
$\dfrac{\text{Assets}}{\text{Equity}}$	$\dfrac{6,686,792}{689,002} = 9.71$	$\dfrac{5,553,582}{538,170} = 10.32$

ROE is the product of ROA and LEV. The bank's liabilities levered up the ROA significantly. Using the DuPont approach, we can analyze HDFC Bank's ROE for 2016 and 2015 as follows (allowing for rounding differences):

Year	Return on equity		Return on assets		Leverage
	$\dfrac{\text{Profit}}{\text{Equity}}$	=	$\dfrac{\text{Profit}}{\text{Assets}}$	×	$\dfrac{\text{Assets}}{\text{Equity}}$
2016	18.60%		1.92%		9.71
2015	19.88%		1.93%		10.32

High leverage is a characteristic feature of banks. Banks depend on deposits and borrowings to a far greater extent than non-financial firms. As you saw earlier, this is an important reason for the stringent regulation of banks. A leverage ratio of 9 times would be unimaginable for a non-financial business. Leverage decreased significantly in 2016. It was a double whammy for the bank because both ROA and LEV decreased, resulting in a lower ROE. As we know from Figure 14.1, profit margin and asset turnover drive ROA. Using the DuPont approach, we can analyze HDFC Bank's ROA as follows:

Year	Profit margin		Asset turnover		Return on assets
	$\dfrac{\text{Profit}}{\text{Sales}}$	×	$\dfrac{\text{Sales}}{\text{Assets}}$	=	$\dfrac{\text{Profit}}{\text{Assets}}$
2016	17.23%		0.1112 times		1.92%
2015	17.77%		0.1084 times		1.93%

This analysis shows that the bank's ROA was a shade lower in 2016. Though margin was lower, the bank benefited from the increase in asset turnover. Now, let us look at these drivers in some detail.

Profit Margin

The PM measures the amount of net profit earned per rupee of revenue. Using the data in Exhibit 14.2, we compute HDFC Bank's margin as follows:

Profit margin	2016	2015
$\dfrac{\text{Profit}}{\text{Revenue}}$	$\dfrac{128,173}{743,732} = 17.23\%$	$\dfrac{107,000}{602,122} = 17.77\%$

The bank's profit margin decreased from 17.77 per cent to 17.23 per cent. We need additional analysis to identify the sources of this decline. As an example of this analysis, let us look at the cost of deposits, the most important cost for banks.

Cost of deposits   Banks pay interest on deposits, their biggest source of finance. High interest costs lead to lower profit margin. We can calculate the cost of funds as the average interest rate paid by the bank. We find from the schedule of interest expense in the annual report that interest on deposits is 291,509 for 2016 and 235,048 for 2015. From Exhibit 14.1, the deposits are: 5,458,733 in 2016; 4,502,837 in 2015; and 3,670,803 in 2014. The average deposits are: 4,980,785 in 2016 and 4,086,820 in 2015. Using this information, we can compute HDFC Bank's cost of deposits as follows:

Cost of deposits	2016	2015
$\dfrac{\text{Interest on deposits}}{\text{Deposits}}$	$\dfrac{291,509}{4,980,785} = 5.85\%$	$\dfrac{235,048}{4,086,820} = 5.75\%$

The cost of deposits went up by 0.1 per cent in 2016. It is determined by the interest rates that a bank offers on its deposits. Interest rates are, in turn, determined by many factors including the RBI's monetary policy and the demand for and supply of funds in the market. The cost of deposits is also affected by the composition of a bank's deposits. You may recall that banks do not pay any interest on demand deposits (mainly current accounts), but pay some interest on savings accounts and higher rates on term deposits such as fixed and recurring deposits. The proportion of deposits in current and savings deposits to total deposits is known as the *CASA ratio*. A larger CASA ratio implies a lower cost of funds. HDFC Bank's percentage distribution of deposits for the last three years was as follows:

	2016	2015	2014
Low-cost deposits:			
Demand deposits	16.18	16.32	16.74
Savings bank deposits	27.06	27.71	28.07
CASA ratio	43.24	44.03	44.81
High-cost deposits:			
Term deposits	56.76	55.97	55.19
Total	100.00	100.00	100.00

The share of low-cost demand and savings bank deposits went down by 1.57 per cent over the three-year period and by 0.79 per cent since 2015. It was 52.68 per cent in 2011 and has fallen consistently since then. It appears to be a trend and needs to be examined.

Sun Bank's deposits for three years were as follows:

TEST YOUR UNDERSTANDING 14.2
Effect of Deposit Mix on Profitability

Type of deposits	Year 1	Year 2	Year 3
Current accounts	₹15,000	₹25,000	₹29,000
Savings accounts	3,000	8,000	12,000
Term deposits	28,000	35,000	38,000
Total	46,000	68,000	79,000

Evaluate the bank's performance in raising deposits.

Credit losses Bad debts are a major drain on a bank's profits. The RBI lays down guidelines called *prudential norms* for classifying loans under various categories for estimating provisions for bad debts. Under these guidelines, every loan must be classified as either a *standard asset* or a *non-performing asset* (NPA). A standard asset is a loan which has not defaulted on principal or interest payments. These assets do not show signs of any problem and carry no more than the normal risk attached to the business. However, banks are supposed to make provision for these too.

An asset becomes an NPA when it ceases to generate income for a bank. For example, a term loan is treated as an NPA if interest and/or instalment of principal remain unpaid for more than 90 days from the due date for payment. Table 14.1 illustrates the RBI's classification of NPA:[3]

Category	Characteristics	Action
Sub-standard assets	1. Remained NPA for not more than 12 months. 2. The current net worth of the borrower or guarantor or the current market value of the security does not cover the dues to the bank.	1. Provide 15 per cent for secured assets. 2. Provide 25 per cent for unsecured assets.
Doubtful assets	1. Remained in the sub-standard category for 12 months. 2. Have weaknesses that make collection or liquidation in full highly questionable and improbable.	1. Provide 100 per cent for the unsecured portion. 2. Provide between 25 per cent to 100 per cent for the secured portion, depending on the period for which the advance has remained doubtful.
Loss assets	Loss has been identified by the bank or internal or external auditors or the RBI inspection but the amount has not been written off wholly.	Write off or fully provide for these assets.

TABLE 14.1
NPA Classification

Analysts pay keen attention to a bank's asset quality. In their anxiety to achieve growth and market share, banks often lend to high-risk customers. A study of NPAs helps us to understand asset quality. HDFC Bank's NPAs in 2016 and 2015 were as follows:

FINANCIAL VIEW
Understanding Asset Quality

	2016	2015
		(in millions)
Gross NPAs		
Opening balance	₹34,384	₹29,893
Additions (fresh NPAs) during the year	57,126	47,901
Reductions during the year:	(47,582)	(43,410)
— Upgradation	13,771	10,767
— Recoveries	14,387	14,130
— Write-offs	19,424	18,513
Closing balance	43,928	34,384
Provisions	30,724	25,421
Net NPAs	13,204	8,923

---

[3] The RBI revises these guidelines from time to time.

NPAs include all loans, investments and foreign exchange and derivatives that are classified as non-performing by the bank. Gross NPAs are before deducting the provisions for NPAs. Net NPAs are gross NPAs net of provisions. Net NPAs were higher at 0.28 per cent of net advances in 2016, compared to 0.25 per cent in 2015. This shows a slight deterioration in the bank's NPAs. The provision coverage ratio (PCR) tells us the extent to which a bank has provided for NPAs and is therefore insulated from the effect of credit losses. It is measured as the ratio of provisions to gross NPAs. HDFC Bank's PCR is 69.94 per cent in 2016 and 73.93 per cent in 2016. Further, HDFC Bank has a low ratio of net NPAs to net advances (i.e. advances net of provisions): 0.28 per cent in 2016 and 0.25 per cent in 2015. This is the lowest among the big banks and possibly one of the lowest among all banks. In sum, HDFC Bank's asset quality is very high and it has provided for probable credit losses.

Source: HDFC Bank 2016 annual report, p. 103.

From the statement of profit and loss, in 2016 HDFC Bank made a provision of ₹23,444 for NPAs, compared to ₹18,682 in 2015. The effect of these estimated bad debt losses on profitability is as follows:

Credit losses	2016	2015
$\dfrac{\text{Provision for NPAs}}{\text{Revenue}}$	$\dfrac{23,444}{743,732} = 3.15\%$	$\dfrac{18,682}{602,122} = 3.10\%$

The ratio increased by 0.05 per cent. This may seem low but analysts follow even small changes to see if they are indicative of a trend.

Overhead efficiency   Overhead efficiency (also known as **cost-to-income ratio** or **cost ratio**) is the ratio of operating expenses to revenue. Operating expenses include salaries and other employee-related expenses, rent and other administrative expenses, but exclude interest expense. It measures the operating efficiency of a bank. The smaller the ratio, the more efficient the bank. Using the information in Exhibit 14.2, we compute HDFC Bank's overhead efficiency as follows:

Overhead efficiency	2016	2015
$\dfrac{\text{Operating expenses}}{\text{Revenue}}$	$\dfrac{178,319}{743,732} = 23.98\%$	$\dfrac{145,775}{602,122} = 24.21\%$

The decrease in the bank's overhead efficiency indicates better utilization of its employees, office space, technology, and other resources. Since most of a bank's operating expenses are fixed or semi-fixed, overhead efficiency is also a measure of its operating leverage. The lower the operating leverage, the lesser the risk of being burdened with fixed costs in the event of a contraction in business.

Net interest margin   Banks make money by borrowing at low interest rates and lending at high interest rates, consistent with the associated risks. **Net interest income** (NII) is the difference between a bank's interest income and interest expense. It is a measure of a bank's ability to control interest rate risk. The higher the net interest income, the lower the interest rate risk. NII is analogous to gross profit. HDFC Bank's net interest income is ₹290,920 for 2016 (interest earned, ₹631,616 – interest expense, ₹340,696) and ₹233,780 for 2015 (interest earned, ₹506,665 – interest expense, ₹272,885).

Net interest margin (NIM) is the ratio of net interest income to interest-earning assets. It measures the rate of net interest income earned on a bank's interest-earning assets. We find from the schedule of interest earned that HDFC Bank earns interest income chiefly from investments and advances. Taking the average of the sum of investments and advances, the bank's average interest-earning assets are ₹5,983,272 for 2016 and ₹4,913,353 for 2015. Using the above information, we calculate HDFC Bank's NIM as follows:

Net interest margin	2016	2015
$\dfrac{\text{Net interest income}}{\text{Interest-earning assets}}$	$\dfrac{290{,}920}{5{,}983{,}272} = 4.86\%$	$\dfrac{233{,}780}{4{,}913{,}353} = 4.76\%$

The higher the NIM, the more profitable the bank. HDFC Bank's NIM increased slightly in 2016. It is possible to generate a high NIM by investing in assets with a high yield, but also highly risky assets such as junk bonds. Therefore, while assessing the adequacy of a bank's net interest margin, we should also consider the riskiness of a bank's assets.

The following information is available relates from Win Bank's financial statements:

	Year 2	Year 1
Interest income	₹1,120	₹980
Interest expense...	830	670
Advances	7,900	7,440
Investments	930	670

Calculate the bank's net interest margin for Year 2.

TEST YOUR UNDERSTANDING 14.3
Calculating Net Interest Margin

Spread Spread measures the difference between the yield on a bank's interest-earning assets and the cost of its interest-bearing liabilities. As discussed earlier, interest-earning assets consist of investments and advances. Interest-bearing liabilities are chiefly deposits and borrowings. HDFC Bank's average interest-bearing liabilities are ₹5,636,994 for 2016 and ₹4,632,195 for 2015. Using the above information and interest income and interest expense from our NIM calculations, we calculate HDFC Bank's spread as follows:

Spread	2016	2015
Yield: $\dfrac{\text{Interest income}}{\text{Interest-earning assets}}$	$\dfrac{631{,}616}{5{,}983{,}272} = 10.56\%$	$\dfrac{506{,}665}{4{,}913{,}353} = 10.31\%$
Cost of funds: $\dfrac{\text{Interest expense}}{\text{Interest-bearing liabilities}}$	$\dfrac{340{,}696}{5{,}636{,}994} = 6.04\%$	$\dfrac{272{,}885}{4{,}632{,}195} = 5.89\%$
Spread: Yield – Cost of funds	10.56% – 6.04% = 4.52%	10.31% – 5.89% = 4.42%

The higher the spread, the more profitable the bank. HDFC Bank's spread increased by 0.10 per cent in 2016. The yield went up more than the cost of funds. The increase in the cost of funds is in line with the increase in the cost of deposits. As with net interest margin, a high spread can be an indication of a bank owning highly risky assets such as loans to risky customers. Therefore, a bank should avoid focusing on spread ignoring risk.

Asset Turnover

The ATO is a measure of a bank's efficiency in utilizing its assets. It indicates how many times the assets were turned over in a period in order to generate revenue. If the ATO is high, we can infer that the enterprise is managing its assets efficiently. A low ATO implies an inability to deploy the deposits. Using the information about revenue and average assets from our earlier calculations, we compute HDFC Bank's ATO as follows:

Asset turnover	2016	2015
$\dfrac{\text{Revenue}}{\text{Assets}}$	$\dfrac{743{,}732}{6{,}686{,}792} = 0.1112 \text{ times}$	$\dfrac{602{,}122}{5{,}553{,}582} = 0.1084 \text{ times}$

In 2016, HDFC Bank earned a revenue of ₹1,112 per ₹10,000 of assets as compared to ₹1,084 in 2015. It indicates improvement in utilization of assets in 2016. This finding is in line with the revenue growth of 24 per cent, that was more than the asset growth of 20 per cent.

ONE-MINUTE QUIZ 14.2
Net Interest Margin

Net interest margin equals
(a) Interest income – interest expense.
(b) (Interest income – interest expense)/Interest income.
(c) (Interest income – interest expense)/ interest-earning assets.
(d) Yield – Cost of funds.

EARNINGS QUALITY ANALYSIS
Non-interest Income

In 2016, HDFC Bank earned 11.17 per cent of total revenue from commission, exchange and brokerage. Interest income requires investment in advances. Non-interest income such as commission, exchange and brokerage requires no investment and frees the bank from credit risk and interest rate risk. Fee income from investment banking, securities underwriting, sales of third party products and so on have greater growth potential. Also, these activities don't consume capital. There are some negatives, though. Lending relationships are built over long periods and are difficult to break. A borrower would stick to its bank that has stood by it during difficult times. Activities that generate fee income don't engender the same loyalty. Also, these activities require high set-up costs and continuing fixed or semi-fixed costs that increase the degree of operating leverage. Therefore, while these activities don't increase financial leverage, they may increase the volatility of earnings. Further, sales of third party products such as insurance and mutual funds could cannibalize the bank's deposits and open the bank to charges of mis-selling.

Capital Adequacy

Learning Objective

LO 7 Understand a bank's need for long-term capital.

A bank should have sources of finance that will be available especially in difficult times. Banks depend heavily on deposits and loans, but these are risky for two reasons.

1. *Dependability:* Debt is a fair-weather friend because depositors and other lenders will want to withdraw their funds at the slightest hint of trouble in a bank. Banks need resources they can rely on when faced with difficulties. Shareholders can't take out their equity capital and retained earnings because equity is not redeemable.

2. *Payment commitment:* Debt carries fixed principal and interest payment obligations. Dependence on debt will aggravate a bank's woes and accelerate its collapse. In contrast, equity has no fixed dividend or capital payment obligations.

Therefore, equity is a permanent source of capital that a bank's depositors and other creditors can count on at all times.

Capital adequacy refers to the sufficiency of a bank's capital in relation to the risks associated with its operations. Capital adequacy measures the shock-absorbing ability of a bank. The greater the share of equity in a bank's funds, the better the bank's ability to survive adverse developments, such as an unexpected rise in bad debts, liquidity problems, troubles in other banks, and volatility in interest rates and exchange rates. Thus, high capital adequacy enhances a bank's liquidity and solvency. Capital adequacy will depend on (a) the availability of long-term capital and (b) the risks associated with a bank's activities.

A bank's regulatory capital is divided into two tiers according to the characteristics of the instrument. Tier 1 capital consists mainly of share capital and certain reserves. It is a bank's high-quality capital, because of its loss absorption capacity. Tier 2 capital consists of certain other reserves and subordinated debt (i.e. unsecured creditors) and its loss absorption capacity is lower than that of Tier 1 capital. Intangible assets, losses in current and past periods, and deferred tax asset are some of the items that must be deducted in calculating Tier 1 capital.[4]

Banks face two major risks: (a) credit risk, and (b) market risk. **Credit risk**, or *counterparty risk*, is the possibility of loss due to default by a bank's borrower, i.e. counterparty. For example, Central government securities carry a lower credit risk than corporate debt, because the government can print currency and levy taxes in order to meet its principal and interest obligations. **Market risk** is the possibility of loss due to changes in interest rates, foreign exchange rates, and equity and commodity prices. **Risk-weight** is a measure

---

[4] The RBI's circular dated March 1, 2016 made the following changes: (1) Revaluation reserve is treated as CET 1 capital at a discount of 55 per cent; (2) Foreign currency translation reserve is treated as CET 1 capital at a discount of 25 per cent; (3) Deferred tax assets are to be deducted in full from CET 1 capital but DTAs relating to timing differences are treated as CET 1 capital up to 10 per cent of a bank's CET 1 capital. The term CET 1 capital is explained later.

of the risk associated with an asset. The higher the risk of owning an asset, the higher the risk-weight assigned to the asset. Thus, corporate debt would have a higher risk-weight than government debt. **Risk-weighted asset** is the amount of an asset multiplied by its risk-weight. **Capital adequacy ratio** (also known as **capital risk adequacy ratio** or **capital ratio**) is the ratio of capital to risk-weighted assets (RWAs).

To understand how risk affects capital adequacy, suppose two banks have assets of ₹1,000 each as follows:

HANDHOLD 14.2
Understanding Capital Adequacy

	Risk-averse Bank	Risk-taking Bank
Cash	₹300	₹100
Government securities	600	200
Corporate loans	100	700
	1,000	1,000

Cash and government securities are risk-free, so they will be assigned zero risk-weight. Corporate loans are risky, so they will have a higher risk-weight. Only 10 per cent of Risk-averse Bank's assets is in risky assets, in contrast to 70 per cent for Risk-taking Bank. Risk-averse Bank can withstand external shocks better than Risk-taking Bank. Therefore, Risk-taking Bank will require higher capital than Risk-averse Bank.

Basel III Regulations

The Bank for International Settlements (BIS) fosters international monetary and financial cooperation and serves as a bank for central banks. The BIS aims "at promoting monetary and financial stability, acts as a forum for discussion and cooperation among central banks and the financial community and acts as a bank to central banks and international organizations." Sixty central banks and monetary authorities (including the RBI) are members of the BIS. Its head office is in Basel, Switzerland. The Basel Committee on Banking Supervision (BCBS), a part of the BIS, lays down standards for the prudential regulation of banks including capital adequacy norms.

Learning Objective

LO 8   Explain Basel III capital and liquidity regulations.

In 1988, the Basel Committee recommended risk-based capital standards for banks (Basel I). Two key elements of Basel I were risk-weighting of assets and minimum capital requirements. Bank assets were grouped into five categories according to credit risk. A minimum capital of 8 per cent of RWAs was required. In 2004, the Basel Committee issued a revised framework for capital measurement and capital standards (Basel II). From March 31, 2009, banks in India have to comply with Basel II. Basel II rests on three pillars: Pillar 1, minimum capital requirement; Pillar 2, supervisory review process; and Pillar 3, market discipline. The total capital ratio must not be less than 8 per cent. Capital requirements should be commensurate with a bank's risk profile and control environment. The amount of capital should be related to the bank's risk management and internal control processes. Basel II required adopting a general disclosure policy and a process for assessing the disclosures. The disclosures required include the bank's capital structure, capital adequacy, risk exposure and assessment, and description of risk management objectives and policies.

Basel III was released in 2010 in the wake of the 2008 financial crisis that resulted in the erosion of the solvency and liquidity of banks. It is the currently applicable set of reform measures to strengthen the regulation, supervision, and risk management of the banking sector. These measures aim to improve the banking sector's ability to absorb shocks arising from financial and economic stress, improve risk management and governance, and strengthen banks' transparency and disclosures. The reforms strengthen bank-level, or *micro-prudential*, regulation to raise the resilience of individual banking institutions to periods of stress and have a *macro-prudential* focus, addressing system-wide risks that can build up across the banking sector. Basel III strengthens the capital framework and introduces a liquidity standard. Basel III is implemented in India in a phased manner from April 1, 2013. Full implementation is expected by March 31, 2019. We'll now look at the capital and liquidity requirements under Basel III.

Capital

The Basel III capital framework addresses the solvency problems of banks that surfaced during the financial crisis. Many banks had excessive leverage, on and off the balance sheet. Strengthening bank capital rests on three pillars:

Pillar 1:   Capital; risk coverage; containing leverage

Pillar 2:   Risk management and supervision

Pillar 3:   Market discipline

Pillar 1 Basel III strengthens the capital base, enhances risk coverage, and introduces a leverage ratio.

Capital Regulatory capital consists of Tier 1 capital and Tier 2 capital.

Tier 1 capital. Tier 1 capital, also known as *going concern capital*, is meant to prevent a bank from collapse. It is the sum of Common Equity Tier 1 (CET 1) and Additional Tier 1. CET 1 capital consists of equity shares that meet the criteria for classification as equity shares for regulatory purposes, equity share premium, retained earnings, accumulated other comprehensive income and other disclosed reserves, minority interest (i.e. non-controlling interest in consolidated subsidiaries), and regulatory adjustments.

The criteria for the classification of an instrument as common shares for regulatory purposes include the following:

1. It represents the most subordinated claim in liquidation of a bank;
2. It is entitled to a claim on the residual assets that is proportional with its share of issued share capital, after all senior claims have been repaid in liquidation;
3. Principal is perpetual and is never repaid outside of liquidation (excluding in a buyback in accordance with the law);
4. The bank does not create an expectation that the instrument will be bought back;
5. Distributions are paid out of distributable items and the level of distributions are not subject to a cap;
6. Distributions are not mandatory and non-payment is not a default;
7. The paid-in amount is included as equity under relevant accounting standards;
8. It is clearly and separately disclosed on the bank's balance sheet.

The criteria are cumulative.

Additional Tier 1 capital consists of instruments issued by the bank that meet the criteria for inclusion in Additional Tier 1 capital (and are not included in CET 1), share premium resulting from the issue of instruments included in Additional Tier 1 capital, instruments issued by consolidated subsidiaries of the bank and held by third parties that meet the criteria for inclusion in Additional Tier 1 capital and are not included in CET 1, and regulatory adjustments applied in the calculation of Additional Tier 1 Capital.

The minimum criteria for an instrument issued by a bank to meet or exceed for it to be included in Additional Tier 1 capital include the following:

1. It is subordinated to depositors, general creditors, and subordinated debt of the bank.
2. It is neither secured nor covered by a guarantee of the issuer or related entity or other arrangement that legally or economically enhances the seniority of the claim vis-à-vis bank creditors.
3. It is perpetual, i.e. there is no maturity date and there are no step-ups or an other incentive to redeem.
4. It may be callable at the initiative of the issuer only after a minimum of five years.
5. Any repayment of principal (e.g. through repurchase or redemption) must be with prior supervisory approval and banks should not assume or create market expectations that supervisory approval will be given.
6. The bank must have full discretion at all times to cancel distributions/payments.

7. Instruments classified as liabilities for accounting purposes must have principal loss absorption through either (i) conversion to common shares at an objective pre-specified trigger point or (ii) a write-down mechanism which allocates losses to the instrument at a pre-specified trigger point.

Tier 2 capital. Tier 2 capital, also known as *gone concern capital*, is meant to provide loss absorption after a bank's collapse. It consists of instruments issued by the bank that meet the criteria for inclusion in Tier 2 capital (and are not included in Tier 1 capital), share premium resulting from the issue of instruments included in Tier 2 capital, instruments issued by consolidated subsidiaries of the bank and held by third parties that meet the criteria for inclusion in Tier 2 capital and are not included in Tier 1, certain loan loss provisions, and regulatory adjustments applied in the calculation of Tier 2 Capital.

The minimum criteria for an instrument issued by a bank to meet or exceed for it to be included in Tier 2 capital include the following:

1. It is subordinated to depositors and general creditors of the bank.
2. It is neither secured nor covered by a guarantee of the issuer or related entity or other arrangement that legally or economically enhances the seniority of the claim vis-à-vis depositors and general bank creditors.
3. Minimum original maturity of at least five years, recognition in regulatory capital in the remaining five years before maturity will be amortized on a straight-line basis and there are no step-ups or other incentives to redeem.
4. It may be callable at the initiative of the issuer only after a minimum of five years.
5. The investor must have no rights to accelerate the repayment of future scheduled payments (coupon or principal), except in bankruptcy and liquidation.
6. The instrument can't have a credit sensitive dividend feature, that is a dividend/coupon that is reset periodically based in whole or in part on the banking organization's credit standing.

Provisions or loan-loss reserves held against future, presently unidentified losses are freely available to meet losses which subsequently materialize and, therefore, qualify for inclusion within Tier 2. Provisions ascribed to identified deterioration of particular assets or known liabilities, whether individual or grouped, should be excluded.

Minimum capital. CET 1 capital must be at least 4.5 per cent of RWAs. Tier 1 capital must be at least be 7 per cent of RWAs. Total capital must be at least 8 per cent of RWAs. Besides, Basel III has introduced two new buffers: (a) a *capital conservation buffer* of 2.5 per cent by reducing dividend payments, share buybacks, and staff bonus payments; and (b) a *countercyclical buffer* of up to 2.5 per cent depending on macroeconomic circumstances. For both buffers, an extra cushion of CET 1 capital needs to be held leading to a CET 1 capital ratio of 9.5 per cent. Table 14.2 summarizes the BCBS and RBI capital requirements under Basel II and Basel III.

	BCBS		RBI	
	Basel II	Basel III	Basel II	Basel III
			(percent of risk-weighted assets)	
(i) Minimum Common Equity Tier 1	2.0	4.5	2.7	5.5
(ii) Capital Conservation Buffer (comprised of Common Equity)	—	2.5	—	2.5
(iii) Minimum Common Equity Tier 1 plus Capital Conservation Buffer [(i) + (ii)]	2.0	7.0	2.7	8.0
(iv) Additional Tier 1 Capital	2.0	1.5	1.8	1.5
(v) Minimum Tier 1 Capital [(i) + (iv)]	4.0	6.0	4.5	7.0
(vi) Tier 2 Capital	4.0	2.0	4.5	2.0
(vii) Minimum Total Capital [(v) + (vi)]	8.0	8.0	9.0	9.0
(viii) Minimum Total Capital plus Capital Conservation Buffer [(vii) + (ii)]	8.0	10.5	9.0	11.5

TABLE 14.2
BCBS and RBI Capital Requirements

Risk coverage It includes specifying higher capital for trading and derivatives activities and securitization and strengthening of the counterparty credit risk framework.

Containing leverage Basel III has introduced a simple, non-risk based leverage ratio in response to the excessive leverage built up in the years preceding the 2008 financial crisis. It supplements the risk-based capital requirements. In the wake of the crisis, banks were forced to deleverage, i.e. reduce debt by selling off assets resulting in further losses and contraction in credit availability. Sudden deleveraging destabilizes the markets for financial and real assets and leads to further all-round selling, thereby worsening the crisis. The leverage ratio is calculated by dividing the capital measure by the total exposure. For the capital measure, Tier 1 capital is considered. The exposure measure is the sum of the values of all assets and off-balance sheet items not deducted for calculation of Tier 1 capital. To start with, a leverage ratio of 3 per cent is proposed.

The RBI has specified risk-weights for various types of assets. Central government debt and Central government guaranteed debt attract zero risk-weight. State government debt attracts zero risk-weight, but State government guaranteed claims attract 20 per cent risk-weight. Claims on corporates, whether owned by the government or not, have risk-weights depending on their credit rating and term. For example, long-term claims have risk-weights ranging from 20 per cent to 150 per cent as follows:

Rating	AAA	AA	A	BBB	≤ BB	Unrated
Risk-weight (%)	20	30	50	100	150	150

Short-term claims have risk-weights from 20 per cent (for A1+) to 150 per cent (for A4 and D). Unrated claims, long-term or short-term, have 100 per cent. Non-performing assets, net of specific provisions, have risk-weights depending on the extent of specific loss provision made for them: 150 per cent when provision is less than 20 per cent of the outstanding amount, 100 per cent when provision is at least 20 per cent and 50 per cent when provision is at least 50 per cent. Off-balance sheet items are also assigned appropriate risk-weights.

Pillar 2: Risk management and supervision It includes addressing firm-wide governance and risk management; capturing the risk of off-balance sheet exposures and securitization activities; managing risk concentrations; providing incentives for banks to better manage risk and returns over the long term; sound compensation practices; valuation practices; stress testing; accounting standards for financial instruments; corporate governance; and supervisory colleges.

Pillar 3: Market discipline Disclosures or improved disclosures are required for securitization exposures and sponsorship of off-balance sheet vehicles and the detail of the components of regulatory capital and their reconciliation to the reported accounts, including a comprehensive explanation of how a bank calculates its regulatory capital ratios.

TEST YOUR UNDERSTANDING 14.4
Capital Adequacy under Basel III

Trust Bank has the following assets:

Asset	Amount
Cash	₹10,500
Balance with RBI	2,000
Central government securities	29,200
Corporate debt, AAA-rated	71,800
Corporate debt, BB-rated	16,100
Non-performing assets (net of 50% provision)	4,200

Calculate Trust Bank's minimum capital under Basel III standards according to (a) BCBS and (b) RBI.

What is the risk weight for a AAA-rated long-term loan given to a Government of India company?
- (a) 0%.
- (b) 20%
- (c) 50%.
- (d) 100%.

Liquidity

While proposing new liquidity rules for US banks, Ben Bernanke, the former Governor of the Federal Reserve said: "Liquidity is essential to a bank's viability and central to the smooth functioning of the financial system."[5] In addition to solvency, banks' liquidity was heavily strained during the financial crisis. In response to the problem, Basel III includes a new liquidity standard introducing two liquidity ratios: (a) the liquidity coverage ratio (LCR), and (b) the net stable funding ratio (NSFR).

Liquidity coverage ratio   The **liquidity coverage ratio (LCR)** is intended to improve the short-term resilience of the liquidity risk profile of institutions, requiring them to hold a buffer of "high-quality" liquid assets to match net liquidity outflows during a *30-day period* of stress.

$$\text{Liquidity coverage ratio} = \frac{\text{Stock of high-quality liquid assets}}{\text{Net cash outflows over a 30-day time period}} \geq 100\%$$

Banks have to ensure that they have at all times sufficient high-quality liquid assets to survive an acute stress scenario lasting 30 days. The scenario may include a significant downgrade of the bank's credit rating, a partial loss of deposits, a loss of unsecured wholesale funding, a significant increase in secured funding "haircuts",[6] and an increase in derivative collateral calls and substantial calls on off-balance sheet exposures.

Stock of high quality liquid assets   The characteristics of *high-quality liquid assets* include the following: low credit and market risk; ease and certainty of valuation; low correlation with risky assets; and listed on developed and recognized exchange. All high-quality liquid assets should ideally be central bank eligible for intraday liquidity needs and overnight liquidity facilities in a jurisdiction and currency where the bank has access to the central bank. There are two categories of such assets: Level 1 and Level 2. Level 1 assets can comprise an unlimited share of the pool, are held at market value and are not subject to a haircut under the LCR. The following are examples of Level 1 assets:

- Cash;
- Deposits held with central banks to the extent that these deposits can be withdrawn in times of stress; and
- Marketable securities issued by the Central government that are assigned 0 per cent risk-weight under Basel II and are traded in large, deep markets.

Level 2 assets are limited to 40 per cent of the stock. A minimum 15 per cent haircut is applied to the current market value of each Level 2 asset held in the stock. The following are examples of Level 2 assets:

- Marketable securities issued by the Central government that are assigned 20 per cent risk-weight under Basel II and are actively traded in large, deep markets; and
- Corporate bonds and covered bonds[7] that have a credit rating of at least of AA and are traded in large, deep markets.

---

[5]   Federal Reserve press release dated October 24, 2013.

[6]   "Haircut" is a percentage reduction of the amount of an asset or a liability usually as part of a debt restructuring arrangement.

[7]   Covered bonds are subject to special public supervision to protect bondholders. Proceeds from the issue of these bonds must be invested in specified assets that would be used, in the event of default by the issuer, to pay the bondholders.

Net cash outflows over a 30-day time period   It is the total expected cash outflows minus total expected cash inflows for the subsequent 30 calendar days. Inflows are capped at 75 per cent of total expected cash outflows. For calculating expected cash outflows, the following minimum run-off rates are to be used:

Retail deposits: These are demand deposits and term deposits placed by a natural person. Term deposits with a residual maturity or withdrawal notice period of greater than 30 days are excluded, if the depositor has no legal right to withdraw deposits within the 30-day horizon, or if early withdrawal results in a significant penalty that is materially greater than the loss of interest.

- Stable deposits, i.e. deposits covered by an effective deposit insurance scheme or an equivalent public guarantee: run-off rate, 5 per cent
- Less stable deposits: run-off rate, 10 per cent

Unsecured wholesale funding: These are liabilities and general obligations that are raised from non-natural persons (i.e. legal entities, including sole proprietorships and partnerships). The minimum run-off rates depend on the category such as stable small business customers (5 per cent), less stable small business customers (10 per cent), and legal entities with operational relationships (25 per cent).

Secured funding: These are liabilities and general obligations that are collateralized by legal rights to specifically designated assets. The run-off rates are 0 per cent for funding backed by Level 1 assets, 15 per cent for Level 2 assets, 25 per cent for a domestic sovereign, and 100 per cent for all others.

Cash inflows are to be calculated depending on the contractual arrangements and the category of the receivables. For example, contractual inflows from retail and small business customers and wholesale non-financial customers are to be taken at 50 per cent of the receivables.

Net stable funding ratio   The **net stable funding ratio** (NSFR) requires a minimum amount of stable sources of funding at a bank to the liquidity profiles of the assets, as well as the potential for contingent liquidity needs arising from off-balance sheet commitments, over a *one-year horizon*. The NSFR aims to limit over-reliance on short-term wholesale funding during time of buoyant market liquidity and encourage better assessment of liquidity risk across all on- and off-balance sheet items.

$$\text{Net stable funding ratio} = \frac{\text{Available stable funding}}{\text{Required stable funding}} \geq 100\%$$

Available stable funding   *Available stable funding* (ASF) is the total amount of an institution's (a) capital, (b) preference share capital with maturity of equal to or greater than one year, (c) liabilities with effective maturities of one year or greater, (d) that portion of non-maturity deposits and/or term deposits with maturities of less than one year that would be expected to stay with the institution for an extended period in an idiosyncratic stress event, and (e) the portion of wholesale funding with maturities of less than a year that is expected to stay with the institution for an extended period in an idiosyncratic stress event. The available amount of stable funding is calculated by first assigning the carrying value of an institution's equity and liabilities to one of five categories with ASF factors of 100 per cent, 90 per cent, 80 per cent, 50 per cent, and 0 per cent. The total ASF is the sum of the weighted amounts. Table 14.3 illustrates ASF factors.

ASF Factor	Examples
100%	▪ Tier 1 and Tier 2 capital; ▪ Preference share capital not included in Tier 2 capital with maturity $\geq$ 1 year; and ▪ Secured and unsecured borrowings and liabilities with effective remaining maturities $\geq$ 1 year.
90%	▪ "Stable" non-maturity (demand) deposits and/or term deposits with residual maturity < 1 year.
80%	▪ "Less stable" non-maturity (demand) deposits and/or term deposits with residual maturity < 1 year.
50%	▪ Unsecured wholesale funding, non-maturity (demand) deposits and/or term deposits with residual maturity < 1 year provided by non-financial corporates, sovereigns, multilateral development banks, and public sector enterprises.
0%	▪ All other liabilities and equity categories not included in the above categories.

TABLE 14.3
Available Stable Funding

Required stable funding Required stable funding (RSF) depends on the liquidity profiles of a bank's assets, off-balance sheet exposures, and other activities. The required amount of stable funding is calculated as the sum of the value of the assets held and funded by the bank, multiplied by a specific required stable funding (RSF) factor assigned to each particular asset type, added to the amount of off-balance sheet activity (or potential liquidity exposure) multiplied by its associated RSF factor. Assets that are more liquid and more readily available to act as a source of extended liquidity in the stressed environment receive lower RSF factors (and require less stable funding) than assets considered less liquid and, therefore, require more stable funding. There are six asset types with RSF factors of 0 per cent, 5 per cent, 20 per cent, 50 per cent, 65 per cent, 80 per cent, and 100 per cent. The total RSF is the sum of the weighted amounts. Table 14.4 illustrates RSF factors.

RSF Factor	Examples
0%	▪ Cash; ▪ Unencumbered short-term unsecured instruments and transactions with outstanding maturities < 1 year.
5%	▪ Unencumbered marketable securities with residual maturities of one year or greater representing claims on claims guaranteed by sovereigns, centrals banks, etc. that are assigned 0% risk-weight under Basel II.
20%	▪ Unencumbered corporate bonds rated AA- or higher with residual maturities $\geq$ 1 year; ▪ Unencumbered marketable securities with residual maturities $\geq$ 1 year representing claims on claims guaranteed by sovereigns, centrals banks, etc. that are assigned 20% risk-weight under Basel II.
50%	▪ Gold; ▪ Unencumbered equity securities, not issued by financial institutions or their affiliates, listed on a recognized exchange and included in a large cap market index; and ▪ Unsecured corporate bonds that are central bank eligible and are not issued by financial institutions.
65%	▪ Unencumbered residential mortgages of any maturity that would qualify for the 35% or lower risk-weight under Basel II; ▪ Other unencumbered loans, excluding loans to financial institutions, with a remaining maturity of one year or greater, that would qualify for the 35% or lower risk-weight under Basel II.
85%	▪ Unencumbered loans to retail customers and small and medium enterprises having a maturity < 1 year. ▪ All other assets not included in the above categories.

TABLE 14.4
Required Stable Funding

Stress testing Managing liquidity under "normal" circumstances is one thing; being prepared to manage liquidity under stressed conditions is a different matter. Examples of stress scenarios include the following: drying of market liquidity; restrictions on currency convertibility; severe settlement disruptions. Stress testing on a regular basis for a variety of short-term and protracted stress scenarios is necessary to identify sources of potential liquidity strain and to ensure that current exposures are within a bank's liquidity risk tolerance. The frequency of stress testing would be higher for systematically important institutions (such as large banks) and in volatile market conditions. The results of stress testing should be utilized to rethink the bank's strategy and operations.

▪ In September 2015, the RBI declared SBI and ICICI Bank as Domestic-Systemically Important Banks (D-SIBs). These banks are required to meet higher capital adequacy requirements.

ONE-MINUTE QUIZ 14.4
Liquidity

Which of the following is a high quality liquid asset? There may be more than one correct answer.

(a) AA- corporate bonds.
(b) AA corporate bonds.
(c) Gold.
(d) Cash.

Off-balance Sheet Activities

Learning Objective

LO 9 Explain the importance of off-balance sheet activities for under standing the financial condition of banks.

Lending and investing are fund-based activities, because the bank uses its funds for these purposes. Increasingly, banks take up non-funded activities that only require the banks to make commitments. Since non-funded activities do not result in liabilities, the balance sheet does not reflect them. These are known as off-balance sheet (OBS) activities. These include issuing guarantees and letters of credit and engaging in treasury operations.

A *guarantee* is a promise by a bank to pay a specified amount, if the party for whose benefit it is issued defaults on its obligation. For example, suppose a construction company gets a contract to build a skyscraper. The builder may be required to provide a bank guarantee for timely completion and work quality. The bank guarantees the performance of the contract by the builder (its customer) and receives a commission. Banks issue guarantees to government departments such as Central Excise and Customs and electricity companies. The customer is liable to pay the amount and the bank steps in only if the customer defaults. Since it is not known whether the customer will default, guarantees are contingent liabilities and they appear outside the balance sheet.

A *letter of credit* (LC) is an undertaking by a bank to the payee (the supplier of goods or services) to pay him on behalf of the buyer (usually the bank's customer) an amount up to the limit specified in the LC, provided the payee meets the conditions in the LC and submits the specified documents. The bank receives a commission for issuing the LC. LCs are contingent liabilities for banks. OBS activities are an important source of fee income for many banks. But they can add to the bank's overall risk exposure.

Treasury operations involve trading in foreign exchange and financial derivatives and they are increasingly a major source of income for many banks. Banks regularly trade in derivatives and foreign currency. Trading involves near-zero initial outlay and is, therefore, an attractive proposition to banks. Treasury products include spot contracts, swaps, options, forwards, and futures.

OBS activities are high risk, high return ventures. The losses can be significant even if the bank takes due care and complies with regulations. These activities are vulnerable to the excesses of rogue traders involving violations of laws that entail not only losses but also regulatory penalties. Barings Bank, SocGen, UBS, and JPMorgan Chase are examples banks that engaged in excessive OBS activities leading to huge losses and fines.

REAL WORLD
Off-balance Sheet
Activities

State Bank of India's off-balance sheet activities on March 31, 2016 included the following:

1. Liability on account of outstanding forward exchange contracts: ₹6,559 billion.
2. Guarantees given on behalf of constituents: ₹2,526 billion.
3. Acceptances, endorsements, and other obligations: ₹1,312 billion.
4. Bills for collection: ₹1,066 billion.

These four items are over *six times* the bank's equity. The magnitude of the off-balance sheet activities looks alarming – enough to wipe out the bank, should the liabilities materialize. However, only a small fraction of them may turn out to be payable by the bank. Increasingly, bank regulators are taking a less cheerful view of these liabilities. Basel III standards require off-balance sheet liabilities to be considered for determining capital adequacy.

Banks are often victims of employee and customer fraud. Unfortunately, they are themselves perpetrators of deception. Let's see some well-known practices.

- *Evergreening loans:* Suppose a customer is about to default on principal or interest payments on a loan. The bank gives a new loan to the customer in order to help the customer pay those amounts. As a result, the bank avoids classification of the earlier loan as an NPA. The bank keeps doing this over and over again, or as is more likely the customer goes bust. Evergreening postpones the day of reckoning for the bank.

- *Understating NPA provision:* The bank suppresses credit losses in order to avoid a big hit to the profit in a quarter or year. This is done by altering the repayment terms or by omitting bad loans outright. Usually, this is done on the direction of the bank's top management.

- *Reporting date window dressing:* This is done to show growth. A few days before the reporting date the bank gives a loan or overdraft to a customer who deposits the amount back with the bank. So both loans and deposits grow and managers meet their growth targets.

- *Overvaluing security:* The security is worth much less than the stated amount. This could be so from the beginning or because of later events such as asset impairment.

- *Cherry picking:* The bank selectively sells investments classified as available for sale, or hold to collect and sell, to recognize gains but keeps investments which have suffered a loss.

- *Value dating:* The presumed date of receipt of principal or interest is taken as prior to the actual date of receipt. This is done to avoid classification of a loan as NPA at the reporting date.

- IFRS and Ind AS classify financial assets as amortized cost, FVTPL and FVTOCI. Currently, they are classified as held to maturity, held for trading and available for sale, according to the RBI's instructions.

- IFRS and Ind AS follow the expected loss approach. Indian GAAP follows the incurred loss approach.

- IFRS and Ind AS don't prescribe a format for bank financial statements. The RBI's circular dated June 23, 2016 has suggested formats for balance sheet and statement of profit and loss different from those in the Third Schedule.

RECAP

- Banks intermediate between savers and borrowers and help direct resources to productive areas. Healthy banks are a sign of a strong economy.
- Banks are strictly regulated because of their significance to the economy.
- The Banking Regulation Act lays down the form and content of the balance sheet and the statement of profit and loss. The RBI issues instructions for the financial statements.
- A bank's capital and liabilities consist of capital, reserves and surplus, deposits, borrowings, and other liabilities and provisions. Assets consist of cash and balances with the RBI, balances with banks and money at call and short notice, investments, advances, fixed assets, and other assets.
- The statement of profit and loss has four heads: income (i.e. revenue), expenditure, profit or loss, and appropriations.
- The return on equity (ROE) is the product of *return on assets* (ROA) and *leverage* (LEV). ROA is driven by *profit margin* (PM) and *asset turnover* (ATO). PM is affected by the *spread* between interest yield and interest cost, credit losses, and operating costs. ATO is driven by the level of business.
- Banks need long-term capital for stable operations. The greater the amount of equity in a bank's capital, the lesser the chances of a bank facing liquidity or solvency problems. The principle is: the riskier an asset, the greater its capital requirement.
- Risk-weights are specified for various asset categories.
- *Basel III*, released in the wake of the 2008 financial crisis, focuses on bank-level and system-wide changes. It emphasizes the importance of equity in a bank's capital structure. *Common Equity Tier 1* capital must be at least 4.5 per cent of RWAs. Minimum Tier 1 capital is 7 per cent and minimum total capital is 8 per cent. Basel III introduced a *capital conservation buffer* of 2.5 per cent and a *countercyclical buffer* of up to 2.5 per cent. It introduced a *liquidity coverage ratio* and a *net stable funding ratio* to strengthen liquidity during stress.
- *Off-balance sheet* (OBS), activities do not require funds and are therefore profitable. Examples are bank guarantees, LCs and treasury operations. However, they can add to a bank's risk.

Review Problem

Vinay Bank has the following balance sheet on March 31, 20XX:

Capital and Liabilities

Capital	₹20,000
Retained earnings	3,250
Deposits	192,850
Borrowings	11,800
Other liabilities	3,150
	231,050

Assets

Cash and balances with Reserve Bank of India	₹3,720
Balances with Banks and money at call and short notice	8,130
Investments	11,280
Advances	205,290
Fixed assets	1,960
Other assets	670
	231,050

Additional information:

1. Cash, ₹1,200.
2. Balances with the RBI include an amount ₹1,670 that can be withdrawn any time.
3. Investments include (a) central government securities, ₹2,980 and (b) AA-rated corporate bonds, ₹6,400. These investments are regularly traded in the debt market.
4. The repayment schedule of deposits (all savings, regarded as stable) and borrowings (all unsecured from less stable business customers) is as follows:

Deposits:

1 to 30 days	₹ 71,380
31 to 60 days	40,350
61 to 180 days	42,800
Less than one year	13,890
One year to two years	12,100
More than two years	12,330
	192,850

Borrowings:

1 to 30 days	₹ 1,300
31 to 60 days	2,010
61 to 180 days	1,450
Less than one year	900
One year to two years	5,980
More than two years	160
	11,800

5. The repayment schedule of advances (all non-financial business customers) is as follows:

Advances:

1 to 30 days	₹ 900
31 to 60 days	58,240
61 to 180 days	17,110
Less than one year	118,250
One year to two years	9,110
More than two years	1,680
	205,290

Required

Calculate Vinay Bank's liquidity coverage ratio.

Solution to the Review Problem

Stock of high quality liquid assets:
Level 1 assets:

Cash	100%	₹1,200	₹1,200
Balance with the RBI	100%	1,670	1,670
Central government securities	100%	2,980	2,980
			5,850

Level 2 assets:

Corporate bonds, rated AA	85%	₹6,400	₹5,440
40% cap of liquid assets, or 2/3% of Level 1 assets			3,900
Total value of stock of highly liquid assets (₹5,850 + ₹3,900)			9,750

Cash outflows:

A. Retail deposits: all demand deposits, stable	5%	₹71,380	₹3,569
B. Unsecured wholesale funding from less stable business customers	10%	1,300	130
Total cash outflows			3,699

Cash inflows:

Non-financial business customers	50%	900	450
Net cash outflows			3,249

$$\text{Liquidity coverage ratio} = \frac{9,750}{3,249} = 300\%$$

ASSIGNMENT MATERIAL

Questions

1. What is the primary role of banks in an economy?
2. What do *commercial banks* do?
3. How are *investment banks* different from commercial banks?
4. What is the main function of the Reserve Bank of India?
5. Why are banks regulated more strictly than non-banking enterprises?
6. Name three laws that banks must comply with in India.
7. Describe the legal framework for the financial statements of banks.
8. List the five groups in the capital and liabilities section of a bank's balance sheet.
9. List the six groups in the assets section of a bank's balance sheet.
10. What is the essential difference between a *demand deposit* and a *term deposit*?
11. Explain the terms: (a) *cash reserve ratio*; (b) *statutory liquidity ratio*; (c) *approved securities*.
12. What is the difference between *money at call* and *money at short notice*?
13. How are *bills purchased* different from *bills discounted*?
14. What are the four heads in a bank's statement of profit and loss?
15. What are the drivers of a bank's return on equity?
16. Explain the terms: (a) *net interest margin*; (b) *CASA ratio*; (c) *spread*.
17. What is *capital adequacy*? Why is it important?
18. What is *Basel III*? Describe the three pillars of Basel III.
19. What is the need for the liquidity coverage ratio in addition to the capital ratio?

Problems

National Bank had revenues of ₹55,900 and expenses of ₹38,100 for the year ended March 31, 20XX. Income tax expense was of ₹5,200.

Problem 14.1
Statutory Reserve ✻

Required

1. Calculate the bank's net profit.
2. How much should it transfer to statutory reserve, if it is (a) a scheduled bank, (b) a non-scheduled bank?

Problem 14.2
Calculating Demand and
Time Liabilities ✳

Secure Bank has the following deposits:

Current accounts..	₹82,000
Savings accounts (payable on demand)...	31,000
Fixed deposits	23,000
Cash certificates	1,000

Required

Compute the bank's demand and time liabilities.

Problem 14.3
Classification and
Presentation of Items in
the Financial Statements
of a Bank ✳✳

Selected items from the financial statements of a bank are as follows:
  (a) Current accounts
  (b) Statutory reserve
  (c) Certificates of deposit
  (d) Borrowings from EXIM Bank
  (e) Bills payable
  (f) Guarantees on behalf of constituents
  (g) Current account with Reserve Bank of India
  (h) Money at call and short notice with Canara Bank in India
  (i) Investments in bonds of Indian companies
  (j) Advance tax
  (k) Term loans given to customers

Required

Using the format given below, state how each of the items will be classified and presented in the financial statements.
  (a) Current accounts   Liabilities → Deposits → Demand deposits

Problem 14.4
Classification and
Presentation of Items in
the Financial Statements
of a Bank ✳✳ Alternative
to Problem 14.3

Selected items from the financial statements of a bank are as follows:
  (a) Advances secured by tangible assets
  (b) Deferred tax asset
  (c) Investment in US government securities
  (d) Balance with SBI in current account
  (e) Staff security deposits
  (f) Liability for outstanding forward exchange contracts
  (g) Refinance from SIDBI
  (h) Recurring deposits
  (i) Revaluation reserve
  (j) Overdrafts
  (k) Savings accounts

Required

Using the format given below, state how each of the items will be classified and presented in the financial statements.
  (a) Advances secured by tangible assets   Assets → Advances → Secured by tangible assets;

Problem 14.5
Explaining the Cost of
Deposits ✳✳

Pinnacle Bank had the following deposits at the end of two consecutive years:

	20X2	20X1
Current accounts..	₹48,200	₹38,700
Savings accounts..	23,100	19,300
Fixed deposits	87,900	61,500

Required

1. Calculate the CASA ratio for each of the two years.
2. Based on the available information, explain how the change in the composition of the deposits would have affected the bank's overall interest cost.

Zenith Bank had the following deposits at the end of two consecutive years:

Problem 14.6
Explaining the Cost of Deposits ∗∗ Alternative to Problem 14.5

	20X2	20X1
Current accounts	₹29,100	₹10,600
Savings accounts	16,200	21,500
Fixed deposits	78,700	97,800

Required

1. Calculate the CASA ratio for each of the two years.
2. Based on the available information, explain how the change in the composition of the deposits would have affected the bank's overall interest cost.

Swish Bank has the following information for three years:

Problem 14.7
Evaluating the Spread∗∗∗

	Year 3	Year 2	Year 1
Interest income	₹ 22,340	₹ 16,910	₹ 12,290
Interest expense	14,500	11,500	9,210
Advances	146,800	134,960	121,870
Investments	3,100	2,600	2,000
Deposits	98,630	81,610	73,980
Borrowings	15,100	14,100	13,100

Required

1. Calculate the bank's spread.
2. Evaluate the change in the spread.

Placid Bank has the following information for three years:

Problem 14.8
Evaluating the Spread ∗∗∗
Alternative to Problem 14.7

	Year 3	Year 2	Year 1
Interest income	₹ 19,250	₹ 17,100	₹13,900
Interest expense	10,470	9,110	8,230
Advances	106,180	102,490	96,130
Investments	2,450	2,190	1,720
Deposits	76,540	72,230	67,810
Borrowings	21,300	19,800	17,100

Required

1. Calculate the bank's spread.
2. Evaluate the change in the spread.

Mass Bank has the following selected information for three years:

Problem 14.9
Profitability Measures∗∗∗∗

	Year 3	Year 2	Year 1
Statement of profit and loss			
Interest income	₹27,800	₹23,900	₹21,430
Other income	340	230	190
Revenue	28,140	24,130	21,620
Operating expenses	11,730	8,160	6,370
Interest expense	17,340	14,910	12,290
Provision for NPAs	4,160	1,740	980
Balance sheet			
Deposits	₹98,630	₹81,610	₹73,980
Borrowings	15,100	14,100	13,100
Advances	146,800	134,960	121,870
Investments	3,100	2,600	2,000

Required

Evaluate the bank's performance.

Problem 14.10
Profitability Measures
✳✳✳✳ Alternative to
Problem 14.9

Fun Bank has the following selected information for three years:

	Year 3	Year 2	Year 1
Statement of profit and loss			
Interest income	₹ 2,440	₹ 1,500	₹ 1,280
Other income	65	45	40
Operating expenses	840	690	600
Interest expense	1,500	1,140	1,080
Provision for NPAs	610	230	160
Balance sheet			
Borrowings	₹ 4,500	₹ 2,900	₹ 2,500
Deposits	11,000	9,000	8,000
Advances	13,000	11,000	10,000
Investments	3,100	2,600	2,000

Required

Evaluate the bank's performance.

Problem 14.11
Capital Requirement under
Basel III ✳✳✳✳✳

Blasé Bank has the following assets:

Assets	
Cash	₹12,100
Balance with RBI	1,800
Central government securities	43,100
State government securities	6,730
Corporate debt, AAA	53,100
Corporate debt, BB	12,900
Non-performing assets (gross, ₹2,000 less provision ₹800)	1,200

Required

Calculate Blasé Bank's minimum capital under Basel III standards. Round the amount to the next higher rupee.

Problem 14.12
Capital Requirement under
Basel III ✳✳✳✳✳
Alternative to
Problem 14.11

Cool Bank has the following assets:

Assets	
Cash	₹7,940
Balance with RBI	2,600
Central government securities	18,100
State government securities	2,720
State government-guaranteed securities	10,100
Corporate debt, AAA	16,430
Corporate debt, BBB	41,200
Non-performing assets (gross, ₹7,000 less provision, ₹4,200)	2,800

Required

Calculate Cool Bank's minimum capital under Basel II standards. Round the amount to the next higher rupee.

Business Decision Cases

BDC 14.1
Gradual Bank and Fast Bank Selected information from the financial statements of Gradual Bank and Fast Bank for two years is given below.

	Gradual Bank		Fast Bank	
	Year 2	Year 1	Year 2	Year 1
Statement of profit and loss				
Interest income..	₹14,980	₹13,450	₹17,210	₹12,190
Other income..	115	100	1,430	90
Revenue	15,095	13,550	18,640	12,280
Operating expenses...	1,910	1,760	3,560	1,210
Interest expense	8,300	8,170	15,130	8,390
Provision for NPAs	940	680	1,920	570
Total expenditure...	11,150	10,610	20,610	10,170
Net profit..	3,945	2,940	(1,970)	2,110
Dividend..	650	600	0	450
Balance sheet				
Equity and Liabilities				
Share capital	₹ 8,055	₹ 8,000	₹ 2,000	₹ 2,000
Reserves and surplus..	15,205	11,910	11,300	13,270
Deposits..	83,200	87,450	106,150	84,160
Borrowings...	3,300	5,100	1,710	1,210
Other liabilities and provisions	170	130	190	140
	109,930	112,590	121,350	100,780
Assets				
Cash and balances with RBI	₹ 1,210	₹ 890	₹ 1,610	₹ 870
Balances with banks and money at call and short notice..	780	490	790	540
Advances...	106,430	110,560	117,580	98,160
Investments..	900	200	980	900
Fixed assets..	480	350	280	260
Other assets	130	100	110	50
	109,930	112,590	121,350	100,780

Required

1. Compare the performance of the two banks.
2. Which one is riskier? Which one is more profitable?

Interpreting Financial Reports

ICICI Bank is India's largest private sector bank. It has a reputation for aggressive growth. Analysts have voiced concern over the bank's loan portfolio and margins. In contrast, HDFC Bank is reputed to be more cautious and more profitable.

IFR 14.1
ICICI Bank

Required

1. Develop an analysis of ICICI Bank's financial statements on the lines of the analysis of HDFC Bank's illustration in the chapter.
2. Is ICICI Bank different from HDFC Bank? In what ways?

Financial Analysis

Study the financial statements of a sample of public sector banks and private banks in India.

FA 14.1
Non-Performing Assets

Required

1. Summarize the position on NPAs in the banks.
2. Do you see any patterns? Explain.
3. Comment on the measures taken by the banks to reduce NPAs.

Study the financial statements of a sample of public sector banks and private banks in India and foreign banks.

FA 14.2
Capital Adequacy

Required

1. Summarize the position on capital adequacy in the banks.
2. Comment on the measures taken by the banks to meet the capital standards.

Answers to One-minute Quiz

14.1 b.
14.2 c.
14.3 b.
14.4 b, d.

Answers to Test Your Understanding

14.1 *Demand liabilities:* Current accounts, ₹50,000 + Demand portion of savings accounts, ₹8,000 + Overdue fixed deposits, ₹1,000 = ₹59,000. *Time liabilities:* Time portion of savings accounts, ₹2,000 + Fixed deposits, ₹19,000 = ₹21,000.

14.2 Sun Bank's deposit growth was 48 per cent in Year 2, but slowed drastically to 16 per cent in Year 3. However, over the three-year period, the bank's CASA ratio improved from 40 per cent in Year 1 to 49 per cent in Year 2 to 52 per cent in Year 3. The bank's low-cost current accounts and savings accounts grew above or at the overall growth rate of deposits, high-cost term deposits grew at rates below the overall growth rate. As a result, the average cost of deposits would have fallen over the three-year period. Raising deposits is important for a bank, but bringing down the cost of deposits is also important.

14.3

	Year 2	Year 1
Interest income	₹1,120	₹ 980
Interest expense	830	670
Advances	7,900	7,440
Investments	930	670
Net interest income	290	—
Interest-earning assets	8,830	8,110
Average interest-earning assets	8,470	—
Net interest margin	3.42%	—

14.4

	Amount	Risk-weight (%)	Risk-weighted asset
Cash	₹10,500	0	₹ 0
Balance with RBI	2,000	0	0
Central government securities	29,200	0	0
Corporate debt, AAA	71,800	20	14,360
Corporate debt, BB	16,100	150	24,150
Non-performing assets (net of 50% provided)	4,200	50	2,100
Total			40,610

Minimum capital: (a) BCBS: 10.5% of ₹40,610 = ₹4,264.05; (b) RBI: 11.5% of ₹40,610 = ₹4,670.15.

CHAPTER 15

Earnings Analysis and Qualitative Information

LEARNING OBJECTIVES

After studying this chapter, you should be able to:

1. Assess earnings quality.
2. Separate operating performance from the effect of financial activities.
3. Describe earnings management and identify motives for managing earnings.
4. Analyze segment performance.
5. Explain pro forma financial measures.
6. Define free cash flow and explain its use and limitations.
7. Understand economic value added.
8. Understand the forces that influence corporate disclosure policy.
9. Describe the implications of the efficient market hypothesis for financial statement analysis.
10. Examine claims in management communications.
11. Understand the importance of corporate governance in financial reporting.
12. Question the role of auditors, analysts and the press in financial reporting.

SPEED READ

Transitory and non-operating items obscure earnings. The effect of financial activities should be separated to understand operating performance. Managers manipulate earnings because of performance pressure. Segment information breaks down a firm's performance. Pro forma measures exclude some GAAP items. Free cash flow is the difference between operating and investing cash. Economic value added is the excess of profit after a charge for capital employed. Companies often provide voluntary disclosures because of market forces. Efficient markets anticipate much of the information contained in financial reports prior to their release. Qualitative information in annual reports is useful in understanding the financial statements. Independent directors, audit committees and auditors are intended to monitor financial reporting. Analysts and the press have influence over the quality of financial statements.

WAH TAJ?

Indian Hotels Limited is the owner of the prestigious Taj hotels in India and abroad. In the year ended March 31, 2016, the company slashed its net loss to ₹605 million from ₹3,781 million in the financial year 2015 and ₹5,539 in the financial year 2014. Remarkable, on the face of it. There is more to it than these numbers might suggest. Revenue grew by a not-so-spectacular 9.6 per cent in 2016 and 3 per cent in 2015. Costs increased by 9 per cent in 2016 and 4.6 per cent in 2015. That should have wiped out the chances of a better performance. The turnaround story is complicated by a number of items in the financial statements. Exceptional items added ₹672 million to the loss in 2016, as compared to ₹3,539 million in 2015. Impairment charges in 2015 totalled ₹3,484 million. In contrast, there was a profit of ₹565 million on the sale of a long-term investment in 2016. This almost offset the loss of ₹250 million from a project written off and the loss of ₹350 million on the sale of a subsidiary. Besides, helped mainly by dividend income from investments other income increased by ₹1,664 million. At best, the numbers tell us that the company is facing up to the bad decisions it made in the past. While it is certainly welcome, it would be a mistake to think of it as a turnaround.

Earnings Quality

A key objective of financial statement analysis is to estimate future earnings from current earnings. Unfortunately, the profit reported in the annual report is a 'noisy' measure of a company's operating performance. The analyst needs to identify the major sources of revenue and profit, such as divisions and product lines, as well as understand the extent to which a company's earnings are dependent on each of them. An important part of the exercise of recomputing a company's earnings is to identify and segregate non-operating items so that the resulting earnings number represents probable future earnings from regular and continuing activities.

Earnings quality refers to the probability of earnings trends continuing and the extent to which earnings could represent distributable cash. Earnings are said to be of *high quality* if they can be distributed in cash, they are derived primarily from continuing operations and the methods used in measuring profit are conservative.

In contrast, earnings are said to be of *low quality* if they have only a small percentage of distributable cash, are derived from non-operating sources, and are computed using liberal accounting methods. Here are some examples of low-quality earnings.

1. Earnings result from change to liberal accounting estimates, e.g. increasing useful life of fixed assets; understating allowance for credit losses.
2. Earnings result from change to liberal accounting methods, e.g. switching to SLM from WDV in the early part of an asset's life; moving to FIFO from WAC in inflationary times.
3. Non-recurring items contribute significantly to results, e.g. gain on sale of a subsidiary; receipt of a large tax refund.
4. Earnings are cyclical, e.g. peak earnings of shipping companies.
5. Earnings are volatile due to uncontrollable factors, e.g. earnings of Indian coffee plantations affected by frost in Brazil.

Let's now see how a company's earnings quality may be affected by the following:
- Choice of accounting policies;
- Changes in accounting methods;
- Changes in accounting estimates;
- Non-operating and non-recurring items.
- Discontinued operations; and
- Prior period errors;

Choice of Accounting Policies

Accounting standards lay down the broad framework for the preparation and presentation of financial statements. Within this framework, management has considerable flexibility in selecting accounting methods and estimating key accounting determinants, such as useful life of assets and the amount of allowance for credit losses. Reported income numbers are often affected significantly by the accounting methods and estimates used. Conservative accounting methods and estimates tend to produce a lower profit. Table 15.1 gives examples of accounting policy choices in areas in which management exercises significant discretion and judgment.

The bewildering variety of accounting policies complicates comparisons of earnings of companies even within the same industry. At a minimum, companies should disclose the measurement bases used in preparing the financial statements (e.g. historical cost, current cost, net realizable value, fair value or recoverable value), accounting policies that are relevant to an understanding of the financial statements, management's judgments and assumptions, and other sources of estimation uncertainty.

Revenue recognition	■ Determining when a sale occurred or a service was provided ■ Allocating fair value to the multiple elements of goods and services to be provided ■ Estimating percentage of completion in construction contracts
Inventories	■ Specific identification, first-in, first-out, and weighted-average cost ■ Estimating net realizable value
Property, plant and equipment	■ Cost of acquisition ■ Revaluation
Depreciation	■ Estimating and revising useful life and residual value ■ Straight-line, written-down-value, production-units and sum-of-the-years'-digits methods
Asset impairment	■ Estimating future cash flows ■ Estimating cost of capital
Financial assets	■ Determining fair value ■ Classifying financial investments as hold to collect or hold to collect and sell ■ Estimating credit losses
Operating investments	■ Determining control, significant influence and joint control
Leases	■ Classifying a lease as an operating or a finance lease ■ Determining incremental borrowing rate ■ Estimating residual value
Pensions	■ Estimating discount rate ■ Estimating expected return on plan assets ■ Estimating life expectancy ■ Estimating salary growth rate
Foreign currency	■ Functional currency

TABLE 15.1
Management Discretion and Judgment in Accounting Policy Choices

To illustrate the effect of alternative accounting policies, suppose two companies, Conservative and Liberal, were set up in 20XX in the same industry. Conservative's accounting policies are: WAC for inventory valuation, WDV for depreciation, and full write-off of product development costs. Liberal Company follows FIFO, SLM, and one-fifth amortization of product development costs. Both companies have identical revenues, expenses, and purchases, and have 10,000 equity shares. Assume a 30 per cent income tax rate. Exhibit 15.1 presents the statement of profit and loss of the two companies.

Statement of Profit and Loss for 20XX		
	Conservative	**Liberal**
Revenue		
Sales	₹1,000,000	₹1,000,000
Expenses		
Cost of goods sold (a)	300,000	200,000
Depreciation (b)	255,000	120,000
Product development costs (c)	100,000	20,000
Other expenses	80,000	80,000
	735,000	420,000
Profit before tax	265,000	580,000
Income tax (d)	96,000	126,000
Profit after tax	169,000	454,000
Number of equity shares	10,000	10,000
Earnings per share	16.90	45.40
Notes:		
(a) Beginning inventories	0	0
Purchases	700,000	700,000
Cost of goods available for sale	700,000	700,000
Ending inventories: WAC; FIFO	400,000	500,000
Cost of goods sold	300,000	200,000

EXHIBIT 15.1
Comparing the Effect of Alternative Accounting Policies

(b)	Cost of fixed assets	800,000	800,000
	Residual value	80,000	80,000
	Useful life	6 years	6 years
	Depreciation: WDV, SLM	255,000	120,000
(c)	Product Development Costs: Full write-off; One-fifth amortized	100,000	20,000
(d)	Income Tax: Sales	1,000,000	1,000,000
	Cost of goods sold	300,000	200,000
	Initial marketing costs (allowed fully in tax)	100,000	100,000
	Other expenses	80,000	80,000
	Depreciation 25% of 800,000	200,000	200,000
	Expenses for tax purposes	680,000	580,000
	Taxable income	320,000	420,000
	Income tax, 30%	96,000	126,000

As a result of its more stringent accounting policies, Conservative reports earnings per share of ₹16.90 versus Liberal's ₹45.40. Clearly, we should keep in mind differences in the accounting methods between the two companies while comparing their results. The more stringent inventory valuation policy has helped Conservative save ₹30,000 in tax (difference in cost of goods sold, ₹100,000 × tax rate, 30 per cent). Thus, Conservative is better off than Liberal by ₹30,000 in net cash flow from operations. From the discussion in Chapter 5, you would know that the effect of the difference will reverse in future years. For example, the higher year-end inventory will have the effect of increasing cost of goods sold next year, thereby decreasing next year's net profit. So Liberal's higher earnings per share is transitory.[1]

In this illustration, the recomputation of Liberal's earnings is not too difficult mainly because all the information required for this purpose is available. Unfortunately, in the real world, much of the information required to make the recomputation is not available since companies don't often disclose all the relevant information. Meaningful comparisons are not possible unless the analyst knows the accounting policies followed and their effect.

Changes in Accounting Methods

We know that an enterprise should follow accounting policies consistently for similar transactions within each period and from one period to the next so that the results of different periods can be compared. For example, if an entity switches to SLM from WDV, the profit in the current period will not be comparable with that in the previous period. Therefore, an entity shall change an accounting policy only if the change (a) is required by an Ind AS; or (b) results in the financial statements providing reliable and *more relevant* information about the effects of transactions on the entity's financial position, financial performance or cash flows. "Reliable" means that the financial statements (i) represent faithfully the entity's financial position, financial performance and cash flows; (ii) reflect the economic substance of transactions, and not merely the legal form; (iii) are neutral, i.e. free from bias; (iv) are prudent; and (v) are complete in all material respects. "Relevant" means that the information that results is relevant to the economic decision-making needs of users. A company's anxiety to maintain a certain level of profitability in a bad year or to lower the amount of income tax expense is not an acceptable reason for a change in an accounting policy.

An accounting policy change may be voluntary or required by an Ind AS. When an entity changes an accounting policy voluntarily, it must apply the change retrospectively. *Retrospective application* is applying a new accounting policy to transactions as if that policy had always been applied. An entity shall account for a change in accounting policy resulting from the initial application of an Ind AS in accordance with any specific transitional provisions in that standard. If an Ind AS does not include specific transitional

---

[1] As an exercise, you may recompute the EPS with deferred tax effect.

provisions, the entity must apply the change retrospectively. When a change in accounting policy is applied retrospectively, the entity shall adjust the opening balance of each affected component of equity for the earliest prior period presented and the other comparative amounts disclosed for each prior period presented as if the new accounting policy had always been applied.

When a voluntary change in accounting policy has an effect on the current period or any prior period (even if it is impracticable to determine the related amount), or might have an effect on future periods, an entity shall disclose (a) the nature of the change in accounting policy; (b) the reasons for the change; and (c) the amount of the adjustment for the current period and each prior period presented for each financial statement line item affected.

Apart from violating comparability frequent changes are perceived by analysts and others as desperate attempts to camouflage serious financial and business difficulties being experienced by an enterprise. Even so, a few companies change their accounting policies to puff the reported earnings. When accounting changes have been made by a company, the analyst has to restate the results of earlier periods so that the earnings series becomes comparable.

Sometimes, accounting changes intended to increase reported profit have the effect of lowering profits in later years because of unexpected changes in the economic environment. For example, in the early 1990s, a few companies began to show their land holdings as inventories so as to take advantage of the boom in real estate prices. These companies transferred the unrealized appreciation in the value of their lands to capital reserve. However, when the property market went into a recession, they got into trouble.

Changes in Accounting Estimates

As a result of the uncertainties inherent in business activities, many items in financial statements cannot be measured with precision but can only be estimated. You have seen examples of estimates of bad debts, inventory obsolescence, the fair value of financial instruments, the useful lives of and/or the expected pattern of consumption of the benefits from depreciable assets, and warranty obligations. The use of estimates is unavoidable. Estimation involves judgments based on the latest available, reliable information. It is important to revise an estimate if changes occur in the circumstances under which the estimate was based or as a result of new information or experience. The revision of an estimate does not relate to prior periods and is not the correction of an error. The effect of a change in an accounting estimate shall be recognized *prospectively*. An entity shall disclose the nature and amount of a change in an accounting estimate, which has an effect in the current period or is expected to have an effect in future periods.

Non-operating and Non-recurring Items

Certain items of income and expense may be large, or otherwise important to users of financial statements in understanding and making projections about the financial performance of a business. The reported results can be considered to be representative if the underlying activities and events in a period are of a normal, recurring nature. The effect of unusual and non-recurring events should be isolated to predict the likely profit for the next year.

For many companies, income from non-operating sources has been significantly higher in recent years. Dividend income from mutual fund investments, interest income for manufacturing and service organizations, foreign exchange gains, and gain on sale of property, plant and equipment are examples of income from non-operating sources, and these appear under "other income" in the statement of profit and loss. Much of "other income" comes from sources other than a company's core business or is related to items of a non-recurring nature. Non-operating income is increasing for many companies and even helping some of them hide losses from their normal business operations.

Here are a few examples of how non-recurring and non-operating items affect profit:

- *HDFC:* Net profit of ₹26 billion for the quarter ended March 31, 2016 included profit on sale of investment in HDFC Life of ₹15 billion.

- *Biocon:* Net profit for the September 2015 quarter doubled to ₹3 billion. It included proceeds of ₹2 billion from the sale of shares in its subsidiary Syngene.

- *Indian Hotels:* Group net loss went down from ₹1,695 million in the June 2016 quarter to ₹268 million in the September 2016 quarter. Reasons for the decrease in loss included: (a) loss on disposal of an overseas operation was ₹1,018 million in June and it dropped to ₹13 million in September; (b) loss on change in the fair value of currency swaps was ₹178 million in June as compared to gain of ₹317 million in September.

- *Emami:* Net profit jumped to ₹880 million in the September 2016 quarter from ₹420 million in the year-ago quarter. Other income rose to ₹250 million from ₹60 million over the period.

HANDHOLD 15.1
Non-operating Income

Sony Corporation reported a net profit of ¥43 billion for the year to March 2013, after non-stop losses for four years: 2009, ¥99 billion; 2010, ¥41 billion; 2011, ¥260 billion; 2012, ¥457 billion. That's good news. Let's take a close look at the numbers. First, the profit was one-tenth of what the company spent on restructuring in the past five years. Also, it expected to spend another ¥50 billion in 2014. Second, gain on sale of investments produced ¥42 billion of that profit. Finally, the improvement came about despite a decline in the profits from the company's core businesses because of the better performance of the financial services business. A return to profitability had some way to go. In 2014, the company reported a net loss of ¥128 billion and followed with a net loss of ¥126 billion in 2015. In 2016, it reported a net profit ¥148 billion, helped by gain on sale of investments of ¥52 billion. The apparent improvement in 2013 and again in 2016 came from non-operating income. Sony's tagline is "make.believe".

Discontinued Operations

Most large companies are engaged in many types of business. The different activities are organized as separate groups of products, services, or customers. Sometimes, a company may discontinue operations in certain major business segments either because they are not profitable or for other reasons. A **discontinued operation** is a business or a component of a business that a firm has already discontinued or plans to discontinue. Typically, it would be a *cash-generating unit* (CGU) or a group of CGUs.

For predicting earnings from regular, on-going activities, the analyst should separate the results of continuing operations. In addition, the analyst should exclude any gain or loss from the disposal of a business segment as a part of recomputation of the earnings. Separate disclosure of discontinued operations is necessary to facilitate evaluation of the ongoing activities of the business. Unfortunately, such disclosures are rare in India.

Prior Period Errors

Prior period errors are omissions and misstatements in an entity's past financial statements. They result from not using or misusing information that was available when the financial statements were authorized for issue. Prior period errors include calculation errors, incorrect application of accounting policies, misinterpretations of facts, and fraud. Examples are inaccuracy in totalling inventory sheets and flawed depreciation calculations arising from the use of incorrect asset lives or omission to consider residual values. Prior period errors are different from changes in accounting estimates (e.g. revision of asset lives or allowance for credit losses), which are inherently approximations that are routinely revised as additional information becomes available in subsequent periods.

An enterprise should correct material prior period errors retrospectively in the first set of financial statements authorized for issue after their discovery. The comparative numbers for the prior periods in which the error occurred should be corrected. Unless it is impracticable to do so, the prior period error should be corrected by *retrospective restatement*.

Retrospective restatement corrects the recognition, measurement and amounts as if a prior period error had never occurred. Prior period errors should be disclosed. The Companies Act 2013 provides for restatement of financial statements with the approval of the National Company Law Tribunal. When there are prior period errors, the analyst should segregate them and recompute the amounts beginning with the year in which the error occurred.

REAL WORLD
Errors

Since the financial statements of large companies are generally audited by reputable accounting firms, it is fair to expect these statements to be free from material errors and omissions. Here are two unusual examples of errors.

- On September 23, 2016, Santander Consumer USA, the car loans arm of Spain's largest bank, announced that it would be restating its quarterly and annual financial statements for 2013, 2014, 2015 and the first quarter statements for 2016 due to errors identified in those statements. The restatements were being made to correct errors associated with the company's methodology for accreting dealer discounts, subvention payments from manufacturers and capitalized origination costs, the company's lack of consideration of net discounts when estimating the allowance for credit losses and the discount rate used in determining the impairment for loans accounted for as troubled debt restructurings. The expected cumulative impact of the errors was an increase to total equity of approximately 1 per cent, as of March 31, 2016. The company's shares were up about 11 per cent in the trading that followed, as the errors were smaller than expected.

- On April 28, 2014, Bank of America announced that it had made an error in calculating its regulatory capital reported to the Federal Reserve but it did not affect its financial statement numbers. The error related to the bonds issued by Merrill Lynch, acquired by Bank of America in 2009. The bonds were acquired at a discount to their original value but some of them were paid off or bought back at higher amounts. The resulting loss should have been reduced from the bank's regulatory capital but was not, in error. Thankfully, despite the loss the bank did not breach any capital requirements. The bank's stock price fell by more than 6 per cent following the announcement.

Prior period errors are seen by investors as the result of weak internal controls.

Which of the following is not an example of an error? There may be more than one correct answer.
(a) Capitalization of R & D costs instead of expensing them.
(b) A change from a useful life estimate when the original estimate was made without considering technical evaluation.
(c) A calculation error in estimating credit losses.
(d) A change in an estimate of credit losses based on information not available at the previous reporting date.

ONE-MINUTE QUIZ 15.1
Accounting Errors

Earnings Quality and Cash Flow

Earnings that are in cash are of high quality. If the gap difference between earnings and cash flow is low, it means that the earnings are rapidly converted into cash. We know that over the life of a firm earnings equal cash flow. The gap between earnings and cash flow indicates the effect of accrual. The ratio of cash flow to earnings is an important measure of earnings quality. Using this measure, DRL's earnings quality is as follows:

Cash flow to earnings ratio	2016	2015
$\dfrac{\text{Net cash from operating activities}}{\text{Profit}}$	$\dfrac{40,476}{21,514} = 1.88$	$\dfrac{25,235}{23,364} = 1.08$

A ratio of about 1:1 would suggest that the conversion of earnings into cash is working fine. DRL's ratio jumped from 1.08 to 1.88. It has to return to about 1.0 soon. High volatility from one period to another would raise questions about earnings quality. An important reason for the decline in profit in 2016 was the foreign exchange loss relating to the company's Venezuela operations (₹4,621). Excluding the effect of this loss, the profit is

₹26,135 and the cash flow to earnings ratio is 1.55. Even this represents a sharp increase from 2015.

Earnings Quality and Growth

Firms that grow by frequent acquisitions are more prone to trouble. Acquisitions are often overvalued. Failed acquisitions leave behind a debris of goodwill impairment loss. Again, firms that enjoy stratospheric growth rates are brought down to earth sooner than later as competition catches up. Further, the earnings of start-up firms are completely unpredictable, since such firms swing from high hopes to great despair on a daily basis. So it is never clear whether they can manage to survive. Recall from Chapter 12 that the price-earnings ratio is an indicator of the market's growth expectations. In addition, the PE ratio can tell us about earnings quality. A low PE ratio could imply that the market suspects the quality of reported earnings and therefore applies a discount to it.

ONE-MINUTE QUIZ 15.2
Transitory Items

Transitory items are most likely in which quarter?
- (a) First quarter.
- (b) Second quarter.
- (c) Third quarter.
- (d) Fourth quarter.

TEST YOUR UNDERSTANDING 15.1
Earnings Quality

Aaron Company's statement of profit and loss for two consecutive years is as follows.

Statement of Profit and Loss	20X6	20X5
		(in million)
Net sales	₹125	₹130
Other income (net)	15	1
Cost of sales	98	135
Operating expenses	30	36
Net profit	12	(40)

Additional information: (a) Other income consisted of gain on sale of surplus land of ₹14 million and interest income of ₹1 million in 20X6 and interest income of ₹1 million in 20X5. (b) Sales to related parties resulted in a profit of ₹8 million in 20X6. There were no sales to related parties in 20X5. (c) A business unit that incurred a loss of ₹9 million in 20X5 was discontinued in 20X6. Closure costs of the discontinued business totalled ₹2 million, included in operating expenses. Has Aaron Company turned the corner?

Advanced Profitability Analysis: Focus on Operations

Learning Objective

LO 2   Separate operating performance from the effect of financial activities.

In our analysis of DRL in Chapter 12, we did not distinguish between operating and non-operating items. This is true of our income measure and asset base:

- Profit after tax includes "other income" that has a number of financial and other non-operating items.
- Assets include financial assets such as investments and bank deposits.

We'll now see how to refine the income and asset measures.

Operating Profit

Since interest expense and non-operating items are determined by factors that have little to do with the efficiency of management of assets, analysts calculate a return measure based on the **net operating profit after tax** (NOPAT). For this purpose, we consider only revenues from sales and cost of operations and exclude non-operating incomes – interest income and other non-operating incomes and exceptional items – and non-operating expenses – principally, interest expense.

We have to adjust for the tax effect of these exclusions. For instance, since interest income is taxable, the reported income tax expense includes tax on interest income. Since operating income excludes interest income, the tax expense should also exclude the tax effect of that income. So we deduct the tax on interest income from the reported tax expense, *as if* there was no interest income. Similarly, since interest expense is tax-deductible, the tax expense includes the tax shield on interest expense. Since operating income excludes interest expense, the tax expense should also exclude the tax effect of that expense. So we add back the tax saving on interest expense from the tax expense, *as if* there was no interest expense. The tax adjustment for other exclusions from net profit follows similar reasoning. For tax adjustment, we apply the marginal tax rate of 34.61 per cent for 2016 and 33.99 per cent for 2015, which were the statutory tax rates in those years. Exhibit 15.2 presents the calculation of NOPAT.

EXHIBIT 15.2
Calculation of NOPAT

DR REDDY'S LABORATORIES LIMITED Reformulated Statement of Profit and Loss For the year ended March 31				
		2016		**2015**
				(in millions)
Revenue from operations		₹156,978		₹150,233
Cost of material consumed	₹24,667		₹28,259	
Purchase of stock-in-trade	11,743		9,420	
Changes in inventories	(1,003)		(558)	
Conversion charges	2,436		1,929	
Employee benefits expense	31,874		29,446	
Depreciation and amortization expense	9,705		7,599	
Other expenses	48,053	127,475	46,801	122,896
Operating profit before tax		29,503		27,337
Tax as reported	(5,237)		(5,632)	
Deduct Tax on financial income	932		932	
Add Tax on finance costs	(285)		(368)	
Deduct Tax on exceptional items	(1,599)		—	
Tax on Operating profit		(6,189)		(5,068)
Net operating profit after tax (NOPAT)		23,314		22,269
Add Financial income	2,693		2,741	
Tax: 34.61%; 33.99%	(932)		(932)	
	1,761		1,809	
Deduct Finance costs	(824)		(1,082)	
Tax: 34.61%; 33.99%	285		368	
	(539)		(714)	
Add Net financial income		1,222		1,095
Deduct Exceptional item	(4,621)		—	
Tax: 34.61%; 33.99%	1,599	(3,022)	—	—
Profit for the year		21,514		23,364

NOPAT increased 4.69 per cent in 2016, slightly better than the revenue growth of 4.49 per cent. This suggests improved profitability of operations. Net financial income was 5.7 per cent of net profit in 2016, up from 4.7 per cent in 2016. This indicates the company's higher dependence on non-business activities shore up the profit. Financial income is subject to interest rate changes, which are outside the company's control. Since financial income more volatile than operating income, it is difficult to sustain any improvement resulting from financial activities. The exceptional loss was 14.1 per cent of net profit in 2016.

Net Operating Assets

Since we have eliminated financial income and other non-operating income, the asset base should have only "operating assets", i.e. assets that are used in the operations. Also, financial investments do not contribute to sales; so there is no reason to consider them as part of the denominator in asset turnover. Current investments, which are investments in financial assets, constitute 11 per cent of DRL's total assets. (DRL's non-current investments are in business operations.) Since the company is not in the business of investing in mutual funds, these are not part of the company's operating assets. Further, DRL has term deposits with banks. These are included in cash and bank balances (original maturity of up to 12 months) and other non-current assets (original maturity of more than 12 months). Though financial assets earn interest, they are not invested in the company's operations. Therefore, we exclude them from operating assets. Exhibit 15.3 presents the calculation of operating assets.

EXHIBIT 15.3

Calculation of Net Operating Assets

DR REDDY'S LABORATORIES LIMITED Reformulated Balance Sheet For the year ended March 31			
	2016	2015	2014
			(in millions)
Total assets	₹200,104	₹185,978	₹160,296
Deduct Financial assets			
Current investments	21,122	21,022	10,664
Term deposits with original maturity of less than 3 months	3,841	1,595	3,864
Term deposits with original maturity of more than 3 months	12,709	12,837	14,298
	37,672	35,454	28,826
Operating assets: Total assets – Financial assets	162,432	150,524	131,470
Total liabilities	83,095	87,447	81,644
Deduct Financial liabilities			
Long-term borrowings	10,690	14,315	20,755
Short-term borrowings	22,718	21,857	20,607
	33,408	36,172	41,362
Operating liabilities: Total liabilities – Financial liabilities	49,687	51,275	40,282
Net operating assets: Operating assets – Operating liabilities	112,745	99,249	91,188
Average net operating assets	105,997	95,219	

Return on Operating Investment

DRL's average net operating assets are 105,997 for 2016 and 95,219 for 2015. Using NOPAT, sales and average net operating assets, we recalculate NOPAT margin, net operating asset turnover and return on net operating assets (RNOA):

NOPAT margin	2016	2015
$\dfrac{\text{NOPAT}}{\text{Sales}}$	$\dfrac{23,314}{156,978} = 14.85\%$	$\dfrac{22,269}{150,233} = 14.82\%$

NOA turnover	2016	2015
$\dfrac{\text{Sales}}{\text{Net operating assets}}$	$\dfrac{156,978}{105,997} = 1.48 \text{ times}$	$\dfrac{150,233}{95,219} = 1.58 \text{ times}$

Return on net operating assets	2016	2015
$\dfrac{\text{NOPAT}}{\text{Net operating assets}}$	$\dfrac{23,314}{105,997} = 21.99\%$	$\dfrac{22,269}{95,219} = 23.39\%$

With these measures, we can understand DRL's operating performance better. We note that in 2016 the NOPAT margin was 14.85 per cent, as compared to 13.71 per cent we calculated in Chapter 12. This is because we exclude non-operating income from the numerator, but there is no change in the denominator, viz. sales. The NOA turnover story is similar: it goes up to 1.48 from the ATO of 0.81 in Chapter 12, because we exclude financial assets from the denominator, but there is no change in the numerator, viz. sales. The RNOA is 21.99 per cent, which is higher than the ROA of 11.14 per cent in Chapter 12. We should compare the return on operating assets with the cost of capital. For instance, if the cost of capital is 10 per cent, DRL is doing very well.

Earnings Quality and Operating Profits

Earnings that are derived primarily from continuing operations that are not volatile from year to year are of high quality. Since non-operating and non-recurring items are volatile, they distort performance. The ratio of operating profit to profit is an important measure of earnings quality. Using this measure, DRL's earnings quality is as follows:

Operating profit to profit ratio	2016	2015
$\dfrac{\text{NOPAT}}{\text{Profit}}$	$\dfrac{23,314}{21,514} = 1.08$	$\dfrac{22,269}{23,364} = 0.95$

A ratio of about 1:1 would suggest that the profit comes from operations. DRL's ratio increased from 0.95 to 1.08. High volatility from one period would raise questions about earnings quality. Excluding the effect of the foreign exchange loss, the ratio would be 0.89. This indicates a deterioration. The higher net financial income in 2016 is another explanation for the difference. Shareholders expect a company to invest in its core or related business (e.g. pharmaceutical products in DRL's case), and not in mutual funds or bank deposits. They can invest directly in such assets and do not need the intermediation of the company.

HANDHOLD 15.2
NOPAT

Manas Company reported a net profit of ₹10,000 for 20X3. It had interest income of ₹700, interest expense of ₹200 and exceptional loss of ₹150. The corporate tax rate was 30 per cent. The company's NOPAT is ₹9,755, calculated as follows: Net profit, ₹10,000 − Net financial income after tax, ₹350 (₹500 × 0.7) + Exceptional loss after tax, ₹105 (₹150 × 0.7).

TEST YOUR UNDERSTANDING 15.2
NOPAT

Lakshman Company reported a net profit of ₹80,000 for 20XX. It had the following items: (a) Interest income, ₹1,000; (b) Interest expense, ₹7,000; (c) Dividend from overseas subsidiaries, ₹900; (d) Impairment charge, ₹3,000; (e) Gain on sale of investments, ₹600; (f) Fair value loss on investments, ₹400. Corporate tax was rate 35 per cent. Compute the company's NOPAT.

Earnings Management

Learning Objective

LO 3 Describe earnings management and identify motives for managing earnings.

You have probably heard this one. In a job interview for a company's accountant, everyone was given financial information and asked, "What is the net profit?" All candidates except one provided the correct answer but none of them got the job. The one who was selected wrote, "What do you want the net profit to be?" **Earnings management** (or *creative accounting*) is using judgment and discretion available in generally accepted accounting principles or making operating decisions in order to produce a pre-determined effect on the financial statements.

The spectrum is very wide from deferring advertisement spending to the following quarter (not a crime) to showing phony sales (a crime), and the causes vary from subconscious hopefulness or doubt without any intention to mislead to outright fraud motivated by fear or greed. We use the term 'earnings management' here to refer to managing items in any of the financial statements, and not only the statement of profit and loss. Earnings management is an academic euphemism for financial reporting manipulation.[2] We consider three types of earnings management: (1) managing accruals; (2) managing real earnings; (3) perpetrating fraud.

---

[2] For a good discussion of earnings management, see Kin Lo, Earnings management and earnings quality, *Journal of Accounting and Economics*, August 2008.

Accrual-based Earnings Management

Accrual accounting requires managers to make critical financial reporting decisions, such as estimating useful lives of property, plant and equipment, determining fair value, selecting depreciation methods, testing for impairment, estimating credit losses debts, and reckoning pension liability. Ideally, their judgment should be neutral and not biased in favour of a particular result. However, decisions involving managerial judgment are the product of conflicting considerations, such as the following:

- Investors expect companies to show superior performance in every reporting period.
- Analysts expect companies to meet or beat the earnings forecast or management guidance.
- Managers don't want to fall short of their own published guidance or earnings forecast.
- Creditors may require early repayment or a higher interest rate for violation of debt covenants.
- The majority shareholder wants to reduce the company's income tax expense.
- Managers are keen to get a larger performance-linked bonus.
- The competition watchdog may impose penalties on companies that earn excessive profits.

In these circumstances, it is not easy for managers to make judgments about financial reporting in a neutral way, more so because they too are interested parties. So managers engage in accrual-based earnings management (AEM). AEM can take a variety of forms depending on the extent to which managers' financial reporting decisions are biased.

The general perception is that managers always attempt to overstate the profit, but there are reasons to understate the profit. Earnings management may either (a) increase income, increase assets, decrease liabilities; or (b) decrease income, decrease assets, increase liabilities. We will now see examples of these actions:

- *Increase income, increase assets, decrease liabilities:* Companies want to appear successful prior to a public issue of equity or debt. So we would expect them to report a higher profit. They may raise the useful lives of assets, lower the allowance for credit losses, recognize revenue for goods sent to distributors but not yet sold, switch from WAC to FIFO in a time of inflation and reduce the warranty liability. Similar pressures exist when they are below analyst expectations. A likely shortfall in the minimum current ratio stipulated in a loan agreement may induce managers to classify a current liability item as non-current. A company that is on the verge of breaching a debt covenant may structure an operating lease as a finance lease.

- *Decrease income, decrease assets, increase liabilities:* Companies want to minimize their income tax expense, especially if they have to pay MAT. So we would expect them to report a lower profit. They may reduce the useful lives of assets, increase the allowance for credit losses, delay recognizing revenue for goods already sold, switch from FIFO to WAC in a time of inflation and increase warranty liability. Similar pressures exist when they have overshot analyst expectations or are facing scrutiny for anti-competitive activities.

Managers may engage in **big bath**, the practice of making big asset write-downs or huge provisions for restructuring or liabilities. As the name suggests, big bath enables a firm to come clean. In big bath, also known as *kitchen sinking*, productive assets and saleable inventories may be written off, large impairment charges taken, and excessively large provisions may be made for credit losses, losses on disposal of assets and redundancy payments to employees. Even if the business does not do any better, the reported profit will go up in the next period because of lower charges for depreciation and cost of goods sold and write-back of the excess restructuring provision to the statement of profit and loss. Big bath is usually done when a new CEO takes over. **Earnings smoothing** occurs when a company evens out the fluctuations in the reported earnings, in order to convey a picture of steady growth. Here managers do not allow the profit to go up or down too much in any one period and use income-increasing and income-decreasing methods opportunistically. An example is the use of *cookie jar reserves* by over-providing for sales returns, credit losses or warranties and using the "reserves" to smooth earnings in bad years.

Acquisitions create opportunities for earnings management. For instance, the acquiree's in-process research and development may be written off at the time of acquisition. This ensures lower charges and higher earnings in the future when the firm benefits from those R & D activities. Goodwill may be overvalued to make up for the write-off of the in-process R & D and for lower fair values assigned to depreciable assets. Since goodwill is not depreciated unlike depreciable assets, future depreciation and amortization expense will be lower. Though most acquisitions fail, these techniques make an acquisition look like a success. Firms unable to grow are more likely to acquire other firms. It is often difficult to discern the effect of an acquisition on profit. So after an acquisition, the acquirer may appear to have done better but it is impossible to tell if this is true. Acquisitions also entail significant provisions for restructuring costs, such as employee separation costs, legal costs, and advisory fees. Analysts usually treat such items as one-off costs and ignore them. So a whole lot of costs – incurred, likely or unlikely – are pushed into acquisition-related provisions. Managers may "bleed back" the excess provisions in later years thus increasing the profits making it appear that the acquisition was a success. This is also true of restructuring.

Whatever may be the motives or the methods, earnings management is bad for the analyst because it makes understanding and forecasting performance difficult. Earnings management produces lower quality earnings. The analyst should be aware of the conditions that trigger earnings management and read the accounting policies, schedules and notes to the financial statements carefully. Understanding the quality of management and the governance arrangements in place including the reputation of the company's board of directors, audit committee and auditors would be useful.

REAL WORLD
Accounting for Nano's
Development Costs

In 2008, Tata Motors launched Nano as an affordable car for Indians. The initial hype about the car soon gave way to despair. Over the years, sales tumbled to a few thousands. In October 2016, Cyrus Mistry after he was removed as the executive chairman of Tata Sons alleged that "historically, the company had employed aggressive accounting to capitalise a substantial portion of the product development expenses, creating a future liability. Beyond this, the Nano product development concept called for a car below ₹1 lakh, but the costs were always above this. The product has consistently lost money, peaking at ₹1,000 crores. As there is no line of sight to profitability for the Nano, any turnaround strategy for the company requires to shut it down." Tata Motors' unamortized product development costs since 2008 were as follows:

Year	2016	2015	2014	2013	2012	2011	2010	2009	2008
Amount (billion)	₹308.21	₹247.68	₹173.96	₹140.30	₹84.72	₹48.80	₹57.76	₹12.90	₹2.37

The company did not disclose how much of the unamortized product development costs related to Nano. We can assume that a significant portion related to Nano. Note that the costs jumped nearly 150 times over the period 2008 to 2016. In a filing with the Bombay Stock Exchange, the company stated that its accounting policies were "in due compliance with the relevant Accounting Standards under IGAAP, IND-AS and IFRS Accounting Standards. These are regularly reviewed by our Audit Committee, Statutory Auditors and appropriately disclosed in our financial statements." It added: "As far as development cost and investments in Nano specific dies and toolings are concerned, these have been significantly written off, in line with the accounting policies over the last several years." According to its accounting policy, the company amortizes product development costs over 120 months for "new generation vehicles on the basis of the highest of the volumes between planned and actuals and on a straight-line method." Since the actual volumes were lower than expected, the company was probably expensing less than required by the failure of the car.

Real Earnings Management

In real earnings management (REM) managers manipulate earnings by modifying operating decisions. Consider these examples of REM.

- *Reducing discretionary expenditures:* Expenditure on R & D, technology acquisition and upgrade, advertising, training, and plant maintenance are not related to production or sales. Management has considerable discretion in deciding on the amount and timing of these expenditures. For instance, a consumer goods company may defer an advertisement campaign to the next quarter in order to improve the current quarter earnings.

- *Offering price discounts to boost sales:* Prices are reduced towards the end of a reporting period. While this may increase revenue in that period, the risk is that customers may expect similar discounts in future periods. Further, customers may defer purchases until the end of a period in the hope of a repeat act by the company.

- *Selling surplus assets at a gain:* Surplus land and buildings may be sold in order to realize the gains. Sadly, the same land and buildings can't be sold again. So the gains will be one-off.

- *Offering generous credit terms:* Customers may be induced into buying more because of easier and cheaper credit. The risk is that customers may get used to diluted standards and resist any tightening later. Also, credit losses may increase because of lax standards.

- *Overproduction:* Increasing output reduces fixed overhead per unit and lowers cost of goods sold. It may be difficult to sell the additional inventories in the next period. Also, inventory carrying costs (e.g. interest, storage, insurance) will increase.

- *Delaying plant commissioning:* Delaying the commissioning of a new plant defers recognition of depreciation expense. The period for interest capitalization may also be extended as a result. So there is a double benefit.

- *Deferring capital expenditure:* Deferring capital expenditure reduces current depreciation expense but would hurt future production capacity.

- *Deferring planned maintenance:* Deferring planned maintenance will reduce current maintenance expenditure but will damage the equipment.

Managing real activities is perfectly within GAAP, yet it may be harmful to firm value. For instance, reduced R & D spending could affect the introduction of new products and result in a competitive disadvantage. REM may be more difficult to detect than AEM, since management's operating decisions are not made public.

Fraud

Fraudulent financial reporting is an extreme form of earnings management. Unlike AEM and REM, fraud involves altering the facts. Fraud is the last resort of beleaguered managers who have exhausted possibilities for AEM and REM. Since it is illegal, it must not be attempted.

Figure 15.1 illustrates the different types of earnings management activities.

Figure 15.1

THE EARNINGS MANAGEMENT CONTINUUM

Earnings management can range from pinching on R & D to falsifying sales.

- No tampering with records and documents. - Perfectly legal. - Involves operating decisions.	- Choices made within the scope of GAAP. - Unethical, though not illegal. - Involves accounting decisions.	- Manipulating records and documents. - Illegal. - Results from an intent to cheat.
Real Earnings Management	**Accrual-based Earnings Management**	**Fraud**

Five days before the end of a quarter the CEO of a company finds that the sales target has already been reached. Which of the following activities is he likely to engage in? There may be more than one correct answer.

  (a) Defer recognition of revenue earned in the remaining days of the quarter to the next quarter.
  (b) Fake sales and receivables.
  (c) Present unearned revenue as revenue.
  (d) Delay delivery of goods to the next quarter.

Rishabh is a turnaround artist. He took over as the CEO of Fortune Company on August 29, 20X5. He plans to do the following things in the September quarter: (a) write down inventories by 30 per cent below market value; (b) take an impairment charge of 50 per cent of the carrying amount of tangible and intangible assets; (c) increase the allowance for credit losses by 25 per cent; (d) increase life expectancy for estimating pension liabilities; (e) write off all on-going R & D projects. What would be the effect of these changes on the profit for the September quarter and for subsequent reporting periods?

Do you think a company that always meets analysts' forecast earnings is a good investment?

ONE-MINUTE QUIZ 15.3
Earnings Management

TEST YOUR UNDERSTANDING 15.3
Earnings Management

QUICK QUESTION
Meeting forecasts

Segment Performance

Many firms operate in multiple businesses and geographical areas. Often, the risks and returns in these businesses and areas are different. For instance, ITC's main businesses are cigarettes, consumer goods, hotels, agri-business, and paperboards, paper and packaging and it exports to 46 countries. Cigarettes are heavily taxed and strictly regulated; consumer goods sell in highly competitive markets; hotel room occupancy and tariff are affected by economic, business, and political conditions; agri-business is affected by weather; paper and packaging products compete with synthetic materials; export revenue is affected by regulations in the importing countries and exchange rate movements. A single revenue or profit number can't capture the complexities of ITC's diverse activities.

An **operating segment** is a part of an entity that earns revenues and incurs expenses and its performance is reviewed by the entity's chief decision maker, usually the entity's chief executive officer or chief operating officer. Operating segments that are similar in products and services, production and operation processes, types of customers, distribution methods and regulation can be combined into a single operating segment. Information about an operating segment should be reported if its revenue (including internal transfers) is not less than 10 per cent of the total revenue of all operating segments, its absolute profit or loss is not less than 10 per cent of the combined absolute profit or loss of all operating segments, or its assets are not less than 10 per cent of the combined assets of all operating segments. For each operating segment financial statements should provide information about, among others, revenues, interest revenue and expense, depreciation and amortization, segment profit or loss and segment assets and liabilities.

Exhibit 15.4 presents the distribution of DRL's segment revenue and profit. The company has reported three segments: pharmaceutical services and active ingredients (PSAI), global generics (GG) and proprietary products (PP). PSAI is in bulk drugs and contract research. GG is in formulations, mostly from expired patents. PP makes the company's own products.

Learning Objective
LO 4 Analyze segment performance.

EXHIBIT 15.4
Segment Revenue and Profit

DR REDDY'S LABORATORIES LIMITED Segment Revenue and Profit For the year ended March 31									
	2016				2015				
	Revenue	Profit	Revenue	Profit	Revenue	Profit	Revenue	Profit
	(in millions)		*(per cent to total)*		*(in millions)*		*(per cent to total)*	
PSAI	₹28,248	₹1,487	17	5	₹32,915	₹1,035	21	4
GG	129,833	33,262	80	116	122,004	30,597	78	116
PP	2,659	(6,340)	2	(22)	1,013	(5,371)	1	(20)
Others	1,685	217	1	1	1,205	(18)	0	0
	162,425	28,626	100	100	157,137	26,243	100	100

GG is both the biggest and the best performing segment. It accounts for 80 per cent of the company's revenue and 116 per cent of profit. PSAI is next with 17 per cent of the revenue and 5 per cent of the profit. While GG's share of revenue increased, PSAI's share decreased. Also, while GG's revenue grew 6 per cent, PSAI's revenue went down 14 per cent. PP's revenue grew 162 per cent, albeit on a very small base. Also, PP was not profitable in both years.

Let's now look at the profit margin (profit/sales) of the three segments.

Profit margin	2016	2015
PSAI	5%	3%
GG	26	25
PP	– 238	– 530

GG has a healthy margin of 26 per cent, a little more than in 2015. PSAI is less profitable but its margin improved. PP is a loss-making business.

The company states that since its manufacturing facilities, development facilities, and treasury assets and liabilities are often deployed interchangeably across business segments, it is impractical to allocate these assets and liabilities to each business segment. Therefore, we are unable to calculate return on assets and asset turnover by segment. By geographic markets, North America accounts for 53 per cent, up from 48 per cent in 2015. So the company's fortunes are significantly linked to the economic, political and regulatory conditions in the US and the dollar-rupee exchange rate.

QUICK QUESTION
Segments

What do you think would be the typical number of operating segments disclosed by companies?

REAL WORLD
Segment Information

Information about the performance of segments tells us about the importance of segments to the performance of the company. Let's take two well-known consumer product companies, Hindustan Unilever Limited (HUL) and ITC Limited.

- In 2016, HUL had four segments: soaps and detergents, personal products, beverages, and packaged foods. Soaps and detergents were the biggest segment generating 47 per cent of the company's revenue but only 39 per cent of the profit. Personal products were the most profitable producing 29 per cent of the revenue but 45 per cent of the profit. Beverages contributed 11 per cent of the revenue and a similar share of the profit. Packaged foods chipped in with 6 per cent of the revenue and 2 per cent of the profit. The rest of the revenue and profit came from other segments not separately reported. HUL depends heavily on its traditional products.

- In 2016, ITC had five segments: cigarettes, consumer products, hotels, agri-business and paperboards, paper and packaging. Cancer sticks churned out 57 per cent of the revenue and a monstrous 85 per cent of the profit. Consumer products and hotels provided 16 per cent and 2 per cent of the revenue respectively but less than 1 per cent of the profit. Agri-business and paperboards brought in 12 per cent and 9 per cent of the revenue but made 6 per cent each of the profit, respectively. What will be left of ITC if the government bans tobacco or smoking goes out of fashion, as has happened in developed countries?

Segment disclosure is often inadequate. Take Tata Motors, for instance. Investors would be keen to know about the profitability of the Nano car, an important initiative of Ratan Tata, the then chairman. The segments disclosed are Tata vehicles and Jaguar Land Rover. "Tata vehicles" includes both passenger and commercial vehicles and Nano's numbers lie buried in that segment. Not terribly helpful to the company's investors.

Companies argue that segment disclosure will aid competitors more than investors. Do you agree?

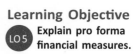

DISCUSSION QUESTION 15.1

....

....

....

Pro Forma Financial Measures

Pro forma literally means "as a matter of form". A **pro forma financial measure** (or **non-GAAP financial measure**) is a measure of past or future financial performance, financial position, or cash flows that differ from a measure defined by applicable GAAP.[3] A pro forma measure excludes (includes) items that are (are not) a part of the comparable measure in the GAAP financial statements. Table 15.2 describes three commonly used pro forma measures.

Learning Objective

LO 5 Explain pro forma financial measures.

Acronym	Expansion	Explanation
▪ EBIT	Earnings before Interest and Tax	Profit excludes interest income and expense and tax.
▪ EBITDA	Earnings before Interest, Tax, Depreciation and Amortization	Profit excludes interest income and expense, tax, depreciation of tangible assets and amortization of intangible assets.
▪ EBITDAR	Earnings before Interest, Tax, Depreciation, Amortization and Restructuring or Rent	Profit excludes interest income and expense, tax, depreciation of tangible assets, amortization of intangible assets, restructuring costs and lease rent.

TABLE 15.2
Common Pro Forma Measures

EBIT, or operating profit, differs from the GAAP measure, because it excludes interest income and interest expense, non-recurring or exceptional items and income tax. EBITDA excludes interest income and interest expense, income tax, depreciation, and amortization, all of which are included in the GAAP measure of net profit. EBITDAR excludes in addition restructuring costs and lease rent. Pro forma measures are "as if" profit calculations.

Pro forma financial information can be useful in explaining the components of earnings. For example, the exclusion of non-recurring gains and losses can help investors focus on earnings from normal or regular operations and facilitate better predictions of future performance. Regrettably, pro forma measures may be used to distract the investor from GAAP numbers when the latter are likely to give an unfavourable impression. For instance, a loss may be cast as a profit by the exclusion of some types of losses. Companies should avoid the temptation of using pro forma numbers to report "EBS" (everything but bad stuff), as Lynn Turner, a former chief accountant of the US Securities and Exchange Commission put it. Also, pro forma measures can become misleading if they are computed differently from one period to another. This is not difficult because there are no standard definitions of pro forma measures.

Pro forma reporting became widespread during the 1990s Internet boom. Many dotcom firms could not report a GAAP profit, but were under enormous pressure from the equity market to report some profit to justify their high stock prices. So they came up with performance measures of dubious value such as EBITDA. Some companies were egregious, even by the lenient ways of pro forma reporting. For example, Amazon.com, the well-known Internet retailer, while discussing its 2000 fourth quarter results in its January 2001 press release, first described its revenue and then cited its narrowing quarterly "U.S. pro forma operating loss" of $16 million. That figure excluded interest expense, losses on equity investments, stock-based compensation expense, amortization of intangible assets, and

---

[3] Synonyms for pro forma measure include adjusted financials, alternative performance measures, anti-GAAP measure, bespoke numbers, custom reporting, and fantasy accounting.

write-downs for impaired assets. This gave rise to a new pro forma measure: EBITDAM (earnings before interest, tax, depreciation, amortization, and marketing expenses); the only major item not added back was cost of goods sold.

Even though the Internet bubble burst in 2001, the pro forma habit remains. In fact, we are seeing new acronyms. Kingfisher Airlines used EBITDAR (earnings before interest, tax, depreciation, amortization, and aircraft lease rentals) in an attempt to come up with some positive measure of earnings. In the quarter ended June 30, 2010, Goldman Sachs added back $550 million in fine imposed by the U.S. Securities and Exchange Commission; the measure came to be known as EBITDAF: earnings before interest, tax, depreciation, amortization, and fine.

Depreciation and interest are as much costs of doing business as the cost of raw materials. Is it proper to exclude them? Those who complain about the rising use of pro forma numbers (some even want them banned outright) are out of touch with reality. Pro forma measures are popular with analysts who refer to them frequently in earnings calls and research reports. They are used in quarterly and annual earnings releases, prospectuses and executive pay contracts. So it may be necessary to regulate their use, so that they don't mislead investors and lenders. The following guidelines for the use of a pro forma measure may help.

- Explain why it is important in understanding the company's business.
- Differentiate it from a GAAP measure.
- Identify it as unaudited or audited.
- Define it in the document where it is used. Don't change the definition unless it is a must.
- Provide a reconciliation of the measure with the nearest GAAP measure.

REAL WORLD
Pro Forma Measures

Some love them. Others frown on them. The extreme reactions are understandable. Those who find them useful draw attention to the one-size-fits-all nature of GAAP numbers that don't fit anyone at all. Those who distrust them emphasize their potential for misleading gullible investors. Consider the following bizarre examples.

- In the second quarter of 2016 Tesla reported GAAP revenue of $1.3 billion and non-GAAP revenue of $1.6 billion. Non-GAAP revenue included, among others, net increase in deferred revenue. GAAP operating expenses were $513 million and included $61 million of non-cash stock-based compensation. After excluding non-cash stock based compensation, non-GAAP operating expenses were $452 million. The second quarter GAAP net loss was $293 million, while non-GAAP net loss was $150 million. GAAP cash flow from operations during the quarter was $150 million, which included the receipt of Model 3 deposits. After adding $143 million of cash inflows from vehicle sales to bank leasing partners, cash flow from core operations was nearly $293 million.
- In the fourth quarter of 2016 Microsoft took a $1.1 billion charge, largely for the former Nokia division. In the same quarter Intel took a $1.4 billion restructuring charge. They excluded the charges from their pro forma earnings. Microsoft has taken billions of dollars in write-downs from failed acquisitions in three of the previous five years and Intel has reported restructuring charges in seven of the past 10 years. Both companies have executive compensation tied in part to operating profit.
- In 2015, Facebook reported a GAAP net income of $10,217 million and a non-GAAP net income of $12,368 million. The reconciliation items included share-based compensation expense of $3,218 and amortization of intangibles of $751 million.
- In the fourth quarter of 2016 Microsoft reported a GAAP revenue of $20.6 billion and a non-GAAP revenue of $22.6 billion. The difference is because of the way in which Windows OEM revenue will be recognized, i.e. at the time of billing rather than the current practice of recognizing revenue at the time installation under the new accounting standard related to revenue recognition that the company expects to adopt effective July 1, 2017, i.e. for next fiscal year.

■ In the third quarter of 2016 Indigo reported a profit after tax of ₹4,873 million and EBITDAR of ₹14,605.

Considering their potential for misleading investors, should pro forma measures be prohibited?

....

....

....

Which of the following statements about pro forma measures is incorrect? There may be more than one correct answer.

(a) They are audited.
(b) They are discussed in earnings releases.
(c) They appear in the statement of profit and loss.
(d) They have no standard definitions.

Free Cash Flow

Free cash flow is the difference between net cash flows from operating and investing activities. It may be positive or negative. *Positive free cash flow* means that the net cash generated from operations is more than what a firm can use in investing in new assets. In contrast, *negative free cash flow* implies that the firm is investing more cash in new assets than the cash generated from operations. We would expect positive free cash flow for firms that have stable levels of operations and normal growth and negative free cash flow for firms that are growing rapidly and are investing heavily in expansion, modernization and renovation of their operations, and acquisition of other enterprises as part of their operations.

From Exhibit 13.11 in Chapter 13, Compass Company generated net cash of ₹72,000 from operating activities. Investing activities comprise all investments by a firm, both in its own business and in the financial instruments of other enterprises. However, for calculating free cash flow, we should exclude financial investments. It invested ₹151,000 in the purchase of plant and machinery net of sale of old assets. Therefore, its free cash flow is – ₹79,000. Since interest received is related to financial investments, we exclude it. We can infer that the company is expanding its operations and that we can expect the current investments to produce additional cash from operations in the future.

Free cash flow is a popular basis for enterprise valuation. Analysts use the free cash flow measure to value firms that produce a stable, positive free cash flow year after year and expect to have a similar trend in the future. They arrive at the value of a firm by discounting free cash flow at an estimated cost of capital for the firm. By deducting likely incremental investment needed to maintain current operating cash flow, free cash flow gives a better idea of sustainable cash flow.

The free cash flow measure is less suitable for valuing high growth firms that are investing substantially in additional capacity year after year or making repeated acquisitions of other businesses as part of their growth strategy. For example, telecommunication firms invest heavily in licences, spectrum, towers, and software. As a result, they have negative free cash flow in those years. In the intermediate term, they would have moderately positive free cash flow with tapering off of incremental investment. In the long term, they expect large positive free cash flow, as their investments start to pay back. However, if we apply the free cash flow method, such firms would be virtually worthless because their free cash flow is negative. On the whole, it would seem that free cash flow is a useful measure for firms that operate in mature markets and industries, where investment is mostly for replacement than for expansion. Note that free cash flow is another pro forma financial measure.

Economic Value Added

Learning Objective

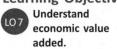 **Understand economic value added.**

Accountants and economists use the term profit, but define them differently. Accounting profit is based on actual transactions. Economic profit uses the idea of *opportunity cost*: the value of the best alternative forgone. To determine accounting profit we consider interest on borrowings but we don't charge any imputed cost for equity. Economic profit is what remains after a capital charge for both borrowings and equity. Accounting profit is the owner's measure of profit. Economic profit is the firm's measure of profit. What matters to the firm is how its resources are utilized; who financed the resources is irrelevant. Since managers are responsible for efficient utilization of the firm's resources, economic profit is a better measure of managerial performance.

The idea of economic profit gives rise to the measure **economic value added** (EVA) or **residual income**. Exhibit 15.5 presents HUL's EVA calculation for 2016.

EXHIBIT 15.5
Economic Value Added

Hindustan Unilever Limited Economic Value Added for the year ended March 31		
	2016	**2015**
	(in million)	
Profit after tax before exceptional items	₹40,780	₹38,430
Add Interest after taxes	0	110
Net operating profit after tax (NOPAT)	40,780	38,540
Deduct Cost of capital employed	5,520	4,740
Economic value added	35,260	33,800

Source: Company annual report

We add back interest in order to arrive at NOPAT, the firm-level measure of profit. Then we deduct a notional charge for the firm's capital. **Capital employed** equals operating assets less operating liabilities. We measure capital employed as the sum of the market value of equity and the market value of debt. The book value of debt may be used if market value is not available. The cost of capital is the weighted average of the cost of equity and the cost of debt. The cost of equity is usually calculated using the capital asset pricing model (CAPM). The cost of debt is the interest rate applicable to debt that is rated similar to the company's debt. The weighted average cost capital (WACC) is used to calculate the notional charge for capital.

EVA tells us how profitable the firm is. The higher the EVA, the better the firm's operating efficiency. EVA is a direct measure of managerial performance. Some companies set internal EVA targets and link managers' incentives to EVA achievement. EVA is a pro forma measure of sorts, since it is based partly on accounting profit.

TEST YOUR UNDERSTANDING 15.4
Economic Value Added

Buzz Company reported a net profit of ₹25,200 for the year ended March 31, 20X2. Interest income was ₹5,000 and interest expense was ₹12,000. The company had bank deposits of ₹100,000 and bonds payable of ₹175,000. The company's equity (5,000 shares of ₹10) was reported at ₹123,000 in the balance sheet. Buzz Company's share traded at ₹140 at the close of the year. The cost of debt was 7 per cent and the required return on equity was 9 per cent. Corporate income tax rate was 25 per cent. Compute Buzz Company's economic value added for the year.

ONE-MINUTE QUIZ 15.5
Accounting Profit and Economic Profit

Which of the following is not considered in computing accounting profit but considered for computing economic profit? There may be more than one correct answer.
(a) Equity dividend.
(b) Interest income.
(c) Interest expense.
(d) Cost of capital.

Corporate Disclosure Policy

Companies must disclose a certain minimum amount of information specified by law and accounting standards. The Companies Act requires all companies to make a number of financial disclosures. Again, listed companies must make detailed disclosures relating to their activities under regulations and rules issued by SEBI. For example, they have to publish quarterly financial results.

Learning Objective

LO8 Understand the forces that influence corporate disclosure policy.

However, many companies voluntarily provide disclosures over and above those specified by law, such as financial forecasts, new customers added, budgets, capital expenditure plans, new products, restructuring, and R&D initiatives. In recent years, **voluntary disclosure** has become an important aspect of financial reporting.

Voluntary disclosures appear in the financial statements, footnotes, management discussion and analysis and press releases and on websites. Managers can use these disclosures to communicate information that cannot be effectively conveyed in the standard financial report because of accounting and regulatory constraints. Voluntary disclosure is particularly important for firms that face high competition, rapid technology innovation, frequent changes in customer preferences, and investment in intangible assets. This is the case with companies operating in the New Economy. Many economic forces drive voluntary disclosure. Here are some of them.

Capital market forces Firms compete for resources in the capital market. Investors and analysts view firms that are more transparent as superior to firms that just satisfy minimum disclosure requirements. You may recall from Chapter 1 that firms entering the capital market risk being considered 'lemons'. The cost of being perceived as a 'lemon' is high – the firm may not be able to raise equity capital or may have to incur a high cost of capital. Firms can overcome this problem by providing relevant additional information. Firms that provide more disclosures carry greater credibility with the investment community and could raise more capital at relatively lower costs.

Product market forces Firms sometimes preannounce their products in order to deter existing rivals and new players. For example, Microsoft announces new operating systems well in advance. Further, prior disclosure helps customers and others prepare and processes. For example, Boeing's new aircraft may require changes in flight schedules and airport infrastructure. Also, customers are more comfortable dealing with suppliers that follow high standards of governance, including extensive voluntary disclosure. A transparent company creates confidence in its customers and enjoys a superior brand image.

Firms are concerned that their competitors can use the disclosures they provide to their shareholders. This will have a detrimental effect on the value of their shares. The existence of competitors creates a potential competitive disadvantage to the disclosing firm. Firms and managers often use this argument to avoid providing additional information to their shareholders. The flip-side of this argument is that if all firms disclose, everyone will benefit from others' disclosures.

Managerial labour market forces Managers make a living by supplying their talent for managing organizations. They manage the funds entrusted to the firm by the shareholders. Their value in the labour market depends as much on their managerial ability as on their being worthy of the trust reposed in them. They can maintain and enhance their reputation for competence and trustworthiness by providing additional disclosures to the shareholders. In return, they get rewards, such as longer tenures, better remuneration, and prospects of better terms in the job market. Failure to provide useful additional information may result in loss of reputation, with unfavourable consequences for their career.

Shareholder litigation In countries characterized by high levels of litigation, the fear of shareholder litigation motivates greater disclosure. For example, in the US, shareholders affected by a material fall in stock prices can sue companies and managers for damages under certain circumstances on the ground that they were not provided with relevant information. In such settings, managers are ever keen to avert the possibility of violating the law and are likely to follow the age-old dictum: "When in doubt, disclose".

Thus, corporate disclosure policy is the result of the interplay of complex forces.[4]

RESEARCH INSIGHT
Disclosure and Cost of Capital

Analytical research in financial economics suggests that greater disclosure by a firm reduces information asymmetry between the insiders (managers and employees) and the firm's shareholders, and thereby diminishes the risk in investing and dealing in its securities. As a result, investors require a lower risk premium for investing in the securities of firms that provide greater voluntary disclosure. Empirical research broadly supports this position. Research by Professor Christine Botosan shows that the cost of equity is decreasing in the amount of disclosure provided by companies in their annual reports.[5] Professor Partha Sengupta finds that the cost of debt is decreasing in the amount of corporate disclosure as evaluated by analysts.[6]

Efficient Market Hypothesis and Financial Statement Analysis

Learning Objective

LO 9 Describe the implications of the efficient market hypothesis for financial statement analysis.

According to the **efficient market hypothesis** (EMH), publicly available information is quickly impounded in stock prices. The publicly available information comprises accounting and other information, whether firm-specific, industry-wide or economy-wide. The EMH implies that an investor cannot profit by having access to information that is also available to others since the stock price already reflects that information. However, profits can still be made using private information, e.g. by an insider such as a director or employee of a company.

Two explanations are offered for market efficiency and both of them have to do with the role of security analysts:

- A large number of security analysts are competing to detect mispriced securities. Therefore, it is highly likely that all significant information will be impounded in stock prices.

- Mistakes of judgment or estimation made by some analysts will be diffused in the price formation process, to the extent that these mistakes are independent across analysts.

For more than four decades, researchers in economics, finance, and accounting have studied the relationship between stock prices and accounting earnings.[7] The following conclusions from this research are important for financial statement analysis and financial reporting:

1. *Accounting information and stock prices:* Accounting information affects stock prices, but much of the price reaction associated with earnings occurs prior to the announcement of annual earnings. Financial reports are only one of the many sources on which markets rely in arriving at prices. Much of the information about major events affecting various companies is received prior to the release of financial reports: new contracts, new financing, legal actions, product introductions, patent grants, capital spending plans, personnel changes, and the like. Still, financial reports provide investors and analysts the assurance that their initial interpretations of company news were sensible and to some degree accurate.

---

[4] For a comprehensive review of research on this topic, see Robert E. Verrecchia, Essays on disclosure, *Journal of Accounting and Economics*, December 2001.

[5] Christine A. Botosan, Disclosure level and the cost of equity capital, *The Accounting Review*, July 1997.

[6] Partha Sengupta, Corporate disclosure quality and the cost of debt, *The Accounting Review*, October 1998.

[7] An excellent review of efficient market studies in accounting is available in William H. Beaver, *Financial Reporting: An Accounting Revolution*, 3rd ed., Englewood Cliffs, New Jersey: Prentice-Hall, 1998.

2. *Accounting method differences:* The market is not 'fooled' by accounting method differences causing earnings to be different, both across firms and over time. Suppose two firms are identical in terms of risk and expected dividend-paying ability, but one of them follows the straight-line depreciation method while the other follows the written-down-value method. The earnings of the first firm will be higher in the early years. Since there is no difference in the dividend-paying ability of the two firms, the market prices of their stocks will be equal if the method of depreciation followed is known. In a similar vein, a change in a firm's earnings induced by a cosmetic change in accounting method will not affect the stock price of the company.

3. *Disclosure regulation:* Mandatory disclosures do not evoke any significant market price reaction. Since the market operates on a "rich" information system, it already has information about certain matters even before they are disclosed following directives from regulatory agencies. Therefore, additional disclosures, such as inflation-adjusted profits and business segment information, have not made much difference to the market.

A passive investment strategy is appropriate if capital markets are informationally efficient. Under this strategy, the investor will hold a diversified investment portfolio to lower stock-specific risks and reduce the number of buy and sell transactions to minimize transaction costs.[8]

Understanding Annual Reports and Earnings Releases

Companies should use annual reports and earnings releases to communicate with their investors. Managers are expected to tell the story of the year or quarter that went by and explain what they did or failed to do to meet the expectations of the investors. Corporate releases should be written in plain language that an ordinary investor can understand. Warren Buffett, the legendary investor, recommends the use of plain English in management communications. Unfortunately, not everyone seems to share Buffett's conviction. Corporate releases often confuse rather than communicate. Corporate jargon, buzz words and catchphrases are used to hide poor performance. Consider the following statement by Biocon when the company reported a 55 per cent drop in its profit for the March 2014 quarter and a 19 per cent drop for the year 2014:

Learning Objective

LO 10 Examine claims in management communications.

> Biocon ended fiscal 2014 on a strong note. We delivered 16% revenue growth along with a healthy EBITDA Margin of 25%. This fiscal we recorded robust performance, an outcome of our efforts aimed at optimising our product mix, augmenting capacities and driving operational efficiencies... We are pleased that a large number of patients benefitted from these two products. We continue with our innovation-led business strategy and look forward to deliver superior value to our stakeholders.

The remarkable thing about this statement and the rest of the press release is that there is not a word about the halving of profit. Ordinary shareholders would be keen to know the reasons for this steep fall despite the impressive revenue growth. They may not understand expressions such as "optimising product mix", "augmenting capacities", "driving operational efficiencies", "innovation-led strategy" and "superior value". They may prefer a statement like this one:

> During the quarter ended March 31, 2014, our revenue increased by 15% but profit decreased by 55%. The reasons for the two moving in different directions are as follows: (1) ...; (2) ...; (3)....

The typical annual report or earnings release mentions competitive advantage, cyber security, headwinds, leveraging, scale, synergy, and value creation. They abound in grandiose

---

[8] Standard texts on investments provide a detailed analysis of the efficient market hypothesis.

announcements like "We live in extraordinary times". Then there are the mandatory references to artificial intelligence, big data, breakthrough, clean energy, climate change, cloud computing, disruption, driverless cars, empowerment, and the fourth industrial revolution, to name a few.

In a Bottomliners comic strip, the boss is seen telling his secretary: "Analysts are complaining about our corporate earnings. Would you please bring me a new batch of excuses?" Companies often give 'creative' reasons for not meeting investor expectations. An unstated convention is to blame external conditions for bad performance but take credit for good performance. The usual reasons mentioned for disappointing results include assassinations, government policies, global competition, inflation, monsoon (early or late, good or bad), natural calamities, oil prices, political turmoil, recession, and the rupee's appreciation (IT outsourcing and exporters) or depreciation (import-dependent companies). In order to sound convincing, the excuse has to be relevant.

- Hindustan Unilever blamed the 1 per cent fall in its sales in the December 2016 quarter on the withdrawal of ₹1,000 and ₹500 notes from circulation. The net profit of ₹10,380 million for the quarter included a gain from the sale of surplus property of ₹1,590 million. Also, the company cut advertising by ₹360 million. Without those, it was less than the profit of ₹9,720 million for the year-ago quarter. This is an amazing case of earnings management and earnings excuse rolled into one.

CEOs claim credit when things go well, but do not hesitate to blame problems on their underlings. Here again, Buffett is different. Consider the following extract from his 2009 letter to Berkshire Hathaway shareholders:

> Charlie [Munger, vice-chairman] and I believe that a CEO must not delegate risk control. It's simply too important. At Berkshire, I both initiate and monitor *every* derivatives contract on our books... If Berkshire ever gets in trouble, it will be *my* fault. It will not be because of the misjudgments made by a risk committee or chief risk officer [Buffett's emphasis].

Given that most companies are not run by Buffett, investors should know how to decode 'management speak'. For the next few years, investors should be ready for new excuses such as tighter US visa rules, new pollution control standards for automobiles, and Brexit.

The analyst should read carefully the chairman's statement, management discussion and analysis (MD&A), directors' report and auditors' report. While a lot of it may be jargon, cliché or hype, sometimes they provide additional information, explain the information in the financial statements or highlight risks. For example, the MD&A in the 2016 annual report of Dr. Reddy's Laboratories mentions the risks from pricing pressure, increased USFDA inspections and mergers and acquisitions by the company's competitors.

Corporate Governance and Financial Reporting

Learning Objective

LO 11 Understand the importance of corporate governance in financial reporting.

The board of directors approves the company's financial statements. The board's report to the shareholders must include a *directors' responsibility statement* (DRS) that contains assurances on accounting standards and policies, accounting records, going concern basis, internal controls, and legal compliance. No-nonsense independent directors and sceptical audit committees underpin effective governance.

Independent directors are part-time directors who are not expected to have any business or financial relationship with the company. They are expected to question the management's proposals and performance. The audit committee consists of board members. It should monitor the integrity of the financial statements of the company and review the company's internal control and risk management systems. It recommends the appointment and remuneration of auditors and reviews and monitors the auditor's independence and the performance and effectiveness of the audit process.

Independent directors and the audit committee have significant responsibilities under the Companies Act 2013 and the SEBI (Listing Obligations and Disclosure Requirements) Regulations 2015. In practice, things don't always work as intended. Independent directors are often selected from within a close network based on social or political connections rather than on business knowledge and competence. They receive substantial amounts in sitting fees and remuneration. Some of them zip from one board meeting to another, at times in exotic lands. It is unrealistic to expect such individuals to have the time, inclination or expertise to ask incisive questions in board or audit committee meetings. For example, many of them are unlikely to understand the accounting intricacies in business combination, consolidation, deferred taxes, fair value, foreign currency translation, impairment, leases, pensions, the percentage of completion, revenue recognition, and stock-based compensation. The analyst should look at the profiles of independent directors. A discount should be applied if the directors are household names and are on multiple company boards, since it is more likely that such individuals are simply lending their names to companies for a fee.

Increasingly, whistle-blowing is recognized as an important method of fraud deterrence and detection. In some countries including the US and the UK, whistle-blowers get legal protection and financial rewards. For example, the Dodd-Frank Wall Street Reform and Consumer Protection Act provides for payments in some cases to whistle-blowers. The listing regulations in India require listed companies to have a whistle-blower policy to report concerns about unethical behaviour, actual or suspected fraud or violation of the company's code of conduct or ethics policy and to protect whistle-blowers against victimization. Whistle-blowers may also have direct access to the chairman of the audit committee in exceptional cases.

Finally, it is down to the "tone at the top." If the board and the top management are seen as ethical, employees are more likely to be ethical. It is said that the fish rots from the head. So do organizations. A former WorldCom employee, who was jailed for fraud, observed: "When boards open the door a crack to unethical behaviour ... then it leaves a lot of interpretation for everyone down the line."

Auditors, Analysts and the Press

Auditors have responsibilities under the Companies Act and other laws. They are expected to exercise oversight of the financial reporting process including the internal control systems. A company's shareholders appoint the external auditors, who report to them on whether the financial statements present a "true and fair view" of the company's financial condition and performance. In practice, the controlling shareholder appoints the auditors. Also, auditors are involved in consulting and advisory activities for the companies they audit. So auditors have a conflict of interest that raises questions about their independence. Auditors' reports are written as boilerplate changing the company's name and the reporting period. The additional report by the auditors on internal financial controls is again bland. If these reports are to be believed, no Indian company has weaknesses in internal control systems. In contrast, many US companies mention weak internal controls after the Sarbanes-Oxley Act of 2002 required them. It is good to know that Indian companies have better internal control systems than US companies.

Analysts in brokerage firms and investment advisory services prepare periodic reports on companies and industries for their clients and sometimes for outsiders. Analysts can question the management in private meetings, conference calls and analyst briefings about internal expectations specified in budgets and other internal documents. Sell-side analysts work for brokerages, banks and research firms and their reports are sometimes available to outsiders. Their recommendations (mostly "buy") are expected to generate commission income for their employers. So sell-side research is conflicted. Buy-side analysts are employed in mutual funds and other investment firms and produce research reports for

Learning Objective

LO 12 Question the role of auditors, analysts and the press in financial reporting.

in-house use by their employers. Analysts are not formally a part of the financial reporting process unlike directors and auditors. Nevertheless, they exert significant influence over the quality of financial statements. If they suspect foul play, they can put a sell on the stock. As mentioned earlier, the pressure to meet unrealistic analyst expectations may result in earnings management including fraud. Analysts are often held responsible for managers pursuing short-term gains at the cost of neglecting long-term success.

Similar to analysts, the press (print and electronic media) are not a part of the reporting process. Business newspapers and magazines and television channels in India report on the working of companies and point to problems. Most of the reports relate to business issues, such as fall in sales, strikes, raw material shortage and so on. Sometimes they highlight bribery, fraud and other unlawful acts. Critical stories about earnings quality and accounting problems are rare, possibly because they are not seen as likely to increase sales or viewership. In contrast, international newspapers and TV channels carry frequent reports, commentaries and editorials on accounting practices and complex accounting issues. There are two concerns regarding the role of the press. One, they are sometimes owned or controlled by large business groups. Two, they depend on companies for advertising revenue. So their neutrality is a question mark.

DISCUSSION QUESTION 15.3

There have been plenty of high-profile accounting frauds reported from around the world. Here are a few examples. *US*: AIG, AOL, Autonomy, Bristol-Myers Squibb, CA, Dynegy, Enron, HealthSouth, IBM, Lehman, Olympus, Sunbeam, Waste Management, Tyco, Valeant, WorldCom. *UK*: BCCI, Mirror Group, Polly Peck, Tesco. *Japan*: IHI Corporation, Livedoor, Kanebo, Nikko Cordial, Olympus, Toshiba. *Italy*: Parmalat. *China*: Alibaba, Caterpillar China, Hanergy, NQ Mobile, Longtop, Sino-Forest. India has had just *one* high-profile accounting fraud all these years: Satyam. Could it be that Indian businessmen, managers, accountants and auditors are far more honest when it comes to accounting?

....

....

....

RECAP

- *Earnings quality* is affected by the accounting methods and estimates used, prior period errors, discontinued operations, changes in accounting policies, and non-operating and non-recurring items.
- In order to understand the profitability of an enterprise's operations, we remove financial items. *Net operating profit after tax (NOPAT)* focuses on operating performance.
- Managers are interested in their company's scorecard since their bonus and career prospects depend on the reported performance to a great extent. Therefore, they may wish to report higher, lower or smoothed earnings depending on the circumstances.
- *Segment information* provides the management's view of how the various part of an enterprise's performance. It helps us understand the performance of the various parts of firm's operations and the associated risks.
- *Pro forma measures* exclude items that are a part of the comparable GAAP measure. Pro forma measures have their place, but they can be sometimes misleading.
- *Free cash flow* is the difference between operating and investing cash. It is a popular valuation basis. It is not a good indicator of future cash flow for growing firms.
- *Economic value added* measures the profitability of a firm's investment. It uses a notional charge for capital employed regardless of whether a firm is financed by debt or equity.
- Companies provide *voluntary disclosures* to communicate information that cannot be effectively conveyed in the standard financial report. Voluntary disclosure is

motivated by capital market pressure, product market forces, the reputation of managers in the labour market, and potential shareholder litigation.

- Market efficiency implies that stock prices reflect publicly available information. Research shows that the market anticipates much of the information contained in annual and interim financial reports prior to their release. The market is also not 'fooled' by accounting method differences. The market has access to more information than that available in annual reports.

- Annual reports and earnings releases are full of jargon, buzz words, and catchphrases. It is important to see through them to find out what the company is saying and not saying.

- Independent directors, audit committees and auditors are a part of the financial reporting process. Their effectiveness may vary from company to company.

- Though analysts and the press are not a formal part of the financial reporting process, they have influence over it.

Review Problem

Consider the following contexts for a firm.
- (a) A new CEO joins the firm.
- (b) The firm faces intense competition in the product market.
- (c) Corporate income tax rate has been reduced effective next year.
- (d) The competition watchdog is investigating the firm for acting in collusion with its competitors.
- (e) The firm is likely to incur huge losses.
- (f) The firm is about to decide on granting stock options to its top management.
- (g) The firm has a large profit in the current quarter but the next quarter is likely to be weak.

Required
What is the likely earnings management behaviour in each context? Consider each context separately.

Solution to the Review Problem
- (a) *Big bath:* The new CEO would like to get rid of past costs and losses.
- (b) *Income-increasing:* This will help the firm to show higher profits despite the low margins because of intense competition.
- (c) *Income-decreasing:* Deferring profits to next year will save tax because of the lower rate.
- (d) *Income-decreasing:* This will help the firm escape regulatory scrutiny.
- (e) *Big bath:* It is better to report all bad news now than repeat it.
- (f) *Income-decreasing:* This will help bring down the stock price at the time of grant, so that the potential gain to the top management increases.
- (g) *Income-decreasing:* The firm can defer some of the current quarter sales to the next quarter.

ASSIGNMENT MATERIAL

Questions

1. What are the characteristics of high *earnings quality*?
2. How do companies benefit from high earnings quality?
3. Is *earnings management* unavoidable?
4. How can stringent accounting standards help in reducing earnings management?
5. Give examples of income-decreasing earnings management.
6. How is segment information useful in analyzing a company's performance?
7. Are *pro forma measures* helpful or harmful?

8. When is *free cash flow* a good basis for valuing a business?
9. How is *economic profit* different from accounting profit?
10. Why do companies make *voluntary disclosures*? Are there any costs?
11. Does the *efficient market hypothesis* necessarily imply that an investor can't benefit from financial statement analysis?
12. What institutional arrangements exist to keep earnings management in check?

Problems

Problem 15.1
Earnings Quality of Statement of Profit and Loss Items *

The following items are included in determining the net profit of a non-financial firm.

(a) Revenue from sales
(b) Dividend income
(c) Expenditure on discontinued project written off
(d) Loss on sale of investments

(e) MAT credit written off
(f) Write-back of tax provision
(g) Fair value gain on investments
(h) Penalty for violation of competition law

(i) Provision for contingencies
(j) Impairment of goodwill
(k) Effect of change in life expectancy used for employee benefits
(l) Interest on income tax refunds

Required

State whether these items indicate high or low earnings quality. Consider each item separately.

Problem 15.2
Earnings Quality of Statement of Profit and Loss Items * Alternative to Problem 15.1

The following items are included in determining the net profit of a non-financial firm.

(a) Revenue from services
(b) Gain on cancellation of forward contracts
(c) Gain on sale of equipment
(d) Shop rental income (for a hotel)

(e) Copyright permission fee (for a newspaper)
(f) Effect of change in discount rate used for employee benefits
(g) Fair value loss on investments
(h) Engineering and services fee (for a construction company)

(i) Scrap sales
(j) Profit on sale of a subsidiary
(k) Impairment of property, plant and equipment
(l) Insurance settlement received

Required

State whether these items indicate high or low earnings quality. Consider each item separately.

Problem 15.3
Alternative Accounting Methods and Profitability Analysis **

Shah Company and Mehta Company sell casual wear. The 20X4 statement of profit and loss of the two companies is as follows:

	Shah Company	Mehta Company
Sales...	₹54,000	₹78,000
Cost of goods sold	25,500	48,000
Operating expenses...	18,000	22,000
	43,500	70,000
Profit before interest and tax...	10,500	8,000
Income tax...	5,000	3,800
Profit after tax	5,500	4,200

Depreciation expense included in cost of goods sold was ₹7,500 for Shah Company and ₹12,000 for Mehta Company. Shah Company followed the WDV method, while Mehta Company followed the straight-line method. Shah Company's straight-line depreciation would be ₹4,500. There were no other differences in their accounting.

Required

1. Compute the profit margin for the two companies using the reported net profit.
2. Recompute Shah Company's net profit and profit margin applying straight-line depreciation.
3. Compare the results in Requirements 1 and 2. Does the difference in the depreciation method affect your evaluation of the two companies?

Sunil Company and Akhil Company make shoes. The 20X2 statement of profit and loss of the two companies is as follows:

Problem 15.4
Alternative Accounting
Methods and Profitability
Analysis ** Alternative to
Problem 15.3

	Sunil Company	Akhil Company
Sales..	₹100,000	₹110,000
Cost of goods sold	60,000	65,000
Operating expenses..	24,000	28,000
	84,000	93,000
Profit before interest and tax	16,000	17,000
Income tax...	4,000	5,000
Profit after tax	12,000	12,000

The two companies follow the same accounting methods except for inventory. Sunil Company follows FIFO, while Akhil Company follows WAC. Sunil Company's 20X2 inventories were as follows: beginning, ₹18,000; ending, ₹15,000. Under WAC, they would be ₹17,000 and ₹12,000, respectively.

Required

1. Compute the profit margin for the two companies using the reported net profit.
2. Recompute Sunil Company's net profit and profit margin applying WAC.
3. Compare the results in Requirements 1 and 2. Does the difference in the inventory method affect your evaluation of the two companies?

The statement of profit and loss of Hafiz Company and Saif Company for two years is as follows:

Problem 15.5
Earnings Quality
Analysis ***

	Hafiz Company		Saif Company	
	20X2	20X1	20X2	20X1
Net sales...	₹12,000	₹10,000	₹10,200	₹9,900
Cost of goods sold	8,400	7,000	7,140	6,930
Gross profit..	3,600	3,000	3,060	2,970
Operating expenses.....................................	2,160	1,800	1,836	1,782
Operating profit...	1,440	1,200	1,224	1,188
Non-operating items: Net interest income..	99	98	300	97
Profit before tax	1,539	1,298	1,524	1,285
Tax expense, 30%...	462	389	457	386
Net profit..	1,077	909	1,067	899

Required

1. Which company is more profitable?
2. Analyze the earnings quality of the two companies.
3. Which company is more likely a better investment opportunity?

The statement of profit and loss of Ajay Company and Vipul Company for two years is as follows:

Problem 15.6
Earnings Management
****

	Ajay Company		Vipul Company	
	20X6	20X5	20X6	20X5
Net sales...	₹15,000	₹12,000	₹13,200	₹12,000
Cost of goods sold	7,050	7,440	7,524	6,600
Gross profit..	7,950	4,560	5,676	5,400
Operating expenses.....................................	1,988	1,824	2,100	1,890
Operating profit...	5,962	2,736	3,576	3,510
Non-operating items: Interest income (impairment)...	(6,100)	100	90	130
Profit before tax	(138)	2,836	3,666	3,640
Tax expense, 30%...	(41)	851	1,100	1,092
Net profit..	(97)	1,985	2,566	2,548

Required

1. Evaluate the profitability of the two companies.
2. At the annual earnings release, Ajay Company's chief financial officer stated that the impairment charge made the company's future earnings "shock-proof because the worst is behind". What would you make of this statement? What questions would you ask the CFO about this item?

Problem 15.7
Free Cash Flow ✷✷✷✷

Arcadia Design Company
Cash Flow Statement
For the year ended October 31, 20X5

Cash flow from operating activities

Cash received from customers..	₹84,000	
Cash paid to suppliers and employees..	(80,600)	
Income tax paid...	(2,900)	
Net cash provided by operating activities...		₹500
Cash flow from investing activities		
Purchase of plant and machinery..	(19,900)	
Proceeds from sale of plant and machinery...	5,000	
Purchase of investments...	(1,900)	
Proceeds from sale of investments	9,600	
Interest received..	1,200	
Dividend received	1,800	
Net cash used in investing activities..		(4,200)
Cash flow from financing activities		
Proceeds from issue of share capital..	8,000	
Redemption of debentures	(4,700)	
Interest paid...	(2,200)	
Net cash provided by financing activities...		1,100
Net decrease in cash and cash equivalents...		(2,600)
Cash and cash equivalent at beginning of period...................................		3,800
Cash and cash equivalents at end of period		1,200

Required

1. Compute the company's free cash flow.
2. What do we learn from the company's free cash flow?
3. Can the business be valued on the basis of free cash flow?

Problem 15.8
Economic Value
Added ✷✷✷✷✷

Win Company reported the following in its financial statements for 20X2 and 20X1 (in millions):

	20X2	20X1
Non-current investments: financial assets and investment in associate	₹800	₹300
Current investments...	1,600	1,100
Cash and cash equivalents	500	450
Non-current borrowings	10,000	9,500
Current borrowings...	3,200	1,300
Equity..	7,100	6,200
Interest expense	550	350
Interest income...	120	90
Net profit...	2,950	2,600

The following additional information is available:

(a) The fair values of the non-current investments and non-current borrowings were as follows:

	20X2	20X1
Non-current investments: financial assets	₹250	₹150
Non-current borrowings	11,000	8,100
Current borrowings...	3,500	1,200

    (b) Cash equivalents included commercial paper of ₹1,400 in 20X2 and ₹950 in 20X1.

    (c) The company had 200 million shares of ₹10 par value fully paid in both years. The share traded at ₹60 in 20X2 and ₹50 in 20X1.

    (d) Cost of equity was 15 per cent and cost of debt was 10 per cent.

    (e) Corporate income tax rate was 30 per cent.

Required

    1. Compute the company's average capital employed for 20X2.
    2. Compute the company's cost of capital.
    3. Compute the company's economic value added.
    4. How would you interpret the economic value added?

Business Decision Cases

On February 21, 20X5, Manish Singhal joined as the new CEO of Western Bank Limited. The bank was established over five decades ago and has been one of India's best banks in profitability, growth, asset quality, customer service and regulatory compliance. Lately, things have not been going well at the bank. Profitability has come down due to intense competition from new banks that have low operating cost and high technology. Growth has stalled because of the subdued demand for credit. The slowing economy has led to rising bad loans. New banks are poaching the bank's borrowers and depositors with superior customer service. For the first time in its history, Western Bank was fined for violation of anti-money laundering laws and know-your-customer guidelines. In short, the bank is in a mess. The board has appointed Singhal for three years to restore the bank to its past glory. Singhal has worked in foreign banks for over 25 years and thinks that Indian banks are "utterly slow creatures". Asked to describe himself in an interview to a business TV channel he said he liked challenges.

BDC 15.1
Western Bank Limited

    Soon after Singhal took over, he met with Sujata Roy the bank's CFO for five years. Roy joined as an officer over 30 years ago and has risen to her current position by sheer hard work and honesty. A bright banker, she has worked in all the major functions of the bank including credit, compliance, internal audit, treasury, risk management, and financial reporting and has been posted in the bank's overseas operations. Roy is cautious by nature and it shows in her work. Her colleagues call her Ms. Straight.

    Feroze Contractor is the chairman of the audit committee of Western Bank's board of directors. Contractor is a senior partner of a big CA firm. He has over 15 years of board and audit committee experience and has a formidable reputation for his uncompromising commitment to truthful financial reporting. He jokes in audit committee meetings that he "loves parks and hates prisons."

    Swaminathan Shankar is an independent director and audit committee member. He is a risk management consultant with five years of board and audit committee experience. He advises major banks in India on their risk management policies and practices. He introduces himself as "completely risk-averse."

    Excerpts from the meetings between Singhal and Roy (Scene 1) and Roy, Contractor and Shankar (Scene 2) are given below.

Scene 1 (February 14 Roy's meeting with CEO)

CEO:	Come in, Sujata. The reason I am meeting you soon after joining is to get a sense of the bank's financials. You are the conscience-keeper of the bank. Do tell me whatever I should know.
Roy:	Yes, Manish, if I may. The bank has loyal borrowers and depositors. Some have been with us for three generations.
CEO:	Glad to hear that.
Roy:	Unfortunately, we have had some problems lately. But I don't think there is anything fundamentally wrong with the bank.
CEO:	You probably know that the board has brought me in with a specific mandate to clean up the place. I am going to wield the broom from now on.
Roy:	As for financial reporting, we are upfront and candid. Especially when it comes to bad news.
CEO:	I like that. So you are going to be my comrade-in-arms.
Roy:	Surely. I ensure that the bank's financial reports are truthful and the controls are strong.
CEO:	OK, let's get going. I want to improve the bank's PCR [provision coverage ratio] in Q4. Today there is a letter from the RBI asking us to increase the provision for NPAs.

Roy:	Yes, I am aware of the letter, though I haven't seen it yet. We have to comply.
CEO:	Can we make the best of this situation?
Roy:	How?
CEO:	We can provide more than what the RBI is asking us to do. I'm sure they too will look at it kindly.
Roy:	We should provide what is necessary. No more, no less.
CEO:	We can use this occasion to clean up our books.
Roy:	Our books are clean. We have not hidden anything. We have a tough external auditor and an even more difficult audit committee chair.
CEO:	You know very well that it is not zero or one in accounting. There is judgment in accounting.
Roy:	Sorry, I don't understand what you're coming to.
CEO:	Let me give a couple of examples. Take pensions. The discount rate, life expectancy, expected return on plan – all these involve discretion. We could use a lower discount rate, longer life expectancy or lower return. After all, bond yields are coming down and people are living longer. This will be completely in sync with your legendary caution.
Roy:	Why now?
CEO:	It has to be done sometime. Let's begin now.
Roy:	What about regulatory requirements? These things will cut into our capital and the RBI inspectors won't like it.
CEO:	Well, we have to balance these things. So we should sell off some of our surplus land, non-core investments, stuff like that. We can revalue the land and buildings.
Roy:	Non-core investments such as what?
CEO:	Take our housing subsidiary. After all these years, it has a paltry four per cent market share. It's an embarrassment, you see.
Roy:	OK. What other investments?
CEO:	We own shares in the National Stock Exchange. I don't know why.
Roy:	We were the co-founders of NSE.
CEO:	But I wonder what sense does it make to keep them now. We can book the gains.
Roy:	Anything else?
CEO:	We're going to spend huge amounts on bringing our IT systems up to date. You know IT benefits can vanish quickly. So why not expense them?
Roy:	When we went to the board for approval, we told them that the benefits will last four to five years.
CEO:	Technology is dynamic. It keeps changing all the time. By writing them off, we'll reduce the balance sheet risk.
Roy:	Anything else?
CEO:	I will jot down ideas and let you know. Think about these from the bank's side and not get bogged down in theory.
Roy:	My last question. When I meet investors, they ask about our growth plans. In fact, a big fund is after me to arrange a meeting with you before the Q4 results.
CEO:	In a dull market like this, growth has to come from acquisitions. I am thinking of buying an insurance company and a brokerage. Actually, someone talked to me about these in my previous job. They are still up for sale. We have to acquire smaller banks if we want growth. They may look pricey. But good things cost money. There are also some troubled banks out there.
Roy:	OK, I have enough to think about. I will be back in a couple of days.
CEO:	Don't think too much. (laughs)

Scene 2 (February 15 Roy's meeting with audit committee chair and audit committee member)

Contractor:	What's happening in the bank? The business is not that good. But your new CEO is a go-getter. Is he keeping everyone on their toes?
Roy:	The bank is staring at a loss for the first time in its history this quarter.
Contractor:	It was expected. Other banks are doing no better. I think everyone understands.
Roy:	That's right. The point about the CEO you made is more worrisome.

Contractor:	What? We had a lot of difficulties getting Manish to join us. We had to offer him a stock option plan to induce him. What's the matter?
Roy:	I have no doubt he is capable. His attitude to financial reporting and controls worries me.
Contractor:	Can you be specific?
Roy:	So far he has not been specific, so I don't know what he wants. He has dropped broad hints about what he wants in the Q4 results.
Contractor:	Such as what?
Roy:	He wants to provide for bad loans more than what the RBI requires or even what may be truly necessary.
Contractor:	Conservatism is a good thing. Isn't it?
Roy:	Ind AS doesn't say so. I did a Control-F search for conservatism and didn't get a single match.
Contractor:	You're right. It's officially out but companies do it still.
Shankar:	I am a bit confused. Has conservatism been banished? When I studied accounting 20 years ago, my instructor must have uttered the C word hundreds of time. He was effusive about the benefits of conservative accounting because you can't trust managers' self-restraint when it came to reporting.
Roy:	The current view is that any kind of bias should be avoided and accounting should be neutral.
Contractor:	No deliberate overstatement or understatement. What other ideas does he have?
Roy:	He wants to play with the pensions numbers. The discount rate, life expectancy,… That sort of thing.
Contractor:	We will go by the actuary's report. But who selects the actuary?
Roy:	The HR department does.
Shankar:	Can the company nudge the actuary into making these changes? That would be unacceptable.
Roy:	There is some scope for discretion in this. The actuary can move within a band.
Contractor:	If the CEO has his way, the bank's capital will take a hit. With the Basel III kicking in we don't have any cushion.
Roy:	He has some ideas for making profits. He wants to monetize the surplus land, housing subsidiary, NSE shares, cut down on IT… Strangely, he wants to expand by acquiring an insurance company, a brokerage, some banks, even some troubled banks. Oh, I forgot. He wants to revalue the land and buildings. It looks like a potpourri.
Contractor:	What else is he saying?
Roy:	I think he has some more ideas.
Shankar:	Is there method in his madness? Some of the changes will decrease profits, some will increase profits. So the net effect will be a lot subdued than going one way.
Contractor:	I have seen this movie many times. It's the new CEO effect. Sujata, you need to be cautious. Go by the accounting standards. Sound out the auditors. Once the changes are clear, inform the audit committee. If the CEO overdoes this sort of thing, we have to restrain him.
Roy:	OK.

Required

1. List the items the CEO has proposed and their effect on the bank's financial statements.
2. Classify the items as involving accounting decisions and operating decisions.
3. Is there "method in his madness"?
4. What "movie" is Feroze Contractor referring to?
5. What should Sujata Roy do next?

Interpreting Financial Reports

Toshiba Corporation is a well-known name in electronics. Its tagline "Leading Innovation" captures the company's wide array of products from personal computers to power generation. It started as a shop-cum-factory called Tanaka Seizo-sho in 1882 in Tokyo and grew to be a $50 billion dollar

IFR 15.1
Toshiba Corporation

business in 2016. The company was the poster child for Japan's efforts to regulate corporate behaviour and even appeared as a case study on governance. In 2013, the group was ranked ninth out of 120 publicly traded Japanese companies with good governance practices in a list compiled by the Japan Corporate Governance Network, a Tokyo-based private organization. Ernst & Young ShinNihon was the company's external auditor.

In January 2015 an accounting scandal involving a company-wide effort to inflate profit by $1.3 billion erupted. It was revealed that Seiya Shimaoka, Toshiba's internal auditor, asked Makoto Kubo the company's chief financial officer to examine the accounts at Toshiba's laptop business. Kubo ignored his requests stating that examining them would delay the company's earnings reporting deadline.

An independent investigation by a committee consisting of external lawyers and accountants said that the scandal happened because of the corporate culture at Toshiba in which it was impossible to act contrary to the intent of superiors and a systematic involvement including by top management. The report highlighted severe external circumstances such as the accident at the Fukushima nuclear plant, the flooding of the company's plant during the floods in Thailand, and the extreme strengthening of the Japanese yen. The committee highlighted the breakdown of controls by the internal audit committee. At a wider level the scandal was seen as a blow to the Prime Minister Shinzo Abe's efforts to reform business and corporate governance practices in Japan.

The methods for perpetrating fraud in the various divisions were as follows:

(a) *Application of the percentage of completion method:* Provisions for contract losses were not recorded in an appropriate and timely manner and profits were overstated due to inappropriate estimates of total cost of contract work because cost reduction measures with low feasibility were factored into those estimates.

(b) *Recording operating expenses:* Provisions were not recorded in a timely manner and costs were recorded in a subsequent period by deferring part of that payment to the subsequent period.

(c) *Overpricing of parts:* Parts are bought in bulk and sold to overseas manufacturers for PC manufacturing. Finished PC products are purchased from these manufacturers. The sale prices were kept higher than their purchase prices.

(d) *Inventory costing:* The standard cost of inventories was not revised regularly. As a result, losses were not recognized in a timely manner when it was expected that sales would no longer be possible or when the net sales price fell below the acquisition cost.

As an illustration of the fraud, we will consider how the percentage of completion method was applied in the Power Systems Company which supplies thermal, hydro and nuclear power generation systems. The method is applied where the estimated contract revenue is Japanese Yen (JPY) 1.0 billion or more and the contract work period is one year or more and some other contracts. Internal control for projects in which the percentage of completion method is used consists of these steps:

1. *Registration of project:* Sales, administration or planning department personnel register the project in the system as a project in which the method can be used. The person's superior confirms and approves the method for the project.

2. *Cost estimation:* Administration or engineering department personnel determine the delivery date and prepare an estimate cost sheet. The operations accounting department, a superior at the administration department examines the contents of that estimate cost sheet closely and approves that form based on documentary evidence. The approved cost estimate sheet is circulated to the sales department. Administration or sales department personnel confirm with the operations, engineering, or procurement department every month or every quarter on whether there has been any change in the estimated costs. When a change is required, it is entered into the system and approved by a superior. Changes in the contract terms are approved similarly.

3. *Calculation of revenue:* Toshiba's percentage of completion system automatically calculates the amount of sales and costs to be recorded based on the percentage of completion method.

4. *Verification of the amount of sales to be recorded:* Planning department and accounting department personnel verify the consistency of the original data (contract amounts, cumulative amounts, and estimated total costs) used in calculations using the percentage of completion method.

5. *Recording of sales:* Toshiba's percentage of completion system automatically journalizes entries and records sales.

6. *Reversing entries of recorded sales:* Upon completion of construction, sales are recorded on the system as the total contract amount. In order to prevent double entries of sales, sales using the percentage of completion method are reversed. When sales are recorded on the system as the total contract revenue, the information is automatically linked to the percentage of completion method system. Revering entries of sales and sales costs are recorded using an automatic link of the percentage of completion method system.

Expected losses from the next period are to be recorded as "provisions for contract losses for orders received." Loss-making projects are identified through an elaborate process involving sales, planning, administration, engineering and accounting departments. In order to ensure that no loss-making project is omitted, the planning department sends to the sales or the administration department each quarter a confirmation list of loss-making projects that lists projects where the contract amount is JPY 1.0 billion or more and the amount of loss is JPY 100 million or more from the list of backlog orders on the system, and will request confirmation from those departments. In addition, the planning department requests the accounting department to prepare the latest "Schedule for Provision for Contract Losses for Orders Received" at the end of each quarter. Provisions are recorded using the Schedule. Finally, provisions for contract losses for the previous quarter are reversed. According to the rules, it is not necessary to report to or obtain a decision or approval from the Division Vice President or President to record provisions for contract losses and procedures for registering in the system total estimated costs of contract work. In practice, provisions for losses cannot be recorded without the approval of the Company President except for the recording of small provisions. It was also necessary to obtain such approval even to change the total estimated cost of contract work.

Project G illustrates how things worked in practice. The orders for the project were received by Westinghouse Electric Corporation (WEC), a consolidated US subsidiary of Toshiba during the period from 2007 to 2009 with a total contract amount of US$7.6 billion to build Power Plant G with delivery dates from 2013 to 2019. Due to design changes and delayed construction work, WEC reported additional recognized risks of US$385 million (impact on profit and loss was negative US$276 million) and US$401 million (impact on profit and loss was negative 332 million) in the second quarter and the third quarter of FY 2013, respectively. After further evaluation by Toshiba, the accounting records US$69 million (impact on profit and loss was negative US$50 million) and US$293 million (impact on profit and loss was negative US$225 million), respectively. For the fourth quarter of FY 2013, Toshiba and WEC agreed to recognize US$401 million in the accounting records. However, the reduction in the second quarter of FY 2013 had no sufficient basis. In the third quarter, Ernst & Young ShinNihon insisted that the company record the amount of US$401 million, but Toshiba accepted US$293 million (impact on profit and loss negative US$225 million). The figure had no specific grounds, so the figure of US$401 million should have been adopted.

It turned out that in August 2013 Yasuharu Igarashi President of the Power Systems Company sent an expert team from Toshiba to WEC to review the estimated increase of US$86.1 million and the team reduced the amount to US$69 million, included in the consolidated financial statements in September 2013. In October 2013, WEC reported to Toshiba that it believed the amount of US$69 was insufficient in light of comments of WEC's auditor, Ernst & Young LLP. By October 24, WEC reported to Toshiba that the estimated increase in the cost of contract was US$385 million, creating a discrepancy of $316 million. Toshiba's Corporate Finance & Accounting Division and the Accounting Division of Power Systems Company and WEC's officers discussed the matter with Ernst & Young ShinNihon. It was agreed that the amount for the FY 2013 second quarter financial statements would be US$69 million. Toshiba's decision was made on the assumption that cost reductions were possible by shortening the work period and that costs attributable to the customer would be recovered. However, there were no supporting schedules for the assumption.

Investigations revealed that Toshiba's President Hisao Tanaka and CFO Makoto Kubo received reports about an increase in the total estimated cost of contract work for Project G by WEC. The Company Accounting Division was responsible for reviewing the data submitted by subsidiaries and the Corporate Finance & Accounting Division was responsible for reviewing the financial statements prepared by the Company Accounting Division and correct them if there was any problem. Where President and CFO were involved in inappropriate accounting for projects such as Project G, internal control was not functioning in those Divisions and the Divisions themselves were involved in inappropriate accounting. The Corporate Audit Division did not raise the accounting treatment for Project G. The Audit Committee raised the matter with Tanaka, Kubo and Igarashi on various dates. Igarashi replied that the matter was being examined. There were no further questions from the Audit Committee. Ernst & Young ShinNihon was provided with information about the estimated increase of US$316 million immediately before the announcement of Toshiba's financial statements on the last day of October. Also, quarterly reviews were conducted by limited procedures as compared to the year-end auditing of financial statements.

Required

1. When is the percentage of completion method to be used? Was Toshiba's use of the method for certain contracts appropriate?
2. What is the role of judgment and estimate in applying the percentage of completion method? What safeguards did the company have against potential abuse of the method?
3. Review the internal control systems for the use of the percentage of completion method.
4. How effective were the internal control systems?
5. What was the role of Toshiba's top management in the accounting function?
6. Did Toshiba's audit committee perform its monitoring role? What could the audit committee have done differently?
7. Comment on the role of Toshiba's external auditor.
8. The case refers to four methods of accounting fraud perpetrated in Toshiba and describes the use of the percentage of completion method. Explain how the other three methods could be used.
9. Examine how culture could have played a role in perpetrating and hushing up the fraud.
10. Comment on the developments in Toshiba's accounting, auditing and governance subsequent to the case.

IFR 15.2
ICICI Bank

ICICI Bank is India's largest private sector bank. It has a reputation for aggressive growth. Analysts have voiced concern over the bank's loan portfolio and margins. For the quarter ended March 31, 2016, the bank shocked the market with a profit of ₹7 billion against a consensus analyst of ₹31 billion. This was a decline of 77 per cent from the year-ago quarter. News reports suggested that this was the lowest quarterly profit in at least 15 years. This is what the bank said in its commentary on the results:

> During the three months ended December 31, 2015, [the] RBI articulated the objective of early and conservative recognition of stress and provisioning, held discussions with and asked a number of Indian banks to review certain loan accounts and their classification over the three months ended December 31, 2015 and the three months ended March 31, 2016. As a result of the above factor, non-performing loans increased significantly in the banking system during the second half of fiscal 2016. [The] RBI also directed banks to make an additional provision of 10% during the year ending March 31, 2017 in respect of restructured loan accounts highlighted by RBI;

The culprit was the line item "exceptional items (collective contingency and related reserves)" for ₹36 billion. Commentators speculated that this could represent losses not recognized in the past in a timely manner and that the bank potentially had severe asset quality issues.

Required

1. Analyze the bank's results for the March 2016 quarter. Comment on the bank's explanation.
2. What was the "exceptional items"? Why did it appear in the March 2016 quarter?
3. Was there more to it than the management's story?

Financial Analysis

FA 15.1
Profit, Cash Flow and Earnings Quality

Study the statement of profit and loss and statement of cash flows of a sample of companies.

Required

1. Prepare analysis of the differences between profit and net cash from operating activities. What do you learn from the analysis?
2. Identify items that reverse in sign over two consecutive years and three consecutive years. What does the sign reversal tell us about the earnings quality of the companies?

3. Prepare a note explaining how your study is useful for analyzing and interpreting financial statements.

Plot the following for a sample of companies: stock returns on the Y-axis; and earnings (net profit) and cash flow on the X-axis. In order to improve the quality of your research, you should select companies from many industries and do this study over several years.

FA 15.2
Earnings or Cash Flow?

Required

1. Prepare a report explaining the results of your study.
2. Repeat the analysis using alternative measures of net profit (such as excluding non-operating items, exceptional items, effect of accounting method and estimate changes). Compare these results with the one above and explain why they differ or do not differ.

Companies present graphs and ratios in annual reports to highlight their performance. While these help investors to get a quick grasp of the big picture, they are not audited. So they are vulnerable to selective use and abuse.

FA 15.3
Graphs and Ratios in Annual Reports

Required

1. Prepare a report on how companies use graphs and ratios in their reports.
2. Comment on whether the use of graphs and ratios is likely to mislead investors.

Study the annual reports of a sample of companies for five years.

FA 15.4
Economic Value Added

Required

1. Compute the EVA of the companies.
2. Analyze the trend in EVA over the period.
3. Plot the following for the companies: stock returns on the Y-axis; and EVA, net profit and cash flow on the X-axis. Interpret the graph.
4. Prepare a report based explaining the results of your study.

Study the annual reports of a sample of companies that have reported losses or low profits.

FA 15.5
Earnings Excuses

Required

1. List the explanations for the loss or low profit from the chairman's statement and the directors' report and management discussion and analysis.
2. Evaluate whether the explanations are justified.

Answers to One-minute Quiz

15.1 d.
15.2 d.
15.3 a, d.
15.4 a, c.
15.5 d.

Answers to Test Your Understanding

15.1 The adjusted net loss for 20X6 is ₹8 million, calculated as follows: Reported net profit, ₹12 million – Gain on sale of surplus land, ₹14 million – Profit from sales to related parties, ₹8 million + Cost of closure of discontinued business, ₹2 million. The adjusted net loss for 20X5 is ₹31 million, after excluding the loss from discontinued business, ₹9 million. The loss came down in 20X6.

15.2 NOPAT is ₹85,135, calculated as follows: Net profit, ₹80,000 + Net financial income, ₹6,000 × 0.65 – Dividend from overseas subsidiaries, ₹900 × 0.65 + Impairment charge, ₹3,000 × 0.65 – Gain on sale of investments, ₹600 × 0.65 + Fair value loss on investments, ₹400 × 0.65.

15.3 The proposed actions would have the effect of reducing the profit for the September 20X5 quarter and increasing future profits.

15.4 Computation of economic value added:

Market value of equity: 5,000 × ₹140		₹700,000
Market value of debt	₹175,000	
Deduct Bank deposits	100,000	
Net debt		75,000
Capital employed		775,000
Weight of equity: 700,000/775,000		0.9032
Weight of net debt: 75,000/775,000		0.0968
Cost of equity (given)		9%
Cost of debt, after tax: 7% × 0.75		5.25%
Weighted average cost of capital: 0.9032 × 9% + 0.0968 × 5.25%		8.64%
Net profit		₹95,200
Deduct Interest income, after tax: ₹5,000 × 0.75		(3,750)
Add Interest expense, after tax: ₹12,000 × 0.75		9,000
NOPAT		100,450
Deduct Capital charge: ₹775,000 × 8.64%		66,960
Economic value added		33,490

Interview with Professor Suraj Srinivasan, Harvard Business School

Professor Suraj Srinivasan is the Philip J. Stomberg Professor of Business Administration at Harvard Business School.

Question: Audit committees are expected to monitor the financial reporting and control systems of companies. What should the audit committee members do to avoid unpleasant surprises?

Answer: The task of audit committees starts with developing a good understanding of the strategy of the business, the key drivers of performance, and the risks in the business model. Directors should ensure that they have a deep knowledge of whether the strategy is ensuring sustainable growth and profitability. This will allow the audit committee to focus on how the company's internal systems are geared to managing the key risks and how external financial reporting communicates the key success and risk factors to investors. Risks can arise from competition, technology, and other factors external to the firm or from internal factors such as weak controls systems, high-powered incentives, and risky investment decisions. The audit committee needs to have a systematic process to consider these risks, ask the right questions, and assess the answers. A focus merely on compliance issues carries the danger of blinding the audit committee to bigger risks that are strategic in nature.

Question: What matters more to external auditors: reputation costs or financial and legal penalties?

Answer: Both the loss of reputation and legal penalties should eventually be manifested as financial penalties for auditors. But for reputational penalties arising from client or market pressure to work effectively, there needs to be a high degree of transparency about audit quality. For example, if an auditor experiences a large audit failure in one client, the other clients of the audit firm need to be able to assess if the failure is the case of a bad apple (say one ineffective audit partner) or a systematic failure of audit quality at the entire audit firm. This is hard to establish and therefore, in practice, we see limited reputational penalties experienced by audit firms for audit failure. Therefore, the onus falls to regulators (in the US these would be the SEC or PCAOB) or to the courts to levy administrative or financial penalties. To progress towards a more market-oriented solution (i.e., reputational penalties) it would be useful to create greater transparency in the audit process. For example, the recent move by the PCAOB in the US to require the disclosure of the lead audit partners name for every company is a welcome move that will allow for greater transparency.

Question: The Sarbanes-Oxley Act has been around for over ten years. How has it improved the control environment in companies?

Answer: The Sarbanes-Oxley Act (SOX) used a few mechanisms to improve the control environment in companies. One instrument was to mandate internal control monitoring by the auditor. Under this, the auditors have to provide an opinion on the quality of internal controls. Another significant development was to get the CEO and CFO to certify the financial statements. The Act also empowered auditors to be more critical in their assurance function by increasing their power vis-à-vis managers and created the PCAOB to monitor auditors. The research evidence suggests that, taken together, the various measures under SOX have led to greater investment in internal controls, fewer cases of weaknesses in control systems, and fewer accounting misstatements. Accounting mistakes, when they inevitably do occur, are less severe than prior to SOX. However, the flip side of the greater attention and investment in internal controls is the concern that these costs are disproportionately higher for smaller companies. And also that greater attention to internal controls can deter risk taking in firms leading to lower innovation and growth. This concern has led to fewer companies going public and has resulted in public companies going private.

Question: How does shareholder activism affect the quality of corporate governance?

Answer: In the ownership model prevalent in the US and other western economies (e.g., UK and Canada), shareholding in companies is mainly owned by dispersed shareholders, mainly large mutual funds and other financial institutions, most of who own relatively small portion of the company's total shareholding. Shareholders notionally elect a board of directors to provide guidance and to monitor professional managers that run the companies. There are two levels of agency problems created by this model – first between the shareholders and the board of directors and secondly between the board and managers. Dispersed shareholders have constraints in ensuring that the board is active and vigilant and that the right directors are elected. And, since the board of directors relies on managers for information and because directors are often selected by incumbent managers, it is unclear whether the board has the ability or willingness to actively monitor executives.

Shareholder activism attempts to mitigate some of these problems. Activist shareholders accumulate significant stakes in companies and this concentrated shareholding provides them with an incentive to question managers and to push for changes in poorly performing companies. Activist shareholders often raise questions about perquisite consumption, excess compensation, poor capital allocation decisions, and weak strategy execution and demand that poorly performing executives and directors be replaced. Research evidence shows that companies that experience activist demands improve investment decisions, shed poorly performing businesses, improve capital structure, and replace poorly performing managers. Evidence also suggests that the threat that activists will target poorly performing companies creates pressure on boards to ask the tough questions of managers even without activists actually appearing on the scene. Therefore, overall governance quality is improved in the presence of an active environment of shareholder activism.

Question: What are the costs and benefits of management earnings guidance? How can they be balanced?

Answer: Corporate executives are best placed to inform capital markets about the business prospects of the company. Earnings guidance provides investors and analysts with the managers' view of the immediate and long-term forecasts of the profit potential of the business. A clear view of future profitability will likely reduce uncertainty about the company resulting in lower volatility of stock prices thus reducing cost of capital for the business. This is especially true for companies that face uncertain market conditions whether due to competition, technological change, or a host of other factors. The benefit of earnings guidance is, therefore, to provide greater clarity about a business to capital markets.

On the other hand, the risk in providing specific earnings guidance (such as Earnings per Share (EPS) target) is that managers and investors become fixated on that one number to the exclusion of everything else. Research evidence suggests that managers are willing to forgo projects that are value adding in the long-term if such investments will affect the ability to meet EPS targets in the short-term. There is also the risk that managers engage in earnings management to meet guidance targets.

On balance, some level of guidance is necessary if the absence of such disclosure will lead to greater volatility in stock prices. However, managers can ensure that the focus of the disclosure is on the long-term strategic direction of the business and less on next quarter's performance. Boards of directors should also pay attention to perverse incentives towards short-termism that can be driven by compensation plans, for example, an over–reliance on stock price or short-term earnings targets in the compensation scheme. A vigilant audit committee that understands the critical accounting estimates underlying the financials can mitigate manager's incentives to manipulate earnings to achieve earnings targets.

Topic	Ind AS	IFRS
The Conceptual Framework for Financial Reporting	None	CF
First-time Adoption of International Financial Reporting Standards	Ind AS 101	IFRS 1
Share-based Payment	Ind AS 102	IFRS 2
Business Combinations	Ind AS 103	IFRS 3
Insurance Contracts	Ind AS 104	IFRS 4
Non-current Assets Held for Sale and Discontinued Operations	Ind AS 105	IFRS 5
Exploration for and Evaluation of Mineral Resources	Ind AS 106	IFRS 6
Financial Instruments: Disclosures	Ind AS 107	IFRS 7
Operating Segments	Ind AS 108	IFRS 8
Financial Instruments*	Ind AS 109	IFRS 9
Consolidated Financial Statements	Ind AS 110	IFRS 10
Joint Arrangements	Ind AS 111	IFRS 11
Disclosure of Interests in Other Entities	Ind AS 112	IFRS 12
Fair Value Measurement	Ind AS 113	IFRS 13
Regulatory Deferral Accounts	Ind AS 114	IFRS 14
Presentation of Financial Statements	Ind AS 1	IAS 1
Inventories	Ind AS 2	IAS 2
Statement of Cash Flows	Ind AS 7	IAS 7
Accounting Policies, Changes in Accounting Estimates and Errors	Ind AS 8	IAS 8
Events after the Reporting Period	Ind AS 10	IAS 10
Construction Contracts	Ind AS 11**	IAS 11
Service Concession Agreements		IFRIC 12
Income Taxes	Ind AS 12	IAS 12
Property, Plant and Equipment	Ind AS 16	IAS 16
Leases	Ind AS 17	IAS 17
Revenue	Ind AS 18	IAS 18
Employee Benefits	Ind AS 19	IAS 19
Accounting for Government Grants and Disclosure of Government Assistance	Ind AS 20	IAS 20
The Effects of Changes in Foreign Exchange Rates	Ind AS 21	IAS 21
Borrowing Costs	Ind AS 23	IAS 23
Related Party Disclosures	Ind AS 24	IAS 24
Separate Financial Statements	Ind AS 27	IAS 27
Investments in Associates and Joint Ventures	Ind AS 28	IAS 28
Financial Reporting in Hyperinflationary Economies	Ind AS 29	IAS 29
Financial Instruments: Presentation	Ind AS 32	IAS 32
Earnings per Share	Ind AS 33	IAS 33
Interim Financial Reporting	Ind AS 34	IAS 34
Impairment of Assets	Ind AS 36	IAS 36
Provisions, Contingent Liabilities and Contingent Assets	Ind AS 37	IAS 37
Intangible Assets	Ind AS 38	IAS 38
Financial Instruments*		IAS 39
Investment Property	Ind AS 40	IAS 40
Agriculture	Ind AS 41	IAS 41

* IFRS 9 will replace IAS 39 from January 1, 2018.
** Includes service concession agreements.

B
Dr. Reddy's Laboratories Limited Consolidated Financial Statements

Consolidated Balance Sheet, March 31	Ind AS	Indian GAAP		
	2016	2016	2015	2014
				(in millions)
ASSETS				
Non-current assets				
Property, plant and equipment	₹46,130	₹46,296	₹41,837	₹37,496
Capital work-in-progress	6,626	6,631	5,290	6,388
Goodwill	4,650			
Other intangible assets	15,946	19,338	11,933	8,912
Financial assets				
Investments	3,297	1,456	1,456	4
Loans	8	5,194	4,181	2,322
Deferred tax assets, net	5,905	2,853	2,450	1,917
Other non-current assets	1,991	135	64	—
Total non-current assets	84,553	81,903	67,211	57,039
Current assets				
Inventories	25,578	25,799	25,699	24,188
Financial assets				
Investments	35,034	21,122	21,022	10,664
Trade receivables	41,250	41,667	41,012	33,253
Cash and cash equivalents	4,920	18,358	18,724	23,006
Loans	206	10,058	10,747	10,989
Others	10,950	1,197	1,563	1,157
Current tax assets, net	1,348	—	—	—
Total current assets	119,286	118,201	118,767	103,257
Total assets	203,839	200,104	185,978	160,296
EQUITY AND LIABILITIES				
Equity				
Equity share capital	₹ 853	₹ 853	₹ 852	₹ 851
Other equity	124,845	116,156	97,679	77,801
Total equity	125,698	117,009	98,531	78,652
Liabilities				
Non-current liabilities				
Financial liabilities				
Borrowings	10,690	10,690	14,315	20,755
Other financial liabilities	2,498	2,498	2,733	1,181
Provisions	947	947	779	563
Deferred tax liabilities, net	537	592	1,407	1,241
Total non-current liabilities	14,672	14,727	19,234	23,740

Current liabilities

Financial liabilities

Borrowings	22,718	22,718	21,857	20,607
Trade payables	9,068	9,309	8,673	8,932
Other financial liabilities	23,230	—	—	—
Other current liabilities	862	24,395	26,244	20,208
Provisions	7,591	11,946	11,439	8,157
Total current liabilities	63,469	68,368	68,213	57,904
Total equity and liabilities	203,839	200,104	185,978	160,296

Consolidated Statement of Profit and Loss For the year ended March 31			
	Ind AS	**Indian GAAP**	
	2016	2016	2015
	(in millions except earnings per share)		
INCOME			
Sales, gross	—	₹154,639	₹147,855
Less: Excise duty		(842)	(829)
Sales, net	₹152,475	153,797	147,026
Service income	—	1,466	1,689
Licence fees	2,233	767	369
Other operating revenues	975	948	1,149
Revenue from operations	155,683	156,978	150,233
Other income	2,950	2,693	2,741
Total revenue	158,633	159,671	152,974
EXPENSES			
Cost of material consumed	26,799	24,667	28,259
Purchase of stock-in-trade	11,743	11,743	9,420
Changes in inventories	(957)	1,003	(558)
Conversion charges	—	2,436	1,929
Employee benefits expense	31,174	31,874	29,446
Selling expenses	11,811	—	—
Finance costs	826	824	1,082
Depreciation and amortization expense	9,389	9,705	7,599
Other expenses	39,260	48,053	46,801
Total expenses	130,045	128,299	123,978
Profit before exceptional and extraordinary items and tax	28,588	31,372	28,996
Exceptional items			
Foreign exchange loss	—	4,621	—
Profit before tax	28,588	26,751	28,996
Tax expense			
Current tax expense	—	6,620	6,242
Deferred tax expense/(benefit)	—	(1,383)	(610)
	7,511	5,237	5,632
Profit for the year	21,077	21,514	23,364
Share of profit of equity accounted investees, net of tax	229	—	—
Net profit after taxes and share of profit of associates	21,306	—	—
Other comprehensive income	(370)	—	—
Comprehensive income	20,936	—	—
Earnings per share			
Basic	124.93	—	137.18
Diluted	124.54	—	136.59

Consolidated Statement of Cash Flows For the year ended March 31	Indian GAAP	
	2016	2015
	(in millions)	
CASH FLOWS FROM (USED IN) OPERATING ACTIVITIES		
Profit before taxation	₹26,751	₹28,996
Adjustments:		
Depreciation and amortization expense	9,705	7,599
Provision for wealth tax	—	2
Profit on sale of current investments, net	(800)	(729)
Dividend from mutual fund units	(53)	(26)
Foreign exchange loss, net	1,211	538
Foreign exchange loss related to Venezuela operations	4,621	843
Loss on derecognition/impairment of fixed assets	155	267
Stock compensation expense, net	455	519
Allowance for sales returns	3,272	3,536
Interest income	(1,403)	(1,054)
Finance costs	824	1,082
Loss on sale of fixed assets, net	112	144
Provision for inventory obsolescence	2,746	3,635
Provision for doubtful debts, net	137	168
Provision for doubtful advances, net	17	16
Operating cash flows before working capital changes	47,750	45,536
Changes in operating assets and liabilities		
Trade receivables	733	(10,935)
Inventories	(2,570)	(5,413)
Trade payables	829	(45)
Other assets and liabilities, net	833	1,556
Cash generated from operations	47,575	30,699
Income taxes paid, net	(7,099)	(5,464)
Net cash from operating activities	40,476	25,235
CASH FLOWS FROM (USED IN) INVESTING ACTIVITIES		
Purchase of fixed assets	(13,879)	(15,315)
Proceeds from sale of fixed assets	84	172
Decrease in deposit accounts (having original maturity of more than 3 months) and other bank balances	321	1,581
Purchase of investments	(55,163)	(37,005)
Proceeds from sale of investments	55,864	27,386
Interest received	1,235	784
Cash paid for acquisition of business units, net of cash acquired	(7,936)	(276)
Dividend received on mutual funds	53	26
Net cash used in investing activities	(19,421)	(22,647)
CASH FLOWS FROM (USED IN) FINANCING ACTIVITIES		
Proceeds from issuance of share capital	1	5
Repayment of long term borrowings	(11,714)	(3,728)
Proceeds from/(repayment of) short term borrowings, net	(273)	4,068
Interest paid	(917)	(1,090)
Dividend paid (including dividend distribution tax)	(4,106)	(3,587)
Net cash used in financing activities	(17,009)	(4,332)
Net increase/(decrease) in cash and cash equivalents	4,046	(1,744)
Cash and cash equivalents at the beginning of the year	5,829	8,624
Effect of foreign exchange loss on cash and cash equivalents	(4,288)	(1,051)
Cash and cash equivalents at the end of the year	5,587	5,829
Notes to the statement of cash flows:		
Cash and cash equivalents at the end of the year	5,587	5,829
Other bank balances	12,771	12,895
Cash and bank balances at the end of the year	18,358	18,724

APPENDIX C

Time Value of Money

Suppose that a person is offered ₹100 today or a year later. He would prefer to receive the amount today than a year later, because the amount available today can be invested to earn interest, so it will increase in value to more than ₹100 in the future. For example, if the amount can be invested at 10 per cent per year, it will increase to ₹110 one year later. The idea that receiving money today is preferable to receiving the same amount in the future gives rise to the concept of **time value of money**. In the above example, the interest of ₹10 which would be foregone, if the payment is received after one year is the measure of the time value of ₹100. Since business enterprises make decisions that involve investing, borrowing, and receiving large sums of money at various points in time, the time value of money is an important consideration in these decisions.

Simple Interest and Compound Interest

Simple interest is interest on the principal amount. The amount of principal and the interest payments remain the same from one period to another. For example, assume that Sachin invested ₹1,000 for three years at 10 per cent per year. He will earn an interest of ₹300, as shown below:

$$\text{Interest} = \text{Principal} \times \text{Interest rate} \times \text{Time}$$
$$= ₹1,000 \times 10/100 \times 3$$
$$= ₹300$$

At the end of three years, Sachin will receive a total amount of ₹1,300.

Compound interest is interest earned on the principal amount and the interest of prior periods. Interest earned in each period is added to the principal, and interest for the next period is computed on this total amount. To illustrate the idea of compound interest, assume that compound interest at yearly rest is payable on Sachin's investment. The interest and the total amount can be computed as follows:

Year	Beginning Balance (A)	Compound Interest (B) 10% of A	Ending Balance (C) (A + B)
1	₹1,000	₹100	₹1,100
2	1,100	110	1,210
3	1,210	121	1,331

The compound interest for the period of three years is ₹331 as compared to the simple interest of ₹300. The difference of ₹31 represents interest earned in the second year on the first year's interest (₹100 × 0.10) plus the interest earned in the third year on the first and second years' interest (₹210 × 0.10).

Future Value of a Single Amount

Future value is the amount to which a sum of money invested today at a specified compound interest will grow after a certain period. The future value of a single amount invested today can be computed as follows:

$$F_{i,\,n} = P(1 + i)^n$$

where

F = Future value
P = Principal
i = Interest rate
n = Number of periods

Using the future value formula, we can calculate the future value of Sachin's investment as follows:

$$F_{10,3} = ₹1,000\ (1 + 0.10)^3$$

$$= ₹1,331$$

The calculations involved with compounding become more tedious as the number of periods increases. Fortunately, there are tables that make it easier for us to compute future values for various combinations of interest rates and periods. Table C.1 shows the future value of ₹1 for various rates and periods.

Suppose that we want to compute the future value of ₹1,000 invested by Sachin using the table. We find the factor in the column for 10 per cent and the row for Period 3. The factor 1.3310 means that if ₹1 is invested today, it will cumulate to ₹1.3310 at the end of Year 3. The cash flows can be represented as follows:

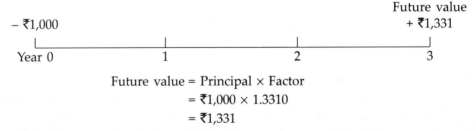

Future value = Principal × Factor
= ₹1,000 × 1.3310
= ₹1,331

In this diagram, Year 0 denotes present time, or beginning of the first year; Year 1 denotes end of the first year; Year 2 end of the second year; and Year 3 end of the third year. Minus (–) denotes outflow or principal, and plus (+) inflow or return of principal and/or interest.

Table C.1 can also be used where compounding takes place more than once a year. In such cases, the number of years is multiplied by the number of times the compounding occurs to determine the number of periods and the annual interest rate is divided by the number of times of compounding. For example, assume that Ravi invested for one year ₹1,000 at 8 per cent per annum, compounded quarterly. From the table the factor for the period of 4 and interest of 2 per cent is 1.0824. Therefore, the future value of the investment of ₹1,000 will be ₹1,082.40. It may be noted that the future value of the investment would have been ₹1,080 with annual compounding.

Future Value of an Ordinary Annuity

An **ordinary annuity** is a series of equal payments made at the end of each period. The future value of an ordinary annuity is the sum of all payments *plus* the compound interest on each payment. For example, assume that Raju deposits ₹1,000 at the end of three consecutive years in a recurring deposit account yielding 10 per cent per year. The cumulative sum can be determined as follows:

Year	Beginning (A)	Compound Interest (B) 10% of A	Payment (C)	Ending Balance (D) (A + B + C)
1	₹ 0	₹ 0	₹1,000	₹1,000
2	1,000	100	1,000	2,100
3	2,100	210	1,000	3,310

The following formula can be used to calculate the future value of an ordinary annuity:

$$F_{i,n} = A\left[\frac{(1+i)^n - 1}{i}\right]$$

where

F = Future value
A = Annuity (periodic payment)
i = Interest rate
n = Number of periods

Table C.2 shows the future value of an annuity of ₹1 for various rates and periods. We find the factor in the column for 10 per cent and the row for Period 3. The factor 3.3100 means that if ₹1 is invested at the end of every year for three years, it will cumulate to ₹3.3100 at the end of Year 3. The cash flows can be represented as follows:

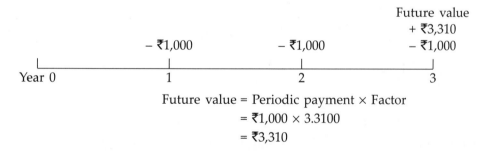

$$\text{Future value} = \text{Periodic payment} \times \text{Factor}$$
$$= ₹1,000 \times 3.3100$$
$$= ₹3,310$$

Present Value of a Single Amount

Present value is the amount that must be invested today in order to receive a certain amount in the future. The process of computing present value is known as **discounting**. The idea of discounting is used extensively in accounting. The present value of a single amount can be calculated as:

$$P_{i,n} = \frac{F}{(1+i)^n}$$

From the formula, it will be seen that future value and present value have a reciprocal relationship. So, the present value factor for a given period at a given interest is the reciprocal of the relevant future value factor.

To illustrate the computation of present value, assume that John wants to have ₹5,000 at the end of three years by investing his savings at 10 per cent. The amount that he must invest today is computed as:

$$P_{10,3} = \frac{5,000}{(1+0.1)^3} = 3,757$$

From Table C.3, the present value factor for three years at 10 per cent interest is 0.7513. This means that an investment of ₹0.7513 today at a compound interest of 10 per cent will produce ₹1 at the end of three years. The cash flows can be represented as follows:

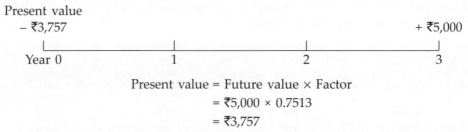

Present value = Future value × Factor

= ₹5,000 × 0.7513

= ₹3,757

The result is confirmed by the following calculation, but for a rounding error of ₹0.57:

Year	Beginning Balance (A)	Compound Interest (B) 10% of A	Ending Balance (C) (A + B)
1	₹3,757.00	₹375.70	₹4,132.70
2	4,132.70	413.27	4,545.97
3	4,545.97	454.60	5,000.57

Present Value of an Ordinary Annuity

The present value of an ordinary annuity is the amount that must be invested today in order to receive a series of equal future payments at the end of every year over a period. The following formula is used to calculate the present value of an ordinary annuity:

$$P_{i,n} = A\left[\frac{(1+i)^n - 1}{i(1+i)^n}\right]$$

where

P = Present value

A = Annuity (periodic payment)

i = Interest rate

n = Number of periods

For example, assume that Velu would like to receive a payment of ₹1,000 at the end of every year for three years. How much would he have to pay today to receive these amounts at an interest rate of 10 per cent? We shall use Table C.4 to compute the present value of this series of payments. The factor is 2.4869, which means that the present value of ₹1 receivable at the end of every year for three years is ₹2.4869. The cash flows can be represented as follows:

Present value

−₹2,487   +₹1,000   +₹1,000   +₹1,000

Year 0   1   2   3

Present value = Future value × Factor

= ₹1,000 × 2.4869

= ₹2,487

The result is confirmed by the following calculation, but for a rounding error of ₹0.20:

Year	Beginning Balance (A)	Compound Interest (B) 10% of A	Payment (C)	Ending Balance (D) (A + B − C)
1	₹2,487.00	₹248.70	₹1,000	₹1,735.70
2	1,735.70	173.57	1,000	909.27
3	909.27	90.93	1,000	0.20

Present Value of an Annuity Due

This differs from an ordinary annuity due because, in this case, the payments occur at the *beginning* of each period rather than at the end. Using the example in ordinary annuity, complete this as an exercise and check your answer from Table C.5.

Table C.1 Future Value of 1: $F_{i,n} = P(1 + i)^n$

i/n	1%	2%	3%	4%	5%	6%	7%	8%	9%	10%	i/n
1	1.0100	1.0200	1.0300	1.0400	1.0500	1.0600	1.0700	1.0800	1.0900	1.1000	1
2	1.0201	1.0404	1.0609	1.0816	1.1025	1.1236	1.1449	1.1664	1.1881	1.2100	2
3	1.0303	1.0612	1.0927	1.1249	1.1576	1.1910	1.2250	1.2597	1.2950	1.3310	3
4	1.0406	1.0824	1.1255	1.1699	1.2155	1.2625	1.3108	1.3605	1.4116	1.4641	4
5	1.0510	1.1041	1.1593	1.2167	1.2763	1.3382	1.4026	1.4693	1.5386	1.6105	5
6	1.0615	1.1262	1.1941	1.2653	1.3401	1.4185	1.5007	1.5869	1.6771	1.7716	6
7	1.0721	1.1487	1.2299	1.3159	1.4071	1.5036	1.6058	1.7138	1.8280	1.9487	7
8	1.0829	1.1717	1.2668	1.3686	1.4775	1.5938	1.7182	1.8509	1.9926	2.1436	8
9	1.0937	1.1951	1.3048	1.4233	1.5513	1.6895	1.8385	1.9990	2.1719	2.3579	9
10	1.1046	1.2190	1.3439	1.4802	1.6289	1.7908	1.9672	2.1589	2.3674	2.5937	10
11	1.1157	1.2434	1.3842	1.5395	1.7103	1.8983	2.1049	2.3316	2.5804	2.8531	11
12	1.1268	1.2682	1.4258	1.6010	1.7959	2.0122	2.2522	2.5182	2.8127	3.1384	12
13	1.1381	1.2936	1.4685	1.6651	1.8856	2.1329	2.4098	2.7196	3.0658	3.4523	13
14	1.1495	1.3195	1.5126	1.7317	1.9799	2.2609	2.5785	2.9372	3.3417	3.7975	14
15	1.1610	1.3459	1.5580	1.8009	2.0789	2.3966	2.7590	3.1722	3.6425	4.1772	15
16	1.1726	1.3728	1.6047	1.8730	2.1829	2.5404	2.9522	3.4259	3.9703	4.5950	16
17	1.1843	1.4002	1.6528	1.9479	2.2920	2.6928	3.1588	3.7000	4.3276	5.0545	17
18	1.1961	1.4282	1.7024	2.0258	2.4066	2.8543	3.3799	3.9960	4.7171	5.5599	18
19	1.2081	1.4568	1.7535	2.1068	2.5270	3.0256	3.6165	4.3157	5.1417	6.1159	19
20	1.2202	1.4859	1.8061	2.1911	2.6533	3.2071	3.8697	4.6610	5.6044	6.7275	20
21	1.2324	1.5157	1.8603	2.2788	2.7860	3.3996	4.1406	5.0338	6.1088	7.4002	21
22	1.2447	1.5460	1.9161	2.3699	2.9253	3.6035	4.4304	5.4365	6.6586	8.1403	22
23	1.2572	1.5769	1.9736	2.4647	3.0715	3.8197	4.7405	5.8715	7.2579	8.9543	23
24	1.2697	1.6084	2.0328	2.5633	3.2251	4.0489	5.0724	6.3412	7.9111	9.8497	24
25	1.2824	1.6406	2.0938	2.6658	3.3864	4.2919	5.4274	6.8485	8.6231	10.8347	25
26	1.2953	1.6734	2.1566	2.7725	3.5557	4.5494	5.8074	7.3964	9.3992	11.9182	26
27	1.3082	1.7069	2.2213	2.8834	3.7335	4.8223	6.2139	7.9881	10.2451	13.1100	27
28	1.3213	1.7410	2.2879	2.9987	3.9201	5.1117	6.6488	8.6271	11.1671	14.4210	28
29	1.3345	1.7758	2.3566	3.1187	4.1161	5.4184	7.1143	9.3173	12.1722	15.8631	29
30	1.3478	1.8114	2.4273	3.2434	4.3219	5.7435	7.6123	10.0627	13.2677	17.4494	30
31	1.3613	1.8476	2.5001	3.3731	4.5380	6.0881	8.1451	10.8677	14.4618	19.1943	31
32	1.3749	1.8845	2.5751	3.5081	4.7649	6.4534	8.7153	11.7371	15.7633	21.1138	32
33	1.3887	1.9222	2.6523	3.6484	5.0032	6.8406	9.3253	12.6760	17.1820	23.2252	33
34	1.4026	1.9607	2.7319	3.7943	5.2533	7.2510	9.9781	13.6901	18.7284	25.5477	34
35	1.4166	1.9999	2.8139	3.9461	5.5160	7.6861	10.6766	14.7853	20.4140	28.1024	35
36	1.4308	2.0399	2.8983	4.1039	5.7918	8.1473	11.4239	15.9682	22.2512	30.9127	36
37	1.4451	2.0807	2.9852	4.2681	6.0814	8.6361	12.2236	17.2456	24.2538	34.0039	37
38	1.4595	2.1223	3.0748	4.4388	6.3855	9.1543	13.0793	18.6253	26.4367	37.4043	38
39	1.4741	2.1647	3.1670	4.6164	6.7048	9.7035	13.9948	20.1153	28.8160	41.1448	39
40	1.4889	2.2080	3.2620	4.8010	7.0400	10.2857	14.9745	21.7245	31.4094	45.2593	40

Table C.2   Future Value of an Ordinary Annuity of 1: $F_{i,n} = \{(1 + i)^{n-1}\}/i$

i/n	1%	2%	3%	4%	5%	6%	7%	8%	9%	10%	i/n
1	1.0000	1.0000	1.0000	1.0000	1.0000	1.0000	1.0000	1.0000	1.0000	1.0000	1
2	2.0100	2.0200	2.0300	2.0400	2.0500	2.0600	2.0700	2.0800	2.0900	2.1000	2
3	3.0301	3.0604	3.0909	3.1216	3.1525	3.1836	3.2149	3.2464	3.2781	3.3100	3
4	4.0604	4.1216	4.1836	4.2465	4.3101	4.3746	4.4399	4.5061	4.5731	4.6410	4
5	5.1010	5.2040	5.3091	5.4163	5.5256	5.6371	5.7507	5.8666	5.9847	6.1051	5
6	6.1520	6.3081	6.4684	6.6330	6.8019	6.9753	7.1533	7.3359	7.5233	7.7156	6
7	7.2135	7.4343	7.6625	7.8983	8.1420	8.3938	8.6540	8.9228	9.2004	9.4872	7
8	8.2857	8.5830	8.8923	9.2142	9.5491	9.8975	10.2598	10.6366	11.0285	11.4359	8
9	9.3685	9.7546	10.1591	10.5828	11.0266	11.4913	11.9780	12.4876	13.0210	13.5795	9
10	10.4622	10.9497	11.4639	12.0061	12.5779	13.1808	13.8164	14.4866	15.1929	15.9374	10
11	11.5668	12.1687	12.8078	13.4864	14.2068	14.9716	15.7836	16.6455	17.5603	18.5312	11
12	12.6825	13.4121	14.1920	15.0258	15.9171	16.8699	17.8885	18.9771	20.1407	21.3843	12
13	13.8093	14.6803	15.6178	16.6268	17.7130	18.8821	20.1406	21.4953	22.9534	24.5227	13
14	14.9474	15.9739	17.0863	18.2919	19.5986	21.0151	22.5505	24.2149	26.0192	27.9750	14
15	16.0969	17.2934	18.5989	20.0236	21.5786	23.2760	25.1290	27.1521	29.3609	31.7725	15
16	17.2579	18.6393	20.1569	21.8245	23.6575	25.6725	27.8881	30.3243	33.0034	35.9497	16
17	18.4304	20.0121	21.7616	23.6975	25.8404	28.2129	30.8402	33.7502	36.9737	40.5447	17
18	19.6147	21.4123	23.4144	25.6454	28.1324	30.9057	33.9990	37.4502	41.3013	45.5992	18
19	20.8109	22.8406	25.1169	27.6712	30.5390	33.7600	37.3790	41.4463	46.0185	51.1591	19
20	22.0190	24.2974	26.8704	29.7781	33.0660	36.7856	40.9955	45.7620	51.1601	57.2750	20
21	23.2392	25.7833	28.6765	31.9692	35.7193	39.9927	44.8652	50.4229	56.7645	64.0025	21
22	24.4716	27.2990	30.5368	34.2480	38.5052	43.3923	49.0057	55.4568	62.8733	71.4027	22
23	25.7163	28.8450	32.4529	36.6179	41.4305	46.9958	53.4361	60.8933	69.5319	79.5430	23
24	26.9735	30.4219	34.4265	39.0826	44.5020	50.8156	58.1767	66.7648	76.7898	88.4973	24
25	28.2432	32.0303	36.4593	41.6459	47.7271	54.8645	63.2490	73.1059	84.7009	98.3471	25
26	29.5256	33.6709	38.5530	44.3117	51.1135	59.1564	68.6765	79.9544	93.3240	109.1818	26
27	30.8209	35.3443	40.7096	47.0842	54.6691	63.7058	74.4838	87.3508	102.7231	121.0999	27
28	32.1291	37.0512	42.9309	49.9676	58.4026	68.5281	80.6977	95.3388	112.9682	134.2099	28
29	33.4504	38.7922	45.2189	52.9663	62.3227	73.6398	87.3465	103.9659	124.1354	148.6309	29
30	34.7849	40.5681	47.5754	56.0849	66.4388	79.0582	94.4608	113.2832	136.3075	164.4940	30
31	36.1327	42.3794	50.0027	59.3283	70.7608	84.8017	102.0730	123.3459	149.5752	181.9434	31
32	37.4941	44.2270	52.5028	62.7015	75.2988	90.8898	110.2182	134.2135	164.0370	201.1378	32
33	38.8690	46.1116	55.0778	66.2095	80.0638	97.3432	118.9334	145.9506	179.8003	222.2515	33
34	40.2577	48.0338	57.7302	69.8579	85.0670	104.1838	128.2588	158.6267	196.9823	245.4767	34
35	41.6603	49.9945	60.4621	73.6522	90.3203	111.4348	138.2369	172.3168	215.7108	271.0244	35
36	43.0769	51.9944	63.2759	77.5983	95.8363	119.1209	148.9135	187.1021	236.1247	299.1268	36
37	44.5076	54.0343	66.1742	81.7022	101.6281	127.2681	160.3374	203.0703	258.3759	330.0395	37
38	45.9527	56.1149	69.1594	85.9703	107.7095	135.9042	172.5610	220.3159	282.6298	364.0434	38
39	47.4123	58.2372	72.2342	90.4091	114.0950	145.0585	185.6403	238.9412	309.0665	401.4478	39
40	48.8864	60.4020	75.4013	95.0255	120.7998	154.7620	199.6351	259.0565	337.8824	442.5926	40

Table C.3 Present Value of 1: $P_{i,n} = F/(1 + i)^n$

i/n	1%	2%	3%	4%	5%	6%	7%	8%	9%	10%	i/n
1	0.9901	0.9804	0.9709	0.9615	0.9524	0.9434	0.9346	0.9259	0.9174	0.9091	1
2	0.9803	0.9612	0.9426	0.9246	0.9070	0.8900	0.8734	0.8573	0.8417	0.8264	2
3	0.9706	0.9423	0.9151	0.8890	0.8638	0.8396	0.8163	0.7938	0.7722	0.7513	3
4	0.9610	0.9238	0.8885	0.8548	0.8227	0.7921	0.7629	0.7350	0.7084	0.6830	4
5	0.9515	0.9057	0.8626	0.8219	0.7835	0.7473	0.7130	0.6806	0.6499	0.6209	5
6	0.9420	0.8880	0.8375	0.7903	0.7462	0.7050	0.6663	0.6302	0.5963	0.5645	6
7	0.9327	0.8706	0.8131	0.7599	0.7107	0.6651	0.6227	0.5835	0.5470	0.5132	7
8	0.9235	0.8535	0.7894	0.7307	0.6768	0.6274	0.5820	0.5403	0.5019	0.4665	8
9	0.9143	0.8368	0.7664	0.7026	0.6446	0.5919	0.5439	0.5002	0.4604	0.4241	9
10	0.9053	0.8203	0.7441	0.6756	0.6139	0.5584	0.5083	0.4632	0.4224	0.3855	10
11	0.8963	0.8043	0.7224	0.6496	0.5847	0.5268	0.4751	0.4289	0.3875	0.3505	11
12	0.8874	0.7885	0.7014	0.6246	0.5568	0.4970	0.4440	0.3971	0.3555	0.3186	12
13	0.8787	0.7730	0.6810	0.6006	0.5303	0.4688	0.4150	0.3677	0.3262	0.2897	13
14	0.8700	0.7579	0.6611	0.5775	0.5051	0.4423	0.3878	0.3405	0.2992	0.2633	14
15	0.8613	0.7430	0.6419	0.5553	0.4810	0.4173	0.3624	0.3152	0.2745	0.2394	15
16	0.8528	0.7284	0.6232	0.5339	0.4581	0.3936	0.3387	0.2919	0.2519	0.2176	16
17	0.8444	0.7142	0.6050	0.5134	0.4363	0.3714	0.3166	0.2703	0.2311	0.1978	17
18	0.8360	0.7002	0.5874	0.4936	0.4155	0.3503	0.2959	0.2502	0.2120	0.1799	18
19	0.8277	0.6864	0.5703	0.4746	0.3957	0.3305	0.2765	0.2317	0.1945	0.1635	19
20	0.8195	0.6730	0.5537	0.4564	0.3769	0.3118	0.2584	0.2145	0.1784	0.1486	20
21	0.8114	0.6598	0.5375	0.4388	0.3589	0.2942	0.2415	0.1987	0.1637	0.1351	21
22	0.8034	0.6468	0.5219	0.4220	0.3418	0.2775	0.2257	0.1839	0.1502	0.1228	22
23	0.7954	0.6342	0.5067	0.4057	0.3256	0.2618	0.2109	0.1703	0.1378	0.1117	23
24	0.7876	0.6217	0.4919	0.3901	0.3101	0.2470	0.1971	0.1577	0.1264	0.1015	24
25	0.7798	0.6095	0.4776	0.3751	0.2953	0.2330	0.1842	0.1460	0.1160	0.0923	25
26	0.7720	0.5976	0.4637	0.3607	0.2812	0.2198	0.1722	0.1352	0.1064	0.0839	26
27	0.7644	0.5859	0.4502	0.3468	0.2678	0.2074	0.1609	0.1252	0.0976	0.0763	27
28	0.7568	0.5744	0.4371	0.3335	0.2551	0.1956	0.1504	0.1159	0.0895	0.0693	28
29	0.7493	0.5631	0.4243	0.3207	0.2429	0.1846	0.1406	0.1073	0.0822	0.0630	29
30	0.7419	0.5521	0.4120	0.3083	0.2314	0.1741	0.1314	0.0994	0.0754	0.0573	30
31	0.7346	0.5412	0.4000	0.2965	0.2204	0.1643	0.1228	0.0920	0.0691	0.0521	31
32	0.7273	0.5306	0.3883	0.2851	0.2099	0.1550	0.1147	0.0852	0.0634	0.0474	32
33	0.7201	0.5202	0.3770	0.2741	0.1999	0.1462	0.1072	0.0789	0.0582	0.0431	33
34	0.7130	0.5100	0.3660	0.2636	0.1904	0.1379	0.1002	0.0730	0.0534	0.0391	34
35	0.7059	0.5000	0.3554	0.2534	0.1813	0.1301	0.0937	0.0676	0.0490	0.0356	35
36	0.6989	0.4902	0.3450	0.2437	0.1727	0.1227	0.0875	0.0626	0.0449	0.0323	36
37	0.6920	0.4806	0.3350	0.2343	0.1644	0.1158	0.0818	0.0580	0.0412	0.0294	37
38	0.6852	0.4712	0.3252	0.2253	0.1566	0.1092	0.0765	0.0537	0.0378	0.0267	38
39	0.6784	0.4619	0.3158	0.2166	0.1491	0.1031	0.0715	0.0497	0.0347	0.0243	39
40	0.6717	0.4529	0.3066	0.2083	0.1420	0.0972	0.0668	0.0460	0.0318	0.0221	40

Table C.4 Present Value of an Ordinary Annuity of 1: $P_{i,n} = \{(1 + i)^n - 1\}/i(1 + i)^n$

i/n	1%	2%	3%	4%	5%	6%	7%	8%	9%	10%	i/n
1	0.9901	0.9804	0.9709	0.9615	0.9524	0.9434	0.9346	0.9259	0.9174	0.9091	1
2	1.9704	1.9416	1.9135	1.8861	1.8594	1.8334	1.8080	1.7833	1.7591	1.7355	2
3	2.9410	2.8839	2.8286	2.7751	2.7232	2.6730	2.6243	2.5771	2.5313	2.4869	3
4	3.9020	3.8077	3.7171	3.6299	3.5460	3.4651	3.3872	3.3121	3.2397	3.1699	4
5	4.8534	4.7135	4.5797	4.4518	4.3295	4.2124	4.1002	3.9927	3.8897	3.7908	5
6	5.7955	5.6014	5.4172	5.2421	5.0757	4.9173	4.7665	4.6229	4.4859	4.3553	6
7	6.7282	6.4720	6.2303	6.0021	5.7864	5.5824	5.3893	5.2064	5.0330	4.8684	7
8	7.6517	7.3255	7.0197	6.7327	6.4632	6.2098	5.9713	5.7466	5.5348	5.3349	8
9	8.5660	8.1622	7.7861	7.4353	7.1078	6.8017	6.5152	6.2469	5.9952	5.7590	9
10	9.4713	8.9826	8.5302	8.1109	7.7217	7.3601	7.0236	6.7101	6.4177	6.1446	10
11	10.3676	9.7868	9.2526	8.7605	8.3064	7.8869	7.4987	7.1390	6.8052	6.4951	11
12	11.2551	10.5753	9.9540	9.3851	8.8633	8.3838	7.9427	7.5361	7.1607	6.8137	12
13	12.1337	11.3484	10.6350	9.9856	9.3936	8.8527	8.3577	7.9038	7.4869	7.1034	13
14	13.0037	12.1062	11.2961	10.5631	9.8986	9.2950	8.7455	8.2442	7.7862	7.3667	14
15	13.8651	12.8493	11.9379	11.1184	10.3797	9.7122	9.1079	8.5595	8.0607	7.6061	15
16	14.7179	13.5777	12.5611	11.6523	10.8378	10.1059	9.4466	8.8514	8.3126	7.8237	16
17	15.5623	14.2919	13.1661	12.1657	11.2741	10.4773	9.7632	9.1216	8.5436	8.0216	17
18	16.3983	14.9920	13.7535	12.6593	11.6896	10.8276	10.0591	9.3719	8.7556	8.2014	18
19	17.2260	15.6785	14.3238	13.1339	12.0853	11.1581	10.3356	9.6036	8.9501	8.3649	19
20	18.0456	16.3514	14.8775	13.5903	12.4622	11.4699	10.5940	9.8181	9.1285	8.5136	20
21	18.8570	17.0112	15.4150	14.0292	12.8212	11.7641	10.8355	10.0168	9.2922	8.6487	21
22	19.6604	17.6580	15.9369	14.4511	13.1630	12.0416	11.0612	10.2007	9.4424	8.7715	22
23	20.4558	18.2922	16.4436	14.8568	13.4886	12.3034	11.2722	10.3711	9.5802	8.8832	23
24	21.2434	18.9139	16.9355	15.2470	13.7986	12.5504	11.4693	10.5288	9.7066	8.9847	24
25	22.0232	19.5235	17.4131	15.6221	14.0939	12.7834	11.6536	10.6748	9.8226	9.0770	25
26	22.7952	20.1210	17.8768	15.9828	14.3752	13.0032	11.8258	10.8100	9.9290	9.1609	26
27	23.5596	20.7069	18.3270	16.3296	14.6430	13.2105	11.9867	10.9352	10.0266	9.2372	27
28	24.3164	21.2813	18.7641	16.6631	14.8981	13.4062	12.1371	11.0511	10.1161	9.3066	28
29	25.0658	21.8444	19.1885	16.9837	15.1411	13.5907	12.2777	11.1584	10.1983	9.3696	29
30	25.8077	22.3965	19.6004	17.2920	15.3725	13.7648	12.4090	11.2578	10.2737	9.4269	30
31	26.5423	22.9377	20.0004	17.5885	15.5928	13.9291	12.5318	11.3498	10.3428	9.4790	31
32	27.2696	23.4683	20.3888	17.8736	15.8027	14.0840	12.6466	11.4350	10.4062	9.5264	32
33	27.9897	23.9886	20.7658	18.1476	16.0025	14.2302	12.7538	11.5139	10.4644	9.5694	33
34	28.7027	24.4986	21.1318	18.4112	16.1929	14.3681	12.8540	11.5869	10.5178	9.6086	34
35	29.4086	24.9986	21.4872	18.6646	16.3742	14.4982	12.9477	11.6546	10.5668	9.6442	35
36	30.1075	25.4888	21.8323	18.9083	16.5469	14.6210	13.0352	11.7172	10.6118	9.6765	36
37	30.7995	25.9695	22.1672	19.1426	16.7113	14.7368	13.1170	11.7752	10.6530	9.7059	37
38	31.4847	26.4406	22.4925	19.3679	16.8679	14.8460	13.1935	11.8289	10.6908	9.7327	38
39	32.1630	26.9026	22.8082	19.5845	17.0170	14.9491	13.2649	11.8786	10.7255	9.7570	39
40	32.8347	27.3555	23.1148	19.7928	17.1591	15.0463	13.3317	11.9246	10.7574	9.7791	40

Table C.5 Present Value of an Annuity Due of 1: $P_{i,n} = 1 + \{(1 + i)^{n-1} - 1\}/i(1 + i)^{n-1}$

i/n	1%	2%	3%	4%	5%	6%	7%	8%	9%	10%	i/n
1	1.0000	1.0000	1.0000	1.0000	1.0000	1.0000	1.0000	1.0000	1.0000	1.0000	1
2	1.9901	1.9804	1.9709	1.9615	1.9524	1.9434	1.9346	1.9259	1.9174	1.9091	2
3	2.9704	2.9416	2.9135	2.8861	2.8594	2.8334	2.8080	2.7833	2.7591	2.7355	3
4	3.9410	3.8839	3.8286	3.7751	3.7232	3.6730	3.6243	3.5771	3.5313	3.4869	4
5	4.9020	4.8077	4.7171	4.6299	4.5460	4.4651	4.3872	4.3121	4.2397	4.1699	5
6	5.8534	5.7135	5.5797	5.4518	5.3295	5.2124	5.1002	4.9927	4.8897	4.7908	6
7	6.7955	6.6014	6.4172	6.2421	6.0757	5.9173	5.7665	5.6229	5.4859	5.3553	7
8	7.7282	7.4720	7.2303	7.0021	6.7864	6.5824	6.3893	6.2064	6.0330	5.8684	8
9	8.6517	8.3255	8.0197	7.7327	7.4632	7.2098	6.9713	6.7466	6.5348	6.3349	9
10	9.5660	9.1622	8.7861	8.4353	8.1078	7.8017	7.5152	7.2469	6.9952	6.7590	10
11	10.4713	9.9826	9.5302	9.1109	8.7217	8.3601	8.0236	7.7101	7.4177	7.1446	11
12	11.3676	10.7868	10.2526	9.7605	9.3064	8.8869	8.4987	8.1390	7.8052	7.4951	12
13	12.2551	11.5753	10.9540	10.3851	9.8633	9.3838	8.9427	8.5361	8.1607	7.8137	13
14	13.1337	12.3484	11.6350	10.9856	10.3936	9.8527	9.3577	8.9038	8.4869	8.1034	14
15	14.0037	13.1062	12.2961	11.5631	10.8986	10.2950	9.7455	9.2442	8.7862	8.3667	15
16	14.8651	13.8493	12.9379	12.1184	11.3797	10.7122	10.1079	9.5595	9.0607	8.6061	16
17	15.7179	14.5777	13.5611	12.6523	11.8378	11.1059	10.4466	9.8514	9.3126	8.8237	17
18	16.5623	15.2919	14.1661	13.1657	12.2741	11.4773	10.7632	10.1216	9.5436	9.0216	18
19	17.3983	15.9920	14.7535	13.6593	12.6896	11.8276	11.0591	10.3719	9.7556	9.2014	19
20	18.2260	16.6785	15.3238	14.1339	13.0853	12.1581	11.3356	10.6036	9.9501	9.3649	20
21	19.0456	17.3514	15.8775	14.5903	13.4622	12.4699	11.5940	10.8181	10.1285	9.5136	21
22	19.8570	18.0112	16.4150	15.0292	13.8212	12.7641	11.8355	11.0168	10.2922	9.6487	22
23	20.6604	18.6580	16.9369	15.4511	14.1630	13.0416	12.0612	11.2007	10.4424	9.7715	23
24	21.4558	19.2922	17.4436	15.8568	14.4886	13.3034	12.2722	11.3711	10.5802	9.8832	24
25	22.2434	19.9139	17.9355	16.2470	14.7986	13.5504	12.4693	11.5288	10.7066	9.9847	25
26	23.0232	20.5235	18.4131	16.6221	15.0939	13.7834	12.6536	11.6748	10.8226	10.0770	26
27	23.7952	21.1210	18.8768	16.9828	15.3752	14.0032	12.8258	11.8100	10.9290	10.1609	27
28	24.5596	21.7069	19.3270	17.3296	15.6430	14.2105	12.9867	11.9352	11.0266	10.2372	28
29	25.3164	22.2813	19.7641	17.6631	15.8981	14.4062	13.1371	12.0511	11.1161	10.3066	29
30	26.0658	22.8444	20.1885	17.9837	16.1411	14.5907	13.2777	12.1584	11.1983	10.3696	30
31	26.8077	23.3965	20.6004	18.2920	16.3725	14.7648	13.4090	12.2578	11.2737	10.4269	31
32	27.5423	23.9377	21.0004	18.5885	16.5928	14.9291	13.5318	12.3498	11.3428	10.4790	32
33	28.2696	24.4683	21.3888	18.8736	16.8027	15.0840	13.6466	12.4350	11.4062	10.5264	33
34	28.9897	24.9886	21.7658	19.1476	17.0025	15.2302	13.7538	12.5139	11.4644	10.5694	34
35	29.7027	25.4986	22.1318	19.4112	17.1929	15.3681	13.8540	12.5869	11.5178	10.6086	35
36	30.4086	25.9986	22.4872	19.6646	17.3742	15.4982	13.9477	12.6546	11.5668	10.6442	36
37	31.1075	26.4888	22.8323	19.9083	17.5469	15.6210	14.0352	12.7172	11.6118	10.6765	37
38	31.7995	26.9695	23.1672	20.1426	17.7113	15.7368	14.1170	12.7752	11.6530	10.7059	38
39	32.4847	27.4406	23.4925	20.3679	17.8679	15.8460	14.1935	12.8289	11.6908	10.7327	39
40	33.1630	27.9026	23.8082	20.5845	18.0170	15.9491	14.2649	12.8786	11.7255	10.7570	40

D Summary of Formulas

Chapter 2

Economic resources = Claims

Assets = Liabilities + Equity

Assets = Liabilities + (Capital + Revenues − Expenses − Drawings − Dividends)

Chapter 3

Effect	Assets, Expenses, Drawings, Dividends	Liabilities, Capital, Revenues
Increase	Debit	Credit
Decrease	Credit	Debit

Chapter 4

Net sales	= Sales − Sales returns and allowances
Net purchases	= Purchases − Purchases returns and allowances − Purchases discounts
Net cost of purchases	= Net purchases + Freight in
Cost of goods sold	= Beginning inventory + Net cost of purchases − Ending inventory
Gross profit	= Net sales − Cost of goods sold
Operating expenses	= Selling expenses + Administrative expenses
Profit before interest and tax	= Gross profit − Operating expenses
Profit before tax	= Profit before interest and tax − Interest expense
Net profit	= Profit before tax − Income tax

$$\text{Gross profit ratio} = \frac{\text{Gross profit}}{\text{Net sales}}$$

Chapter 5

$$\text{Inventory turnover} = \frac{\text{Cost of goods sold}}{\text{Average inventories}}$$

$$\text{Average holding period} = \frac{360}{\text{Inventory turnover}}$$

Chapter 6

$$\text{Depreciation expense, SLM} = \frac{\text{Cost} - \text{Residual value}}{\text{Useful life}}$$

$$\text{Depreciation rate, WDV} = 1 - \sqrt[n]{\frac{\text{Residual value}}{\text{Cost}}}, \; n \text{ being useful life}$$

$$\text{Depreciation rate, SYD} = \text{Cost} - \text{Residual value} \times \frac{k}{\text{Sum of the digits, 1 to } k},$$

$$k \text{ being useful life}$$

$$\text{Depreciation rate, Production-units} = \frac{\text{Cost} - \text{Residual value}}{\text{Useful life}}$$

Chapter 7

$$\text{Receivable turnover} = \frac{\text{Sales}}{\text{Average receivables}}$$

$$\text{Average collection period} = \frac{360}{\text{Receivable turnover}}$$

Chapter 12

$$\text{Profit margin} = \frac{\text{Profit}}{\text{Sales}}$$

$$\text{Asset turnover} = \frac{\text{Sales}}{\text{Assets}}$$

$$\text{Return on assets} = \frac{\text{Profit}}{\text{Assets}}$$

$$\text{Return on equity} = \frac{\text{Net profit}}{\text{Equity}}$$

$$\text{Earnings per share} = \frac{\text{Net profit}}{\text{Number of equity shares}}$$

$$\text{Current ratio} = \frac{\text{Current assets}}{\text{Current liabilities}}$$

$$\text{Quick ratio} = \frac{\text{Quick assets}}{\text{Current liabilities}}$$

$$\text{Debt-to-equity ratio} = \frac{\text{Current debt} + \text{Long-term debt}}{\text{Equity}}$$

$$\text{Liabilities-to-equity ratio} = \frac{\text{All liabilities}}{\text{Equity}}$$

$$\text{Interest cover} = \frac{\text{Profit before interest and tax}}{\text{Interest expense}}$$

$$\text{Price-earnings ratio} = \frac{\text{Market price per share}}{\text{Earnings per share}}$$

$$\text{Dividend yield} = \frac{\text{Dividend per share}}{\text{Market per share}}$$

$$\text{Price-to-book ratio} = \frac{\text{Market price per share}}{\text{Book value per share}}$$

Chapter 13

Cash received from customers = Sales + Decrease (− increase) in gross receivables − Written-off

Cash paid to suppliers and employees = Cost of goods sold
+ Selling and administrative expenses
− Non-cash expenses
+ Increase (− decrease) in inventories
+ Increase (− decrease) in prepaid expenses
+ Decrease (− increase) in trade payables

Income tax paid = Income tax expense + Decrease (− increase) in income tax payable

Net cash from operating activities = Profit before tax + Non-cash charges
+ Non-operating expenses and losses
− Non-operating incomes and gains
+ Decrease (− increase) in gross receivables
+ Decrease (− increase) in inventories
+ Decrease (− increase) in prepaid expenses
− Decrease (+ increase) in trade payables
− Income tax paid

Chapter 14

$$\text{Cost of deposits} = \frac{\text{Interest on deposits}}{\text{Deposits}}$$

$$\text{Overhead efficiency} = \frac{\text{Operating expenses}}{\text{Revenue}}$$

$$\text{Net interest income} = \text{Interest income} - \text{Interest expense}$$

$$\text{Net interest margin} = \frac{\text{Net interest income}}{\text{Interest-earning assets}}$$

$$\text{Spread} = \text{Yield} - \text{Cost of funds}$$

$$\text{Yield} = \frac{\text{Interest income}}{\text{Interest-earning assets}}$$

$$\text{Cost of funds} = \frac{\text{Interest expense}}{\text{Interest-bearing liabilities}}$$

$$\text{Liquidity coverage ratio} = \frac{\text{Stock of high-quality liquid assets}}{\text{Net cash outflows over a 30-day time period}}$$

$$\text{Net stable funding ratio} = \frac{\text{Available stable funding}}{\text{Required stable funding}}$$

Chapter 15

$$\text{Earnings quality ratio} = \frac{\text{Net cash from operating activities}}{\text{Profit}}$$

$$\text{Earnings quality ratio} = \frac{\text{NOPAT}}{\text{Profit}}$$

Answer Hints for Selected Problems

Important Note: Hints are given only for selected problems or parts of problems. The Online Study Guide provides problem sheets for evaluating complete answers.

Chapter 1

1.1 Annamalai's net deficiency = 6,000
1.2 Shankar's net surplus = 10,000. Tanvi insolvent.
1.3 Raj's net deficiency = 1,000
1.4 Ramesh's net surplus = 39,000. Anand insolvent.
1.5 Violation: (a), (c), (d), (e). No violation: (b)
1.6 Ahmed's net surplus = 55,000. Others insolvent.
1.7 Harish's net surplus = 30,000. Tanmay insolvent.

Chapter 2

2.2 Balance sheet total = 75,200
2.3 Balance sheet total = 211,400. Profit = 70,000
2.4 (f) Paid for past purchases of supplies.
2.5 (b) Received full refund for supplies returned.
2.6 Cash = 24,000. Capital = 44,500.
2.7 Cash = 19,900. Capital = 15,700.
2.8 Cash = 24,350. Capital = 37,350.
2.9 Cash = 10,900. Capital = 20,200.
2.10 Cash = 33,900. Capital = 43,300.
2.11 Cash = 12,200. Capital = 24,200.
2.12 Profit: February = 11,200. March = 3,200.

Chapter 3

3.1 (d) Debit Trade payables; Credit Cash.
3.3 Trial balance total = 19,800.
3.4 (d) Debit Suspense. Credit Trade payables. 6,300.
3.5 (c) Debit Equipment. Credit Cash. 9,000.
3.6 Trial balance total = 7,950.
3.7 Trial balance total = 28,400.
3.8 Trial balance total = 37,330.
3.9 Trial balance total = 56,080.
3.10 Trial balance total = 24,570.
3.11 January trial balance total = 50,930.
3.12 August trial balance total = 38,650.

Chapter 4

4.1 1. Fee revenue = 22,510.
4.2 (b) Debit Rent expense. Credit Prepaid rent. 2,500.
4.3 Balance sheet total = 29,800. Profit = 2,000.
4.6 Operating loss = 38,000.
4.7 (e) Debit Sales commission expense. Credit Sales commission payable. 1,400.
4.8 (d) Debit Salaries expense. Credit Salaries payable. 24,400.
4.9 June 18: Debit Trade payables 5,700. Credit Cash 5,586. Credit Purchase discounts 114.
4.10 Sep. 8: Debit Purchases. Credit Trade payables. 4,200.
4.11 Revenue (million): 20X3, 105; 20X4, 77; 20X5, 70.
4.12 Profit = 9,780.
4.13 Profit = 9,285.
4.14 Profit = 290.
4.15 Profit = 1,485.
4.16 July profit = 125. August profit = 920.
4.17 November profit = 3,230. December profit = 1,680.
4.18 Profit = 5,770.
4.19 Profit = 8,567.
4.20 Profit = 10,930.
4.21 Profit = 21,700.

Chapter 5

5.1 FIFO = 12,850. LIFO = 13,800. WAC = 13,320
5.2 FIFO = 560. LIFO = 680.
5.3 Cost of good sold: FIFO = 560. LIFO = 605.
5.4 Item-by-item = 26,400. Group = 30,920.
5.5 Net profit: FIFO = 103,000. LIFO = 98,000. WAC = 100,650.
5.6 Net profit: FIFO = 21,000. LIFO = 17,000. WAC = 19,100.
5.7 Ending inventory: FIFO = 22,050. LIFO = 21,830
5.8 Ending inventory: FIFO = 3,760. LIFO = 3,680
5.9 Item-by-item = 267,610. Group = 178,096.
5.10 Item-by-item = 168,880. Group = 176,450.
5.11 Ending inventory: 20X7 = 5,280. 20X8 = 5,610.
5.12 Ending inventory: 20X3 = 73,700. 20X4 = 54,900.
5.13 1. Net profit: FIFO = 147,000. LIFO = 101,500.
     2. Net profit: FIFO = 147,000. LIFO = 45,500.
5.14 1. Net profit: FIFO = 351,400. LIFO = 337,400.
     2. Net profit: FIFO = 351,400. LIFO = 310,100.

Chapter 6

6.2 Cost of acquisition = 605,000
6.4 3. Gain = 3,200.
6.7 35,642

6.8	Net profit = 665,000. Cash flow = 745,000.
6.9	Land = 517,000. Land improvement = 35,000. Buildings = 675,000. Equipment = 600,000.
6.10	Land = 1,740,500. Land improvement = 115,700. Buildings = 2,079,300. Equipment = 1,849,000.
6.15	1. 11,440,000. 2. 30,720,000.
6.18	1. Profit = 2,227,500. Cash flow = 2,727,500.
6.21	4. Equipment 1,020,000.
6.23	Revaluation gain = 200,000.

Chapter 7

7.2	(a) 589,085. (b) 1,000,025. (c) 1,172,900.
7.6	Bad debt expense = 69,827.
7.7	Bad debt expense = 38,651.
7.12	2. Impairment loss = 9,524.
7.13	2. Impairment loss = 13,889.
7.14	1. Impairment loss = 900.
7.15	1. Impairment loss = 500.

Chapter 8

8.1	Goodwill = 160,700
8.2	Goodwill = 142,000.
8.3	Full goodwill = 390,000. Partial goodwill = 320,000.
8.4	Full goodwill = 870,000. Partial goodwill = 642,000.
8.5	1. Joint operation.
8.6	1. Joint operation.

Chapter 9

9.4	MAT expense = 5,000
9.7	Asif: CGST = SGST = 250. Veena: IGST = 700.
9.8	Jain: CGST = SGST = 1,250. Arihant: IGST = 3,200.
9.9	1. Product warranty expense = 7,430.
9.10	1. Product warranty expense = 3,190.
9.11	1. Current tax expense = 657. 2. Deferred tax assets = 555. Deferred tax liabilities = 630.
9.12	1. Current tax expense = 468. 2. Deferred tax assets = 162. Deferred tax liabilities = 120.
9.13	1. Pension expense, Year 3 = 1,387

Chapter 10

10.1	(a) 589,085. (b) 1,000,025. (c) 1,172,900.
10.3	Share premium = 132,000.
10.6	Quarterly lease rental expense = 24,000.
10.13	Part III: Finance lease.
10.14	Part IV: Finance lease.

Chapter 11

11.1	1. Year 3 equity dividend = 10,000.
11.4	7.
11.9	1. 20X1 (a) equity dividend = 37,000.
11.10	1. 20X4 (a) preference dividend = 22,500.
11.11	1. 1.95. 2. 2.03. 3. 1.22
11.12	1. 0.91. 2. 0.95. 3. 0.77

Chapter 12

12.4	Profit margin: 20X6 = 13.95%. 20X5 = 15.49%
12.5	Current ratio: 20X2 = 1.51. 20X1 = 1.09
12.6	Increase: (i). Decrease: (b). No effect: (q).
12.7	Increase: (g). Decrease: (k). No effect: (o).
12.9	Asset turnover: 20X2 = 1.48. 20X1 = 1.76.
12.11	Current ratio: 20X6 = 2.49. 20X5 = 1.94.
12.12	Inventory turnover: Granny = 5.86. Home = 1.76.
12.13	Receivable turnover: Cute = 18.2. Smart = 29.55.
12.14	Profit before tax = 3,500. Inventories = 16,500.
12.15	Net sales = 92,000. Trade payables = 14,000.

Chapter 13

13.1	Operating: (d). Financing: (j). Non-cash: (i).
13.2	1. Fee received = 21,710.
13.3	7,000.
13.4	4,700.
13.5	(21,500)
13.8	Operating: (h). Investing: (m). Financing: (r).
13.9	Operating: (d). Investing: (j). Financing: (s).
13.12	Operating = (24,500). Investing: 17,300.
13.13	Operating = (1,200)
13.14	Financing = 1,100.
13.15	Operating = (7,100).

Chapter 14

14.1	2. (a) = 3,150. 2. (b) = 2,520.
14.2	Demand = 113,000. Time = 24,000.
14.3	(k) Assets Advances Term loans.
14.4	(b) Assets Other assets Deferred tax asset
14.5	CASA ratio: 20X2 = 45%. 20X1 = 49%.
14.6	CASA ratio: 20X2 = 37%. 20X1 = 25%.
14.7	Spread: Year 3 = 1.70%. Year 2 = 0.35%.
14.8	Spread: Year 3 = 7.02%. Year 2 = 6.59%.
14.9	Yield: Year 3 = 19.34%. Year 2 = 18.28%.
14.10	Yield: Year 3 = 16.43%. Year 2 = 11.72%.
14.11	RWA = 31,170.
14.12	RWA = 47,906.

Chapter 15

15.1	High: (a). Low: (e).
15.2	High: (e). Low: (i).
15.7	Free cash flow = (14,400).
15.8	EVA = 959.

Index

Accelerated depreciation, 222
Account, 74
Accounting, 21
    controls, 95
    cycle, 146
    equation, 47
    estimates, 535
    information system, 22
    measurement, 30
    policies, 35, 532
    principles, 30, 34
    profit, 333
    standards, 33, 34
Accrual system, 115
Accrued expenses, 123
Accrued revenues, 123
Accumulated depreciation, 121
Accumulated other comprehensive income, 390
Acid test ratio, 436
Acquisition, 303
    method, 304
Adidas, 176
Adjunct account, 138
Adjusted trial balance, 126
Adjusting entries, 119
Adjustment process, 119
Administrative controls, 95
Administrative expenses, 140
Advances, 505
Adverse selection, 19
Ageing schedule, 268
Agency costs, 20
Akerlof, George A., 19
Amazon.com, 455
Ambuja Cements, 250
Amortization. See Depreciation
Amortized cost, 280, 360
Analysts, 24, 555
Annual reports, 60, 553
Annuity due, 371
Apple Computers, 131
Appropriation, 390
Articles of association, 16
Asset turnover, 56, 432, 513
Assets, 47
Associate, 313
Audit committee, 17, 554, 569
Audit report, 60
Auditing, 36

Auditor, 17, 60, 555
    rotation, 418
Authorized capital, 385
Autonomy, 39
Average collection period, 276, 437
Average holding period, 199, 438
Axis Bank, 25

Bad debts, 267. See Credit losses
Balance sheet, 47, 55, 58, 500
Ball, Ray, 38
Bank financial statements, 500
Bank of America, 537
Bank of Baroda, 2
Bank regulation, 498
Barclays, 360
Basel regulations, 515
Basic earnings per share, 401
Basket purchases, 218
Basu, Sudipta, 193
BCCI, 28
Bear Stearns, 11
Beaver, William H., 552
Berkshire Hathaway, 328
Beta, 443
BHEL, 203, 347
BHS, 2
Bhushan Steel, 24
Bias, 36
Big bath, 542
Bill and hold sales, 149
Bill of exchange, 272
Bill payable, 330,
Bills receivable, 272
Biocon, 173, 317, 553
Blockchain, 94
Board of directors, 16
Bonds. See Debentures
Bonus shares, 396
Book value. See Carrying amount
Borrowings, 501
Botosan, Christine, A., 552
BP, 250
Bribery, 39
Bristol-Myers Squibb, 243
Brown, Philip, 38
Buffett, Warren, 328, 404, 553, 554
Business combination, 303, 305
Business model, 278

Business organizations, 12, 13
Business transactions, 30
Buy-side analysts, 555

CAG, 33, 46
Capital. See Share capital
    adequacy, 514
    employed, 550
    expenditure, 230
    market ratios, 441
    redemption reserve, 389
    reserve, 389
    structure, 401
Capitalization, 216
Carrying amount, 122, 335
CASA ratio, 510
Cash, 266
    discount, 134
    equivalents, 266, 460
    flow ratios, 477
    generating unit, 247
    reserve ratio, 503
    system, 115
Central banks, 498
Central Board of Direct Taxes, 27
Certificate of incorporation, 16
Chartered accountant, 33
Chartered corporation, 383
Chart of accounts, 74
Chief executive officer, 17
Chief financial officer, 17
Cipla, 203
Closing entries, 148
Cloud computing, 94
Cognizant Technology, 424
Commercial banks, 498
Common-size statements, 429
Common seal, 383
Company, 383
Company secretary, 17
Comparability, 193
Competition Commission of India, 27
Components of assets, 218, 229
Compound entry, 88
Compound financial instruments, 366
Conditional sales, 149
Conservatism, 192
Consignment, 149, 185
Consistency, 193

Consolidated financial statements, 302, 305
Construction contracts, 151
Contingent liabilities, 346
Contra account, 121
Contractual cash flow characteristics, 279
Control, 300
Controller, 17
Conversion ratio, 146
Convertible debentures, 361, 366
Convertible preference shares, 388
Cookie jar reserves, 543
Corporate governance, 7, 20, 554, 570
Corporate organization, 16, 383
Correcting entry, 91
Cost flow, 187
Cost
    of acquisition, 216
    of goods available for sale, 136
    of goods sold, 131, 136
Coupon, 278
Covenants, 24
Credit, 76
    balance, 77
    losses, 267, 511
    note, 133
    risk, 266, 514
Credit Suisse, 2
Currency translation reserve, 393
Current
    assets, 58, 182
    liabilities, 330
    ratio, 435
    service cost, 345
    tax, 333

Days sales outstanding. *See* Average collection
        period
Debentures, 361
    issue expenses, 364
    redemption, 365
    redemption fund, 365
    redemption reserve, 389
    retirement, 365
Debit, 76
    balance, 77
    note, 138
Debt-to-equity ratio, 57, 439
Debt instruments, 278
Dechow, Patricia, 125
Deductible temporary difference, 339
Deferral, 119
Deferred tax, 335
    asset, 339
    liability, 336
Defined benefit plan, 345
Defined contribution plan, 345
Definite liabilities, 330
Depletion, 243
Deposits, 501
Depreciable amount, 220
Depreciation, 121, 219
    methods, 221, 228
    myths, 236
    for tax, 232
Derecognition, 75, 233
Derivative financial instruments, 283

Deutsche Bank, 60
Diluted earnings per share, 403
Diluted eps, 401
Direct method, 465
Directors' responsibility statement, 554
Disclosure policy, 551
Discontinued operation, 536
Disney, 154
Dividend, 48, 397
    yield, 442
Donated assets, 218
Double-entry system, 76
Dr. Reddy's Laboratories, 427, 545, 574
Drawings, 53
DuPont analysis, 433, 434, 508

Earnings
    excuses, 554
    guidance, 570
    management, 541
    per share, 401, 434
    quality, 152, 514, 532
    releases, 553
    smoothing, 542
Eastman Kodak, 426
Ebbers, Bernie, 39
Economic value added, 550
Effective interest method, 360
Effective tax rate, 337
Efficient market hypothesis, 552
Elements, 53
Employee benefits, 344
Enron, 39
Equity, 48
Equity instruments, 278
Equity method, 313
Errors, 36, 91
Essar Oil, 355
Estimated liabilities, 332
Ethical issues, 38
Expected losses, 267
Expected return on plan assets, 345
Expense recognition, 118
Expenses, 48, 114

Facebook, 548
Face value, 361
Factoring, 271
Fair value, 265, 360, 418
FASB, 34
FIFA, 28
FIFO, 188
Finance lease, 151, 369
Financial
    accounting, 23
    assets, 58, 265
    flexibility, 476
    instruments, 265
    investments, 277
    leverage, 439
    liabilities, 360
    statement analysis, 424
    statements, 48
    year, 113
Financing activities, 460, 471

Finished goods, 182
Fixed-asset turnover, 248
Fixed assets. *See* Property, plant and equipment
FOB terms, 185
Foreign currency, 390
    transaction, 390
    translation, 390
Forensic accounting, 37
Forfeited shares, 387
Fraud, 24, 37, 38, 39, 60, 97, 153, 202, 249, 286,
        317, 347, 374, 404, 444, 478, 523, 544
Free cash flow, 549
Freight in, 138
Full cost method, 244, 246
Fully depreciated assets, 229
Functional currency, 390
FVTOCI, 281
FVTPL, 282, 360

GAAP, 30
Gains, 114
General
    journal, 87
    ledger, 74
    motors, 31
GMR Infrastructure, 31
Going concern, 31
Goodwill, 242, 304
Government accounting, 37
Gross margin. *See* Gross profit
Gross profit, 131
    method, 196
    ratio, 146
Group, 300
GST, 331
Guarantee, 522
GVK Group, 423

HDFC, 413
HDFC Bank, 287, 506, 511, 514
Hindustan Unilever, 266, 545, 554
Horizontal analysis, 427
Hypothecation, 272

IAS/IFRS, 33, 34
IASB, 33
ICAI, 33
ICICI Bank, 153, 294, 529, 566
IFAC, 33
Impairment, 247, 284
Income measurement, 113, 130
Income tax, 333
Incurred loss, 270
Ind AS, 33, 57, 418
Independent directors, 554
Indian GAAP/Indian accounting, 32, 33
Indian Hotels, 1
Indigo, 549
Indirect method, 467
Information asymmetry, 19
Information systems auditor, 37
Infosys, 132, 287, 458
Instalment sales, 150
Intangible assets, 239

Interest cover, 440
Internal
    audit, 17, 37
    control systems, 95
    rate of return, 280
Intrinsic value, 399
Inventoriable costs, 186
Inventories, 182
Inventory
    error, 183
    losses, 139
    profits, 190
    turnover, 199, 437
    valuation, 191
Investing activities, 460, 469
Investment allowance reserve, 389
Investment property, 249
Invoice, 132
IOSCO, 33
IRDAI, 33
Issued capital, 385
ITC, 545

Jet Airways, 71
Joint
    arrangements, 311
    control, 311
    operation, 311
    venture, 312
Journal, 87

Kingfisher Airlines, 2, 37, 356, 456

Lanco Infratech, 260
Larsen & Toubro, 203
Layaway sales, 149
Leases, 150, 369
Ledger, 74, 89
Lehman Brothers, 39, 380, 499
Lemons principle, 18
Letter of credit, 522
Leverage, 509
Liabilities, 47, 329
Liabilities-to-equity ratio, 439
Lifetime expected credit losses, 268
LIFO, 188
Limited company. *See* Company
Limited liability, 15
    partnership, 16
Liquidity, 266, 435
    coverage ratio, 519
Logitech, 202
Long-lived assets, 215
Losses, 114
Lower-of-cost-market, 191

Machine learning, 94
Madoff, Bernard, 20, 39
Major inspections, 230
Major repairs, 230
Management accounting, 23, 37
Manchester United, 155

Manufacturing costs, 198
Manufacturing organization, 12
Marginal tax rate, 337
Mark-to-market accounting. *See* Fair value
Market interest rate. *See* Yield
Market risk, 514
Maruti Suzuki, 200, 237
MAT, 334
Matching principle, 118
Materiality, 90
McDonald, 25
Merck, 243
Microsoft, 548
Ministry of Corporate Affairs, 32
Ministry of Finance, 33
Mistry, Cyrus P., 1
Money laundering, 39
Money measurement, 32
Moral hazard, 20, 399
Mortgage, 368
Murthy, N. R. Narayana, 5

National Financial Reporting Authority, 33,
    418
National Spot Exchange, 211
Natural resources, 243
Net cost of purchases, 137
Net interest income, 512
Net interest margin, 512
Net margin, 146
Net present value, 235
Net profit, 48, 113
Net realizable value, 191
Net stable funding ratio, 510
Neutrality, 192
Nobles Crus, 295
Nominal accounts, 146
Non-cash activities, 460
Non-controlling interest, 58, 302, 400
Non-current assets, 58, 182
Non-current liabilities, 58
Non-operating/non-recurring items, 535
Non-performing assets, 511
No-par stock, 386
NOPAT, 538
Normal balance, 80

Off-balance sheet financing/activities, 372,
    522
Oil and gas accounting, 243
Olympus, 326
Operating
    activities, 460, 464
    assets, 539
    cycle, 182, 200, 438, 440
    expenses, 131, 139
    lease, 371
    leverage, 440
    liabilities, 329
    profit, 146, 538
    segment, 545
Ordinary
    annuity, 371
    repairs, 230

Other comprehensive income, 390
Overhead efficiency, 512

Pacioli, Luca, 76
Paid-up capital, 385
Parent, 300
Partnership, 14
Par value, 385
Payout ratio, 57
Pensions, 345
Percentage of completion, 151
Period expenses, 186
Periodic inventory system, 137
Periodicity assumption, 32
Permanent accounts, 146
Perpetual existence, 383
Perpetual inventory system, 196
Phar-Mor, 202
Physical flow, 187
Physical inventory, 185
Ponzi scheme, 20
Posting, 88
Preference shares, 364, 387
Prepaid expenses, 120
Present value, 280
Press, 556
Price-earnings ratio, 441
Price-to-book ratio, 443
Principles-based system, 34
Prior period error, 536
Private company, 15
Product costs, 186
Product financing arrangement, 373
Production-units method, 224
Profitability analysis, 431
Profit margin, 56, 431, 510
Pro forma measures, 547
Property, plant and equipment, 215
    turnover, 248
Prudence, 192
Public company, 15
Punjab National Bank, 2
Purchase discounts, 134
Purchase returns and allowances, 138
Purchases, 137

Qualifying asset, 217
Quick ratio, 436
Quindell, 2

Raju, Ramalinga, 97
Ramesh, P. R., 417
Ratio analysis, 431
Raw materials, 182
Real accounts, 147
Real earnings management, 544
Realization principle, 115
Realized reserve, 389
Receivable turnover, 436
Recognition, 75
Recoverable amount, 247
Red flags, 60, 154, 203, 249, 286, 317, 347, 404,
    444

Reebok India, 176
Reliance Industries, 303, 343
Reporting
    currency, 390
    entity, 30
    period, 113
Research and development, 242
Reserve Bank of India, 27, 500
Reserves, 389
Residual value, 220
Retail inventory method, 194
Retained earnings, 48
Return on
    assets, 56, 432, 509
    equity, 57, 434, 508
    investment, 56
Revaluation reserve, 238
Revenue, 48, 114, 131
    expenditure, 230
    recognition, 115
    reserve, 389
Reversing entries, 148
Ricoh India, 39
Rights issue, 386
Risk-weighted asset, 515
Rules-based system, 34

Sale and repurchase, 150
Sales, 132
    discounts, 134
    general and administrative, 139
    returns and allowances, 133
Sales-type lease, 151
Santander, 537
Satyam, 39, 97, 417
SEBI, 33
Securities premium, 48, 389
Segment performance, 545
Self-constructed assets, 218
Sell-side analysts, 140, 555
Selling expenses, 140
Sengupta, Partha, 552
Separate financial statements, 316
Service organization, 12
SFIO, 27
Share-based compensation, 398
Share buyback, 394
Share capital, 48, 384
Share premium. *See* Securities premium
Shares, 16

Shiller, Robert, 442
Siemens India, 424
Signalling, 19
Significant influence, 313
Sinking fund, 365
Sino-Forestry, 39
Skilling, Jeff, 39
Smith, Adam, 21
Software, 243
Sole proprietorship, 14
Solvency analysis, 438
Sony, 536
Special journal, 88
Specific identification, 187
Spence, Michael, 19
Spread, 513
Srinivasan, Suraj, 569
Standard cost method, 195
State Bank of India, 497, 522
Statement of cash flows, 55, 59, 459
Statement of changes in equity, 55, 59, 400
Statement of profit and loss, 55, 59, 506
Statutory
    corporation, 383
    liquidity ratio, 504
    reserve, 389, 501
    tax rate, 337
Steel Authority of India, 348
Stock-in-trade, 183
Stock option plan, 398
Stock split, 397
Straight-line method, 220
Stress testing, 521
Subscribed capital, 383
Subsidiary, 300
Substance over form, 300
Successful efforts method, 244, 246
Sum-of-the-years'-digits, 223
Sun TV, 154
Suzlon Energy, 1, 441, 494
Sweat equity, 386
Syndicate Bank, 24

T account, 76
Take-or-pay contract, 373
Tata Motors, 1, 299, 303, 424
Tata Sons, 1, 316
Tata Steel, 1
Taxable profit, 333
Taxable temporary difference, 336

Tax base, 335
TCS, 109, 132, 287, 347, 384
Temporary accounts, 146
Tesco, 38
Tesla Motors, 20, 548
Throughput contract, 373
Time value of money, 278
Toshiba, 39, 563
Trade discounts, 134
Trade receivables, 266
TRAI, 27
Transfer of receivables, 372
Treasurer, 17
Treasury stock, 394
Trend analysis, 429
Trial balance, 90

Unbilled revenue, 123
Unconditional purchase obligation, 373
Unearned revenue, 122
Unicredit, 295
Unlimited liability, 14
Unrealized reserve, 389
Unused tax credit carryforward, 342
Unused tax loss carryforward, 341
Useful life, 220
US GAAP, 34

Valeant Pharmaceuticals, 175
Verrecchia, Robert E., 552
Vertical analysis, 429
Vodafone, 250, 401
Voluntary disclosure, 551

WAC, 189
Warranties, 332
Wells Fargo, 38
Whistle-blowing, 555
Work-in-progress, 182
Worksheet, 126, 140
WorldCom, 30, 220
Written-down-value method, 222

Yield, 280, 361

Zero-coupon bond, 361